THE LETTERS OF RUDYARD KIPLING

Rudyard Kipling by John Collier, 1891.
According to Mrs Kipling, Collier's was "far and away the best" portrait. Kipling's friend Count Robert D'Humières wrote that the Collier portrait "alone gives the frank, open and youthful expression of the original". (Portrait in oils at Bateman's)

The Letters of Rudyard Kipling

Volume 1
1872–89

Edited by
THOMAS PINNEY

WILTSHIRE
COUNTY COUNCIL
LIBRARY &
MUSEUM SERVICE

MACMILLAN

Rudyard Kipling's letters © 1990
by The National Trust for Places of Historic Interest or Natural Beauty

Selection and editorial matter
© Thomas Pinney 1990

All rights reserved. No reproduction, copy or transmission of
this publication may be made without written permission.

No paragraph of this publication may be reproduced, copied
or transmitted save with written permission or in accordance
with the provisions of the Copyright, Designs and Patents Act
1988, or under the terms of any licence permitting limited
copying issued by the Copyright Licensing Agency, 33–4 Alfred Place,
London WC1E 7DP.

Any person who does any unauthorised act in relation to this
publication may be liable to criminal prosecution and civil claims
for damages.

First published 1990

Published by
THE MACMILLAN PRESS LTD
Houndmills, Basingstoke, Hampshire RG21 2XS
and London
Companies and representatives
throughout the world

Typeset by Wessex Typesetters
(Division of The Eastern Press Ltd)
Frome, Somerset

Printed in Great Britain by
Billing & Sons Ltd, Worcester

British Library Cataloguing in Publication Data
Kipling, Rudyard
The letters of Rudyard Kipling.
Vol. 1: 1872–89
1. English literature. Kipling, Rudyard—
Correspondence, diaries, etc
I. Title   II. Pinney, Thomas
828'.809
ISBN 0–333–36086–9
Set of first 2 volumes ISBN 0–333–52450–0

Contents

List of Illustrations	vi
Introduction and Acknowledgements	vii
List of Abbreviations and Short Titles	xxiv
Family Tree: Kiplings, Macdonalds, and Balestiers	xxvi
Chronology of Rudyard Kipling's Life, 1865–1936	xxviii

The Letters, 1872–89

I	From Schoolboy to Journalist: Westward Ho! – Lahore, 1872–87	1
II	Making a Name: Allahabad, 1887–8	145
III	The Road Back to England, 1889	273

Register of Names and Correspondents	382

List of Illustrations

Frontispiece: Rudyard Kipling by John Collier, 1891. According to Mrs Kipling, Collier's was "far and away the best" portrait. Kipling's friend Count Robert D'Humieres wrote that the Collier portrait "alone gives the frank, open and youthful expression of the original".

1. John Lockwood Kipling and Alice Macdonald Kipling at the time of their marriage, 1865.
2. Facsimile of Kipling's letter to Moberly Bell, 8 May 1897 (Library of Congress).
3. A page from Kipling's letter to the Reverend George Willes, 17 November 1882 (Dalhousie University).
4. Cormell Price, headmaster of the United Services College, Westward Ho!, 1874–1894.
5. Georgiana Burne-Jones and her children, Philip and Margaret, *c.* 1883.
6. Alice Macdonald Kipling (Mrs J. M. Fleming), Kipling's sister "Trix", in 1892, aged 24 (Macdonald Collection, Special Collections, University of Sussex).
7. Rudyard Kipling and his father in India, 1883 (Macdonald Collection, Special Collections, University of Sussex).
8. Edmonia and Alex Hill in the garden of Belvedere House, Allahabad (Library of Congress).

Introduction and Acknowledgements

KIPLING IN HIS LETTERS

As a letter writer Kipling has three, at least, of the requirements for excellence: he is copious, he is various, and he is always interesting. Kipling was not one of those writers who are jealous of their powers, or fear to waste their energies on anything but the highest efforts. Though they were quickly written and quickly sent, his letters exhibit the same abilities as his more carefully planned and frequently revised work for publication. They are, for example, full of his marvellous descriptive power: the telling phrase, the vivid term, the precisely selected detail, the rapid compression of complex scenes and events into a few memorable strokes, evoke Kipling's alert and lively interest in the world around him. That world was wide and various far beyond the ordinary: people and places, animals and things, the animate and inanimate, all are perceived and described with a fresh and distinctive power of realisation.

There is also a great deal of rhetorical violence in the letters, especially when politics are in question, as they more and more were as Kipling grew older. The history of Kipling's political convictions has recently been traced with great clarity and persuasiveness by Michael Brock,[1] and the letters closely follow the pattern that Professor Brock has described. Throughout his Indian years, Kipling was not much troubled by ideas about empire; he echoed the received notions of those among whom he lived and worked, and amusedly satirised the scandals and ineptitudes of the ruling classes. On his return to England a change swiftly occurred. Provoked by the indifference or even hostility of the English at home to the work and values of the English abroad, Kipling became the apostle of the Imperial gospel to the gentiles of England: "And what should they know of England who only England know?" To instruct those who only England know is the overriding purpose of his work in the great creative decade of the 1890s.

[1] Michael Brock, "'Outside His Art': Rudyard Kipling in Politics", *Kipling Journal*, LXII (March 1988) 9–32.

Then came the Boer War; it revealed the inadequacy of English preparation, both individual and communal, to meet the challenges of the empire, and so gave a new form to Kipling's political mission. He took up enthusiastically, even obsessively, the cause of national training, national preparation, national efficiency. England was surrounded by jealous and unscrupulous powers, and must depend upon its own exertions for safety. Worse, there were enemies within the citadel, so Kipling imagined. From the time of the Boer War onward, Kipling's suspicion of conspiracy and betrayal in all forms of politics opposed to his own becomes more and more prominent. After the disasters of World War One and the dislocations of the postwar period, Kipling's isolation from and mistrust of all parties and leaders was nearly complete. Indeed, his view of politics became more theological than political: it was a drama of saints and sinners, angels and devils, with the demonic part assigned variously to the Germans, the Irish, the Americans, the Indian nationalists, and the English liberals. Those who were fighting the good fight were hardly more than a saving remnant. All of this, which is perfectly compatible with clarity of view and great shrewdness of judgement in particular cases, is fully written down in the letters. The relation that Kipling's troubled fascination with politics holds to his art is far from being understood; the letters provide abundant material for the study of the question.

The letters show a very different side of Kipling as well, the side he presented as a friend. Here we see Kipling at his most attractive, always seeking to give pleasure or encouragement to the people he cared about; more remarkable, he is always at pains to be courteous to people about whom he has no reason to care at all and, frequently, good reason to find annoying. Some of his most studied letters are efforts to please and interest his friends by the exercise of his narrative and descriptive art – certain of the letters to Conland, for example, or to Colonel Feilden. Though his friends were of all sorts, Kipling seems able to enter into an interested and generous relation with them despite their very great differences. They include fellow-craftsmen, whether relatively obscure, like Edward Lucas White, or successful, like Rider Haggard; they include a number of older men, to whom Kipling, with no apparent trace of affectation, assigned a sort of patriarchal role – Sir Walter Besant, Charles Eliot Norton, and Colonel Henry Wemyss Feilden are the leading exponents of this role, apart from Kipling's actual father. In the realm of state affairs Kipling also looked for fathers: Rhodes played that part in South Africa, and after him, Lord Milner. Others among his friends were playmates, men of solid professional ability who could nevertheless enter unreservedly into the adventures of games-playing in formal camaraderie that Kipling loved and never seemed to have had enough of: Kay Robinson in India, Dr Conland and W. Hallett Phillips in the

United States, Perceval Landon and H. A. Gwynne in England.

The subject of Kipling's development as an artist has attracted capable critics (headed by J. M. S. Tompkins); but it is a subject that will sustain and repay much fuller study than it has so far had. It must of course be learned from the record of his work; but the letters will provide a valuable supplement. They contain much information about Kipling's reading, his literary admirations, his various projects realised and unrealised, and his judgements on his own work – all matters about which much would otherwise remain unknown and unsuspected. A close analysis of what Kipling has to say on matters of literary art in his letters would provide, I think, a fairly extensive and coherent account of his convictions. In the main, these seem to be an interesting combination of the high Victorian aesthetic of realism with a deeply rooted conviction that the forms of art are primitive, anonymous, and communal.

Kipling avoided the confessional mode in his published writings, and the same avoidance is evident in the letters. He does not write about the history of his opinions, the doubts and uncertainties that he has had to go through in working out his beliefs; he does not philosophise, except in the tersest and most epigrammatic way; he does not meditate on the big questions. As in the stories and verses, the letters often work by indirection, contriving by situation, image, allusion, gesture, and other means to suggest what is left unsaid. Only very rarely, and then in only a hasty and summary way, does Kipling talk about religion. The letters do not even exhibit that fascination with the occult that is so prominent and suggestive an element in Kipling's verse and prose. Apart from this large exclusion, the letters present Kipling the man and artist with an intimacy of detail and an immediacy unmatched by any other source – if they do not quite reveal the "inside of things" that Cardinal Newman looked for in a published correspondence, they come as close to doing that as one can imagine for a writer so determinedly reticent on personal matters as Kipling.

I have touched on only a few of the salient points of interest in Kipling's letters. As I began by saying, they are copious, various, and always interesting: it is therefore certain that different readers will find different elements to engage their curiosity and challenge their powers of interpretation. It is no part of an editor's task to say what these should be or how they should be understood, especially with a writer like Kipling, about whom so much remains problematical and disputed. I may, however, express the hope that has helped me through all of my work on this edition: that it may stimulate a newly curious and open attention to Kipling, both the man and the work, now so long abused in unexamined terms and so little regarded with that intelligent sympathy which is the basis of the only criticism worth having.

KIPLING'S LETTERS: THE MATERIALS

Rudyard Kipling's literary career belongs to the era of fully developed world-wide communications. Even at the beginning of his career the commerce of literature had become large-scale and international: newspaper syndicates, popular magazines, continental and colonial reprints, translations, adaptations for the theatre, musical settings, and other forms of the market besides conventional book publishing, all offered access to audiences far larger than had ever been imagined before. The literary agent had been invented by the 1870s and had quickly become an indispensable part of publishing. When Kipling achieved his precocious fame at the beginning of 1890, this machinery for promotion and large-scale publishing was already in place and operating. In the next year, the passage of the first copyright agreement between England and the United States made English-language publishing aimed at both sides of the Atlantic lucrative and attractive as never before. By the end of Kipling's career, sound recordings, films, and radio were fully established, and the first glimmerings of television had been seen.

For forty-five of his seventy years, Kipling was a famous writer in these conditions of mass marketing; and, on the calendar of literary history, all of this took place only yesterday. Given these conditions – the length, the scale, and the recentness of Kipling's fame – it is no surprise that his letters survive in very large numbers. One should also add that the "cult" of the autograph letter (as A. N. L. Munby has called it) was fully established by the time that Kipling arrived on the scene. So, too, was the fashion among the very rich of collecting modern manuscripts: Henry Huntington, J. P. Morgan, and Harry Elkins Widener, to name no more, were all in the field around the turn of the century. Most of this fraternity collected Kipling, and letters were part of the game they sought.

Finally, Kipling lived in an age that had not yet abandoned letter-writing. The telephone was taking over, but Kipling's life coincided with what Frank Kermode has recently called the "great age" of letter-writing, the "terminal flowering of the genre".[2] Paper and ink were cheap and good; postage cost little; the mail service was quick and efficient; and people were still accustomed to writing with a pen – for Kipling, indeed, the physical act of covering white paper with black ink was a sensuous pleasure, though most of his letters are hasty and inelegant enough regarded merely as manuscript. Kipling kept no telephone in his house. He did learn to type at a fairly early point in the advance of the typewriter into literary territory (at least as early as 1891 and perhaps earlier), and a small proportion of his extant letters is composed in his

---

[2] *London Review of Books*, 15 September 1988.

mistake-ridden typing. He remained to the end one of that generation for whom letter-writing was a habitual and agreeable activity.

I have in hand the texts of about 6300 letters in manuscript, copy, or printed form, drawn from 138 collections, public and private, and from 135 printed sources; they date from 1872, when Kipling was still a miserable child in the care of his awful "Aunty" Holloway, to 11 January 1936, seven days before his death in Middlesex Hospital. There is, as well, an uncounted number of letters whose existence is established by sale catalogues or other records but which I have not succeeded in tracing. How many more letters may still be extant but are not yet entered on any form of public record may never be known. The available letters are of every kind (almost: there are only one or two ostensible love-letters, and letters of personal confession may be said not to exist). They are written to a wide variety of correspondents: to members of the family, to intimate friends, to admired elders, to professional and political colleagues, to acquaintances made through his many activities, and to the miscellaneous members of the huge general public that afflicts a famous man. It is not easy to say which of all these is the most interesting category. The earlier letters, predictably, are the more open and unrestrained; and those letters written to correspondents who had Kipling's confidence are of course more revealing than mere formal replies can be. But Kipling could, at any time and on quite unpredictable occasions, warm up into energetic expressiveness and say something interesting and notable.

Given all the causes making for their preservation, Kipling's letters tended not to be lost to the usual forces that annihilate our ordinary transactions – indifference, inattention, haste, and the (usually correct) judgement that a thing is not worth saving. A letter from Kipling, after the establishment of his fame at an early age, was not likely to be treated indifferently, and if any of his letters were lost, then they were lost through deliberate acts of destruction. Many in fact were, and the main agents were Kipling himself and his wife. Kipling was a determined destroyer of personal papers, animated by a fierce resentment of the fact that his privacy was always subject to invasion. After the death of his father in 1911 (his mother had died the year before), Kipling, left in charge of an accumulation of nearly a half a century's family papers, indulged in an orgy of burning. His sister wrote many years later of what she called the "frenzy of burning any letters or papers connected with his youth" that overtook Kipling after the death of his parents.[3]

---

[3] To Mrs Bambridge, 15 June 1940 (Sussex).

The result is that we have but a pitiful handful – four altogether – of the letters that Kipling wrote to his parents over four decades. Since as a child he had been separated from them for nearly twelve years of residence in England, and since, apart from the years 1882–7 in India, he did not live with them regularly thereafter, Kipling's connection with his parents was kept up by correspondence. There is no point in speculating about what we have lost through this destruction; but in estimating Kipling as a letter writer it is only fair to keep in mind the fact that we do not have anything from what would certainly have been among the most interesting letters that he ever wrote. It is, of course, impossible to be certain about the fate of things that have simply disappeared, and so it is within the realm of possibility that Kipling's missing letters to his parents will turn up some day. But for now, at least, one may conclude that they went up in smoke through the chimney of The Gables, Tisbury, in the winter of 1911.

A second work of destruction that seems confirmed by the circumstantial evidence is of Kipling's letters to his uncle, Sir Edward Burne-Jones. These were destroyed, or at least the "saucy ones" were destroyed, according to Sir Sydney Cockerell, who had good means of knowing.[4] Burne-Jones was, among other things, a man of the widest reading and information, whom Kipling loved to consult; he was also, when he chose, a gifted writer of nonsense and mockery, and nothing is more likely than that all of the correspondence between the two men, uncle and nephew, was of the "saucy" variety. In any case, I have found no surviving letter from Kipling to Burne-Jones. Kipling helped his Aunt Georgiana Burne-Jones in the composition of her *Memorials of Sir Edward Burne-Jones*, but the collaboration, far from leading him to contribute anything to the book from his correspondence with his uncle, probably confirmed him in destroying it. That, however, is only a guess.

Kipling's destructions also included most of the letters sent to him. A good many such letters do, in fact, survive, but they tend not to be from his most obviously interesting correspondents. Kipling was frequently asked if the letters to him from such people as Mark Twain, Hardy, Stevenson, Henry James, or Theodore Roosevelt might be published or used for the purposes of a biographer; he invariably refused, and each such request must have reminded him that the only real protection against such curiosity was to destroy the material desired.

Mrs Kipling was, if anything, an even more dedicated destroyer than her husband. No letters between him and her survive (except for some letters of travel written by Kipling in 1915 and 1917) and it is a safe conjecture that she destroyed them. Three further instances of her destroying her husband's letters are on record.

---

[4] Wilfrid Blunt, *Cockerell* (New York, 1965) p. 61.

One of the intimate friendships that Kipling formed in his mature years was with the journalist Perceval Landon, whom he first met when both men worked together briefly on the Bloemfontein *Friend* in 1900 during the Boer War. Landon was, by virtue of this connection, sealed a member of the Society of "Friends", the little club that Kipling organised to perpetuate the Bloemfontein experience. Thereafter he and Landon saw much of each other, and in 1912 Landon became the Kiplings' tenant at Keylands, a house that they built for him on the Bateman's estate. Landon was frequently absent on his journalistic travels, and he and Kipling thus had many opportunities to write. So far as I have been able to find, no letters survive either from Kipling to Landon or from Landon to Kipling. According to Miss Cecily Nicholson, Kipling's secretary during the 1930s, Mrs Kipling had persuaded Landon, who died in 1927, to will his Kipling letters to her. He did so, and she destroyed them.[5]

Kipling's letters to his wife's mother, Mrs Anna Smith Balestier, written over a period of nearly twenty-five years, came, after Mrs Balestier's death, into the hands of her son, Beatty, whose violent quarrel with Kipling in 1896 had driven Kipling from Vermont, never to return. Since Mrs Kipling, as well as her husband, was estranged from her brother through the quarrel, she could not hope to get access to these letters while her brother lived. But Beatty died in 1936, and his needy widow was forced to put the Kipling letters up for sale. Mrs Kipling thereupon bought them and, given their subsequent disappearance from the world's knowledge, she must have destroyed them.[6] Some parts of these letters have survived and show them to have been full of richly detailed narratives of domestic life not matched by any of the surviving correspondences.

Mrs Kipling also succeeded, after Kipling's death, in buying and destroying the letters that her husband wrote to Mrs Edmonia Hill from 1887 to 1890; but her purpose was, in this case, largely frustrated. Mrs Hill, the American wife of an Englishman in India, met the young Kipling in Allahabad towards the end of 1887. They were quickly attracted to each other, and Kipling was, for a time, a guest in the Hills' house. In 1889 he and the Hills travelled together from India to the United States via China and Japan. For the two years of their intimate

[5] Editor's interview with Miss Nicholson, 12 August 1980. According to Caroline Kipling's diary, Landon willed his letters and papers to RK himself (31 April 1927). The Somerset House record of Landon's death, however, reveals that he died intestate, so that both Miss Nicholson's statement and CK's diary entry must need some modification. However it may have happened, I think it very likely that the Kiplings did get hold of RK's letters to Landon and that they were destroyed. I owe the information about Landon's intestacy to Mr Peter Lewis.

[6] Flora Livingston, cited by Howard Rice, "Kipling's Vermont Period, Notes, II", 199 (typescript, Marlboro College). The catalogue of the Balestier sale is American Art Association, Anderson Galleries, 14–15 April 1937.

acquaintance, Mrs Hill was Kipling's main correspondent, to whom he narrated the story of his daily life and to whom he presented his work for advice and judgement. Their relation was abruptly ended in 1890, perhaps because Caroline Balestier, who was to become Mrs Kipling, had already entered the scene. Though she outlived Mrs Kipling by many years, not dying until 1952, Mrs Hill endured a long widowhood in gradually straitening circumstances. In the 1920s she was discovered living in Baltimore by an enthusiastic Chicago collector named William Carpenter; Mrs Hill was then persuaded by her poverty to sell her Kipling papers to Carpenter, which she did over a period of several years. The material that she thus sold included Kipling's letters to her. Carpenter himself died in 1931, and at some time after this his widow offered the Hill letters to Mrs Kipling. She bought them and, presumably, at once destroyed them.[7]

Unknown to Mrs Kipling – one supposes – was the fact that Carpenter had made typed copies of the Hill letters and that these remained with Mrs Carpenter. Ultimately, at some time unknown, the copies came into the hands of Kipling's daughter, Mrs Elsie Bambridge, who was just as eager to preserve what her father had written as her mother had been to destroy it. There is every reason to believe that the originals no longer exist; but the copies of the Hill letters that Carpenter made are now a part of the Kipling Papers preserved at the University of Sussex. They are, unfortunately, not very good copies: the transcription of the text is full of evident errors, many copies appear to be incomplete, and it has been necessary to rearrange and redate a good many of them. They nevertheless provide the lengthiest and most interesting part of Kipling's early correspondence that survives.

Mrs Kipling was by no means an indiscriminate destroyer, though she was evidently determined to annihilate as much of the intimately personal as she could. In her opposite capacity, as custodian of her husband's career, she did much to preserve and arrange her husband's papers. In this she was assisted by her daughter Elsie, who continued the work after Mrs Kipling's death. The Kipling Papers, the great collection of Kipling's private papers, may be thought of as the work of the two women, mother and daughter. The daughter, Mrs Bambridge, willed the Kipling Papers to the National Trust. Following her death in 1976 the Trust placed the papers in the University of Sussex Library, where they now are. One further major work of destruction was still to be done, however. Mrs Kipling's diaries, begun in the week before her marriage to Kipling in January 1892 and kept down to the day of his death in January 1936, were inherited by Mrs Bambridge. She left

---

[7] Lucille Carpenter to C. J. Paterson, 13 April 1953 (Cornell University). Mrs Livingstone says that it was Carpenter himself who offered Mrs Hill's letters to Mrs Kipling: Flora Livingstone to Mrs Bambridge, 22 October 1941 (Sussex).

instructions in her will that the diaries should be destroyed, and it is reported that they were burned by direction of her trustees. Something of this 45-volume document survives, however, in a typescript of extracts from and summaries of the diary volumes made by C. E. Carrington in 1953 when he was writing his authorised biography of Kipling. I have been able to make use of Carrington's typescript in preparing this edition.

Apart from the great collection at Sussex, there are a good many other important Kipling collections, including large numbers of the letters; several of these collections continue to grow vigorously. With regard to letters, certainly the most important Kipling collection is now that in the Library of Congress; it is founded on the gift of W. R. Carpenter's collection, and has been recently greatly enlarged by the letters collected by H. Dunscombe Colt. In Canada, the Kipling library assembled by James McG. Stewart now at Dalhousie University is rich in Kipling's letters; so is the New York Public Library, and so, too, are the libraries of Syracuse University, Columbia, Harvard, Princeton, and Cornell. In England, the British Library and the Bodleian have important holdings. But by no means all of Kipling's letters are in institutional libraries. It is still possible for the enterprising private collector to hunt the field, as, to take two notable examples, Mrs Lisa Lewis of Wallingford, England, and Miss Matilda Tyler of New Haven, Connecticut, have both done and are doing.

PREVIOUS PUBLICATION OF THE LETTERS

Both Lord Birkenhead and C. E. Carrington, the biographers who worked with the authority of Kipling's daughter, Mrs Bambridge, and who thus had access to the Kipling papers, published selections from Kipling's letters in their books.[8] Morton Cohen published Kipling's letters to Rider Haggard in *Rudyard Kipling to Rider Haggard: The Record of a Friendship* (London, 1965); and in 1983 Elliot Gilbert published a selection of Kipling's letters to his children Elsie and John under the title of *"O Beloved Kids": Rudyard Kipling's Letters to his Children*. One might add such an item as "Letters from Rudyard Kipling to Guy Paget 1919–1936", privately printed in 1936; but this, in an edition of twelve copies, is exceedingly hard to find, even in the largest of libraries, so that it has hardly achieved publication in the ordinary sense. Such is the record of publication of Kipling's letters until now. There have

---

[8] Lord Birkenhead, *Rudyard Kipling* (New York, 1978); C. E. Carrington, *Rudyard Kipling* (London, 1955).

been, of course, many scores or hundreds of the letters published in newspapers, magazine articles, and books over the period of what is now nearly a century since Kipling began to be a subject of print. These are a valuable contribution to the record, and sometimes provide the only extant texts of the letters in question. But in their scattered form they are available only to the most dedicated searcher.

The fact that Kipling's letters have remained largely unpublished is by no means a comment on their interest or value but is entirely owing to the fact that Mrs Bambridge did not wish her father's letters to be published casually or piecemeal and yet could not quite make up her mind to have them published *in extenso*. She discussed the possibility of such a publication with Morton Cohen when he was at work on the letters to Rider Haggard; and earlier she and C. E. Carrington had considered the idea at some length while he was at work on the authorised biography. Nothing came of either of these tentative explorations. It was not until after Mrs Bambridge's death in 1976 and the transfer of the Kipling Papers to the University of Sussex, where, under the direction of John Burt, they have been arranged and catalogued, that it seemed possible to undertake the work with any confidence that it might be carried through. The basis established by the collection at Sussex has in recent years been greatly extended as other important collections have made their way into institutional libraries. This edition is, then, the first comprehensive collection of Kipling's letters; by far the greater part of the letters it contains are published for the first time.

THE SCOPE OF THIS EDITION

Though it aims to be generous and fully representative, this is a selected, not a "complete", *Letters*. When I began my work I began with the intention of publishing everything that I could find, but it did not take long to modify that intention. Inevitably, many of Kipling's surviving letters are simple practical notes – instructing his publisher to send a book to such and such a friend, for example, or ordering paint from a dealer in Vermont. A great many letters are simply social notes, declining or offering invitations or introducing friends or the like. All such letters are the equivalent of a phone call, and it is hard to see that they can have much more general interest than most phone calls. Many more letters, though of considerable intrinsic interest, go over ground covered by some other letter and are therefore largely repetitious. And even more letters are *pro forma* responses to people whom Kipling does not know or about whom he cares nothing but who have, for one reason or another, sought to put themselves in touch with a famous man. It can certainly be argued that for the sake of the record, and for the sake of the detail that only completeness can provide, everything available ought to be published. But, while admitting the force of the argument, I conclude in favour of selection over completeness for the reasons given; to them may be added quite cogent practical reasons of size and expense.

Here, at the beginning of publication, it is not possible to state confidently what proportion of the total number of extant letters this edition will ultimately contain. For the first two volumes, the number is 459 of 1333 available. It is more important, however, to know what principles of selection I have followed than to have the mere numerical tally of those selected. I have aimed, first, at providing a kind of biographical narrative through the letters, marking out the important divisions of Kipling's life, the succession of his different activities and interests, and the changes that went with them. I have not hesitated to include letters that did not seem to me notably interesting in themselves but that provided information not otherwise given about some point in the biographical sequence. I have taken for granted that the main interest in Kipling's life is his literary career, and in illustrating this I have included letters that document the details of the composition and publication of his works – matters not, perhaps, of great general interest, but matters of fact such as must underlie all valid history and interpretation. I have regarded any letter that discusses a question of his art or expresses anything of his more general artistic ideas as privileged, having a special claim to inclusion.

I have also tried to illustrate all of the important personal relations in Kipling's life, so far as the letters allow that to be done. Much is missing. The letters to his parents and to his wife are, so far as can be known, destroyed; no letters have been found from Kipling to Florence Garrard, the girl with whom he thought himself in love for the better part of a decade and who certainly troubled his emotional life. Only one letter (and that a mere formal document) has been found to Wolcott Balestier, the young American who so powerfully affected Kipling and whose death constituted one of the great crises of Kipling's life. And there are other gaps of the kind. From the many remaining letters, however, I have, when other things were equal, preferred the letter that showed Kipling in touch with some person who would not otherwise be documented in the edition, or in some role not otherwise illustrated.

I have not knowingly sought to exclude any side of Kipling from the selection. Much that he has to say on political subjects, especially as he grows older and more bitter, one might wish had been left unsaid. But I have made no attempt to defend Kipling against himself, as it were, and his political ideas and prejudices are very fully documented in this selection.

EDITORIAL METHOD: TEXT

In preparing Kipling's letters for publication I have aimed at giving as accurate a transcription as possible. The conversion of any manuscript into print, however, is an act of translation, and like all translation it must alter what it begins with. I have also made some changes in the interest of the convenience of the reader accustomed to twentieth-century punctuation and other typographical conventions. The main changes that I have imposed are described in the following summary.

Punctuation

Kipling often uses a dash in the place of a period. When such a dash is unambiguously followed by a capital letter and the beginning of a new sentence, I have transcribed it as a period. If, as sometimes happens, Kipling omits to put a period at the end of a sentence, I supply it.

Kipling often omits the apostrophe from such contractions as "don't", "can't", "won't", and from possessives: "England's" or "Ruskin's". I have uniformly supplied the apostrophe when it is missing.

When Kipling begins a quotation with quotation marks but omits to provide them at the end I supply the missing marks; so too with parentheses.

Sometimes Kipling does not indicate the beginning of a new paragraph by indenting. I have uniformly indented all beginnings of paragraphs.

Abbreviations

Kipling does not make very extensive use of abbreviations. The most common is the ampersand, and then the &c for "etc." Very occasionally he uses "wh." and "ye." Since these are clearly abbreviations, the intention of which is to be understood as *and, etc., which,* and *the,* I have transcribed them in expanded form. Abbreviated titles and proper names are sometimes expanded within brackets for clarity: e.g. P[all] M[all] G[azette], L[ieutenant] G[overnor].

Kipling's fairly frequent superscript letters, as in M^r and M^{rs}, are a comparable matter. I have taken them as a sort of abbreviation and have transcribed them as *Mr* and *Mrs*.

Spelling

Clearly inadvertent misspellings – such as *that* for *than* or *of* for *off* – have been silently corrected.

Capitalisation

One source of frequent puzzlement has been over Kipling's capitalisation. It is often impossible to determine from the shape and size of his letters whether he intends a capital or not. In such cases I have followed this rule: if the word in a doubtful case is one not ordinarily capitalised, or one that may be but need not be capitalised, then I have transcribed it in lower case: *sea, east, lord*. Conversely, words that must be capitalised but that Kipling writes in doubtful form have been uniformly capitalised: *Mediterranean, South Carolina, Sir John*.

Extra elements

The placement of postscripts and other elements apart from the main text of the letter has sometimes raised questions. If the item is clearly a postscript – something added after the letter was thought to have been completed – then I put it at the end, after the signature, even though it may be written at the top of the first page. In other cases, such as Kipling's frequent use of the injunction "private", I put it, as a rule, between the dateline and the salutation. Addresses and dates put at the end rather than at the beginning of a letter are left just as Kipling placed them.

Lineation

For the sake of saving space I have run together in a single line the headings, including printed letterheads, of Kipling's letters, using a slash to indicate the original line endings.

Overscored material

Overscored material – a word, a phrase, or a line – I disregard unless it seems to have some special interest. In most cases, Kipling is clearly revising for the sake of clarifying or pointing his expression, not because he is changing the substance of what he has to say.

Letterheads

Printed or embossed letterheads I have transcribed in *italic*. I have not felt bound to transcribe the whole of any given letterhead, but only enough to establish clearly its identity: thus, I transcribe *Hotels Cattani / Engelberg / Grand Hotel* rather than *Hotels Cattani Sommer-Saison*

Mai Bis Oktober / Wintersport: November Bis Marz / Altitude 1019 Mtr / Engelberg / Hotel Titlis / Grand Hotel / & Kuranstalt.

For an immediate illustration of many of these editorial practices, consult the facsimile of Kipling's letter of 8 May 1897, reproduced as plate 2.

Apart from such editorial smoothings, the text of the letters has been treated according to the strict rule of "follow copy". Thus spelling has been left unaltered (except for clear inadvertences, as noted above). Kipling wavered between English and American practices in such sets as *honor/honour*, *color/colour*, or between such permitted variants as *surprise/surprize*. Kipling of course makes mistakes about proper names, and, though he was a confident and accurate speller, he gets the odd word wrong now and then.

All such inconsistencies and mistakes of spelling should be understood by the reader to belong to Kipling's text. So also with any irregularities of punctuation that remain after the regularising practices described above have been applied. In writing a series, for example, Kipling quite commonly will put a comma after one item but a semi-colon after another in the same series; or a semi-colon after one but a colon after another. Sometimes he adds a dash after a semi-colon or colon or period. Whatever his practice, I have made no attempt to alter it for the sake of consistency. Kipling's punctuation of the date-lines and the salutations of his letters is markedly inconsistent, but, since this seemed to me to present no problem to the reader, I have faithfully followed it. I have also followed his erratic practice in treating the titles of books, articles, and musical works: sometimes they are put within quotation marks, sometimes they are italicised, and sometimes they are not distinguished at all. Occasionally I have signalled with the editorial [sic] that an irregularity or error in the text is Kipling's, but I have tried to keep such intrusions to a minimum.

The text of letters that I know only from copies (manuscript or typescript) or from printed sources has been followed with the same exactness as the text of letters in Kipling's holograph. Since one is entirely at the mercy of the copyist or the editor in dealing with copies or printed sources (magazines, books, newspapers, dealers' and auctioneers' catalogues), it is not possible to make the kind of educated guesses about textual points that one can make with the authority of a holograph letter. For this reason I have passively accepted the text of letters in copies or printed form. It follows that I have accepted in such texts many details that I know to be incorrect – dates, proper names, quotations, and the like – but I have made the appropriate corrections in my notes.[9] I have not felt bound to follow the typographical style of the printed sources, however, and have disregarded such elements as bold-face type or italic initials.

EDITORIAL METHOD: ANNOTATION

I have tried to identify in brief but exact form the explicit references of Kipling's letters. The people that Kipling writes to, the people he talks about, the books that he reads, the events of his literary career, the quotations he makes, the public events and the private occasions that figure in the letters: these and other such particulars are the subjects of my annotation. I have also tried through my notes to provide a sufficient biographical context for the letters to be read connectedly.

I have not, as a rule, allowed myself to annotate what might be called the implicit references of the letters, and for this I would ask the reader to admire my restraint rather than to condemn my omissions. Nothing would be easier – and for an editor no temptation is more powerful – than to overwhelm these letters with commentary on the many people and events that the notes refer to, or on the relation of details in the letters to Kipling's life and work. Thus, when a reader wonders why I do not point out the connection between some reference in a letter and some one of Kipling's stories – connections that will constantly occur to even the most casual student of Kipling – the answer is, once started on that line there would be no stopping: the fountains of the great deep of commentary would be broken up and all would be inundated. I have contented myself with the less gratifying but I hope more serviceable exercise of supplying the immediate expository information that the letters seem to require, so far as I can.

"Seem", of course, is the operative word. No editor can know what any one of his present readers, let alone any future readers he may be fortunate enough to have, will need to know. He can only imagine an audience, and hope that experience tempered by good sense will assist his imagination. As a rule, I do not identify the very famous: Queen Victoria, for example, or Dickens. Very often, however, a famous name will occur in some special relation to Kipling. It then becomes a fit subject for a note explaining that relation: Theodore Roosevelt, Henry James, and Georges Clemenceau are instances.

I have tried, with only limited success, to identify all of Kipling's

---

[9] The typed copies of the Hill letters make an exception. They are sometimes so confused – conflating parts of letters of different dates, for example – that to print them in every case as they stand would require an impossibly complex annotation to correct them.

quotations. But I have, for the most part, left alone the allusions and echoes that run in a strong current just below the surface of his letters, as they do through all of his prose and verse. To have marked every point at which an allusion can be detected, or strongly suspected, would seriously overburden the annotation and would also, I think, have the effect of making the editor stand between the reader and the letters instead of discreetly at the side, where he ought to be.

One of the main interests of the letters is their record of Kipling's literary career, and I have aimed to clarify this record by providing titles, dates, and other bibliographical details wherever the letters present the opportunity to do so.

Kipling's vocabulary appears to be one of the most extensive among English writers, drawing as it does upon several languages and a variety of dialects, literatures, and trade or professional jargons. "Bobbery", "flyte", "gaff" (place of public amusement), "garron", "glair", "honing" (to pine or long for), "howked", "plowtered", "popattes", "raxed", "scrattel", "scutter", "slatting", "slummock", "sobbled", "squog", "territs", "thole", "thrang", "wannion", and "werish" are instances from the letters. This is a matter on which it is clearly impossible to be certain whether a reader will need any help or not, and I am mindful that most will have dictionaries. I have therefore considered many strange words as candidates for annotation, but I have in fact written notes on relatively few of them

ACKNOWLEDGEMENTS

When I think over the long array of friends, fellow-scholars, and institutions on whose help I have depended, the names of a group of enthusiastic Kiplingites gathered together in the Kipling Society stand first: Lisa Lewis, Margaret Newsom, John Shearman, Matilda Tyler, and George Webb have become my collaborators, whose encouragement, advice, and expert knowledge I could always count on. Professor Andrew Rutherford, Warden of Goldsmiths' College of the University of London, stands in a special relation of patronage to this edition. His edition of Kipling's short stories, published by Penguin in 1971, was decisive, when I read it, in determining me to undertake my work on the letters; and his recent edition of Kipling's *Early Verse* has provided a much-needed model of careful, expert editorial work on Kipling. I am grateful to him not only for the example of his scholarship but for the information and assistance I have had from him through conversation and correspondence both.

Charles Carrington has put all students of Kipling in his debt by his authorised life of Kipling, which has now stood the rigorous test of more than a generation's use; I have been privileged as well in having had the benefit of his acquaintance and of his direct personal encouragement.

Other scholars on whose work I have relied include the late Reginald Harbord and his collaborators on that remarkable work of amateur devotion, a monument to the enthusiasm and learning of the Kipling Society, *The Readers' Guide to Rudyard Kipling's Work*; Flora Livingston, J. McG. Stewart, and A. W. Yeats, whose bibliographies have cleared a way through the bibliographical jungle of Kipling's writing; and J. H. McGivering and Arthur Young, the compilers of the indispensable *Kipling Dictionary*.

My dependence upon librarians all around the world can be acknowledged only in the most summary form, and even that must be postponed until the final volume of this edition, in which a list of the sources of text will appear. Here, however, I must at least name John Burt, formerly Assistant Librarian at the University of Sussex, who, as the cataloguer and curator of the Kipling Papers, presided over the most important single collection of biographical and bibliographical information about Kipling. His work in arranging the collection and his unrivalled knowledge of its detail have materially simplified my task. I am grateful, too, to the many private collectors of Kipling's letters who have generously allowed me to make use of their property.

I have had essential support in this enterprise from several institutions, support for which I am deeply grateful. A fellowship from the National Endowment for the Humanities made it possible for me to carry out the first stages of my work in 1980; a sabbatical leave in 1985 was supported by a Guggenheim Fellowship and by a grant from the American Council of Learned Societies. My own institution, Pomona College, has steadily provided indispensable assistance to my work through its research fund and travel grants. Dean R. Stanton Hales, who administers the college's research funds, has been unfailingly understanding and helpful.

Jo Thompson, formerly the secretary to the Department of English at Pomona College, initiated me with patient forbearance into word-processing. Colleen Goya and Fielding Buck, then students at the Claremont Graduate School, helped me at the beginning to work out the questions of organising and transcribing Kipling's manuscripts. I have been fortunate in having had the help of three Pomona College undergraduates who have worked with me as research assistants over the past five years: Min Yi, Heidi Beck, and Lisa Umscheid.

To my wife I make no formal acknowledgements here, since her assistance is beyond acknowledging; but I would like her to know that I am aware of a debt not to be calculated.

List of Abbreviations and Short Titles

[ ] Matter supplied by the editor. When an item in square brackets in the text of a letter is followed by a question mark, that indicates a conjectured reading of an illegible or indecipherable word or phrase.
AK Alice Macdonald Kipling.
AL Autograph letter.
ALS Autograph letter signed.
Carrington, *Kipling* Charles Carrington, *Rudyard Kipling* (London: Macmillan, 1955; rev. edn., 1978).
CK Caroline Kipling (Mrs Rudyard Kipling).
CK *Diary* Typescript extracts and summaries by C. E. Carrington from the diary of Caroline Kipling; the original, now destroyed, in 45 volumes (1892–1936). Copy, University of Sussex.
CMG *The Civil and Military Gazette* (Lahore).
DNB *Dictionary of National Biography*.
Harbord, *Readers' Guide* Reginald Harbord (ed.), *The Readers' Guide to Rudyard Kipling's Works*, 8 vols (privately printed, Canterbury and Bournemouth, 1961–72).
Hobson-Jobson Henry Yule and A. C. Burnell, *Hobson-Jobson: A Glossary of Colloquial Anglo-Indian Words and Phrases*, ed. William Crooke (Delhi, 1968 [1903]).
JLK John Lockwood Kipling.
RK Rudyard Kipling.
OED *Oxford English Dictionary*.

Pinney, *Kipling's India*	Thomas Pinney (ed.), *Kipling's India: Uncollected Sketches 1884–88* (London: Macmillan, 1986).
Rutherford, *Early Verse*	Andrew Rutherford (ed.), *Early Verse by Rudyard Kipling 1879–1889* (Oxford: Clarendon Press, 1986).
Stewart-Yeats, *Bibliographical Catalogue*	James McG. Stewart, *Rudyard Kipling: A Bibliographical Catalogue*, ed. A. W. Yeats (Toronto: Dalhousie University Press, and University of Toronto Press, 1959).
Sussex	Kipling Papers, University of Sussex.
TLS	Typed letter signed.
USC	United Services College, Westward Ho!, North Devon.

Note: References to RK's works are, unless otherwise specified, to the English trade edition, the so-called "Uniform Edition", published by Macmillan beginning in 1899.

The place of publication of all other works cited, unless otherwise specified, is understood to be London.

Family Tree: Kiplings, Macdonalds, and Balestiers

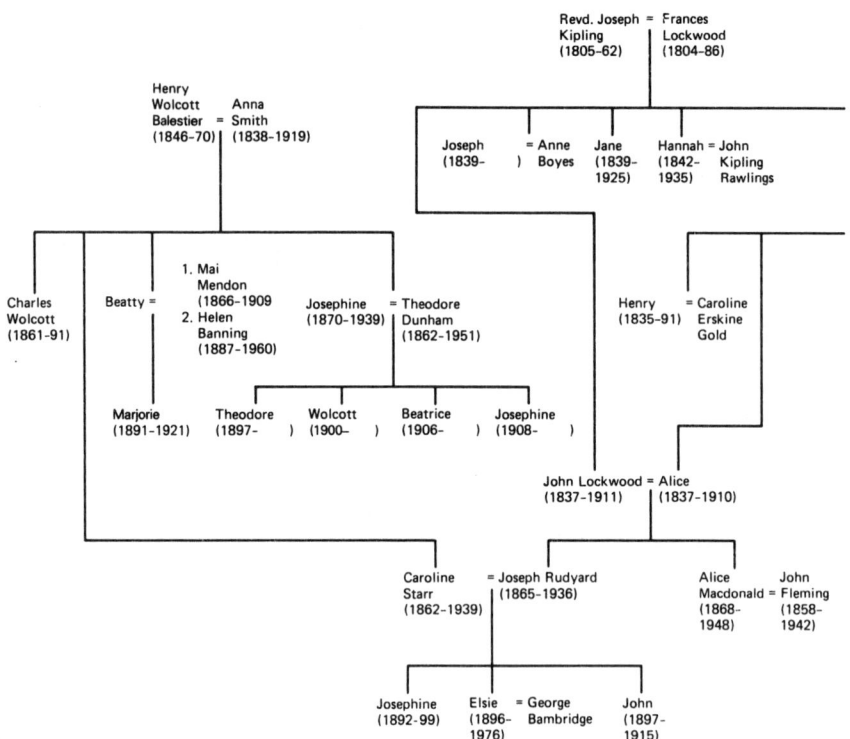

xxvii

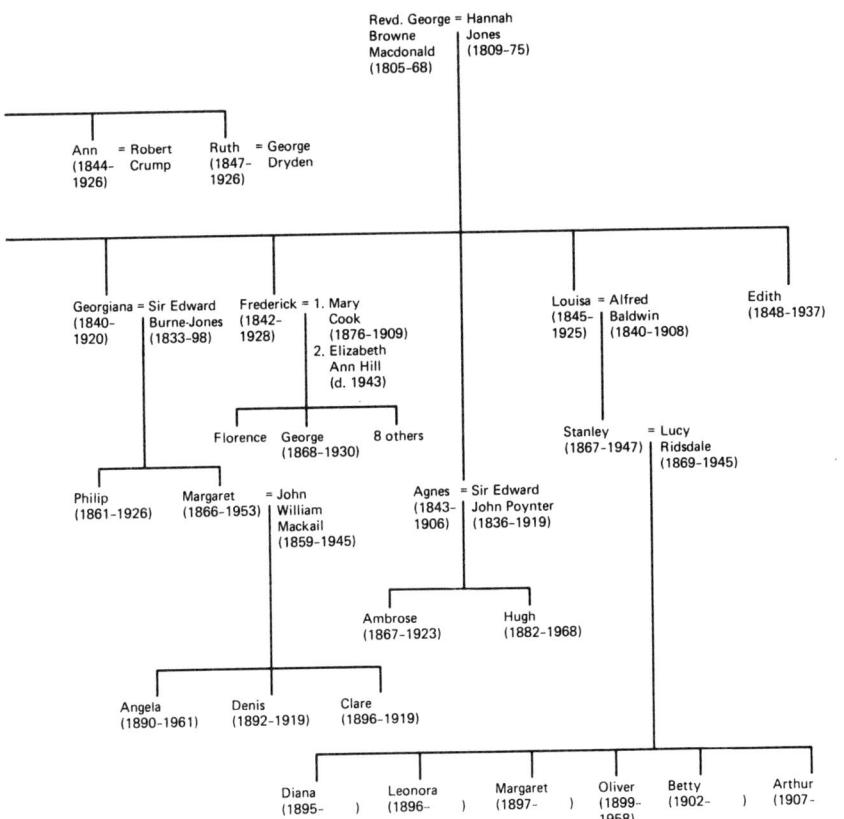

Chronology of Rudyard Kipling's Life, 1865–1936

1865	18 March	John Lockwood Kipling and Alice Macdonald married.
	12 April	JLK and Alice Kipling sail for India, where he is to be Professor of Architectural Sculpture at the government School of Art in Bombay.
	30 December	Rudyard Kipling born.
1868	early	RK accompanies Alice Kipling to England.
	11 June	Alice Macdonald Kipling ("Trix"), RK's sister, born in London.
	7 November	Alice Kipling and her two children leave England for return to Bombay.
1871	15 April	All four Kiplings leave Bombay for England.
	14 October	Alice Kipling takes her children to Southsea to be cared for by Mrs Pryse Agar Holloway.
	18 November	JLK and AK sail for Bombay.
1873	*c.* Christmas	RK visits The Grange, Fulham, the home of his uncle Sir Edward Burne-Jones and Aunt Georgie. He will visit The Grange regularly thereafter.
1875	April	JLK and AK move from Bombay to Lahore, where he is director of School of Art and curator of Lahore Museum.
1877	*c.* April	AK arrives in England (where she remains for the next three years); takes her children from the care of Mrs Holloway. They spend

Chronology of Kipling's Life, 1865–1936

		a summer near Epping, Sussex, and then take lodgings in London.
1878	16 January	RK enters the United Services College, Westward Ho!, North Devon.
	June	JLK arrives in England; RK sees him for the first time since 1871. They go to Paris, where JLK is in charge of Indian exhibit at the Paris Exhibition.
1880	c. Summer	Meets Florence Violet Garrard. By the time RK returns to India he regards himself as engaged to her.
1881		Edits United Service College's *Chronicle*. *Schoolboy Lyrics* privately printed in Lahore.
1882	20 September	Sails from London to join parents in Lahore and begin work on *Civil and Military Gazette*.
	Late October	Arrives in Lahore; resides with parents; assists his father in Lahore Museum.
	c. November	Begins work on *CMG* as assistant to the editor, Stephen Wheeler.
1883	July	AK leaves for England to bring Trix back to India.
	July–August	First visit to Simla.
	18 December	AK and Trix arrive in Lahore: the Kipling family reunited as "the family square".
1884	February	At work on a novel.
	March	RK writes series of special reports on "The Viceroy at Patiala", his first important independent work for the *CMG*.
	July	Engagement to Florence Garrard broken off.
	August	At Dalhousie with family.
	c. August	*Echoes*, a volume of verse parodies by RK and Trix, published.
1885	7 March	Conceives idea of "Mother Maturin", his never-published novel of India.
	March–April	Special correspondent of *CMG* at meeting

		of Viceroy of India and Amir of Afghanistan in Rawalpindi.
	April	To Simla on sick leave.
	30 April–10 May	Walking tour in Himalayas.
	16 August	Returns to Lahore.
	19 December	*Quartette* published; the work of all four Kiplings.
1886	5 April	Joins Masonic Lodge "Hope and Perseverance", no. 782, Lahore.
	c. May	*Departmental Ditties.*
	3 July–c. early August	At Simla.
1887	August–September	At Simla.
	c. November	Transferred to *The Pioneer*, Allahabad.
1888	January	*Plain Tales from the Hills.*
	May	Determines to return to England in February 1889.
	May–June	In Lahore as acting editor of *CMG* in Kay Robinson's absence.
	14–20 June	At Mussoorie with Mrs Hill.
	21 June–July	Last visit to Simla.
	July	Moves into Belvedere, the Hills' house in Allahabad.
	End of year	*Soldiers Three*, first of the "Indian Railway Library" series.
1889	9 March	RK and the Hills leave India from Calcutta, en route to Japan and the United States.
	15 April–11 May	In Japan.
	29 May–25 September	Travelling across United States, writing the *From Sea to Sea* letters.
	5 October	Arrives in Liverpool.
	9 October	Engaged to Caroline Taylor.
	17 October	Makes flying trip to Paris to see Mrs Hill.
	23 October	Arranges to take rooms in Embankment Chambers, London.
	25 October	Mrs Hill and Caroline Taylor leave London for India.
	November ff.	Stories and verses appear in *Macmillan's* and *St James's Gazette*. RK now sought after

Chronology of Kipling's Life, 1865–1936

		by London editors.
	c. November–December	Retains A. P. Watt as his literary agent.
	End of year	Introduced to Wolcott Balestier.
1890	January	"Indian Railway Library" stories republished in England, beginning with *Soldiers Three*.
	Late January–early February	Severe illness; engagement to Caroline Taylor broken off.
	February	Meets Flo Garrard again.
	25 March	Subject of leading article in *The Times*.
	May	JLK and AK arrive in England on furlough, to stay until September 1891.
	24–8 May	In Paris visiting Flo Garrard.
	September	Ill from overwork.
	October	Voyage to Naples.
	November?	First meets Caroline Balestier.
1891	March	Complete edition of *The Light that Failed*.
	June	Travels to New York and back with Uncle Fred Macdonald to see Henry Macdonald, who dies before they arrive.
	August	*Life's Handicap*.
	22 August	Sails on world tour.
	10–25 September	Cape Town.
	18 October–6 November	New Zealand.
	12–25 November	Australia.
	c. 17–18 December	Arrives in Lahore.
	c. 24 December	Learns of Wolcott Balestier's death and at once returns to England.
1892	10 January	Arrives in London.
	18 January	Marries Caroline Balestier.
	3 February–26 July	On honeymoon tour: United States, Canada, Japan.
	March	*Barrack-Room Ballads*.
	June	*The Naulahka*.
	July	Takes up residence in Brattleboro.
	29 December	First child, Josephine, born.
1893	June	*Many Inventions*.
	August	Move to "Naulakha", house designed and

xxxii   *Chronology of Kipling's Life, 1865–1936*

		built for them north of Brattleboro.
1894	3 April– 5 August	Trip to England: London, and Arundell House, Tisbury, Wilts.
	May	*The Jungle Book.*
	25 July	Makes speech at Westward Ho! on Cormell Price's retirement.
	August	Return to Vermont.
1895	26 February– 6 April	In Washington, DC.
	9 July–14 August	In England: Tisbury, Wilts.
	November	*The Second Jungle Book.*
	November–December	Upset over Venezuelan question: expects to return to England "for some long time".
1896	2 February	Elsie Kipling born.
	6 May	Quarrel with Beatty Balestier: RK has him arrested.
	12 May	RK appears at hearing and is humiliated.
	1 September	Sails for England.
	September	They take up residence at Rock House, Maidencombe, Devon.
	October	*The Seven Seas.*
1897	12 May	They leave Rock House for London.
	2 April	Elected to the Athenaeum.
	2 June	To North End House, Rottingdean.
	30 June–c. 8 July	On naval manoeuvres aboard a cruiser.
	17 August	John Kipling born.
	25 September	Move to The Elms, Rottingdean.
	October	"*Captains Courageous*".
1898	8 January– 30 April	Takes family to Cape Town; RK sees much of Rhodes and Milner; visits Kimberley, Bulawayo, Johannesburg.
	1–12 September	On naval manoeuvres with the Channel Fleet.
	30 September	*The Day's Work.*
	December	*A Fleet in Being.*
1899	25 January	Sails with family for New York. Children all ill on arrival.
	20 February	RK falls ill.

Chronology of Kipling's Life, 1865–1936   xxxiii

	6 March	Josephine Kipling dies.
	14 June	Family sails for England; RK never returns to US.
	June	*From Sea to Sea.*
	October	*Stalky & Co.*
	6 December	Hires his first automobile.
1900	20 January	To South Africa.
	19 March–1 April	In Bloemfontein on staff of *The Friend*.
	11 April	Return to England.
	8 December	To South Africa; they live at "The Woolsack" on the Rhodes estate.
1901	17 April	Return to England.
	20–31 July	With Channel Fleet on manoeuvres.
	October	*Kim.*
	21 December	To South Africa.
1902	16 April	Return to England.
	September	*Just So Stories.*
	3 September	Move to Bateman's, Burwash, Sussex.
	27 December	To South Africa.
1903	25 March– 5 April	To Johannesburg and Pretoria.
	22 April	Return to England.
	October	*The Five Nations.*
	12 December	To South Africa.
1904	March	Trip to Kimberley.
	13 April	Return to England.
	October	*Traffics and Discoveries.*
	10 December	To South Africa.
1905	5 April	Return to England.
	23 December	To South Africa.
1906	March	To Johannesburg and Pretoria.
	18 April	Return to England.
	October	*Puck of Pook's Hill.*
	17 December	To South Africa.
1907	6 April	Return to England.
	24, 27 June	Receives honorary degrees at Durham and

		Oxford.
	20 September–24 October	Canadian tour: Quebec, Montreal, Ottawa, Winnipeg, Calgary, Vancouver, Toronto.
	November	Awarded Nobel Prize.
	7–15 December	To Stockholm and back.
	28 December	To South Africa.
1908	15 April	Return to England: they do not visit South Africa again.
	17 June	Honorary degree from Cambridge.
	c. July	*Letters to the Family*.
	4–22 August	Motor tour through north of England.
	29 December	To Engelberg, Switzerland.
1909	2 March–13 April	In Rome.
	October	*Actions and Reactions*.
	c. November	*Abaft the Funnel*.
1910	January	In Engelberg.
	March	In Vernet-les-Bains, where CK takes sulphur treatment.
	26 March–2 April	Return to England by car through France.
	4 May	Death of Cormell Price.
	October	*Rewards and Fairies*.
	22 November	Death of Alice Kipling.
	29 December	To Engelberg.
1911	26 January	Death of John Lockwood Kipling.
	18 February–25 March	Vernet-les-Bains.
	25 March–8 April	Return to England by car through France.
	July	*A History of England*, with C. R. L. Fletcher.
	4–18 August	Tour in France with Mr and Mrs Max Aitken.
	17–24 October	Tour in Ireland with CK: Dublin, Belfast.
	28 December	To Engelberg.
1912	14 February–20 March	In Florence and Venice.
	20–27 March	Return to England via Paris.
	September	Motor tour in west of England.
	October	*Songs from Books*.
	26 December	To Engelberg.

Chronology of Kipling's Life, 1865–1936   xxxv

1913	7 February–15 March	Voyage to Egypt and up the Nile.
	15 March–7 April	Return to France; by car across France on return to England.
	April	RK's play, *The Harbour Watch*, produced.
	24 August–10 September	At Kessingland Grange, Norfolk.
	22 December	To Engelberg.
1914	4–7 February	Return to England via Paris.
	22 February–18 March	Vernet-les-Bains.
	18 March–17 April	Return to England by car through France.
	16 May	Speech on Ulster at Tunbridge Wells.
	23 July–10 August	At Kessingland Grange.
	10 September	Secures commission in Irish Guards for John Kipling from Lord Roberts.
1915	February	*The New Army in Training*.
	April	Bath.
	12–26 August	Visits French front.
	27 September	John Kipling reported wounded and missing. His body is never found.
	29 September	RK has gastritis: onset of permanent illness (duodenal ulcer).
	October	*France at War*.
	December	*The Fringes of the Fleet*.
1916	February	Bath.
	December	*Sea Warfare*.
1917	February	Bath.
	17 April	*A Diversity of Creatures*.
	May	Visits Italian front.
	August	Trip to Edinburgh.
	September	Joins War Graves Commission.
1918	February–March	Bath.
	c. April	*The Eyes of Asia*.
	10–24 September	Visit to Newquay, Cornwall.
1919	10 February–early March	Bath.
	April	*The Years Between*.

	3–29 September	Motor tour to Scotland.
1920	January	In Bath.
	21–25 February	To Isle of Wight; on return they visit Lorne Lodge, Southsea.
	16 March–24 April	Tour in France.
	June	*Letters of Travel.*
	8 July	Honorary degree from the University of Edinburgh.
	21 July–4 August	Visit to French battlefields, including Chalkpit Wood, where John Kipling was lost.
1921	18 February–23 March	To Algiers.
	23 March–4 May	Motor tour through France.
	3–27 September	Motor tour to Scotland.
	19 November	Receives honorary degree from the Sorbonne.
	27 November	Honorary degree from the University of Strasbourg.
1922	March–April	Tour to Gibraltar and Spain.
	10–15 May	Visit to French cemeteries; they hear King George's address at Boulogne.
	August	In London nursing home for examination.
	15 November	Has abdominal operation.
1923	Late January–February	Bath.
	30 March–23 May	By sea to Toulon; at Cannes, then return by car through France.
	April	*The Irish Guards in the Great War.*
	10 October	Rectorial address at St Andrew's.
	November	*Land and Sea Tales.*
1924	11–18 January	Trip to Paris.
	5–9 February	Bath.
	March–April	To Spain via Gibraltar; return to England by car through France.
	26 August–8 September	In France and Belgium; visits cemeteries.
	22 October	Elsie Kipling marries George Bambridge.

Chronology of Kipling's Life, 1865–1936 xxxvii

1925	1–9 February	Brussels, Amsterdam, Rotterdam.
	12 March–21 April	Motor tour in France.
	13–15 May	Brussels.
	3–9 October	Motor tour through west of England.
	10–17 November	Brussels and Paris.
	December	Seriously ill with pneumonia.
1926	5 February–17 May	By ship to the south of France; return to England by car through France.
	September	*Debits and Credits.*
	22 December	To Paris.
1927	6 January	Return to England.
	27 January–28 April	Voyage to Brazil; on return they land at Lisbon and drive through France to England.
	30 September–22 October	In France; RK at opening of Indian War Memorial.
	24 December	To Paris.
1928	8 January	Return to England.
	16 January	RK a pallbearer at funeral of Thomas Hardy.
	4 February–3 May	Voyage to Sicily, Italy, and Spain. Return to England by motor tour through France.
	March	*A Book of Words.*
	5–18 September	Motor tour to Scotland.
1929	1 February–April	Voyage to Egypt; visit war graves in Egypt and Palestine; return through France.
	28 October–6 November	Paris.
	20–7 December	Torquay.
1930	4 February–mid June	Voyage to Jamaica; CK falls ill; to Bermuda, where she is hospitalized. They return via Canada, avoiding the US.
	4 August	At dedication of monument, Dud Corner, Loos, to the missing (including John Kipling).
	October	*Thy Servant a Dog.*
1931	5–27 January	Bath.
	19 February–5 May	Voyage to Egypt; return by motor tour

	29 June–c. 3 July	through France. Paris.
	11–22 October	In nursing home for examination: doctors conclude against an operation.
1932	4 January– 10 February	Bath.
	29 February–17 April	To Monte Carlo and Cannes. Return via Paris by train (they have "put down" their cars).
	April	*Limits and Renewals.*
	28–30 May	Cambridge; RK made honorary fellow, Magdalene College.
	22 August– 4 September	Tour of the Midlands in new Rolls Royce.
1933	1 February–8 May	To Monte Carlo and Cannes; on return, in Paris, RK is diagnosed (5 May) as having duodenal ulcer.
	30 May	Visit to Elsie Bambridge at Wimpole Hall, Cambridgeshire.
	26 June	Elected to Institut de France.
	July	*Souvenirs of France.*
	7 July	To Wimpole Hall.
	22 December– 5 January 1934	Bath.
1934	29 January–11 May	Cannes.
	14 August– 4 September	To Channel Islands.
	October	*Collected Dog Stories.*
1935	31 January–3 May	Cannes.
	1 August	Begins his autobiography.
	15 August– 10 September	Marienbad.
1936	12 January	In London, RK taken ill.
	18 January	Dies in Middlesex Hospital.

Part One
From Schoolboy to Journalist

Westward Ho!–Lahore
1872–87

INTRODUCTION

We have only a few letters from Kipling's boyhood: one written when he was seven, another when he was thirteen, and then a few from the last years of his school life at the United Services College. The narrative of his life as presented in the letters does not properly begin until Kipling reaches India, aged sixteen, towards the end of 1882. Beginning in November of that year, within a month of his taking up his work on the *Civil and Military Gazette*, Kipling's letters thereafter provide an almost continuous narrative of his life down to the end (there is a break in the sequence in 1887: for reasons unknown to me, only four letters survive from that year).

The first note of Kipling's letters from India is that of excitement at entering into man's estate, and, indeed, the sudden transformation from schoolboy to responsible adult, operating in strange places under strange conditions, must have been startling enough: "Altogether, I find that this sort of life suits me down to the ground [he had been reading Mark Twain]. I have about seventy men to bully and hector as I please and am liable to bullying if I don't do *my* share of the business properly" (30 December 1882): this was written on a day when Kipling had had to take over the operation of the newspaper after his editor had suffered an accident, and is therefore not an account of his daily experience: but that such extraordinary circumstances could and did occur was a fact of his life in India from the beginning.

The first excitement wore off rather quickly: after all, Kipling's work was mostly routine, and a routine held down to the lowest level of interest by a suspicious and grudging editor. After a long stretch of newspaper drudgery, and after his first experience of the hot weather, Kipling had lost much of his first exuberance. His verse letter to his aunt at the end of 1883, though no doubt exaggerated for the sake of effect, is probably close enough to what he must often have felt:

> Do you think you could understand
>   What it is to live in the plains,
>   (The doleful dusty plains)
>   Alone, like hermit crab,
>   Where gas is never seen
>   And there's half the world between
>   Yourself and a hansom cab?

A new expansiveness, however, came with his increasing maturity and increasing responsibility. In 1884, Kipling began to be entrusted with important work for his paper. He began contributing original pieces in verse and prose; he wrote a column on local affairs, and he proved himself as a correspondent on special assignments, beginning with a trip to the native state of Patiala to cover a state visit of the Viceroy to the Maharajah (see 4 April 1884). After this, despite some local vicissitudes, his career in India moved in a steady upwards curve. The proprietor of Kipling's paper in Lahore, George Allen, was also the proprietor of a larger, more important, paper in Allahabad, the *Pioneer*; before the end of 1884 Allen had recognised the abilities of his young sub-editor and correspondent in Lahore (17 September 1884). It was only a matter of time before Kipling would be promoted from the smaller to the larger paper. Meantime, he overflowed with new ideas: he and his sister Trix published a volume of parodies called *Echoes* in 1884; he was planning and writing his never-finished, never-published Indian *magnum opus*, "Mother Maturin", and developing the idea of India, both native and British, as a subject for literature. At around the same time he was discovering and shaping two other of his distinctive Indian subject-matters: the British soldier, and the intrigues of Simla. In the process, he was acquiring the experience and the attitudes that would later find expression in his imaginative presentation of the empire. At the end of 1885 appeared *Quartette*, a special number of the *Civil and Military Gazette* entirely produced by the Kipling family: it included Kipling's "The Strange Ride of Morrowbie Jukes", one of the early masterworks of Kipling's Indian career. In the next year, 1886, appeared the collection of Kipling's light verse called *Departmental Ditties*. By the end of that year he was beginning to publish the series of short stories called *Plain Tales from the Hills*, in which Kipling's first, light-hearted version of Anglo-India is fully established, but which includes some sympathetic stories of native life as well: "Lispeth", for example, and "The Story of Muhammad Din".

To Louisa Baldwin,[1] [December? 1872?]
ALS: University of Sussex

The Grange[2] / North End / Fulham.

My dear Auntie,
Thank Uncle Alfred[3] for that nice Robinson Crusoe which he sent me. Thank Stan[4] for his card he sent me. I am going to draw a picture of Cordelia: – From your affectionate nephew Ruddy [drawing of "Cordelia" with "Ruddy" and "Stanley"; on reverse a map, with "Lilliput"; at top and "Bromdignag" written on one section].

p.s. Cousin Phil[5] has given me several suggestions in this letter.

Notes
1. Louisa Macdonald Baldwin (1845–1925), third of the four younger sisters of RK's mother; she married Alfred Baldwin (n. 3, below) in 1866.
2. The house where RK's aunt Georgiana, second oldest of the Macdonald sisters, had lived with her husband Edward Burne-Jones and their children since 1867; the house, on North End Road, just south of Kensington High Street, had belonged in the eighteenth century to Samuel Richardson, the novelist, who wrote *Pamela*, *Clarissa*, and *Sir Charles Grandison* there. To RK it was one of the holy places of his childhood, the house where, he wrote, he entered "paradise" for a month each year, when he stayed there with his aunt and uncle in the December holidays (*Something of Myself*, 1937, p. 11). (Sir) Edward Burne-Jones (1833–98), was the most distinguished and best-loved of RK's uncles.
3. Alfred Baldwin (1840–1908), the son of a prosperous iron founder with establishments in Worcestershire and Warwickshire. Baldwin combined skill in business management with religious intensity and interest in public affairs. Towards the end of his life he was chairman of the Great Western Railway and MP for Bewdley.
4. Stanley Baldwin (1867–1947), first Earl Baldwin of Bewdley, only child of Louisa and Alfred Baldwin; he succeeded his father in business and then, in 1908, in his seat for Bewdley. Baldwin's first cabinet office was in 1921 under Lloyd George; in 1923 he succeeded Bonar Law as Conservative Prime Minister. Defeated in that year, he was twice again Prime Minister, 1924–9 and 1935–7. Baldwin, a much-indulged only child of wealthy parents, educated at Harrow and Trinity College, Cambridge, and free to follow his own tastes, gave RK much to envy. Later Baldwin and RK disagreed on some important political points, but despite such strains their close cousinly relationship was never broken.
5. Philip Burne-Jones (1861–1926), 2nd Baronet, elder child of Edward and Georgiana Burne-Jones. He grew to be a gifted painter but a disappointment to himself and his friends through his lack of confidence in himself, his unlucky love-affairs, and his distractions in society.

To Stanley Baldwin, 20 December 1878
ALS: University of Sussex

[London]

Dear Stan

I am going to send you a sort of tale here about the pets we have at School[1] and the way we manage them. I'll begin with jack-daws first. We get them in the midsummer term when they are quite young and keep them like dogs as no one ever thinks of getting a cage for a jackdaw as they have their wings clipped and a servant or some farmer keeps them for you (for a consideration). One of our fellows had a jackdaw that he had got from the nest and it followed him where-ever he went as he never cut its wings. One day he left it at Sherborne[2] and came on to Bideford. The bird flew from Sherborne to Westward-Ho. He has got it now and is very proud of it. I think it is almost his only friend. He goes all over the place with this bird sitting on his shoulder or flying round and round him and then coming down on his cap.

You can get mag-pies as well but they arn't half so jolly and one fellow had five young hawks that he got out of a wood no end of a way off. Sometimes a fellow gets a squirrel and very often fellows get dormice. You keep those sort of animals in your play-box but they want a great deal of looking after. I got a mole once but they are very stupid and so are white and shrew mice, but sometimes a fellow goes in for them and then his play-box is anything but nice. I had a couple once and fed them on bread and milk, they smelt so I couldn't stand 'em. You can get young thrushes and black birds by the dozen but they are rather troublesome and you have to get a cage. The pets I like best are blind-worms, they take very little trouble to keep as they only want fresh moss every day. They look very pretty if you have a lot of them. I had a couple and they became very tame in a week or two. I am going to keep a lot of them next term. If you want some I think I could manage to send a pair to Slough,[3] if you haven't got that sort of creature. We keep silkworms a good deal, some fellows get more than a hundred cocoons from one season. By 100 cocoons I mean 100 for silk only. Do you have many silkworm keepers at your school? I am very glad you got all those prizes. I got one for English this term but that isn't much. Last term one of our fellows had a Bull-terrier that is about the largest description of pet we have. I got a "diver" last term it swam inshore into the shallows and so I got between it and deep water and "nabbed" it. I have got the skin some where. There are Herons and doves here. Sometimes a fellow gets a pair of doves but for my own part I dislike them they are so stupid.

There are lots of rabbits at Westward Ho but we never keep them for pets. I am very sorry to hear you have got chicken pox. I have had my attack some time ago. I suppose you will be able to be out by Xmas. I have had some very troublesome boils this term but they are all right now. I have been amusing myself by making traps (springles) this term. I only meant mine for tits, finches, and the like but a blundering black bird or thrush got in and smashed my horse-hair nooses and did no end of damage and finally bolted with a yard or two of horse-hair about his claws and body. I hope he liked it. I haven't got much more to say except I hope you will get quit of your chicken-pox and to wish you a merry Xmas and a Happy New Year.

              Your affecte. cousin
              Ruddy
              20 Dec. 1878.

Notes
1. In January 1878 RK entered the United Services College, a boarding school founded in 1874 by a group of retired officers to provide inexpensive education for their sons. It was located at Westward Ho!, an unsuccessful resort on the shores of Bideford Bay, North Devon, where a row of brick lodging-houses bought at bargain rates housed the school. Preparation for the Army examinations dominated the work of most boys, though others were preparing for different careers, including the Indian Civil Service. The first headmaster was Cormell Price (see 30 December 1882), a friend of RK's parents.
2. Presumably the Sherborne in Dorset.
3. Baldwin attended Hawtrey's Preparatory School, Aldin House, Slough.

To Mary Mapes Dodge,[1] 22 August 1879
Text: Catharine Morris Wright, "How 'St Nicholas' Got Rudyard Kipling", *Princeton University Library Chronicle*, XXXV (1974) 259

To the editor –
St. Nicholas Magazine

Dear Sir:
 I send with this a little poem[2] which I hope you may think suitable for St. Nicholas Magazine.
 I am an English schoolboy, thirteen years old and the verses describe an episode in last term.
 I believe American schoolboys are wisely allowed more liberty than we enjoy and may perhaps sympathize with the difficulties of our dusky crew.
              Yours truly,

J. R. Kipling³

United Services College.
Westward Ho
North Devon
England.
22 August 1879

Notes
1. Mrs Dodge (1831–1905), the author of *Hans Brinker*, had been editor of *St Nicholas*, a highly successful monthly for children, since its founding in 1873.
2. "The Dusky Crew", seven stanzas describing how three schoolboys are caught in their off-limits lair and punished; it is the earliest evidence for the existence of the Dunsterville–Beresford–Kipling combination at the centre of *Stalky*. Mrs Dodge rejected the verses, which appear in *Schoolboy Lyrics*.
3. A very rare instance of RK's using the initial of his first name, Joseph.

To Edith Macdonald,¹ [c. January 1881?]
Text: Copy, University of Sussex

U.S. College

Dear Auntie

I promised to send you some more of my scribblings as soon as I had written them. Here is the latest batch.² Please give me your opinion on them as soon as possible. I've got one on hand now and your verdict on *these* will have a great deal to do with it.

How did Stanley manage to get down to Slough? We were six hours late coming down and had to flounder about with the snow up to our waists, looking for a public-house. It was very exciting work for there was a river lying about somewhere and as it was pitch-dark and no parapet worth speaking of to keep us on the bridge, we had to go slowly. We found a house at last and stayed there four mortal hours while they were clearing away the drifts. Afterwards it all seemed like a bad dream, but it was a new experience anyhow. I was never block't up before, in the snow – and I never want to be, again.³

The weather has been very bad for the last few days and there was a body found on the beach last week. Several ships have gone to pieces on Morte Rock⁴ and they say there are nearly thirty-five men missing. That means a good deal to some bodies in Bideford and Appledore. Bideford Quay was covered with little knots of men talking over the news and the way the widows "took it". One old fellow in a jersey was terribly upset, I never saw anything so strange in my life. He was as grey in the face as the river and shaking like a leaf.

I have got something swollen in my neck, they say it's a gland and

I'm regularly blistered with iodine in consequence. It makes your neck look like crocodile-skin and utterly ruins your temper.

Notes
1. Edith Macdonald (1848–1937), youngest of the sisters of RK's mother. She never married, and spent her life living with one or another of her sisters, especially with Louisa Baldwin. Like most of the Macdonalds, she wrote, though she published almost nothing. She was evidently one of RK's earliest and most sympathetic critics: see 12–13 June 1883.
2. Two poems by RK, "Requiescat in Pace" and "Credat Judaeus!" are copied out at the end of the letter. Both appear in *Schoolboy Lyrics*, with many variations from the texts accompanying this letter. They are probably among the very earliest of RK's surviving verses. It was after his second year at school – that is, in 1880 – that "the tide of writing set in" on RK (*Something of Myself*, p. 33).
3. This perhaps refers to what RK later called "the 'great snow' that paralysed all England from the 18th to the 24th of January in 1881" (*CMG*, 30 December 1886).
4. Just up the coast towards Ilfracombe from Westward Ho!

To Edith Plowden,[1] [August 1881][2]
ALS: University of Sussex

                                            c/o Mr. Durrant / Sorrell Farm / Fittleworth[3] /
                                                                             Tuesday afternoon.

My dearest Miss Plowden

Many thanks for letter and order enclosed.[4] Am at present rather worried – Listen. You know I possessed a photo of Miss Garrard,[5] for some time past I've missed it, of course I *couldn't* make a noise about the business and have to do all the searching by myself. It just struck me, that it might be in my book of Poems.[6] I've looked every where I can think of. *Please* send it along as soon as possible if you have found it.

                                                                                          Ruddy.

Notes
1. Edith Plowden, daughter of an Anglo-Indian family, was a friend of both the Macdonald and Kipling families. She lived in Lahore with her brother, a judge, in the 1870s, when she saw much of RK's parents; her MS recollections of this acquaintance are now at the University of Sussex. Miss Plowden never married; she studied art, and published some stories towards the end of the century. In her old age she was a principal informant for Lord Baldwin when he wrote his biography of RK's mother and aunts, *The Macdonald Sisters* (1960). Her note on this letter says that she had many letters from RK before this one, "but destroyed and returned [sic] to him later by his wish."
2. So dated in a note by Miss Plowden on this letter.

3. I cannot explain this address, except to note that RK was on his school holidays at this date. Fittleworth in in West Sussex.
4. Probably for a subscription to the *United Services College Chronicle*, the school magazine that RK edited from June, 1881: two numbers had appeared under his editorship at this point.
5. Florence Violet Garrard (1865–1938). Little is known of her, though she was a powerful influence on RK's life. She lived as a paying guest at the house in Southsea where RK had been before her. RK's sister Trix (*see* 28 January 1882) appears to have continued to visit Southsea, and it was in calling for Trix that RK met Flo, in 1880 (Carrington, *Kipling*, p. 41). By the time he left for India in 1882 he considered himself engaged to her; the affair, if it can be called that, was not decisively over until 1890. All the coolness seems to have been on Flo's side. After studying at the Slade School, and in Paris, she exhibited regularly in London and in Paris. She lived in Chelsea, where she kept a collection of cats, taught painting and drawing, and dressed in mannish style. Maisie, in *The Light that Failed*, derives from Flo Garrard.
6. One of the MS books of RK's poems that circulated among family and friends in the early 1880s. Four, at least, of these survive, three at Sussex and one in the Berg Collection of the New York Public Library; they are somewhat later than the date of this letter, however. Many of RK's early verses have Flo Garrard as their addressee or their theme.

To Mrs John Tavenor Perry,[1] 25 January 1882
ALS: Huntington Library

U.S. College. / Jan. 25th. 82 / "The Cuckoo's Nest."

Dear Mrs. Perry,

In the words of the poet "you see before you" a youth in his shirtsleeves, eating cake and driving Coco[2] to the verge of insanity. As far as I remember that is all I have been doing all the term – as yet. By the way I have got an imposition to vary the monotony of existence, but as I don't intend to do it I feel as dull as it is possible for me. The "other two"[3] are out china hunting.[4] Yesterday I got rather a pretty liquer glass (after a long hunt) with white curls up the stem [drawing of stemmed glass]. It's nearly a century old.

As you don't know the place I'm afraid I couldn't convey to your mind any idea of its flatness and dullness generally. Nevertheless I am hardened enough to prefer it to Warwick gardens.[5] [drawing of Peak Frean biscuit box]

I send you a sketch of a piece of bric a brac in the window. It has completely spoilt my view and since I am too lazy to rise from my chair I am pelting it with cinders and coal. This is [drawing of blackened left hand] a view of the hand I'm writing with – (Done the wrong way) so don't be astonished if the paper is a trifle smudgy. When I got in yesterday the two other devils worse than myself has [*sic*] discovered an infernal machine –

A. is a pair of bellows
B. India rubber tubing
C. A penny whistle [drawing of bellows, tube, and whistle] Of course you can see that the power of noise is almost unlimited and as it can be worked by the foot you can inconvenience your neighbours with very little exertion. We "laid on" that instrument to a next door study like this [drawing showing "our study", bellows and whistle, "next floor", and party wall] and we got it through the ceiling by a little hole in the corner. For nearly two hours they could not make out where the row came from. I condescend to practical jokes you see when I am at school.

They have decided to let me have my own way as regards pictures in the Chronicle. Can you get the address of the Lithograph Machine Seller from Mr. Perry? I've forgotten it. Moreover I've forgotten that it is close on post time and I must finish this note.

More next time. You ought to have your next letter on study paper with a device of our very own.

Ruddy

[the signature ornamented with faces in the loops of the letters and a fish in the tail of the "y"]

I'm going to post

[drawing of RK carrying oversize letter accompanied by small barking dog]

Notes

1. Mary, the wife of John Tavenor Perry (1842–1915), an architect who retired from a successful practice in 1891 to devote himself to writing studies in architectural history. I have not learned anything about his wife or about their connection with RK. Presumably it came about through some professional acquaintance with JLK. Mrs Perry was only 32 years old in 1882 (Census of April 1881).
2. RK's terrier.
3. As RK's study mates are called in the refrain of "The Dusky Crew": "me and the Other Two". They were George Charles Beresford and Lionel Charles Dunsterville. Beresford (1864–1938), the M'Turk of *Stalky*, of an Irish family, had entered USC in 1877. He studied engineering at Cooper's Hill College and went to India in the Public Works Department but returned because of ill health. He studied art at the Slade School, took up photography, and made a professional career of that; he also became a successful antique dealer. After their school years RK saw Beresford hardly at all, but Beresford was an early and active member of the Kipling Society and published *Schooldays with Kipling* in 1936, a rather strained and cranky memoir.
    Dunsterville (1865–1946), the original of Stalky, was at USC 1876–83; he was in Pugh's house with RK, and was his study mate together with Beresford for the last two years of RK's residence at Westward Ho! Commissioned in 1884, he retired as a Major-General in 1918; in 1925 he became the first president of the Kipling Society. He published a series of casual and good-natured memoirs after his retirement.

4. See the account of the mania for "curios" in Beresford's *Schooldays with Kipling* (New York, 1936) pp. 151–65.
5. Where Miss Winnard and the Miss Craiks lived: see 28 January 1882.

To Alice Macdonald Kipling,[1] 28 January 1882
Text: Copy, by JLK, University of Sussex

[Westward Ho!]

Given from the Cuckoo's nest to the Beloved Infant –

Greeting

I sit in the midst of my study
   With cake crumbs adorning my hair
My boots are confoundedly muddy
   And are leaving wet marks on the chair
That supports the fair feet of your Ruddy
   As he rests with stale cake in his hair.

I am full of a sense of importance,
   Of lobster, cream, pilchards and cake
And I feel in my – bosom grim portents
   That herald the course of an ache
I remark I am racked with grim portents
   That usher abdominal ache.

Yet I write you this letter fraternal
   I indite you this brotherly note
Tho' my tortures are waxing infernal
   I write as I ever have wrote
Observe that my tone is fraternal
   And I write as I ever have wrote.

Be it known to you fairest of females
   That dulness is dominant here
And there's little to interest we males
   Whose smallness is lesser than beer
I complain that in spite of our three mails
   Per diem there comes nothing here.

To Alice Macdonald Kipling, 28 January 1882

Moreover the weather is wondrous
   And skies that should rain only shine
We have dry chalk and gravel roads under us
   And the sun is at work before nine
I may state as a fact still more wondrous
   I too am at work before nine.

And further to tell you, the Kingsley
   Memorial College[2] is built
And throughout it strange carpenters' things lie
   And paint-pots are lavishly spilt
Id est they are fitting the Kingsley
   With boardings and carvings and gilt.

By a special train chartered at Bristol
   The guilt [*sic*] comes, some two hundred strong
The sons of land-owners who missed all
   Their rents when the Green Isle went wrong.
To be plain, all the boys come from Bristol
   By the packets of Vermouth and Long.

We have purchased some tea-pots of delft ware
   We found in a Bideford shop
That crammed on the back of a shelf were
   (Mrs. Morten's – she takes things to p-p)
In a shop where a friend and myself were
   Knocking round as we do in a shop.[3]

I have got three most quaintest of glasses
   For Miss Winnard,[4] (I'll send 'em along)
Whose shape all description surpasses
   And I purchased them all for a song
Which means that the price of those glasses
   Was entirely other than long.

And now since the sun is descending
   I must finish my brotherly note
I must make of beginning an ending
   I must finish this versified note
Take a picture I've drawn[5] as an ending
   Most fit for a metrical note.

                               January 28th 1882

Notes

1. Alice Macdonald Kipling (1868–1948), afterwards Mrs John Fleming, always called Trix, RK's sister. Like RK, she was taken to England in 1871 and left with him at Mrs Holloway's in Southsea. She remained there some time after his departure for Westward Ho! and then went to school in London, where she was at the time of this letter. "Trix", short for "Tricksy", was a nickname given by her father: it has misled many writers into calling her Beatrice or Beatrix.
2. The Kingsley Memorial College, occupying a terrace almost next door to USC, opened in 1882; it was set up in consequence of troubles in Ireland, most of the students migrating from the region of Portarlington. The school aimed to provide for the sons of lawyers, clergymen, and doctors the sort of education that USC gave to the sons of military men.
3. This is perhaps the Bideford shop described by Beresford, *Schooldays with Kipling*, pp. 151–4. "Pop" means "pawn".
4. Miss Winnard was one of three maiden ladies with whom Trix lived at 26 Warwick Gardens, Kensington; the other two were Mary and Georgiana Craik, daughters of the writer George Lillie Craik. Through common friends, the Kipling family was put in touch with the "ladies of Warwick Gardens" (as RK called them) and entrusted their children to them after the Southsea years: RK spent more than one holiday with them, and Trix lived with them during the years that she was at school nearby. The tone of the house was literary: the Craik sisters had memories of their father's association with Carlyle and were themselves acquainted with Jean Ingelow and Christina Rossetti. Georgiana was a prolific writer of novels, composed "on her knees, by the fireside" (*Something of Myself*, p. 21).
5. The picture is not in the copy.

To Mrs John Tavenor Perry, 31 January–1 February 1882
ALS: Huntington Library

> Tuesday Eve. / [a?] 24 / U.S. Coll. / Jan. 31st "82" / From the Cuckoo's nest / [on scroll in upper right corner: PUNCTUALITY IS THE THIEF OF TIME]

Dearest Mater,

A thousand thanks for your voluminous epistle which came at tea time and which I am answering fairly punctually!!!!!!!!! If I can dig up my store of stamps from the clutches of the rapacious Dunsterville this ought to reach you on Thursday. I'm up to my eyes in work and am a reformed character entirely. The Chronicle is bothering me awfully. Every Editor wishes to do right in his own eyes – (that's misquoted I'm afraid)[1] and I most certainly protest against it. The result is that I'm nearly at my wits end to make the three pull together – as I haven't the faintest intention of going to the wall.

Cocoa seems to be awfully unwell, I'm afraid she's poisoned by some stuff she took on a poaching expedition. Huntlea[2] says she poached terribly in the Holidays. Moral – Thus we see that it is safest to poach where there is no poison. Poor little beastie! I made her drunk to day

To Mrs John Tavenor Perry, 31 January–1 February 1882

and it seemed to do her a little good. She revived thus [sketch of reclining dog]!

Edwardes³ has left here and his address is

> 5 Derwent Road
> Annersley

As you know, I'm certain they would be most delighted to come to you.

WEDNESDAY [   ]⁴ OR NINE

The new Kingsley Coll has put in an appearance. They are a loosely made, undersized set of Irish Kernes – and they wear forage caps [sketch of comic head with forage cap]!!! The rest of their uniform is very nondescript. Thank Tav from me for the promise of the circulars. The other editors are awfully set against the idea. I had a P.O.O.⁵ from the parents today enclosing £2. Wherefore I am in a good temper and smile [self-portrait head smiling]. It's very difficult to draw on this kind of paper but that's a fairly faithful photo.

Properly speaking I ought to be at work on History but I'm not. Hence we see – Honesty is not the best Policy. You seem to be indulging in a regular butterfly round of festivities since I left. Existence here is "healthy, regular, and dull –" (a Chronicle phrase).⁶ I'm trying to get up a little diversion this afternoon by going in for some single-stick with a fellow. After this fashion [sketch of masked head, holding stick]. One gets knocked about a little but it's a mild form of fun and does no one any harm. Remember me to every one at Putney.⁷ How does Miss Davy⁸ take to the dead languages? I have a vision of her being schooled to decline and conjugation – I will refrain from putting that vision on paper.

Ruddy

How long was Tav down with his malady – you never told me how he was at all.

Notes
1. Perhaps RK has Proverbs 12:15 in mind: "The way of a fool is right in his own eyes."
2. A College servant?
3. Stanley Malcolm Edwardes (1863–1937), who briefly shared a study with RK before the era of Dunsterville and Beresford. He entered the Indian Army in 1884 and retired as a Brigadier-General. He is the original of "Dick Four" in *Stalky & Co*.
4. Word illegible.
5. Post Office Order.
6. If so, I have not found it in RK's contributions to the *Chronicle*: "School life seems . . . regular and monotonous enough" occurs in the *Chronicle* of 30 June 1881.

7. The Perrys lived at 12 The Terrace, Putney.
8. Elizabeth M. Davey was the governess living with the Perry family.

To Alice Macdonald Kipling, [c. early February 1882]
Text: Copied in Alice Macdonald Kipling to Edith Plowden, 8 March 1882 (ALS, Sussex)

[Westward Ho!]

Est ce que mes Tantes sont donc folles?¹ Suppose the other Aunts indulge in second editions! Shan't we become venerable! At first I had a confused idea that I was an Uncle or a grandpapa, but on mature reflection I find that I am only another cousin. Never mind. I ain't cut out of any expectations and I wish her joy. Can you imagine Uncle Edward's face?²

Notes
1. RK's Aunt Aggie – Agnes Macdonald Poynter (1843–1906) – had just had her second child, Hugh, on 28 January, almost fifteen years after the first. According to Mrs Kipling's letter, RK had just seen notice of the event in the *World* of 8 February.
2. (Sir) Edward John Poynter, PRA (1836–1919), in his youth one of the Paris group described in du Maurier's *Trilby*, became a steady and distinguished contributor to the Royal Academy for nearly sixty years. He worked in a variety of forms and media, but was particularly known for paintings of classical and historical subjects. He held a remarkable sequence of high professional positions: he was the first Slade Professor, Director for Art of the South Kensington Museum (as it then was), and Director of the National Gallery before succeeding Millais as President of the Royal Academy in 1897. Poynter was a man of impressive dignity; his wife was the beauty among the Macdonald sisters. Producing children was expected of neither.

To Mrs John Tavenor Perry, 9 March 1882
ALS: Library of Congress

U.S. College / March 9th. 1882

Dear Mater,

I'm afraid I've been terribly behind hand in answering your last letter. The fact is, my hernia has been playing all sorts of little games of late and for a fortnight or so I have been doing no work. Blissful condition isn't it? I'm as well as can be now – to testify to my complete recovery, I went to Bideford a day or two ago and got chased back by an irate farmer because I wrote a verse on the back of his tax-cart[1] [drawing of RK being chased] "Conceive me if you can" something after this fashion. The farmer was very bandy legged and I got away.

Today – Thursday – I have been doing a lot of work – very unusual thing for me – and am resting on my laurels, which means that I'm not going to do nothing at all for the rest of the day. By the time this reaches you, you will be just getting your last "duds" together I suppose. A pleasant trip to you. When do you come back again.

I spent some portion of the time during which I was incapacitated, in hatching out a metrical sentimentality. It has no very special merit about it – but I send it along nevertheless.

> Greeting.
>
> What comfort can I send thee sweet,
>   Save that pain is – we know not why,
>   Save that pain lives – and will not die
> What comfort? I can but repeat
>   Our old philosophy.
>
> Bear and be patient oh my sweet
>   Pain is – but is all pleasure over
>   Pain lives – but am I not thy lover.
> Through all the changes we shall meet,
>   And all new years discover.
>
> What comfort can I send thee sweet
>   Pain is – and none may flee from it,
>   Pain lives – nor softens any whit
> A fire with a constant heat
>   Our birth sees firstly lit.
>
> Bear and be patient oh my sweet!
>   Pain is – and none may tell us why;
>   Pain lives – and dies not till we die, –
> Till the last pulse has ceased to beat.
>   And after – then come I.[2]

What's your opinion of it? Yesterday saw the Chronicle go to press – so there's one great load off my mind. It will be a very large number this time and has the first portion of a serial in it.[3]

I hope to get it out in a week or so, but the men about here are most abominably slow. I have to trot in to Bideford nearly every day and explain how the thing is to be done. Sometimes I [drawing of RK at type case] have to set the type myself and tell them how I want it spaced. They are very dull. On Wednesday we were enlivened by a wreck – two men and a boy – all three saved but the ship went to pieces after a bit. Wrecks are awfully prosaic things when you look at them. I am convinced that to get a proper idea of the sea, one should only read about it.

It's astonishing to think how quickly we are through the term. Here are seven weeks gone already and I've scarcely had time to breathe. Entre nous – I don't quite like the idea of the holidays coming round again so quickly.

The school – to put it mildly – is intensely amused with the attempt of the Queen's life.[4] I'm afraid we are scarcely loyal and patriotic enough – but anyhow three parts of us laughed and the Democratic quarter seemed to be sorry. At all events we got a holiday on the strength of it. So I am very well contented. Long live the Queen.

On looking over this letter it strikes me as being an extremely I-y one. You must make allowances for a person who has had no one but himself and his seediness to meditate on, for some twenty days.

The month's housekeeping falls on me – That's to say I look after the study commissariat. Here's an order – a week old

    30 lbs sugar must
    6 tins condensed milk
    3 lbs coffee
    2 lbs cocoa
    2 lbs oat meal
    7 lbs biscuit

There are only three of us. Did you ever come across such a lot of little pigs!

There is some talk of having a cabinet photo of the study – it would be great fun if we do.

                Ruddy

[drawing of RK with packages on his back]

                          The way we live now

Notes
1. An open, two-wheeled, one-horse farm cart.
2. Four copies of these verses are at Sussex, one sent by RK to Edith Plowden, one in Alice Kipling's hand, and two in RK's hand in notebooks filled with early verse.

3. "Ibbetson Dun", two parts of which appeared in the USC *Chronicle*, 20 March and 3 June 1882 (uncollected).
4. A young man named Maclean fired a shot at Victoria as she went from the train to her carriage at Windsor station on 2 March. RK's "Ave Imperatrix" was a school exercise on the event, published in the *Chronicle* of 20 March.

To Mrs John Tavenor Perry, [29] April 1882
ALS: Huntington Library

U.S. College, / Saturday night, 8.30, / My Den in an awful mess.

Dearest Mater,

This is just a line to open the Correspondence between us again. You can answer when you please. I got in last night about Seven oclock – awfully hungry and very cross. My charge young Richmond[1] had come without an overcoat, so I had to wrap him up in my old brown "wopper" during a three mile ride in the "brakes." There was no end of a wind on, and I'm paying for my insane generosity with a severe cold in the head. Thus we see that generosity is *never* the best policy. Where's my nose rag?

We – that's my study mates – have been eating cheese and biscuits by the pound. I feel awfully stuffy and very much inclined to go to sleep. I can't say that anything extraordinary has happened since I came down. The Kingsley College boys seem to have got into rather a scrape. One ran away and I think two more were expelled. Not bad work for about ten weeks of a spring term, is it?

The greater part of the day has been spent in getting our stores into order – 30 lbs of sugar and a seven pound tin of biscuits occupied us for a long time as we didn't quite see how to stow them. At last we managed to cram them away somehow [drawing of overstuffed cupboard]. Our cupboard bulges a wee bit but that doesn't matter. I was a good deal occupied with that young Richmond. His greenness is something wonderful. I am a sort of a nurse to him. The red streaks on the paper were caused by boiling a stoppered bottle of red ink over the gas. Like the barmaid in the Hans Breitmann ballads it "burst with a bang."[2] – I was almost drenched with the ink, and I feel moist and bleeding all over my head. The ink looks very melodramatic as it trickles down my manly brow.

I must shut up this epistle now, as I've got to grind away at the Chronicle. Write soon if you can find time. I can answer at once.

Ruddy

Notes
1. Francis George Richmond (1868–1933), oldest son of the painter Sir William Blake Richmond. He had come down with RK in order to enter USC, where he stayed only briefly.
2. *The Breitmann Ballads* (1869), by the American Charles Godfrey Leland, were among RK's favourite schoolboy reading.

To Mrs John Tavenor Perry, 22 May 1882
ALS: Huntington Library

U.S. College / May 22nd 82

Dearest "Mater,"

I'm afraid I've been almost as long in answering your letter as you were over mine: the fact is that I've been rather unwell and upset of late. It is the heat of summer that always takes it out of me like this. Moreover I've been up to my eyes in work – articles for local newspapers and gas and sewerage comments, poems, schoolwork, Russian, Chronicle, and stories flying through my head like a railway train.[1]

It may amuse you to know that everything that has ever existed between myself and the fair F.G.[2] *is entirely at an end*. Draw what conclusion you will from this statement. Aren't I a queerly constructed youth. Reckless is a mild way to put my present state of mind. I'm making it *very* lively down here just to work off steam and par consequence – am always in hot water. Every Thursday Friday and Sunday I've got to attend an hour's Choir practice and the constant la-la-la-la-la-la-la-la-la-la-la-la-la-la brings out all sorts of queer notes. I can't make out where I get 'em from. The high ones come over the back of my head, or out of an ear, or somewhere under my scalp. I believe I'm getting on fairly well – but I can't take much interest in the business.

I must apologize to Miss Davy for quitting Putney in so unceremonious a fashion – it was entirely unintentional I assure you. My head is aching awfully and the letters are hopping about in front of my eyes. Excuse this most villanous scrawl. Write soon and I'll send you a longer one in return.

Ruddy

Notes
1. RK studied Russian briefly under Cormell Price (*Something of Myself*, pp. 36–7). RK's contributions to local newspapers remain elusive, though there is plenty of testimony to their existence, including this letter and that of 28 May. JLK reported to Cormell Price, 17 June 1882, that RK "is writing nonsense about sanitation etc. in some local paper – terribly fluent and diffuse – but altogether wide of any useful purpose" (copy,

Lorraine Price). Stephen Wheeler remembered JLK showing to him in India in 1882 a "leader" by RK "on the misdeeds of the local vestry or something of that sort" (5 July 1899: MS, Harvard); and Dunsterville recalled that "when we were hard up we used to rush him into our study and sit over him until he dashed off an article for the local paper, for which he got ten bob" (*Kipling Journal*, December 1940, p. 23). The local paper was doubtless the *Bideford Gazette*. RK refers to his "stuff" in that paper in a letter to Dunsterville, 20–1 January 1927 (MS, Sussex). Several likely items appear in the *Gazette* between February and June 1882, but nothing that can be definitely attributed to RK.

2. Florence Garrard.

To Mrs John Tavenor Perry, 28 May [1882]
ALS: Huntington Library

My Den. / 10.30. / Sunday Morn. / U.S. College. / May. 28th.

Dear Mater,

Many thanks for your note which was a good deal "better than nothing." You are becoming quite a regular correspondant. As for the meaning of my letter it amounts solely to this – A youth has just swallowed his first bitter pill: and you must excuse him if he finds it a little harsh in his mouth. My own selfishness prevents me from going to the Devil at once – besides this is merely a temporary "flick" which, in all probability, is the forerunner of half-a-dozen more. Very sorry if I have disturbed you in any way by anything I might have said in a moment of weakness – but I'm all right now.

As to how it all came about that, of course, is a very minor evil. The thing's done *now*, and, as far as I can see, there remains no chance of improvement. I must e'en "grin and bear it." I'm free to confess that I feel very little equal to "grinning" now, but the rest is fairly easy.

I am rather amused – to my shame be it said – that your man and wife should take flight again so swiftly. Does this involve another excursion to the Soho Bazaar? If so, I feel for you deeply. Isn't there some writer or other who says that a man and his wife in service have opportunities for hatching diabolical plots on the wine cellar and larder. I think it's Douglas Jerrold.[1] Perhaps – I don't wish to be uncharitable – but perhaps it's just as well that they are going away. –

My eyes are feeling a little weak this term – but I think it's only on account of the heat. They still serve me very well to write with – and that's about all I want. Otherwise, I am in rude and robust health and shall astonish you by the strength of my frame when, (like Yankeedoodle) I "come to town." By the way, talking of coming to town reminds me of one of Miss Winnard's letters – wherein I learn that they are going to Switzerland for their Holidays, and that we – Trix and I – shall spend that time at Skipton,[2] the Grange and with *you*. Is that really settled? If so, there will be something well worth going home for – but I wouldn't mind betting that you will be awfully bored with me before half the time is over as I suppose that my frame of mind won't be quite the happiest in the world. You must turn me out into the garden to recover myself there. Seriously though – I can think of nothing I should enjoy better or *wish for more* than a visit to Putney. By the way where will Tav be for that time? I've got a lot of my newspaper articles I wish to shew him, and he might as well be driven insane in midsummer as later on. On the next page I send you a set of three sonnets I have written. They aren't up to much and perhaps they *might* be called "reg'lar downright bad," but it's possible that they will interest you: – wherefore I send them.

Their Consolation.

Alas! Alas! it is a tale so old.
  Alas! Alas! it's pain is very new.
  It is a strange, hard, thought for me and you
That warm limbs and strong hearts should e're grow cold
  That ever Life should cease within our eyes,
  And silence for a season fall on each,
  And, for a season, Loving, ended be
Ah! sweet, what need to follow phantasies
When Love's best fruit lies hard within our reach,
And nought disturbs immutability.
Trust me, when weak the heart and faint the hand,
  And Death, our master little tarrieth,
Then, through Death's own blow shall he understand
  How Love, is stronger than all Earthly death.

Discovery.

We found him in the woodlands – she and I –
  Dead, was our teacher of the silver tongue,
Dead, whom we thought so strong he could not die,
  Dead, with no arrow loosed, with bow unstrung.
And round the great, grey blade that all men dread,
  There crept the waxen-white convolvulus –
  And the keen edge that once fell hard on us
Was blunt and notched and rusted yellow red.

And he, our Master, the unconquered one,
Lay, in the nettles of the forest place,
With dreadful open eyes and changeless face
Turned upward, gazing at the noon day sun.
Then we two, bent over our old, dead, king,
Loosed hands, and gave back hope and troth and ring.[3]

Escaped!

Peace for a season in the heart of me,
   That peace which springs from very weariness.
As one, wave rescued, looketh on the sea
   So look I on the time of my distress –
A powerless power stretching forth weak hands
   To take me, who am fled from out its reach –
An angry breaker beating on the beach
To die in spume streaks on the level sands.
   Yea, peace is come to me and I am free,
   And all the past is dead and will not rise,
   And that which shall be sheweth fair, untrod,
   As one wave rescued turneth from the sea,
   Landward, to rest him, so I turn my eyes
From past things to the future, thanking God.[4]

For the past week I have been scribbling away at all sorts of stuff – gas and sewerage and love stories, all in a jumble together. It is no end of a distraction for me – so I go into it – with all my heart, I was going to say, but I'll alter the expression, – with no end of energy. Perhaps Trixie will have shewn you some thing I did. This week's mail ought to bring something from the people in India about the German scheme.[5] I could scarcely tell you how I hope the notion will be practicable. At the present moment I would give up almost everything I have, for the mere chance of getting out of England for a year or so. Today I've been at Choir practice, and my throat is as hoarse as a crow's. *Moral*, – Never sing *too* loudly and *too* long as you're sure to suffer for it afterwards. We are preparing for a concert. Think of that!!!!! And the miserable tenors are driven from morning till night. I'm getting a little sick of it – but it's doing me no end of good. The weather has been abominable and our athletic sports were postponed in consequence. This is a truthful view of the field

N. view   N.E. view   S. view   W. view
         [slanting ink lines of rain]

There isn't much variety about it but that's as near as I can get it. Write soon.

> Ruddy

P.S. Don't think it was the girl. What you think about me doesn't matter.

Notes
1. The English humorist (1803–57); but it has been suggested that RK is thinking of Scarron's *Roman Comique*, ch. 16.
2. Where RK's Kipling grandmother lived.
3. Miss Winnard offended RK by thinking that this sonnet was about a dead canary (Lord Birkenhead, *Rudyard Kipling*, New York, 1978, p. 54).
4. None of these sonnets was ever published by RK, but "Escaped!", revised, is part of "Concerning a Jawáb", *CMG*, 6 August 1887 (Rutherford, *Early Verse*, pp. 148, 384).
5. I do not know what this may have been.

To The Reverend George Willes,[1] 17–[18] November 1882
ALS: Dalhousie University

> Civil and Military Gazette.[2] / My office! (ahem) / Lahore /
> Friday Nov 17th 1882

Beloved Padre,

I write, so to speak, between the horns of the gum pot and the scissors. For the last two hours I have been putting together the bulk of our paper and correcting proofs of all kinds but just at present there is a lull for tiffin so I am free to write to you. The weather is magnificent but rather cold and I am wearing rather more winter wraps than I have ever done in England. There is sometimes 100° difference between the day and the night. This is trying but luckily it doesn't give me fever.

My working hours are from 10 till 4.15 or earlier if I can manage it. One isn't working all the time but it is necessary to be on hand for special telegrams and visitors between those two times. Besides this there is a lot of work out of office hours, telegrams come to my house at any time of the day and night. These have to be seen to. Special telegrams are generally full of abusive matter which might land us in a libel case and so on. One of the first things a sub editor has to learn is to altogether give up original writing. I have not written three words of original matter beyond reports and reviews since I have joined the staff. The actual business which I am learning is intensely interesting and does not become monotonous in any way for you never meet the same thing twice. Some thirty papers go through my hands daily – Hindu papers, scurrilous and abusive beyond everything, local scandal weeklies, philosophical and literary journals written by Babus in the style of Addison. Native Mohummedan, sleepy little publications, all extracts, Indigo papers, tea and coffee journals, jute journals and official Gazettes all have to be disembowelled if they are worth it. Moreover I am responsible for every scrap of the paper except the first two pages. That is to say, I bear the blame of correspondents' blunders – it is my duty to correct them – misprints and bad lettering – it is my business to find them out – vulgarities, bad grammar and indecency – we get *that* sometimes! – have to be looked to carefully and I have a large correspondence all over India with men of all sorts. All local notes come to me and have to be digested, and I must pick up information about approaching polo matches, garden parties, official dinners and dances, to insert in the local column. For this work my remuneration is Rs. 150 per mensem for the first six months, Rs. 200 for the next six, Rs. 250 for the next six and after this – this isn't stated officially but it's true – they will double the screw if I prove myself capable of working the paper for the eighteen months of low pay. That means I shall be drawing Rs. 500 a month at the end of eighteen months. As my expenses, living with my parents, amount to very little—you can see that the salary is by no means a bad one. Taking into consideration my passage the proprietors will have spent something like £330 on me for the first year. I never knew that I was worth so many shillings to any one.

After this long 'personal statement' as we call it you may be interested to learn that the Punjab University has been inaugurated by the Viceroy.[3] I went to see what could be seen. There were no end of Rajah's – Bahawulpore, Kuperthulla and many others literally stiff with gems. I'll send you an account of it soon that you may see wherein an University of Oriental learning differs from an English one.[4] Just imagine a brown legged son of the east in the red and black gown of an M.A. as I saw him. The effect is killing. I had an irreverent vision of the Common room in a Muhammedan get up. At the end of the proceeding an excited bard began some Urdu verses composed in Honour of the occasion. It was a tour de force of his own – but I am sorry to say he was suppressed, that is to say, they took him by the shoulders and sat him down again in his chair. Imagine that at Oxford!

This old cuss was a Sikh who had got a degree and a wife who had got a degree – but as she couldn't appear in public she was in a little side room in modest retirement [two sketches of native in academic gown and cap]. The "press" was under a balcony, where one of them drew sketches of the viceroy as he appeared in the viceregal chair. This is the sketcher sketching [sketch of RK seated in chair].

Now, I must wind up this letter. I expect one fully as long from you in return. I wrote to Baits[5] from Port Said – why hasn't he answered. –

Tell him this and just see if you can stir the old dreamer up. Once more remember me to every one around and believe me always

Yours sincerely, (and in any
other fashion you choose)
Rudyard Kipling

Notes
1. Willes (1844–1905), a graduate of Christ Church, Oxford, was chaplain at USC, 1879–94, and is the original of the Padre in *Stalky*. According to Beresford, Willes was RK's best friend among the masters at the College.
2. The daily paper published in Lahore for the English residents of the Punjab. RK's parents had been in Lahore, the capital of the Punjab, since 1875, where JLK was principal of the new Mayo School of Industrial Arts and curator of the Lahore Museum. RK's appointment had been arranged by JLK, who knew the proprietors of the *GMG* and who, with his wife, was a regular contributor. The principal proprietor of the paper, George Allen, had interviewed RK in England early in 1882. Leaving England on 20 September RK arrived in Lahore about the last week of October. After some days assisting his father unofficially at the Lahore Museum he entered upon his newspaper work in November and kept at it for the next six and a half years.
3. The inaugural convocation of the Punjab University, presided over by the Viceroy, Lord Ripon, was held on 18 November.
4. The report of the inaugural convocation in the *CMG*, 20 November 1882, is very unlikely to be by RK: in places it suggests his father's style.
5. "Baits" – more usually "Bates" – was a nickname for Cormell Price.

To Edith Macdonald, 24 December 1882
ALS: Library of Congress

Lahore. / Dec 24th. 1882. / Christmas Eve. Sunday. 8.30 P.M.

Dearest Auntie –

At length an epistle from a graceless nephew who is worried out of his little existence. You must know that Christmas Day is recognised as a holiday in the office and this is my only holiday till Good Friday, when I get another day. I was just rejoicing over having a Monday free when a note comes from Stephen Wheeler's wife telling me that he had fallen off his poney and was stunned but that no bones were broken.[1] Of course I at once drove over, this was about an hour and a half ago. I found him insensible, in bed and quite daft when he tried to talk. He didn't know me in the least. I naturally volunteered, since he was my Editor and a good fellow into the bargain, to sit up with him and generally make myself useful but the woman seems to consider him just a bit shaken only and wouldn't hear of it. So I drove over to Doctor Laurie's[2] at once to see what he thought of the business. He said that Wheeler oughtn't to go to work for another ten days at least and that he couldn't at all say how matters might turn out. So I said some evil little words and dashed around to the managing proprietor's[3] and had a peg and a long confab with him. Ultimately we came to the conclusion that we must pull through somehow. This somehow unfortunately means that the whole burden and alas the responsibility of the paper will rest for a week or so on my youthful shoulders. I shall have to drive over to office tomorrow and slave like a nigger and above all, give up the big Club Ball on Tuesday. On Wednesday however I am going to a big Masonic Banquet where in default of my Seniors I shall have to return thanks for the Press in a Speech.[4] Just now I intend holding a council of war with the parents to see how on earth we are to tide over the abominable accident to the paper. They are all well up in *the* business and will be of no end of use to me.

What an abominably selfish letter I have written. It's nothing but I, I, I, all the way through. Tell me everything about everybody when you answer this epistle. How is Aunt Louie,[5] I heard lately that she has been rather unwell poor darling, I only saw her once at the Hotel and I straightway fell in love with her. She is better now isn't she. Give me full particulars about the cousins for in spite of the home life here which I enjoy intensely, I feel very much that I am in a strange land. Now for the council of war. Goodnight and Goodbye for a season from

Your graceless
Ruddy

Notes
1. Stephen Wheeler (1854–1937), editor of the *CMG* until his return to England in 1887. Wheeler wanted a strictly disciplined assistant and treated RK in a stiff and discouraging way. RK was afterwards to say that he owed whatever accuracy and discipline he had to Wheeler (*Something of Myself*, p. 41) but he plainly disliked Wheeler so long as he had to work under him. Wheeler, in return, never thought much of RK. As he wrote to a would-be bibliographer of RK in 1899, "I am afraid I do not share your views as to his place in literature" (MS, Harvard). He had the grace, however, to refrain from putting anything about RK in print, though he no doubt had many invitations. After his return to England Wheeler became librarian of the Oriental Club, and helped to edit the letters and poems of Walter Savage Landor.
2. E. Lawrie, MB (Edinburgh, 1867), surgeon and Professor of Anatomy and Surgery at the Lahore Medical School. He is mentioned in *Something of Myself*, p. 64.
3. Lieutenant-Colonel (later Sir) David Parkes Masson (1847–1915).
4. The occasion is not reported in the *CMG*, which rarely bothered to print such details of local activity. This is the first recorded contact between RK and Freemasonry. He joined the Lahore Lodge ("Hope and Perseverance" no. 782) in April 1886 by special dispensation, being yet under-age, and was a faithful member during the rest of his years in India (see Harry Carr, "Kipling and the Craft", *Ars Quatuor Coronatorum*, LXXVII (1964) 213–53).
5. Mrs Alfred Baldwin. Edith Macdonald was now a permanent resident of the Baldwin house.

To Cormell Price,[1] 30 December 1882
ALS: Library of Congress

> Lahore. / December. 30th. 1882 / Saturday evening / 6.30.

Dear *Uncle* Crom –

Now that I am over seven thousand miles away I can go back to the old term without it being too much audacity – Both parents have gone to the Jaipur Exhibition[2] for ten days and I am altogether alone in the house. Moreover, Wheeler the Editor has fallen off – and under – a jibbing pony so for the past week the whole burden of the C.M.G. has rested on *my* shoulders. I spent Christmas day – my one yearly holiday – with the exception of Good Friday in office and I have been working eight hours a day and shall work again tomorrow. The managing proprietor is much too busy to help; the only other proprietor handy has gone out for a day or two to shoot – and he has prolonged that day or two a good deal. However, just before he went he gave me a Christmas present which I value a good deal. He said that "he had the fullest confidence in me owing to the energy with which I had thrown myself into the breach caused by Wheeler's accident." I have grown at least six inches since then. Seriously tho', it was by no means a small compliment for a youngster. By the way, India knocks the *illegitimate* conceit out of a boy in no time. I have had my lessons and I hope I shall profit by them. Within the last month I have been promoted to writing reviews and editorial notes – as a reward for doing the scissor work well, and this too I am extremely proud of in a small way.

Altogether, I find that this sort of life suits me down to the ground. I have about seventy men to bully and hector as I please and am liable to bullying if I don't do *my* share of the business properly. This is quite as it should be and I take any bullyings with a good grace. The father has made me a present of a very handsome roan stallion "Joe" and just now he is the very apple of my eye and is a very personal friend. He takes me to and from office with the sober trot of a cavalry charger. He was originally in the 19th Bengal lancers. If it were not for one's work the weeks would be ghastlily dull – as it is they fly past, quicker even than at School and one day is an exact repetition of the other. On looking over this letter I find it disgustingly sloppy and egoistical – but a boy's letter is invariably after that fashion and you will have had so many of them that you know what to expect when an ex pupil writes – all the credit to themselves, if they get on; and abuse unlimited of their School if they don't. How grateful I am to you for what you have been to me and done for me within the last five years I can hardly say. Now however I must go to bed and have a smoke – it's two in the morning for I have been out to dinner since I began this screed and I have done two good hours of leader since I left[3] – but there's no good in night work.

Ruddy.

Notes
1. Price (1835–1910), headmaster of RK's school, idealised in "The Head" of *Stalky*. He had attended King Edward's Grammar School, Birmingham, where his closest friend was Edward Burne-Jones. Henry Macdonald, the elder brother of RK's mother and aunts, was at the same school; through him both Price and Burne-Jones were introduced to the Macdonald family. Price's acquaintance with RK's mother thus antedated her marriage. At Brasenose College, Oxford, he and William Morris were close friends. Price began the study of medicine in 1860 but soon gave it up and accepted a private tutorship in Russia. In 1863 he became Master of the Modern Side at Haileybury, and held this post until 1874, when he was appointed first Headmaster of the United Services College. The twenty years he spent in that post coincided with such prosperity as the College had. In his relation to RK, Price managed to combine the roles of family friend ("Uncle Crom") and of schoolmaster ("Sir") with a success always gladly acknowledged by RK, who describes Price as "a lean, slow-spoken, bearded, Arab-complexioned man" (*Something of Myself*, p. 21).
2. An exhibition of the arts and industry of Rajputana opened on 1 January 1883; the reports describing it in the *CMG*, 10 and 12 January, were by JLK.
3. RK is writing on a Saturday; presumably the leader on "Indian Jails" in the *CMG*, 1 January 1883, is meant.

To Cormell Price, 18 March 1883
ALS: Library of Congress

Lahore / March. 18th. 1883.

Dear Uncle Crom,

In case I haven't acquainted you with the fact – it may be as well to tell you that all the Indian papers know where S. H. Powell came from.[1] You see I got the information some time before your letter came and, with a view to doing a good turn for the Coll, I wrote at once to Madras and Bombay papers, so that from the Madras Times it was copied into every paper on the E. coast of India and from the Bombay Gazette into every paper on the west coast. Here are a few of 'em. *Times of India, Madras Times, Englishman, Indian Daily News* etc. You will always find me *very* willing to do anything for you in any way out here. I am thinking of arranging an O.U.S.C. annual dinner in India. Do you consider that the experiment would be worth trying?[2]

Since I last wrote to you I have learnt to run alone, and have an office and separate authority of my own. The proprietors are good enough to say that they are thoroughly satisfied with me, and, in every way, act up to their expressions of approval. Wheeler, my Ed. – to make a vile pun my (h)ed – has given me a good 'report' as well as one or two rather uncalled for compliments. By the time that this reaches you I shall be drawing £20 (English money) a month besides occasional 'extras' – one of these is the editing of a guide book to Lahore. Of course my father helps me and between us we get Rs. 500 for our trouble.[3] Besides these I am "telegraphic correspondent" to a sister paper and this brings from Rs 40 to 50 a month extra.[4] I have put down these items in a rather coldblooded way I am afraid but it is in order to give you some idea of the conditions of life. Of course one has to work for this, and I am at it from 9.30 to 5 on weekdays and for two or three hours on Sunday. It is a standing wonder to me how I go on at my work as I have done. Somehow it never seems to pall on one and it's never twice alike in any point.

This is just the shortest of short scribbles – if you will be good enough to send over an advt – it will cost very little and you have a splendid field for advertisement.[5]

I send you our contract rates. Seeing the extent of our circulation – from Peshawur to Delhi, and from Karachi to Simla you will see it's not a high charge.

Ruddy.

Notes
1. Sidney Henry Powell (1866–1945), a student at USC, had passed first in the December examinations for Woolwich; he served in the Royal Engineers in India, Egypt, and France, rising to Major-General. Powell shared a study with RK at one point and is said to be the original of Tertius in *Stalky*.
2. I have found no evidence of any such dinners.
3. I cannot find that any such book was ever published. JLK published a guide to Lahore with Thomas Henry Thornton (*Lahore*, published by the authors, 1876); it seems likely that a revision of this book was the project that RK speaks of.
4. The *Pioneer* of Allahabad, under the same ownership as the *CMG*, had been founded by George Allen, the senior proprietor, in 1865; it was the most important English-language daily outside the Presidency cities of Calcutta, Bombay, and Madras. I have found twenty-four items reported from Lahore in the *Pioneer* between 17 March 1883 and 11 March 1884. There is no evidence for RK's authorship other than the statement in this letter that he is "telegraphic correspondent". A few of these items, however (e.g. 5 and 10 January 1884), are certainly by RK.
5. See 1 June 1883.

To The Reverend George Willes, 24 April 1883
ALS: Dalhousie University

Lahore / April 24th '83.

Dear Padre

What on earth is the meaning of your long silence? I have piped – several times – and you have altogether refused to dance. Please answer this and let me know something about the old Col. I am busy advertising for the names of all O.U.S.C.'s in India, with a view to getting up an annual Westward Ho! dinner somewhere in Calcutta – or wherever is most convenient. Murray[1] and Young (N.E.)[2] have been consulted on the subject and Stratton[3] Craster,[4] Fenton,[5] Grinston (R.E.)[6] and Willes[7] and one or two others have been asked to help. I myself am red hot about the idea, (By the way red hot is not such an exaggeration as it sounds. The thermometer is 86°, under the Punkah, 108° away from it and 167° in the sun) and want it to turn out a success. What do you think of the notion? I have very little of any interest to tell you – work goes steadily on and I have been promoted to an office of my own, and absolute control – as well, unfortunately, as absolute responsibility – is in my department. Pay too has 'riz' which is pleasant – and I have ordered a dog cart. Can you imagine me in barnacles[8] steering doubtfully over the grey plains of Lahore in a bamboo cart? Here are four views of the Country from my office [sketch of flat plains]. I must admit that they are just a little bit monotonous – but the Punjab has 90,000 square miles exactly like this. In spite of this dullness of scenery life is very pleasant out here and the heat keeps me in beautiful condition. For the past six months I have never known what it was to have an hour's seediness and at school if you recollect I was always seedy or – to my shame be it said – shamming to be so. There! The murder's out and my Latin master[9] may make the best of it. How is he? I don't exactly like to rush into a correspondence with him, without a word of warning but, if he would care to write me a line or two, occasionally, I should be only too happy to send him some in return and, if he has a weakness for strange Indian carpets and brass ware, of a kind that do *not* find their way to English markets – I can get them for him – but this is in the nature of a bribe so I'll change the subject. Tell him tho', that I should like him to write – "With all their faults we love our Peers."[10] You know I can't send you much of a note as the mail is on the point of going out. Remember me to the Camps Common Room, individually and collectively – 'Soc' Dunsterville, (never mind about his prefectorial dignity – He'll get all those notions out of his mind when he has been in India a week) heavily for not writing to me and believe me

Yours always
Rudyard Kipling

P.S. What has happened to the Chronicle? I was anxiously looking out for a lot of school news but it never came. Do you think you could get me a light – 12 or 14 bore breechloader – for about 10 or 15 guineas. I can't get one to suit me out here. One barrel modified and the other full choke. If you can – and I know no one with whom the choice can be better left than with you, I will send you out a cheque on your writing – but don't do it if you find it a nuisance. We have splendid quail and partridge shooting about here and, as I am at work pretty nearly all day long, I find this my one great amusement in the early morning. The other day my servant nearly blew off my head. I gave him a gun, on half cock to carry for me – it was a breech loader. He promptly lowered the hammer on the nipple – (as he afterwards explained to keep the *cap* dry) and the next thing I knew was a flight of quail shot singing past my ear and lodging in a tree trunk. The natives are wonderfully careless, so get a gun with safety bolts if you can padre.

Notes
1. John Henry Murray (1860–?), at USC 1876–80. The *OUSC Register* records only that he was "in the service of the Eastern Bengal State Railway".
2. Norman Edward Young (1863–1902), at USC 1875–80; in Pugh's house with RK, and nicknamed "Satan"; served with Egyptian Army, 1892–8; died of fever at Bloemfontein.
3. Wallace Christopher Ramsay Stratton (1862–?), at USC 1875–9; commissioned 1881 in Royal Artillery; retired as Lieutenant-Colonel in 1916. He served in the Political Department, 1885–1917.
4. Shafto Longfield Craster (1862–1943), at USC 1874–9; served in the Royal Engineers in India, retiring as Colonel in 1919.
5. Raymond Rooke Fenton (1862–?), at USC 1876–80; went out to India as an indigo planter in Bihar.
6. Colonel Sir Rollo Estouteville Grimston (1861–1916), at USC 1876–9, in Crofts's house; commissioned 1881; held staff appointments, including that of ADC to the Viceroy, 1893–8.
7. Of the three Willes brothers at USC in RK's day this might be either Francis Charles (1860–?) or Arthur Herbert (1864–96).
8. Spectacles.
9. W. C. Crofts: see 14 November 1883.
10. Gilbert and Sullivan, *Pirates of Penzance*, I: "with all our faults, we love our House of Peers".

To Cormell Price, 19–21 May 1883
ALS: Library of Congress

Lahore / May. 19th. 1883

Dear Uncle Crom

It may interest you to hear that I have had a letter from Campbell (H.V.)[1] of the W. Riding Regt now at Nowshera. He is quite enthusiastic about the O.U.S.C. gathering and sends me several more or less unpracticable suggestions. I am beating up for recruits all over the country and hope to get a respectable number by Xmas. If we *do* have the dinner, it shall be reported in the C & M Gazette in a prominent situation and I'll send you a copy.[2]

My chief Wheeler wants a month's leave and I am told that I shall officiate for him, and, as far as I can learn, for myself as well in a great measure. This will give me a lively time of it but, since I have suggested that extra work demands extra pay, it ought to bring me a in a little profit besides the Kudos attaching to the management, for a short time, of the "second journal in India" – Latterly I have been translating a good deal of the *Journal de St Petersbourg* for the paper – and just now I am at work on a fascinating little novellette in the same paper.[3] These frivolous Anglo-Indians prefer novellettes to blue books and a down country paper is working almost identically the same vein, so I have to be as brisk as ever I can with my translations to forestall it. Half the pleasure of my work is to steal a march on the other papers when there is any news going, and to dress it up prettily before they do. A good deal more than half the annoyance is to find out that they have headed you off, or else deliberately accuse you of having obtained information "through improper and unauthorized channels." The Calcutta dailies, on the principle of "setting a thief to catch a thief" are very much given to this form of attack and they are such tough skinned reprobates that it's difficult to hit 'em on the raw with any certainty of their wincing visibly. When, however, they are once properly "drawn," you can get a good deal of amusement and some instruction out of their wriggles.

Monday. I have been writing this letter by fits and starts for the better part of four days and now the mail is going and I haven't said half I want to. Don't trouble to answer this letter.

Ruddie.

Notes
1. Lieutenant Henry Vincent Campbell (1864–89), at USC 1879–81; commissioned 1882; died of fever in Burma.
2. No report appears.
3. It is not clear just what items these may be, since nothing in the *CMG* around this time

is credited to the *Journal de St Petersbourg* and there is no trace of a novelette in the paper. Possibilities are such things as "Musketry Practice in the Russian Army", 9 May; an item on the explorations of Lieutenant Naziranoff, 14 May; and a summary of a paper on explorations in Merv, 24 May. Translating continued to be one of RK's more tedious duties under Wheeler: see *Something of Myself*, p. 49.

To Edith Macdonald, [May? 1883?]
ALS, *incomplete*: Library of Congress

[Lahore]

When are you going to Rottingdean? There are times when I feel as if I would give all the world to be cavorting over those downs with you again.[1] Home sickness is bad enough when you are within two hundred miles of any "haven where you would be",[2] but to get it in all its beauty you must be seven thousand miles away from anywhere, and then you realize what it is to be properly, completely and thoroughly "home sick". I only hope that you may never know what the full bitterness of it is. One advantage of the emotion is that it makes you work like a nigger to shake it off and it is only *through work* that you ever get the better of it.

Yet, you know, my lines have been cast in pleasant enough places and barring my inability to get any leave this year,[3] I have really nothing whatever to complain of. All the same, India isn't England and a thermometer at 168°[4] in the sun isn't calculated to bring about a resemblance. Let us talk of more pleasant things – I have a new and toy like dog cart which is the apple of my eye. It came from Lucknow a few days ago, and gives the "Sober One" ("Joe") an altogether dissipated and rakish air.

[drawing of dog cart]

This is a diagram of it, without wheels; it's nothing but tough male bamboo canes.

My files are waiting for the shears in long rows so I must wind up this note – which is a meagre and padded one at the best but I have written it slowly and it is nearly eleven oclock now. The Parents should be coming home soon – we break up early in the Punjab and I must get work over before I go to bed. My Love to all the relatives and to you first of all.

Your own
Nephew

[drawing of wall]

View of the outer wall of my room. Half our office verandah fell down the other day. Supposed to have been loosened by an earthquake.[5]

Notes
1. Rottingdean, a village four miles east of Brighton, has the most extensive associations of any place with RK and his family, beginning when the Burne-Joneses bought a house there in 1880; thereafter it became a regular holiday place for the cousinhood of Kiplings, Burne-Joneses, Baldwins, Poynters, and Macdonalds; Edward Burne-Jones and Cormell Price are buried there, Stanley Baldwin took a wife from the village, RK's son was born there, and for five years RK lived in The Elms, at the centre of the village.
2. *Book of Common Prayer*, Psalm 107:30: "haven where they would be".
3. Yet he did get leave, and spent a month at Simla in July and August (see 14–17 August 1883).
4. The "Meteorological Observations" in the *CMG* included readings made not only in the shade but in the sun's rays: on 19 May, for example, the reading was 166.7°; on 21 May, 168.7°.
5. I find no record of an earthquake around this time in Lahore, but RK may refer to some earlier one.

To Cormell Price, 1 June 1883
ALS: Library of Congress

Civil and Military Gazette, / Lahore. / From the Assistant Editor. /
1-6-83

Dear Uncle Crom,

Bless you for that last long letter on our present Indian policy – it gave me some material for an editorial note – I can't trust myself to write calmly about that "Bill".[1] Old stagers say that race feeling has never run so high since the Mutiny. If there should be a rising, the present Government are directly responsible at least so every one says. There is a proclamation just now spread all over the Punjab which is quite incomprehensible and *therefore*, may be considered seditious.[2] At any rate the Government's attention has been drawn to it. Have you heard anything at all about it?

The Secretary's advertisement has arriven, and goes in tonight I fancy.[3] I am off to Amritzar next Sunday to call upon N.E. Young and arrange further details about the O.U.S.C. dinner. When everything is ready, there will be a note about it in the C.M.G. drawing attention and so on.

My chief has broken down with fever and goes away to Simla for a month. This is likely to make my work very heavy for the time, but they have telegraphed for an assistant from Kurachi and he will take a good deal off my shoulders. Latterly, I have been doing a good deal of scrap writing, owing to Wheeler's collapse, and some of them, tho' I say it as shouldn't, were quite respectable scraps.[4]

There's nothing else to tell you this week. My dog-cart is a 'joy for ever' to me, and enables me to go about a good deal more than I did. I am off to the Club tonight for the lottery night. Our local races come off tomorrow and needs must, since I can't attend the racing, that I must get what I can of information from the sporting members of the community.[5]

Remember me to the whole of the Common room, and believe me
Yours always
Ruddy.

Notes
1. A bill identified with the Legal Member of Lord Ripon's Council, Sir Courtney Ilbert, to allow native judges to try British subjects (or, as RK put it, "that Native Judges should try white women", *Something of Myself*, p. 50). It was introduced in February 1883, and the outcry against it filled the Indian newspapers until its passage, in much modified form, a year later. A leader on the bill, perhaps by RK, appears in the *CMG*, 2 June 1883.
2. The proclamation was printed in the *CMG*, 17 May; it proclaims the imminent end of the world and commands the duty of the Faithful so that "all may be prepared for that day". On the 26th a note in the *CMG* concluded that "there is nothing so distinctly seditious in its character as to call for Government interference". But the *CMG* continued to pay uneasy attention to the subject for some time (e.g. 4 June).
3. The advertisement for the United Services College first appears on 5 June; it states the school's terms (from 60 to 75 guineas per year) and reports its current successes.
4. These cannot be certainly identified. By "scraps" RK means the miscellaneous "notes" to which a large part of the front page of each day's paper was given over and which were the outlet for a good part of the staff's own writing as opposed to the telegraphic news and the reprinted items of "exchange" that made up the bulk of the paper. An attack on the behaviour of the liberal government at home (28 May, p. 1c) and a note on the Muslim proclamation mentioned in this letter (30 May) are no doubt by RK. Perhaps that on Matthew Arnold's article on "Isaiah of Jerusalem", 1 June, is too.
5. An account of the 2 June meeting appears in the *CMG*, 5 June: it is too circumstantial to have been written *in absentia*.

To Edith Macdonald, 12–13 June 1883
ALS: Library of Congress

Civil and Military Gazette Office. / Lahore / June 12th 1883

Dear Auntie, your parboiled nephew reclines with his feet on a chair,

To Edith Macdonald, 12–13 June 1883

Watching the punkah swing through the red hot fly-full air;
For, when work is nearly at end and the telephone ceases to ring
Then the soul of the poet awakes and the "Stunt"[1] begins to sing.
Sings, as Sterne's starling wailed, watching the blazing sun
"I can't get out"[2] – at least, till after the sunset gun;
For the heavens are red hot iron and the earth is burning brass,
And the river glares in the sun like a torrent of molten glass,
And the quivering heat haze rises, the pitiless sunlight glows
Till my cart reins blister my fingers as my spectacles blisters my nose.[3]
Heat, like a baker's oven that sweats one down to the bone
Never such heat, and such health, has your parboiled nephew known.
May the Gods forgive my boasting, but nearly a year has fled
And I haven't been seedy once in liver or stomach or head.
An inference thence I draw that, given a daily fill
Of work, I've no time to waste in loafing and "feeling ill."
But what are my liver and lights and other organs to you?
We've all of us got 'em, I know and some of us badly too,
Let me off to another subject – that joy of my youthful heart
A varnished dream of delight, my *beautiful* bamboo cart,
With a *real live* horse attached, and a whip with no end of a lash
And a groom to sit behind, in *case* I should meet with a smash,
A fearful and wonderful way is the fashion wherein I drive,
But the Pater's been driven by me – and the pater is yet alive.
And after the cart comes the Club – I am honorary member:
Waiting for *pukka** election by ballot in next September
And this is a pleasant thing and pleasant it is to stray,
Down to the gossip and "coolth" at the end of a busy day
Pleasant to breakfast or dine there, pleasant to chat there – and that recalls
A fact to my mind, I'm engaged, just now, on some Station theatricals
This is exciting work and calculated to slump any
Man in the world, to deal with an amateur acting company.
Every one wants "best part;" every one slurs the fact,
That unless we rehearse at times we shall never be able to act.
Nobody comes to rehearsal – every one says "all right
We're a wee bit shaky now but we'll struggle through on the night."[4]
Wednesday; I went for a ride this morning, before it was light
Down to my office to see the "weekly edition" put right
In the hush of the dim, dark, dawn as the night began to retreat
And the jackal dashed to lair, at the sound of my horse's feet;
When the great Kite preened its wings, and called to its mate from the tree,
And the lilac opened its buds 'ere the sun should be up to see;

* Regular [RK's note].

And the trailing rose clumps thrilled with the sparrows' pent up strife
Oh! a ride in an Indian dawn there's no such pleasure in life!
(Solemn and sober my trot (for I haven't a jockey's hold)
But the freshness woke up Joe, who frisked like a two-year-old
Snorting and stamping and neighing, as he thought of the decade or two
Since he ran by his mother's side at Wazirabad or Bunnoo)
But the sun rose only too soon, and at seven I came back, yet
My saddle was (saving your presence) as black as my boots with sweat
And my face was a dripping horror and Joe a reeking offence –
When I gave him his slice of bread, in the garden, and staggered thence
To my room for a *tunda ghuzul* (which means a refreshing tub)
Then went to my proofs till nine, and at nine o'clock went to my grub.
Verily, this is a rough written, empty aimless screed . . . .
I can only ask you Aunt Edie to take the will for the deed
Had I time, as inclination, I would send you a twenty page budget
But the needs of the paper are many and therefore this letter I fudge it.
The sound of our thundering presses comes up like the surge on that shore
We sat by and talked together six thousand miles from Lahore.[5]
If I shut my eyes and the parrots were hushed in the palms outside,
I might fancy myself for a time by some wholesome English tide.
But the hot air puffs in my face, and you are away from me
While the punkah puddles the heat of an office at ninety three
White, limewashed glaring walls are *not* like a white chalk cliff
And only my daily work and never a breeze is stiff.
So I end my dolorous ditty with a howl of wild despair
As I write in my sodden shirtsleeves, with feet put up on a chair.
Oh! what is "two hundred a month," and half year "rises" to come,
To a fellow with hairs in his pen, and lizard-tails in his gum;
His ink putrescent and loathsome, a paste of corrupting flies,
His spectacles dimmed and steamy, and goggles over his eyes.
"Oh give me a London *trottoir*, some byewalk damp and muddy.
In place of this wholesome heat" is the cry of your washed out
Ruddy

Notes
1. "Assistant" as reduced by Indian pronunciation.
2. "The Passport. The Hotel at Paris", *A Sentimental Journey*.
3. The *CMG* reports the temperature as 114° in the shade on the 12 June.
4. If this reached production it received no notice in the *CMG*.
5. Aunt Edith's special function for RK was to receive his poems and his talk of literary ambition; in the summer before he sailed for India he was with her at Rottingdean, writing poems and talking to her about them: some dedicatory verses entitled "A Memory of Our Sojourn by the Sea" in a MS volume of verse at Sussex recall that time.

To Edith Macdonald, 14–17 August 1883
AL, *incomplete*: Library of Congress

Lahore. / August 14th. 1883.

Dearest Auntie,

Your "expansive" note greeting me on my return from Simla[1] where I had been spending a month with one of the proprietors[2] to my own exceeding delight. Privilege leave, as I may have told you before, gives you the pleasant duty of enjoying yourself in a cool climate for thirty days and being paid £20 for that duty. The Walkers, with whom I was staying, are angels without wings and did their level best to make things comfortable for their guests. The month was a round of picnics, dances, theatricals and so on – and I flirted with the bottled up energy of a year on my lips. Don't be horrified for there were about half a dozen of 'em and I took back the lacerated fragments of my heart as I distributed my P[our].P[rendre].C[ongé]. cards and returned the whole intact, to Flo Garrard's keeping as per usual. I was nearly eight hours a day in the saddle and at the end of the month found out that I could actually ride anywhere without turning giddy. Simla is built round the sides of a mountain 8400 feet high and the roads are just ledges. At first they turned my head a good deal but – in a little I was enabled to canter any how and any where. Now of course Lahore is as level as a billiard table and Joe had no work for a fortnight when I came back, so you can imagine what a time we had. There are 9 men and 2 ladies in the Station and most of these are going away. Practically I am living at the Club. I dine there every night and go home to the big house to sleep. The dullness is something hideous after all the bustle of Simla, but I have come back with a healthy appetite for work which prevents me feeling it as much as might be. I shall be alone for another six weeks or so, and then the Pater may drop in, for a few days, on his way to look after the Calcutta Exhibition[3] I think. Meantime my life here is, to put it mildly, slow. Out of office that is. In office the cholera telegrams[4] and the Ilbert Bill keep us lively enough. I get up at about seven, as the mornings are ever so much cooler than they used to be, have Joe saddled and canter down to the race course to school him over some jumps. This always ends in my coming off ignominiously and in Joe executing a war dance on his own account. It is of no use running after him or attempting to catch him in the ordinary way, so I wait till he has got his back turned and then run away home. Presently there is a terrible clatter behind and Joe comes up trotting his hardest with the reins dangling all anyhow between his feet. I pretend to cut him and turn into the Lawrence gardens[5] to sit down (as I am usually pretty well blown after this horse play). After I have been there a minute or so Joe comes and waits at the back of the seat trying to get me to notice him. When he's near enough, I grab the bridle and struggle up and make tracks home for breakfast. I have always some one to bear me company at that meal. After breakfast I go off to office in the big carriage and work till five. At five go to the empty house to load cartridges and shoot parrots from my hammock for an hour, then afternoon tea and a ride to the hall, where we sit (9 of us) round drinking strange iced drinks and feeling bored. Then home again to change for dinner at the Club, which is a terribly dull ceremony. Then a game of billiards or whist and back to bed. The programme does not sound pleasant but I get a certain amount of fun out of it and it makes me work very comfortably. The heat is quite pleasant only 103° in the shade and 73° on the grass at night.

Friday. I have been writing this letter just as I had time and now the mail is going out with about half of it blank. Really dear I haven't a thing to tell you except that I am very busy and very happy.

Would it interest you to know that I have to keep an eye on household affairs and my Khansamahs [. . . .]6

Notes
1. A resort town in the Punjab, 7000 feet up in the lower Himalayas and the seat of government in India for the summer – the "hills" of RK's *Plain Tales*. The Supreme Government of India, the Government of the Punjab, and the Commander-in-Chief of the Army all had Simla as official summer headquarters.
2. (Sir) James Walker (1845–1927), manager of the Alliance Bank of India and a proprietor of the *CMG* and the *Pioneer*; he was a friend of RK's parents. In later years, on his return from India, Walker took a house not far from Burwash and was thus a neighbour of RK's. It was apparently Walker who first suggested the offer of a job in India to RK.
3. The Calcutta Exhibition, the first attempt to hold an international exhibition in India, opened on 4 December 1883 and closed on 10 March 1884. The Punjab exhibit was the responsibility of JLK; his catalogue and notes prepared for the exhibit are noticed in the *CMG*, 8 January 1884. Either RK or JLK might have written the notice.
4. Cholera broke out in Egypt that summer, had reached Bombay, and was watched anxiously from the rest of India; the *CMG* published an almost daily telegraphic report on its progress.
5. The public gardens surrounding the assembly hall and theatre in Lahore.
6. Usually translated "butler": a house-steward, "the chief table servant" (*Hobson-Jobson*).

To Cormell Price, 29 August 1883
ALS: Library of Congress

Lahore / August. 29th. 1883

Dear Uncle Crom
 Your last letter was a short one indeed but I suppose that the end of

the Summer term always leaves a good deal on your hands. Glad to see that Dunsterville has passed for Sandhurst.¹ This must be a blow to W.C.C.² who prophesied the blackest outlook for him. India is threatened with something very like a famine in the Punjab, N[orth].W[est].P[rovinces]. and northern portions of the Bombay Presidency. Indirectly this gives me a great deal to do, as I am told off to string together reassuring fibs evolved out of the weekly crop and weather report. This isn't easy work and one is hardpressed at times for a *really* original lie.³

I got a half holiday, a few days ago, which I spent in reporting a Criminal charge of Adultery case to keep my hand in. Finally, it got so bad that on my own responsibility, I refused to let the sheets through the press; to the intense indignation of the only two Lahore ladies – India is a queer place for that sort of thing and, as these cases are almost always heard in Camera, Council and witnesses speak in a delightfully open manner.⁴ Beyond this there isn't much to tell you – I am going in for the "Lower Standard" Urdu⁵ and to that end have a munshi⁶ every morning at 7 o'clock to give me an hour's work before I go out for my morning ride. Urdu is a difficult tongue to write, at least I find it so, and an easy one to read. By this time the Mother is in England:⁷ I suppose you will see something of her won't you? Where do you go for the few days you allow yourself in the long holidays – to Rottingdean as usual? Murray is coming down to meet me soon and I hope to be able to lay hold of Young (N.E.) for a season as I am living all alone while the pater is cutting me out of the hearts of all my old flames at Simla – that's the worst of a family I find.

This is the merest scrawl of a note and will, of course, tell you nothing but there is nothing to tell with only 11 people in the station – 9 of them men. I wonder if you could realize the utter desolation of a "plains Station" in the months of August and September. The heat is pretty bad but we are gradually getting on towards the cool weather and in another six weeks or so shall discard punkahs and put on heavy things. Meantime it is 107° in the shade and 78° on the grass at nights.

With these interesting statistics I must come to an end. Remember me to the Common Room and old schools fellows generally.

Yrs always
Ruddie

Notes
1. Of his entrance into Sandhurst, Dunsterville wrote: "My success at my first try at the Army Entrance examination startled every one, myself no less than the others" (*Stalky's Reminiscences*, 1928, pp. 56–7).
2. William Carr Crofts: see 14 November 1883.
3. E.g., an item in the *CMG*, 21 August, saying that a famine is not possible: "the worst that can happen is high prices". There are only a few items in August at all resembling RK's description.

4. The *CMG* for 25 August merely reports discreetly that Mr Hart, proprietor of the Lahore Livery Stables, had brought a charge against Vere Alston, a Lahore barrister, under Section 497 of the Penal Code: readers doubtless knew that this was the section covering adultery. The case was adjourned to the next month, when full reports appeared in the *CMG* for 26, 27, and 28 September. The paper for 3 October reports that Alston was found not guilty, by reason of the unreliability of the chief witness against him.
5. The lower and higher standards were Army examinations required of officers in the Indian Army and open to others.
6. Usually translated "clerk"; here, a native teacher of languages.
7. Alice Kipling left for England at the end of July; she returned with her daughter in December.

To Mrs James Walker,[1] [September? 1883]
ALS: Morgan Library

[Lahore]

In Memoriam[2]/July–August. 1883.

If I have held my peace so long
   Here, in the bosom of the plains,
   Trust me – 'tis but because my brains
Would yield no echo of a song.

A peaceful lot is mine to sing,
   In dullness deep my lines are laid
   Save when – to please some sporting maid,
I tilt (and tumble) at the Ring.

Three black cheroots the day beguile;
   Week follows week – the long month goes,
   And Adlard[3] sends his bill for "close"
Which I receive and promptly – file.

No longer flies the fiery steed
   Ramping (on two rupees per diem,
   To be refunded if you buy 'em)
Across the Annandyllic[4] meads.

No longer by the Jhampan's[5] side
   I frisk along the crowded Mall
   From half past four till even fall,
Or by Peliti's[6] take my ride.

To Mrs James Walker, [September? 1883]

No longer through the stately pines
   The soft Hill breezes come and go,
   No longer, in the dusk below
The merry 'Rickshaw's'[7] lantern shines.

For Jakko's[8] woods are far away
   And, in the place of Combermere,[9]
   Across the muddy *Chick*[10] I hear
The rain that "raineth every day."[11]

Unharrowed is my tender Soul
   By M-ss O'M-R-A's[12] bold black eye –
   For, far from any passer by
I hear the sullen presses roll.

The foul *chaprassi*[13] in his lair
   Sits silent as a turban'd Sphinx:
   And all the city's million stinks
Float inward on the frowzy air,

And so I rest a graceful boot
   Upon the table's inky baize,
   And think of other – happier days
And sob above my cheap cheroot.

I dream of lotos eating days,
   Of pleasant rides in pleasant places,
   Of half a hundred pretty faces,
Of Solan beer and Henry Clays ———[14]

"A change" like that which Byron wrote,
   Comes "o'er the spirit of my dream;"[15]
   I hear the restless parrot scream,
And watch the gay thermantidote;[16]

Too moved for words, its wings I study, –
   Wipe well each glass protected eye
   And, ere I throw the inkstand by
Subscribe myself yours truly,

                            Ruddy.

P.S. Dear Mrs Walker,

I was a young sinner not to write before but even if I were to go on writing till Christmas I doubt if I could tell you within that time how grateful I am for that month's pleasure I owe you and Mr Walker. I suppose a Journalist (with a capital J) ought to be able to put his feelings on paper but here I'm afraid I can't. I can only write Thank you – and leave you to fill in the rest.

News of any sort here – there is none, except that Miss Coates and her fiancé Walker,[17] "go on" in an appalling fashion! *I've* tanned my skin blushing so frequently so it must be bad you see. They are to be married next month people say.

Remember me to every one at Kelvin Grove,

Yours always
Ruddy.

Notes
1. Lizzie Marion Hogan (d. 1892), first wife of James Walker, the owner of the *CMG* (see 14–17 August 1883); RK spent his Simla leave at their house, Kelvin Grove.
2. RK has borrowed the stanza form as well as the title of Tennyson's poem for this letter.
3. W. Adlard, civil and military tailors, Lahore and Dalhousie (advertisements in *CMG*).
4. The race track at Simla was on a meadow called Annandale.
5. A sedan or portable chair used by women in the hill stations; "a jolting, back-breaking abomination" (Buck, *Simla Past and Present*, Calcutta, 1904, p. 157). Simla roads were so narrow that carriages were generally prohibited.
6. The favoured confectionery shop and cafe of Simla, operated by Signor Federico Peliti.
7. 'Rickshaws (abbreviated from Ginrickshaw) were new in Simla, where they displaced the Jhampan.
8. The hill dominating Simla.
9. The ravine crossed by the bridge first built by Lord Combermere.
10. A sun blind or screen of split bamboo.
11. See the Clown's song, *Twelfth Night*, V. i.
12. Miss O'Meara appears as a "Bohemian Gipsy Queen" at the Simla fancy dress ball in September (*CMG*, 18 September 1883); perhaps the daughter of the only O'Meara in the *Bengal Directory* (1883), a resident engineer on the Oudh and Rohilcund Railway. RK also appeared with a Miss O'Meara at Lahore in February 1885 in a play called "Up a Tree" (*CMG*, 4 February).
13. A messenger.
14. Beer from Solan, near Simla; and a kind of cigar.
15. A recurring line in Byron's "The Dream".
16. An air-cooling device fitted in a window, in use in India since the 1830s. It combined a fan with wetted grass mats, so that the air was cooled as it was stirred. The thermantidote was the second line of defence against the Indian heat, after the punkah was no longer sufficient.
17. (Sir) George Casson Walker (1854–1925), Bengal Civil Service, married Fannie Coates on 6 October (*CMG*, 9 October); Sir George ended his career as Financial Adviser to the Nizam of Hyderabad.

To W. C. Crofts,[1] 14 November 1883
MS: University of Sussex

            Lahore, / November 14. 1883.

Dear Sir
 A few days since I came across a man who said that he knew you in England; this has reminded me that, for the past twelve months I have hardly held any communication whatever with the college – and none whatever with you. When you gave me the Tauchnitz "Aurora Leigh,"[2] you were good enough to suggest that I should write to you occasionally from Lahore; and, at the end of a year, you see I have taken you at your word.
 My Father has gone down to Calcutta on work connected with the Calcutta Exhibition[3] and, for the next two months or so, I shall be living entirely alone in the house. It isn't exactly pleasant; especially when I am down with dysentery or Lahore fever, but, as the opening of the cold weather is always a busy time, it has advantages. My work is anything but light and lasts all through the week; as Sunday comes in convenient for finishing off arrears of work. Just at present my Editor has gone sick and I am alone on the paper – there are only two of us on the staff and this is a drawback. Your theory about "giving a boy more work than he can do and he'll do it" works beautifully out here, though I didn't believe it in the Latin set. I have nearly always a little more than I can do on my hands and consequently it gets done. The chief's illness, however, has given me an early rise of pay – I draw £300 a year[4] for the next six months when I am told that I'm to get another six month's rise. As the Editor has £1000 a year and I may be called upon every now and then to take his place for a week or two – as he isn't strong – I suppose this arrangement is fair enough; and it *must* be a good deal more than I am worth – but the climate, and the chances against Insurance companies, cover the margin. Englishmen in India are tender folk and seem to require a good deal of looking after. I am enclosing some specimens of the stuff I write daily[5] – will you pass sentence upon them, in due form, in some answering letter? I have nothing to say in self defence, and all the work is about at the same level. Amusements aren't many – one dances occasionally, plays tennis every day, and rides always. I have gone in for Polo and volunteering[6] – as it's impossible to "fug" out here. On an average my horse spills me once a week but polo is a fascinating game all the same. Private theatricals and moonlight picnics make up the rest of unofficial diversions; and time goes as quickly as it ever did at School.
 You see I have no home news to go upon and am compelled to send an egoistical scrawl in its place. If you should ever have the time or the

inclination to send me a line or two from Westward Ho! I should be more grateful than I can say. Even a month's exile out here would show you the value of English letters and news. Except from the home journals I get very *very* little of either now.

Yours sincerely
Rudyard Kipling.

Notes
1. William Carr Crofts (1846–1912), RK's classics and English master, the model for King in *Stalky*. Educated at Brasenose College, Oxford, he joined USC in 1875, remaining there until 1893. He was a powerful swimmer, a champion rower, having twice won the Diamond Challenge Sculls at Henley, and a semi-professional photographer. He drowned in a cove on the coast of Sark in 1912. RK makes fun of his self-importance and his quick temper in *Stalky* but pays special tribute to Crofts in *Something of Myself* for his brilliant invective and his scholarly devotion to literature: "one learns more from a good scholar in a rage than from a score of lucid and laborious drudges" (p. 32).
2. By Mrs Browning, 1856. RK's reading of it appears in certain motifs in *The Light that Failed* (Carrington, *Kipling*, rev. edn, p. 215).
3. See 14–17 August 1883.
4. Up from the £240 he was receiving in March (see 18 March), itself an increase over his original salary (see 17 November 1882).
5. Presumably these specimens included the few items from 1883 in the so-called Crofts Collection, some twenty-three items cut from Indian papers, initialled, and sent to Crofts by RK; they were preserved by Crofts and sold after his death. The collection contained these brief untitled items from the *CMG* in 1883: on Lord Truro and Indian crime, 9 August; on the Dasera festival, 2 October; on the volcanic explosion in Java, 2 October; on the Viceregal tour in Cashmere, 16 October; and on William Morris's "The Day Is Coming", 7 November. The list of the Crofts Collection has long been taken as evidence of RK's authorship, but it should be noted that RK later denied writing all but the third of these five items, at least under the titles that had been added to them by the bibliographers. He of course wrote far more in his first year than has been identified.
6. RK was a nominal member of the 1st Punjab Volunteers, of Lahore, but is said not to have attended to his duty (Colonel H. R. Goulding, *"Old Lahore": Reminiscences of a Resident*, Lahore, 1924, p. 19).

To [Edith Macdonald], [December 1883]
ALS: Library of Congress

[Lahore]

At the End of a Year.

This is the end of a Year
Auntie dear;
Drear –
(Horridly, hopelessly drear)

To [Edith Macdonald], [December 1883]

    As I write
    In the night;
  (From the depths of a frosty night)
I've little to show for the year,
    I fear,
In the book of the Bank or the Heart.
  (In cash or Flo's heart.)
I'm twelve months older it's true –
    Entre nous,
That's all I can truthfully write
    Tonight –
Painful, but painfully true.

I'm drawing three hundred a year
    Out here,
  But it's queer
I'd barter the "bloomin' lot"
    On the spot,
    (If I could)
    For the wood
Pavement of Kensington High –
  Street, and a London sky,
And the noise of the local trains,
  (Those merry city trains)
And the flashing theatre lights,
    In the Strand,
  And the bustle and stir o' nights –
  And "the touch of a vanished hand."[1]

      3
(Do you think you could understand
  What it is to live in the plains,
   (The doleful dusty plains)
    Alone, like a hermit crab,
  Where gas is never seen
    And there's half the world between
    Yourself and a hansom cab?)

So I dream of a thousand things,
(As I scribble and smoke and think)
Of months with leaden wings,
  Bedraggled with printers' ink,
Of chalky Sussex cliffs,
  And how – were it not for the "ifs" –

(Those pestilent practical "ifs")
   I would pack up my traps and go
   By the bounding P and O;
     And quit Lahore tonight
But that is impossible *quite*.

5

For the facts of the case are this
   (The prose of my being is this)
   On the table beneath my hand,
   (In a neat little tape-bound row)
   Are the proofs which the printers expect
   (The proofs which this child must correct)
     For tomorrow's issue you know.
And, in case I should be remiss,
   This legend is writ for a guide: –
   (On their fat little backs for a guide)
   "Sir. Bearer is waiting outside
   "Please arrange. Sir, – Yours to command"
   "Badshee Shah" – So you *see* I am tied
     Verily, tight am I tied
         To the land.

And the moral hereof is plain
    I maintain
I've lost my first love and the heat
   Of much primal conceit
(*Nota Bene*. There's lots of it yet
   You bet).
I've lost all the fun of the college,
   And half my school knowledge,
I've lost my first trust in all men,
   From Colombo to Quetta,
I've lost (shall I find her again?)
My Love from the place where I set her.[2]

I've gained what is called a "good start"
   A horse and a cart
   A gun and a few suits of clothes
     And a stock of "strange oaths",[3]
   A place at the Club
     And my grub. That is – if I face all the ills
    Of fevers and chills,

> And, once in two years, take a tolera-
> Ble chance of a spasm of cholera.
> In view of which facts I may safely assert
> That I'm bound to Lahore till – I turns to its dirt.
> And some fifteen years hence may be gaily employed
> In spreading the germs of malignant typhoid
> Or, with cowdung and straw, duly plastered and set,
> I may guard my successor's young head from the wet

Ruddy.

Notes
1. Tennyson, "Break, Break, Break", l. 11.
2. If there was an explicit break with Flo Garrard now, this is the only evidence for it.
3. Shakespeare, *As You Like It*, II.vii.150.

To Margaret and Philip Burne-Jones, [1] [c. 1883?]
MS: University of Sussex

Civil & Military Gazette. / Lahore

A Cousin's Christmas Card.

A demi-official communication compiled at the office of the C.M.G. for the benefit of other Cousins. With marginal notes and official translations.

1.

As coming from an Eastern Land,	The cousin premises
I'd have the cousins understand,	of the beauty of
T'is absolutely stiff with speeches,	his poem,
An Eastern printing office teaches,	and of its
And rich with Hindu mystery	extreme subtility
In Tamil, Urdu and Hindi.	in parts

2

For instance – when the loathsome *"tar"*[1]	1. telegram
Calls the *"chuprassi"*[2] from afar	2. messenger
And at your *"hookum"*[3] swift he goes	3. order
A *"tunda moorghie"*[4] – minus clothes	4. cold fowl
Across the *"Maidans"*[5] icy space	5. heath
With *"Kummels"*[6] clouted round his face	6. heavy clothes

    This to the English mind –
      I'm sure –
    Might seem a little bit
      obscure
    But to *this* Anglo-Indian   [drawing of rising sun]
      one   "And the day shall have a sun
    It shews his labour is   That shall make thee wish it
      begun.   done."

3

Moreover, when the *"admis"*[1] sit	1. men	and continues
With Rook-ud-din's most greasy *"chit"*[2]	2. note	his tale yet further
And to your *"Kia hai"*[3] some grunter	3. What is it?	in mystic wise
Growls *"Gurebpurwan Jawaib Munta,"*[4]	4. Protector of the poor, an answer is wanted.	

    This to the cousins might
      indeed
      Appear a Jabberwocky
        screed:-
    But to the tortured
      Rudyard's soul
    It shews his foreman's   and
      in a hole.

To Margaret and Philip Burne-Jones, [c. 1883?]

4

And further – when all work is "*chuck*"¹	1. done with	with a
And boss and "*stunt*"² sit round and "*buck*,"³	2. Assistant 3. talk	display of great
And through the "*chics*"⁴ the *tattoos*'⁵ neigh	4. blinds	wisdom
Comes clearly from the near "*Serai*",⁶	5. poneys'	in his
Then rising cry we "*Syce bolow*"⁷		
Snatch up "*terais*"⁸ and *Juldee Jao*.⁹	6. stable	poesie
This *may* appear – but I'm resolved	7. call the groom	
It shall not seem the *least* involved	8. sun hats	
And so I tell you, for your knowing,	9. go quickly	
These six lines show the staff when going.		

5

Yet once more – by the "*chillag's*"¹ light	1. wick in oil
When "*wallahs*"² wake you in the night	2. men
With *Hakim sahib ke gher khan hai?*	3. Where's the Doctor's House? The Memsahib is ill.
Memsahib bemar"³ – and you reply	
Half wakened "*Memsahib bahut bemar*"?	4. Is the lady very ill? Haven't you a mounted messenger to send?
*Tomara pahs ne hai sowar?*⁴	
This in a London city read	
Would prove the poet off his head	[drawing of unidentified structure]
But in an Anglo Indian Station	
It means – increase of population.	with an illustration

W.O.P.²

And he hadn't time to finish an otherwise perfect epic. Shew this to Miss Plowden and she will find out one or two mistakes.

W.O.P.

Notes
1. For Philip Burne-Jones see [December? 1872?]. Margaret Burne-Jones (1866–1953), afterwards Mrs J. W. Mackail, was RK's cousin, and his play-fellow from the days of RK's school holidays spent at the Grange, the Burne-Jones house in Fulham.
2. A play-name probably originating in some deliberate mispronunciation: at least Margaret thought so (Harbord, *Readers' Guide*, p. 5060). She and RK had come across a letter of Dickens in which he called himself the "Sparkler of England"; this suggested "The Wop of Albion" for her, and, when RK went to India, "The Wop of Asia" for him. Dickens was evidently an important experience in common between the two.

To [Edith Macdonald, 26–8 January 1884][1]
ALS, *incomplete*: Library of Congress

[Lahore]

[. . .] and enjoy it immensely from 7.30 to 10 p.m. daily. We two[2] "frivol" like babies and the Parents are delighted to think us so. Nearly every morning, for the past week Trixie and I go out for rides, i.e. I am teaching Trixie to ride. She enjoys the fun immensely. This morning she and I went out into the open and trotted back as hard as we could come (T. bumped a good deal but that's only natural). If you had seen her with the colour in her cheeks, her hair down and blowing about in the wind, and her hat jammed at the back of the head you would have seen her at her loveliest – and that's a big order. We are all spoiling the maiden sadly – but she won't spoil easily and brightens up the domestic shanty like a "Swan's incandescent".[3] She'll make a good horse woman in time as she seems fearless, and has a pair of very good hands.[4] Old Joe in his sullen way is very fond of her and stands like a rock while she is arranging her habit. Apropos to beasts here is a list of domestic pets exclusive of two horses

    T's Persian cat
    " fox terrier pup.   } They all hate one another
    The Pater's Raven[5]
    My "Buz", bull terrier

The mother doesn't take kindly to pets as a rule, but she has grown to be very fond of the cat and takes her on her lap at times – this is a GREAT concession.

Yesterday the Punjab Club gave a big dinner to our retiring Honorary

Secretary, who is going to be married. There were about forty at table and I had to reply for the Press of India – it was my maiden speech so that fact must be my excuse for quoting it as the reporter showed it to me. As a matter of fact it wasn't anything half so polished as I was in the middle of a "hoss-trade" with a friend when my name was called. Wheeler had sloped silently and left me to pull through as I could. This is what I am said to have said: –

"Gentlemen (I know that's all right) "This is a flattering and I confess, a most embarrassing honour. So far as a youngster of my position and *in*experience can claim to represent the Press of India believe me I thank you most heartily for the toast you have just drunk. You know the proverb about the "strength of the chain being its weakest link," and that "little boys should be seen and not heard." May I ask you to 'take in the chain' and forgive the baldness of my maiden speech? It may sound a startlingly original sentence but I am "*unaccustomed* to public speaking."[6] This little bit of nonsense took very fairly and they all made a big row and beat upon the table with their fists. So I'm through my baptism of fire in the public oratory line.

Monday Morn. What a changeable thing is life in this country. Last even there sprang up a warm wind (which by the way was not due for three months) and literally blew me over. I had had a twenty mile ride that morning but felt none the worse till the wind came and then I curled up like a withered rosebud. I'm still a good deal wilted and weak and have got through my "trivial round and daily task"[7] in a rather perfunctory style. Beyond letter writing I feel that I'm not equal to original composition of any kind. Apropos to that, here is a versified cutting I wrote some days ago, which tells its own tale.[8] I need only explain that I too was once nearly shot while riding down the Mall, and the "Poet's mind" was, consequently, vexed by the "shallow wit"[9] of volunteers who could miss a mark at two hundred yards and nearly hit a man at two thousand. There is no more fearful wild fowl than your Martini-Henri rifle.[10] The 1st P.V.R. are seeking the blood of the person who wrote the verses.[11]

This has been a long and not particularly amusing letter and now I must go over to the press and attend to a long murder case which is being brought in, by bare legged messengers, slip by slip from the High Court.[12] Love to all the relations.

            Always your loving Nephew
            Ruddy.

P.S. Did I tell you that I'm special correspondent to the Pioneer, which brings me in £7 a month extra to mine income? At the end of the year, if I am not bowled over by the hot weather I shall be touching £400 per annewum – and after all what earthly good is it?
                       R.

Notes

1. Date added to MS in another hand.
2. Trix and her mother returned in December to India, a country that Trix had not seen since leaving it at the age of three.
3. A match.
4. Trix wrote in 1937 that "my brother and I seldom rode together, for his prophetic eye always saw me returning with some terrible injury, even before I was settled in the saddle" ("Some Reminiscences of my Brother", *Kipling Journal*, December 1937, p. 120).
5. JLK says that he once "reared from the nest a pair of hill crows, – ravens in all but size. . . . They were miracles of naughtiness . . . especially given to torment a little dog who hated them" (*Beast and Man in India*, 1891, p. 31).
6. This is not reported in the *CMG*.
7. John Keble, *The Christian Year*, "Morning"; "The trivial round, the common task."
8. "A Beleaguered City", *CMG*, 28 January 1884, signed "Blank Cartridge" (Rutherford, *Early Verse*).
9. Tennyson, "The Poet's Mind", ll. 1–2.
10. The standard issue to the British army. RK's "Black Jack" turns on its peculiarities.
11. P.V.R. = Punjab Volunteer Rifles. Since RK is writing in the morning and the paper containing his verses would not appear until the afternoon, his remark is strictly prophetic.
12. Private William Day was charged with the murder of Private Roan in the preceding November; Day shot the sleeping Roan following a fight between the two men. He was found guilty and hanged (*CMG*, 30 January).

To Edith Macdonald, 4 February 1884
ALS: Library of Congress

Lahore. / Feb. 4 1884.

Dearest Auntie,

Verily India is a strange land, and its people are still stranger. Yesterday morning I got an invitation to come to an old Afghan's house somewhere in the city. You must know that we have more than one of the Afghan Sirdars who fought against us in the war,[1] as prisoners at Lahore. They are under no sort of surveillance but they *have* to stay here and keep quiet. When I got the note – couched in flowery English and flowerier Persian – I rode off into the City, wondering what on earth the old sinner could want with me. He was a Kizil Bash[2] if that conveys any meaning to you.

In the end, I was shown his house and rode into the square courtyard with the Sirdar's mounted follower at my heels. Then we went up stairs – *such* filthy stairs – to Kizil bash's room a dirty place but stuffed full of embroideries, gold cloth, old armour and inlaid tables. The old

To Edith Macdonald, 4 February 1884

boy, who was sitting at one end of the room, rose to meet me and made me sit down after enquiring how I did. We conversed in Urdu, to the following extraordinary effect: –

(K.B.). Your honour's health and prosperity are they well assured?

(I). By your favour, Khan, they are so.

(K.B.). I have heard of the fame of your honour, so far north as Peshawar – that you have the ear of the Lat-Sahib (our Lieutenant Governor) and that he fears your *Khubber-Ke-Kargus* (newspaper) more than God or the Sheitans. Therefore, (this with the air of a King) I have *sent* for you, Sahib.

Here I began to feel rather uneasy and answered "The Khan honours me too greatly. Who am I that I should know the heart of the Lat-Sahib or that the Lat-Sahib should fear me. It is true (here I couldn't help advertising the CMG.) that my Khubber-Ke-Kargus, is heard from Karachi and Scinde to Benares, and from Peshawur to Delhi – but it is a little thing O Khan. How should *I* help you?" Then the old boy began in a low tone about the iniquity of his being a prisoner in Lahore. "My wives and my women are at Cabul, but I am here. Write in your Khubber Ke Kargus Sahib that I will do anything they ask me, write that it is cruel and unjust to keep me here." Write (and so he went on for about twenty minutes like a madman and finally wound up by throwing me a bundle of currency notes and asked me to count them. I did so and I found them about Rs 16,000 – that is to say about £1300). These I was told would be the price of merely recommending him to be released, a thing I might have done in ten lines on the front page any day if I had only known of his case. Of course it wasn't possible to do anything after an insult like that, but I daren't give him a piece of my mind in his own house for fear of accidents – fatal ones may be – so I threw back the notes and told him that the years had impaired his eyesight and I wasn't a Bunnoochi or a Baluchi (two races the most covetous on earth) but an English Sahib. Then he pulled up and thought for a few moments. Finally he blurted out that we English were "fools" and didn't know the value of money but that *"all* sahibs knew how to value women and horses". Whereupon he sent a small boy into an inner chamber and, to my intense amusement, there came out a Cashmiri girl that Moore[3] might have raved over. She was very handsome and beautifully dressed, but I didn't quite see how she was to be introduced into an English household like ours. I rather lost my temper and abused the Khan pretty freely for this last piece of impudence and told him to go to a half caste native newspaper walla for what he wanted (all the same I'm afraid I kissed the damsel when the Khan's broad back was turned). At the end of my harangue I found that I couldn't make a dignified exit as I had intended, 'cos the door was shut and bolted. Then I pulled up and told the old gentleman to open the door. It was a funny scene to think over afterwards because, all the time I was talking to the Khan [he] was shrugging his shoulders and waving his hands in protest, and I could hear the devil's own noise in the courtyard – sounds of horses and men. Never having been in a position like this I, naturally, began to sweat big drops, and cursed the Khan's female relatives in a manner which made the Cashmiri titter. It seemed that the man only wanted to get his horses out to show me and when that was done he went down to the yard – I followed – and saw about seven of the most beautiful beasts it has ever been my lot to look on. There were two bay Arabs, one Kathiawar mare, and four perfect little Hagara country breds. Then I'm afraid my resolution began to waver, 'specially when he said I might pick any three I liked – they were such beauties and had such perfect manners. However I explained very gravely that I wasn't going to help him a bit and he ought to have known better than to "blacken an Englishman's face" in the way he had done and if I had had my own way I'd keep him in Lahore till he died. When I come to think of the way in which I slanged him, I'm rather astonished to think he didn't stick me then and there. No one would have been any the wiser and there would have been one unbeliever less. However he kept his temper very fairly and told me to come upstairs again and have a smoke and some coffee. If I refused I knew he would think I was afraid of poison, and if I accepted I was afraid I should get some *dhatura*[4] with the coffee. However I accepted the offer and we went up stairs again and here began the cleverest part of the old man's policy. I saw when I came in that he meant no bodily harm, for the money was out on the table, from my couch in the window I could see the horses being marched to and fro in the yard and the Kashmiri was superintending the coffee and getting my pipe ready. The Khan took his seat out of sight of me and left me there to sip and smoke, and watch, if I chose the money, the horses, and the girl. This went on for nearly half an hour, and I was so thoroughly indignant with the old beast that I resolved to inflict myself upon him for a time till I sobered down. When I had smoked out one pipe, drunk my coffee and talked Oriental platonics with the Kashmiri I rose up to go and my host didn't attempt to hinder me. He had lost about three cups of coffee, one smoke, and a couple of hours of his time (but that didn't count) and had heard some plain truths about his ancestry. Of course I couldn't do anything for him – tho' his case is a hard one I admit – but I can mention the subject to Wheeler, and he can, if he likes, take notice of it, so that I shan't be concerned in the affair. When I mounted my old Waler[5] (he *did* look such a scarecrow) I found that beneath the gullet plate of the saddle had been pushed a little bag of uncut sapphires and big greasy emeralds. This was his last try I presume and it might have seriously injured my brute's back if I hadn't removed it. I took it out and sent it through one of the windows of the upper story where it will be a good find for somebody. Then I rode out of the city and came to our peaceful civil station just as the people were pouring out of church – it seems so queer an adventure that I went and set it down and am sending you the story thereof. I haven't told anyone here of the bribery business because, if I did, some unscrupulous beggar might tell the Khan that *he* would help him and so lay hold of the money, the lady or, worse still, the horses. Besides I may be able to help the old boy respectably and without any considerations.[6]

Wasn't it a rummy adventure for a Sunday morning.[7]

Your
Ruddy.

Notes
1. The Second Afghan War, 1879–80.
2. A member of the Shiite Persian community in Afghanistan – "a Persianized Turk" (*OED*). RK's verses at the head of ch. 14, *The Light that Failed*, are attributed to *Kizilbashi*.
3. Tom Moore, the Irish poet: "The Light of the Haram" in his *Lalla Rookh* abounds in beautiful Kashmiris.
4. The thorn apple, producing an intoxicant used on their victims by Thugs.
5. Horses imported from New South Wales, hence "Walers". They were big, and so suited for cavalry use. This was not "Joe" but another, unnamed horse: see 2–7 June 1884.
6. Nothing about him appears in the *CMG*.
7. RK makes no mention of this story in *Something of Myself*; his "first bribe", he says there, was offered at Patiala in March of this year (p. 45).

To Cormell Price, 19 February 1884
ALS: Library of Congress

Civil & Military Gazette / Lahore / Feb. 19th. 1884.

Dear Uncle Crom,

Herewith a certain poor poem for the Chronicle[1] – if that paper is still going on. Like the last one,[2] it is written at the parents rather more than the boys but no one will know that if you don't say so. Anyhow it may please some of the parents and 'specially those who have been in this land. I'm very busy indeed just now, having a lot of special correspondence[3] and, in my spare moments (which are not many) a novel of sorts,[4] or I should write to you a good deal more regularly than I have done. Moreover there are a good many private theatricals going forward[5] and in all these things I am more or less directly concerned.

Lord Ripon[6] has landed himself into a rather curious hole. Since the mutilated remains of the Ibert Bill were passed[7] he has been as it were "cut" by the Bengal, Bombay and Upper India press and you shall see a real live Viceroy talking by the yard and perambulating all Madras, with only two or three papers taking any note of his movements or speeches.

This is curious and also true.

Ruddy.

Notes

1. "On Fort Duty", published in the USC *Chronicle*, 28 March 1884, and signed "Z.54.R.A." (Rutherford, *Early Verse*).
2. "The song of the Exiles", USC *Chronicle*, 15 October 1883, signed "Gigs" (Rutherford, *Early Verse*).
3. Not identified. There is a long review and abstract of the Punjab Administration Report for 1882–3 occupying eight columns in the *CMG* of 16 February, three more on the 18th, and four more on the 22nd. But RK may mean something quite different.
4. This is perhaps the earliest reference to the novel, never published, that RK called "Mother Maturin". However, RK's diary for 1885 (Harvard) records on 7 March 1885 that "the idea of 'Mother Maturin' dawned on me today". If this is to be taken literally to mean that "Mother Maturin" had no existence before 7 March 1885, then the "novel of sorts" referred to here must be another work, of which nothing more is known. For "Mother Maturin", see 30 July–1 August 1885.
5. Notice of plans to perform W. S. Gilbert's *Sweethearts* and a play called *Checkmate* "sometime" in March appears in the *CMG*, 19 February, but there is no further word of them. Gilbert's *Palace of Truth* was performed on 14 and 15 April; RK was cast as Chrysal in this and got as far as the dress rehearsal but missed both performances owing to "a very sudden indisposition" (*CMG*, 16 and 18 April).
6. George Frederick Samuel Robinson (1827–1909), second Earl and first Marquess of Ripon, Liberal politician; Viceroy of India, 1880–4. He was highly unpopular among official Anglo-Indians for what were regarded as his unconsidered and dangerous concessions to the natives. RK shared the general dislike, calling Ripon "a circular and bewildered recluse of religious tendencies" (*Something of Myself*, p. 50). Ripon was a Catholic convert.
7. On 25 January 1884.

To Edith Macdonald, 4 April 1884
ALS: Library of Congress

Lahore / Friday Even. April 4th. 1884

Sweetheart Auntie,

Don't you wish you were a nice little assistant editor playing all alone in the office for ten hours a day, with your chief blind with ophthalmia and the blessed English mail coming in in tons? Please say yes and I'll change places because I've been at work since eight this morning, and I'm a wee bit tired and sick at heart with it all. And the heat is creeping upon us like Tennyson's beast of prey behind the ever-dying fire;[1] only, in our case, the fire is being stoked up daily. Bless you a hundred thousand times for your letter; for it came when I was in a vale of "dock dispare" as "Helen's Babies"[2] would say sitting like Marius over the ruins of disembowelled papers from home[3] – myself sorely homesick too. Since I last wrote I have won my spurs as a descriptive special correspondent and even elicited approval from the far off Simla hills where my proprietors dwell. I was sent down to Pattiala a native state two hundred miles away. Lord Ripon our Viceroy was down there on a visit and I was told to write as much as I could[4] – ask Miss Craik[5] what I wrote as I have sent her the proofs for circulation among such of my friends as care to see them; but, however much I wrote I couldn't describe the jewels, the champagne, treachery, intrigue, princely hospitality, elephants, fours in hands etc. I came across. Fancy I had one elephant, one four in hand and as many horses as I could use *daily* at my disposal and lived like a prince of the blood royal, with sentries, guards of honour and everything except the salute, from which I was debarred on account of my non-official position. You may say what you like about the decadence of India, but, in a purely native state you see what a blaze of jewels and colour India must have been. At the close of my visit I was presented with fruits and nuts and, as I had expected, a douceur of Rs. 1000 at the bottom of the fruits. So I had to stride off in the blazing sunshine and my shirt sleeves to the Durbar and slang the Council of Regency, the Prime minister and the Finance minister for treating me like a servant instead of a friend. The C. & M. Gazette is the one paper that Pattiala State (the Maharajah is a minor) funks, as being read by our Lieutenant Governor and I had hoped they wouldn't have insulted one of the staff in this manner. Result was apologies all round and a return of the greasy notes to the finance minister, but before I went the Commander in Chief, a splendid old Sikh, insisted on giving me a silver mounted Remington rifle, and his blessing.[6] He was the best purely native native it has ever been my luck to come across and I took his present and his blessing in full Durbar and gave him my silver hunting spurs in exchange swearing that from that time forth I should look on him as a father. They are queer people these Sikhs but they do hold by the English and old Buckshi Gunda Singh fought against us at Chillianwallah[7] for which I like him.

Two other newspaper men were down with me and they cleared something like Rs. 2500 each I'm told by douceurs only – but they were half castes and, as I tenderly explained to one of them, it's "Like getting money from your father." I managed to cut down these gentry and get my letters into the papers before any other journal could get ahead of us, by a starlight ride of sixteen miles, to the nearest railway station, and sixteen miles back. The story is a long one to tell here and involves a lot of technical details but anyhow, I left Pattiala station at 9.20 one night (on a borrowed horse belonging to a native lancer) caught the half past ten train to Lahore and got my letter in. Then my horse shut up and I had to hunt about the platform of Rajporra station till I found a trooper of the irregular horse asleep with his beast picketed in the sand. I didn't wake the man but took his horse and tied my tired one to the lance and fled back to Pattiala – covering the 32 miles in a trifle less than two and a half hours and getting my letter into the paper next day – to the disgust of the other men.[8] [. . .][9] So heigho for economy and the cutting down of all beyond necessaries and with £20 clear to my credit we shall begin to set the "ball a rowling." May I live till it comes to "hunder poun" which should be at the year's end, and then I shall begin to flap my little wings and crow. This sobers the youthful mind and, as an intensely original remark, is "a spur in the sides of his intent"[10] – witness my long ride described over leaf whereto I verily believe I was urged solely for my far off little woman's sake. I think you can understand the sentiment, tho' it *did* end in flaying me where skin is *most* necessary to a horseman. I fear me this long rigmarole has told you nothing important but that really isn't my fault. I have to write two columns a week on what has happened, or rather what hasn't happened in Lahore,[11] and this sort of business can be done once and once only in the seven days. I couldn't write the blessed thing twice out even for the dearest Aunt in Christendom. My best love to that Godmother of mine in Wilden. It's a strange fact that I have never written to her for years – but you must even pass on the pith of my scribblings. Kitty Pullen,[12] if I recollect, was a little bit of a body who, once upon a time, kissed me at Bewdley when I was four.[13] You see, I am not forgetful of past favours. Now I am going to bed – a hot, – a red hot bed in a red hot room.

Your Nephew
Ruddy

Notes
1. Cf. Tennyson, "Locksley Hall", ll. 136–7.
2. See ch. 12 of John Habberton, Helen's Babies: "dokdishpair".
3. The General Gaius Marius, in old age a fugitive among the ruins of Carthage.
4. The Viceroy was at Patiala from 17 to 22 March. RK produced a four-part account, "The Viceroy at Patiala", CMG, 20, 21, 22, and 26 March (uncollected, except for the part of 22 March, in Pinney, Kipling's India).
5. Mary Craik: see 28 January 1882.
6. RK tells a very different version of the episode in Something of Myself. He returned the gift, he says there, by the hands of a low-caste camp-sweeper, so that his servant feared that RK's life might be endangered by the insult (p. 45).
7. The battle of Chillianwallah, 1849, in the second Sikh war.
8. There is perhaps a reminiscence of this ride in ch. 12 of The Naulahka.
9. Five and a half lines have been irrecoverably deleted by an unknown hand.

10. *Macbeth*, I.vii.25–6: "I have no spur/To prick the sides of my intent."
11. The earliest known of RK's columns entitled "A Week in Lahore" appeared in the *CMG*, 7 May 1884. He wrote the column irregularly until June 1886, when it disappears from the paper.
12. An orphaned cousin of the Macdonald family who lived with RK's grandmother.
13. Where RK's Macdonald grandparents lived. RK's first visit to England was in 1868; his second, in 1871: "when I was four" fits neither date.

To Edith Macdonald, 28 April 1884
ALS: Library of Congress

Lahore / April. 28th. 1884

Dearest Auntie

This has been a dolesome week for us all. T. went down with fever for thirty six long hours and was in bed for two days but she is up and about now. I myself have, for the last seven days, suffered from pains in the head – *not* a head-ache understand – and all sorts of disturbances in my eyes but, like T., I'm recovering and the medical man hints that I shan't hurt myself if I "go easy" until it is time for my flight to the hills, as he is inclined to think that I've been overdoing it of late. Wheeler and I have made a compact therefore to work the paper at the lowest possible pressure throughout the hot weather, which is "best for him and best for me." Nearly every one who can get leave has gone away and this little go of fever is a not too delicate hint to Mrs. Kipling to take her daughter to Dalhousie[1] as soon as may be. I'm only anxious to get them well away for the next four months as we shan't have a particularly healthy hot weather – measles and typhoid and small pox among the natives in April are pretty certain to grow unpleasant in July and August. As you are seven thousand miles away I don't mind telling you that there has been a case of sporadic cholera already and, as this is the third year since we had the last epidemic, we are anticipating a festive season later on.[2] It's very funny to watch the progress of any disease. It begins like an engagement with dropping shots, falling no one knows where and gradually settling down into a steady roll – a death roll if you please. But this is a gruesome subject. Lock it up in your own bosom therefore and, if you write to the Mother, I charge you, an you love me, not to tell her anything unpleasant about Lahore 'cos she'll be at the hills and it will only upset her. I'm looking forward to taking up what the Mother calls my "bachelor" life again, with the Pater, in a few weeks. It's a collarless, cuffless, bootless paradise of tobacco, unpunctuality, and sloth. We both enjoy it and roam about the house like bears in just any garment that comes handiest.

This "Poet's mind" has been vexed by the "shallow wit"³ of the Lahore Municipality and the result, as you will see, is duly enclosed.⁴ Maybe it will amuse you. The Municipality are fairly wrath, the more so as most of the other Indian journals are copying the doggrel. After much vexation of spirit I have at last, got my – or rather our – little book of verse under way.⁵ It is composed exclusively of parodies and has taken up more time than it is worth. Our big Scotch foreman,⁶ into whose hands I delivered the copy with solemn injunctions to make "a good thing of it," has waxed quite enthusiastic over the job. This afternoon he assured me with oaths and curses that I might throw the book at his head if it wasn't a ―――― success as far as his department went; and he *is* undoubtedly learned in type and printers craft. He declares that it is to be out in a fortnight from now and the cost to your humble servant will be just nothing while he has the pick of some tons of the newest type. *Moral.* Be a journalist and you can publish as you please. It's a tiny little book but we hope to get it decently reviewed and as it's anonymous no harm will be done. Be assured that I will send you a copy. And now good bye. It's a skimpy letter but I ain't up to my usual form and Wheeler has gone down with ague.

Your loving nephew
Ruddy.

Notes
1. Since Trix at sixteen was too young for a Simla season her mother took her to Dalhousie, a less fashionable and less expensive hill station than Simla. RK joined them in August, the only time that he did not spend his hot-weather leave at Simla while he was in India.
2. A quarantine had already been imposed on ships from India at Mediterranean ports, but the *CMG* says nothing of an epidemic in the next few months.
3. See [26–8 January 1884]. This was evidently a joke between RK and Edith Macdonald.
4. "The Ornamental Beasts", *CMG*, 26 April 1884 (Rutherford, *Early Verse*); the verses make fun of the Municipality's authorising the purchase of two tiger cubs for the local zoo at a time when there was general outcry against the state of the town drains.
5. *Echoes, by Two Writers* (Lahore, 1884); the first book that RK published on his own initiative (*Schoolboy Lyrics* was produced without his knowledge by his parents), a collaboration with Trix. The thirty-nine poems in the book are mostly parodies or imitations but not exclusively. Some arise out of RK's personal experience rather than his reading, and of these most date from just before his departure for India.
6. The printer was J. M. Chalmers.

To Edith Macdonald, 2–7 June [1884]
AL, *incomplete*: Library of Congress

June 2nd. Inkpot has been upset over the top of page.

Dearest Auntie

At last the hot weather has come upon us handsomely. As I write under the Punkah it is 95°, and an ill omened pillar of dust is skirmishing about outside under an orange coloured sky. The clouds are so low down and so metallic in appearance that one feels as if they could be rapped with the knuckles, and if this were done that they would ring like saucepans.

Our great consolation through it all is to hear the Mother at Dalhousie talking of velvets and plush and wood fires far away in the Hills. Thank goodness she and the child are out of it, which is well, for the Abominable has come into the station and it seems as though she would stay with us for a month or two or three. I saw her, the other day, knock a man down. He died in a trifle under two hours, and his friends told me that it was the "will of God." I was never so angry with any one in my life before as I was with those dusky mourners. *Just* think, a human life (not that that is of any importance in this densely crowded land) thrown away before one's very eyes through rotten melons and bad *arrack*! But I was a fool all the same and defrayed the expenses of the funeral (3s. 8d in your money) because I rather liked the man. He was one of my orderlies. All this may sound unpleasant to Western imaginations, but I assure you that an English East wind is more deadly than most epidemics of Asiatic cholera.

I went down with a touch of fever seven days ago. It laid hold of me for forty eight hours and then let me go uninjured. My only dread is lest I should get a severe go and so be forced to take my month's leave some time before the worst gets to the worst – in August or September that is – 'specially September.

Tuesday. The clouds broke last night in rain and wind. Such rain and such lightning – thirty flashes to the minute and the sky as it were disembowelled at each flash. It has cooled us down a little but not much.

The unpleasant consequences of allowing even an old horse a week's holiday showed themselves yesterday in the case of my waler. He has been luxuriating for eight long days and, even as Jeshurun did, so he waxed fat and kicked.[1] I hadn't been equal to riding him for some time by reason of my fever but yesterday evening methought I would just take him out of stables and trot him round the compound. To this end I didn't trouble about slipping on the saddle but just clambered up and commenced drumming on his aged ribs with my heels – as is my wont.

The old boy threw me at once, into a clump of hardy annuals, with all the *verve* of a two year old. I wasn't hurt a bit and as soon as I had stomached the insult I felt proud that my gee was so festive. This evening I intend that he shall be ridden – excessively and indubitably ridden by me until he has recovered his tone for it's much too hot to ride a bobbery horse in this weather. Now that there are so few folk in the Station I am a good deal thrown back on my horses' society. You see in this country, living as they do with natives, you can have 'em out and about the place like dogs and a "naked horse" in the garden is great fun. The waler will canter after me and pretend to shy when I wave a whip at him. Joe I can't trust because he bites when occasion offers and, if the two are loose together, they fight. (A horse fight by the way is one of the most impressive things out. They worry each other like dogs and scream like a regiment of women). The other evening I went to sleep in a hammock in the garden and the waler walked out of his stable to see how I was getting on. His voice in my ear woke me up but as I didn't want to play I turned round and slapped him over the nose – a proceeding which he chose to regard as a signal for romps. He shoved his thick head under the hammock and before I could stop him, regularly nuzzled me out on to the path below. I fancy it must have been intention on his part, at all events I rose up and drove him away to his own quarters and he returned in a few minutes to try to repeat the game.

Wednesday. The weather has been delightfully broken up by a blustering, almost cold, wind which came on yesterday even. Four of us, two couples, went out for a ride on the dusty alkali plains between Lahore and Miran Mir[2] and "revelled in the blast." The ride degenerated into a sky lark after a dog on the horizon and we came in at eight o'clock singing and shouting along the deserted roads like children out for a holiday. The beauty of Lahore in the hot weather is that you can carry on as you will and there is no one to say "don't."

Friday. The mail came in last night with never a word for either of us poor wretches down here, and we had instead the melancholy satisfaction of packing off the weeks *dâk*[3] to Dalhousie for the mother and child. By the way, that portion of the family move into a bigger house to set it in order against the time that we come up from below on our respective leaves. That's the mischief of a family; you have to keep a double establishment up for half the year, and any average woman in the hills must have five or six men *solely to carry her about*. Our family square is, thank goodness, well enough able to bear the financial strain, but it comes cruelly hard on people who have a big family and an inelastic income. I know scores of 'em in this distressful country, and whenever the Pater mourns, as he does sometimes, bless him, that he has nothing for me to "come in to" save his name, I remind him, (coarsely at times, seeing that we live alone and lose, in a great measure, the graces of speech) that he has only one female to look after in addition to Mrs. Kipling, who might so easily have presented him with half a dozen girls and a boy or two in by gone days. I fancy the argument comforts him a little, but people will always find something to growl at however comfortable they may be. Now that I am out here and am "doing for myself" here, the Pater would fain have me twelve years old once more and to that end talks of my screw as "that boy's pocket money," and if I let him, would I believe pay all my bills. *Entre nous* I have been disgracefully petted and spoiled and that at a time when I ought to have my head bumped against all sorts of unpleasant things besides heat and hard work. But I fear me that the family □ will have to be broken up one of these days so I enjoy its shelter and its comforts while I may.

Saturday. This letter really must come to an end today. I have taken it up at odd moments and scribbled at it till it has grown to three sheets of elaborately expressed nothings which are hardly likely to interest you. I was counting on a holiday today but the Sind Punjab and Delhi railway needs must derail a train and slay thirteen coolies and there was no reporter handy *of course*, when the preliminary inquiry opened. It's not the least use being above any sort of work in this land so I had to ride over to the court and report as best I might. The heat was terrific, the court crowded with natives; and I don't expect you to believe me when I tell you that the thermometer marked 128° on the wall behind me. I was there for four hours, took down four columns of matter – cross examinations, and technical details for the most part – re copied it from shorthand to long, and am wailing [waiting] now for the proofs to turn up in time for tonight's paper.[4] A two mile ride with the thermometer at 172° in the sun has skinned my nose, and the iron of my giglamps has burnt a blue horse-shoe over the bridge of it, but there are times when Life is really worth living and those half a dozen hours of high-pressure work came in as a tonic to the regular office routine. My chief has complimented me quite unreservedly – a rare thing for him as he believes in "sitting on" the young idea when possible. Consequently I am in a peaceful frame of mind, in spite of the heat. It's curious to notice how the weather trains one down. Just now I am 8st. 5 lbs and the Pater chaffs me about my slimness. He calls it "leanness" which is vulgar. I prefer to consider it hard condition. This evening at six we have our fortnightly races. They are great fun as we are all Gentlemen riders. I am entered for the Musical Stakes – prize a jews harp. A quarter mile scurry for all ponies, bonafide hacks – the rider to play a musical instrument and to come in playing it. Old Joe doesn't mind what you do on his back so I have arranged a tambourine on the pommel of my saddle thus [drawing] and shall drum on it with my whip butt. Last fortnight every one rode every one else's tat;[5] the winner to come in last. Joe won this race easily – my mount bolted with me and ran about half a mile ere I could get a pull on her. Her owner told me she had a snaffle mouth – an infamous fib – and when I pointed out that she had no mouth at all he blandly answered – "Oh I forgot to tell you that you ought to have put on a *chain* snaffle and a standing martingale." This arrangement I may tell you is a good deal more severe than an ordinary curb, and I rode in a smooth bit that was about as thick as a healthy knitting needle. The moral of which is never ride a strange horse in a race without trying it first. Perhaps "racing," as you understand it in England, sounds rather shocking to you. Here are a list of the prizes for your information. *A two mile steeple chase*, A pewter mug. *A half mile flat* handicap, a whip. *The musical stakes* – a jews harp. A *cheroot and umbrella race* – (you smoke the cheroot and keep the "brolly" open), a cigar holder – *and a postilion race* – riding one horse and driving another – a card of Honour [the rest is missing].

Notes
1. Deuteronomy 32.15.
2. The cantonment three miles east of Lahore.
3. Mail.
4. A two-part article on the preliminary inquiry, "The Railway Accident", appears in the *CMG* not on Saturday but on Monday and Tuesday, 9–10 June. Four articles on the trial, "The Late Railway Accident", appeared on 14, 16, 17, and 18 June. There is no evidence apart from this letter that they are by RK.
5. Short for tattoo, a country-bred pony.

To Margaret Burne-Jones, 10 June 1884
ALS: University of Sussex

                    Lahore / June 10th. 1884 – 9.45 in the Evening

Dear Wop

"I wants to make your flesh creep"[1] with a description of our unholy weather just now. It's not that I wish to be pitied, because I am disgustingly well, but I take an interest and a deep pride in everything that Lahore produces. To begin with; for the past seven days we have not seen the sun, and thrice in that time the lamps have been lit at our office at high noon. As you look out of window the land seems to have been smitten with a black frost and fog, and the view ends in mist at fifty yards range – it might be London in November but for the heat, and that is really terrifying. At six o'clock in the evening the butt of my riding crop is too hot to hold, and I can feel the heat of the stirrup-irons through the soles of my boots. All through the day the air is perfectly dead and smells hideously – the smell of sulphur, old brick fields and charnel houses. In the evening, at seven punctually, a burning wind cracks our skin for an hour and then dies away in thunder and a flash or two of summer lightning and the thermometer stands as high at night as it does in the day. All sounds are deadened as if the skies were hung with wool and there are awful half hours towards the end of the day when you feel as though the "Twilight of the Gods" had begun. At nine in the morning you twist a handkerchief round your dog cart reins before you can lay a finger on them and you are lucky if in your evening ride or drive a blast of the hot wind doesn't make your nose bleed. It cuts into the nostrils like a razor and has more than once sent me home with all the appearance of a severely wounded warrior. I ain't proud but *can* your country produce anything like this?[2]

The oldest inhabitant says that he remembers nothing like this, because by rights we ought to have a sky of brass over our heads and a *clean* heat withal. No one seems to know what it means but all are agreed that rain *must* come ere long. You in the West who talk so much about the weather can't understand what it is to wait for a drop of water to cool your torments. Here's a faithful copy of a conversation holden this evening between two residents – men *bien entendu*.

"How's your room? Mine's 96°."

"You're lucky. Can't keep mine below 100°. Any hope of rain?"

"Don't know. There's been heavy rain in the Hills but the River's low. Looks bad. How's your liver?"

"All right. Had six hours fever yesterday from sleeping in the thermantidote though."

"Ah! you should avoid thermantidotes like pork and pegs. How much quinine pulled you through?"

"Fifty grains in the day. My head's all jumpy now. Come and have a drink. What'll you take?"

"Sulphuric ether peg; and you?"

"Tonic and bitters, thanks. Boy, bring a punkah."

Then they collapsed but I took down the conversation *verbatim* on my sleeve cuff, but it was all spoken with immense deliberation and the regular hot weather drawl that we all get into. It took about fifteen minutes to deliver. Sulphuric ether pegs are nasty things to take but a chlorodyne one is worse and a tonic and bitters vilest of all. Every mixed drink with soda water is a peg[3] – but they don't necessarily include whiskey.

All this time, though, the Mother and the Sister are far away in a cool climate where they wear velvet and plush and fear neither the "pestilence that walketh in the darkness or the sickness that destroyeth in the noonday"[4] and their daily letters full of stories of cold wet rains and bitter thunderstorms fill us two with peace. Every evening as the budget is read and the cheroots are brought on the table we go through our chorus of thanks giving. The Pater, with his head in a bowl of hot charcoal trying to light his smoke: – "Well, (puff) praise the (puff, puff) Lord *they* are out of it." The Son meditatively from the depths of a cane chair: –

"Yes," – then, as a happy thought strikes him, "and they are best where they are." The formulae of Father and Son seldom vary and the expression comes to our lips almost mechanically. I have badgered the Pater into taking a ten days "privilege leave" at the end of this month because I fancy the weather is telling on him. He has a report to write which I have bound mysef by solemn oaths to finish for him.[5] His three months holiday begins in August but the extra leave won't do him any harm. Now, have I made your flesh creep sufficient? because I'm going to put myself to grill on a heated stove falsely called a bed, while the fetid air is puddled up to some semblance of a breeze by an inefficient punkah and I have no more time to spare on my revered cousin. The sheet is as warm as though it had been freshly ironed – verily the "Land of Regrets"[6] is a sweet place.

Your shrivelled
Wop of Asia

The queer fist is because I'm writing with a blistered paw – effects of a thin bridle and a strong horse on Saturday – so I write gingerly and with the extreme end of the pen in my hand.

Notes
1. Dickens, *Pickwick Papers*, ch. 8.
2. Between the first and the tenth of the month the maximum temperatures varied from 100° to 113°, and six days were either misty, hazy, or dusty.
3. *Peg* is from the English, not from any Indian source. Chlorodyne, a patent medicine, was advertised as a cure or treatment for diarrhoea, ague, dysentery, fever, lockjaw, cramp, colic, snake bite, prickly heat, sunstroke, and cholera (e.g., *CMG*, 30 September 1884).
4. Psalms 91:6, *Book of Common Prayer*.
5. Perhaps the Annual Report of the Lahore Central Museum for 1883–4; it is reviewed in detail in the *CMG*, 2 July 1884.
6. The title and refrain of a poem about India by Sir Alfred Lyall, collected in *Verses Written in India* (London, 1889).

To Edith Macdonald, [10–14] July [1884]
AL, *incomplete*: Library of Congress

Lahore / July. 11th.

"At Cromer by the sea coast all alone she longed to be."[1] And did you find yourself better after your visit to that funniest of out of the way health resorts? Jean Ingelow's heroine, if you recollect, heard the gulls there talking about all sorts of unpleasant things and incontinently wrote certain exceeding bad verses to celebrate the occasion. This is a warning.

The Pater and I have struggled through the worst of the hot weather together and at the end of the month we go up together to Dalhousie where the Mother is anxiously awaiting us. For Mr. Kipling the hot weather is practically over as he won't have to return till October. I have September to face, alone, but as that month *can't* be so awful as the past one I care not.

I assure you Auntie, that for one weary week my fear in the daytime was that I was going to die, and at night my only fear was that I might live to the morning. I wasn't seedy but I was washed out and boiled down to the lowest safe working point, had lost my sense of taste, my temper and all desire to keep alive a moment longer than was necessary. The Pater had gone to Dalhousie for a week and as soon as I was alone in the big dark house my eyes began their old tricks again,[2] and I was so utterly unstrung (*you'd* be as bad if you sweated twenty four hours a day for three weeks on end) that they bothered me a good deal. I could only avoid the shadows by working every minute that I could see, and I can say with my hand on my heart – I mean my head – that I cured myself by going sixteen hours grind a day at office, at original matter and much precis writing – *videlicet,* condensing a Bill which has been introduced into the legislative council, from ten columns to two, and writing the grimmest sort of stuff and nonsense about its possible scope or probable inefficiency.[3] It cured the blue devils but it about used me up. Wheeler came back some days ago from his trip to the Hills; he's not much better I fear and talks about getting a month in September during which time I shall be again in charge of the old rag and after my holiday ought to do her and myself justice.

Nota Bene. This is the way that holiday will be spent – I, Rudyard Kipling, swear it. Get up at 9.30, or later and eat heavily. 10–2. lie on a sofa, smoke cheroots and make Trixie read me *my own poems* till I go to sleep. Tiffin heavily. Lie on my back in the sunshine after tiffin, smoke and sleep some more. Dine at eight and go to sleep under two thick blankets! Elevated and soothing isn't it? I intend to leave every scrap of work behind; never to look at the C.M.G. and to abstain from anything more intellectual than tobacco. I wonder whether you can understand the intense need for physical and mental rest that comes over one at the end of eleven months straight on end labour – otherwise you'll scoff at my "menew" drawn up above.

Friday Morn. A wet and sodden evening yesterday and I went down to the station to see a couple of ladies off to England. One of 'em was the fair Miss Webbe, the girl that [. . .]⁴

Sunday Morn. Wheeler is pronounced to be ill with "ulcer of the cornea" and fever – videlicet partial blindness and complete prostration. For me it has been a weary ten hour day of almost hopeless work and unspeakable confusion and worry but the blessed old rag came out all serene, tho' I did have to write the greater part of it. It rests me to pour out the story of my bothers into your ear, and to know that you'll know exactly the right thing to write in return. May you be spared the inevitable filing down and defilement of temper and spirits that is the birthright of such a worm as I, but in spite of that I would sooner be baited by incompetent subordinates, and drunken proof readers out here——

Monday – and here I fell fast asleep but I meant to have written than any other possible walk of life – which isn't grammatical but I trust you see my meaning. Wheeler is awful blind still and goodness only knows when he will be better: so today again has been nothing but toil and weariness of spirit and I have just seen to the last page of my old rag comfortably locked up and put to bed on the main press – to my exceeding satisfaction for the stars in their courses came down and fought with me.

Starlight by the way reminds me of a moonlight picnic held at the Shalimar rose gardens a few days ago – one of the loveliest places under Heaven.⁵ There were eight of us and a full moon forbye. A young Subaltern and myself were the hosts and, tho' I say it as shouldn't, I have a notion that the picnic was one of the pleasantest entertainments of the season. We rode down in couples to the Gardens in the moonlight. The gardens themselves looked like fairy land. Great sheets of still water, inlaid marble colonnades, and carved marble couches at the edge, thick trees and lime bushes and acres of night blooming flowers that scented the whole air. The scene was really past all description and I couldn't give you any better idea than by referring you to Tennyson's description of the garden of the princess Ida by moon light. We just sat round and talked and then the women began to sing *naturally and without pressing* and the voices came across the water like the voices of spirits. This is strong I admit but not beyond what the occasion demands. I wonder how all the scene would have impressed you. In the end we deluged our partners with bouquets and wreaths of Marshal Niel roses and I drove the party back in the small hours of the morning. A big picnic is a mistake as the thing can only be done at all well between

To Edith Macdonald, [10–14] July [1884]

people who know one another well and thoroughly. Once more, I wish you had been there. That was a most pleasant interlude in a week's worry.

Trixie and I have been hard at work lately on a book of "Echoes" which is to be printed some day. It's all parody work for which T. shows a great facility being her mother's daughter where verse is concerned. I have written a psychological poem on Jack and Jill, in Browning's vein, and made an Idyll of the King, out of the rhyme of King Stephen.[6] Tennyson lends himself to parody only too quickly: –

> A weed, one weed and only one had I,
>   One weed the weediest one of all my store
> One weed, with but one match to light it by
>   A weed was mine that now is mine no more.

> A weed, a weedy weed was mine to smoke
>   Oh ay! ay oh! the match that burns and dies
> My true love garmented in russet cloak
>   Ay oh! oh ay! the flickering flame that flies.

> And one went out and one refused to burn
>   And one expired, and t'other would not draw.
> And both have failed me – whither shall I turn
>   For withered weeds that shall be mine no more.[7]

But this is frivol and drivel and my letter must come to an end. Being busy I write a long letter which is natural.
    Love to you all and a big heartful from your
                              Nephew all for yourself.

Notes
1. Jean Ingelow, "Requiescat in Pace!", ll. 22–3.
2. Perhaps something like what he describes in *Something of Myself*, p. 17: "I imagined I saw shadows and things that were not there." According to RK it was at this time, too, that he heard from Flo Garrard breaking off their "understanding" (see 3 May–24 June 1886).
3. The précis is "The Reorganisation of the Punjab Commission", *CMG*, 3 July 1884. An article on the scheme, 30 June, and one on its possible effects, 4 July 1884, may also be by RK.
4. A page of the MS appears to be missing from this point until the continuation of the letter on "Saturday Morn". I have not identified Miss Webbe, though it is probable that she is the Miss Marian Webb who played the part of Azema in the Lahore production of *The Palace of Truth* on 14 April 1884: see 19 February 1884.
5. Four miles east of Lahore, laid out in 1667 for Shah Jahan; they covered about eighty acres at the time of RK's writing.
6. "The Flight of the Bucket" and "The Cursing of Stephen" in *Echoes*.

7. This parody of Tennyson's "Pelleas and Ettare", ll. 391–400, does not appear in *Echoes* (Rutherford, *Early Verse*).

To Edith Macdonald, 14 August [1884]
AL, *incomplete*: Library of Congress

Maryville / Dalhousie / August. 14th

On Leave

In these days have I returned to my Nursery and Trixie is with me, so that for one blessed month I am become a child again. Dalhousie is one of the loveliest places on the face of the earth – it is also one of the rainiest and from a social point of view the dullest;[1] but we four have been very happy. In the daytime it is my *business* to go a walking or a riding when the weather permits; to play hop scotch with Mr. Kipling; to shoot with an air gun at a target, to drink bottled beer (a thing impossible in the plains) and to write poems; – at the rate of one gem per diem. Once a day, too, the Civil and Military Gazette comes up from below and I spend a jovial half [hour?] with a B.B.B. pencil, making scornful marginal notes as to the way in which my department is now managed. In a fortnight I shall go down stairs and Wheeler will come up for a month and then *he'll* make marginal notes of exceeding bitterness on my work. So that we are both kept up to our mark.

Yesterday Trix dragged me out to the Rubicon, a mountain stream cutting across a two foot road over huge boulders of granite and down into the valley below three thousand good feet. There we danced on stepping stones; picked flowers and sailed boats of bark down the current, finally the game grew so fascinating that my only match box was converted into a boat which gave us amusement and excitement for ten [   ][2] minutes before it dropped out of sight. Then [   ] came across a mother lizard who had la[   ] five crimson eggs on the ground [   ] of the cliff and we watched [   ] for an [   ]; patting and arranging [   ] scraping sand over them. It's [   ] I have ever assisted at. The mist in front of us rose like a wall and we seemed to be at the end of the world. All round us the mountain streams were thundering down to the plains (and in the confined spaces of these huge valleys every stream sings like a bell) but quite distinct from the big noises we could hear the tiny "lick lick lick" of the little creatures' claws in the stones. Trixie and I went away big with the knowledge that we knew of a lizard's nest right away among the Himalayas. Then we unearthed a monstrous Eft[3] at least a foot long and him we chased into a granite crevice with the ends of our umbrellas lest he should discover his wife's eggs and eat them; when the economy of nature had been put straight, so far as lay in our hands, we went home singing at the top of our voices, for the pleasure of hearing how far the sound carried. Fancy a place where you can sing and play at swimming boats in your oldest garments, no man making you afraid!

Today Trix went out for a ride on old Joe who was sent up here for my pleasure but who is to remain for hers. I bought her a side saddle so that she is independent of every one, and that side saddle wants a lady's stirrup. Just now she is using one of mine but I've sent off to Simla for one, and the saddler's, with a fine sense of what is needed in the Hills, have sent me the invoice of a patent Ladies' safety [ ]kel plated abomination (doubtless contrived [ ] a mouse-trap) which will throw [ ] gear into the shade. Trixie is [ ] with [ ] horse at her disposal. [ ] is spoiling Joe as [ ] be [the rest is missing].

Notes
1. "Dullhouses", as Trix said it was called (11 April 1945: *ALS*, Sussex).
2. Word or brief phrase missing from damaged MS, here and from other bracketed places.
3. Tennyson, *Maud*, I.iv.31: "A monstrous eft was of old the Lord."

To Miss Coxen,[1] 2 September 1884
ALS: Library of Congress

Lahore/Sept. 2nd. 1884

Dear Miss Coxen

Herewith my long promised but much deferred booklet.[2] The *Pioneer* has been good enough to write all sorts of complimentary things about it but, as my preface says, it is your opinion and not the Pi's that I value.

My month at Dalhousie ended in the death of Joe. He fell out of his stable one night (thanks to the carelessness of the *sais*),[3] rolled over the khud[4] and broke his back. *Me voici* at present confined to the wee white pony that used to support Miss Shegog's weight. This is melancholy news to end a note with but Lahore is ghastly dull and I must be forgiven for catching the infection.

Yours very sincerely
Rudyard Kipling.

Notes
1. Miss Coxen played the part of Palmis in the production of *The Palace of Truth* at Lahore in April 1884 in which RK had the part of Chrysal (see 19 February 1884). RK evidently saw much of her in the spring and early summer of this year: see his verses on her leaving Lahore in Rutherford, *Early Verse*, pp. 219–20.
2. *Echoes*. The book, in an edition of 150 copies, was published in August.
3. Groom.
4. Steep slope or hillside; the hill-station roads were often cut into the *khud*, and falls were frequent.

To Edith Macdonald, 17 September 1884
ALS: Library of Congress

Lahore / Sept. 17th. 1884.

Dearest Auntie,

Like the hardened wife beaters of Bow Street, your nephew has put in his fourteen days "solitary confinement with hard labour." There are yet five more weeks ere the family come down from their various summer refuges. Trix is on a visit at Dalhousie; (107 miles off) the Pater and Mrs. K at Simla (240 miles) and as for me I'm watching the hot weather die out down here. Things are not so bad as they were last year – or I'm more used to the business – but living as utterly alone as I do neither sweetens the temper or soothes a bothered soul. There's hardly a soul in the Station and in spite of our efforts to keep going, we are very very dull. But I'm afraid I speak with prejudice. As a matter of fact, I haven't been quite well and look on creation as through a glass darkly. Last night I was shot out of my little bed with spassims in my tummy and all sorts of aches forbye. Threshing around in a pitch dark empty house and calling for servants who won't hear, and hunting for medicines one can't find isn't the pleasantest thing in the world. When I had dug up my man he lit a lamp and took a look at me and straightway bolted out of the house. This made me fancy that I must have got a touch of the "sickness that destroyeth in the noonday"[1] as distinguished from the other article and I poured myself out a pretty stiff doze of chlorodyne and sat down to await the march of events and pray for the morning. I had hardly rolled on to the floor however before my man turned up for the second time with a naked oil lamp, a little bottle and a queer looking weapon in his hand. The fellow had brought me opium and a pipe all complete and then and there insisted upon my smoking as much as I could. Well I wasn't in a condition to argue so he rolled the pills and I set to. Presently I felt the cramps in my legs dying out and my tummy more settled and a minute or two later it seemed to me that I fell through the floor. When I woke up I found my man waiting at the bed side where he had put me, with a glass of warm milk and a stupendous grin. After the milk I felt much clearer in the head and got up to breakfast and office. Mind you I merely felt awfully dull and thick headed but I must have looked queer for Macdonald,[2] my help from Allahabad, declares that I came into the office with every sign of advanced intoxication. This however has worn off and left me almost well – an evening ride will put me straight I trust. My man is awfully pleased with himself and walks round me as though I were a rare and curious animal, occasionally putting his hand on my shoulder. You may guess how grateful I am to him for his prompt action. He vows and declares that I was going to have a touch of the sickness that is loose in our City now. Whether he is right or wrong I know not but he certainly cut short a spell of the acutest pain I have ever experienced in my life and no woman could have tended me more carefully than he through those three terrible hours between eleven and two.

Nota Bene. In the ordinary affairs of life he lies beyond your imagination and will swindle me whenever he has a chance. They are a queer people indeed. I haven't written a word to the mother about last night's experiences; she would worry and fret and mayhap come down to Lahore – a place where she could neither help me nor I her if any thing went wrong. In October – at the end of it that is, everything will be safe for both of them – Mother and child – and I shan't have the least compunction in hurrying them up or rather down.

A Paternal and muddle headed Government (whose sworn foe am I) have called the Pater up to Simla to "consult" about the London Exhibition of next year. It is more than possible that he may be sent home to look after it while it lasts – a matter of perhaps four months.[3] He'll enjoy that I fancy for like the costermonger's donkey, an Exhibition is "a little 'oliday to 'im."

A propos to removals I am rather exercised about my own chances in that line. Allen,[4] our main proprietor and the man who looks on me very much as the work of his hands, is very keen on getting me off to Allahabad on the *Pioneer* and has been again talking to the Pater about it at Simla. Allen says truthfully enough it will be close upon £500 a year for me, let alone the dignity of being on the boss paper of Asia. All this I admit but on the other hand I find that Allahabad is 800 miles from Lahore and I should be as completely out of the family as though I were in England, a thing that I certainly don't desire till the time comes – my own time that is. The Parents of course are torn two ways and the Pater says "E'en settle it yourself." So I've consumed about half a pound of tobacco in the momentous question and hinted as politely as possible that I'd rather stay where I am. I'm beginning to know the Province. Wheeler goes sick often enough to give me a good many temporary Editorships – rather more than I require indeed, and anyhow I'm well up in the business of the paper. To this Allen says in effect, "Quite true my son but we must have you on the Pioneer, in twelve months at the outside. You'll get Rs 400 a month and a lot of valuable experience." I'm afraid this doesn't please me any the more. Now here's a professional secret. The Pioneer makes a *clear profit* of £12,000, *not* rupees per annum, whereas the C.M.G. is worked at an annual loss of £1,000. Any fool can help run a paying paper but the beauty of the business is to work up an unprofitable one, by making it attractive if possible. This I have been steadily trying to do when my hands are free and I'd cheerfully do it on a hundred a year less – just for my own personal satisfaction. If they get another man in to fill my place he'll want a salary nearly twice as big as mine for doing the same work. Our proprietors can't drop the C.M.G. because in spite of a loss which they can well afford to pay, it ranks next the *Pi* and absorbs all the *clientêle* of the Punjab and Northern Bengal. Why not then work it on the cheap for a bit? Excellent as my arguments are, I'm afraid I shall have to leave my first love just when I've got all the reins into my hand and begin again on another paper where all the work is done differently and in all the minutiæ of newspaper "fixings" there are vast differences. Consequently I am a wee bit wrath, but the Pater vows it's a grand step and it only remains therefore if all goes well to make our last year together as pleasant as may be.

Ask Stan what it's like to get his remove into a higher form and though the cases aren't exactly parallel I fancy he'd tell you what my sentiments are. Not a man on the Pioneer and there are four of 'em is under seven years' experience and I shall have to unlearn what little I know. Now that the matter seems settled I intend having a final flare-up on the old rag and am starting a set of weekly articles whereof the enclosed is a specimen.[5] Another one on an opium den in Lahore[6] has stirred up the easy going clericals here to a state of virtuous horror, and a parody of Locksley Hall,[7] which please find with this, has disturbed the Pioneer who wanted to say something nasty about Lord Ripon's retirement but only came out with a ponderous leader no one read. I chuckle a good deal over the week's work and am meditating a whole series of fresh assaults. Macdonald, who is a *Pioneer* man, sent to relieve Wheeler, is doing his share of galvanising the paper into vitality and I fancy our month together will be a festive one. But Lord! Lord! what vanity is this. Here am I, just helped by my servant out of something exceeding unpleasant to say no more, and with my head still ringing like a bell from the fumes of that infernal opium, plotting and planning and crowing on my own little dunghill as though I were one of the immortals.

Midnight. Just in from a dinner with the wife of one of our railway magnates and, as usual, abominably restless, and wide awake. Wherefore I must finish off this letter and then seek comfort in the smoking bowl – of my pipe. Everything is ghastly still and the night is as black as pitch. I am correspondingly cheerful but I won't inflict my mirth on you.

Love to all the Aunts and relations. By the way I hear that a photo of Stan has reached the parents and this reminds me that I have no up to date photo of your sweet face. My only one, in front of me now, represents you as a girl of twenty,[8] and I fain would get another. Bear this in mind and send one swiftly to your

Always loving Nephew.

Notes
1. Psalms 91:6, *Book of Common Prayer*.
2. Andrew Macdonald (1852–99), assistant editor of the *Pioneer*. He was afterwards editor of the Calcultta *Englishman*.
3. The Colonial and Indian Exhibition at South Kensington, 1886. JLK did not attend it, but he was responsible for the Punjab exhibit.
4. (Sir) George William Allen (1831–1900) founded the *Pioneer* in 1865; CIE, 1879; KCIE, 1897. JLK knew him from an early period in his Indian years and contributed to the *Pioneer* regularly, both from Bombay and from Lahore. Allen's gift was in finding good people to write for him.
5. "The Tragedy of Crusoe, C.S.", *CMG*, 13 September (uncollected) is probably the item in question; it is not attested by any external evidence except for the signature "Jacob Cavendish, M.A.", a pseudonym that RK used at this time, and no one else on the *CMG* could have written it. It did not lead to a "set of weekly articles". It is, however, the earliest known of RK's imaginative prose compositions in the *CMG*.
6. "The Gate of the Hundred Sorrows", *CMG*, 26 September. Since it had not yet been published, the reaction of the "clericals" is imaginary.
7. "Lord Ripon's Reverie", *CMG*, 15 September (Rutherford, *Early Verse*).
8. She had turned thirty-six three days before the date of this letter.

To Elizabeth Davey,[1] 2 October 1884
ALS: Mr Jeffrey Young

Lahore / October. 2nd. 1884

Dearest Lizzie,

When I say that I'm a blackguard of the deepest dye in the matter of not answering your last letter, you will, I trust, agree with me. I was on leave when your note came, among the mists and rains of damp Dalhousie and rejoiced as much as you could to read of the Fairy Prince who had turned up, at last, from far Cathay. No one that I know deserves a piece of good fortune of this kind better than Miss D[avey][2] and if, by chance, it should turn out that your fairy prince stayed I should rejoice exceedingly. There are very few of the kind out here and, for matter of that Princesses either.

For the past month I've been alone in Lahore, which was practically deserted, struggling with the old rag. The life was by no means a pleasant one, but it paid me well as my owners have given me a *dowsuer*, which is French I think for a tip, of £20 and have raised my salary to £30 a month i.e. £360 a year. Did I tell you how my little book of poems[3] has come to be a success – I might almost write a great success. The papers have given me some really handsome Reviews – Here are a few gems: – A brilliant little book of rhymes. Excellent examples of spontaneous grace and nicety of diction. Touching off the humours of Indian life with dainty felicity. Also they said I had the grace of Praed[4] the classic rhythm of Mortimer Collins[5] and a whole host of other diseases insomuch that I shall have to issue a second edition.[6] From a financial point of view the little venture did more than I could ever have anticipated and enabled me to buy a new horse, who is the delight of my play time. He rejoices in the name of *Deadly Sin*, by reason of an especially malignant eye, and has come to follow me around like a dog. But this is a detail which won't interest you I fancy. Trix and Mrs K. are at present at Dalhousie where the former has grown in "beauty and favour before God and man – especially man"[7] – only she won't have much to do with them – as is only proper.

I have plunged merrily into the small "vortex" of society here – People are gradually beginning to drift down again as the weather gets cooler – and thanks to Trixie have made my debut as that most unenviable of beings a "dancing man." It means late hours and dress boots – two things which my lazy "sole" (if you'll forgive the pun) abominates. But the details of Indian life are so trivial that, with the best will in the world I couldn't make anything like a letter out of 'em. This is a scurvy return for your lengthy communication dear – but the best I can give just now. Write soon, for my home letters are few and far between and I'd give up everything I have for an hour in Boltons.[8] My best love to that best of women Mrs P[erry].[9] she owes me a letter by the bye. Remind her of this. And believe me

Yours always
Ruddy

Notes

1. The governess in the Perry family (see 31 January–February 1882); her age is given in the Census of April 1881 as twenty-five.
2. The letters of the name after the initial have been inked out.
3. *Echoes*.
4. Winthrop Mackworth Praed (1802–39), a notable writer of *vers de société*.
5. Collins (1827–76), writer of much light verse among other work.

6. No second edition of *Echoes* is known, though RK was still planning one a year later: see 19 November 1885.
7. Perhaps an echo of Luke 2:52.
8. The Perrys now lived at 25 The Grove, The Boltons, West Brompton.
9. All but the initial letter of the name has been inked out.

To Edith Macdonald, 21 November 1884
ALS: Library of Congress

Lahore. / Nov. 21. 1884

Dearest Auntie,

The beginning of your last letter cut me to the core of my somewhat leathery conscience; for, as a matter of fact, I haven't sent you a line since you acknowledged the receipt of Echoes and so wildly mistook the dedication thereof.[1] No dear I did *not* write those verses for Flo, and if I had should certainly not have sent you a duplicate. Pope was the only man who ever did that and he came to a bad end.[2] I must confess that at first I was a good deal hurt at the mistake but accidents will occur in the best regulated families and I suppose your error was one of 'em. By the way that book has been most favourably noticed all round India and the whole edition is sold out. *The World* too was good enough to give me a nice little notice and I'm proportionately pleased.[3] There was only one paper – The Indian Review – that cut 'em up savagely and by way of showing that I bore no malice I cut out the slashingest parts and put 'em into the advertisement[4] – the consequence was [that] all the world and his wife when they heard that the poems were vicious sent in orders for the book and we scored hugely. The event of the past month has been Trixie's *very own* horse – a present to her from that best of parents her Pater. He – Brownie – is a dark brown waler pony (i.e. an Australian) and the most perfect ladies' horse I know – with a long flowing mane and tail, a mouth like silk and paces like an armchair. Unfortunately the sister bless her (though she hasn't an atom of nervousness) rides in a casual manner that makes me sweat with funk whenever I go out with her and I have suggested that she should get some style into her riding as soon as may be. Meantime lest Brownie shouldn't have enough work I take him out every morning on to the race course and introduce him to Lahore. At present he is rather out of his element and doesn't know his way about but for all that I am charmed with his style and manners. You know the sort of beast ladies delight in – a neck arched, tail switching prancer that foams at the mouth and pretends to be jumping out of his skin on the least provocation and that really is as quiet as a sheep. Well, that's Brownie and for further particulars you had better ask Trixie. If my own white rat couldn't gallop his head off I'm afraid I might be envious especially as B. cost nearly four times as much as the frivolous Deadly Sin who does all my work. But I'm going to have 'em both photoed and you shall see for yourself.

Like you I've been writing a story in my leisure. It has only taken me three months and is only six pages long but I've never fallen in love with any tale of my own fashioning so much – not that it has any merit.[5] I'm trying to work it off on some alien paper to get myself pice thereby. Now that I'm allowed to write to any rag I please I find that I can always get a few odd pounds a month for myself apart from my screw and incidentally can get myself a little bit known in our small world out here.[6] Of late however I have been wildly busy as the Chief hasn't been up to the mark and has let me do a lot of his work confound him! It's good for me of course but I find it cuts down my few hours of playtime most unpleasantly. The Pater went off on Wednesday on a visit to the Duke of Connaught[7] at Mirat taking with him, as usual, a little cold. I trust that the "Ryal Dooke" may be of some use to him. He seems an affable sort of cuss – especially his wife who can really ride very prettily. This is an empty headed sort of letter I'm afraid but there's really nothing to write about except the weather and crops – and they won't interest you. My love to Aunt Louie and Uncle Alfred. It's curious to think how little I've ever seen of the two – and my salaams to Stanley. I'd give something to be in the Sixth at Harrow as he is with a University Education to follow.

Always your loving Nephew

P.S. I'm promised two months next year and intend taking a sea trip to Ceylon and Madras and coming back via Bombay going round India.[8] Isn't it richness?

Notes
1. RK's presentation copy of *Echoes* to Edith Macdonald is now at the University of Sussex. The dedicatory verses RK has written read:

> Though the "Englishman" deride it
> Though the captious "Statesman" chide it,
> Your dear judgment shall decide it
>   Yours alone.
> For the good that in each line is,
> From the title page to Finis,
>   Is your own.

2. RK must be thinking only vaguely of Pope's literary duplicities.
3. "A clever little book", the *World* reviewer calls it (22 October 1884, p. 22), and singles

out "Nursery Rhymes for Little Anglo-Indians" and "The Sudder Bazaar". The *World* had a special appeal for RK: according to Beresford, RK had some acquaintance with Edmund Yates, the editor (*Schooldays with Kipling*, p. 109), and the first work he ever sold was to the *World*, which printed his "Two Lives", 8 November 1882.
4. An advertisement for *Echoes* in the *CMG*, 17 November 1884, quotes from the favourable reviews in the *Pioneer*, *CMG*, and the *World*, but adds this from the *Indian Review*: "Some of them (including the worse than senseless 'Appropriate verses on an elegant landscape') ought never to have been published at all . . . the humour is rather forced."
5. Not certainly identified, but probably "The Strange Ride of Morrowbie Jukes", on which RK is known to have been working by 8 December 1884 (RK's diary, 1885: Harvard).
6. This permission indicates that RK had by now gained recognition of his abilities: the steady flow of his Indian work – at least that part of it so far identified – dates from the end of 1884.
7. The Duke (1850–1942), third and favourite son of Queen Victoria, had been appointed to command the Meerut military district in 1883. His acquaintance with the Duke was later of some importance to JLK, for he was engaged by the Duke to decorate in Indian style the billiard-room of the Duke's Bagshot house. This work led, in turn, to a commission from Queen Victoria for JLK to arrange and supervise the decoration for a suite of rooms at Osborne *à l'Indienne*.
8. RK did not make this trip.

To Edith Macdonald, 30 July–1 August 1885
ALS: Library of Congress

North Bank. / Simla.[1] / July. 30th. 1885.

Beloved Aunt (or should I not rather say "Venerated Orientalist and experienced Traveller in the Far East"). My crimes of omission are great but I honestly and truly have been driven like anything during the past eight weeks and the faculty of private and domestic writing has departed from me. So you are really back and have seen Cairo, the Pyramids and the Sphinx! These things were not my fortune. One only sees mirage in the putrid ditch falsely hight the Suez Canal. I envy you your lazing, loitering, look-into-a-shop-go-a-few-doors-down-and-look-into-another voyage. But oh the nerve that must have sustained you in the Bay of Biscay racket. It pitches P. and O. liners about like corks, so I can imagine what it would do with smaller craft. There is, to landsmen, one hideous moment (which recurs about thirty five times in the hour) when the nose of Her tilts into a green-grey sea, and the stern of her points starward; while the screw kicks like a demented pony. This is called "plunging" and produces all the effect of sinking by the head. There is another moment (which occurs twenty five times within the hour) when first one side of the deck and then the other lies flush with the sea and you begin to suspect that She will never get up again. This is called "rolling through all the angles;" and ends in upsetting a soup-plate into the bosom of your dress while an infuriated portmanteau is clamouring for your life in the cabin. Great and wondrous is the sea and its motions. Marvellous also the adaptability of the human sto – mind to all varying conditions. As things stand it is best perhaps that you did not extend your visit to Lahore. We shouldn't have let you go under the year and you might have disliked that. Seriously though, best of Aunts, what would you say if I were to ask you at some future time to come out and keep house for me through a season at Allahabad? When the evil day of my transfer comes as come it must if I go on happily. *Some one* will have to look after me. I'm helpless as a babe by myself; and I have fended off the prospects with the direst threats of instant matrimony whenever it has been discussed. I think we might manage a six months together fairly successfully! You would find the "glowing" East a hideous delusion but you might enjoy one or two of its beauties if you were blessed with the knowledge that you were going home in a few months. I would give something for the certainty that I should see England again in the next ten years or even before I die at the regulation insurance age – 33 1/2 years. But it's no good wishing with half a hundred things to be done at once and one's life daily more taken up with the interests of the people of the land. Thank Heaven my face is cured though I am scarred for life.[2] The photo that I shall send you in a few weeks won't show my scars at all as they will have been skilfully "touched out" but the sunken brands and red tracings exist. They are perfect bliss compared with the mental misery caused by the actual sores – with health has come back a regular flood of outside work of every kind, sort and description. I'm here at Simla with the Mother and Trix as Special Correspondent for the Civil and Military Gazette. I told you that for my work at the Durbar[3] they raised my screw to £420 English or £35 a month. For that sum I try to give my paper as near to £40 a month of editorial notes; reviews; articles and social Simla letters.[4] That in itself is fairly lively work and – tho' this may sound strange to you – entails as much riding, waltzing, dining out and concerts in a week as I should get at home in a lifetime.[5] Then I have been working on Indian stories for other papers – notably the *Pioneer* which has professed its willingness to take anything I might choose to send. I've sent them a mixed assortment of verses; and some prose stuff.[6] All of which have taken the public's somewhat dense soul and been largely quoted. (By the way a tenth-rate journal of yours called the *Times* I think calmly "bagged" an article of mine upon the geology of a little known part of Central Asia without a word of acknowledgement.[7] Next time you meet Mr. Buckle[8] tell him with my compliments that I object to special information being utilized in this way. 'Tis n't professional unless it's quoted and not used as original matter. But I'm going astray). Also the *Calcutta Review* has written very sweetly about a poem of mine – in blank verse –

To Edith Macdonald, 30 July–1 August

which appears in the August number and is going to
story of a wholly novel type.⁹ Like the Quarterlies th
read but it gives one a certain amount of prestige to
Further I have really embarked – to the tune of 237 f
my novel – Mother Maturin – an Anglo Indian episo
"it growed"¹¹ while I wrote and I find myself now con
volume business at least. It's not one bit nice or prope
grim sort of a moral with it and tries to deal with the unutterable horrors of lower class Eurasian and native life as they exist outside reports and reports and reports. I haven't got the Pater's verdict on what I've done. He comes up in a couple of days and will then sit in judgement. Trixie says it's awfully horrid: Mother says it's nasty but powerful and I *know* it to be in large measure true. It is an unfailing delight to me and I'm just in that pleasant stage where the characters are living with me always. The Parents say "publish it at home and let it have a chance." I hold that India would be the better place and have already received one offer for the book from an Indian Paper. A few years ago one Proprietor offered my Mother Rs 1,000. for an Anglo Indian story. If he renews the offer to the son I close at once and Mother Maturin, whatever her after fate, shall appear in weekly parts. Then maybe, I might be able to struggle home for six weeks with what I've got already. Fancy six whole weeks at home. Luckily for you you can't guess how the thought makes the pen fly.

Saturday. The household expects the Head up this evening and is rejoiceful accordingly. Trix and I with truely tender consideration have migrated into the room which is to be the Pater's workroom and are having a house warming. That is to say she has brought in all her M.S.S. and I've brought in all mine.

*Kelvin Grove.*¹² The other end of Simla. The Pater came up from Lahore as fit as a fiddle in spite of the ghastly heat that has been his portion and I promptly left the house for a month's visit to one of the Proprietors of the paper. He and his wife are a couple of angels in every possible way. I stayed here for a month two years ago. The house is full of people – all of whom understand how to talk nonsense cleverly and you may imagine what a madcap sort of a time we are having. Northbank won't hold all four of us without crowding the workrooms inconveniently and I would sooner sleep ten in a hay loft than have my office doubled up with the Pater's. Them's his sentiments also and the moment there is any danger of papers mixing I bolt.

I go back to Lahore on the first of September when it will be quite cool enough to be comfortable and there I "resume my Assistant Editorial duties." Before that date however there is much to be done in the way of dances and dinners. I am booked for two of the former and three of the latter within the next week. And here will I tell you a secret. The

From Schoolboy to Journalist

best way to sicken a youth of frivolity is to pitch him neck and crop into the thick of it on the understanding that he is to write descriptive matter about each dance, frivol etc. Were it not for my love of waltzing I should abominate the whole business. As it is, it is the dullest of dull things to be *chroniquer* of a Gay Season in the hills. And we are supposed to be very gay indeed.

My face is said to be cured but I am still in the doctor's hands and he has certified that it would be very unwise of me to go down to Lahore just now as there was some talk of my doing. I'm not a hog on it as you may fancy – and in fact even after four months of a cool climate don't feel quite as fit as I ought to do. It's the want of spring and go that bothers me and I feel more certain every day that I shall never get it or any part of it back again. This isn't a very lively letter is it but I am not over lively myself and must turn off to a heap of Russian journals which are "awaiting disposal."

Always your loving
Ruddy.

Notes

1. North Bank was a house belonging to Sir Edward Buck. RK had been in Simla perhaps as early as April and certainly by May as the representative of the *CMG*; the arrangement may also have been a sort of sick leave.
2. "Lahore sores are common just now, and Ruddy has one on his cheek. . . . These wretched things last for months and doctors haven't a notion how to treat 'em" (JLK to Edith Plowden, 16 March 1885: MS, Sussex). The affliction, now treatable, is caused by the parasite *Leishmania*.
3. That is, at the meeting of Lord Dufferin, the new Governor-General, with the Amir Abdurrahman of Afghanistan in March 1885. As special correspondent, RK produced articles for the *CMG* on 24, 26, 28, and 31 March, and on 1, 2, 6, 7, 8, 9, 10, and 14 April, written from Rawalpindi, Peshawar, and Jumrood, on the far north-western frontier (31 March, and 1, 2, 7 and 8 April appear in Pinney, *Kipling's India*; the rest are uncollected). This was the occasion when RK wandered into the Khyber Pass and was, he thought, shot at by a tribesman (Carrington, *Kipling*, p. 59): see also 30 January 1886.
4. Only a fraction of these can be identified.
5. RK learned to dance for this assignment: "His proprietors told him . . . he must waltz well; – so what we at home couldn't persuade him to like, became a duty" (JLK to Edith Plowden, 16 March 1885: MS, Sussex).
6. The prose stuff includes "Dis Aliter Visum", 4 July; the verses, "After the Fever", 22 June, "My Rival", 8 July, and "Possibilities", 13 July.
7. Not identified.
8. George Earle Buckle, editor of *The Times*.
9. RK's blank verse "Vision of Hamid Ali" appears in the October – not August – number of the *Calcutta Review*. If his ghost story also appeared it has not been identified.
10. RK's never-published novel. He seems to have designed it as a receptacle for all of his Indian impressions, and it grew to many hundreds of pages. According to Mrs Hill, "it is the story of an old Irish woman who kept an opium den in Lahore but sent her daughter to be educated in England. She marries a Civilian and comes to live in Lahore – hence a story, – how Govt. secrets came to be known in the bazar and vice versa" (note accompanying RK to Mrs Hill, 8 April 1902: Sussex). Parts of "Mother Maturin" no doubt worked their way into other stories – it was mined for

Kim, for example – but evidently it never satisfied RK. The last reference to it as an extant MS is in August 1904 (RK to Robert McClure: MS, Columbia); the present location of the MS is unknown, and perhaps it has been destroyed (see Carrington, *Kipling*, p. 359).
11. Harriet Beecher Stowe, *Uncle Tom's Cabin*, ch. 20.
12. The home of James Walker: see [September? 1883].

To Cormell Price, 19 September 1885
ALS: Library of Congress

Lahore. / Sept. 19th / 1885.

Dear Uncle Crom:

The bustle and bother of the past month have prevented me answering your last very pleasant letter till now; though, as far as the "old Coll" is concerned I have not been altogether idle. A Captain Sandys[1] of the Commissariat Dept. in Mian Mir, three miles off, has a son whom he wishes to put to school – a youth of about nine and a half.[2] He was talking the matter over with me and I, of course, went all I knew on Westward Ho! I laid myself out royally to describe the place where six[3] of the happiest years of my life have been spent, with the result that Sandys wanted the prospectus, terms and all the rest of it. Unfortunately I don't keep these and I want you to send me them as soon as you can. There has been some discussion about the college in the *Times of India* at Bombay where a Lieut. Col. Sparkes has expressed his willingness to give any one full particulars about the place.[4] I have placed Sandys in communication with this gentleman ('guess he's Sparke's father[5]) and am leaving the rest to the workings of Providence. All the same I should be grateful if you wouldn't mind sending me a few of the papers for I come across a whole lot of people in travail about their sons' future and tho' I can work 'em up to interest and enthusiasm I can't of course make them clinch the matter straight off. Perhaps the papers would. At any rate if you like to send them I'll try; and will see if the after dinner conversations of anxious fathers can't be made to take practical shape. *Nota Bene.* The paternal mind is captivated by compulsory cricket: the maternal by full details of the "Preparatory" where the absolutely unique and high spirited Teddie, Tommie, or Gussie will receive a mother's care. Therefore, if you see fit, Sir, send me those papers.

By all means let the Chronicle do what it will to "Echoes," the more the better.[6] I should prefer you to review them; or failing this let the . . . humm – Cane be handed over to my respected Latin Master.[7] He loathed me as to Latin (and he had good right) but I think we came together on one or two points of the wide fields marked Upper School English. (5–6 30.) I told you did I not how the demand for "Echoes" has made me put a second edition, bigger, better, and bound, in hand. At least Thacker Spink & Co of Calcutta insisted upon my doing it. Well, we quarelled(?) for various reasons and I wound up my communications by a series of caricatures of a violent and personal kind. Then "all smiles stopped together;" and, as I chuse "never to stoop"[8] *Echoes* has come back to my own office where, with the help of £5000 worth of fresh machinery, the Scotch foreman vows it shall turn out in such guise as to make T.S. & Co green with spite, and to this Christian wish I say Amen with all my soul.[9] I couldn't very well avoid the row (tho' I *might* have helped the caricatures but they were irresistable) and it stops all chance of the firm publishing a novel of Anglo Indian life that I have – three quarters finished – in hand. Moral. Make friends with the Mammon of Paternoster row even in India. The *Calcutta Review* that most sober and dignified quarterly has let me into its staff and I appear next month in some peculiarly blank verse. Thereafter a prose article about as blank as the verse.[10] They don't pay on that estimable old ragbag but a certain amount of dignity is supposed to attach to writing for it and I am sadly deficient in dignity. Also I have been supplying a contemporary with a set of poems entitled the "Bungalow Ballads."[11] I didn't sign 'em for which I'm sorry as they took; and a purblind world has set them down as Sir Auckland Colvin's[12] work. I chuckle but as yet have made no sign. They will appear in Echoes (2nd Edtn.) and confound the unbelievers. It is whispered that A.C. himself has not denied the impeachment. I think scorn of him in consequence. Further I am under contract to turn out for my own rag a Christmas supplement[13] – the which is a new departure for the average Indian organ. Have three months to do it in and find that I shall want every day of that time. My owners – who are absolutely the most liberal men I know – have raised my pay again to Rs. 400 a month. Thanks to the inscrutable American Mystery,[14] which has nearly addled my brains as well as reducing my income by a quarter that means only £400 a year. Is there *any* hope for the depreciate Rupee Sir? We have got it down to 1/6 at sight and "How far oh Catiline" etc.[15] is the wretched coin to sink? When one sends home for a £15 gun and has to pay £20[16] the mystery presses heavily on brain and pocket. Have been living alone for the past month in Lahore as my four month holiday at Simla came to an abrupt end – the mischief of printers' deviltry is that your tail is a telegraph wire and you can be yerked thereby from Olympus to Hades at an hour's notice. My family, who seem to be enjoying themselves mightily at Simla, don't come down for another month and I've been improving my leisure by an attack of fever. It's bad enough being ill in company but alone in an empty house without a soul to bring you a

To Cormell Price, 19 September 1885 87

glass of water is something ghastly. Have just had three days of it and feel as weak as a kitten. Enclosed please find some stuff I've turned out lately which may interest you. It isn't up to much and is under the curse of being written to fill up space. I have to turn out things of this kind about once a week.[17] My best respects to the Common Room – there *are* no boys who remember me now – at least the Chronicle shows no familiar names.

Yours always
Ruddy.

Notes
1. Captain E. C. C. Sandys, Commissariat Department, Assistant Commissary General at Mian Mir (*India List*, 1886).
2. No one named Sandys appears in the *OUSC Register*.
3. In fact four and a half: from January 1878 to about July 1882.
4. Lieutenant-Colonel John Barnes Sparks (d. 1893), Public Works Department, port storekeeper, State Railway Department, Bombay. Sparks's article in *The Times of India*, 12 September 1885, reported the success of the College in modern language instruction.
5. James Noel Sparks (1869–1950), at USC 1880–5; BA, Jesus College, Cambridge; a consulting civil and metallurgical engineer.
6. *Echoes* was reviewed by Crofts in the USC *Chronicle* of 2 July 1886: see 14 September 1886. RK presented a copy to the school common room, with a dedicatory poem (Rutherford, *Early Verse*).
7. Crofts.
8. Browning, "My Last Duchess", ll. 46, 43.
9. No second edition of *Echoes* is known.
10. Not identified.
11. A series of six verses in the *Pioneer* of Allahabad, between 15 August and 5 September (mostly uncollected).
12. Colvin (1838–1908), after important work in India and Egypt, was now financial member of Council, 1883–8; he was Lieutenant-Governor of the North-West Provinces from 1887 until his retirement in 1892. In 1899 Colvin accepted the dedication of the early study of RK by G. F. Monkshood.
13. *Quartette*: this was the work of the entire Kipling family, but dominated by RK: "The Phantom 'Rickshaw" and "The Strange Ride of Morrowbie Jukes" first appeared in this.
14. RK means the question of American silver, current theories of bimetalism, and the sinking exchange value of the Indian rupee against sterling. These were standing topics in the Indian newspapers.
15. Cicero, *Against Catiline*, I.i.1.
16. Perhaps the gun requested in 24 April 1883.
17. "The City of Dreadful Night", *CMG*, 10 September (*Life's Handicap*). If he turned out such things "about once a week" they have not been identified. He cannot mean the column entitled "A Week in Lahore" that he produced at infrequent intervals between 1884 and 1886, for that did not appear between March and December of 1885.

To Margaret Burne-Jones, [27] September 1885[1]
ALS: University of Sussex

                                        Lahore. / Sept. 26th. 1885.

Sunday.
Dear Wop,

As my faithful servitor says when I tell him to do some thing his soul abhors: – "*Bahut Accha.*" Very good. I'm glad you liked it. Proof that it must have taken your fancy and is therefore good. Only wait till the cold weather lets me into the slums of our great city and the Pater and I 'ull dig you up some old silverwork.

That was a grand letter of yours and goes up to the Maiden at Simla this very afternoon. Hence my zeal in answering it. There'd be the biggest sort of a row if I kept eight pages of your peculiarly-impressive-but-just-the-least-little-bit-in-the-world-difficult-to-decipher script all to myself. Which reminds me that Maiden of Mine has been and gone and written a tale and told me to go and print it.[2] This I've done and – no, the Maiden shall send you a copy herself. She's got nine and thirty of 'em available for circulation and I won't take the edge off her pleasure.

Now how am I to tackle your letter properly: throwing in the "dear me how interesting" at the proper time. I will e'en turn it upside down and work backwards. Para. two from the butt end asks me if I know The City of Dreadful Night.[3] *Do* I know it? Oh Wop! Wop! What a question. Here's one portion of your answer and to my mind one of the sweetest and truest quotes going abroad: –

> And since he cannot spend nor use aright
>   The little time here given him in trust
> But wasteth it in weary undelight
>   Of foolish toil and trouble, strife and lust,
> He *naturally claimeth to inherit*
>   The everlasting future that his merit
>   May have full scope – *as surely is most just.*[4]

Furthermore, did I not, one month ago, spend one weary weary night on the great minar of the mosque of Wazir Khan, looking down upon the heat tortured city of Lahore and seventy thousand men and women sleeping in the moonlight; and did I not write a description of my night's vigil and christen it "The City of Dreadful Night." Go to – Go to Uncle Crom and ask him for a copy of that article. I sent it to him a week or two syne.

Believe I knew that pack of hounds. Their kennels are about a mile down the Lewes Road; and they used to wake up as one hound and sing hymns to the moon. Don't generalize hastily Wop dear. Them hounds want *no end* of keeping in order to break 'em of "skirting" and "rioting." It isn't so bad in England but imported hounds out here get fearfully demoralized – by the climate or something – and then you really *do* see some healthy "thonging". *Please* don't stop that man Wop. For aught you or I know we may get drafts from that pack to make up the Station one this cold weather; and to chase the agile jackal over the young bajra[5] as it sprouteth. *You've* never been pulled up five miles from anywhere with both boots full of India because the hounds owned to a hare or worse still a black buck and there was no whipping them off. Tell the "walker" to hit 'em hard and give him my love. From hounds to horses is easy. I call my own beloved, "Dolly Bobbs" because she bobbs mightily. It isn't a shy but simple pirouetting (looks misspelt that!) and ducking and curtseying all over the road. Not an atom of vice of any kind but simply feminine nervousness. I really expect to hear her say one of these days when she is specially on the keen edge, "Lor! *what* a start that gave me to be sure!" You'd laugh at her if you saw her, for a child's poney in England and she does the work of two London horses. First say for a long morning ride in company with a lady whose only idea of pace is to bucket across the fields all she knows. Then hot and quiet to breakfast and thereafter in my dogcart to office. Home again at four and stripped for a long ride either alone or in company, a spin round the race course or – but I'll tell you about that later. Into cart again to take me to the Club two miles off and bring me back at eleven or twelve at the very top of her trot which isn't a slow one. Trixie's waler has turned out no good at lady's work and I have the Pater's instructions to sell him. Have discovered that he is no end of a jumper and plays polo as nearly perfectly as I could wish. So does Dolly – not so well as Brownie but with less pulling. Now I am forbidden polo by the powers above: *and* I have two horses who love the game. Also, I have been alone for a month with precious little to do. Can you wonder then that I have fallen from the paths of virtue? I did all I could to keep straight but I couldn't help it and I play surreptitiously twice a week on Brownie and my beloved. With my weight up B. can play for ever without feeling the strain. Dolly can stand the one ten minutes [*sic*]. I cut in on her at the end of the game when my bridle hand is tired and we have a lovely time. You mayn't believe me but I assure you Dolly knows all about it and her little ears go forward and she begins to move as if she was on hot bricks as soon as I get her on the ground. Then she follows the ball like a cat a mouse and whenever I miss my stroke nips round with a snort so quickly that unless I'm sitting tight I find myself hanging on to her neck. But this is a deep and Wopsome secret and I trust to your sisterly honour not to divulge it. The Mummy thinks polo is dangerous and I *never* play when she's down.

What a marvellous thing is feminine insight. Your paragraph about my keeping my "old eyes open" made me blush all to myself in the empty house. For it is a lamentable fact that I, R. Kipling, have been done, dished, had, taken in, made an ass of, bamboozled – anything contemptible you please by a "Daughter of Heth in Silk Attire". And it served me jolly well right for I was attempting to work the D of H to my own and the Old Rag's ends. She knowed it all along and I got a note – a delicately spiteful one such as only a woman could write – from her hand the other day pointing out exactly where I had failed. It's a long story and of no interest to anyone but the Principals but oh Lord! Lord! how I have abased myself in sackcloth and ashes and sworn never to pit my poor wits against a woman again. The sin of this generation Wop is conceit and I can only repeat that it served me perfectly right. I told the Mummy of course – I believe I can, honestly, say that Polo is the only thing I keep from her and by the same token the only thing outside office work that she hasn't the fullest authority in and uses it bless her – and she wrote that she would have done just the same if she had been the woman.

Well, all that blissful, bustling, frivolous flirting time is over and done with and there's a month's solitary confinement behind me and another to face or ever my Family return. Pay's riz as I told you but the Lord he hath taken it out o' me in fever. Had a three days go of it a fortnight since and my faithful henchmen, recognizing that I was off my head, departed and had a concert in the compound. Shouldn't ha' minded if they'd left me the iced water but they didn't and I had a ghastly time. My note to the doctor miscarried and he didn't turn up for thirty hours. When he arrived (he told me this afterwards) I cursed him fluently and offered to race him for Rs. 500 a side. I suppose I must have been fairly lively but it was the getting better alone that breaks the heart of man or boy. Never a soul to come nigh one and the whole house full of noises and whispers, and sighs and groans and chuckles from headachy dawn to delirious dusk. I wrote to the Mummy that "a return of this would drive me into instant matrimony or some officiating arrangement until your return". Honestly Wop I assure you that, as I was threshing my way out of the nightmares, if I had been alone in the country, say at Allahabad, I should have straightway applied for the £100 a year that the Pater has promised to give me when I marry and have laid my aching bones at the feet of the first disengaged white girl who would have taken me. I began to understand faintly why so many good men perpetrate matrimony. It's temporary insanity superinduced by intermittent fever. Well what's the proverb about the Devil and his disease?[6] I got all right, was made much of at the Club when I reappeared and scoffed at my idle visions. All the same living alone is in every way abominable. One feels it most on Sundays when the work *won't* be spread thin enough to cover the whole day. Had a subaltern in to breakfast this morn[7] (He turns up nearly every Sabbath to glower at me for an hour or two over his cheroot) but he's gone and it's only two o'clock. There's no one to call on; it's too hot to ride: I can't go on with the novel: I've done all my proofs and shooting parrots is wicked – almost as bad as sleeping in the middle of the day. Luckily I have the blessed distraction of writing you a letter and I intend making the most of it. It may disgust you by its length at the other end but I shall like that. Let me turn to your epistle and see what further remains to be answered therein.

Oh! about that sentence you couldn't quite follow. Maybe I wrote at Random but what I meant was this. You see in our best of all possible worlds – read India – there are whole hosts of abuses oppressions and unthinking wrongs that may one of these days be set right if you hammer long enough. Understand clearly that I don't mean the sort of Indian wrongs that Crom Price writes to me about – the extended employment of natives out of Hindustan etc. – because my views on that subject would shock you a good deal and C.P. bless him doesn't know that any native of any caste would flatly refuse to cross the "black water" unless he had received a purely English education and had been *outcasted*. What I mean is that the population out here die from purely preventible causes; are starved from purely preventible causes; are in native states hideously misgoverned from their rulers' own folly and so on. Let me make my meaning clearer by an instance. Say that a district as big as Yorkshire near Delhi lies out of the reach of the regular rains and that consequently for three years out of seven the villagers are face to face with starvation. A system of what we call *bunds*, dams, channels and embankments would at least store water and stave off drought for a year. Well that means saving so many men and so many cattle, easing the work of the Deputy Commissioner and improving the land. Find out, if you can, how many bunds could be raised for how much money; where retrenchment or an extra cess elsewhere could raise that money: consult specialists and nearly every Civilian in India is strong either in settlement work, crime repression, canals, public buildings or something of the kind[;] get all your information into a taking form – never mind if you have to delay a month or even two, and then begin to hammer away about this district through the paper as hard as you know how. Keep on hammering. Get good men to write you leaders about it: get lesser men to write letters about it; get statistics and drive ahead. Ten to one nothing will be done at first but other papers take up the matter; the Deputy Commissioner of the District is asked first, tentatively, by the Provincial Government if he thinks anything can be done and whether these suggestions of yours are any good. Perhaps he can perhaps he can't. Maybe he'll raise one *bund* to see how it works. Then as soon as the villagers begin to realize that a *bunded* tehsil (parish) turns out better crops than an unbunded one they'll go into the business with a will. Same thing with drains; supply of horses for the Punjab; village debts; prevention of fever; outstation dispensaries and a thousand thousand other things. Just now Lady Dufferin's fund for the Medical education of native women is exciting a good deal of comment.[8] A Bengal native paper, whose editor I should like to lick till he couldn't stand, begins talking a lot of nonsense about "we should have preferred an extended movement on a national basis dealing with the primary education of womenkind" and discounting the scheme all it knows. We might wait till Doomsday till the Bengalis educated their native women: meantime they are rotting in the zenanas, for sheer want of medical attendance; English docs you know aren't allowed to see a zenana woman in her last agonies. Well, that's a piece of flatulent wind baggery that might do mischief to a notion that if properly carried out will do infinitely more good than all the "Associations for advancement" [of] "National Progress" (that is national foot and mouth disease) in the Empire. Your duty clearly is to combat that paper with all your power. Rake it with statistics; tall writing; appeals, and finally "chaff" – no Asiatic understands "chaff." If prose doesn't go home hack out some verses with a lilting refrain that will take and catch the public ear and you have helped to scotch a snake. Same with "widow remarriage." Thank Goodness you haven't any notion of the horrors of enforced widow hood out here. The agitation is as old as the hills but our progressive Aryan brother, the Oxford B.A. who'll eat with you, ride with you and talk to your wife won't *dare* to fly in the face of his "custom." Hammer away at that in prose and verse and see what comes of it. The danger of course specially with a young writer lies in overstating the case. This must be guarded against by rigorous checking and pruning; for however powerful the press may be at home, it is infinitely more powerful out here where a paper can be suppressed at any moment. Queer Paradox ain't it? But it is so. Personally I'm death on Drains and water supply – that doesn't lend itself to verse – and every now and again I have a chance of wiring in to some municipality where the cholera returns are higher than they should be. People won't stir quickly for abstracts of reports. Go down and look at the place yourself and write all you know on the running pen. Serve hot and something is sure to come of it. I had a rare chance the other day, though it didn't concern men as much as horses. I left Simla by an "ordinary" mail cart in company with a lot of natives. Well, the native officials treated those passengers like pigs and turned out, in the darkness, chafed, galled and bleeding horses. I went round with a lantern and inspected the whole lot quietly and explained my views to the native contractor. Got in to

To Margaret Burne-Jones, [27] September 1885

Lahore and gave an unimpassioned account of the whole journey in the paper.[9] Ten days later comes a Government letter to the contractor with my account cut out and an intimation for him to "explain his conduct in writing". Better still, the Vet whose duty it is to inspect the line woke up to a sense of his duties and made things extra lively for the contractor. Result not a single galled horse on the road and more consideration for native passengers. That's a small business of course and not half so important as the bunded district. If we can get that really forced into the public (or rather the Supreme Govt's notice) we shall have done something worth the doing and I shall chortle like a Boojum. You see, if you once set the ball a rolling you can generally get two or three men infinitely better than yourself with twenty years' experience to help it along. They only want the prodding and therefore it is your bounden duty, for the performance or nonperformance of which your conscience holds you answerable, that you shall keep your pen-point sharp and *clean* and try all you know to get a style that commands attention and the power of writing facilely. It mayn't be literature (there's ample time for that in the next world, where one of the delights of Paradise will be printing your poems on rubbed rough edged paper and reading laudatory reviews of 'em in the *Celestial Intelligencer*) but it may save men and cattle alive and lead to really tangible results. There's no finer feeling in life than the knowledge that a year's work has really done some living good, besides amusing and interesting people, for a Province that you are genuinely interested in and love. Then again there's nothing more sobering than the knowledge of the enormous mass of work that remains to be done and the utter hopelessness of doing one tithe of it. Also the knowledge that you have been entrusted with the control – for an assistant editor has far more real control over his paper than an editor – on the same principal that a first mate navigates a P and O steamer – of a big power that can make even Lieutenant Governors and Viceroys "sit up" to use a vile *slangerie*. Curiously enough I have written to you more freely, my sister, than I have *even spoken* to any one I know. But I believe, or rather I am certain, that you will understand me and forgive the egoism and conceit of youth that crops out several times in the last page or two. You want a "gude conceit of yourself" to stand the roastings of other papers. I get a fair share of it and whenever by chance I miss an attack on R.K.'s "illiberal and narrow minded effusions," some "damned officious friend" is sure to send it in with red chalk drawn round the most offensive passages.

Well, to get back to that same old sentence. Seest thou what I mean Wop by saying that the Cretans (some of 'em are mentally cretins but that's a detail) want prodding up with a pen if you can't use a thick stick. The stick would be best in many cases I admit but the Lord he hath not dowered me with one.

As the Wop truthfully observes writing letters is one thing and writing books another. Still the Wop who can describe a coast guard as she did is in my humble opinion perfectly competent to go ahead on books – or anything else she pleases. In spite of what I've written above I hold devoutly, with Lowell, that Literature (*with* the L) should not be immolated on the alter of "high moral Purpose", "inculcating valuable truths" and so on. It's immoral and degrading and futile. Surely your *shouk* (Anglice bent or turn) should be Literature with the L sooner or later – novel or story or more probably Review. I write of course in ignorance inasmuch as three years ago (and alas! I've been out three years and a week today) you never did me the honour to talk to me about these things. Wherefore I prophecy and my prophecy is this. I give you three years – thirty six calendar months – wherein to turn out something and a half year over. If at the end of that time you have *not* turned out any thing I shall go to Trix and say "Hi! you know that Wop of Europe don't you?" And Trix'll say "Yes, 'Cousin o' sorts I write to. Don't you mean." And I shall answer: – "Exactly. Don't you write to her never a line no more. We've disinherited her and cast her off for a Blazing Fraud. The Wop of Europe is dead. Let us bury her deeply." And Trix will again make answer: – "Thou fool. She has been married for the last year or may be two and she has passed beyond your knowledge and comprehension and understanding. Verily the Wop of Europe is dead indeed and there is arisen another and a greater Wop. Go to! Turn thee to thy club again!" And I shall lift up my voice and wail and wonder secretly whether the Wop *has* fulfilled her destiny and whether my Sister's words be true. Which things are an allegory and by mine Halidome Wop I believe that the top of my head has been softened by fever. But I will abide by my prophecy and await its issue. And writing of the Maiden reminds me that her bust is in the Simla Fine Arts Exhibition[10] (*vulgo* "The Wattle and daub show") and she herself is even more admired than the bust and hath Goodness only knows how many new dresses. But I rejoice with an exceeding great joy to think that these trifles disturb her not and she clings healthily to the inkpot as of yore. *You* being a mere woman can't understand my intense anxiety about the Maiden and my jealous care lest she should show signs of being "touched in the heart."

The slang of the stables is vastly convenient at times. So far nothing has shown itself but I live on "tenter horns" from day to day. Of course we can't hope to stave off the Inevitable but I promise that unless he is a most superior man, I'll make it desperately uncomfortable for the coming man – *when* he comes. I want two years more of her if I can get it – and I shan't stop short of hunting crops to attain mine end. Here too I trust to her strong sense of humour to keep her on the straight and easy course of unmarried life but – as I've said The Lord knows what will turn up and I live in fear. The whole four of us have got a magazine in hand for Xmas – a collection of Indian stories published as some sort of a supplement to the Old Rag. 'Makes people take an interest in the paper you know. Of course you'll get a copy. Your news about Master Phillup is good indeed. I wish he could come out here for a three month's tour. Given the passage it's about as easy as staying at home. He would put up with us for as long as he liked and we could pass him along, as is the custom, from friend to friend in most of the cities he would care to visit. Begin say with the Jain Temples at Mount Abu, where he'd sit down flat and gasp, go on to Jaipûr and see the Dead City of Ambèr from elephant back and some of the most marvellous dresses in the world. Come on to Lahore thence exeunt with the Pater and myself to Amritsar and the Golden Temple; Peshawur, a day and a night up the line to the mouth of the Khyber, every step of the way full of the maddest scenery and incident, Lucknow, Agra, Delhi, Allahabad where there are usually a few hundred thousand pilgrims, and thence either to Calcutta which is not interesting or across central India to Bombay, or back to Lahore and to the Hills and the snow. From October to March the climate anywhere is as lovely as he could wish and an intelligent Bombay servant who spoke English could make everything easy for him. We don't get men who can paint out here often and when they do they don't know where to go. Of course I suppose the notion is impossible for his side; but *we* should like it dearly and I think Phil would. He'd come back and say India had the finest climate in the world and I should want him back to fry for a little between May and August. He can't go on grinding for ever and (tho' that's not his fault) he doesn't know what light and colour and sunshine are. There's much to be said in favour of the notion. Think over it. Sunday must be my excuse for such a portentously long letter but an' you were alone all day in an empty house you also would pour out the vials of your idleness on your friends. An interview with my landlord (just fancy, the whole house is *mine* now by right o' rent) has been the only break. I want him to build me a small bungalow on my own plan, helped by the pater. Say's he would have been delighted but there are no good sites and I suppose I shall have to wait. Dolly Bobbs waits without and I'm off for a ride with a most energetic lady who gallops as long as she can and as hard as she can. Calls it exercise. I call it Purgatory but as she can't get any one else she insists on my coming.

          Always your faithful Brother
          The Wop of Asia.

Notes
1. Sunday was the 27th in 1885; this date is confirmed by RK's diary for 1885, which records a "long letter to Margot" on 27 September (Harvard).

2. Not identified. Her "Haunted Cabin" was just about to appear in *Quartette*.
3. The poem by James Thomson, published in 1874. RK used the title at least four times for his own work.
4. "The City of Dreadful Night", XIII.22–8, very slightly misquoted. RK uses the passage as the motto to *Under the Deodars*.
5. Millet.
6. "The devil was sick, the devil a monk would be; the devil was well, the devil a monk was he."
7. His name was Drake: RK's diary, 27 September 1885. He was perhaps Lieutenant F. R. Drake, Royal Artillery, stationed at Lahore.
8. The prospectus of the fund appears in the *CMG*, 17 August. RK's "The Song of the Women" (1888) was written in support of Lady Dufferin's Fund.
9. I have been unable to find any such item in the *CMG*.
10. A terracotta bust by JLK (*CMG*, 7 October 1885).

To Margaret Burne-Jones, 28 November 1885–11 January 1886

ALS: University of Sussex

Lahore. / November. 28th / 85.

Noble, fluent-penned, Excellent wop of Albion!

Thirty seven and eighteen of that sweet Roman hand make five and fifty pages, and rejoicing in the house of Kipling. This morning's breakfast table was littered with flying pages and Trix and I both read aloud such extracts as took our fancy at the same time. It was a lively meal and we said with quadruple voice: – "how *thundering* good is the girl's description of that fire." It must have been a festive time for you and yours and, you will forgive this I know, the run round Hammersmith in search of the gardener was a *man's* business and should never have been allowed to fall to the lot of my blessed Aunt.[1] It would be enough to kill her. Anyhow I rejoice that it was over safely with nothing worse than the destruction of a little beef and suet pudding. Fires never operate as a warning to Jerry builders; but there is a place prepared for Tebbs and glue hotter than burning £40 tenements one brick thick. I shall be there officially, and for your sake shall put on some extra kerosine.[2]

In the wealth of your letter I am bewildered. At which end shall I attack those six Baronial sheets and the twelve Knightly ones in a strange script? Shall I say that I agree with you about the manners of the Young Man of the present day? I will. He is a lazy, ill mannered beast *but* he is better out here than with you. Reason why. We put a higher value on our women folk 'cause they be scarcer and I fancy are a trifle more deferential to them than in England. We may speak to them or ride with them smoking *but*, the man who did not bestir himself to do everything he could for a woman travelling – yea even to giving up his seat in the mail cart to a soldier's wife, and taking her ticket etc. for her, would, an his friends knew of his conduct, be sat upon, in our particularly frank and brutal manner. 'Give you another instance. Man whom I knew and who had been out here for seven years went home the other day for three months. Average sort of a man. Holding forth in the Club on his return he said: – "'Tell you what upset me. Having white women to wait at table. 'Made an ass of myself again and again by jumping up when the servant girl brought round the dinner. When I dined at hotels I always waited on myself. 'Can't stand an Englishwoman doing what's properly khitmagah's[3] work." And, would you believe it, we said with one voice: – "Quite right". Your system of men being waited upon by women would strike me very queerly if I came back and so it would any man who had been out here long. No, I think we are, in many ways more courteous to our women kind than our brethren in the west; tho' the Lord he knoweth how little that is.

On the second count We the young men of India stand wholly absolved. The "neat ease of mockery and disrespect" with which your young friends hide their "nobler natures" – the young imps – and the want of seriousness doesn't exist here *except* among a few army men and boys fresh from [sic] India. The diseased vanity which leads to this sort of moral prevarication is born in a large measure from idleness and (of course) youth. It's like distemper in pups and the best cure is making 'em work all they know. With us that particular form of cant does not exist. Everyone of us, from the youngest, has to be dealing with men and things – not sitting down and curling his downy upper lip in scorn at their ways – but actually going down into the thick of the business and working. It knocks that special sort of lunacy on the head *jut put*.[4] We don't cultivate it; priding ourselves rather on our "Earnestness" – which in English means an infinite capacity for boreing the other man with details of your own work *or* driving the government wild with appeals for more money for your district. A man who tried the "nothing new nothing true, don't matter a d—n business" would be simply laughed at for a fool. There's so much true; so much new; and the *mattering* is a question of life and death sometimes. You may tell 'em with my love that there is a God. You see him work out here which in your fenced in, railway ticket, kind of life at home you can't well do.

Better still send some of the boys out here to catch murderers; or run canals; or make railways. It would tan 'em and clean their rotten little brains a little. My faith! How angry have I grown over naught. Let me turn to the second part of your letter with its enquiries about "natives."

When you write "native" who do you mean? The Mahommedan who hates the Hindu; the Hindu who hates the Mahommedan; the Sikh who loathes both; or the semi-anglicized product of our Indian colleges who is hated and despised by Sikh, Hindu, and Mahommedan. Do you mean the Punjabi who will have nothing to do with the Bengali; the Mahrattha to whom the Punjabi's tongue is as incomprehensible as Russian to me; the Parsee who controls the whole trade of Bombay and ranges himself on all questions as an Englishman; the Sindee who is an outsider; the Bhil or the Gond who is an aborigine; the Rajput who despises everything on God's earth but himself; the Delhi traders who control trade to the value of millions; the Afghan who is only kept from looting these same merchants by dread of English interference. Which one of all the thousand conflicting tongues, races, nationalities and peoples between the Khaibar Pass and Ceylon do you mean? There is no such thing as the natives of India, any more than there is the "People of India" as our friends the Indian delegates would have you believe. You may rest assured Wop that if we didn't hold the land in six months it would be one big cock pit of conflicting princelets. Now "do the English as a rule feel the welfare of the natives much at heart." Oh Wop! If you had met some of the men I know you would cross out the sentence and weep. What else are we working in the country for. For what else do the best men of the Commission die from overwork, and disease, if not to keep the people alive in the first place and healthy in the second. We spend our best men on the country like water and if ever a foreign country was made better through "the blood of the martyrs" India is that country. I couldn't now tell you what the men one knows are doing but you can read for yourself if you will how Englishmen have laboured and died for the peoples of the country. Wop dear have you ever heard of a "demoralized district"; when tens of thousands of peoples are panic stricken say, with an invasion of cholera – or dying from famine? Do you know how Englishmen, Oxford men expensively educated, are turned off to "do" that district – to make their own arrangements for the cholera camps; for the prevention of disorder; or for for famine relief, to pull the business through or die – whichever God wills. Then another man, or may be boy takes his place. Yes the English in India do do a little for the benefit of the natives and small thanks they get.

(Wednesday: Mein Gott Himmelsneeskenherrenheddof! *What* a gorgeous cold I've started, cultivated and overcome since I last wrote. 'Made me miss the mail too while Trixie sent off an apoplectic envelope of twaddle. She's a bad girl is Trixie. Don't you have nothing to do with her. She makes me hand over all your letters to me and won't let me have a glimpse at your letters to her. Stay! Where was I? 'Um – yes, as Jingle[5] would say. 'Cold fever, Cataplasm. 'Sister sitting on bed, slapping hot plaster on throat askin' if it stung. Throat like superannuated organ pipe – Jus' so. Camphor, Rubinis and balsam of quinine – no balsam aniseed and Rubini's quinine – no Coleman's pectoral quinine and rubini's plaster of aniseed – I give it up. Ta-ta. 'See you again presently.)

But to return to our cousins I have endeavoured to put forward feebly the fact that the English have the welfare of the natives at heart. One year out here would show you how much truth I have *not* written. Then you demand: – Have we any interests in common? *Werry* few dear old Wop – the bulk of us – d—d few. And 'faith if you knew in what inconceivable filth of mind the peoples of India were brought up from their cradle; if you realized the views – or one tenth of the views – they hold about women and their absolute incapacity for speaking the truth as we understand it – the immeasurable gulf that lies between the two races in all things you would see how it comes to pass that the Englishman is prone to despise the natives – (I *must* use that misleading term for brevity's sake) – and how, except in the matter of trade, to have little or nothing in common with him. Now this is a wholly wrong attitude of mind but it's one that a Briton who washes, and don't take bribes, and who thinks of other things besides intrigue and seduction most naturally falls into. *When he does* – goodbye to his chances of attempting to understand the people of the land. (It's rather a Pott and Slurkian[6] thing to do but I send you herewith my "East and West"[7] an almost verbatim repro. of my confab with an Afghan gentleman (who by the way is an old friend of mine) on my way up from Rajputana the other day.[8] It may bear on what we are talking about). Underneath our excellent administrative system; under the piles of reports and statistics; the thousands of troops; the doctors; and the civilian runs wholly untouched and unaffected the life of the peoples of the land – a life as full of impossibilities and wonders as the Arabian nights. I don't want to gush over it but I do want you to understand Wop dear that, immediately outside of our own English life, is the dark and crooked and fantastic, and wicked, and awe inspiring life of the "native". Our rule, so long as no one steals too flagrantly or murders too openly, affects it in no way whatever – only fences it around and prevents it from being disturbed. I have done my little best to penetrate into it and have put the little I have learnt into the pages of "Mother Maturin" – Heaven send that she may grow into a full blown novel before I die – My experiences of course are only a queer jumble of opium-dens, night houses, night strolls with natives; evenings spent in their company in their own homes (in the men's quarter of course) and the long yarns that my native friends spin me, and one or two queer things I've come across in my own office experience. The result of it all has been to interest me immensely and keenly in the people and to show me how little an Englishman can hope to understand 'em. I would that you could see some of the chapters of Mother Maturin and you would follow more plainly what I mean. But this is a digression. Again you want to know whether the natives feel "affectionately" towards Europeans. No, they don't take to a European 'cos he *is* a European – but when they take to a man because they like him their attachment is rather striking. In this country every thing is done by personal influence – the personal influence of the Englishman. Only our government doesn't recognize the fact and goes centralizing and centralizing at Simla until the District officers – the little kings of the counties – are reduced simply to machines for compiling statistics and lose touch with the people. A man who has the confidence of the natives can do *anything*, whether he is Civilian or Unofficial. Let me give two humble examples. The Mahommedans in the city know my Pater and almost worship him in many ways, for things he's done – 'specially for his kindness towards poor Mahommedans (frankly both he and I prefer Mussalmans to Hindus; they're a better lot roughly speaking). Pater is collecting exhibits for the Indo Colonial Exhibition[9] and can get through about twice as much work as other men simply because he knows the people, they know him and he handles 'em properly. Beyond a certain point however they refuse to go. They won't send valuables for exhibit across the black water *unless* they know my Pater goes with 'em. If he did they'd send *lakhs* worth on his simple assurance that they would be returned uninjured. But the Pater can't go and to his assurances that everything will be safe in the hands of the other Sahibs they simply reply: – "Ah! but what do those Sahibs know about us or we about them. Go you yourself Sahib and you can take anything you like". Pater can't go: so much the worse therefore for the Exhibition as far as the Punjab is concerned. They (the peoples of this country) are by birth and training suspicious but if you get their confidence they'll do anything. With a few exceptions all the Englishmen who have to deal with 'em get their confidence and to do that they have to be handled like children or young horses. Another small very small instance. My own men, about 170 altogether, have rather a belief in me – primarily because I am my father's son (and in this country everyone is the son of some father – and writes his father's name down when he writes his own) and nextly because I've laid myself out to try and understand 'em. The last three years have just shown me how hopeless and how interesting the task is, but also how my *wish* – *not* my order – can make the whole gang buckle to and work double tides or overtime for nothing so long as they understand it was for the Chota Sahib.[10] And yet, if these men weren't paid for an extra half hour's work, under ordinary circumstances, they'd *cry* like children. A queer people indeed. Touchy as children; obstinate as men; patient as the High God's themselves; vicious as Devils but always loveable if you know how to take 'em. And so far as I know, the proper way to handle 'em is not by looking on 'em "as excitable masses of barbarism" (I speak for the Punjab only) or the "down trodden millions of Ind groaning under the heel of an alien and unsympathetic despotism", but as men with a language of their own which it is your business to understand; and proverbs, which it is your business to quote (this is a land of proverbs) and bywords and allusions which it is your business to master; and feelings which it is your business to enter into and sympathize with. Then they'll believe in you and do things for you, and let you do things for them. *But* (and here you will think me wrong perhaps) never lose sight of the fact that so long as you are in this country you will be looked to by the natives round in [sic] you as their guide and leader if anything happens. Therefore comport yourself as such. This is a solemn fact. If anything goes wrong from a quarrel to an accident the natives *instantly* fly to a European for "orders." If a man's dying in the road they won't touch him unless they have an Englishman to order 'em. If there's a row in the city the native policeman will take his orders from the first wandering white man he sees and so on *ad infinitum*. This is only the sober truth. They will go to their own District officer first and if they can't get him to the nearest Englishman. I had almost forgotten another instance of "confidence." The financial management of the funds of the "Durbar Sahib" – the big temple at Amritsar which is the centre of the Sikh religion was till recently "bossed" by an Englishman on the urgent request of the Sikhs' priests. Now I believe they have a native treasurer but that Englishman is always called in if there's any hitch. It comes to this then – The natives aren't "affectionate" to Englishmen *qua* Englishmen but they have a belief that they can be trusted implicitly to speak truth and keep accounts straight – all of 'em. When they believe in any particular Englishman affection is a mild word for their feelings. They worship him almost. At the same time they'd perjure their immortal souls to cheat him to the extent of d/1/2 English money. You can reconcile these manifold contradictions Wop as you please. But they are all pretty near the truth. Have I answered your questions at sufficient length think you?

So you approved of the City of Dreadful Night and paid me the compliment of making it better.[11] Now Infidel I have thee on the hip. Just attend for a moment. Your epistles show me that you have a style about seven and a half times better and more powerful than mine as you have a handwriting incomparably finer. That much I know of the Wop of Albion *unofficially*. But with all these advantages I have never seen Miss Margaret Burne Jones in print anywhere and consequently when she tells me calmly that she has been doctoring my prose I cock my assistant editorial nose and cry: – "'Odds scissors and paste pots! Who the this and that *is* this Miss Margaret Burne Jones who takes a pen in her hand and ploughs over the work of a journalist of three year's standing?" You can't get out of it Wop dear. I never met you in print – don't know who you are – "don't recogn'ze y'r 'thority Mishter" as the drunken Volunteer said. You must come down from your eclectic pole and write too, and then I'll say: – "Hum! 'Margaret Burne Jones'! Writes deucedly good prose but by Jove you should see her letters: 'Girl has an absolute genius for correspondence. *I've* got some of her best work – description of a coast guard."

Though you are a Resplendent Wop and though I value your criticisms more than any one else's *I'm blessed* if you shall be allowed to play round outside and beautify the alligators in the tanks without stepping in yourself. Go upstairs to your own room and write something and Trix and I will welcome you as a Sister and a Fellow Worker in large capital letters. What says the poet:

> Murder the Wop and he never objects
> "But (until you have gone and become "one of us"
> Mr. Wenus) keep your pen from wandering casually
>   over his text.[12]

Which reminds me Trix has contributed a story to Quartette[13] which has filled me with woe. As a neat bit o' work 'tisn't half bad. As a proof it's simply [   ][14] as Hafiz says. Ram Dass, excellent Hindu that he is, brings me pages on pages each viler than the first: – "Sar I cannot understand" says he; and I have to go through it all again. If *Quartette* comes out without a howling misprint in every other line it will be by the blessing of Providence alone. I never met such awful proofs in my life. Thank Heaven that *Quartette* only comes once a year. Otherwise my eyes (what's left of 'em) would shrivel out. Imagine 513 mistakes in one galley of five pages! The family seem to be rather amused than afflicted by "those absurd misprints" but it's anything but fun for me.[15] When you die and Gabriel offers you the choice between editing a Christmas magazine and another situation elsewhere say to him: – Gabriel – You mean well I dare say but I'd prefer the other *nokri*.[16] Bring along the kerosine and strap me down on the gridiron.

Tuesday. 8th. Thereupon there was a tempest which raged for three days and has just blown over. All about Quartette of course. I've staked what little reputation is mine on getting it out by the 15th of this month and Ram Dass tells me that I am his Father and His Mother but it can't be done. *Told* me rather I should say on Friday of these things and I set myself to prove that he lied through the greater part of last Sabbath. Came at eight in the morning ere the frost was off the ground and set to correcting proofs. 'Tisn't the nicest thing in the world to proof read with driving gloves on and fingers numbed with cold and Ram Dass sulkily defiant (he objected to early hours) and the coolies deaf and dumb and snuffed out with chill. But we spent a lovely sabbath together he and I and have holpen Q. amazingly – which pleased me mightily.

Queer beggars these men are, as I've told you about forty times already Wop. Ram Dass was cold and unhappy and it was all I could do to keep him to his work. Hadn't had his breakfast (this was a lie) wasn't well (another) didn't see where the necessity for hurry came in (Number Three). I waited till I had a knot of Mahommedan compositors round me and spake thus: – "Oh Ram Dass! I have been now three years eating the salt of this newspaper and I though (lit: it was in my mind) that the Hindus worked as well as the Mahommedans. But I now find that I have made a mistake and that the Hindus are weak and childish without spirit (ûkhàl is difficult to translate exactly – it means all that goes to make up a Man) and (this hurt his feelings most of all) nearly as worthless as a Bengali babu." Now if there is one thing Ram Dass prides himself upon it's his being a Panjabi of the Panjabis and my words stuck. I hadn't no more bother that Sunday about "Quartette" and when we'd done I told Ram Dass in the floweriest tongue at my command that he had worked like an elephant. And, here I howked in a Punjabi proverb: – "As is the shoulder of the elephant so is the weight of his labour. Therefore O Ram Dass you and I will have much and heavy work to get through together." The idea of myself delivering these little homilies on the sanctity of toil upsets me sometimes as an excellent jest and thus my finest reproofs are marred by an illtimed grin of self derision. I think of Price and Westward Ho! and the enormous energy which I devoted to shirking my work and it – doesn't help me.

Thanks for your dialogue of the diseased youth. Trix and I have rapturously added it to our stock of household sayings and quote it about seven times a day. It's all very well to scoff Wop but I assure you that many men marry for no higher motive than: – "Lady I am unwell. My bones ache etc." The mother's care and (Oh bother your fist I can't stick to it[17]) attentions have completely demoralized me and after much grave thought I have decided that when I marry it must be a lady well versed in domestic knowledge, not less than twelve years my senior, and by preference, some other man's wife. Thus only can I hope to pass gracefully from the comforts of the foursquare hearth to the comforts of my own. Six years hence when a terrific scandal agitates upper India and I have to bolt into Cashmere with my bride you at least will understand that the elopement was due to no overwhelming passion beyond my own desire for comfort and that having found my pearl of great price – the housekeeper as sweet and as perfect and almost as old as my mother – I have taken her away from some man who couldn't appreciate her, for my own benefit. Who in is his senses would buy a young four year old raw from the dealer's hands, unlearned in the niceties of polo; mouthless; paceless and mannerless; ignorant of hacking and resentful of harness and keep him for ever till he died? And yet the (cat and) dog-cart matrimonial is sometimes harnessed to – but the question is a deep one. I have always regretted that I parted with my unhandsome but perfectly trained charger, the fifteen hand, fifteen rupee *John Anderson*.[18] It shall never occur again. I promise myself. Dolly Bobs is fair to look upon but has lately taken to shying in a way that crisps my hair. She nearly walked into a brougham on Thursday in a futile attempt to flee from a dog, dimly visible on the horizon. I pulled her out and she went through the rest of the journey with never more than two legs on the ground at the same time.[19] (Pretty sort of decorative frieze if you reduce her plump little person to straight lines) and yet I should be the first to complain bitterly if a young and untrained person conducted herself with the casualness of Miss Dolly Bobs, while I owned her. You see I couldn't hit her between the ears with a whip butt; or tie her head down with a short martingale; or wrap an old glove round her bit-port; nor cut her daily allowance of food without all my friends calling me a wretch. We are a disgustingly illogical people we English.

The first of our series of fortnightly Cinderellas[20] comes on the day after tomorrow – 17 dancing men to 39 dancing women. Rather a cheerful look out for the women I fear me. Specially as we male hopsters have that vile habit of dancing *only* with five or six ladies at the utmost – and in a dance of 15 dances take 3. from each.

Sunday/6th. Why *will* the Pater use my note for drawing on?[21] I'm sure it isn't fit for water colours in spite of the beauteous vision below. (We are nothing if not versatile in our hand writings).[22]

Wednesday 16th. A murrain on Quartette and every soul saving us four therewith connected. Ram Dass has broken down helplessly, the Scotch foreman has been smitten with fever and the clerk in charge of the accounts [is] more hopelessly incompetent than any native I have yet had dealings with – and that's saying a good deal. I've been doing my level best with the thing – working in office till seven or eight at nights and taking a large share of the business arrangements on myself to ease 'em off and here's Q. two days late already. Remember Wop in spite of what good lies in the native he is utterly unable to do anything finished or clean, or neat unless he has the Englishman at his elbow to guide and direct and put straight. Remember when you hear the educated gentlemen of colour (who by the way are much less in sympathy with the natives than we) tell you of the enormous progress made by India of late years that every step of that progress is boosted on both sides, and propped up from below and held up from above by Englishmen who take the blame if anything goes wrong and gloss over the shortcomings and that without that aid – you would get – well anything mismanaged, ill directed, scamped, helpless, and careless that you please. And a mismanaged nation is not a sweet thing I believe – 'never had one myself tho'; Ram D. and his kin taxing my patience and long suffering to the verge of lunacy. They are all willing enough but, in addition to their natural incapacity to understand, so ghastly careless and casual. What on earth do you think of a Head Printer – a man who has been as long at his business as you have been alive – telling you calmly that he did not see the "necessity of having words spaced apart at equal distances." And R.D. told me that three days ago and I called him a "child" and a "child's child" and a speaker of "baby's talk." 'Faith it makes me indignant to think of it even now and here am I yarning away about office worry as though you knew R.D. and cared one little, little cuss for his iniquities. Let us attack less technical ground. Did Trix tell you about the big Club ball on the 28th and the little Cinderella on the 24th. I'm one of the hosts at the Club hop and worse luck don't expect to be able to attend either function – albeit my cards are neatly filled from no. 1. to extra no. 3. Still the exchange is a most delightful one. James Walker and his wife (J.W. is one of our proprietors) wanted me to spend Xmas with them knocking about on tour to Agra, Bundrabund, and may be Bhurtpore for a week or ten days in company with another married couple very dear friends of mine. I told 'em months ago that the matter rested with my chief and this evening comes a letter to "Dear Ruddy" from Mrs. Walker – who is a delightful lady and as clever as she is – must I write the bitter truth to clear your mind of any suspicion that may be therein? – unlovely, telling me that "Jim" had written to Wheeler demanding the body of the Assistant Editor for as long as he could be spared and that if he let me go I was to "come and be made much of for my letters on" – various things in the old rag. W. ain't likely to refuse a request that has nearly all the force of a Royal Command, and besides it won't hurt him to work my 'workins' a while and see what it feels like. Though I *should* like to have those two dances all the same. If his answer's satisfactory – and I shall know tomorrow morn – I meet the party at Umballa on the morning of the 24th and go down with 'em to Agra – where lies the desire of my eyes the Taj. Of course I shall be obliged to write an account of the business. I shouldn't be happy if I didn't either in myself or in my duty to the Rag – bless her. But was ever so unworthy a "Dowb" so well "looked after". Followest thou the allusion Wop?[23] The Pater hails the trip as a step in my Indian Education – he's great on my seeing the land when I can and most generously offered to take the financial part of it off my shoulders. 'Can't accept of course but I'd like dearly to bear him off with me.

Quartette will be off my mind and the getting out of the long delayed 2nd Edition of *Echoes* (still in demand I beg you remember) a thing postponable till my return. When *that's* out I can turn to Mother Maturin in my bits of spare time as I please.

The Mother – who is never seedy – has been down this week with a severe go of rheumatism in her left shoulder and Trixie has profited by the occasion to show herself in the light of a grand nurse. We are afraid the Mother caught a chill at the last dance and instead of turning to bronchitis or fever the thing went for the muscles. Anyhow it has kept her in bed for three days and to her own room for as many more and she is not equal to going out yet. Personally I am rejoiced that it's only temporary paralysis and not fever or anything serious but the Mummy says tho' it may be nothing to boast of it has hurt her a good deal and she would exchange for any minor honourable disease. The stiffness has nearly all gone now thanks to the attention of Doctor Elizabeth Bielby[24] – our new lady doctor and a dear, round, tubby, darling she is: – and Trixie's attendance: but we don't want the Mother to come out of her own room and begin to take the reins again just yet. As Miss Bielby put it to her: – "Only do a half of anything you've a mind to" and this is what we are taking care that the prop of the family shall do. Trix is housekeeper enough to see that everything runs smoothly and, saving that our meals are not graced by the Mother, things go just the same.

Thursday Dec. 17 Midday – and I've been working by lamplight ever since ten. It's bitterly cold, wet, blowing and cloudy – the past four months' dust clammy mud and the mud walls melting like sugar. Rained all last night and has been showering at intervals all day. But for everything around me save the weather I should feel as though I were in London with a fog atop o' me. The Mother's all right today though still stiff; but it's much too cold for her to leave her room. I left Trix in attendance when I came away and oh how the cold blasts tickled little Dolly. In the press the men are shivering like Italian greyhounds, and even over here I find that a huge fire at my back and a big lamp in front is hardly enough to keep me warm.

Praise be to Allah but Quartette will be through this evening – finished and completed so far as these imperfect instruments will permit. The Scotch foreman is recovering from his fever and has buckled to once more, while the Unspeakable Ram Dass in his delight at the prospect of ridding himself of my importunities has done his level best. After all he *did* work well tho' he is a Splended Ass. 'Came early to office this morn for the purpose of overhauling accounts and found that the register of "Quartette" subscriptions had been missing for two days past and that the Bengali Babu in charge hadn't thought fit to tell me a word about it or to book the additional orders. That's how we work in the Punjab. He was a Bengali so I didn't feel called upon to let him down easily and he was insolent which didn't improve his case in the least. He was a native B.A. and reminded me of the fact. I had forgotten it but increased the fine on that count. Brutal wasn't it Wop! Seeing that he knew Goldsmith's Deserted Village from beginning to end and more "advanced arithmetic" than I shall ever attain to in this life. And on my word that's about as fair a sample of the results of English educational top-dressing on the native subsoil as you could get. – Knows fractions and decimals – can't keep the register of two hundred orders correctly or neatly – Remembers the *Deserted Village* and mislays an account book. – Thirdly and lastly – Lies – Like a Bengali – to get out of the mess. The whole to be purchased in bulk or retail for Rs. 35. per mensem with trademark of the Calcutta University attached. In an evil hour for himself did Laljee Mull say that he was a B.A. He has a wife and three kids and is at least twenty one. What hope is there of a man or boy rather of that stamp – the representative of a class ten thousand strong. – Broken down – used up – played out – before they are men and through the very weakness of their physical nature morally rotten and untrustworthy. A-a-a-Men. I'm becoming a regular preacher in my old age.

Which reminds me the Pater has drored a Xmas card for you and set me to hammer out poetry. A murrain on all verse – I stick to blank so you mustn't criticize those halting lines too hardly. The picture's dead truthful: so are the lines but the Picture has the more merit.

Friday. December. 18th. 10 in the morning. Still working by lamplight with a general impression that I've been doing nothing else for the past thirty six hours. "This evening" did I say in the pride of my heart – "This morning" was Quartette cleared away at five before the dawn had broken and when the rain was coming down hard. 'Twas a merry merry night. I got four copies out for the people at home *minus* advertisements and the one or two last touches at seven last night and left the foreman with a bottle of brandy and my blessing – for I knew what was coming. He had kept on forty odd men besides binders to keep Quartette going. When I got home the people read it and counted printer's errors – about twenty I think in 125 pages – made, for such is the innate clumsiness of my men – *after* my corrections. On the whole – though I said it as shouldn't – I felt that my struggles with the proofsheets had been rewarded. We four crowed jubilantly and at ten I retired to rest – the Mother – bless her – petting me after the wont of Mothers and saying that I was tired out. In my bedroom I remembered Chalmers the Scotch foreman and his forty thieves and wondered what the end would be. Wondered so much that I left the house secretly and plashed over to the press. As I thought the men were on the verge of mutiny – saying they wouldn't work any more and C. was tearing his hair over the advertisements. Ram Dass said he was cold and hungry and eyed the brandy bottle. Now a man – any man except an assistant editor – when he works overtime is paid for his labour but there is no law which enforces his working all night – and that was just what I meant my friends to do. And oh *how* you would have laughed to have seen the situation. The big hall where the presses are faintly lit by scores of candle ends: – our architect never contemplated working at night – full of bobbing shadows and reflections; the mob of white and red and green turbans tossing round the raised platform in the centre of the room and clamouring to be let go and Ram Dass, Chalmers and myself in great coats standing above the mob and reducing them to order by argument. I suppose the effect was artistic and picturesque but we weren't on the look out for that. Chalmers led away Ram Dass and – so he says – gave him a heavy tot of brandy. Anyhow R.D. came back in a good temper with moist eyes and goodwill in his heart. Meantime from the dais I was haranguing the press men. Took me nearly twenty minutes to prove to their satisfaction that as they had engaged to work overtime they *must* go on till Quartette was finished. God only knew when that time would be but they could see for themselves that myself and the head of the printers — "a man who knew everything" (lit. a sub-janta wallah) – would remain with them as long as they did even till the next day if need. Then I made concessions because it was a case without precedent. They might bring in their hookahs and smoke ten at a time over the big charcoal braziers and talk and go to sleep in half hour shifts and (here I clinched the business) I myself would supply the tobacco. That had 'em where they were weakest. One shilling English money supplied me with about *twelve pounds* of the hideous mixture of cow dung and dried grass they delight in. I sent a man to knock up a shopkeeper in a hut about a quarter of a mile away; got the weed; told off the stand easy gang and put in all I knew with the rest. And what a mad night it was. Something went wrong with the two colour title page. The type in "Civil and Military Gazette" was worn out and wouldn't come up properly. With gum and bits of paper and paste and brown paper I "packed the lay" with these lilly fingers – stuck bits of paper behind the piece of paper that is pressed against the type in order to bulge out the paper into the face of the worn letters. I don't know whether that's clear enough to your mind. It was a long and dirty job and I got foully mired with the droppings of candle ends and paste. Chalmers was correcting proofs of advertisements, standing over the men to see they did it – and I assure you that by the inadequate candle-light and under the hands of asinine punjabis proofs were uncommon queer. As soon as I got the title page moderately decent – it looks pretty well but a practised eye could tell I'd been "faking it" – I placed myself under Chalmer's orders for the rest of the time. So when I wasn't correcting proofs of superior saddles and watches and medicines – *not* the outpourings of my mighty genius – I was going round from shift to shift and keeping 'em in good temper and chaffing the men who were smoking and patting the children – for that's all they are in their tempers – on the back and telling 'em how such a work was never before produced in India and how the Calcutta printers would think shame of themselves when they heard that Panjabis worked all night like elephants. Never have I seen Ram Dass toil as he did in the early hours of this morn and never did he handle his men so neatly. It must ha' been the brandy I suppose. About two o'clock something went wrong with the title page *again* and the impression went bad. Got that corrected and kept on. And the lights bobbed, and the native tobacco stank; and I smoked many cheroots; and Chalmers tramped up and down the shifts; and I tramped and read proofs and Ram Dass was heartened a second time with the bottle and it grew colder and wetter and more dismal and the clock struck five. Then was Quartette born and we laid her aside reverently and departed into the dark each our several ways saying that – Never since the Old Rag began had it been party to such a proceeding as ours. And we felt mighty proud and sleepy. I got to bed at 5.30 a.m. and was exceeding late for breakfast. "My boy" said the Pater eyeing my weary eyes and disheveled locks: "If you would only get up in the mornings and do your work you'd be ever so much better." I hid my head behind a coffee cup and chuckled. Luckily the office routine work today hasn't been heavy for I fancied there would be some difficulty at the last moment and filled up the bulk of the paper beforehand. But I feel awfully sleepy and tired and have been on my feet a long time looking after the binders. These too are unfathomable idiots and but for strict watching would misbind. Thank goodness the copies are off to the papers for review and we shall get the 250 ordered away tonight.

All this may seem a tremendous pother over so small a thing as a Christmas annual – a booklet that drops in dozens from the English presses as easily and as quietly as snow flakes in December. Out here things are different as I learnt in my midnight struggle with the title page and throughout the whole of the time I was correcting those unspeakably hideous proofs. To quote the indefatigable Chalmers as he departed at five: – "Seein' the stupeedity o' those men an' conseederin' the material at our deesposal I may say Mister Kipling that we have done vara weel."

December 19th. A day of solemn and holy joy tempered only by office work and the knowledge that my chief can't spare me to go to Bhurtpore with the Walkers. After all I'm not surprised and as I stand on velvet either way I don't much care. A dance and a ball are fair equivalents – almost – and I'll debit the deficiency to my Chief the next time he wants a holiday and asks me to take the paper on alone. It's a fact in Natural History that the Editor *can't* work without the assistant, whereas the assistant *can* make shift without the Editor. Men on other papers have told me the same thing. The Pater has been writing – on *my* pet paper too, bad pens and ink to him – whole sheaves to Aunt Louie. It seems that he has a notion that Stan ought to come out to India for a while and see things. He seems about as keen on Stan's travels as I am on Phil's. Lord! Lord! If we were as we wish to be what a procession of globe-trotting cousins would we bring to Lahore and take about India. I don't for an instant suppose that Aunt Louie would let that paragon with a horror of fast girls go away for a year but if financial arrangements didn't stop it, 'twould be a grand thing for the boy – I beg his pardon 'Varsity MAN! Honestly Wop, do you think that he will ever put on the irons after having been to college – and resign himself cheerfully to Wilden near Stourport until such time as he becomes an M.P.? Odds luck and fortune! if I had that youngster's education and physique and money at the back on't there would be a new daily paper running in India before a year was over – either here or in North Borneo[25] a land for which I have a wholly illogical affection; believing that the North Borneo Company are destined to grow and increase and dig drains, and docks, and export fat sacksfull of wares and grains and much teak and maybe precious stones. It would be well to start a paper in that new land and advocate sewers and wharfs and schemes of local self-government. But after all one has work enough in so raw a province as the Punjab and I mustn't let my enthusiasm for a new land run away with me. Thanks mainly to our old rag there's a big arrangement started for supplying country bred remounts to the Bengal cavalry – a good business which should employ many dealers and save money.

Jan 11th. Only five weeks over this letter. Not bad for me. I really *must* send it off this mail – it's getting as ridiculous as your bangles – the enamelled ones Trix is always sending and never sends. I'll write crampsome on this page and wind up.

The Mother is ever so much better and the Beilby duck says so. So looks the Mother which is better still. And odds gush and gabble! *how* Quartette has been reviewed by the Indian papers. Christmas annuals are a novelty here I know but I never expected the unadulterated butter that Q. got. Fancy the Wop of Asia compared to Wilkie Collins for having written the strange ride of Morrowbie Jukes! And this is what the grave and sobre Bombay Gazette said. I should like to break Grattan Geary's[26] head for profanation – All the same Q. has been a thundering success – financially which is the great thing and thanks to it my screw has once more been raised. Doesn't make me feel very happy though because the Government of India is poor and I have to pay income tax £12–10s per annum *on the top of a rupee at 1/5 7/8*. Isn't it abominable. However I have the consolation of abusing the financial policy of the Government with the big big WE. And that's worth a few rupees as a safety valve.

I've gathered together a few things I've done o' late and am sending 'em to you. They may possibly interest you only mind Wop not a line do you cut until you've appeared in print yourself.

And now at the end of this awful pile of M.S. to ask you a favour, and a big one. In the course of your wanderings do you ever come to know any thing about the Slade Art School and the students there – the female ones I mean of course. Circumstances over which I have not the smallest control prevent my going home and seeing the school myself. There is or was a maiden there of the name of Garrard – Flo Garrard – and I want to know, *how* she is and what she is doing.[27] So far as I know you're the only person who's likely to be able to find this out for me, and if possible I want you as quietly and as unobtrusively as possible to learn all you can about the girl. It's a cool sort of request to make isn't it? And I shouldn't ha' done it but that I am at my wits end for news in this particular instance. If I said that for *any* information you gave me you should have anything in my power to give "even unto the half of my kingdom" you would naturally be offended so I appeal humbly to the Wop of Albion to help me for old sake's sake. I only want to know if the girl looks well and – so far as your eyes can judge – happy. Thereafter if I can serve you in any way you know who to go to.

Yours expectantly
THE WOP OF ASIA

Notes
1. Georgiana Macdonald Burne-Jones (1840–1920), Margaret's mother and RK's aunt, second of the five Macdonald sisters. It was Aunt Georgie who presided over the domestic life at The Grange, so important to RK as a lonely schoolboy. Of all the good things at The Grange, she was, he wrote, "best of all, immeasurably" (*Something of Myself*, p. 12). Though they later differed sharply over politics their personal affection was never impaired. At the very moment when feelings ran highest over the Boer War, which Aunt Georgie opposed, RK was helping her to write the biography of her husband, *Memorials of Edward Burne-Jones*.
2. A fire at a coffee-house just south of The Grange had occurred on 23 October.
3. Waiter's (usually *khitmatgar*).
4. Immediately.
5. In Dickens, *Pickwick Papers*.
6. The rival editors in the Eatanswill election: Dickens, *Pickwick Papers*.
7. *CMG*, 14 November 1885 (uncollected).
8. Where RK had been on 7 November to report the Viceroy's opening of Mayo College: "The Viceroy at Ajmir", *CMG*, 11 November, and "The Opening of the Mayo College", 12 November, are both by RK (uncollected).
9. See 17 September 1884. JLK's design for the Punjab exhibition is described by RK in *CMG*, 3 February 1886 (uncollected).
10. "Little lord", i.e. Kipling junior.
11. See [27] September 1885. Writing to Margaret on 31 January 1886 JLK says "Ruddy let me see your note on his City of Dreadful Night and I was delighted to mark your advice. . . . The temptations to vulgar smartness, to over emphasis and other vices are tremendous" (MS, Sussex).
12. Cf. the fractured ballads of Silas Wegg in Dickens, *Our Mutual Friend*, e.g., ch. 40.
13. "The Haunted Cabin".
14. RK has here attempted a phrase in Persian: it is indecipherable except for the word "garden".

15. "I remember how we laughed together over the proofs of 'Quartette' – a sonnet of my mother's which ought to have been called 'Parted' came back headed 'Putrid'!" (Alice Fleming, "Some Reminiscences of My Brother", *Kipling Journal*, December 1937, p. 126).
16. Employment.
17. RK has been imitating her hand from the beginning of the paragraph.
18. Joe, as in "John Anderson, my Jo". But Joe was killed in a fall at Dalhousie: see 2 September 1884.
19. Here RK has drawn a frieze of stick-figures, showing horse and rider in violent motion.
20. Dancing parties that end at midnight.
21. JLK has drawn a trumpeter in turban and native costume down the left side of the sheet.
22. The first part of the paragraph imitates JLK's hand, the rest, Margaret's.
23. "Take care of Dowb" is a catchphrase dating from the Crimean War. A politician having a nephew named Dowbiggin serving in the army sent a telegram to the general urging him to "take care of Dowbiggin". This was garbled in the transmission to "take care of Dowb" and became public knowledge in that form. See the *Oxford Dictionary of Proverbs*.
24. Elizabeth Bielby, MD, Professor of Midwifery, Lahore Medical School, and Lecturer to female students. She had come to Lahore in October from Lucknow, the first woman doctor in the Punjab. Trix attended her lectures.
25. Administered by the British North Borneo Company since 1882; made a British protectorate in 1885.
26. Grattan Geary (?–1900), editor and proprietor of the *Bombay Gazette*, 1880–1900.
27. Flo Garrard was at the Slade School, 1884–7, after which she went to Paris for further study.

To W. C. Crofts, 20 December 1885
Text: Copy, University of Sussex

Civil and Military Gazette/Lahore, Dec. 20: 1885.

Dear Mr. Crofts,

I have sent you by this mail a copy of a Christmas Annual which I have had the misfortune to start and edit. Editing when Punjabi compositors are in question is not pleasant. You will note that the thing is not free from misprints and is badly inked, but it is the first venture of its kind and has been very well received by the Indian public for whom we wrote.[1] The "Quartette" is, of course, my Father, Mother, Sister and myself. I have marked my share by a dot on the contents table.[2] Some of it may perhaps interest you, and if you could spare a moment or two on mail day, I should be glad of a *written opinion* on it.

Yours very sincerely,
Rudyard Kipling

Notes
1. RK must refer to the sales in advance of publication. The printing of the book had been finished only two days before this letter, and no reviews had yet appeared.

2. RK is said to have marked in the Crofts copy all the items now assigned to him and, in addition, "My Christmas at the Ajaibgaum Exhibition". The attribution was picked up by the bibliographers, but except in the one instance of the Crofts copy, RK consistently denied that the work was his. It seems clear that it was written by JLK.

To Louisa Baldwin, 24 January 1886
AL: Library of Congress

[Lahore] Jan. 24th/86

Dearest Auntie

The Mother promises me a seat in her envelope to you so I write. There's nothing on earth to record – except heavy rain – and I dare say the mother has told you this at length. Trix is in the next room writing to Margaret – she writes enormous letters does "our Miss Bailie" – the Pater is out and I've just come in from a drive to church at Mian Mir five miles out.[1] Imagine a cloudless blue sky, a brilliant sun, and weather and wind so chilly that you must wear a thick ulster while you drive and wadded gloves lest your hands numb! That's a very fair sample of a January day in Lahore.

You find the mother's account of her "man housemaid" amusing. I wonder how you would like to have your groom come to me, as mine did yesterday and ask for a loan of £5 because he was going to get his eldest son – aged 12 – married. The man's pay is something under fourteen shillings a month. I have not lost the opportunity of expressing my views most forcibly on child marriage and argued the matter with him this morning as I drove. "It's quite true" said he "my son is a child – but it is the custom of our country and he must be married." Small wonder that the people are hopelessly poor and in debt. He hinted gravely that if I didn't lend the money, the marriage could not take place. Whereupon I was so rejoiced that I flatly refused the loan and threatened both father and son with my eternal displeasure if this foolery took place. It will though I know and my groom will live and die deep in debt and his son after him. The fiancée by the way is 9. By this time a copy of Quartette should have reached you. Has the mother told you that the Indian Press have reviewed it most favourably – said all manner of sweet and gushing things – and that if all goes well we shall get another out next year. We have had several solemn consultations on the subject and the stories, and have settled one or two. Christmas annuals aren't pleasant things to edit by any means – specially with native printers.

Glad to see from your letter to the mother such good accounts of Stan. He is a cousin that I should have liked much to have known at home but we saw so little of each other. Don't you think a trip to India would be a suitable preliminary to his settling down to the business. Have it after he takes his degree and sen[d] him up here. We can give him letters to most places and he might make an enjoyable six months of it. Thus: – Bombay, Mt Abu, Ajmer, Jaipur, Lahore, Peshawur, Lahore, Amritsar, Simla, Agra, Allahabad, Cawnpore, Lucknow, Benares, Calcutta – by steamer to Madras and Ceylon and up again through Southern India to Bombay. My word, what a trip I could make out of it for him if I could only get away for half a year from the office. I went down to Ajmer on business – special correspondent – in November,[2] and it was lovely but I hadn't time to "laze" through the country as Stan ought to do. I suppose the notion's an impracticable one so you'd better not mention it to him. The tiffin gong has just tinkled and I fly – ravenously hungry after the open air and my wrestles with a naughty little horse who got frightened by a train. Love to Aunt Edie – she owes me a letter. Remind her – and Uncle Alfred. My salaams to Stan.

Always your loving God Son

Notes
1. Where RK was flirting with the daughter of the Revd W. H. Duke, "an awful military chaplain . . . who has a lovely daughter – like the picture of Lady Hamilton, says Ruddy" (JLK to Margaret Burne-Jones, 31 January 1886: MS, Sussex).
2. To report the opening of the Mayo College: see 28 November 1885–11 January 1886.

To Lionel Dunsterville, 30 January 1886
ALS: University of Sussex

Lahore. / Jan. 30th / 86

Dear Old Man –

(On second thoughts – You unmitigated old Blackguard).

I saw your name in the trooper list but never a hint as to your destination and I've been cursing you fluently ever since.[1] Of course if you had rheumatic fever I don't mind forgiving you but the next time you drop into India in this casual manner just you let me know, or the consequences will be serious. So you're at Nassik[2] are you. Hum! There's a big house on the top of a hill there where Proctor Sims[3] the Engineer

To Lionel Dunsterville, 30 January 1886

lives or used to live – close to the river. Make a reverent pilgrimage thither O my Son and reflect that in those walls did the Saintly Gigger spend the fourth and fifth years of his life – many ages ago. If you know P. Sims he'll tell you. A lovely spot is Nassik. You know the rhyme of course –

> There was a young lady of Nassik
> Whose attire was graceful and classic
>   For all that she wore
>   Both behind and before
> Was a wreath of the roses of Nassick

I didn't know that your sister was down there.[4] At least I wasn't sure. She has been good enough to write to me from Haiderabad (Sind) and I guess one of my reply letters must be knocking about that forsaken spot still. Nor did I know that another of your sisters was here in Lahore though Dr. Beilby dined with us last Sunday. She (the Beilby) is a delightful woman – pleasant plump and professional exceedingly.

The record of my time is not a lively one. I've been to Peshawur, Ajmir, and one or two native states[5] as special correspondent within the last year besides putting in four months at Simla on the same work. Now I am back in office cursing the Punjabi coolie who is the veriest ass God ever made and drawing the princely income of Rs 400 per mensem in return for which I have to work a little harder than I did before – at College say. Young *mi* is at Ferozpur,[6] Satan[7] has left here, Boileau[8] is quartered at Mian Mir, Davies[9] *mi* comes in from Sealkôt to visit some friends of his here. Murray[10] came in from Jhelum 'tother day and spent a day with me. He's a man and a good one at that. I don't think that there are any more O.U.S.C.'s within hail though I dare say if I had gone down to Delhi to the camp of exercise I should have seen scores. They are as thick as blackberries in upper India. What the deuce is Johnnie Baugh[11] doing in Bombay? I didn't know he was in Her Majesty's service at all. Never mind, you shall tell me as soon as you come up. And look here. You won't be fit to travel up to Pindi without a break my son, after rheumatic fever. So you'll come and put up with us for as long as you can and I'll see if you are fit to be sent on. Pindi's chilly and if you are the same careless ruffian as you used to be ten to one you'll come north with insufficient bedding and wraps. Anyhow you will report yourself to me on arrival at Lahore and I will take charge of you. I am living en famille with my father, mother and sister – all of us – so that you won't have to put up with the tender mercies of a bachelor's establishment. Having made that point clear I pass on.

Sorry to find you haven't even a medal for your manly breast. Do you know I believe, if in a weak moment Government gave you such an article, you'd go and pop it somewhere – that is to say if you haven't outgrown our old instincts in the little study. Loss of batta[12] is more serious. However you may get your chance of something festive up here. The Bonerwals have killed a man – a Colonel Hutchinson – and I fancy they will be expeditioned.[13] *Nota Bene.* Never close with an Afghan; plug at him from a distance. There's no glory if he sticks you and precious little if you pot him. I had an experience at Jumrood which brought this home to me.[14] I stood afar off and heaved rocks at mine adversary like David did and providentially smote him on the mouth insomuch that he lost interest in me and departed. He had a knife and seemed to object to my going on foot towards the Khaibar. Narrow minded sort of a cuss who couldn't appreciate the responsibilities of journalism. That's been all the active service I've ever seen and I didn't like it. I tried to go to Burma[15] for the paper but I couldn't be spared. By the way did you see that poor Dury[16] was killed by those swine? There's £1800 worth of education gone to smash and a good fellow with it.[17]

I must turn to my labours again and tug at the lever of the Universe. Hurry up and come along. I'm anxious to see you as you may guess. Give my best salaams to your sister, wear flannel next your skin, take sufficient warm kit for the journey north and hasten to

Thine Ever
Gigger

P.S.   Your handwriting is damnable. Take a lesson by mine.
P.S.   Ain't Quartette thrilling – There's a Jenny say qwai about that Phantom Rickshaw that positively haunts me. I have built up a reputation in the Punjab as a chartered libertine on the strength of it.

Notes

1. Dunsterville had been in Egypt but was now assigned to the Punjab, "where we arrived in January 1886. Rheumatic fever bowled me out *en route* and I had to be left behind, sick, in Deolali" (*Stalky's Reminiscences*, p. 66).
2. The summer resort frequented by Bombay civilians, about a hundred miles from Bombay. JLK's family spent the hot months there when RK was a child in Bombay.
3. R. Proctor Sims, CE, Public Works Councillor in the native state of Bhaunagar, Bombay Presidency (*India Directory*, 1890, 1893). The Kipling family stayed with him in August 1870, when JLK was ill with fever (Alice Kipling to Mrs Rivett-Carnac, 28 August 1870: ALS, Sussex).
4. Dunsterville had five sisters.
5. There is no evidence to identify these.
6. Arthur Frederick Young (1866–88), at USC 1879–84; in Pugh's House; Captain of School, September–December 1884; commissioned in East Lancashire Regiment, 1885; died of fever at Ferozepore, 1888.
7. See 24 April 1883.
8. Lieutenant-Colonel Herbert Edward Boileau, Indian Army (1861–?), at USC 1878–9; commissioned 1881; retired 1909.

9. Colonel Charles Henry Davies (1867–1927?), at USC 1877–80; Indian Army 1885; retired 1920.
10. John Henry Murray: see 24 April 1883.
11. Major Mackenzie Walcott Baugh, Indian Army (1862–1931), at USC 1878–81; commissioned 1883, Lancashire Fusiliers; retired 1907.
12. Extra allowance for field service.
13. Colonel Hutchinson died of wounds after a skirmish with the Bonerwals on the Peshawar frontier, 8 January: the Bonerwals escaped an expedition.
14. This must be the episode that RK mentions in *Something of Myself*, p. 44, when he was shot at in the Khyber Pass; note that here he speaks of a knife, not a gun. The occasion was the Durbar of March 1885: see 30 July–1 August 1885.
15. King Theebaw of Upper Burma had been defeated in two weeks' fighting in late 1885; on 1 January 1886 Upper Burma was added to the Empire.
16. Lieutenant Robert Dury, Indian Army (1863–85), at USC 1878–81; commissioned 1883; killed in Burma, 17 November 1885.
17. Cf. "Arithmetic on the Frontier", published in *Departmental Ditties* this year:

> A scrimmage in a Border Station–
> A canter down some dark defile –
> Two thousand pounds of education
> Drops to a ten-rupee *jezail* –

To W. C. Crofts, 18–27 February 1886
ALS: Dalhousie University

Lahore: / Feb. 18th / 86.

Dear Mr. Crofts,

So it *was* you who sent me the Feristah!¹ We held a family council over it and solemnly decided that it must have been one of my many aunts and her I thanked effusively. She denied all knowledge of the gift which puzzled us a good deal and we gave up the search as hopeless. However I'm rejoiced to find that it was you, and if I had only thought or, better still if you had only written a letter just to keep touch with me I might have *known* to whom I was indebted for a present of that kind. But *why* didn't you put your name to the book?

And now to thank you for your letter – a most unexpected pleasure. I saw the address and – goodness knows I was far enough away from such things at the time – thought in a hazy sort of way about a "notice in the corridor" – so you see I remembered the "sweet Roman hand." Then I opened and hunted for the signature and lo! it was a signature that I had shuddered at any time between '78 and 82. I was glad enough to see it and only wished that I had had Dunsterville with me at the time. That youth turned up from Suakim on his way to Rawil Pindie and his regiment about four days ago and stayed with me eight and forty hours. He is absolutely unaltered – 'hasn't even begun to think of a moustache – 'stumbled out of the train with the cheerful announcement that he had only the clothes he stood up in, having lost his luggage somewhere within the limits of the Indian Empire, annexed a pair of my trowsers, captured all my cigars, derided the notion of my being anything else but "Old Giger", and went to bed with the old announcement: – "Look here Giger if you snore I'll throw a boot at you." I made much of him and we talked College till we were tired and double tired. It seems that after I left he used to do private "tu" in Latin with you and so came to know and swear by you – a thing which amused me a good deal as our Study used to spend a good deal of prep devising atrocious tortures for our Latin Master.

However, I confess that I was too deeply indebted to you for the run of your library – I'd give something for the privilege now in this land where books are so dear – to hate you with more than a strictly limited and Latin hate. Well, we talked and talked of the fellows and the masters, and, in the course of the long conversation, Dunsterville pointed out a little fact to me which has made me rabidly furious against M.H.P.[2] You will not recollect that he once changed my dormitory – just before I left – and insisted upon the change with an unreasoning vehemence that astonished me. Thereafter followed a row I think. I objected to be transferred because my little room was a snug one, had no prefect, and allowed me room to spread my books and kit. I took to reporting my dormitory – the new one – making life a burden to M.H.P. and, finally, in one big row, falling upon the members of the new dormitory with a small pen knife at least three quarters of an inch long in the blade. About this time M.H.P. – who must be a very Stead[3] in his moral and virtuous knowledge of impurity and bestiality – transferred me to my old room; clearing out the other two boys who occupied it. It never struck me that the step was anything beyond an averagely lunatic one on the part of M.H.P. – I was not innocent, in some respects, as the fish girls of Appledore could have testified had they chosen – but I certainly didn't suspect anything. Dunsterville told me on Wednesday, in the plain ungarnished tongue of youth, the why and the wherefore of my removal according to M.H.P. and by the light of later knowledge I see very clearly what that moral but absolutely tactless Malthusian must have suspected. It's childish and ludicrous I know but, at the present moment, I am conscious of a deep and personal hatred against the man which I would give a good deal to satisfy. This to your private ear only. Shake the slumbering reminiscences of my past misconduct which are sure to linger in the hirsute bosom of that over zealous guardian of youthful morality and see if I am right. If so, tell him with my compliments that it will be a source of lasting regret to me that I did not set to work in earnest to make myself ten times a hotter handful than I was. I knew he thought me a liar but I did not know that he suspected me of being anything much worse. However I have my consolation. He shall be put into my novel – that novel which is always growing and is never finished; and to finish the revenge I'll marry him to a woman who shall give him something else to think about! But 'tis an unsavoury subject and a *most* unsavoury man. Let us drop him off the pen point and burn incense to cleanse the room.

The fall of the Kingsley College was a question of time only.[4] You can't run an educational establishment on a pair of bathing drawers, a bugle and a big drum – even though Wall[5] pound the latter and buttress his speculation with tinned salmon. 'Lacks the elements of permanence you know like our financial policy. I chuckled a good deal over the downfall and was almost inspired to write a poem – but I hadn't the time.

You ask have I seen any O.U.S.C.'s. The land's alive with 'em. F. Young at Ferozpur, Viper Berry[6] at Nusserabad (I stumbled on him in a tent when I was down Rajputana way doing special correspondent), Berry *ma* at Peshawar, Campbell H.V. somewhere in that direction making love to every girl he meets and taking more liquor than is good for him; N.E. Young just gone south after a year in Lahore fort; Stratton a political assistant in Rajputana – a handsome boy fully aware of the fact – Stockwell[7] adjutant of a highland regiment, very curly about the head and desperately angry if he is called "Dolly." R.E. Grimston a shining light of Simla society last year; J. Murray working like a good one on the Railway coming in to see me every now and then with a six inch moustache; Boileau in Lahore till lately but being poisoned by oysters compelled to take a sea voyage; Cunliffe,[8] a trooper in the 9th Lancers now gone home but not before he paid me a visit; Maxwell[9] at Allahabad; Armstrong[10] somewhere south; Cheyne[11] in the Cheshire – a big pink boy with no end of side and many many others. I only mention a few I've seen or know of. Ranken[12] and Mammoth Green[13] both came within my range a little while since. Dunsterville has met dozens of others – but he says they don't change and I find that he is about right.

For myself I am getting unpleasantly bald and feel an old old man – The work of an Indian paper isn't exactly play you know but it's work I love, and above all it pays. *Me voici* in receipt of the stupendous income of £500 per annum, and fairly well known in Upper India as a scribbler. *Quartette* has been splendidly reviewed but I snorted a little when one writer compared my three stories to Wilkie Collins – slightly to the disadvantage of W.C. There *are* limits even to laudatory reviews. But of these things "more anon" to quote the prurient minded Pugh. Shades of Zola, Sodom and Onan! What a hideously corrupt moral interior that wretched man has painfully built up for himself. And yet he too must have been a babe ere he was a housemaster. Pity it is that he was not smothered in the caudle. If you believed in the doctrine of transmigration of souls I could furnish you with M.H.P.'s pedigree for the last two thousand years. However this has nothing to do with anything wholesome.

Writing of morals though reminds me of Boucher[14] and the way your nose curled in afternoon church at some specially awful inanity when the conduct of the row did not justify your sleeping. Allah be praised I do not have to attend church – and therefore I go. Which is a perfectly plain paradox. But you must hear the whole story and pity me – She had the face of an angel, the voice of a dove and the step of the fawn. I worshipped her blindly till I found she was the Cantonment Chaplain's daughter. My love was proof against this also and I said; – "I will go and listen to her Papa on Sundays." I went once and covered myself with glory by producing a card case instead of a prayer book and dropping a whist voucher into the collection bag. He preached. I went a second time for I saw that She was lovely and I hoped peradventure that her Papa might have been drunk. But he preached a second time and I drove home – it was a five mile drive and bitter cold – and laid the mangled heads of Her Papa's sermon before my Papa. And he said: – "My Son – there must be hereditary insanity in that family. Avoid it." And I avode for I was of the same opinion as my Papa. That was a month ago and it was the only time I went to church for four years.

A hasty hunt through my shelves shows me that I haven't anything on hand that would be worth sending for your inspection – unless indeed it's my Rupaiyat of Omar Kal'vin[15] – a parody on that magnificent – but absolutely untruthful – version of Fitzgerald's. Curious fact sir that the whole of the Rubaiyat in the original Persian hasn't anything in it like the Rubaiyat one knows in the English. There's the "eat drink and be merry for tomorrow we die" tone running through it of course – but that's all. I've been through the book with a persian scholar – a native who writes persian verses – and gave it up in despair as a fraud. However to return to the Rupaiyat it was a skit on our present financial policy and procured me the great satisfaction of a delightful note from Sir A. Colvin our finance minister complimenting me like anything and saying "that it was a joy to find that the days of wit and delicate humour are not yet dead in the land." As the whole poem was levelled at him it's very nice of him. I wonder how long I should have had to wait at home before the Chancellor of the Exchequer congratulated me on an attack on his financial policy — a year or two. Imagine the awful cynicism of a man who writes an attack on his own measures. This is what Colvin has done; capping my Rupaiyat by a parody of Solomon's proverbs.[16] I rushed a Victor Hugo skit into a Calcutta paper in revenge and I send 'em to you.[17] They aren't very intelligible unless you know the country and the indecent haste with which the Income Tax was passed but they serve to show what takes in this country.

Also I enclose a leaderette on my pet subject – infant marriage and enforced widowhood.[18] I'm a hog on both these things – and drains. Drains are a great and glorious thing and I study 'em and write about 'em when I can. My experience of "widdies" is extensive and peculiar. The virgin widow takes to prostitution in seventy five cases out of a hundred – 'cos she can't remarry. I suppose that the weakness for drains is a survival of the "worm-twap" instinct the late H.J.C.[19] used to condemn in me with such fervour. I loves 'em and so far they haven't bowled me over.

Further I have to report that I am under contract to write a Comic Operetta on an Anglo Indian subject for Simla this season.[20] I've got it all out in the rough and it only needs pulling together – a longer business than one expects. It's very very Anglo Indian and I don't think it would be intelligible at home. However my fellow worker – the man who is setting the music – says it's pretty certain to take here. Anything amuses a land of people who are always at work.

I see by this week's P[all].M[all]. Gazette that the worthy William Morris has been giving his opinion on the Hundred best books. Lord! Lord! what a lying world it is. He has gravely stuck down the Mahabarât and I will wager everything I have that he hasn't the ghost of a conception what he means when he advises the study of that monstrous midden. Imprimis it's a colossal undertaking even in the English *and* the only translation which would be intelligible to the ordinary English reader has just begun and is coming out in monthly parts – semi occasional parts I should say – here.[21] Well, I have patiently perused all the Mahab. I could lay my hands on and I assure you that a more hopeless, aimless, diffuse drivel (tempered with puerile obscenity) it would be hard to come across. Yet Morris gravely puts it down – and the Shah-nameh[22] as well. I wonder that he didn't stick in the Ramayana of Tulsi Dass and the Rig Veda to crown the lie. I see every now and then at home some man who hasn't touched 'em lifting up his voice in praise of "the golden mines of Oriental Literature" and I snort. There are one or two things worth the reading but to get at them one has to wade through a muck heap, and the vast bulk of the stuff that is as a matter of duty belauded and extolled to the skies is so much waste of paper and ink. Get hold of a translation of the Rig Veda Sir and by the time you've ploughed through a few thousand verses reiterating one monotonous whine for horses, cattle, corn and strong drinks you will heave the book out of window and go a hunting for the blood of Monier Williams.[23] But I suppose we must accept the dictum of William the poet and it would be flat blasphemy to hint that one decent primer on Sanitary Engineering and sewage disposal is worth more than all the tomes of sacred smut ever produced. Young India – in the shape of the educated Bengali – has a clear notion that a study of English and surveying pays better than anything else and when he is exhorted to "study the classics of his glorious land" he smiles. He knows all the dirty yarns in 'em from his youth up, for they make the staple of the songs of the people and the lullabies of the mothers. What more does he want? Imagine ten folio pages filled with stuff like this: – "I adore the toe-nails of the sacred guru whose breath is like the breath of the kine of India. I prostrate myself making the seven abasements and the four lesser genuflexions before the dust of his feet which are like unto the young lotus. Oh Indra! give us sons – fair men. I worship Indra with the prescribed ceremonies and the navel of the illustrious Guru!" Am I exaggerating? Don't condemn me till you've tried to swallow some of the big fraud yourself Sir.

By all means send me all the photoes of the college you can spare. I only wish you could see the photoes of my walking tour a year ago in the Himalayas.[24] The last one was taken 16,000 feet above sea and the mountains in front took three full plates to reproduce – one above the other you know. It was a bungling bit of work but gives you some notion of the eternal snows. I met three bears in the course of the outing and fled like Elisha's scoffers – was it Elijah or Elisha[25] – I'm shaky in scripture history. Anyhow I ran merrily for about half a mile and was mortified to find that the brutes never even stopped feeding (they grub about like huge swine on the mountain sides) or shown the least inclination to come after me. Yesterday – (this is 27 Feb) I was wandering through the public gardens here and came across Molesworth[26] – (mi) – a full blown subaltern in a regiment. He seemed altogether unchanged. 'Hadn't even grown broader across the shoulders, and his voice was as uncertainly squeaky as of old. I *do* wish one or two OUSC's would grow up just to show one that the thing is possible.

Kay Robinson[27] – one of the *Pioneer* press men and brother of Phil the Indian garden man[28] – has been staying with me for a few days. He had a name of sorts by reason of an article in the 19th Century on "the Man of the future."[29] Do you recollect it Sir? We had a lively four days together and I made discovery that neatly as he writes he is a still neater shot with a chunk of brick where crows are concerned. You may see therefore how intellectual and refined were our amusements. Ever since a memorable night when I saw an Under-Secretary to the Supreme Government in the Home Department "toboganning" down the staircase of the Simla Club on a table top I have ceased to believe in the dignity of man and hold him nothing better than an average school boy.

This is a long letter written out of gratitude for your note and in the hope that it may drive you to write another. Also you shall flap these sheets under the nose of my beloved Padre, Will[e]s, and shall point out to him that they are the reward of virtue – (There's not the least necessity to give him your private opinion on the rambling scrawl.) Possibly he may be smitten with envy and send me a line or two but matrimony is a sad destroyer of correspondence. (What did the grave digger say about the corpses?)[30] Remember me to all the Common Room who have not forgotten me and I pray you tell the Man of Morals – whom I shall assuredly put into my novel – that while there is breath in this poor body I shall *never* forget him. Lastly believe me

Yours always very sincerely
Rudyard Kipling

Notes
1. Browning, *Ferishtah's Fancies* (1884).
2. Matthew Henry Pugh (1852–1914), taught mathematics at USC, 1876–93, and was RK's housemaster. He is caricatured as Prout in *Stalky*; the story of "The Impressionists" in which Prout's suspiciousness is played upon evidently owes something to the episode described in this letter.
3. William Thomas Stead (1849–1912), editor of the *Pall Mall Gazette* and founder of the "new journalism".
4. The Kingsley College (see 28 January 1882) closed in December 1885.
5. The Revd F. Hewson Wall, headmaster of Kingsley College.
6. This name seems to be Berry in the MS, but no one of that name is listed in the USC Register. There were four Berney brothers at the College; of these, only Captain Thomas Hugh Berney (1866–1900) seems to fit the terms of this letter.
7. Colonel George Clifton Inglis Stockwell (1863–1936), at USC 1876–9; commissioned 1882; retired 1916; promoted honorary Major-General, 1919.
8. Brigadier-General Frederick Hugh Gordon Cunliffe (1861–1955), at USC 1876–9. RK mentions this visit in *Something of Myself*, pp. 66–7.
9. Lieutenant-Colonel William Lockhart Maxwell (1862–1914), Indian Army; at USC 1876–80.
10. Major Richard Armstrong (1862–99), at USC 1875–9; commissioned 1880.
11. Lieutenant Charles Cheyne (1863–?), Indian Army; at USC 1877–8; retired 1893.
12. Brevet Colonel George Patrick Ranken (1859–1924), Indian Army; at USC 1875–7; commissioned 1879; retired 1911.
13. Either Ernest Frederick Green (1861–?), USC 1875–7, Indian Police, Bombay Presidency, 1885–1916; or Charles Douglas Green (1869–1928), USC 1880–6; he does not appear to have served in India at this time.
14. The Revd Charles Estcourt Boucher was curate of Northam, Bideford, 1879–85. The USC boys regularly attended services at Northam.
15. *CMG*, 30 January 1886, an attack on the financial policies of Sir Auckland Colvin (*Departmental Ditties*).
16. "Proverbs of Sillyman" by Ibn Evil'un, *Pioneer*, 5 February. The *Pioneer* printed this as a "pendant" to RK's "Rupaiyat", reprinted from the *CMG*. The "Proverbs" have in consequence been mistakenly attributed to RK.
17. "The History of a Crime (after V-CT-R H-GO)", *The Englishman*, 3 February 1886 (uncollected). In the standard bibliography of RK this item is wrongly stated to have appeared in the *Pioneer*, 5 February 1886 (Stewart, *Bibliographical Catalogue*, ed. Yeats, p. 538).
18. An untitled note in *CMG*, 13 February 1886.
19. Thus in MS, but perhaps for E.J.C., i.e., Edward James Campbell, chaplain at USC and RK's first housemaster. RK detested him.
20. I have found no trace of this except for a remark in a letter of JLK that a Mrs Le Mesurier at Simla is getting RK to "write either a new libretto or to alter the old

Contrabandista – which she is getting up" (to Edith Plowden, 27 July 1886: MS, Sussex).
21. Pratap Chandra Roy, *The Mahabharata* (16 vols, Calcutta, 1883–96).
22. Epic poem by the Persian poet Firdausi.
23. (Sir) Monier Monier-Williams (1819–99), Professor of Sanskrit at Oxford.
24. In May 1885: see Carrington, *Kipling*, pp. 60–1, and *Something of Myself*, pp. 58–60.
25. II Kings 2:24. It was Elisha.
26. Lieutenant George Nassau Molesworth (1865–86), at USC, 1875–83; he died at Cherat, Punjab, in July of this year.
27. Edward Kay Robinson (1857–1928), born in India, where his father was a journalist and at one time editor of the *Pioneer*; educated at Cheltenham; worked on the *Globe* before returning to India and the *Pioneer*; edited the *CMG*, 1887–95. He then returned to England and made a living as a writer on nature subjects and editor of *The Country-Side*. His first meeting with RK was on this visit to Lahore, though they had corresponded previously.
28. Philip Stewart Robinson (1847–1902): *In My Indian Garden* (1878).
29. *The Nineteenth Century*, LXXI (May 1883) 759–64.
30. *Hamlet*, v.i.186–90.

To Andrew Macdonald,[1] [February? 1886]
ALS: Ray Collection, Morgan Library

"Civil and Military Gazette," / Lahore. / Editor's Office.

Dear Macdonald:

My congratulations on your home trip first and my regrets for not acknowledging Englishman "quotes" after. In that respect I am to blame for I see that I calmly lifted your Harbans Sahai note[2] without acknowledgment. 'Twas my only fault tho' for as a rule I'm extremely punctilious in acknowledging – more so than that bahaduring[3] official pimp the *Pioneer* who seems to think that the honour of its acceptance ought to be enough for any one *without* acknowledgment. However it shall not occur again and I apologize.

You were perfectly right about the Hugo Skit[4] – "whitey brown" is a dangerous epithet anywhere within the limits of the Indian Empire. I was rather relieved to see you hadn't gelt it a little more.

Sorry to say that I haven't any rhyming fireworks in stock just now; all my attention being concentrated on my Departmental Ditties and front page scraps. However I'll do all I can to accommodate you in a few days. When do you go – Let me know the date or perchance I might be firing a carnal chit to your address and it might be read by one who knew not Joseph – which happens to be my name. I've got a craggy sort of Epic coming out in the Calcutta Review[5] an estimable and virtuous production which appears to be able to digest my blank verse. Heaven forfend that I should speak ill of it. Our weather is simply bestial –

Heavy wet, and wind. Kay Robinson of the *Pi* trickled down here for a few days. He is a nice youth and a merry – a little like his brother of unsavoury memory. Send me a line ere you depart and believe me

Yours always
Rudyard K.

Notes
1. The editor of *The Englishman*: see 17 September 1884.
2. Not identified.
3. *Bahadur* means "great man": "bahaduring" suggests pomposity or self-importance.
4. "The History of a Crime" (see 18–27 February 1886). It does not include the phrase "whitey brown".
5. "The Seven Nights of Creation", *Calcutta Review*, LXXXII (April 1886) 464–7 (uncollected); the *Review* had earlier published RK's blank verse "Vision of Hamid Ali" (see 30 July 1885). In the *CMG* of 10 April 1886 RK published a notice of the April *Calcutta Review*, including this remark on his own poem: "The poet's corner is occupied by Mr. Rudyard Kipling, in whose hands the Talmudic theory of the origin of all evil things is presented in an Indian shape, as supposed to have been told by 'Yussuf, the potter, in the cool shadow of the Bhatti Gate.'" Thirty-six of the 144 lines of "The Seven Nights of Creation" appear in *Schoolboy Lyrics* and in *Early Verse*; another twenty-five appear in JLK's *Beast and Man in India*, but the whole is to be found only in the *Calcutta Review*.

To E. K. Robinson, 30 April 1886
ALS: University of Sussex

Lahore. / April 30th. 86

Dear Kay,

You ought to know better at your time o' life than to knock a youngster off his legs in this way. How do you expect anyone will be able to hold me after your letter.[1] (Small honour has a Prophet in his own land. My sister found one phrase in your letter which she whittled sharp and stuck into me. I am now hailed as a "tender cynic" and the ferules of parasols are jabbed into my ribs to test the tenderness. Barring this one consequence it was a delightful letter and I thank you many times for it.)

About that notion, which is abroad, that scraps delight me not nor routine work either.[2] Allen said the same thing and then I sat tight, he being a full mouthed man and one [of my] owners to boot. Now I'll speak distinctly as the drunkard said. The whole settlement and routine of the old rag from the end of the leader to the beginning of the advertisements is in my hands and mine only; my respected chief contributing a blue pencil mark now and then and a healthy snarl just to soothe me. The telegrams also and such scraps as I or my father may write are my share likewise; and these things call me to office half one golden hour before, and let me out, always three quarters, sometimes a whole hour behind, my chief. My Sabbath is enlivened by the official visits of the printer and my evenings after dinner are made merry by his demands. So much for the routine to which I am averse. Of the scraps it is no profit to speak. They are pasted into a book with the days marked over them and are ready to be shown up the next time I have the "aversion" brought officially to my notice.[3]

On my word I fancy Allen must think I write my "skits" in office hours. This is not so. You may bet your journalistic boots that if my worthy chief found any portion of the work which he did not conceive to be his share falling on his shoulders I should hear about it pretty sharply. The rhymed rubbish and the stuff like "Section 420. I.P.C."[4] is written out of office for my own personal amusement – (I don't play tennis or whist or ride and my driving is no pleasure to me) – and then – O my friend – is damned as waste of time and only put in with a running lecture on the sinfulness of writing such stuff. Roughly speaking an extra half column of scraps is necessary to prevent a talking to and ensure the reception of a "special." Under these conditions is my "play" writing printed. When it is rejected – as happened in the case of my "Other Side of the Question"[5] I send it to the *Englishman* and get Rs 30. Otherwise of course I am not allowed to write for other papers.

I can't put what you call my "higher flights" aside any more than $\begin{cases} I \\ you \end{cases}$ can put aside the occasional woman which is good for health and the softening of ferocious manners. It's my amusement and like all amusements the nicer for being discouraged. If you find the "notion" floating about any where where you can combat it tell 'em like a good fellow that if I *was* averse to routine and scraps they'd know it in an unmistakeable way – from Wheeler, who would point out that he was "doing all my work," or else (his trump card) "that I was making things hard for him." He lives in nervous dread of these things. I chuckle, because I am unregenerate. He's a good man is my chief but he'll never burst a blood vessel through hauling.

Would you be astonished if I told you that I look forward to nothing but an Indian journalist's career? Why should I? My home's out here; my people are out here; all the friends etc. I know are out here and all the interests I have are out here. Why should I go home. Any fool can put up rhymes and the market is full of boys who could undersell me as soon as I put foot in it. Recollect that at present I serve in my own stud for Rs 400 a month. Where would a colt get Rs 400 for his services on a home farm? Besides I was bought out of the stockyard on trust. Bitted, mouthed and broken to saddle polo and harness on spec. Very well. I shall begin to pay for my breaking in a few years. Then it will take some time to refund that expenditure. Then there is my personal and purely unprofessional gratitude to the gang who selected me, which gives the gang a further right to my services – for as long a time in fact as they may choose to retain them. London journalism – you have some years of it behind you – is a great and grand thing but it seems to me, I speak in ignorance; that out here one lives and writes more in the centre of history with one's hands on everything than in a land where by reason of its hugeness every one is on the outskirts of everything; watching ministers, policies and financiers from afar. What do *you* think?

However if I live I'm young enough to change my opinions many times over; but I shall have to go through a rough time of it if I prefer a life that I don't know to the broad margins, uncut edges and pleasant type of my daily existence in this land.

For another thing I am deeply interested in the queer ways and works of the people of the land. I hunt and rummage among 'em; knowing Lahore City – that wonderful, dirty, mysterious ant hill – blind fold and wandering through it like Haroun Al-Raschid in search of strange things. "Section 420. I.P.C." (originally called "in the House of Suddhoo") is the outcome of some of these researches but the bulk of my notes and references goes to enrich a bruised tin tea box where lies – 350 f.cp. pages thick – my "Mother Maturin." The novel that is always being written and yet gets no furrarder.

You – I know – don't care for this sort of thing and I daresay you wonder what's the good of "perugin'" among bunnias[6] and prostitutes (the aliteration would be coarse). Naturally. You made your mark at home and you want to go and chalk it over again. I'm in love with the country and would sooner write about her than anything else. Wherefore let us depart our several ways in amity? You to Fleet Street (where I shall come when I die if I'm good) and I to my own place where I find heat and smells of oil and spices, and puffs of temple incense, and sweat, and darkness, and dirt and lust and cruelty, and, above all, things wonderful and fascinating innumerable. Give me time Kay – Give me seven years and three added to them and abide the publishment of *"Mother Maturin."* Then you shall sit down in your gas lit, hotwater pipe warmed office, at midnight, and shall indite a review saying that the book ought never to have been written. And perhaps I shall agree with you then.

After this peroration let us take a cheroot and think. What else was there to answer? Something about the "friendly hand." *Bahut accha.*[7] This much will I do. I will write a poem – next Sunday – if I can, and you shall read him, and if he's any good you shall send him to the Philistines even as Pendennis's friend vended his children.[8] Do what you like with him and if there's any question of payment see that I get none. I may sell rejected matter for lucre but new stuff I won't. 'Tisnt in the bond. That's the great merit of that obese antediluvian (board-school spelling there) the *Calcutta Review*. She never pays. I'm hatching out the Story of Scindia's ride for her in rhyming verse.[9] He was chivied from Panipat to the Delhi ridge (forty miles) after Ahmed Shah Duraini "eat up" his men and he didn't like it. He mentions the fact in elegant verse as he jabs his sobbing beast over the sand and the *ber* bushes, which is very likely and realistic, and calculated to do much good.

That reminds me. Apropos of vain tales. D'you know how the Devil got into the Ark? It's a talmudic legend but on mine honour it came Irish some how as I tried to work it out: –

'Twas whan the rain fell stiddy
An' the Arrk was pitched an' ready
That Noah got his orders for to take the stock below;
He grabbed em all together
By the horn an' hide an' feather
An' all except the donkey was agreeable to go.

Thin Noah shpoke him fairly
Thin talked to him sevarely
An' thin he cursed him squarely – to the Glory av the Lorrd.
"Devil take the ass that bred you!
An' the silly fool that fed you!
Devil go wid ye ye spalpeen!" – An' the Donkey wint aboard.

But t'was most onaisy sailin'
Or the wind was always failin'
An' the ladies in the cabin cudn't stand the stable air.
An' the bastes betwixt the hatches
They tuk an' died in batches
An' Noah sid: – "There's wan av us that hasn't paid his fare!"

He heard a flusteration
Mid the bastes an' all Creation,
The bellowin' av elephants an' trumpetin' av whales
An' he saw forninst the windy
Whan he wint to stop the shindy
The Devil with his pitchfork was bedevilling their tails.

Now Noah knew him slightly
So axed av him politely
For what was he indebted to this pleasint visitation.
And the Devil gav' for answer: –

"Evict me af ye can sir!
"For I cam in wid the Donkey *on yer Honour's invitation.*"[10]

With this abomination which has been appropriated by my Pa for an article he has written,[11] I'll end.

Yours always
Rudyard Kipling

P.S. This isn't my fault. One W.R. Lawrence,[12] a bald headed diplomat from Rajputana, now on duty down here, recently married, aged 29 years and a delightful fellow told me at the club last night he knew you. He seems to have been connected with the darker episodes of your life – 'was present when you were arrested for stealing apples at Cheltenham. Sat on the same bench (whether felon's or schoolboy's I know not) and desires to be much remembered: Let the board of Rescripts take notice. I'm off to Jummoo on Saturday night to sing the Saga of Kashmir's installation.[13] If Chesney[14] wants a telegram from thence he might let me know by wire and I'll send.

R.K.[15]

P.P.S. I was averse to routine was I? It rankles in my stomick. On Saturday afternoon I gloriously fainted in office ere the work was well begun and did no more that day. Observe the old rag for that date. Maybe the sad deterioration is visible to no eye save mine. I maintain it exists none the less.

K

Notes

1. Robinson "urged [RK] to go to England, where he would win real fame, and possibly wealth" (Robinson, "Kipling In India", *McClure's Magazine*, July 1896, p. 100).
2. Robinson was just about to take over, temporarily, the editorship of the *CMG* from Wheeler and had been told that RK was bad at newspaper routine (see also 4–5 December 1886). This notion persisted long after RK had left India and appears in a number of statements about his Indian career.
3. These scrapbooks are now at Sussex.
4. The title under which "In the House of Suddhoo" was published in the *CMG*, 30 April. "I.P.C." = Indian Penal Code.
5. This has not yet been traced.
6. Merchants or moneylenders.
7. Very good.
8. Perhaps ch. 41 of Thackeray's *Pendennis*: "This youth will fetch some price on the market; for he is a comely lad, though not over strong; but we will fatten him up, and give him the bath, and curl his hair, and we will sell him for a hundred piastres to Bacon or to Bungay."
9. "With Scindia to Delhi"; it did not appear in the *Calcutta Review* but was first published in *Barrack-Room Ballads* (1892).
10. Published, somewhat revised, as Part II of "The Legend of Evil", *Barrack-Room Ballads*.
11. The verses first appeared at the head of ch. 4 of JLK's *Beast and Man in India*.

12. (Sir) Walter Roper Lawrence, 1st Baronet (1857–1940), educated at Cheltenham and Balliol; entered Indian Civil Service, 1877, and was now, after political service in Rajputana, Under-Secretary to the Punjab Government. He afterwards held various high positions in India, including membership of the Council. RK helped Lawrence to write his memoirs, *The India We Served* (1928).
13. RK reported the installation of the Maharajah in two articles to the *CMG*, 13 and 14 May (uncollected).
14. George Maclagan Chesney (1858–1926), joined the *Pioneer* in 1880 and edited it, with intervals, 1888–1915; from 1915 to 1926 he represented the *Pioneer* and *CMG* in London.
15. Beneath his signature RK has drawn a tiny pair of spectacles that he sometimes used as his sign.

To Margaret Burne-Jones, 3 May–24 June 1886
ALS: University of Sussex

Lahore. / May. 3rd. 6. P.M. Grey twilight / 1886

Dear Wop,

It's very sickening and if I weren't ashamed of myself as it is I'd throw up my head and howl. The Mother and the Maid have just left the house for Simla – gone till the 15th of October and Trix covered herself with glory by weeping. Pater's gone with 'em to the Station. I've got office work coming on in half an hour so I can't go – can't do anything but sit down in the half emptied house with the punkah creaking and the thermantidote throbbing and pour out my woes to you. Yah! how I loathe and abominate the hot weather and the necessity of sending away one's women folk for six months of the twelve. Here's the Pater and me thrown back on bachelor life again; dining at Clubs, knocking about alone with never a lady at the head of the table or Trix to make fun of us, or anything decent at all. You don't know – for which thank your God – the sinking when the heat shuts in and the women folk go off. I like it less each year. 1883 was moderate; 1884 was not nice, for Trix and the Mother were at Dalhousie; '85 was all right because I was only adrift for two months and three weeks.¹ This year is horrid – I shall be all right in a day or so when I've returned to the desolate freedom of the wild ass and linked on to the hot weather group of men who talk of nothing but their work and go to sleep directly after dinner. But oh Lord! Lord! how bad I feel now.

That's a manly way of shutting up under discomfort. It was Trixie's fault. She sat down and yowled and the Mother was nearly as bad. Pater didn't mind. He joins 'em in six weeks, I hope and pray for his sake. The vials of the family pity were turned on me because I shouldn't get off for three months at the lowest estimate and if I *did* get away

To Margaret Burne-Jones, 3 May–24 June 1886

before it would be on sick leave.[2] 'No pleasing them *any* way! I shall do all I know to take my holiday in August, if I live so long, and try to screw a ten day's run out of my chief by getting some man to do my work.

Wednesday 5th. Feeling decidedly better. Can acknowledge with many thanks O Wop your glorious epistle which was ravished from me by Trix. I mayn't touch a line from you to her but if I keep back one single pen wiggle from you to me it's murder. I wish you didn't write to me just at dinner time. I have to read it out aloud to the Family while they eat and my vittles get cold. It's awfully sad and makes me thin. Couldn't you catch me in office or between meals somehow. I should like it better. All the same I'm grateful. As the Pater said when I turned the soup-plate upside down and spread your royal script in layers atop; – "There's some use in having a letter writer like that girl."

June: 1. A nice long interval of close upon a month but I couldn't very well help it. I was bundled off to Kashmir to report the installation of the Maharajah[3] and found all my work in arrears when I got back. Then I fell foul of the Lahore Municipality for the filthy state of Lahore City and every moment I could spare from routine work was devoted to abusing them and pointing out a few trifling foolish defects in their drains and sanitary arrangements.[4] Whereupon they – the City Fathers – turned the weekly native paper the *Tribune* on me and that excellent organ devoted three columns to abuse of me and the "private malice and petty spite" which actuated me.[5] As I don't know any of the Municipal members except the English Secretary[6] – who is a sworn ally of mine – I don't quite see where the malice comes in. I've managed however to get a few neglected evils looked into and startled the old President – Nawab Nawazish Ali Khan – almost into energy. By the same token my wanderings into the lesser known lanes and gullies of the city made me most amazing sick – and the sickness wasn't helped by my last three day's work. On Friday night at midnight the roof of our Lahore High School tumbled in and killed three poor boys asleep underneath. Saturday's paper doesn't come out till midnight and my chief for which I won't forgive him sent me off at 6 in the evening to turn up facts about the disaster. With my usual luck where thing's horrible are concerned I came in just before the funeral and to my horror in the next room to the wrecked one lay the three bodies waiting for the coffins. It was the most ghastly business I've ever had to deal with. In front a huge room with one third of the roof down and the beams and earth lying three and four feet deep on the floor; on the left a heap of smashed beds – no fragment a foot long, boots, boys' hats and clothing, and on the right a view into the next room of the three swathed figures on the cots, the sound of the midwives who had laid them out, whispering together, and the smell – the death smell of carbolic acid. I was tired with my work, thoroughly angry at having been told off for such charnel house work, and used up with the heat. Consequently I nearly broke down as I stood. However I got the additional facts and went to office where I unburdened my soul and was violently sick.[7] One of the boys was eighteen poor lad and I knew him. I haven't reached that philosophical pitch of taking horrors as they come and I had a fair notion of what would be in store for me that night. You know my peculiarity about eyes.[8] It recurs whenever my tummy's out of order or I'm overworked or unstrung and it came back in full force that night. If I'd been a convicted murderer I couldn't have been more persistently followed by those things on the beds. What with the heat and the worry and the eyes I spent as unpleasant a night as you'd hope for in another and worse world. However next morning the trouble went and I got my balance till next time which will be when I'm next out of sorts. Disease and deaths from disease I can stand because I've seen both often and it's in the working of life but an accident like this one is horrible – ghastly – unnatural – and I would, if I could, avoid it.

June. 4th. A sudden spell of chilly weather has overtaken us and the thermometer stands at 80° in the house while it is possible to sleep without punkahs. Seeing that our just measure of heat should be 110°–116° in the shade with a minimum at dawn on the grass of 84°–89° the cold is startling.

June. 10th. It didn't last long enough to kill us did that heat. The last three days have been ghastly hot – the regular business. Thick clouds [shutting?] down above, white glare from the earth below, and orange dust haze in the air and furious unreasoning heat over all. The Pater as I may have mentioned hasn't been well. At least he has had a bad cold and slight feverishness and oh how he is sorry for himself! It isn't seediness so much as the knowledge that he has no women folk to pet him – no one except an irreverent son whose temper is worn to fiddlestrings. Poor Pater! He's worried about his leave – the month's holiday he has applied for and is afraid he won't get. As I irreverently put it yesterday when my own bothers had made me half crazy he "went on like a child". Whereat there was dissension in the house of Kipling for fully twenty minutes. Then we smoked the cheroot of peace together and went off to dinner. Do you know what hemi crania means? A half head ache so – [drawing of head with line dividing it from top to bottom]. I've been having it for a few days and it is a lovely thing. One half of my head in a mathematical line from the top of my skull to the cleft of my jaw, throbs and hammers and sizzles and bangs and swears while the other half – calm and collected – takes note of the agonies next door. My disgusting doctor says it's overwork again and I'm equally certain that it rose from my suddenly and violently discarding tobacco for three days. Anyhow it hurts awfully – feels like petrifaction in sections and makes one write abject drivel.

Many thanks indeed, dear, for the trouble you took with me about Flo Garrard.[9] Was the advice you gave about Miss Winnard[10] intended to link on to the first case. I fancied it might be read that way possibly but I wasn't sure. Thank you all the same but I'm even a bigger idiot than you take me for. I got my *jawâb*,[11] (the natural and most lawful ending of a boy and girl attachment) two years ago. The only drawback to the excellence of the thing was that I couldn't disentangle as quickly as my little lady; and the consequence was that I was very unhappy and, being young, held that the bottom had tumbled out of the Great Universe. I don't quite believe that now but I'm as far from disentanglement as I was in the year of grace 1884 – July. (Only two years of course but they seemed long ones). One of these days if I live long enough I shall grow out of the whole affair and look back on it in much the same light as Flo, I conceive, looks on it today – wherever she is. But take my word for it Wop it hurts while it lasts and at no time more deeply than in the hot weather when you've done all the work you can, can't go out, can't read, can't do anything but sit in the big dark rooms and think. (For that reason Sunday is the worst day of the week. It's so full of unmanageable hours between 4. and 7. in the evening). May be I exaggerate, being full of my own little troubles, but I shouldn't care to have my worst enemy go through some of the evenings I've gone through. You see the folly has been kept and nursed too long and has grown accordingly. I get tiny little scraps of news about Flo from time to time (have got them rather) and one learns to be wondrous quick at securing news of that kind; and on that information do I think. Dignified and manly isn't it? But some men have the blessed gift of taking their *jawâb* standing up and with a light heart. I can't and at this moment if I fancied there were the faintest chance of getting my little woman back would throw up the whole of my career in India if she'd ask me to come home. Which would be prudent.

June 11th. I shall have to knock off letter writing until I've got some sleep again or I shall be writing lunacy. Couldn't rest last night because of my head; couldn't get any sleep the night before and by this time I'm nearly crazy.

Tonight, thank Heaven, I'm assured of rest for a few hours. My doctor says I've got to be hypodermically syringed – morphia or something of the kind.

June. 17th. I spoke rashly. What a lively time I've been going through! Something was wrong with the morphia and it didn't act so I didn't sleep. Then I had some more medicines to soothe me and they made me livelier and more wide awake than ever. That was Saturday night.

On Sunday I was for administrative purposes a lunatic as I had been on Saturday when I did my office work – Lord knows how. The *mean* temperature of Sunday was 100°–116° in the shade, 176° in the sun, and 83° on the grass. That made me worse. I spent the blessed Sabbath afternoon trying to make some coquettish leeches stick on my temples but they wouldn't and I begged the doctor if he loved me to give me enough morphia to put me to sleep for ever. He didn't. He gave me enough to drug me and one way and another I was bolstered up enough to face office on Monday with big Ben tolling in my head and no sensation in my hands or feet. Monday's mean temperature was 100° also. It was lovely; but I got better as the day went on, and got some sort of sleep at night. On Tuesday a lot of fresh *dawai*[12] was administered and I suppose one of the powders or portions [*sic*] must have touched the right spring for the ache departed almost at the same time as my Father left on his 33 days' holiday for Simla. He looked seedy and I had some trouble in preventing him from staying down to look after me. I slept right round the clock on Tuesday night from 9.30 to 9.30 and was so delighted at having my rest I forgot to bother about the heat which is seasonable – too seasonable. Three soldiers died in Cantonments last night of heat apoplexy and they've been having a funeral nearly every day for a fortnight. But Tommy *is* so careless. He drinks heavy beer, and sleeps at once after a full flesh meal and dies naturally. Did I tell you a rather grim story of what I saw the other night when I went round the guards in Fort Lahore[13] with the subaltern of the day. I'd been round often before but never on a night like this. It was pitchy black, choking hot with a blinding dust storm out. Fort Lahore is wickedly hot always as I've learnt to my cost before now. I went into the main guard at midnight (it marked 97° in the guardroom verandah) and I saw by the lamp light every man jack of the guard stripped as near as might be *sitting up*. They daren't lie down for the lives of 'em in heat like that. It meant apoplexy.

However none of my men – the gunners are the ones I know most of – have collapsed so far. Personally I'm in the lap of luxury. My bedroom even at midnight which I consider the hottest time of the twenty four hours never goes beyond 86° but that means six men are working night and day in relays to keep it cool. They are queer fellows my coolies. They talk to me in the evening and tell me about their crops and families. Half the year they cultivate and the other half they come into the cities and hire out as Punkah coolies. It's worth while petting the men who keep you cool. They have a child's weakness for sweets (serves 'em instead of flesh meat) and 3 1/2d gives them all oceans of sticky sweet cakes.

'Strikes me this letter is even more egoistical than the bulk of my correspondence but oh Wop if you were the centre of a large black empty house and eat alone and drove alone and talked alone and had no one to see you'd be as bad. I know exactly what is in store for me by nasty experiences and I find after nearly four years I have less heart to stand against the heat and less stomach for bacheldordom [sic] than ever I had. This year however I have a companion – the faithfullest of all she friends – my Vic. I misremember if I've told you about her. She is a very fine bred fox terrier, biddable as is no woman I have yet had the pleasure of meeting, with a ridiculous fondness for me and no one else. The way a dog voluntarily cuts itself off from its kind to associate with man amuses and touches me. Vic doesn't associate with her own race at all; being a dog of routine and cultured habits. In the morning she wakes me up by sitting on my chest and shares my chota hazri;[14] my breakfast and the inside of the day's post. Then to office on the child's seat of the victoria, specially her own, then sleep until I shut the box at five. Then home for her evening saucer of milk and a rat hunt round the garden. She kills anything that she can put her teeth into. Then out with me to the Hall[15] and then if I dine at the Club home by herself in the carriage on the back seat and then at ten out in the carriage again to fetch me back. The coachman told me the other day in fun as I thought that he pulled up opposite my side of the house and the little body hopped in. I find from the other servants that this is a fact and that Vic gravely drops off my bed, goes out into the verandah and gets in "just like a memsahib." Anyhow she comes somehow with the air of owning the blessed conveyance. To really appreciate a dog you should live alone with it and talk to it because there's no one else. Vic knows by the change of my tone whether it is expedient for her to throw herself into my lap and croon – she croons like a cat or a tea kettle – or whether a nap under my chair is the sounder policy. I've never had to raise my voice to her once in the three months I've owned her. Just now she is very seedy with the heat and puts her head on my shoulder like a tired child and cries. I prescribe rats for depression and they work marvellous. But to return to severer things.

The fame of Phil's Grosvenor picture has penetrated to the wild Northwest and the art critic of the *Pioneer* Mowbray Morris devotes many lines to it.[16] The Pater has written to congratulate Uncle Ned and I send you the cutting. M.M. hates your father, calls him the "Good Jones" for which I want to kick him so his praise of Phil is the more valuable. *Apropos* you would be amused to see how much the Indian journals contain about your Father. Blessed if our London sporting correspondent of all people of earth didn't fly off at score about his "Mermaid and Mariner."[17] The S.C. had been to see it and it had impressed him wonderfully. He was desperately in earnest but he mixed up all sorts of epithets in his desire to make clear how he had been thrilled.

Thanks for your criticism on my stuffs Wop. It's dead true about the slang – a vice of youth luckily which the Pater says I shall outgrow. I wonder what you'd think of the last little booklet I've published – to look as nearly as possible like an official envelope and called "Departmental Ditties and other Verses."[18] Half of it would be Greek to you and the other half you'd take a "scunner"[19] at. Yet I wrote it with a purpose and for a moral end arrived at in a rather odd way.

June. 24th. I wonder when on earth this letter is ever going to get itself finished. I've had another attack of head – not a very bad one luckily and this has compelled me to lay aside the letter for a little. Trix from Simla writes that she has had a long communication from you. That young woman appears to be enjoying herself much and I'm glad of it, for life for a girl out here is desperate dull. See now Wop I'll tell you a secret which, for obvious reasons, must not be told to Trixie. I haven't mentioned a word about it to the Parents because I didn't want to worry them and held myself perfectly competent to deal with the matter on my own hook. A youngster, he's only eight and twenty, a brother journalist from the Northwest wrote to me some weeks ago telling me all about his "feelings" in regard to Trixie and goodness knows what else and asking me if I thought the case hopeless. The audacity of some men beats me. He had only seen T. for four days and had certainly not impressed her in the least. Personally I liked the man – would even have gone so far as to back his bill for him (which is the highest proof of friendship you know) but that didn't prevent me from sitting down and sending him a brief and courteous epistle of an exceedingly unpleasant nature. Unofficially of course I was sorry for him because I knew how he'd feel but, officially and as a Brother, I was at some pains to thoroughly sit upon and end him. You can't realize how savage one feels at a thing of this kind – an attempt to smash the Family Square and the child barely eighteen too! If after my lucid reasoning he chooses to write to the Parents and get *their* verdict he has only himself to thank for what follows. I shall declare war against him to the knife and Trix will laugh at him. A horrid nuisance it is being a Brother. I shall be afraid to ask any man of my acquaintance to dinner if they go off their heads at such slight provocation. Thank Heaven I haven't half a dozen sisters. But it was audacity wasn't it Wop? And it deserved a stern reproof didn't it?

Now with this other page methinks I shall bring this letter to an end. For the next three months at any rate there will be nothing to record. The rains broke about a week ago and we had five inches in twenty four hours whereat the house leaked horrid. Today I am a raw red lump of prickly heat – the direct result of the damp moist air. With the rain has come sickness all down the Line and I fancy that we shall have a troublesome season of it. In all likelihood, unless I break down before,

I go to Simla in September that month being a pleasant one in the hills and a foul one in the plains. The People want me up in July for my holiday but it's no good leaving work as long as you can keep to it.[20]

This is a rambling futile profitless sort of letter but I pray you remember that I haven't more than half my wits about me and not one tithe of my rightful go and strength. Never come out to India Wop – even on a pleasure trip. It's a fine place to write about but bad to live in. Give my love to your Mother and remember me to Phil and Uncle Ned.

Yours languidly
The Wop of Asia.

Notes
1. By "adrift" RK presumably means apart from his family, rather than "left behind in Lahore". He was in Simla from about May until mid-August 1885, and thus alone in Lahore only from mid-August to mid-October.
2. In the event, RK left for Simla on 3 July and returned around 12 August. He had, he says, broken down from overwork and insomnia (4–5 December 1886).
3. "The Installation at Jummu": see 30 April 1886.
4. Topics in RK's "Week in Lahore" column, CMG, 5 and 17 May 1886. The Lahore Municipality was notable in India at this time as being composed entirely of native members.
5. I have not been able to find a file of the paper. It was a weekly devoted to "advocacy of the interests of the people of India" (India Directory, 1886).
6. His name was David Johnston.
7. The article did not appear until the Monday: "Fatal Accident in Lahore", CMG, 31 May 1886.
8. See 10–14 July 1884.
9. See 28 November 1885–11 January 1886.
10. One of the ladies of Warwick Gardens: see 28 January 1882.
11. Dismissal.
12. Medicine.
13. The Fort and Palace of Lahore, begun by Akbar; it was garrisoned by detachments from Mian Mir. "Fort Lahore, where Runjit Singh's wives lay, was a mausoleum of ghosts" (Something of Myself, p. 42).
14. Early (before breakfast) tea.
15. Either the Lawrence Hall or the Montgomery Hall, both in the Lawrence Gardens.
16. Philip Burne-Jones's first exhibited picture, of a subject taken from Henry James's "Madonna of the Future", is called "an uncommonly clever little work" and commended for not looking like a Burne-Jones painting (Pioneer, 8 June, p. 2c). Mowbray Morris (1848–1911), son of the manager of The Times, was dramatic critic for that paper to 1885, and editor of Macmillan's Magazine thereafter. His role as art critic for the Pioneer was carried out by mail.
17. I cannot find this in either the CMG or the Pioneer. The painting is The Depths of the Sea, in this year's Royal Academy exhibit. It was the only picture that Burne-Jones ever sent to the Royal Academy show.
18. It was just published but had already sold out; an advertisement in the CMG, 9 June, promises that it "will be republished shortly".
19. Disgust.
20. He went in early July: see n. 2, above.

To W. C. Crofts, 14 September 1886
ALS: Cornell University

Lahore. / Sept. 14. 86

Dear Mr. Crofts:

Have I to thank you for the review of *Echoes* in the last number of the Chronicle?[1] It is an extremely complimentary one and were the booklet on the market now I should promptly use [it]. By the way the second thing – Departmental Ditties – which I sent to the common room has got into its second edition – 750 copies – revised, enlarged and in real book form and from what my publisher in Calcutta tells me I fancy I shall touch a third before the year is out. The Indian public like reading about what they know and do themselves. Herein I suppose they resemble publics all the world over.

I am sending you with this mail a bundle of stuff I've written lately to fill up back columns of the newspaper. The Mythology of "Ixion"[2] is a trifle mixed but one can't combine Olympus and the East without some sort of sacrifice. Perhaps Mr. Price would like to have a look at them.

If you *have* a spare moment Sir I should be much obliged if you could, first, send me a letter and secondly stir up Mr. Willes to some remembrance of me. He is married I know but I have seen "four and twenty leaders of revolts"[3] – I mean to say I have seen within the last thirty months eighteen men married, and do not understand why this should interrupt the course of correspondence. I am out of touch of the old school altogether and this last Chronicle contained no name I knew.

Yours always sincerely
Rudyard Kipling

Maxwell goes to Burmah with his regiment.
Molesworth G.N. has died of typhoid fever at Cherat near Peshawur. Cherat is a *sanitarium* where typhoid is nearly always present.
Ranken has been ordered off to Burmah to join the transport there.
"Toby" Fitzgerald and *"Nelly" Gordon* are at Umballa with the Queen's Bays.
Dunsterville in the Murree Hills with the 107th is reported to be spending his time "gardening." He says that the "Gwubby" instinct has returned to him.
Philips ("butcher" of that ilk) is with the Commissariat at Umballa.
For "Chronicle"?

Notes
1. He had: see 9 September 1885.
2. Published as "From Olympus to Hades", *CMG*, 12 August 1886 (uncollected).
3. Browning, "A Soul's Tragedy", last line.

To Edith Macdonald, 4–5 December 1886
AL, incomplete: Library of Congress

Lahore. / Dec. 4th: 86

Dearest Auntie,

That I have been a grievous sinner I know well. That I am without an apology to offer for a year's silence I know better. That it is my duty – and a great pleasure also – to sit down and write a letter to you at once in reply to a reminder more convincing than folios of letters I know best of all.

For the last year I have been up to my eyes in work but this should be no excuse for my silence. Now take a chair and a lamp and sit down in the one and light the other and I'll tell you all about it. *Imprimis* there was the regular work which goes on from day to day and seems to grow as it goes on. Secondly there was my novel a thing that is always growing and is never finished. Then in the third case was my book or rather I should say books for I have attained to the dignity of a second edition and my publishers talk of a third. In early Spring I wrote a set of twelve rhymes, bad rhymes and cheaply cynical, dealing with Anglo-Indian life in the Plains and these were added to others and christened "Departmental Ditties and other Verses" and sent out into the world in a cover imitating an official docket which you know luckily nothing about. The official docket is bound about with red tape and is a foul thing to look on and a fouler to read. Then a strange thing happened. The little booklet just hit the taste of the Anglo-Indian public for it told them about what they knew. The first 500 copies sold off like smoke in less than a month and I got some lively reviews comparing me to Mortimer Collins, Lowel and all sorts of people whose shoe-latchets I am not worthy to unloose.[1] Then I had the book published by a Calcutta firm as a book – I send you a copy with this mail.

Vanity Fair reviewed it.[2] Andrew Lang in Longman's[3] said some of the work was worthy of Bret Harte and again the public bought, and people quoted my things in leading articles and still quote them and Thacker Spink and Co write to say that the second edition is nearly exhausted. Seeing how small the reading public out here is, this is not so small as it looks. The Viceroy and divers others great people have written and said all sorts of sweet things to me about the book and, best of all, a Bombay paper devoted a column and a half to proving that my verse was no great shakes after all and that I had better choke off for a couple of years;[4] being still an infant and of mean understanding. I was mistrustful of the praise but when the abuse began I made no sort of doubt I had builded better than I knew. Some people say the book is inherently bad and vicious; some say that it conveys moral lessons if people would look for 'em, some say it was written with a purpose and others that it is aimless and futile and vile. I guess all sides are wrong and I leave your discernment to unravel the threads and see how far the most intentionally unpleasant rhymes are meant to carry meanings. However the fact remains that I have made a mark – I say it with all the modesty that a youngster who has had a fill of butter can say so. Everyone in the sets I know, had read or heard about the Departmental Ditties, and strangers in trains, and hotels and all manner of out of the way places come up to me and say nice things. Also – last proof of notoriety – people turn their heads and look and ask to be introduced to me when I dance or dine in strange places beyond my district.

By the way, how is my revered Cousin Stanley? Why don't you send him on a year's furlough round India or the world in general, before he settles down to his father's business and the girls of Stourport and Kidderminster set their virgin caps at him? He will be worth marrying will Stanley and – here I go only by the weird specimens of young civilians imported into our part of the world – a University education whatever its advantages may be doesn't seem to help a boy in looking after himself, one little bit. Tell Uncle Alfred this blasphemy and see him laugh. Now what further remains? Oh – to revert to shop once more. I've got a new editor[5] – a *Globe* man – in place of my old chief who went home on five months leave. Between the two of us we've been making the *Civil and Military Gazette* hum. He is a young man an enthusiast and most delightful to work with. While the family was away at Simla he lived with me, and we spent the hot weather nearly all the time in office. It was grand while it lasted but the End was that I broke down with *insomnia* again and after a merry course of leeches and morphia injections went to Simla. Then he shut up with over work and dysentery and substitutes had to be called in while we rested: but as soon as my leave was up and he was better we sailed in anew and had a fine time. On one memorable occasion we worked for fifteen hours on end with only breaks for meals. The thermometer was between 84° and 86° all the time and we registered a solemn vow never to do it again. They say the paper is immensely improved under the new direction. We certainly have freshened things up all round and cut down expenses simply because we used to write the greater part of our paper ourselves. Now Robinson – he is a brother of Phil Robinson who wrote *"In my Indian Garden"* – goes in a few days and Wheeler returns. He is eminently respectable and horrid dull with a *penchant* for most of the aged frauds in the Punjab commission. What he will think of the "policy of the paper" on his return goodness knows. He will have some difficulty in making his and Robinson's views join and I fear more difficulty in keeping me to the sober paths of précis and abstract writing wherein his soul delights.⁶ Robinson gave me an absolutely free hand and consulted me about questions of "views" and "lines" and "policies" so that in his Consulship I got a greater insight into the higher workings of a paper than ever before.

Also, during my month at Simla I worked – for another paper under the same ownership as ours – under one of my proprietors – the managing one who built himself a fortune out of the *Pioneer*.⁷ He had got a notion from Wheeler that I had an aversion to routine. It was my business to disabuse him and I fancy I did. Robinson was also kindly told of my weakness about "routine", and came, he admits it now, with the intention of giving me a dose of it. He says that he erred and was deceived and that I have even an offensive partiality for routine. Goodness knows I gave him and myself enough steady mechanical "grind" at the old rag. I wanted to clear my character from what I thought was an unfair slur – though I feel sure Wheeler did not mean it unkindly – and I trust he [sic] succeeded.

It has been a pleasant *interregnum* this work with a man in every way congenial and bright and witty, with unlimited powers of work and a shameful levity of disposition. In our more frivolous moments when the paper was put to bed, we had sumptuous rat hunts in the office with our three terriers and decorated the walls with huge caricatures of the "office" "putting sparkle into the paper." Robinson's orders were to "put sparkle into it" and he had done it nobly. Our owners say nice things about both of us and there is a chance of Robinson returning again.

But I've run off at score on "shop" again. It's the only thing one thinks about – or almost so; so it dribbles out on paper. I am running a series of Anglo-Indian social stories: – "Plain Tales from the Hills."⁸ I enclose some samples. They ain't worth publishing in book form but lots of people have written for them to be so treated. However I *don't*. No more books for another year unless it be some additions to the third editions of *Departmental Ditties*.

December. 5th. This letter may catch the home Mail but I fear that the books and cuttings won't. I don't know quite what I am sending you as I am making a general collection of stuff I've done lately just to show you what lines I'm working on. I shall be a good deal astonished if you approve or even admit the necessity of a good deal of my out-turn but most of it was written – as I have already said – with an object or purpose; tho' it is for you to find out what these are [the rest is missing].

Notes
1. The *Bombay Gazette*, 5 July 1886, compared RK to the Lowell of the *Biglow Papers*. The comparison to Mortimer Collins (1827–76) I have not found. See 2 October 1884.
2. 11 September 1886.
3. October 1886: "The story of Giffen . . . is worthy of Bret Harte."
4. Perhaps RK means *The Times of India*, 6 October 1886.
5. Kay Robinson (see 18–27 February 1886).
6. Wheeler's return was not for long. He resigned in March, 1887, and was replaced by Robinson, who remained to edit the *CMG* until 1895.
7. George Allen. The only certainly identified items by RK in the *Pioneer* during his stay in Simla this year are "Cupid's Department", 20 July, "The Simla Exodus", 5 August (both uncollected), and "Out of Society", 14 August (Pinney, *Kipling's India*).
8. The series began in November.

To Mrs Maunsell,[1] 10 June 1887[2]
ALS: Library of Congress

[Lahore] June 10/87

Dear Mrs. Maunsell,

Thanks – many thanks for disorganizing a quiet evening – with the thermometer at 95° by the way – I don't get many Home letters and this particular one was in a handwriting I knew, unfortunately, a good deal too well. Whereat I, suspecting all manner of things the most unreasonable and impossible, opened it in a whirl and found it was . . . . you. Then I lifted up my voice and swore, for a likeness of face is bad enough but an identity of handwriting is too bad. Seriously I never knew anything so insane in my life. But to return to the substance – not the form – of your letter. I am grateful for it though, to put it mildly, it was rather long in coming and, unless I am much mistaken took two days to write.

In regard to those "confessions of a jhampani"[3] fragments of them have been done – but that is all and I fear they will never be finished. But I am always up to my ears in work and the last thing is a new book which has just been finished.[4] It is called Plain Tales from the Hills and is a collection of thirty nine stories of Simla and the plains – among others, "On the Strength of a Likeness."[5] Let me have your Home address and I'll send you a copy. The thing may interest you as one who knows Simla. It has certainly amused people here. After that is through the publisher's hands I turn to a certain never ending novel[6] which I have by me. I saw your husband's transfer in the Gazette.[7]

Meerut is a gay station. Next year, if I live so long and at present I am supposed by an uneducated faculty to be very seedy, I shall be in Allahabad or thereabouts. The ghost may turn up as you say, but I don't think it is likely and I most certainly shall not put myself in the way of meeting it, though methinks I should like just one more rattling swinging waltz. I haven't danced for three months and this is preying on my soul. By the same token I haven't ridden. The heat is infernal. And that reminds me.

The latest news of Mr Hill,[8] in upper Burma, was that he was being eaten up by mosquitoes in a village with an unpronounceable name and his house was a stable which he shared with *"Lady Flo"* – an excellent mare but inconvenient I should say as a sleeping companion.

That again reminds me that the other day I met Mr Dancey's mare – lame but still happy. She let out at me in quite the old fashion – for old sake's sake I suppose. In July, if I can hold out till then, I go up to Simla and the dear old life thereof for one month. The new Townhall is opened and the season promises well – seven women per head of male population. Amen.

By the way if in the course of your travels you should meet at Canterbury the terrible Mrs. Crawford,[9] I charge you strictly to say no word about me. She is a wonderful woman with an offensive persistency of purpose which makes me wild. She wants me to do something for her and a deadly silence on my part fails to choke her off. On second thoughts tell her I am dying: it may lead her to refrain from troubling my last moments with epistles; but whatever you do, don't say I have written to you. There are no other folk in the big world of England that are likely to know of me.

If you have time and inclination answer this rambling screed as soon as may be. It is possible that you may, out of your kindness, be able to render me a service later on. In the meantime believe me

Yours very sincerely
Rudyard Kipling

Notes
1. Perhaps the wife of Colonel John Richardson Maunsell, Royal Engineers, in the Public Works Department, Bombay. He was on furlough in 1887.
2. For some reason unknown, hardly any of RK's letters from 1887 have been found. He was productively at work in Lahore for most of the year and must have written a great many letters.
3. I have found no trace of these.
4. The last of the "Plain Tales" appeared in the *CMG* on this day. When the volume appears in 1888 RK had added eleven stories not in the original series and excluded ten that were.
5. *CMG*, 10 January 1887.
6. "Mother Maturin".
7. Colonel Maunsell disappears from the *India Directory* after 1887.

8. A. P. Hill, of the Telegraph Department, was then superintending railway construction in Upper Burma.
9. Perhaps the wife of Charles Edward Gordon Crawford, CS, Registrar of the High Court of Bombay, on furlough at this time.

To Isabella Burton,[1] 26 October 1887

Text: Composite from exhibition catalogue, "Rottingdean through the Ages" (Rottingdean, 1951) item 319, and R. E. Harbord, *The Readers' Guide to Rudyard Kipling's Work*, I (1961) 5

Lahore, Wednesday Oct. 26/87

Not mad exactly, but very wrathful, I refrained even from good words. . . . 'Twere unfair to spring a dedication on you without warning. . . . If I put on the title page, *sans* initials or anything, just this much, "To the wittiest woman in India I dedicate this book" will you, as they say in the offices, "initial and pass as correct?"[2] . . . . However, if you have the faintest doubt about mixing yourself up even indirectly with "a new man's bid" for public favour you can always, with that convincing candour which is one of your most startling attributes, promptly deny the dedication and turn your nose up at it.

Notes

1. Mrs Burton (d. 1916), the wife of Major Francis Charles Burton, is identified with Mrs Hauksbee, the clever, witty, and cynical heroine of a number of RK's Simla stories. She must have been wholly a Simla acquaintance, for the Major was never stationed at Lahore in RK's day. Major Burton was a staff officer with the 1st Bengal Cavalry at Peshawar in 1887; he later commanded the 2nd Bengal Lancers, and returned to England in 1901. Mrs Burton was Irish, dressed by preference (it is said) in yellow and black, and was the mother of four sons and two daughters, none of whom survived her. RK acted with her and her husband in *A Scrap of Paper* (an adaptation from Sardou) at Simla in September 1887, the earliest documented evidence of RK's acquaintance with Mrs Burton. But that acquaintance must precede 17 November 1886, when the first of the Mrs Hauksbee stories ("Three and – an Extra") was published.
2. The dedication to *Plain Tales from the Hills*, published at the beginning of 1888, reads just as RK gives it here, but Mrs Burton evidently declined to receive it. At any rate, a copy of the third edition is inscribed by RK to his mother as "The Most Excellent Lady of the Dedication/from/her unworthy son:/June. 1890" (Wimpole Hall). In 1923 RK wrote that "P.T's was dedicated to my mother in '88 tho' Mrs. Burton claimed it" (MS note, 5 April 1923: Sussex).

Part Two
Making a Name

Allahabad
1887–8

INTRODUCTION

Kipling had been marked by his superiors as a candidate for promotion to the *Pioneer* of Allahabad as early as 1884, but the move did not take place until the end of 1887 – just when is not known exactly, but he had left Lahore by mid-November 1887 and was writing for the *Pioneer* by early December. The move allowed him to leave behind most of the routines of journalism that he had had to practise in Lahore for five years and to enter into a new phase as an established writer, whose name was increasingly recognised among the English in India.

Allahabad was a different world for Kipling: it was Hindu, as Lahore had been Moslem, and he did not much like the change. It had, however, one notable compensation, apart from his new standing as a star journalist. Very shortly after he arrived in Allahabad, he met Mrs Edmonia Hill, the wife of Professor Alexander Hill of the Muir Central College. Kipling and Mrs Hill were at once attracted to each other, and were quickly close friends: Kipling consulted her on his work, submitted it to her for her judgement, and confided to her his hopes and plans: she was muse, collaborator, and confidante all at once. In the summer of 1888 he moved in with the Hills as a paying guest in their Allahabad house.

Meantime, he was kept busy on special assignments; Rajasthan, Calcutta, Jamalpur, the Giridh coal fields, were among the subjects of his special articles for the *Pioneer*. At the beginning of 1888 he was put in charge of a new supplement to the *Pioneer* called *The Week's News*, for which he was expected to supply a steady stream of fiction as well. Thus began the stories that, later in 1888, were collected in the series called "The Railway Library" and that, in no very long time, were to make him famous: the series includes such titles as *Soldiers Three, In Black and White, Under the Deodars*, and *The Phantom 'Rickshaw*. So abundant was the flow from Kipling's pen in these months of 1888 that the *Pioneer* could not absorb it all and a good part of it continued to be diverted to the pages of *The Civil and Military Gazette*.

Kipling now saw that he must return to England; he had achieved everything that lay within the scope of Indian journalism, and if he was to move beyond those limits it would have to be in cosmopolitan London. The thought must have occurred to him often enough before, but by the middle of 1888 he had definitely made up his mind to make the venture. A return to Lahore in the hot weather of 1888 to edit the *Civil and Military Gazette* in Kay Robinson's absence confirmed Kipling in his decision: in Lahore, the scene of his apprenticeship and first success, he found everything *"connu* and triply *connu"*. It was, clearly, time to move on.

To Edmonia Hill,[1] [c. late December 1887?]
Text: Copy, University of Sussex

[Allahabad][2]

Dear Mrs. Hill.

Can you imagine me bounding round in a badminton net?[3] I've been trying to draw you a rough sketch of my appearance – but it couldn't be done. T'was too horrid for anything.

American – and more particularly the tongue of Pennsylvania – is the *one* language I have long and ardently desired to learn. May I come on Sunday afternoon. You see today is my Sunday and not tomorrow. Mebbe I'll see you at the bandstand this even.

Yours sincerely
Rudyard Kipling

Notes
1. Edmonia Taylor Hill (1858–1952), the wife of Samuel Alexander Hill, Professor of Physical Science at the Muir College, Allahabad. Mrs Hill, called "Ted", was an American, the daughter of the President of Beaver College for women in Beaver, Pennsylvania, near Pittsburgh. She and RK first met not long after his transfer to Allahabad and the acquaintance very quickly became a friendship.
2. RK's long-expected transfer to the staff of the *Pioneer* in Allahabad was finally made in mid or late November, 1887. The first item of his in the *Pioneer* that can be identified after the transfer appeared on 9 December ("The Investiture at Oodeypore", dateline 4 December: uncollected).
3. According to Mrs Hill, RK was "quite good at badminton" ("The Young Kipling", *Atlantic Monthly*, April 1936, p. 407).

To Margaret Burne-Jones, 25 January–24 March 1888
ALS: University of Sussex

Jamalpur (900 miles and more southerly of Lahore) / Jan:25:88:

Sweet and trusty Wop. How far has your letter wandered! Four times has it crossed the Holy Ganges, going westward twelve hundred and southward a thousand miles ere it caught me amid the lush green of Bengal Proper, south of the miles of wheatfields of Mokana, south of

Benares, south of every place I have ever known – in a land where tigers come and roar – blood curdling thought! – among the low hills of Kajna. But of this change and of what led to it, more anon. In the first place, thanks for your consolation which is the consolation of a sweet spirit and of a knowledge calmer and deeper than anything whereto I have attained. Thanks also for a certain subtle feminine irony that comes as a tonic and is wholesome. Bless you Wop, for what you have written! Did I say cynicism? I made a mistake, for God knows that I laugh at myself and not at others, for my mistrust. You have seen into the root of the mischief in hinting that it were well for me to work with my hands, and so take my fellows on this earth simply – as people, and not as studies or things to be boiled down and used up or treated and developed. It is a phase as you say and will pass in time: but the fit irks while it is on me. 'Curious question that of yours about believing in Trixie. I do. Oh yes immensely. How does your Latinity go? "She is alive who was dead and behold she lives for ever, holding the keys of death and hell."[1] Excellent 'i faith! One little drawback mars the full felicity as you will have heard ere this. The whole thing is broken off – so far as I can learn at this distance, – on the ground of incompatibility of temper; and – trust a woman for prolonging the agony out of misplaced pity – the wretched worm upon the hook, Jack Fleming,[2] is still allowed to write to the girl whereby, methinks, he will enjoy in full those torments which were my share when I received a somewhat similar permission from Flo Garrard close upon four years ago. Now in respect to Jack Fleming I do not care one straw. He may be stretched on a rack and consumed by slow fire if my maiden be in any sort benefitted thereby; but I am sorry for the lingering death of the beast, and my faith in the excellence of my sister's judgment – whereon, if I mistake not – I dwelt at some length in my last letter – is a little shaken. There was no compulsion, and there was ample time to choose. *Therefore*, she seems to have made a choice, in the settling of her affections, which has not endured three months. I do not know what she has told you. I daresay you have the story at length. I am a little sorry for Fleming – not because he is *jawâbed*[3] but because he is suffered to torture himself with vain hope; and a little disgusted at the bursting of the heaven-hued bubble. However let us trust that the next lover from the skies, the man among men etc. etc., will be better. This I write for your eye only. For my little maiden I have nothing but sympathy because she is very sorry and upset in her poor little mind. I have read Chaucer and I know through him what a woman should be. I have read other books, bound in different textile fabrics, and I do not know what a woman is, but have had some glimpses at what she can be. I will wait for the rising of the morning star to disperse these mists and then I will write and say: – "I have the keys of death and Hell". But whether you will be

To Margaret Burne-Jones, 25 January–24 March 1888

pleased at my way of putting it is quite another matter. I fancy from what I can make out of the movements of my folk in the north, that I shall come home next year for a while and then we will sit in the mulberry tree and hide pieces of bread and pork dripping under the dining room sofa and slide down the drawing room table and flatly deny the existence of any such objectionable being as "Mr. Rudyard Kipling" or of so womanly wise a soul as "Miss Margaret Burne Jones." But the matter in hand is not womankind but work. Hear now while I speak. Since November last I have been a vagabond on the face of the earth. But such a vagabondage! Did I tell you how the *Pioneer* took me over and bade me go out for a month into Rajputana – the home of a hundred thousand legends and the great fighting pen of India. They gave me did my generous masters Rs 600 a month and paid my railway expenses. Ach Himmel. Was there anything like that dissolute tramp through some of the loveliest and oldest places upon the face of the earth. I wrote a series of letters called "Letters of Marque" – by the way it is running still[4] – and I railed and rode and drove and tramped and slept in Kings' palaces or under the stars themselves and saw panthers killed and heard tigers roar in the hills, and for six days had no white face with me, and explored dead cities desolate these three hundred years, and came to stately Residences where I feasted in fine linen and came to desolate way side stations where I slept with natives upon the cotton bales and clean forgot that there was a newspapery telegraphic world without. Oh it was a good and clean life and I saw and heard all sorts and conditions of men and they told me the stories of their lives, black and white and brown alike, and I filled three note books and walked "with death and morning on the silver horns"[5] and knew what it was to endure hunger and thirst. When I came out of the wilderness, having touched the edge of the Great Indian Desert, and seen many wonderful and awful things, I found the railway stations blazing with my name coupled with that of another author – you may have heard of him – Bret Harte. In my absence, the *Pioneer* had started a new weekly paper and I, as the author of *Plain Tales from the Hills* was advertised as the writer of a series of "Anglo Indian Studies".[6] On my return to Allahabad – the place where the *Pioneer* is printed – I had to turn to and hatch out stories; for they had told me nothing of this new departure. One of my proprietors[7] made me welcome for a month and I worked like a nigger, because I love him, and would do anything for him and went to all the dances and dinners that were going for thirty days. Then they cut me adrift afresh, bidding me chuse my own ground for exploration. I have taken the 19th century and the Railway colonies in India, and the opium factories and the out of the way life of Calcutta, and Benares, and a relic of the Mutiny for my subjects[8] and am come here to Jamalpur, which is a sort of Crewe[9] of Eastern India, where men make locomotives and control many hundreds of miles of lines.

Jan. 26th. 'Been out on business all day in soft warm drenching rain and return to you now, having competely lost the thread of my egoistical argument. Where was I? At Jamalpur. It's a wonderful place and I see that I shall have my work cut out to describe it. I've got my first harvest of notes and have been writing out for three hours continuous. Consequently my hand is getting shaky and crampsome. Say Wop. If you had your name placarded up and down 2,200 miles of line and written big in every newspaper in India and were yourself invited to dinner parties for people to look at and ask "how do you write those – er – things?" you wouldn't feel happy. I am just now overtaken with an immense discontent and dissatisfaction with all that I have turned out and the Plain Tales have put the coping upon my unrest.[10] They are horrid bad and I feel that they should ha' been so much better. I am sending you a copy of 'em. Be merciful and remember that

> "my way is parted from thy way
> out of sight, beyond light."[11]

Your friends I believe write pretty things. Mine are ugsome, and unimpressive at that. You can see from the printing how vilely books are got up in India. I invented the hieroglyph at the top of the title page for the Wop of Albion. It is impressive and grew out of a blot on the word "Madge".

Jan. 27th. 'Be shot if it is. The blot has runned away all down the page and I'll get you another as soon as ever I get to Calcutta if I live. I've had a riotous day cutting about over the "shops" and inspecting 120 diseased locos, a quarter of a million of pound's worth of stock and goodness knows what all. It's all down in a notebook somewhere but I'm too dead fagged to write it out (and there is an "interesting" tale for the week after next to be written) and so I fly to you for consolation. Tomorrow I go to a big meeting of the local Masonic Lodge. Curious thing to think that though I've come south 980 miles I am certain tomorrow of finding men who will talk to me as though they had known me all their lives on subjects on which both I and they will be able to discourse about with freedom and *camaraderie*. Let us hope they'll give me some decent material for Studies. I'm in low water again.

You want a fantastic tale *mon amie*. The night is yet young. I'll tell you some. Here is one that I was mixed up in. Last month I was right away on the other side of India; not 400 miles from Bombay. Now I am less than 300 from Calcutta. You can see the stretch on the map. When I was on the borders of Bhilwarra (look that out on the map) I met a man who was also a mason. "Ships upon the sea" are nothing compared to our meetings in India. He said to me "A friend of mine is coming across the Empire from the East (Assam way) touching at Bombay and going Home. I cannot stir from here to meet him though he will pass within less than 300 miles. Your road towards the Great Indian Desert will cross his if you go by such and such a train, just on the borders of the sands, if he keeps to his timing. Take me a message, to this man, which I do not wish to write." The message was perfectly unintelligible to me and would, I imagine, have been equally so to any man who did not know to what it referred. My brother gave me this message and I went up and up northwards from the western side of India till I came to a junction on the edge of the desert and was set out of the train at five on a bitterly cold winter's morning with all the stars blazing overhead and a wind fit to cut you in two blowing off the sands. The Calcutta train – i.e. the train from Agra bearing the Bombay mails came in and a man in one of the carriages opened a window and looked out sleepily. I didn't want to go threshing all down the train – there were three Englishmen on it, in search of my unknown, so I went towards the window and behold, it was the man I was told to find; for he also (doesn't this sound mad?) was also a brother of mine. I bent over him and gave the message and he said sleepily: – "Tha'anks. I know what it means. You needn't repeat it. Tha'anks." Then I went away and the Calcutta train went off to Bombay and I set out into the desert on my journey. Now *remember* I didn't know the name of the man who gave me the message. He didn't know mine. I didn't know the man who received it and he didn't know me. Wasn't it odd and out of the world? I felt like the Camorri and the Brothers of Mercy[12] and all sorts of veiled and mysterious things for at least five minutes. Is that quaint enough for you?[13] Here is another tale. Right away in the Desert there is a city set in 150 miles of sand, ruled by a mad king and smitten with a grievous water famine so that the city is empty. No one ever goes there: it is a semi independent native state and Englishmen are unknown to the inhabitants. A low caste servant of an Englishman about four hundred miles east of this place wearied of his inactive life and stole some money from his master *and* a Treacher's price-list. Treacher is a the big general merchant at Bombay and his lists resemble the fat books of the Co-operative stores. Armed with this book, the native hired a fleet camel and went away into the desert. When he came to a village he said, waving the price-list: – "There is a big war at Cabul and the British Government says that every able bodied man must go up and fight. How many have you available. I am Mahommed Suruf Kahn, a servant of the British government." Naturally, these poor devils who cling to their little oases as a Swiss to his mountains said: – "For God's sake, get out of this with your terrible book and we'll give you money to report that we have no fighting levies." By the way all our soldiers are volunteers and we have the pick and flower of the land. He used to take the bribe and go on, on his camel to another village, pretending to write men down in his book, taking money and scaring the souls out of the men of Jeysulmir. Presently, the Native State got wind of his proceedings and sent out a man on a fleet camel to catch him. Try to catch a wild bunny on the Grange lawn to realize what hunting one man across the desert means. However they caught him just when he had rooked enough to retire on and – mark the sequel as a purely Oriental bit of justice. He got three months for obtaining money under false pretences and frightening all the countryside *but* he got one year for pretending to be a Mahommedan of good family when he was only a low caste Hindu. He was caught by a Mussalman state you see. The case never came into Our jurisdiction at all for the man knew better than to go into British territory where he would have been laughed at by the first village headman.[14]

Mar: 7:th: Allahabad.
Never mind the rest of the idiotically egoistic letter I'd written. A casual line from the Mother informs me that you are engaged to a man whose name I don't remember[15] – anyhow he's not half good enough for you – and a first class scholar. All luck and good fortune, peace and contentment go with you and with him for your sake, now and for ever. Take the Yogi's blessing as the wandering priests deliver it: – So long as the water flows down hill, and the cloud brings the rain and the rain the increase of the earth, while the Gods are above the earth and the Devils below, to reward the good and to punish the evil, while the yoke presses the bullock's neck, the rein the horse's, the gold star the forehead of the bride, and the logs of the burning ghat the limbs of the dead, good luck go before you as a runner before the face of the King, good fortune shadow you as a canopy the Presence of the King, and good fortune come after you as an army in its strength follows the elephant of the King. The four elements be gracious to you and the Gods give you the desire of your heart. Ganesh dwell above your door and Lakshmi within the house, and the great Vishn who is over all guard you against the snake by night and the wild beast by day, the rotten beam, the scattered fire, the poison of foes and the flattery of friends, the dangers of field and jungle path, of river and ford, of desert and drouth, of famine and pestilence and the loss of sons. In the name of the Great One who is above all the Gods, all the Heavens and all the Hells, who was and is and will be, this I have asked on your head and your house and your childrens' – that the light may never go out with you or yours. That's a comprehensive sort of blessing isn't it, and I have excised the luxuriance of detail with which it is adorned. In plain English: – "God bless you my Wop" for you are only one shade less dear to me than my own sister. I am sorry now that I told you what I felt when she got

engaged. Anyhow you won't remember it, for I am certain that you are so certain of all felicity that the remembrance of it has passed. And who is a beast like myself to meddle with a maiden's dreams? I know that you must love the man, because I cannot imagine your contracting an engagement without giving your whole heart first. And you are additionally lucky in having your mother's so full approval. Aunt Georgie has told us that he is "the one man on earth she'd ha' liked you to have chosen." Let him prove himself so. I can't say that I'd care to entrust you to any man I know or have heard of – but then I feel pretty much on that point as I did about Trixie's – experiment shall we call it? One small wee piece of advice let me, in my ignorance, give.

March. 24th. Great Scott, who am I to give advice. I've just been making an egregious ass of myself. This letter really must be finished for this mail or it will be held over to the days of your grandmotherhood and then the congratulations will be a trifle stale. A letter from Aunt Louie reminds me that I am desperately in arrears with my home correspondence: also my Indian – but this if you only are dumb for a sufficient length of time answers itself. But I am up to my ears in work and plans and schemes, and must stop. My Wop, I envy you very bitterly, and I am pleased for your sake. Take my Wopsome love and – don't turn up your nose in scorn – if ever the time comes when you want help of any sort I, if I be above ground, am your servant and brother. Whereon the Wop laughs in great security and saith: –"I am alive who was dead and behold I live for ever holding the keys of death and hell." So may it be.

The Wop of Asia.

Notes
1. Cf. Revelation 1:18.
2. Captain John Murchison Fleming (1858–1942), commissioned in the King's Own Scottish Borderers, 1879; seconded to Survey of India Department 1885; Superintendent of Survey, 1898, retiring as Lieutenant-Colonel in 1911. He and Trix were engaged in 1887; she broke it off, but they were engaged again in the summer of this year, and married in the next. The marriage was childless and unsatisfactory to both parties. Trix and Fleming appear to have been spiritual opposites.
3. Dismissed.
4. It began on 14 December and ran to 28 February 1888.
5. Tennyson, *The Princess*, vii.189.
6. The new paper, which RK edited, was a supplement to the *Pioneer* called the *Week's News* and began publication on 7 January 1888. It was largely a "re-hash of news and views" (*Something of Myself*, p. 71) but offered a page of fiction each week that RK was glad to fill, and did so with the stories that later went into the Indian Railway Library. The advertisement that RK mentions appears in the *Pioneer*, 24 December 1887: it offered both Bret Harte's "The Argonauts of North Liberty" and the "Anglo-Indian Studies" of Rudyard Kipling in the new publication.
7. George Allen.
8. "Among the Railway Folk", "In an Opium Factory", "The City of Dreadful Night", and "The Bride's Progress", the first four items of which RK refers, are all collected

in *From Sea to Sea*; the fifth, "The Little House at Arrah", an episode of the Indian Mutiny, appears only in the suppressed edition of *The Smith Administration*.
9. Crewe was the site of the main locomotive works of the London and North Western Railway and is a major railway centre.
10. *Plain Tales* had just come out in book form (Calcutta, 1888).
11. Cf. Rossetti, "Song of the Bower", concluding lines.
12. The Camorra was a secret terrorist society flourishing in nineteenth-century Italy; I do not know what he means by the Brothers of Mercy. Perhaps the Fathers of Mercy?
13. RK used the episode to open "The Man Who Would Be King".
14. This story RK used in "Recruiting Extraordinary", *CMG*, 9 January 1888, reprinted as "The Great Census" in *The Smith Administration* (suppressed edition).
15. John William Mackail (1859–1945), a highly distinguished Balliol graduate and an official of the Board of Education, mainly known now for his literary work, including many classical translations and editions, and a *Life* of William Morris; Professor of Poetry, Oxford (1906–11); President of the British Academy (1932–6); Order of Merit (1935).

To F. Koenig,[1] 22 March 1888

Text: Harry Carr, "Kipling and the Craft", *Ars Quatuour Coronatorum*, LXXVII (1964) 224–5: dated Allahabad, 22 March 1888

Dear Sir and Worshipful Master,

It is with great regret I have to inform you that I am now permanently transferred to Allahabad and therefore forced to abandon any active connection with my Mother Lodge. I write to ask you to forward a Clearance Certificate to enable me to join 'Lodge Independence with Philanthropy' at this Station, and also to send my Grand Lodge Certificate to the Master of that Lodge when it arrives.[2] I have of course no intention of withdrawing my name from the Lodge Roll and shall be obliged if you would have me put down as an Absent Brother.

I send herewith Rs. 24 P.M., subscription and shall always look back with keen pleasure to my Masonic life in 'Lodge Hope and Perseverance', and, if at any time, I can do anything to further its aims and objects, am entirely at your disposal. Convey my warmest and most fraternal regards to the Brethren and

Believe me

Yours faithfully and fraternally,
Rudyard Kipling.

Notes

1. Identified only as the then Master of RK's Lahore Masonic Lodge, "Hope and Perseverance". RK joined the Masons by special dispensation – he was not yet twenty-one – in April 1886 and was active in the Lodge until he left Lahore. He is known to have given two lectures on Masonic subjects to the Lodge, and he served as Secretary from January 1887. RK resigned from his Indian Masonic Lodges after leaving India,

and, though he continued to take an interest in the Craft and held various honorary memberships, there is no evidence that he was ever again a practising member of any Lodge (Harry Carr, "Kipling and the Craft", *Ars Quatuour Coronatorum*, LXXVII (1964) 215–53).
2. RK joined the Allahabad Lodge on 17 April 1888 (Carr, "Kipling and the Craft", p. 225).

To Edmonia Hill, [22] April [1888]
Text: Copy, University of Sussex

Allahabad at 94°/ in the shade / Sunday the something / of April

This morning an evil minded firm of publishers sent me a batch of aniline dye publications purporting to be the Third Edition of the Departmental Ditties[1] – whereof a copy was promised you some – months or years was it? – centuries ago. The little book is not well printed and appears to have been bound "cock-eye" – twisted malevolently in the press. At times it reminds me of one of those elementary primers on "heat," "food" or, the "steam engine" so dear to your husband's Department. No – I am not pleased with it – inside or out; but such as it is, it is yours if you will stoop to the taking. There are new poems of sorts to the extent of about a dozen scattered up and down its ill-trimmed pages. Let us hope the dear public will swallow it as it has swallowed the others.

And so the letter which you were kind enough to let me right – (am I *quite* mad that I forget my spelling?) opens. There is nothing and less than nothing to tell for with a sky like a greasy soup tureen shut down on a gasping land life does not move swiftly. One small incident that happened almost before your train was clear of the station[2] moved me to laughter; but I was awfully angry all the same. I returned to my humble ekka gharri[3] and was aware of a raw boned red horse backing and filling all across the road. Behind him was a certain brougham and in that brougham sat one native, another native and I think three Aryan brats but there may have been more. They were going home in state in the Memsahib's *gharri*. I didn't moralize any; I let 'em go on their stolen drive. Didn't s'pose t'was any concern of mine what they did to that brougham. May be they all enjoy a hawa-khana[4] in it every evening.

11.30. a.m. So much for the plans of men! Here's a letter in from Lahore announcing that Kay Robinson goes on leave on the 5th of next month. That means I have to go up and nurse the baby – the *Civil & Military* for a month, returning to this hole about the middle of June. This is de-lightful but I'd sooner get my month's editorial work over now than later on when I shall want my days and my hands clear. You never had to "run" a daily rag alone – for which be joyful. Tisn't quite as amusing as stoking a P & O liner in the Red Sea but it's a good deal hotter and combines excitement with education. If the Lahore Organ about three weeks hence, comes out "all face" as the little children say, you will understand that the Editor – where are we without capital letters! – has suddenly departed this world or lost his reason. Pray that I may run the show without any grievous breakdown or palpable blunder. There won't be a human soul in Lahore and the heat will be worse than down here.

Remind me that I bear a grudge against Mrs. Ross.[5] She has insulted [me] by sending the English version of Madame Bovary embellished by bad Woodbury or autotype pictures.[6] To mark my deep contempt I have thrown it at the lame black cat who is my constant companion and from her language I gather that she approves of Flaubert as little as I do. Happy thought! Perhaps Flaubert had indigestion and that suggested killing his crazy heroine with arsenic. You've read the thing haven't you? Didn't you resent it? Twasn't so bad in its French but when I unearthed it in all the bald brutality of the British tongue I kicked . . . . as the black cat knoweth.

Apropos. I sent you the Sermon on the Mount – what *am* I writing of? – the Hill of Illusion[7] on Saturday. Now that it is fairly off my hands and I have looked at it objectively I cannot say that I am as much in love with it as I was. There are bald patches in it which I try to persuade myself are due to the crampedness of the space permitted. Except in real life it is difficult to throw a very real tragedy, on one side or the other, into the space of half an hour's speech. See the misfortune of permitting a pen and ink egoist to write to you!

Here am I choked up with half a dozen plans, ideas and stump outlines of stories and never – so help me – in my need – *never* one sympathetic soul between here and the limits of my tether to discuss 'em with and see how they will work. Can a man take a black cat into his confidence? She looks deceitfully sympathetic and purrs applaudingly but I am afraid that her heart is with her kittens under the almirah.[8] Is a punkah coolie to be trusted? Alas! He only turns on his side, scratches himself and says *garibbarwar*.[9] This is a stony hearted world.

I spent Saturday alternately browsing over a pipe and trying to hack out a *causerie intime* between two girls at Simla.[10] If I can successfully take the public into the innermost recesses of a young ladies' boudoir I don't know what I shan't arrive at or where I shan't go in the end. It's very difficult, with the limited amount of knowledge at my disposal, to get the hang of conversation between girls. Could I trespass on your kindness so far as to ask you on some idle afternoon to look over and check the thing in proof? You shall have the widest of margins as befits the wisest of Censors and your commands will be obeyed. I should be grateful if you would do this kindness.

Went to the Bandstand in the afternoon and O Hades it was warm and I was in the worst of tempers. Possibly for this very reason four men insisted on my dining with them. Three I scorned but went off with Bayliss[11] to the Fort[12] for the first time since the sing-song and dined with him and a nice Captain who unless I am mistaken is doing his best to qualify for consumption, and we sat under the stars after dinner and swapped stories of incident and accident by land and by sea. The drive home through the fort gates disgusted me mightily as Pepys said – or did not say. It was stuffy and in every sort abominable.

Seeing the small size of the booklet that I send, 'seems to me that this letter is about long enough. Forgive its rampant egoism and the store of nonsense with which it is filled. I must turn my feeble intellect to a forecast of the arrangements necessary for the C & M. *Entre Nous*, I would far sooner go to sleep . . . through the hot weather if possible.

When you have time and inclination send a line in my direction and bear in mind the present that you were good enough to promise me. May the season be a pleasant one to you, and all good fortune go with you. I can afford that wish for the Lord he knoweth that I have no luck of my own.

Yours
R.K.

Notes
1. Calcutta, Thacker, Spink and Co. (1888), containing ten poems not previously collected.
2. Mrs Hill had just left for Mussoorie, a hill station not far from Simla, for the hot weather.
3. A one-horse, two-wheeled native carriage: "a tea-tray on wheels" ("The Sudder Bazaar").
4. Outing.
5. The wife of G. E. A. Ross, advocate in the High Court, Allahabad (*India Directory*, 1888).
6. Both processes for photographic reproduction.
7. First published *CMG*, 28 September 1887; reprinted *Week's News*, 21 April 1888 (*Under the Deodars*).
8. Wardrobe or chest of drawers.
9. "Protector of the Poor".
10. "Poor Dear Mama", *Week's News*, 26 May 1888; the first part of *The Story of the Gadsbys*.
11. Lieutenant Eustace Granville Bayliss, East Surrey Regiment, Allahabad.
12. Built by Akbar in the sixteenth century and rebuilt by the English in the nineteenth: see 3 May–24 June 1886.

To Edmonia Hill, [24? April 1888]
Text: Copy, University of Sussex

[Allahabad]

Same old Place of Torment – half past ten of a moonlit night:
April of the Year One.[1]

Of course you could not be at Mussoorie by this time: hence, equally of course, no answer to my letter. Thirdly and lastly as a natural consequence to the above, I take up the Office Pen – a chewed and battered exponent of my poor ideas – and begin a letter which may or may not be finished and when it is finished, may not be posted. When one had done, said, written and thought nothing for eight and forty hours past, there is a certain amount of comfort in covering the helpless paper with scrawls. You need not read them you know; but I should be flattered if you did.

Imprimis I have walked fifteen miles, more or less, up and down the garden path smoking the pipe of unrest. Reason – a beast of a snake who came between the wind and my nobility this afternoon. 'Never knew such a place of peril as Allahabad. I slew him with a stick – grievously – and he was not pretty to look at by the time I had finished; but I felt that I at least had done my duty. You know the superstition that the creatures travel in pairs? They have done this ever since the day of the Temptation when Satan's helpmate in the lamentable little business that deprived you and me of our wings and harps was the snake woman Lilith – for whose ways and works consult Rosetti – D.G. of that ilk.[2] I have been looking for Lilith with a stick but she has not appeared. 'Wonder if she will make her way into my room in the night and avenge the slaughter of her husband.

Secundo. There has been a storm – a fine storm that has lowered the temperature and sent all Allahabad rejoicing to the Club, to compare sensations, like frogs after a rain. Even the large and stately (or straightly ought I to say?) Mrs. Straight[3] was there; and we all pretended with great pretence that this was "quite as good as the hills." I pretended most of all; for the reaction after a long and severe course of truth telling has made me reckless.

In the matter of Straights. I owe the husband[4] a grimly sensational evening. I dined with him at the Club on Monday and the talk turned on the everlasting battle between the Law and the criminal. For one hour and a half from the coffee to the second cheroot Straight unburdened himself of anecdote after anecdote – each one more grisly than the last. He has been concerned in most of the more distinguished murder trials of the past twenty years and "what he don't know aint hardly worth the knowin'." I learnt how the Condemned receive their death sentences and how they stood at the last moment; how one hair and an overlooked blood spot supplied a chain of evidence strong enough to draw a man to the gallows – and a score of other equally fascinating and equally horrible things till, at last, as Hawthorne says, "Me seemed that I should never draw a breath of pure air again." I am not much in love with my own mind – it's a scrubby grubby sort o' thing but my faith! 'tis cream laid, wire wove, triple glazed, ivory bank post note paper compared to the mental condition of one who has sat in judgment professionally upon his fellow men. Straight completed his tale of wrong doing by attempting to describe Peace[5] – (surely you have heard of Charley Peace our pet English murderer, the man who played the piano and kept tame rabbits when he was not engaged in assisting the Souls' flight of his fellow creatures.) "He was a stumpy little man" Straight began. "Yes" said I, with immense interest, "And what was he like to look at?" "Well" said S. with genial frankness "He was very like you about the head." I collapsed while the rest of the table roared. Now I see no fun in being compared by a cold eyed judge of the high court to a notorious murderer. Wouldn't he be prejudiced if I came before him professionally – *his* professionally, I mean; not mine?

Notes

1. Of his life in Allahabad? Of his acquaintance with Mrs Hill? From this letter on, most of the copies of RK's letters in India to Mrs Hill have salutations and closings only by way of exception. Perhaps Mrs Hill deleted them from the originals when she sold them. The copies are unsatisfactory in many others ways as well, but whether by design or accident who can say?
2. Sonnet 78 in *The House of Life*.
3. Mrs Douglas Straight (see next note). According to Mrs Hill's note, Mrs Straight was the heroine of "Three and – an Extra".
4. (Sir) Douglas Straight (1844–1914), a lawyer with a large London practice in criminal law before going to India: Judge of the High Court of Judicature, Allahabad, 1879–92.
5. Charles Peace (1832–79) was executed for a murder committed in 1876.

To Edmonia Hill, [c. 25 April 1888]
Text: Incomplete Copy, Cornell University

[Allahabad]

"[. . .] To Lady Dufferin"[1] – See how the Viceregal taint creeps out! He's[2] had so many addresses that he calls a poem,[3] prompted by any one in the world but Lady D. an address. This "Address" then has "moved me very much." It is so full of feeling and in such perfect good taste. So he thanks me "in my wife's name and my own" and asks me [to] "accept the accompanying volume of mine which will be followed by a very good photograph of Lady Dufferin as soon as the supply which we are expecting arrives". Wah! Wah! They'll be making me the Poet Laureat of Peterhoff[4] next – Up to date neither book nor picture has arrived. I s'pose that the one will be letters from High Latitudes[5] and the other, A faithful presentiment of Mrs. D. scowling under her tiara. She has a most baleful and malevolent glare due to short sight.

Well, what do you an untrammelled and republican American think of it all?

There is little news.

Notes
1. Hariot Georgina Rowan Hamilton (1843–1936), married Lord Dufferin in 1862.
2. Frederick Temple Hamilton-Temple Blackwood (1826–1902), first Marquess of Dufferin and Ava, Liberal politician and diplomat. He was Governor-General of Canada, Ambassador to Russia, Ambassador to Turkey, and Special Commissioner to Egypt before succeeding Lord Ripon as Viceroy of India, 1884–8; he was afterwards Ambassador to Italy and to France. Dufferin was a man who, in Carrington's words, had "done everything, met everyone, been everywhere" (*Kipling*, p. 64); through it all he retained his Irish charm.
3. "The Song of the Women", *Pioneer*, 17 April 1888, written on behalf of Lady Dufferin's Fund for the medical education of Indian women (see [27] September 1885).
4. The Viceroy's residence at Simla.
5. Dufferin's account of his voyage to Iceland and Spitzbergen, published in 1856.

To Cormell Price, 26 April 1888
ALS: Library of Congress

N.W.P. Club[1] / *Allahabad* / April 26 / 88

Dear Uncle Crom

Your letter enclosing the second advertisement received; and since I am now on the *Pioneer* I have sent the slip into the *Pi* – by far the larger paper of the two.[2] The other advertisement[3] shall be stopped – it has been religiously running since you sent it to me – as soon as ever I get back to Lahore. I am off on Sunday night to take charge of the *Civil and Military Gazette* for a month while the Editor is on leave. I wonder how your home journalists would like being shifted off at 48 hours notice on a nine hundred mile journey. As a matter of fact I am on the Pioneer permanently and haven't seen my people for six months but as the two papers belong to one proprietary I go to be a *locum tenens*.

Just at present I am in all the agonies of reviewdom for my new book[4] is out and the papers have discovered that I am a "moralist" and the Lord only knows what else beside. However the thing is selling like wildfire and so I can afford to despise attacks on my virtue.

I have spent the winter on a couple of the most fascinating tours (in Rajputana and lower Bengal) that the mind of a literary loafer could have imagined: and the proceeds are twenty things entitled Letters of Marque which I am arranging to publish as soon as may be.[5]

I send you a sample of my book by this mail and I pray you deal mercifully with it.

Give my most special salaams to Mr. Crofts and my beloved *padre*,[6] and convey my undying detestation of mine ancient Housemaster[7] to him if he still lives (which I trust he does not) and believe me

Yours in haste but always affectionately
Ruddy.

Notes
1. The North-West Provinces Club.
2. The new advertisement was for the USC preparatory school, the junior school of the college, for boys aged seven through twelve (e.g., *Pioneer*, 5 May).
3. A regular advertisement in the *CMG* (e.g., 3 March 1888); it gives the enrolment (200), the staff (15), and a record of recent successes in the army examinations.
4. *Plain Tales from the Hills*.
5. They did not appear until 1891, when unauthorised Indian and English editions were printed, but were then suppressed by RK. A revised text of the letters was published by RK in *From Sea to Sea* (1899).
6. Willes.
7. Pugh.

To Edmonia Hill, 30 April 1888
Text: Copy, University of Sussex

Allahabad: 30: 4: 88:

'Stonishing how calm a man can keep in the midst of chaos if his mind is at ease. Here am I ordered up to Lahore[1] – with all my arrangements superbly incomplete and fragmentary, not a scrap of "copy" available, half a dozen agonizing telegrams pulling me three different ways at once, an ice box which will do everything but hold ice with decency and sobriety and I am mooning around with a pipe in my mouth smiling like the Cheshire Cat. "Worthy friends, fellow labourers and faithful servitors be calm" is the burden of my song. "What *have* you to fash yourselves about? Take example from me." I am off on an eight hundred mile trip. Do *I* swear and cavort and behave unseemly?

But they won't be calm and they worry me with their complaints and their requisitions. Peace, babblers and let me write my letters. I will attend to you later on.

Your note has come in and I am pleased to know that Mussoorie and the Sermon on the Mount[2] content you. You will enjoy yourself mightily ere the season is over – and will return I trust cured of those savage headaches, and ready to face the horrors of the Rains.

You ask what did Mrs. Kipling say to it – the Sermon. She didn't say much but she wrote a good deal. Here's an extract from her letter. "It's clever and subtle and all that and *I* see the morality in it but, O my boy, how do *you* know it? Don't tell me about "guessing in the dark." It's an insult to your old Mother's intelligence. If Mrs. Hauksbee[3] enlightened you I'm not sorry that she has gone home." Mrs. H's departure to other and better climes was postponed from the 13th to the 27th and now that I have read the passenger list of the steamer of that date I see why.[4] Well, she was very kind to me in her curiously cynical way and I owe her thanks for half a hundred ideas and some stories. A hasty pencil note from Bombay gives me her farewell and her opinions. She says: – "Good bye and cultivate humility. Your last[5] is not bad – very bad – but it lacks depth and you have made a mistake in not marking the change between the moods, towards the end. They should slide into one another, whatever they may do in real life. You have painted them without transition and the effect is streaky. Otherwise it is passable. I leave you to make my peace with the infuriated amateurs who will have read "All these men and women merely players." My barque is on the strand and my ship is on the shore and, please God, I shall not return." That "Play Acting"[6] in the Pioneer was hers and already I hear from the Station that it jibed at that the people are *very* angry. Poor dears! I've been so pressed for regular work that I haven't had time to frivol except as Elephaz the Temanite,[7] and that was written when I was "down in the gulf of dark despair" as Budge said.[8]

No. Lahore is not a nice place and I am lucky only in going back to the best and most genial of Fathers, to smoke the pipe of sweet council with him and to see if my hand has lost touch of the pencil, or his forsaken the pen. We shall be all alone together and we shall enjoy ourselves grimly in front of the thermantidote. All the station has changed within the past few months and the new pastures, if any there be, may lie as fallow as the plain of Gomorrah so far as I am concerned. So from the 5th May to the 5th June I shall be at Lahore and then I shall take my leave and then – H'm. I guess for a little time Rachel will be heard weeping for her children. Anyhow my present desires are limited to pulling through the next month – *not* on American papers, O Scoffer.

Do you suppose that this unfortunate edits

To Edmonia Hill, 30 April 1888

>   A Weekly county paper –
> The *tuck*[9] may be acquired in a day
> Advertisements from butcher, quack and draper
> At contract price your printers bill will pay;
> And, as for news, you coolly light your taper
> At any useful lamp that sheds a ray.
> Thus doubly armed with pastepot and with scissors
> You may defy the hordes of vulgar quizzers.

No! I am low but not so low as all that.

Don't you read the C and M though. Twon't be good enough, and I shan't feel happy.

Many thanks for your courtesy in stooping to look through my proofs.[10] They shall come up as soon as a gang of reluctant hirelings can be induced to type-set. I've stuffed up the weekly with tales for the next seven weeks, in the order as under

His Majesty the King (baby)
Sleipner-late Thurinda. (sporting)
A Supplementary Chapter (Simla)
The Solid Muldoon. (barrack room)
"Poor dear Mamma" (that's yours)
From the Egg to the Fruit. (Simla)

and another unnamed bantling. I'm most anxious about the fifth.[11]

Now for the tenth time Kadir Baksh[12] has come with tears in his eyes to point out that unless I depart I shall miss the train. All right. Jam everything into the trunks and I'll stamp on 'em till they shut. That's the best way of packing.

Oh the photograph![13] The mischief and all of a photograph. It's come and it's about two feet square and dwarfs everything else in my humble quarters. I believe she sent it with her own sacred hands. It's a whale of a panel photograph. But I forget that you don't know anything about it. Read the letter I wrote a few days ago. I send it in all its horrifying bulk, and you will understand. I'll pack it up into my dress suit – this advertisement-hoarding of a photograph.

In regard to the other letter – don't wither me with your indignation. Once more I remind you of your permission to me to write if there was anything on my mind. I haven't got a mind but it's all the same and a man must have a confidante I suppose. Now I go forth with this letter – that is to say if I can ever get my packing done before six o'clock. My salaam to your husband.

Yours just at present packingly
Rudyard Kipling

Notes
1. To replace Kay Robinson as editor of the *CMG* in Robinson's absence.
2. "The Hill of Illusion": see [22] April [1888].
3. Mrs F. C. Burton: see 26 October 1887. Mrs Burton left India from Bombay on the SS *Sutlej*, 27 April (*Pioneer*, 2 May 1888); Major Burton's name is not on the passenger list.
4. The reason was presumably Sir Lepel Griffin: see 8 May.
5. Possibly "The Strange Adventures of a Houseboat", *CMG*, 16 April 1888 (uncollected).
6. "Play-acting", *Pioneer*, 27 April 1888, initialled M.E., describes the vanities and stupidities of a provincial group of amateur actors.
7. The pseudonym (from the name of one of Job's comforters) with which RK signs "New Songs and Old", *Pioneer*, 30 April 1888 (Rutherford, *Early Verse*, pp. 402–4).
8. Not Budge but Toddie, in Habberton's *Helen Babies*: see 4 April 1884.
9. Thus in copy: "trick"?
10. Of "Poor Dear Mamma".
11. "His Majesty the King", *Week's News*, 5 May; "'Sleipner,' Late 'Thurinda'", *Week's News*, 12 May; "A Supplementary Chapter", *Week's News*, 19 May; "The Solid Muldoon", *Week's News*, 9 June; "Poor Dear Mamma", *Week's News*, 26 May; "From the Egg to the Fruit" was published as "The Tents of Kedar" (part three of *The Story of the Gadsbys*), *Week's News*, 18 August. The "unnamed bantling" is perhaps "With Any Amazement", *Week's News*, 9 June, the fourth part of *The Story of the Gadsbys*.
12. RK's servant, whose name is used in several stories. "He is tall and commanding in appearance and is wholly dependable" (Edmonia Hill, "The Young Kipling", p. 411).
13. Of Lady Dufferin: see [c. 25 April 1888].

To Edmonia Hill, 8 May [1888]
Text: Copy, University of Sussex

Lahore. May: 8: of the year one.

A cool day – the Punkahs stopped, the dust laid – "on earth peace and good will towards men."

Expect neither reason nor sanity under this hand today. "I am not mad most noble Festus"[1] but only a little exalted, and that does not mean elevated though it is ten o'clock o' the night. The reasons for this will appear later on if you have the patience to read them. Your very kind note came in last night: a mort of thanks for it. I am among my own people once more and but for no trace being left of the old home I could imagine that I had never gone away. And yet, for many reasons, not altogether clear some folk are dead – some have gone away and I am both dead and alive but chiefly dead. As a great and special concession you are, if you care to, free to write to me. This editor doesn't bite. He is gummed into an office chair from eight in the morning till six at night and has to work after dinner – in all a full twelve hours a day solid going with nothing in the wide world to show for it except a stodgy and indigestible paper, which most people throw down with the genial remark: – "Oh! Nothing in the C & M. – as usual." I ain't mad as I may have remarked before but do you know Will Carleton's bitterly true lines: –

"Is your son a small unbound edition of Moses and Solomon both?
"Can he compass his spirit with meekness and strangle a natural oath
"Can he courteously talk to an equal, or browbeat an impudent dunce,
"Can he keep things in apple pie order and do half a dozen at once?
"Does he know when to stir up his virtue? Can he put a check rein on his pride,
"Can he carry a gentleman's manners inside a rhinocerous hide?
"Can he know all and do all and be all, with cheerfulness courage and vim?
"If so, then, *perhaps*, we'll be making an editor outen of him."[2]

As you know, they've made an "editor outen of me" for the last week, and I am ruefully contemplating Carleton's ideal by the light of my many shortcomings. However I don't care. I'll tell you my reason later on, when I've answered your note and can turn from things frivolous, such as the running of daily rags to things of importance such as . . . . but I spare you for the present.

You say? What say you? Let me see. Hm – hm – hm – Oh! You find *"Dray Wara Yow Dee"*[3] beyond your comprehension or – violent beyond your comprehension. How could it well be otherwise? If you understood how Pathans think you would be in as evil a case as I; and in that for your own sake I would never desire you to be. I am back among my own folk – the savage, boastful, arrogant, hot headed men of the North; and after the frog like *purbeahs*[4] of the Northwest I like the change. Since my return the Club where I am now staying has been infested with vagrom loafers, snaky locked and vulture eyed, trailing around to pay me their respects. When a ruffianly Biluch or Eusufzori[5] Pathan comes to do this in a not too spacious room he comes with a gift and I am the richer by a quaint silken Bokhariot purse, come down from the Lord and the wanderer who bought it, only know where and a quainter jade necklet of Yarkand beyond the snows. Now what earthly use can I have of a plasma necklet? I know what to do with the little *Kurhesh* I think.

Also, one burly sinner has given me an amulet of rare device and when I told him that I was charmed against all evil he swore outlandish oaths and said – but you would not understand the proverb were it repeated. I am rejoiced to be among the men I understand again. They are not saints but I like them and they pretend to like me – which, after all, is the utmost that a man can expect in this "best of all possible worlds." If you saw these Ishmaelites you would see how my tale is no way overdrawn and, by the way, the incident of the killing is bodily cribbed from a frontier murder case deposition. Jealousy racks them as any violent passion does people with strong feelings, the stronger for being cloaked under the whitened mask of respectability. Read the C and M of the 9th, leader and first page article if you would see what sort of creature the Pathan is.[6] I wouldn't recommend our leading articles as a rule, nor would I counsel you to read the Rag while under my direction. In my zeal of disclaimer, I have dropped a large blot which "please see under" as the Babus say.

Incidentally it may be mentioned that the tucker of a sleeve-edge is open coarse lace that they sew into the neck and wrists of a small boy's clothes.[7] Any fringe or lace at the neck can catch in an earring or the like in the [sketch] same way that a sleeve fringe can. And now are you sufficiently enlightened madam? I have a very *very* tender corner in my heart for little children but it is not often that I have an opportunity for showing it. You see, society does not expect these things from a young man and therefore I am discreetly dumb. The next W[eek's].N[ews]. tale[8] is a cut and thrust sort of sporting yarn devised for the benefit of the "officer butchas who know so much about horses." I hope to have the proofs of *"Poor dear Mamma"* shortly and these go to you for check and countersignature if you will take that trouble. The 5th[9] is the one that I am most anxious about and it rests with you whether the 5th is to be a success or not. I depend herein upon your clemency.

You do well to suggest that the Pi should be whacked for its impertinence in putting in insulting international comparisons.[10] Most improper, I agree with you; but I have been in my readings and training an American for so long that I am perhaps prejudiced.

And so you know who Mrs. Hauksbee is, do you? Mark the sequel of the tragedy! The steamer was that of the 27th and all was well until he, hoping to be sent to Hyderabad (he has all the cheek of a child) hung back for a week and so left on the 4th.[11] It may have been her advice; for she is one of the few women in the world who have a man's ambition beating in a 23-inch figure. Anyhow I know that, knowing what I do of her temper, I should not care to be her neighbour at the saloon table during this voyage. By all things that all men value most, if she had been twenty years younger, and I fear that she will not see forty six again, but what did Tarrion say to Mrs Hauksbee after she won him his appointment?[12]

Notes
1. Acts 26:25.
2. "The Editor's Guests", *Farm Ballads* (New York, 1873).
3. *Week's News*, 28 April 1888 (*In Black and White*).

4. "Easterners": RK's point of view is relative to the far north-west of the Punjab.
5. Thus in copy: the Yusafzais are one of the many Pathan tribes.
6. The first-page article is "Fitzhardy's Murderer"; the leader is "Across the Border. XVIII. The Peshawar Pathan of the Present". Neither is by RK.
7. RK uses "tucker" in "His Majesty the King": in the story as collected in *Wee Willie Winkie* the word is altered to "open work".
8. " 'Sleipner,' Late 'Thurinda' ".
9. "The Valley of the Shadow", *Week's News*, 23 June 1888; in the collected form of *The Story of the Gadsbys* it comes seventh.
10. A leader in the *Pioneer*, 28 April, on Matthew Arnold's "Civilisation in the United States", maintains that no Englishman of taste would wish to live in the US.
11. The "he", according to Mrs Hill's note on this letter, was Sir Lepel Griffin. The topic is the relation between him and Mrs Burton, who sailed from Bombay on the 27th April without her husband (see 30 April 1888), presumably expecting Sir Lepel to be among the passengers. Sir Lepel's name is, in fact, on the passenger list of that sailing printed in the *Pioneer*, 2 May; evidently RK had later information that he was not, after all, on the boat.

    Sir Lepel Henry Griffin (1838–1908) joined the Indian Civil Service in 1860; Chief Political Officer in Afghanistan, 1880; Agent to Governor-General for Central India, 1881–8; retired 1889. He enjoyed a reputation as writer, speaker, and wit. Sir Walter Lawrence calls him "the best known Civilian of his time, able, brilliant, and scornful" (*The India We Served*, 1928, p. 17). Griffin served in the Punjab Government for many years and would have been well known to JLK. He did not marry until 1889, shortly after his return to England and retirement.
12. Presumably not what Tarrion said to her but about her: "If Mrs. Hauksbee were twenty years younger, and I her husband, I should be Viceroy of India in fifteen years" ("Consequences", *Plain Tales*, last page).

To Edmonia Hill, [9–11?] May 1888

Text: Copy, University of Sussex

Lahore

Wednesday morn. *Cras ingens iterabimus aequor.*¹ Driving the old bulgine² afresh and this dear sweet genial station has given me already a fine old headache and a touch of common or Laurence Hall Garden fever. I don't care. It's bound to go off and it has only put in its appearance because I was too lucky yesterday.

This morning's dak bring me proofs in the rough of "Poor Dear Mamma" one copy whereof comes with this to you. I have marked the places where I was more than usually uncertain about my ground but your eye will show you more weaknesses. It's my first attempt at light dialogue and it drags and would bear cutting. Do anything you are minded to with a big bold pencil and be sure I shall obey. I don't want the thing to break down through glaring inaccuracy in trying to reflect a girl's mind. It's an averagely impudent attempt all things considered and I rather wonder what my lady³ will say to it when it comes out.

She writes me by the way – bless her for it – that she approves of the Dufferin business.[4] Therefore it must be good and right and proper you know. My esteemed Parent is grieved to see that I set so little store on that rolling-board of a photo. He is devising a frame for it. It's hardly necessary to point out to him that if my Lady ever sees fit to send me Her photo, out comes Lady D. tiara, pink sash and scowl, to make room for a girl whose shoe strings she isn't worthy to untie. I have exhorted Mr Kipling to make a scrumptuous frame, and I'll take good care that it has an adjustable back to take any size of photo.

A lady for whom he has a tender and viceregal regard has shown Lord D[ufferin]. the *Hill of Illusion* and I grieve to say that his remarks were noteworthy more for breadth than depth. Truth to tell he said something amusing but wrong – wrong as it well could be.

Anyway I don't write for one eyed Viceroys except on occasion.

Something in your letter – two things – have upset me horribly and I demand full explanation. In the first place what makes you hint that that "Incomparable She" is in any way like Tillie Venner.[5] She isn't – she isn't and if she were she has a perfect right to be anything she pleases so long as she is mine. She cannot be aught unlovely and to be sweeter than she is would be a hard task even for her whose foot is set upon my neck. She can't care for all the stuff I turn out. I shouldn't like her to understand it all or to be in sympathy with it. If she cares for a little it is more than I deserve. Again what on earth or out of it is the line you refer to "in the same metre" as the Browning quote which refers to a thing known while the other is only guessed at.[6] Maybe tis your *metier* to hurl cold water à la Gummidge[7] on rhapsodies to the Unknown Her: but I don't like it. Let me have that quotation swiftly for it worries me and just now I am worried with a hundred things. Maybe I did wrong to guess and maybe I arrogated too much to myself when I wrote the quotation. I suppose I *was* over confident and you did well, as an impartial outsider, to remind me of it. But, my faith, it is difficult to be properly grateful for your kindness. Tell me, then, what is "the thing known" and tell me by return of post for the trifle sticks a good deal in my mind – and the more so because I cannot write and tell her. I was thinking about it half last night and that wasn't wise for Reuter had been doing all sorts of things to popes and emperors and such like cattle and I was supposed to have an opinion on the subject. He might ha' murdered every crowned head 'tween here and Panama and I shouldn't ha' cared. Bother that missing quotation! I'll think no more about it for a little time.

Our station is empty swept and garnished and all who have not gone are going to flit. As a wilderness it has its points. As the capital of the province it is rather a fraud. A piano, a violin and a banjo have their home in the Club and when all three are in full blast, I do not feel happy. Piano is a hardened performer but fiddle and Banjo are new and when one is picking out "Marching through Georgia" and t'other forgetting a step-dance life is a Paradise. Three nights ago they vexed me so that I besought them all to join their forces and serenade a sleeping friend. I wanted him to taste a little of my torment. Piano couldn't come but he brought some bones, and between the four of us we made Rome howl to the tune of "When Shepherds watched their flocks by night." Would you believe that the man for whom we had poured out our soulfullest high c's, slept through it all and turned up at mess next morning placidly ignorant! This it is to be a public character and strive to make the world better.

Other than this small incident, there's nothing to tell. I have returned to the old, wearying, Godless futile life at a club – same men, same talk, same billiards – all *connu* and triply *connu* and, except for what I carry in my heart, I could almost swear that I had never been away. However it will pass in time and I look forward as I have never looked to anything in my life for its ending and the relief. Constitutionally I am "of an immense idleness" as the French say and twelve hours a day treadmill don't suit my views at all; but as it all fits with my plans it must be got through and now that I have the Gift I don't care.

"That name was ruler of the dark – Isolt."[8] Tisn't Isolt but it's something even prettier; and Tennyson put the situation beautifully. However you aren't interested in quotation and you are much too good in submitting to be bored by letters of this inordinate length. I believe I *am* a busy man though this outpouring wouldn't seem to imply it but the time is stolen and stolen things, they say who have taken 'em, are always the best.

The twilight has come and the paper has been put to bed with all its imperfections on its head and this letter has been hanging on the stocks for three days. D'you know the length of it? As nearly as may be, two and three quarter columns of the third page of the C. & M. Gazette.[9]

Give my best salaams to your husband and thank him for that most suggestive little telegram. There is a tale in it; but just now there isn't a tale in me: It shall be done later:

Yours very sincerely,
Rudyard Kipling.

P.S.: I have just been called, on paper, an "idiotic scribbler." by an excited correspondent who wants my blood or something of that kind. I am so penetrated with the justice of this remark that I cannot treat it harshly. "They are a queer folk a man – many of him – is the public"

Notes
1. Horace, *Odes*, vii.32: "Tomorrow we set out once more upon the boundless sea."

2. Engine.
3. The first appearance of the unidentified girl whose relation to RK occupies much of the letters for the next month; she then disappears. Mrs Hill treats her as actual. In a note on the letter of 29–30 May she writes: "About RK's love affair – which he got bravely over. The girl was not worthy – she wouldn't marry such an 'ineligible'." Carrington, *Kipling*, p. 112, doubts her existence and suggests that she may be an invention allowing RK to express what he cannot say to Mrs Hill herself.
4. RK's "Song of the Women"?: see [c. 25 April 1888].
5. The frivolous and stupid beauty in "Wressley of the Foreign Office" (*Plain Tales from the Hills*).
6. Probably refers to the passage from Browning's "Any Wife to Any Husband" at the head of "The Tents of Kedar".
7. The "lone, lorn creetur" in Dickens, *David Copperfield*.
8. Tennyson, "The Last Tournament", l. 601.
9. The copy of this letter is evidently imperfect. The text shows no evidence of the passage of three days, and two and three-quarter columns of the *CMG* would contain about 2700 words, rather more than twice the length of this copy.

To Edmonia Hill, [12–14] May 1888
Text: Copy, University of Sussex

[Lahore]

Saturday: "With his best leader hitched to a letter that enquired if he wrote it or who."[1]

I am persecuted by Padres – whoppers – who are firing off texts at me and accusing me of being irreligious.[2] *Moi!* They ask me to refer to Matthew, Mark, Luke and John – but especially Matthew. I *won't* look not for all the Padres in Padredom. I'm going to write a letter; and if fifteen hours continuous in office deserves a reprieve I've earned it. We print late on Saturdays and always try to stuff all we can into the hog-trough – Result: congestion, indigestion, suggestion [sic] and disgust. I've been here since seven and the clock hands are near eleven now. The Rag is horrid unsatisfactory and the men are half asleep and wholly sulky.

A queer sight is an Indian press room on a hot weather night. Ours is about as big as the Mayo (dancing) hall[3] and is lit by flickering dips with a hurricane lamp here and there. The half naked men who turn the big presses look very picturesque in the uncertain light as they loll against the black walls and wait for their call, just like supers at the theatre. Even the old presses look mysterious and ghostly and from right away at the far end of the "chapel" comes the death-watch *tick tick tick* of the type being set up by white sheeted yawners.[4] The ghosts of the dead carry tapers you know. So do these and if they tilt their candles too much the grease gutters on to the type and makes printing impossible. Two or three little boys, who evidently have not the least business here, have curled themselves up on one of the big tables and gone to sleep; the native foreman is nodding at his desk (his turban will get into the candle if he doesn't take care) the office pi-dog that has attached himself to me has followed me across and is sleeping at my feet, and I have settled myself down at an unclean table to wait for the last telegrams, and take the last proofs. It isn't a cool night by any means and there is a mixed flavour of printers ink, baled paper, deodar wood and hot coolie that is not sweet. My own office across the compound is polluted with a day's steady smoking and I felt so creeply in there with the muskrats[5] cutting about the wainscot that I removed myself as much for company as supervision. Can you wonder that these poor beasts misprint? They are all half drunk with sleepihead and they are looking at me reproachfully as they mangle the wisdom of Reuter and blunder among my spider-tracks. Phew! It's hot and I am anything but happy!

Monday. The Revised Budget Estimates turned up at mirk midnight but what could I do with 'em?[6] I wasn't thinking of anything half so uninteresting. Anyways the paper came out; which after all is an immense step in advance when you come to think of it. See now how good providence is to an unworthy person. Yesterday was a day of grief to me. I was troubled with all sorts of fancies and ideas and the more I thought the less happy was I. The weather was vile, the rooms were stifling and I had had no word from My Lady for very long. I couldn't work comfortably and my temper was not that of the angels. So I crowned my misdeeds by a night at Poker[7] – a select poker party in my room – whiskey and baccy and stifling hot lamps – I went out hand after hand and consoled myself with the old proverb about the compensation of being unlucky at cards – I am *always* unlucky. Last night I was thinking of something else and in that abstraction mistook threes for a full hand .... but these things would not interest you. Next morn, this morn, came my reward and I am willing on those terms to lose nightly at that fascinating game. But it would be useless alas! and my plunge into the green cloth is only intended – you know I have a cold-blooded trick of turning most things and experiences into print – to give me material for a poker-tale.[8] To return. My Lady has sent me comfort for the week to come and now I fear no thing. I have a hundred things to tell her but this pen and ink (who *was* the beast who invented 'em?) shakes all. It seemed to me that it was ages since I had last heard anything. The letter came with the heavy double dâk from the South – the main-stay of the paper and that dâk had to wait until I was done – whereby the C & M today is thrown back in all its branches and I have a considerable idea that we are going to miss the mail. Who cares? But as a mere matter of curiosity I should like to know *who* edits the paper,

My Lady or I? I am not quite certain. There's a quaint little turn in *Lorna Doone* where John Ridd vows that he cannot even kill a pig or sell a rick to the factor without asking himself: – "What would Lorna do? What would Lorna think?"[9] I don't kill pigs much but very few things go through my hands without my mentally referring 'em to the Supreme Court – My Supreme Court of arbitration. She'll never see and she'll never know but it is pleasant to do it.

Apropos. Such a queer thing happened this morn. I was deep in the Letter (praise be to Allah My Lady writes a fair hand!) and the "rags" were lying round in unsoiled confusion, when my revered Parent dropped in on his way to *his* office. He's a disgustingly observant man and saluted me with a quotation from one of my own rhymes that I could well have spared: –

> "God save the lad, whence comes the licht
> That wimples o'er his face."[10]

I made answer: – "I'm just settling the first dak and if you bring no "copy" avaunt, *Mon père!*" "Hmph" said Mr Kipling shaking his beard: – "D'you always settle the first dak with that sort of head on you? Journalism must be a finer profession than I thought." Then I heaved the *Gazette of India* at him and he fled. I hate being interrupted in mine Editorial Functions and now, at the risk of boring you atrociously let us be serious. I am compounded of evil elements as Shakespeare saith.[11] Here is My Lady writing to me that she is well and – yes, thinks of me I think – and she is going to amuse herself "as surely is most just"[12] and – well, *do* you think I ought to be so down upon the wretched printer folk just because I am a fool and a jealous fool at that? I don't think she [would?] like me any the better if I mentioned it to her and since it cannot interest you I'll e'en drop it. There is no sense in wishing every personable man dead is there? or desiring that the very wind should not touch her cheek, or that the earth should not look at her. And, *entre nous*, I fancy that she would be the first to open those perfect eyes of hers – (I know now what "fish-pools of Heshbon"[13] mean though I will *never* forgive the singer for the meanness of his comparison –) and say: – "Good gracious! What nonsense." And to this I would answer – "Nonsense indeed. Amen." Let it go then.

Now let me return to reason and see what my scanty budget has to offer to amuse you. Would 94° in the office interest you? It has no charms for me – any more than another weary weary dinner at the L G's[14] for which I am let in tomorrow night. The last was on Friday. There were only six of us and I was prompted of the Devil to scandalize Lyall. However he wouldn't be scandalized and was, for him, almost amusing. Now that his women folk have gone away and he only gives bachelor parties he thaws perceptibly. We have few ladies here and they don't appear in public much. Perhaps that was why I was so [   ][15] left to myself on Saturday evening when one of them said to me "Oh, *do* get me something to drink." I hadn't spoken to any one except men since ten days, and I answered: – "*Certainly, Khitmatgar peg lao.*"[16] Then she went away in a huff and a gang of acquaintances called me a Barbarian. How on earth was I to know whether she wanted water or lemonade or what? She should have named her poison before bothering me. It is well known throughout the station that I have returned "in financial difficulties." That is why I am of an unamiable temper. Ain't they clear sighted these dear Anglo-Indians!

Marsh – Marsh – Let me think![17] Ye – es. Met in Simla, '86. She is a lady of a circular figure with children – lived on the second floor of the Dovedell. Husband in Slawah[18] in those days. Bought my book from the publishers, and asked me to write my name in it, as inscription witnesseth, cribbed photo from my Mamma who keeps 'em in permanent stock I believe. May or may not assert that I gave it her. No use to ask her, as she would tell a fib. If you would like to see her turn pink enquire across the table: – "Usen't Mr. Kipling to tell very amusing stories?" She was an eminently respectable lady with a curious taste for *risqué* yarns. Saw her first at a tiffin at the Simla Bank, and last at Umballa station, making up a bed for the babies on the floor of the carriage which vastly resembled a nursery. Knew her for eleven days in all and found her dull in every one of 'em. *Est-ce que vous voulez des renseignements particuliers?* There's a nice amount of information put into your hand! but I can trust you not to mis-use it. She wouldn't care to look over your shoulder and see, and I certainly don't want to have her angry with me, three and twenty days hence,[19] for my all too candid exposition of her merits.

They are suggesting at Simla that I act in something this year if I can only come up in time. Don't know who suggests or what company but I am remarkably certain that whatever happens I do *not*. I give neither promise nor pledge conditional or unconditional in any more directions and I am today writing to explain in response to an invitation to stay with some folk at Simla that my movements will be so uncertain that I put up at Harding's[20] – that will be near my own folk and not too far from the C[ommander]. in C[hief's]'s where I have some work to do.

But oh me! How long, how bitterly long and hopeless are the days: and the nights are all but as long. 'Tisn't becoming to a man to whine but one does feel so diresomely wretched at intervals. (By the way, it is *quite* decided that we miss the mail this afternoon, and if any ⁎ ⁎ ⁎ ⁎ ⁎[21]

Here came Munshi Newal Kishore[22] all the way from Lucknow with a long long tale of a Manager that he wants for a paper-mill. Blow M.N.K.!: Does he s'pose I keep Mill Managers on the premises. I have soothed him with soft words and sent him off, to my Father on whose head he will sit for three quarters of an hour. Ha! Ha![23] Thus I shall be revenged for this morning's surprisal. The paper has come out and the ferocious blare of a tin horn announces that the old dak horse is going his hardest upon the road that I may not travel – the road to the station. It's a full paper, done with a fuller heart and may the Unpunishable Cherub,[24] whom I have thinly disguised in the similitude of an allegory, forgive me for its blunders.

Notes
1. Will Carleton, "The Editor's Guests".
2. A leader in the *CMG*, 5 May, on religious disturbances in Madras, held that "the plain duty of the Government in India to-day" is "to abstain altogether from active encouragement of conversions to Christianity". RK does not seem to have allowed any correspondence on the subject.
3. The public hall of Allahabad, built in 1879, opposite the Club.
4. This effect is recalled in the opening pages of "The Man Who Would Be King".
5. The Indian muskrat is related to the shrew but is the size of a rat and has a strong musky odour (*Hobson-Jobson*).
6. They appear in Monday's paper, the 14th.
7. When he went to Allahabad at the end of 1887 RK found that "Poker had just driven out Whist and men gambled seriously" at the N.W.P. Club (*Something of Myself*, p. 70).
8. If he wrote one it has not been identified.
9. See the opening of ch. 17.
10. "The Fall of Jock Gillespie", *CMG*, 10 November 1886 (*Departmental Ditties*).
11. He does not. This is perhaps a sample of the "Shakespeare" that RK used to manufacture freely (Alice Fleming, "Some Reminiscences of My Brother", *Kipling Journal*, December 1937, p. 120).
12. Thomson, "City of Dreadful Night", xiii.28.
13. Song of Solomon 7:4.
14. Sir James Broadwood Lyall (1838–1916), Lieutenant-Governor of the Punjab, 1887–92.
15. Blank in copy.
16. "Steward, bring a drink."
17. The wife of H. Marsh, executive engineer, Public Works Department, at Etawah (*India Directory*, 1887–8).
18. Thus in copy, for Etawah.
19. When RK expected to be at Mussoorie, where Mrs Marsh evidently was staying. Since RK was earlier (see 22 April) expecting to return to Allahabad directly from Lahore, he must have had his leave advanced.
20. Harding's Hotel, Simla.
21. Thus in copy.
22. Owner of a large printing press at Lucknow, and of the newspaper *Oudh Akhbar*; called the "Indian John Murray" for his active publishing program, including many translations of Western literature (*CMG*, 2 January 1886).
23. Thus in copy, but RK almost certainly wrote "Wah! Wah!"
24. "The Unpunishable Cherub", *CMG*, 15 May 1888 (uncollected); the cherub is Cupid.

To Edmonia Hill, 15¹ May 1888
Text: Copy, University of Sussex

[Lahore]

Oh! *How* good of you! I've just unearthed the returned proof of "Poor Dear Mamma," embellished and adorned, winding up, characteristically enough, with a lash at my Hindustani.² It is bad, Madam, I admit. If I had only spent upon it the time that I have devoted to other things it would have been better. I should have studied it at Allahabad. All your orders in margin, shall be obeyed, for they are all good and wise ones and give the poor thing a semblance of tone that it did not possess before. "More especially" as the church service says³ "do we thank thee for the allusion to the impossibility of darning, and the right words of the girl who is in difficulties with her dress." *Who* said riding habits lace up the back?⁴ Not I. I'm blind but that at least I know. I meant . . . . Well I've taken it out now, and will deal with the others as directed. Also, very many thanks for the quotation which has relieved me.⁵

Has not the inanity of the past letters impressed upon you that one in my condition is, in some points, stupid beyond words. I can't write and tell my Lady that the matter is all cleared up because she would wonder what in the world I had been doing. And I could only say: – "Been a fool as usual" which is not a pleasant statement to make, however nice it may be to hear. I'll write to her and use the last four lines of "Love among the ruins"⁶ and she can make what she pleases of them can this – Tillie Venner! I am statelily glad to find that you apologize for that but it will be long ere I can forgive you. *Eccolo!* It would seem that she has a certain appreciation for one form of literature for she writes me that it is long between my letters. There's glory for me! You'll only laugh and depart to another picnic, but I am rich. "Long between my letters" or words to that effect. "Tisn't much," think you. "May have been only a rhetorical flourish put in to soften the sting of something that went before." I am not going to believe that and you, Madam, are a cynic. Look you, the first woman in all the world has said that it is long between my letters, and I envy no writer now. My public isn't a *very* large one – I think that I could put my arm round it if I tried very hard, but since the days when "Dante once prepared to paint a picture" (Browning tells the story in his dedication)⁷ there was never public like to mine. What am I to do? What shall I tell her? An I consulted my inclinations I should write every day and all day, till she grew as utterly wearied of the sight of my fist as I am sure you are. As a matter of fact I have to write nearly all day, but it is the other public – the pigs of the Punjab, and they wouldn't quite understand if my office maunderings got mixed up with other things. I shall tell her that it is all her own fault for not writing oftener and then, if she really cares, methinks that will extract an extra letter or two. Prettiest of all, but it is far too sweet to rewrite in cold blood, is what she says of the waiting for the letters. I believe she means it – I know she means it and I bless her for saying it.

I don't wait for her letters. I get one and go on till I get the next, my nose to the grindstone for fear of thinking. When a horrible Sunday comes and I am thrown back upon myself I know how long I have waited and then I get all the arrears of suspense in one gloomy lump. I have written and told her that, save and except her letters, I have nothing – absolutely nothing, and that is a fact. Wonder what my Mother would say if she read that confession! With that touching faith that mothers have in the worst of children, she has written me that "she really thinks the tone of the paper has improved." Bless her dear heart what does she know of the tones of papers? I am here and she sees with the rose coloured spectacles of Love, work that I look at with profound disgust, except when I think of My Lady and go on. But the drawback of that sweet soul's letters is that they are in no sense keepable. I'd as soon think of filing them in my box as I would of putting a seraph under a bell-glass. Therefore, when they are gotten by heart they are reverently burned, anything might happen you know and if a nimble karait[8] captured my toe tonight all the unsympathetic puds[9] in the province could rummage my papers without coming on anything more exciting than M.S. cuttings and old cheroots. And at the same time I would give the little that I am worth to keep 'em. What does Mrs Proudie say: – "Men's insides is made so comical, God help 'em!"[10] I can't imagine a man deliberately keeping sacred letters. If it all died, they would hurt more than any woe. If it lived he would have the reality and the memory. That is if he could repeat the letters off by heart as I can. You will see from this that My Lady does not favour me with any lengthy outpourings. She doesn't gush and I try in my letters to her to keep myself within that decent insular reserve that is the hereditary mask of the Englishman. It's difficult and therefore I come to you in your patience, to set down the many things that I may not write to her.

Hello! The twilight has come again and I must go to take "my ease in my Club."[11] Both are very bitter mockers.

Monday Night: After dinner: a good, old fashioned Punjab evening. Praise be, I've worried through another day somehow and the night is near, wherein – how does the quotation go? – "No man can sleep."[12] A dull dinner enlivened with duller talk until some ruffian started the Shakespeare–Bacon controversy and I rose and fled from the room. Now they're playing billiards next door and a bevy of mild gamblers have just been informed that if they want to play poker tonight they mustn't come into my room to carry out their gambols. A telegram

1. John Lockwood Kipling and Alice Macdonald Kipling at the time of their marriage, 1865; both were then 27.

Telegrams. St Marychurch
Station. Torre.

Rock House,
Maidencombe,
S! Marychurch.

May. 8. 97

Dear Bell —

All I need is the book rights of the Lady of the Snows. I want letters to quote it like anything. The more the merrier. Please let 'em! I didn't know Wallace was doing the Thessaly letters but it caught my mind as a very good bit of work. Races who use revolvers promiscuous are apt to go off at half-cock and incidentally to recoil and blow off backwards. As to the Jubilee, I loathe it. It's about a lot of costers disconnected bits of verse like macaroni, and I can't string 'em on one thread to save myself. After all, it's Cecil's job. Like a fool I've used up my best notions of a scheme in "A Song of the English." But I will try till the last minute

Ever yours
Rudyard Kipling

2. Facsimile of Kipling's letter to Moberly Bell, 8 May 1897.

This old Juno was a settler who had got a degree — and a wife who had got — a degree but as she wouldn't appear in public — she — in a little side in modest schema. The press was under a balcony where one of them drew sketches of the balcony as he appeared in the newspaper chair. This is the ×Kodak Sketches

3. A page from Kipling's letter to the Reverend George Willes, 17 November 1882.

4. Cormell Price, headmaster of the United Services College, Westward Ho!, 1874–1894.

5. Portrait by Sir Edward Burne-Jones of Georgiana Burne-Jones and her children, Philip and Margaret, c. 1883.

6. Alice Macdonald Kipling (Mrs J. M. Fleming), Kipling's sister "Trix", in 1892, aged 24.

7. Rudyard Kipling and his father in India, 1883.

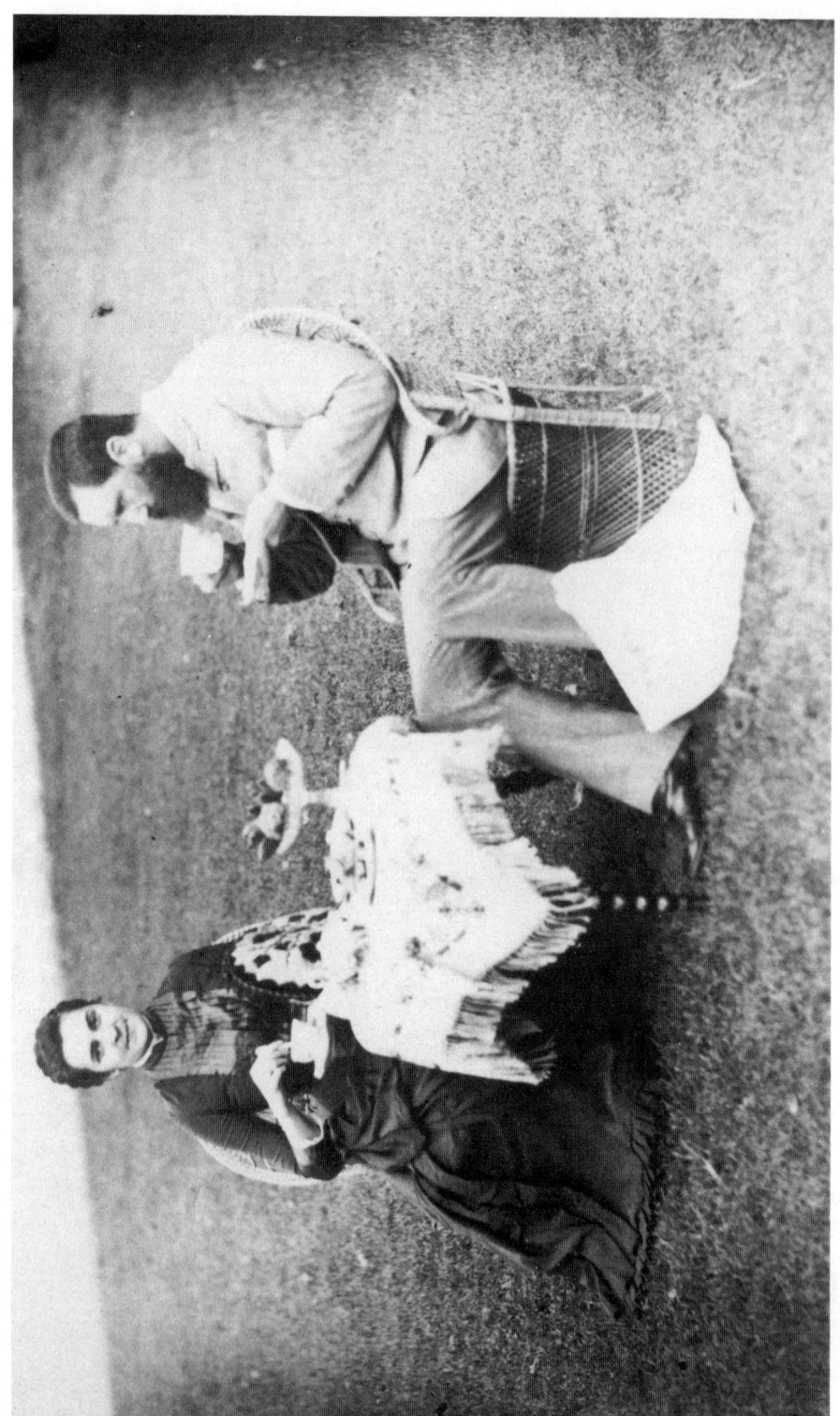

8. Edmonia and Alex Hill in the garden of Belvedere House, Allahabad.

announcing Lord knows what of wars and rumours of wars has just tumbled in. The Jamshidis of Herat have expressed a desire to become Russian subjects and that stormy Petrel Alikhanoff[13] is on the wing again. I s'pose I shall have to grind out something about it later on.[14] What in the name of commonsense have I to do with Jamshidis and complications across the border? I was hundreds of miles away when that pestilent Reuter turned up and he is trying to pull me back again, into the slough.

I won't come. The stint of the day is over and I hold myself as free as one can be when he is tied by the leg and both arms to this sort of toil. Where were we when I broke off – on an intolerably threshed out subject weren't we? Let me go back to it, for in my eyes the world holds nothing better. Tell me how I can tell my Lady to write to me more than she does? It is a large thing to ask for she of course has her own plans, arrangements and diversions; and may be forgiven if my destitution sometimes slips her memory. I had never thought that I should come to live so entirely upon one idea – I never knew that it was in my nature and the knowledge has a little of the bitter in all the sweet. Again and again, I come back to the old question: – "Does she know what her power is over me and if she guessed would she think more lightly of me?" My own pride has kept me back from writing to her point blank: – "For pity's sake write – if it is only a line to let me know that you are still under the same sky as I." She could say with perfect propriety: – "My dear Sir, I write quite often enough" and I suppose looking at it from a philosophical and impartial point of view, My Lady does. Unfortunately I and philosophy have long been strangers. I cannot even be certain that we ever met unless it was in those three dreary years of '85, '86 and the greater part of '87, when I was strong in my own conceit and thought that I knew all that was worth knowing of most things in this world. There is this strange quality in Love that it has in common with Death – the curious and unquenchable remorse for carelessness in the past, for pique and misunderstandings that ravaged the golden time. I don't know whether I ever told you this before. Some time ago I lost a very dear friend in England[15] and, above all the personal sense of loss was the bitter regret for every unkind or unsympathetic thing that I had ever said – for brutal sentences launched with intention to hurt (which is the most despicable form of cruelty) and for a host of other things. I had fancied that those experiences had been put away and would not come back. Here as in many other matters, I am mistaken for I see now in the long nights down here, the whole long list of my shortcomings in respect to My Lady. I have been told – tell me that it is not true – that a woman never forgets whatever and however she may pretend to misremember as the Irish say. I can count up now, under the punkah, time after time when the imps of malice, and perversity have driven me, against my will I know, to say and to do things that hurt – at least I intended at the time (though I repented afterwards and repent now) that they should hurt. What my training may have had to do with this I can't say but that is no extenuation. I am sorry, more sorry than I can say but how am I to make her understand? Face to face I could explain but this paper (I should be ashamed – what *am* I talking of? I do not choose to say, how many sheets of it I have sent to her) stands between. Once or twice she has done me the honour to be a little – just a little (and she had a perfect right to do it and you, forgive me saying so, are not a judge beteween us) severe towards me. Maybe I do wrong in judging the sting of anything I have said by the measure of the pain I received at her hands. There is no equality between us. Hers is the better and the larger soul and exactly as I recognize its superiority, by so much am I humbled for having grieved it. But, you will admit, one can't put these things before a girl even though she be fairest and dearest of all the daughters of Eve.

That last page is enough to bore the eyes out of one's head. You'll get a headache from trying to read it. Let me finish up with a page of sanity.

Yes Madam I have read Cape Cod Folk[16] and it's what they call genre work. Can't say that I care for it much but then my taste in literature is queer. Just now it has been principally confined to blue books of a gay and festive nature – all about export and import tonnage and the racial difference between an Aka and a Madan Kheyl or skittles of that kind.[17] But I've been trying once more to plough through The Descent of Man[18] and every fiber (observe the American way of spelling) of my body revolted against it. To believe in that it is necessary never to have – Hullo! Where is this one-idea'd pen going off to anew. Also I've been taking up some French stuff of sorts – rummy old French books written in the blanking style that I've always associated with the march of the priests in Athalie.[19] But I haven't much time for reading, though you would hardly say so to see the way in which I am writing at length here. By the way I did you a slight injustice in saying that you only had to read three columns of the C & M to get the length of one of my scrawls. This chit, ought to be almost line for line the length of a two-col yarn in the W.N. i.e. 404 lines of about nine words each. This it is to be a pressman and to know mechanically the print-size of your handwriting.

I must turn to and give "Poor Dear Mamma" her final polish by the light of your corrections which have only been jotted down so far. And that shall do [go?] in week after next I think. The next one is a continuation of Otis Yeere[20] and like all continuations of stories inadequate.

So the two on a hill didn't mean anything – didn't they, I wonder, I wonder, I wonder. But if I do that I shall go on wondering far into the night and the Jamshidis are still on hand. This is a thrice-stupid letter but (if this be any consolation) it is no more inane than the one I have written to My Lady – one can't say anything on paper but all the same when one wants to say much the eye of Faith can sometimes catch a glimmering of the meaning. Pray for my sake that my lady will see what I would say and pray – o excessively – that she may not be bored at the extreme prolixity of the saying. You are I know and I conclude. May your life be as pleasant to you as mine is a burden upon me just now. I have raised a headache, and have sent you to sleep I should think.

Yours in all sincerity
Rudyard Kipling.

Notes
1. The copy is dated the 15th, and that date is consistent with all the internal evidence. However, a part of the letter is dated "Monday Night" – that is, on the 14th, 21st, or 28th of May, all of which dates are incompatible with other letters in the series to Mrs Hill. I conclude that "Monday Night" is the copyist's error for "Tuesday Night" – i.e. the 15th. This explanation is the simplest available, and is supported by what seems a more than usual number of doubtful places in the transcription.
2. The story ends with a Hindustani sentence.
3. "Prayer for all Conditions of Men", *Book of Common Prayer*.
4. All this refers to the opening scene of "Poor Dear Mamma"; the bit about riding habits does not appear in the published text.
5. See [9–11?] May 1888.
6. Browning's poem, concluding "Love is best!"
7. "One Word More", l. 32: "Dante once prepared to paint an angel."
8. Among the most poisonous of Indian snakes.
9. (Small) hands.
10. Proudie in copy, but this is George Eliot's Mrs Poyser in *Adam Bede*, not the Mrs Proudie of Trollope's *Barchester Towers*. RK quotes this as one of the mottoes to his "Susannah and the Elder", *Pioneer*, 12 November 1888 (uncollected).
11. Cf. Shakespeare, *Henry IV, Part I*, III.iii.93.
12. Cf. John 9:4.
13. A Moslem soldier (Ali Khan in English style) in the service of the Russians and prominent in the campaigns in Central Asia at this time. His war diaries, which RK translated for the *CMG*, figured in RK's delirious visions during his illness in 1899: see *Something of Myself*, p. 49.
14. "The Rumoured Trouble at Herat", *CMG*, 17 May 1888 (uncollected).
15. Not identified.
16. Sarah Pratt Greene, *Cape Cod Folks* (Boston, 1881).
17. RK produced two leaders on "Indian Trade Returns", *CMG*, 26 and 31 May (uncollected). I have not found anything on the Aka and Madan Kheyls – these were tribes against whom the Black Mountain expedition was about to be mounted.
18. Charles Darwin, *The Descent of Man* (1871).
19. From Mendelssohn's incidental music for Racine's drama.
20. "A Supplementary Chapter", *Week's News*, 19 May; a sort of continuation of "The Education of Otis Yeere", *Week's News*, 10 and 17 March 1888.

To Edmonia Hill, 19–21 May 1888
Text: Copy, University of Sussex

[Lahore] Saturday: even: May: 19:

Now what in the world could ha' happened to that particular C & M? In the best of my knowledge and belief – Lord knows though that I don't quite know what I'm doing these days – I haven't missed a day's rag though I may have missed a dak – perhaps twain. However it doesn't matter. I've come to the end of my first fortnight here and so far as I know and can see, the clouds are beginning to lift. It's most amazing warm and the last few nights have given us a taste of what Lahore can do in its most festive moods. 96° at midnight in a room that was supposed to be cool is rather a scorcher. Howbeit, as I've said before, it has to be put in somehow minus "dancing theatricals tennis and badminton" whereof I trust you are finding as much as you desire.

What's the news? None except that one has died in our station and another is deathly sick, and the rest are talking scandal the one of the other. That's the normal state of Lahore.

By the way what did I say of Mrs M?[1] She was the lady with the babies that I saw off from Umballa two years or two centuries ago and remember that I did more in my last letter than ever a woman did – I spoke the truth. Check every statement of mine by hers and see if they don't tally. By the same token she did not give me her photo.

When I said that you had done me a great service in checking *poor dear Mamma* I meant it. You'll see when it comes out how implicitly I have followed your directions – but in the name of everything *un*quotable *what* portions of it do or did you feel inclined to quote and to whom did you feel inclined to quote? I've got the rough plot of the sequel to it entitled *"With any Amazement"*[2] but as that is purely masculine and deals with a subject wherein I know my ground fairly well you need not be pestered with it unless you choose to ask for it.

As you know I am up to my glaring gig lamps in work of sorts – newspaper idiotcy and yarns – and the more I get into collar the more urgent do the demands of work seem to be. This day I have just come off a fifteen hours spell with my loathing for the occupation ten fold increased and I guess that tomorrow's rag will be rather a curiosity. There are four columns of telegrams lying loose about it somewhere but if I were stretched on a rack of torture I could not at this hour declare what in the world they were about.[3] Now what has happened to my fist! That comes of using a crow-quill.

An ass of a man writes from London saying that he is going to review my last book in the Daily Telegraph – that was a week ago – and asking me whether I am afraid of being slated.[4] Another idiot wants to know whether he can transfer all the soldiers' yarns into a regimental paper – *the Dragon* at Ranikhet.[5] I have told both of 'em that they can do what they "darn please" so long as they leave me alone. Another loon has sent me an anonymous letter complaining of the "flagrant immorality" of the P[lain] T[ales] and asking me where I suppose that I shall go to when I die. I think that I shall write: – "I've made my own arrangements" or better still leave him alone in his glory over a Lost Soul.

That makes all the event[s] of the week save and except a killingly funny invitation to Simla. First comes a letter: – "We've a wing of the house at your disposal" (this is a second invitation, not the one I referred to) "pray consider it at your disposal when you come up." Back goes my answer: – "Thanks awfully but no bandobust,[6] no permanent settlement, no nothing, can't trouble you." And that *chit* crosses a second. "*So* sorry rooms put at the disposal of some cousins." Seeing that the exact date of my arrival ain't known this rather tickled me. I *do* think that people ought to know their own minds when they issue invitations.

Which brings me, prematurely perhaps, back to a very old subject. You ask how things are getting on generally as regards the matter nearest my heart? Many thanks for your kindness seeing all that you have gone through in respect to my ravings. (But I am being made a confidante of now. I'll tell you of that later). I cannot say "excellently well i' faith" for that would be vanity. I will not say "evilly" for I suppose that My Lady is treating me with all the consideration that I deserve. She has sent me another letter and either I, which is very likely, am an ass or she is the least little bit in the world wearied. There seems, or I have ploughed through the letter again and again until there seems, a certain appearance of strain about it – a spacing out of the lines (that's a professional term) and a touch of padding. *Aren't* I an idiot? But a man in my singularly sane condition is never too wise.

I s'pose she was wanting to get away to something else and the letter wound up with a quaint formal turn that at first nearly made me laugh and later on, quite took my breath away – so strange was it to me. There's no breach of confidence in quoting it, so here you are to judge between Her and Me.

"Hoping sincerely that you are not working too hard, though I very much fear it, I am etc. etc."

It's all right I suppose. You know more about these things than I. What do you think of it? The "hoping sincerely" somehow sort o' made me gasp, and the rest of the sentence finished me off. I ain't a judge in these matters 'cause any correspondence that I may have had has always been of one type, the downright direct work business, and Mother

Hauksbee was the only woman who used to write to me en permanence. She neither began, ended nor signed nor dated her chits worth speaking of, and I could use 'em *en bloc* for guidance in anything that I had in hand at the time, in the inkpot line. But Her letters aren't epistles to be desecrated that way and frankly I own that I am the least little bit troubled. Whatever my wisdom in the past on the theory of letter writing, and I believe that I was no end wise – in my own conceit – I confess that this sort of thing was by no means what I had intended, desired, or . . . even deserved. I have written to her in the bitterness of my heart saying: – "What has happened and what have I done or haven't done? Are the letters a bother to you child, or haven't you the time to write 'em" with much more to the same effect – all of which, whether I be right or wrong she'll laugh at – of *that* I am almost sure, and yet I believe that in writing this I do her a great wrong. What in the world ought I to do? Tomorrow, praise Allah, is the Sabbath and I shall have time to get away from that thrice-objectionable paper and think the matter out calmly. You know the thing in the scripture about the generation who "seek for a sign"?[7] I guess that I am pretty much in their predicament, and that my complaint is the absence of the "sign" – of any word that gives me hope to hang on to? or perhaps I am *exigeante*, or perhaps I am a copper-bevelled, nickel-plated, double thonged, lockstick, repeating action FOOL, which is the more likely. But before I forget it all in my own worriment let me tell you the story of my Visitation and Boredom last night and the night before from 9.30 till 1.45 each night.

This in strict confidence 'cause the poor beast hasn't written to his Pa yet!

It was a man[8] of course – a man I used to know very well. He had just come down from Simla where he had been to attend a wedding and in the ten days of his leave – Things had Happened. He called on me at the Club under the pretence that he had just seen my Mother and Sister and wanted to give me latest news. Of course I asked him to dine with me. "Thanks" he said "I'm fiendishly" – but he used the stronger word – "uncomfortable where I am." Seeing that where he was was the mess of his own Regiment I put up my eyebrows and waited developments. My misfortune is that whenever a man is in a row or in love or sick or something he invariably flies over to me to unburden himself whereby my knowledge of the quainter side of Humanity is increased and I am made the repository of many odd secrets – which I keep faithfully as you see. Well he fed with me and I filled him up with Beaune for my own base ends. Sure enough after dinner the murder came out. He'd been and seen and been conquered – had never been so knocked over before and was *quite* certain that it was *pour toujours*. I let him squirm all unassisted until he got to the point 'cause I wanted to note how a man works when he is under stress of an emotion that he is trying to hide. I needn't ha' been so particular for under the influence of a whiskey peg the fountains of the great deep were broken up and he talked! I beg his distinguished pardon, he raved, and all that I had to do was to light pipe after pipe and say "go on my son." He's only six and twenty poor *butcha*[9] and he has it bad – awfl'ly bad and she's the most perfect angel that ever stepped and – Oh ye Gods and little fishes! – She is only seventeen. He amused me immensely in his guileless abandon. "D'you know" said he "I've only been to Simla for ten days and it seems as though I had been out of the station for years and years." "'Don't mean to say so" said I. "How strange now!" "Ah! You can't understand these things" he answered pityingly tramping up and down my room like a caged wolf. He was desperately restless. He recounted to me the details of a little incident which ended in the girl giving him a passion flower – he had that passion flower about him somewhere – and while he talked I strove to keep a decent semblance of gravity. "Have you spoken yet" I said. "No I'm going to wait a month. I don't know what has come over me – D'you know I haven't sworn for *four* days? – and if I find I'm as bad then as I am now I shall go up to Simla if it's only for three days and see what she says." "Are you sure of your answer?" I said. "Pretty sure" he said wagging his head and I groaned for My Lady hadn't sent me a letter for an eternity and a half and I am not of a hopeful temperament – then he descanted afresh on her merits – *his* merits (voilà ce qu'est bien curieuse mais fort naturelle), his people's possible views, his views, his intentions in the future (involving nothing less if you please than a complete change of life and an abandonment of the old regiment) his hopes, his fears for the future (*not* as regarded the girl. He was pretty sure of that) and so on *da capo da capo* till I took him by the shoulders and gently cast him into the outer darkness.

Last night there was evening music – (9.30) at the bandstand and he was dodging around trying to get hold of me. At last I said: – "Come on, then, you maniac" and took him to the club where he began all his lunacy afresh and wound up by dragging out of his shirt-front a quaint old diapered locket in which he had stuck her photo cut out of the wedding group. "It's horrid uncomfortable" he said frankly "but I feel that it's next my heart when it knocks up against me. I can take it out and look at it now and then y'know." Here I went off "pop" for my neck has become used to the thrum of gold lace that carries a certain little bag and I should no more dream of hauling it out to "look at" in "quires and places where they sing"[10] than I should of prancing around on my head. So I laughed and he cussed me for a "brute" and explained to me at great length, the huge and singular advantages of being in his state – all with an air of infinite pity and condescension. And he was so young – oh he was so young! He turned pink and pretty and carried himself as one who had all creation under his foot and incidentally (for he seemed bound on making a general confession of past sins) told me a lot of things about other people in no way connected with this seventeen year old passion-flower kid. In conclusion he said: – "It's so refreshing to get hold of a man who can talk" and I exploded again for I had, contrary to my wont, which is jabbersome, said about ten sentences all through the night.

But the worst came when for the second time I urged him to take himself out of my rooms. He spun round in the verandah and began beginning[11] to congratulate me on *my* engagement! That was too much. "Oh I heard it at Simla" he said and gave me the name of an aged vestal[12] as old as he and though this is mean I'll *swear* that she might have stopped the rumour at once if it ever came from any other mouth than hers. "You ought to sympathize with me" he said hooking my hands. (There is absolutely no limit to this insanity). "I do" said I "for it is manifest that you are not only mad but drunk." Then he went away and left his forage cap behind. He is coming in tomorrow afternoon to pick it up. I shall stay in because I want him for a story[13] (he'll work in beautifully) though some of the things he says are very hard to hear without wincing. From the desperately earnest manner in which he assures me that I am the first person that he has told, I should fancy – (knowing what I do of the man) that his precious Secret is shared by about two thirds of his acquaintances. So far to do him justice I have heard no rumour of it.

This evening (I saw him for a minute) he said that "he was just as bad as ever." He measures his feelings by the flux of *hours*! Wonder what he'd do if he had no confidante except an office table, a hundred hundred[14] chances against him, a barrier to break down and – a woman's scorn at the end of it all. He'd enjoy himself.

Sunday night. The end of an unpleasant day – enlivened by the "Loo", our hot wind, worse than anything that we know in Allahabad, and a dreary drive with a man who is very sick and thinks fit to inflict his sickness of heart on me. So we drove to the burning Mian Mir cantonments and managed completely and effectually to lose our way among the straight drawn roads while my companion called upon the sky to strike him dead. It was a mad sort of drive. The pony was fresh and ran away and we wound up after an exciting stampede by a ten mile trot through an avenue of dusty tamarisks straight into a burning sun-set and a whirling cloud of dust. When I parted from my Jehu he said: – "Pray that I don't live till next morning" and – what could I do? I believe that he is dying of some hideous internal complaint and now and again, his speech shows that he is desperately anxious to hang on to life. My trouble was not as heavy as his; but I could not give him any comfort. I let him talk and I was sorry for him – sorrier than I could say. We have been living next door to each other for a fortnight and up till this time he has never (though I have known him on and off for four years) spoken so freely to me.

And the evening has ended in a mad sort of dinner which in its turn ended by a gabble and babble, and certain men lifted up their voices and swore that there was neither Honour in man nor faith in woman. Luckily for you, you do not know the savagely despairing tone of men's talk at clubs. I heard – what I had often heard before and given no heed to – and it hurt me a good deal. I have just come away from it – forgive my bothering you with my own thoughts – my head in a whirl. "The clubs all over India" – somehow or other that sentence kept ringing in my head as I listened. I know a few of the clubs from the well ordered stateliness of Bengal to the happy go luckydom of Peshawur and I am out of conceit with them all. They may talk and you may laugh – as I verily believe you will – and whatever you or they may do I make my plans as My Lady chooses without regard to any other living soul. If she sends me word – but not without that word – I am hers to command and as I have been in the past. If she says nothing I shall do nothing . . . at least I believe I shall. In her hands – just fancy if she knew – rests the ordering of my life so far as it pleases her to take an interest in it. Down here in the darkness and the heat one is able to think over the matter as calmly as one's nature allows and the conclusion of my thinking is, simply this. As my gay young friend, who is so certain of his ground, says: – "I have never been like this before"; but I write with better reason than he for he has told me – bless his innocent soul! – of all his experiences in the past and I know what mine have been. If I have as I know that I have, so completely come under her power (this again would [not] be a nice thing to admit except in the way of a jest, to a girl) she shall have no cause to complain of my obedience; and, as I have said to her, she makes my plans. What she tells me to believe I will, so far as there is trust in me, believe, and what she bids me do, so far as my poor faculty goes, I will do. I can tell her no more can I? You know how these things go? What ought I to say to her? I dare not insult her with my doubts. I cannot – for she would think me overbold – tell her my hopes. She is a Maiden that I do not pretend to understand and to whom I can only say: – "As you order, so be it –, and if you fail me may the Lord help me." I have learnt in my waiting – more than I ever learnt before – the measure of my absolute dependence upon her. And I was only a few centuries ago dependent upon no one except my own head and my own hand, and the fragmentary literary councils of Mother Hauksbee.

The queerest part of it all is that I have no right to ask whether my trust is misplaced – and that is the hardest burden of all. I must take anything and everything that she does or says as a favour and not as a right and – I am not well used to this. If you have any kin that you take an interest in, pray that they may not go through the time I am enduring now.

Today marks the fifteenth day – one half of the month and every day after is on the right side of the account.

Monday morn: 7 o'clock and a dead still day. Have been up fighting with the week's mail and re-reading all the rubbish that I have written here, and seeing that I have rather a full day before me I'll – in mercy to you – end this scrawl early and despatch it. But I am selfish in this. In my last letter to Her I begged my lady to answer at least six foolish questions that I put to her and by this hand, she has answered never a one. I am going to despatch an urgent line imploring her to write – and write – and write and write freely that I may know that I am wrong in the suspicion that in exact proportion as my fetters are being rivetted on to me so hers are being loosed from her fair hands. Can't you imagine what a cheerful – an invigorating – and consoling belief this is to begin the week with.

Give me what your ideas on this may be – I don't know whether I shall believe 'em if they are consoling and am quite certain that I shan't if they are cynical; and please do not regard me as a more than average idiot.

Yours sincerely
Rudyard Kipling

Notes
1. Marsh: see [12–14] May.
2. *Week's News*, 9 June; this is the sequel to "Poor Dear Mamma" in the periodical publication but is the fourth story in the collected *Story of the Gadsbys*.
3. By "tomorrow's rag" RK presumably means the Saturday, 19 May, number: the CMG came out late on Saturday and so reached its readers on a Sunday. There is only one column of telegraphic news so-called in the issue of 19 May.
4. I have not found a review of *Plain Tales* in the *Daily Telegraph* of this period.
5. Ranikhet was a military sanitarium high in the hills, north-east of Delhi.
6. Arrangement, settlement.
7. In all the Gospels; for example, Matthew 12:39.
8. David Beames (1862–?), commissioned Lieutenant, 19th Bengal Infantry, 1882; promoted Captain, 1893; Major, 1901; retired 1902; disappears from *Army List*, 1910.
9. Young one.
10. Rubric after Third Collect, Morning Prayer, *Book of Common Prayer*.
11. Thus in copy.
12. Miss Parry Lambert: see [25–7] May.
13. Carrington, *Kipling*, p. 99, supposes that RK used Beames for *The Story of the Gadsbys*, but since the parts of that dealing with courtship were already written by this time some other purpose must be in question.
14. Thus in copy.

To Edmonia Hill, [25–7] May 1888
Text: Copy, University of Sussex

[Lahore]

Friday.
 By the way. Have you ever been thoroughly and heartily ashamed? 'Tisn't often that I indulge in that luxury but this night I am and I come to you with the burden of my penitence since – for obvious reasons – I am debarred from writing it to My Lady. I am humiliated, which is not much, and I am thoroughly disgusted with myself.
 I'm a brute. Do you remember what I told you last week about my lunatic ideas in regard to My Maiden of Maidens. Being by nature a cussed idiot I must needs go and write to her almost if not quite as strongly as when I put the case before you. And I've got an answer which in the language of your country makes me "feel mean". She points out and to do her dear head justice she is uncommonly right in what she says that mistakes and misunderstandings are bad enough when they can be set right by verbal explanation.
Saturday. Midnight. Whewww!
 That must stand for a sigh of relief for I have just put a rabid friend of mine into his cart. Your letter of Friday noon has arrived. So many thanks – Indeed "tha'anks awf'lly" for it! The man was a fiction was he? I've had him under the lens since 8:15 this evening. Now for wholesale breaches of confidence! His name is Beames – David Beames – son of Beames,[1] Commissioner of Burdwan or who was before the Babus got him jumped on. He is Adjutant and Wing Commander in the 19th B[engal]. (or P.) L[ancers]. stationed at Mian Mir: went up to Simla to attend the marriage of his oldest friend Captain Saunders to a Miss Temple, daughter of Dr. Temple, V.C., Secretary to the Surgeon General and, while up there, fell in love with Miss Ethel Temple aetat. 17: a maiden with untidy hair, sallow complexion and large bovine eyes for I have seen her photo, which he wears about his foolish, foolish neck. I do not say that the names are fictitious. You have done me sufficient honour already in calling the whole a lie. (Nasty word that, but it takes up less space than "fiction") and you may check 'em by the Army list.
 B. is not mad. He is generally insane and to the best of my belief (who am I to pass judgments on men?) will continue to be so till the 17th or 18th of next month when by hook or by crook he goes up, so he swears with perfectly uncalled for blasphemy, to speak his mind. I have been listening to him patiently at this table and he has given me a fair amount of good material, for he was more than usually expansive. The quaintest thing – though that I was prepared for – was to watch the boy's Pride kicking against his love, and to hear the everlasting

cuckoo cry: – "She's only a girl of seventeen – she's untidy – she isn't very pretty – but she's the only woman in the world for me." I heard again from his lips all the extravagancies that I had read of in books, and was immensely edified at his *naif* astonishment at the fact that all the world had changed for him and the glory of his old pursuits had departed. "There's *the Duchess* going to foal" he wailed "and I don't care – I don't care. I'd been looking forward to have the best colt in the Punjab . . . only eleven and a half days ago. I don't care for my dogs – I don't care for my horses." Then he cussed tremendous!

I set down some of his more excruciating sentences for future use – they'll all be worth weaving in some day – but these I will forbear to bother you with. They were as mad as anything I have ever heard for he was learning Humility and a lot of other strange things and sweated and winced like a colt under the cavesson[2] for the first time. I was in no mood to spare him for many reasons – *imprimis* because I had had my own words thrown in my teeth with an *imprimatur* more terse than flattering and less truthful than either. May be I shall be punished later on but I gave myself up to the full enjoyment of the moment and tried to see how far my words had weight on his mind. I might have worked on so much sculptor's clay. First I pointed out gravely and seriously the "excessively ephemeral existence" of all attachments, the chances of other men mashing round the place and taking that young heart, and the Honourable Necessity of allowing a young girl her choice before forcing a hasty passion on her. Thereat he squirmed for the gift of speech came down upon me and I wanted to see what would happen if I used it. In the end he snorted which is as near as a man gets to sobbing and, while admitting the cold justice of my arguments, called me all the evil names under the sun. I had flicked him on the raw neatly and to the full of my power.

Then I changed my tune and sang a prettier song – sketching the Primrose Path of Dalliance step by step from the tonga flying up hill to the cool of the snows, to the hot-headed avowal at the back of Elysium (verily I told him the quietest spot to go to) and the end of all things – the Glassy Sea of a Perfect Matrimony. And he rejoiced – the idiot – and slapped his leg and swore just as vehemently as before (his four days abstinence from evil language seems to have sent him on with fresh zest) but this time more cheerily and having played him through the moods I let him rest and talk; though I was sorry that I had not hurt him more in the first *chukker*.[3] I believe that I was possessed of one or two devils. I know that when I put him out on the stroke of twelve I went to my room and, as the Amer – as people say – "kicked myself" for having been a brute and a Judas. "It's so awfully good of you old man to let me pester you in this way" he said. But he has given me the material I want and if I can catch him after his engagement (men are entirely different to women in their almost brutal outspokenness) his carcass will give me more flesh for the dissecting. The pity is that he's a common type and unless I run a silver thread through the web, even the cloth I shall spin will look poor and commonplace. However it's great good luck just when I'm running low for subjects. He's dining with me again on Tuesday – he, D. Beames, Lt. 19. P.L. whom I am treacherously deceiving with a false sympathy and a lying condolence.

And the other story was also a "fiction"? Shall I ever be able to discharge my full debt of gratitude to you? The tale went that I was engaged to Miss Amy Parry-Lambert daughter of Colonel Parry-Lambert R.E., in the P[ublic].W[orks].D[epartment]. accounts – an animal who can dance divinely but whose teeth are all false. I remember the time when they were tusks till her stricken Mamma[4] had 'em pulled out and "Amy" looked more presentable. That was a year after pretty Mrs. P.L. went to meet her daughter at Bombay and wrote ruefully to a friend "Amy is with me – and Amy will always be with me." Unless there be bolder men in the world than I have ever met "Amy" always *will*, for she is a judgment of the Lord sent to punish her Mamma, and the horror is that through all the grotesque ugliness of the daughter shows a faint and distorted likeness to the handsome well preserved mother. Barring this one accomplishment of dancing – learned at the expense of subalterns who wished to keep on good terms with her Mamma – there is nothing in the curiosity. She can neither sing, ride, play, play tennis, walk gracefully or talk of anything and she is verging upon spinsterhood being several years older than I. The only fiction in this case is the set of false teeth – but even they are pathetically patent.

Perhaps I ought to have had more forethought but forgive me. It is not every day that one gets the lash of a lady's riding whip across the mouth . . . . and it stings. In future be assured that you shall not be troubled with any more "fictions".

Sunday morning. Now what have I done? Squabbled with the only confidante who takes the trouble to read my ravings. Mrs. Hill, I apologize humbly before I go any further. Will you overlook the rudeness and hear what I have to say about My Lady. She, if you will believe it, is no fiction. Did I say two pages back that her answer had made me feel mean? I spoke the truth but she has sent me another letter that has – never mind. I have tried to be soberly and seriously calm over it, but it's no use and I don't think that I should like to be calm if I could. She is of all people created the sweetest and the best and, again and again I'll write it, I am her servant. Am I altogether a lunatic in your eyes as the luckless David Beames is in mine? I wrote hard things about her and – which was much worse – to her last week and she has repaid me very prettily first by making me penitent and after by lifting me up to her side and making me happy – ever so much happier than I deserve.

And her second letter – think of that second letter! – is as delightfully womanly as she is herself. But I can't write what I feel. My pen won't obey me today. It has its little fits and starts you know.

Remind me that in future I must comport myself with seriousness and gravity; because I love and (now descend upon me with all the scorn you can compress into one letter) because I am loved again. My Heart and I are both, I fancy, changed since last we met but changed in one respect only – for we have grown more serious. At least so it seems to me. Looking back now even to the latter stages of the new life, I can see that much of my passion was leavened with insincerity and doubt, and – here the unfortunate gift came in – scorn and distrust of myself. I didn't know it then but I know it now because the doubt has gone and with it the insincerity and I find myself standing nearer to her than ever I did before. I don't know whether you will see exactly what I'm trying to express. Let us see for a moment whether what Mrs Malaprop calls "an allegory on the Banks of the Nile"[5] would make it clearer. Once upon a time there was a lily – not a common lily like those in your garden – but a splendid tiger-lily and it grew, contrary to the wont of most lilies, on the walls of a house. And a man came by that way and saw the Lily several times and it interested him for he was an amateur botanist in a small way. "It would be nice" he said "to add that Lily to one's collection" and he waited for the Lily and told it the truth that it was the loveliest flower under heaven. But there came a day, when a warm wind blew and the moon was nearly at full and this Royal Tiger Lily bowed her head for just one short instant and the man saw down and down and down into the golden heart of the Lily. And that cured him of any desire to "add the specimen to his collection". He discovered that he belonged to the Lily and the Lily said: – "I belong to you" and then, to anticipate, there was a shine in the tents of Kedar[6] for the Tiger Lily was . . . . gone.

Allegories are unwieldy things. I've got mine all mixed up and, after all, you couldn't understand.

I will be rational and reasonable for a short time. Let me see what your letter says.

You're quite right about the unreality of A Supplementary Chapter.[7] It was written mainly to drag in all the moral or immoral reflections on things in general and Simla in particular, but there was a case not very long ago when a woman of Mrs. M's stamp got a man out of a very tight place by giving him a piece of private information that she had wormed out of a member of Council – old General Wilson[8] I think it was. But these things belong to the old days and: – "I shall never again be friends with roses"[9] as the song says.

Very many thanks for the interest that you so kindly take in my scribblings. Here's a programme card: This week "Poor dear Mamma":

To Edmonia Hill, [25–7] May 1888

next "With Any Amazement" being a faithful pourtrayal of the agonies of Captain G's wedding day – dialogue between himself and his best man. Third, "The Garden of Eden",[10] to conclude the Gadsby set – an audacious sketch of the Mahasu dak bungalow five days after Captain G. has taken the bride there and the two young creatures are settling down to face life together and stand all bewildered and alone. The quotation for that is "And ye shall be as – Gods."[11] Later on when it's republished in book form people may like it. The W.N. is only the experimental medium and but for one pair of eyes, I should knock off the series. After that will come either a rude Barrackroom yarn, or the "Ballad of Boh Da Thone"[12] – both of which I'll send to you in advance. I'm running 'em fine in point of time and may not be able to incorporate all your suggestions but please mark on the duplicate proof and I'll treasure it against the book form.

Here comes the W.N. and I see afresh how much your hints have improved the "P.D.M." I had to cut it down by two inches to fit the bed of Procrustes. It's nice to dance in fetters. "Give us sentiment, give us fun, but . . . keep within 404 lines." Those are my riding-orders. Behind those stories ought to come a three-panel sketch of a native state – "The redemption of Gokral Seetarun" giving a few interesting facts about the inner life in such a state as Patiala for instance.[13] I think it will be rather queer reading. All these things will be sent away in time for the time is near when I mustn't be bothered with proofs littering round the place.

Then – to sweep up all the fragments – my publishers write that the P.T.'s and other books are selling like anything and the Times of India – who has no reason to love me – gives me a decent review as per sample enclosed.[14] "Feminine delicacy of style" tickles me when I think of some of the things that I have put into Mulvaney's mouth. Furthermore, Hunter my own W.W.[15] has risen in the West and wishes to be taken *au grand serieux*. Tisn't good for Hunter to be so taken and I am preparing a little *bandillero* for him which will appear in the *Pi* and will hurt him a few.[16] He'll know my skin on a bush as the Irish say for in the old days he was good to me and showed me one or two tricks of the pen and once he struck at me and got me very neatly. I like, I admire Hunter immensely but . . . . not as a statesman.

You'll see what sort of stuff it is and I fear that you won't approve of it any more than my Lady will. Of course the old rag has been pounding on as usual and I've had my hands full of "rubbish and filling up stuff" as an indignant missionary writes. You've no notion how the missionaries hate me. One lunatic wrote me a letter proving the evil state of my soul, and the vileness of the C & M for not putting in a sectarian letter of his. He wound up with: – "But the missionaries do not require the support of any paper or individual who plays the contemptable (*sic*) roll (crossed out and *role* put in) of a 'pleaser of men' for they are strong in the support of the Holy Ghost. Yet woe to the individual or paper etc." I wrote back referring him to the support of the Holy Ghost as I regretted that the C & M's support was pledged to the preservation of the Queen's peace. He's hopping mad now and says I'm a blasphemer. But what *could* I do? The man was altogether unfit for publication. Many gay and festive letters have I had but that was about the funniest.

There's no news from Simla – no news from anywhere except an occasional growl at the heat. You say it's hot enough in all conscience with you. The heat here is maddening and gets worse at night. In the day one can force oneself into work and not notice it but in the night there is no such relief and so one kicks and knocks about "till the day break."[17] I never was particularly lovely to look at but I am not nice now, being a sort of delicate sea green turned up with purple. It doesn't look so irridescently prismatic as it reads. However today marks the entry into the fourth week and I count the hours to the end. My chief is somewhere at Darjiling and I expect a letter from him daily advising me of his movements. Today is the 27th – there are thirty one days in May aren't there. With each dak comes a line from Simla sketching with singular force the beauties of a meeting with my mother who writes very sweetly and prettily. There'll be some fun later on at Simla. "And I beheld great Heie's [Hera's] angry eyes."[18] How does the quotation go?

But Beames is the man whom I pity most now. He heard about a man going up to Simla to have three dances with Miss Temple, at least that was the way her married sister put it. Do you know what that demented loon did. He dragged out one of his ponies, this was at 10.30 p.m., and rode about the country till two in the morning – from Mian Mir to Lahore twelve miles. The pony was naturally indignant at being hauled out of stable at that ungodly hour and David had to fight with it most of the way. He said that it did him good for every time he gave the pony a rib-binder he felt that he was taking it out of the innocent harmless Blennerhasset.[19] Next day he discovered that Blennerhasset didn't know any one except the Temple girls in Simla and that the three dances were *not* part of a conspiracy to wreck his hope, his peace and what I am led to believe he calls his heart. Your view of the reticence to be observed in these matters is perfectly just from the woman's point of view. But as I have already said men are largely otherwise and this Beames boy has I believe told me as much about himself and his feeling as he himself knows. To me this is curious because my first instinct under similar goading would be to lie, and lie, and lie. So far as I can see from his case and others, my temperament is exceptional. There is another fiancé (a pukka one) in the station. One Reuter[20] of the Forests just engaged to a *not* too young girl who has gone to England to get her *trousseau* and he is as placidly pleased with himself as Beames is alternately exalted and depressed. "We are going to Dalhousie and shall be in Chumba for four years at least. We are going to have a house in the backwoods etc. etc." I envy that man's frame of mind when in the interval of Beames's visitation he walks me round the bandstand and burbles confidently.

But, you ask, why do men tell me these things? I can only answer because they do – somehow or other since the days of my first tail-coat men of all kinds have shot rubbish into my patient ear . . . and I have turned that rubbish into the shekels of the money changer time and again; for it is wrong that a man should waste time and attention and pure priceless sympathy over a *man* for nothing. Is there by the way any euphemism for "skunk" in the English tongue. I wanter walk around an' "yit git a holt uv that word Maise."

Great Scott! Here's dak time already and I've no end of other things to write about. Can't miss this dak though: so it goes with all its imperfections upon its head and I'll write and bore you to extinction tomorrow.

Yours sincerely:
Rudyard Kipling

Notes
1. John Beames (1837–1902), Indian Civil Service, 1858–93; he had been reassigned to a lower position in 1887 when he was shown to have accepted loans from a native, against the rules of the Civil Service.
2. A nose band used as a curb.
3. A period of play in polo.
4. According to Mrs Hill, Mrs Parry Lambert was the original both of the older woman in RK's "My Rival" and of the "Venus Annodomini" in the story of that name.
5. Sheridan, *The Rivals*, III. iii.
6. For the "tents of Kedar", see Song of Solomon 1:5.
7. Published in the *Week's News*, 19 May.
8. Lieutenant-General Thomas Wilson (1819–86), a hero of the Indian Mutiny, was Military Member of the Supreme Council, 1881–6.
9. Swinburne, "The Triumph of Time", stanza 45.
10. Not published until 16 June, nor does it conclude *The Story of the Gadsbys*.
11. Genesis 3:5.
12. "The Solid Muldoon", *Week's News*, 9 June; "The Ballad of Boh Da Thone", *Week's News*, 1 September 1888.
13. I find no evidence of this.
14. 17 May 1888.
15. Sir William Wilson Hunter (1840–1900) was in charge of the statistical survey of the Indian empire, which produced the *Imperial Gazetteer* and made Hunter an expert on all points of Indian information. He was on the Supreme Council, 1881–7. He retired to England in 1887 and was much consulted as an authority on India.
16. "To the Address of W.W.H.", signed R.K., *Pioneer*, 1 June (Rutherford, *Early Verse*).
17. The title of a sketch just published by RK in the *CMG*, 19 May, describing heat and fever-tormented sleeplessness (Pinney, *Kipling's India*). Cf. Song of Solomon 2:16.
18. Tennyson, "Oenone", l. 190.

19. No likely Blennerhasset appears in the *India Directory*.
20. A. M. Reuther, assistant conservator, Jhelum (*India Directory*).

To Edmonia Hill, 29–30 May 1888
Text: Copy, University of Sussex

[Lahore]

May: 29:
There was another letter threatened yesterday but – for which O be joyful! – I could do nothing except stoke the Rag, and that inefficient well. The last few days have been real fine old Lahore scorchers and as a natural consequence I have been anything but fit. Worry and bother and waiting and such like don't improve the health but why they should attack the heart I really am at a loss to see. I've been enjoying a royal series of Palpitations. They are great fun. As a rule they begin in the middle of the night when the heart gives a slam like a shutting door and retires from its duties. Then you sit up, literally and figuratively, and wonder whether it ever intends to beat again. When you have quite decided that it is the entrance to the Valley the thing kicks and you feel as though a railway train were being shunted in your left breast. So – Bumpp! After two or three such stunts the heart begins to make up for lost time like a watch with the spring out of order. Then you get up and gasp and walk about and think of anyone you ever loved or hated until the rush slows down and . . . . you are let off this time. Worst of all is the want of sympathy from the Doctor to whom you appeal for digitalis and so on. "Heart!" says he. "That's not heart! You've got indigestion and you're overworked. Go slow and don't worry." That's an easy prescription for a man to give. T'ain't so easy to follow.

And all these eccentric performances account for my not writing yesterday. I'm worried – every way that a man can be – in a small line; and if I thought that press work was to be taken seriously I'd be much more worried. But these things don't matter. They'll pass in a few days more at the outside.

Wednesday night. Is this epistle ever going to be finished and is the weather going to relent? I believe Lahore has beaten its record for the past seven years and am quite sure that it has beaten me. 90° at four in the morning is not fair. But what was it I started to write about – or rather to continue my letter about? My Maiden's letter I think if that be what has been in my mind for the past five days. I have reflected long, deliberately and, so far as in me lies, calmly, and the heft of my conclusion is that I am more than ever in Love with her; because I believe that I have done her a wrong in doubting her. You say in your letter that it is ungenerous of a man to doubt. Be it so but in your judgment make some allowance for my training. I have not been brought up to believe and my own nature is a miserably self-torturing one – perhaps because I was put through a trouble generous enough for a strong man at a time when I should only have been thinking about my books. I have written My Maiden a letter and come to you to be told whether I have written aright. In effect I have said – "I am wrong and believe that I am wrong and it is for you to forgive me if you will; but my excuse must be that we have been very very long apart and the pen is an untrustworthy servant when there is anything of real moment to be explained." I have said a good deal more than that but I spare you. You see – I can only repeat an old argument again – that she has a deeper hold upon me than I had ever expected for, in spite of the professional tendency to gush that means nothing, I am very loath to "give myself away" as your country folk say.

Now I have given myself away to My Maiden Peerless as I have never given myself away before. And the natural pride of a man (that it is a pitiful thing God knows) makes him exacting in proportion to his surrender of himself. I have tried to make her understand this in my very bald and disjointed explanation and if she does not understand – so much the worse for me. But I think she will because she is as clever as she is lovely and has all the insight of a cultured woman quickened by whatever measure of liking she may have for me. Is that vanity to assume that she does care a little? I suppose that I shall never know until the end whether she does or whether she does not; and it is a serious undertaking to ask one who has so much to give up to consent to come to me. You see that my notions are as comprehensive as they are magnificent – so far as I myself am concerned. What is your opinion about 'em. Never mind the other points that I have referred to you for consideration. Answer me simply that. In your opinion is it worth while for a man to change the whole tenor of his life and his views – whatever they may have been – for the future of a girl's sake. I have not much to offer and a woman is as quick to see that as a man. I dare not even believe that I have in the years to come even a name for the making; for I have too profound a distrust of myself. Would she be justified – knowing what depends upon her answer in saying – always sweetly and graciously: – "Not good enough" or words to that effect? You know these things better than I do. What is your opinion? My own I know but if I can sufficiently command myself I have no intention of making it known until I am in a position to say: – "I can keep to India or put it behind me as you think best to order me." And that will be, if all goes well, after I have done my work in Bhamo[1] and go home in February of next year.² It is a fairly severe test, but if she comes through it unflinching I have no great doubt that I myself shall be found wanting.

You see the awful result of being alone down in the plains. Here am I building castles in the air at a rate that would disgrace a Clapham Jerry-builder and every one of those castles can be knocked into nothing by her sweet breath – if she chooses. It's rather a grim alternative isn't it? But it's always best to look things in the face.

Here comes a wire from Simla announcing that I shall be relieved on the 9th and able to get away on the 10th. I am a bit curious to know whether I shall ever be relieved for my *budli*³ is at Darjiling – hundreds and hundreds of miles away and they say that there is a strong attraction of some kind to keep him there. Isn't it shocking in this century of respectability and Light?⁴ But this is a secret.

I must send him a wire to see if he is really coming and then resign myself to five days more of torment than I had anticipated. How beautiful a thing it is to be the bondslave of a daily rag and the servant of a fair maiden at the same time! I was looking over the file of the C & M the other day and checking it by my own sensations. *I.E.* The leader on Indian trade returns⁵ appeared when I thought in this manner about Her: and the Dragooning of the Native Cavalry⁶ when I thought in that manner of Her till at last it seemed that the whole paper blazed with the secret and I shut it angrily with something very like a blush upon my expressive jowl. I am – no I am not a fool but I am not what I was. She has made me something quite different. Now I really must address myself to the serious consideration of the dak. Ugh! The beastly, naked, official dak! Give me when you have time a verdict upon all that I have written above and remember if in your mind I am (to use a vulgarism) counting my chickens before they are hatched I have at the least allowed an ample margin of time before the process of hatching out and the subsequent flitting from the nest begins, and judge me leniently for Her sake. I don't suppose that I amount to much anyway but I'll wait until I know what she thinks of my qualifications or otherwise and stand or fall by them.

Write soon, for I have rather a wish to learn what you think and believe me

Yours sincerely
Rudyard Kipling

P.S. Thank your husband many times from me for his photo-article which appears in a day or two and pray him to send yet another of the same.⁷ They are sure to be interesting and to lead the amateur into the paths of knowledge.

Notes
1. In northern Burma; much in the news after the Burmese expedition of 1885 and still the scene of guerrilla fighting. Evidently it was intended to send RK there as a reporter.
2. It is not clear how long ago RK had formed this plan: in *Something of Myself* he puts the determination to try his fortunes back home as early as 1886 (p. 65), though in his letter to Kay Robinson of 30 April 1886 he denies any such intention. In any case, it seems to have been understood between him and Mrs Hill from an early moment in their acquaintance that he would make the attempt, and he stuck to the decision.
3. Substitute or relief.
4. Robinson had been married in 1887.
5. "Indian Trade Returns", *CMG*, 26 May (uncollected).
6. "Dragooning the Native Cavalry", *CMG*, 14 May (uncollected).
7. Hill contributed three articles under the title "Amateur Photography in India. (By 'Full-Plate.')", *CMG*, 1, 9, and 12 June.

To Edmonia Hill, [1] June 1888
Text: Copy, University of Sussex

Civil & Military Gazette, / Lahore.

Dear Mrs. Hill.

Many thanks for your last note enclosing verdict on "poor dear Mamma" whereat I laughed a great deal. If the public will only wait till it reads "With Any Amazement" and then goes on to the "Garden of Eden" there will be some fun methinks. Meantime there'll be no tale this week, because they're putting in C. Russell's Death Ship[1] in big lumps and that squeezes me out. However I shall take my revenge with a gross barrack room yarn[2] as soon as the road is free.

What I wanted to tell you is this, not altogether inopportunely, for I have a whole bundle of yarns that I should very much like to discuss with you. I am at issue with a man at Mussoorie pahar[3] about those thrice objectionable plain tales. The story would be a long one to tell but the heft of it is that he don't answer my letters and I'm afraid of the tales being quoted in the Beacon "which is a rag I don't see; thereby causing me damage in sterling rupees".[4] Now I value my dibs and shall also value the opportunity of seeing something of you and pestering you with notions. This is the sad result of being clever and professing a mild interest in my work such as it is. I've written to your husband asking him if he could tell me where to put up. I guess he'll know that I should hardly take rides in a red-hot tin omnibus for the sake of getting speech of a hill-paper editor only. If not, show him this letter.

As to when I come up I cannot say. My chief is wiring wildly for an extension of leave but I don't suppose he'll be later than the 12th anyhow and I shall be able to argue with Dr. Hawthorne[5] (a nice name for a nasty man) a few days later; and by the same token to submit to your critical eye a notion for my next new book,[6] now being builded up. I have won an enemy in the Pi this day by my nonsense about Hunter and to-day's C & M will win me some more.[7] This is a sad thought and reminds me that I must return to the Rag.

Yours very sincerely
Rudyard Kipling

P.S.   Please incite Mr. Hill to finish the photo articles ere I leave.

Notes
1. The story, by W. Clark Russell, was advertised in the *CMG*, 7 May, as being "specially written" for the *Week's News*.
2. "The Solid Muldoon".
3. According to Harbord, *Readers' Guide*, p. 282, "chee chee [that is, Eurasian] for the hill station of Mussoorie".
4. I do not know what RK may be quoting; nor have I been able to find a file of the Mussoorie *Beacon*. It is described as a weekly, "a serio-comic journal of Social, Political, and Literary Topics" (*India Directory*, 1890).
5. Dr R. Hawthorne, BA, FCSC, PhD, editor and proprietor of the *Beacon*.
6. *Soldiers Three*.
7. "To the Address of W.W.H." in the *Pioneer*. An article on "The Industrial Era in India", *CMG*, 1 June, makes fun of Hunter and of Sir George Birdwood; the ideas of both men were opposed to those of JLK, who might just as well as RK have written the article, and perhaps did.

To Edmonia Hill, [5–6] June 1888

Text: Copy, University of Sussex

[Lahore]

Tuesday night.

Many and rather edifying have been my experiences in the last few days. The dust storms and a go of the real fine old crusted Lahore fever have been rather dwarfed by what came after. But in some measure I was prepared for it.

I told you what I had written to My Lady – did I not – some days ago? I have been honoured with an answer over which my heart was a good deal cut into, and my head chuckled rather grimly. What I wrote was, from one point of view, insanity and, from another, system. I preferred to look at it from the last stage and My Lady – who shall blame her for this? – from another. So she answered me in a spirit of pure wisdom which did her infinite credit. I could hardly have expected more and indeed might have received a great deal less. "Did I understand you aright" she says in effect "and have I answered you according to your folly." Follows a direct imputation of "hedging" which is instructive as showing the amount of confidence which she – for whom I would willingly die though I *know* that would do nothing – has placed in me. Luckily for you, Mrs Hill, you have no concern, as you need have no sympathy with, the incidents of a not too quiet youth. Nor have you any grave sins for the repenting, so it is useless to advise you to pray that you may not have your *laches* in the past paid back with compound interest when you would give your soul to be honestly believed.

Wednesday: night: No, I will not growl. After all – had I a right to expect anything more. There's an old English proverb which says: – "He yt playeth at Bowles must need meed rubbes." Proverbs aren't comforting but it's good to have a saw to fall back upon in time of need.

However these are details with which I shall take leave to bother you when I come up to Mussoorie. K[ay].R[obinson]. is here on the 12th and I have to wait a day to get him comfortably settled in the editorial chair leaving on the 14th morn and arriving at Mussoorie pahar on the 15th. Giving over a daily rag demands alas! six hours continuous talking. Think o' that now! I grieve to find that I have conducted the C & M on the simple rule of destroying everything – important or otherwise. Now I have a pack of yelping correspondents round my heels. *Mais je m'en fiche*. What do I care for correspondents of papers? As a poet of your land says:–

> "What to him was joy or hope?
> What to him was love or care?
>
> He'd slipped on a keg of washing soap
> The girl had left on the stair."

I walk with my feet in several thicknesses of clouds and my head! Mon Dieu where *is* my head? I don't know. I think I must have left it in the C.M. office. Simla pahar yawns before me after I have settled with the festive Hawthorne at Mussoorie. By the way. How should I know what the hotel arrangements of Mussoorie are? "Gallio cared for none of these things"[1] and again saith Tennyson: –

> "Ye think the rustic cackle of your bourg
> The murmur of the town."[2]

Am I *very* mad? You also would be mad Madam if you were coming out of the Desert into green fields with the thirst of centuries it seems, upon your tongue. I am going up to Simla *foi de gentilhomme* to make love to Miss Edge!!!![3] Hereon my mother with brutal frankness: – "I shan't hinder you but she's a yellowish green just at present and like a daguerreotype only shows in certain lights. It doesn't say much for your taste."

But to return to calmer scenes. The fifteenth sees me at Mussoorie and I am writing today about my rooms which I book for the 14th in case my chief arrives on the morning of the 12th when I shall gabble over my instructions and flee on the morning of the 13th. Hope I shall be in time *not* to see those tableaux.

You do me too much honour in your allusion to the W.N. I told you why it was crowded out and I told you – did I not – of the public that I write for. Next Saturday brings an unadulterated barrack room horror as vivid a contrast to Poor dear Mamma as I can make; I fear that my public will say: – "Ugh! the little beast. Where *has* he been" just as one rebukes a dog that goes into muddy places. After that I sketch the life of Captain and Mrs Gadsby down to the time where she nearly dies[4] – I've been occupied in her killing for some days – and that is a nasty scene in a death-room, with her husband, and she alone in the face of death. I don't know whether you will see anything in it but I'll guarantee the authenticity of a certain amount.

Hunter's verses were alas! marred by the *us* instead of the *E*.[5] I own it with grief but you – "What do you know of Dicksee's pictures?"[6] It came to me like a flash when it was all over and Chesney who is a scholar had not corrected it. I sit corrected but it will hurt all the same. At least if it don't it will be the first thing meant to hurt that had failed in my hand. Observe the vanity of youth?

I can't write any more because I am too restless for anything, but send me an answer to this letter as soon as possible. I shall have a good deal to tell you when I come up if you can spare me the time and most of all I need to take council with you about my maiden's letter. You will have to advise me upon it and be assured that I will follow your advice. But all my trouble in that matter is not easily to be put down on paper.

Yours sincerely,
Rudyard Kipling

Notes
1. Acts 18:17.
2. "The Marriage of Geraint", ll. 276–7: "the murmur of the world".
3. Ethel Laura, elder daughter of Sir John Edge, Chief Justice of the High Court, Allahabad; she married Major Stuart George Knox in 1893.
4. "The Valley of the Shadow", *Week's News*, 23 June.
5. In the final line of "To the Address of W.W.H." RK writes "*Doctor doctissimus*" for "*doctissime*".
6. Minnie says this to Captain Gadsby when he compares her hair to something in "one of Dicksee's pictures" ("Poor Dear Mamma"). Sir Francis Dicksee (1853–1928), popular painter of subject pictures and portraits, especially of women.

To Edmonia Hill, 12 June [1888]
Text: Copy, University of Sussex

[Lahore] June: 12:

I have been sitting in the midst of a web of letters and wires – chiefest those of a person called Wutzler[1] (nice vegetarian name, something like turnip-tops) who has booked my rooms at the Charleyville from the 14th to the 21st. A-men! My chief came in this morning – not much the better for his month – five week's outing – and to him I have given over amid scenes of wild confusion. Now I've to drag my duds together somehow and clear away tomorrow morn. When does this land me in Mussoorie pahar? Shortly after the arrival of this note I think, for I am hardly likely to stop to play on the road. By the way there is a thunderstorm at Simla accompanied by heavy rain and much lightning. I hope it is clearer in Mussoorie. I am more than sorry to learn that you are not quite well and was surprised to find that you had retreated from those tableaux. Howbeit let us hope that you will be better ere long for, by my faith, I have a many things that I should like to discuss with you if you have the time. But of these more later. I've got to pack. And goodbye till Thursday morn.

Yours very sincerely
Rudyard Kipling.

Note
1. H. Wutzler, a Swiss, was manager of the Charleville Hotel, Mussoorie, where Mrs Hill and her husband were now staying, and where RK spent 14–21 June, on his way to Simla. Mrs Hill describes it as "one of the best places in India, wonderfully situated in the Happy Valley with glorious views of the mountains and with the snowy range always visible" ("Extracts from Hill Diaries", typescript, Cornell).

To Edmonia Hill, 22 June 1888
Text: Copy, University of Sussex

At. "Craigsville": Simla: 22:6:88

One gasps after a plunge through cold water – and boiling hot air is much the same. I had no idea when I turned myself into a coy tobacco-scented purdanashin[1] in that unspeakable dandy,[2] what torment was brewing for me below. The dun[3] was not so bad albeit there was a heavy mugginess upon all the land which I mistrusted. It was in the Siwaliks that the trouble began and one by one I shed all the least important portions of my raiment till I sat "clothed in white samite mystic wonderful"[4] on the box seat of the dak gharri[5] and smoked the cheroot of memory and deep thought. Have you ever come through the Mohun pass by the light of a three-quarter moon? It is like hurrying through miles and miles of platinotype photoes[6] – all as soft as velvet mixed with cream. I don't know my geography a little bit but on one side of the road ran what in happier times had been a big river. It was nearly dead and its bed was as white as a bleached skull except where one little surviving trickle of water wandered in a Godforsaken whereshall-I-go? what's-the-next-turning? sort of a way all alone under the moon and whenever we halted to give the horses breath this miserable torrent – current rather – moaned and sobbed and chuckled till I felt that if I didn't do something I also should follow suit. So I seduced the driver by dint of rupees and sweet words into letting me have the reins and seldom I should think has a gharri been more queerly steered through the Mohun pass. Once we were nearly wrecked on a culvert and once we nearly managed to get into the river ('twasn't *my* fault – the horses wouldn't turn the corner decently) and once we fell among bullock carts but nothing serious happened and we dropped into the burning heat of the Saharunpur plain much earlier than was either right or proper. I had two hours of fierce heat to pull through at S. Station and I filled 'em up by language neither refined nor polite.

There was no sun at Umballa – nothing but a thick venomous haze of burning heat. The landscape – if three bullocks and a stretch of mud can be so honoured – showed as through a November fog but the brasses of the gharri burnt, the paint blistered and the heat struck both from above and below. Then I remembered with a great distinctness that it was the longest day in the year and – so it was. Can you imagine me spread like a mayonnaised lobster and very much the same colour in an air-tight coffin pouring *chagals*[7] of water over myself. They didn't do any good for the heat dried up everything twenty minutes after application. I passed the stream where I was all but washed away last year[8] and it was a bar of white powdery dust adorned with sullen sunbleached boulders. There was no coolth anywhere till I was close upon Simla and never once in all my journey did the low trailing dun clouds lift themselves. I guess when the end of the world comes it will be in that sort of burning vapour.

Howbeit right *at* Simla there was relief though the clouds shut out all view and I seemed to have come into a land of ghosts. Two of 'em were very real – my Mother and sister to wit – and those dear women received me with joy and torrents of questions that never waited for replies and replies that were drawn forth by no questions and kisses that had nothing to do with either questions or replies. It was a pleasant home coming but what touched me more than all was the folly of my small terrier – parted with and forgotten seven months ago.[9] She heard my step, this fat white waddler, and was the first to come to me with ecstatic wriggles and jumps and bounds and fawnings such as dogs use to fill in their lack of speech. Then she promptly foreswore her allegiance to both mother and maid who had petted her and fed her as no dog has been fed I am sure, and for the rest of the evening would have nothing of any one but me whom she nuzzled and whimpered over, thrusting her nose into my hand and demanding imperiously that I should notice her. None of us thought that she would remember and I own that I had quite forgotten; but she belied us all – dear little beast. In a moment of expansiveness I said egotistically: – "I shall think better of myself henceforward." "Hear him!" said the Mother. "Anyone but a man would have said that he would think better of the dog." Whereby I knew in verity that I had come back to the old life and the ways thereof. But not wholly, for it is owned that I am no longer ownable and only a visitor in the land. The Mother says that is so and the Sister too and their eyes see far. "You belong to yourself" says the Mother and the Maiden says: – "You don't belong to us at any rate" and even in the making of this confession we come together after the wreck of the old home on a new and pleasant platform. My main anxiety – forgive my boring you with these details – was to see that they were comfortable and herein I find everything good; for they have settled in a pleasant nutshell which they have made pretty – though they complain of the defilement of my tobacco smoke (the 4 [sic] have been knocked off) and the litter of my office boxes. My rooms of address are at Hardinge's hotel but since Craigsville is next door I do not stay in them.

There's nothing on in Simla beyond little things because the Court – Gawd's trewth the Court! – is in mourning till the 7th January – so far does the death of an Emperor reach.[10] There won't be any dancing till that time by which I shall be thinking of turning my face Allahabadwards! Saw Allen this morning deep in affairs of newspaper policy and did gravely talk business with my tongue in my cheek and the Smile of the Respectable Dependant upon my brow. Saw the Daguerreotype[11] – whity green – coming down the hill. "So glad to see you – Come and help me to make some horrid calls." Nothing would give me greater pleasure said I and so waited until the 'rickshaw had dropped well down the hill and then fled in an opposite direction to write my name in the L[ieutenant].G[overnor].'s book and devise means whereby I should not meet Ethel Edge for the rest of the day. Trix confided to me that she (Miss E. *not* my sister) had caught a rheumatic cold through sitting in a wet saddle (touch o' comedy in that) and was "absolutely unintelligible besides being nearly invisible dear boy." It needed no Ghost from Heaven to tell me that. Called also on Mrs. Napier[12] whereof you have heard and she was out as was the Great Mrs. Allen,[13] and then retired to Peliti's to refresh. There I learnt that the conceit of the men in Simla this year was "positively disgusting" and if a woman wanted a man to go for a ride she generally addressed him thus: – "Would you care to go for a ride with me Mr. So and So if you have time this afternoon and have nothing else to do." Simla is progressing. I remember in '84[14] when the supply exceeded the demand men used to grovel around for rides a week ahead and think themselvs awfu' lucky if they didn't charge down the Mall four abreast. Haven't seen the Crusher[15] anywhere but am likely to meet him this afternoon when I'm told off to escort duty with my Sister and Peliti's at the end under pain of death. She's going to use me a good deal she says while I'm up and I am quite amenable to her discipline. In another week or so I'm out at Mashobra at Buck's place[16] – a pleasant country house where we shall eat strawberries and cream all day long. Meantime I have a small pile of dinner-invites to sort out and arrange and a fair collection of Simla yarns. This casual note is only to let you know that I am more or less arrived here and shall be grateful for any sort of a letter from your hand. So far Simla don't bite on the tongue to use a disgusting smoker's simile. Do you think it's likely to improve?

Notes
1. A woman in *purdah*: screened or curtained.
2. A sort of traveller's chair, like a hammock slung from a pole and carried by two or more men; used in the Himalayas. The traveller sits sideways or lies on his back (*Hobson-Jobson*).
3. The Dun (or Doon) is a great valley lying between the Siwalik hills and the outer escarpment of the Himalayas, on which latter Mussoorie stands. The distance from Mussoorie to the railroad at Saharanpur is 55 miles.
4. A line that recurs in Tennyson's Arthurian poems, e.g. "Morte d'Arthur", l. 31.
5. Mail cart.
6. Prints in platinum-black, by a recently developed process.
7. Water bags.
8. Described in RK's "The Longest Way Round", *CMG*, 30 September 1887 (Pinney, *Kipling's India*).
9. This was Vic or Vixen: the "seven months ago" marks his departure from Lahore to Allahabad in November 1887.
10. Frederick II of Germany died on 9 March. "January" in this sentence may be a copyist's error for July.
11. Miss Edge.
12. The wife of Lieutenant-Colonel George Vernon Coleman Napier (1843–90), 1st Dragoon Guards; commanding at Rawalpindi in 1888.
13. The wife of RK's proprietor, George Allen; they were married in 1876.

14. RK was at Dalhousie rather than Simla in 1884; the mistake may be the copyist's.
15. According to Mrs Hill's note on this letter, this was Tom Edwards, an officer in a Border regiment.
16. Sir Edward Buck (1838–1916), in the Indian Civil Service since 1862; Secretary to the Government of India, 1882–97.

To Edmonia Hill, [24–5] June 1888
Text: Copy, University of Sussex

[Simla]

Sunday.
When will these hotly vaporous clouds lift? I am anxious to see the sun again once more and oh it is anything but cool in these parts!

There's nothing to tell unless the Diary of a bad boy be of any interest. Today I ought to ha' been picnicking at Mashobra with the Allens – and a walk home in the moonlight with "Maudie" (Mrs. Allen) who is getting disgracefully stout and [   ]¹ the Baby² ought to ha' made her younger. However I declined because of my Mother and Sister who, to tell the truth, refused to hear of my going. Never were two severer Janitors³ to welcome one after long absence, and not often two sweeter.

An extensive tramp by the side of my mother's rickshaw yesterday afternoon made me the richer by several priceless tales and – alas! most of the scandal of Simla. Here's one moderately tame anecdote the flavour of which is lost in the putting upon paper: – They were two half-castes of excessive scrubbiness and she wore a Miss McMullen habit with a violet-lake or crimson madder tie. Anyhow 'twas a blood thirsty combination and startled her True-Love's horse when they rode along the Ways insomuch that the beast bolted – bolted savagely. She followed after, bumping and panting and, just before the adored of her heart was neatly shot into some body else's garden she was heard to murmur plaudly:⁴ – "Ge-orge! Ge-orge! I wish you would not go so par-tic-u-lar-ly fast!" To appreciate this properly you should understand the nature of the half-caste and this I am rejoiced to think you do not do.

Also, there is a Demon of a child here who has picked up Language from her Pa and uses it with a deadly facility and fluency. In vain has her mamma tried to check her. She persists in the speech of the bargee and her last performance rose to the dignity of drama. She was alone – a stone got into her tiny shoe, and, the Devil tempted her. She stopped in the middle of the road and said gravely to her nurse: – *Dam! Dam! Dam! 'Ell! 'Ell! 'Ell! Now* you may tell Mamma." Would you believe that "Mamma" smacked her horribly.

Last night Mrs. Napier whom you know by name came in for coffee after dinner with a budget of the letters of Lord Dufferin's mother[5] (he's making a collection of 'em)[6] which she was under oath not to reveal. Naturally she read 'em to us and we shouted for they were of a grave absurdity. (That's a healthy blot but I always was untidy.) One particularly fetched my coarse soul. A key had been lost and the loser wrote to Lady Dufferin about it. That Lady gravely excused herself from any search on the grounds that she had left the big house-door key perdu among the lesser bunches – with the result that all the keys in the house had amazingly increased and multiplied! She would segregate the big key and *then* investigate.[7]

The excuse for writing this fantastically absurd farrago of nonsense was "that she had several important business letters to write and no time to devote to 'em." I liked that. It reminded me of many of my excuses for equally long letters. That book will be amusing when it's finished. I was told off to walk home by Mrs. N's 'rickshaw under a gorgeous moon but she preferred walking on her own feet and wouldn't wear a hat – all of which was very pretty and nice but I couldn't help thinking that a woman who would betray a viceroy's confidence for fun couldn't be *exactly* the woman to begin talking to by moonlight. So I clamped myself up and she discoursed amazingly on the various emotions of the soul, the supreme necessity of truth in Literature (she didn't say daily life) and a host of other things. When I had carted her into her hotel I departed and sat upon certain railings bareheaded and in evening dress, and smoked out a cheroot and a half while I reflected on things in general and particular. I'm glad that she has begun this season's acquaintance by a breach of confidence – the door-key of that witty Irishwoman shall shut all doors and more than Mrs. N. ever intended.

This evening I'm to go to tea there to meet a "globe-trotting heiress". I can understand a man globe trotting *for* an heiress but I can't see why the dooce an heiress should want to globe-trot. Is she so awfully ugly that they must export her to "India and the Colonies" before anyone will look at her? Seems like it somehow; but I shall be enlightened in an hour!! Other than this I have nothing to tell. There's a woman here who has been christened the "Vulgarian Mendacity" – she's all that and I commend the name to your notice in case you ever want anything hard to fling at a friend. We've a good stock of nicknames up here – the Virgin Mary (!!) Sis Cow (this is brutal) Alphonso the Page, Alonzo and the Fair Imogene, The Shadow and the Substance (a thin man and Mrs Marshall that large woman) and many others; but my egoism makes me forget that they would not interest you. I'm out of everything now and shall be till the end and unless the Domestic Tyranny under which I groan runs me out to *Bluebeard* at the Chief's tomorrow, don't go to the theatres. By the way Hobday[8] *is* so funny! You know what we heard at Allahabad fort one night – The *Silver Wedding* etc.? Well, that and the *Happy Fatherland* and *Gunga Din*[9] appears to be his repertoire and Simla is finding him out. I came up to find that Trix knew all his songs – had heard the *Silver Wedding* three, and *Gunga Din eight* times at various houses and had in vulgar parlance been pulling that young man's leg till he said enthusiastically: – "Oh! It is a *glorious* thing to have gifts. You know I'm not only a mere musician I'm a painter too etc. etc." Then said Trix: – "And there's the Anglo-Indian novel of the future to be written". "Ah yes" said H. "I shall do *that too* someday when I have time." Then my sister crumpled up and laughed but he never saw. But Simla, exacting Simla, says that they want something new from him (you must always give Simla something new if you expect her to take an interest in you. In that regard the city is feminine) or they will go on. I hope Bluebeard which he has already given on the piano all over Simla will be a success, for his sake.

Monday. Hi! She was an Heiress undesirable! A Miss Deighton[10] or some such name who will never see thirty three again. She is deeply impressed with the East and is a most matter of fact female with a penchant for Zenana Missions[11] and an inexhaustible stock of wonder for the trivialities of our daily life. Says that our surroundings are "all so scriptural." I had my nose in a tea cup when this bolt came from the blue and deserve the V.C. for not incontinently choking and disgracing myself. Thereafter along the Mall by the side of my sister's rickshaw meeting acquaintances at every step for all Simla was going [to] church. Among others the divine, the radiant Miss P.L.[12] who turned a dainty brick-red when I saluted her with empressement. The Boojum has (in a moment of weakness such as a tender maiden of seven and twenty summers is liable to) asked the Maiden how she would like her (grammar is mixed I fear) as a sister in law? "Very much indeed" said the Maiden "if I had a lot of brothers – to spare." Now there is a coolness between the Boojum and Trix. The former says that the latter laughed at her. I think that there is some truth in the charge.

You see I am babbling of the merest frivolities and those not even interesting. By the way do you know the rhymed version of the epitaph on Lady Edge's tombstone.[13]

> Here Lies L —— a E —— e
> Who tried to be good.
> 'Was inclined to be naughty
> Though *much* over forty
> And – did all she could.

I think it's rather brutal myself but when a lady gives herself away in double handfulls what can one do? Mrs. Allen who is Miss Edge's nominal chaperone does not very much approve of having that colourless potato on her hands – and Miss E. sees this and leads a lonely bib-and-tucker life somewhere upon the higher spurs of Jakko with a governess and a baby – or is it two babies?

P.S. Holy Moses! I've forgotten my share in the dance![14] Who was that long *janwar*[15] who sat opposite me at table, next to a little woman with a strawberry and cream complexion? I've forgotten their names but he appeared to run the show and I want to know what I owe. Please ask.

R.

Notes
1. Passage obscured by ink blot, according to note on copy.
2. Perhaps one of the Allens's three daughters.
3. In the sense of "door keepers".
4. Thus in copy. The word is not in the *OED*.
5. Helen, Lady Dufferin, one of the three famous and beautiful Sheridan sisters, granddaughters of Richard Brinsley Sheridan. The other two were Mrs Caroline Norton and the Duchess of Somerset.
6. Lord Dufferin wrote that he hoped to "publish a selection of my mother's letters" but I cannot find that he did (see his introduction to Lady Dufferin's *Songs, Poems and Verses*, 1894, p. 3).
7. Cf. Lady Dufferin's "A Few Thoughts on Keys": "a very small bunch of [keys] left in any confined space during a few months' absence on the part of their owner, will be found, on his return, to have colonised the whole drawer" (*Songs, Poems, and Verses*, p. 281).
8. Captain (afterwards Colonel) Edmund Arthur Ponsonby Hobday (1859–1931), Royal Artillery; ADC to Lord Roberts at Simla, 1888–9; author of *Sketches on Service during the Indian Frontier Campaigns of 1897* (London, 1898); retired 1911; rejoined army in 1914. He was the author of *Bluebeard*.
9. The first two of these were by George Grossmith; who wrote "Gunga Din" I do not know. A writer in the *Kipling Journal*, December 1934, remembered an "old Indian service's song" called "Gunga Din". Kipling's verses of that title appeared in June 1890.
10. I have not identified her.
11. "Zenana" means women's quarters.
12. Parry Lambert: see [25–7] May 1888.
13. Sir John Edge, the Chief Justice, married Laura Loughborough in 1867; she died in 1936.
14. At Mussoorie.
15. Animal.

To Edmonia Hill, [25–6] June 1888
Text: Copy, University of Sussex

[Simla]

Today brung me the Garden of Eden which has been accepted by Mrs. K as "extensive and peculiar." It will have to be altered again I fear before it is fit for book form – but that I should like to talk over with you. I'm doing absolutely nothing with pen and ink just now – am in short forbidden to bother. It's an easy thing to a man of my temperament to lie in a big verandah amid a regiment of skew-eyed geraniums and look across the hills and – do nothing. I like it awf'lly – oh yes horrid much. You know that quote from Tennyson: –

> They hoard and eat and sleep,
> And oft some brainless Devil enters in
> And drives them to the deep.[1]

I feel like the Gadarene swine sometimes when I reflect on the number of hours that each day carries in its bosom, and the unpleasant trick, that each hour has of being composed of exactly sixty minutes – neither more nor less. Maybe the time will go more speedily at Mashobra, whither I take my way on Thursday and remain till Monday or Tuesday. Mashobra is our city of refuge when Simla gets hot and stuffy and dusty as it is now.

Tuesday. Something is going to happen to the weather. There is a mutter among the hills and the clouds are piling up like dissolute cotton balls. It's abominable stuffy. Last night went to *Bluebeard* at the Chief's with the Maiden and we both behaved disgracefully – laughing rudely and immoderately. In truth 't was very quaint and funny and Hobday deserves all credit. Spent all this morning writing a critique for the C & M[2] until at tiffin Mrs. Napier turned up with some more of the Dufferin letters and made me laugh till it was time to go out and lunch at the Allens where I met one of the Allen boys – they're all so alike that I don't know the differ – and a Mrs. Nicholson[3] well known in Simla and generally called "Victoria by the grace of God" on account of her exceeding stateliness, a Colonel of sorts and The Inexhaustible Baby, over whom A. drivels fatuously. He looks older and more bloodless than ever and she is taking a marvellous likeness to her hook nosed brother[4] – the cuss in the Indian Council.

It was a dreary dull tiffin only enlivened by an attempt on the baby's part to be vehemently sick. I guess that it felt that the company needed excitement so it stirred up its little inside with the stalk of a hollyhock flower and . . . . *apres moi la deluge,* or a fair imitation of it. Babies are horrid little brutes and I don't approve of 'em. They should be suppressed by all the appliances of civilization. In the afternoon went for a walk with the dog and met the Viceroy coming back from tea with Mrs. Napier. He was beastly affable in his dim shortsighted way but I wondered what he was going to do about the Residentship of Kashmir. Ten minutes later he buttonholed Gordon-Young[5] – but this is becoming professional. I'll stake my ears that Mrs. N. made him take Parry Nisbet[6] the Commissioner of Pindi – a barge built old Colonel who adores her – for Kashmir. She's a woman who never forgets anyone who has bowed at her shrine. None the less, I may have libelled her wickedly.

It's evening now and the English mail has come in. I've just seen it at the library. That foul sink the Pall Mall Gazette has quoted, all incorrectly, a fragment from my *Song of the Women*,[7] – at least I think it's this week's paper but I've forgotten all dates except a few.

10.30.p.m. Your letter at last. Came in just before dinner when I thought that all the daks had been delivered and that you had undoubtedly fallen sick of a headache or gone to a sketching club or something nice and sociable of the same order. Where shall I begin to reply? At the blind avenues that were never trodden by my remarkably cornsome feet or how? As you say there was no time – at least none that was not otherwise employed and seeing the extent to which I bored you I hardly regret that our explorations were not wider in scope. Assuredly they led us far enough. There is an idyllic touch about your eating blackberries which amused me mightily. Fancy the stately Mrs. Hill – "her pretty lips with blackberries were all bestained and dyed and when the darksome night appeared they laid them down and died," as the ballad of the Children in the wood says.[8] Surely it's rather early for blackberries and I myself disapprove of staining one's mouth – except with tobacco. Here in Simla we eat strawberries and cream. Sir E. Buck hath promised me all I can absorb at Mashobra, on Thursday – just a week since I reached Simla. By the way tonight is one week since the Charleville hop and by a curious coincidence a subscription dance at the Town Hall (Simla refuses to mourn for Frederick however much it be ordered to do so). Our house stands in the great inarched trend of the main Simla hill where all the lights shine like the lights of Gibraltar. Just now I can see the Town Hall lit up joyously and every now and then the wind brings the grunt or pant of a waltz across the valley. By my faith, I was better employed at eleven o'clock seven short days syne. Mrs. Allen was surprised to find that I was put off tonight's dance and being a genuinely matronly woman put it down to the sudden transfer from the plains to the Hills. "No Marm" sez I "Corns!" and "Victoria by the Grace of God" looked shocked. It's very funny to hear a dance going on by fits and starts from afar.

Your sketch of the American girl is delicious and has made me chuckle.

You have, I regret to see, only put in her queries and none of your replies which must ha' been much more edifying. A scene from "Patience" did she say? I'm thinking it was more a scene from "The Pirates." *Qu'en pensez vous*? Deuce knows you were anything but pleased when your dress was torn but – this is a man's saying – 'twas all your fault. By the way talking about Americans there was a girl of your nationality here last year who was tipped out of her 'rickshaw spinning round a sharp corner. Our men go as fast as they can and a swiftly turned 'rickshaw is very liable to tilt. Well she turned out like Australian mutton from a tin and a man dropped from his horse and hastened to pick her up. She wasn't mad – not very that is. She wiped the dust from her maiden cheek, surveyed the overturned contraption and the apologetic coolies with deep disfavor and said icily: – "Ha-ow pahltry," meaning thereby "How Paltry!"[9] Her assistant, he told me the tale, exploded with laughter where he stood. It exactly described the unnecessary gêne of the situation, the smash and the abandon of flying raiment and the ignominious thud upon the Mall. There are no Americans in Simla this year but they say that one is coming later, a mission female o' sorts.

Here's the last sheet of my second page of nothingness and *won't* you be wearied? I've got to breakfast somewhere or other tomorrow. Mother knows. *I've* forgotten and have to dine at the Simla bank and meet a lot of variegated idiots, winding up with a second visit to *Bluebeard* if my Mother is well enough to go. Otherwise I am let off – to smoke peaceably in my own room and go on with my operetta.[10] Those be all my engagements except a tramp to Viceregal Lodge tomorrow forenoon to call and tell lies! Which, as a matter infinitely more important, reminds me that you consider me a "fiend." May be I am – may be I'm not. My profession don't lead to the cultivation of the higher virtues – at least not many. I don't know what I had said about the dog in Allahabad. Certainly I had forgotten her (not *him* as you write her down) long or ever I had reached Simla. But she is awful devoted and refuses to let me out of her sight and my conscience pricks me therefore.

But, all the same I *had* learned humility and oh it is a hard lesson for a young man to get by heart!

The Crusher[11] ain't here. I s'pose he's gone to Murree. Tell Miss R. this and see her hop. What was the draw at Murree that that giddy butterfly should fly north five hundred miles to look for it? You know, I believe. I know that I don't enlighten.

I have left myself no space to refer to the Scheme.[12] *Am* I still for it? You know that, if it is possible, I most assuredly *am*. By all means and every means Yes, a hundred times and let what may be, be. I too shall be glad when my time comes, tho' at present I have all the ordered felicity of our domestic life to content me, and our queer brutal interchange of thought and work to enjoy. But I have made a discovery – that thought is little and work less; and this is a dark saying. I want rest somehow and here in Simla I think that it is not easy to come by. A great wind is lashing our pines with a sound like the sound of the tide on the beach and it smells as if there would be a storm before the morning. I've a notion that the revellers in the Town Hall are about at their seventh dance for the show didn't begin till after ten and it is now hard upon midnight. They'll all get very wet before they reach home.

I know "Paul Sterne."[13] 'Tisn't a wholesome book by any manner of means. Have you read any of George Macdonald's[14] works – or Besant's[15] whose disciple I am? One is mystical and the other practical and G.M. is the mystic. But the night wears and behold I have touched the eighth page without a single line worth reading. That comes of being away from the chastening discipline of the collar. All salaams to your husband. Here comes the rain across the Hills. Good night.

Notes
1. Parodied from "Ulysses", l. 5.
2. This appears in "Social Simla", *CMG*, 30 June (uncollected). RK quotes a quatrain from the piece – "a recent Simla burlesque" – at the end of "The Man Who Was".
3. The former Victoria Dillon, wife of Major W. G. Nicholson, now Assistant Adjutant-General at headquarters in Simla, later promoted general and knighted as Chief of General Staff.
4. Sir Charles Arthur Turner (1833–1907), Member of the Council of India, 1888–98.
5. Colonel George Gordon Young, Commissioner of Jullunder; he succeeded Parry Nisbet at Rawalpindi (see next note).
6. Lieutenant-Colonel Robert Parry Nisbet (1839–1916), Commissioner of Rawalpindi. The *CMG* had already published a statement that Parry Nisbet was to be resident of Kashmir, a report that was denied. A week later the *Pioneer* said the air was "full of rumours" on the subject (7 July). Parry Nisbet was then appointed.
7. *Pall Mall Gazette*, 31 May, p. 14, prints five of the poem's eight stanzas; seven words are altered from RK's text. By "foul sink" RK must mean W. T. Stead's "new journalism".
8. Misquoted from stanza 15.
9. RK uses this in "A Second-Rate Woman", *Week's News*, 8 September 1888 (*Under the Deodars*).
10. Not identified. See the reference to a projected operetta in 18–27 February 1886.
11. Tom Edwards: see 22 June.
12. To return to England to make his way as a writer.
13. A novel by Cicely Powell (1885).
14. George Macdonald (1824–1905), best remembered as a writer of children's stories, including *At the Back of the North Wind*, but a novelist too. *David Elginbrod* is "mystical".
15. (Sir) Walter Besant (1836–1901), novelist and miscellaneous writer, the founder of the Society of Authors. RK regarded his reading of Besant's *All in a Garden Fair* (1883) as a turning point in his life: "it dealt with a young man who desired to write; . . . and with the reading and rereading it became to me a revelation, a hope and strength" (*Something of Myself*, p. 65).

To Edmonia Hill, 27 June 1888
Text: Copy, University of Sussex

[Simla]

Wednesday afternoon: 4.30.
"Oh what a surprise!" Have you patience to listen to a tale of woe, lamentation and sickness? It's a bit mixed.

In the first place, Chesney who has been ailing for a few days has suddenly gone down with small-pox at Allahabad. The news came in today by wire together with a despairing appeal for help from Parke[1] who is very seedy having hurt his knee or something of the kind and can barely carry on the paper. Result is that Hensman[2] has been sent down – ordered rather for he leaves here on Friday – in relief and on my shoulders comes the special correspondence, Simla letters etc. – same as I did in '85. I don't much object to this but Robinson on the Lahore side is bad with dysentery and – oh it's all a glorious muddle. But before I go any further pray you get yourself vaccinated ere you come down. The case is a purely sporadic one but once "vacced" one is absolutely on the safe side.

Well we held a tiffin-of-war Allen, Hensman and I today amid a wilderness of telegrams and letters. It was a queer grim sort of show for we laughed at the dramatic completeness of the smash and told stories of the tight times when we had run the papers single-handed amid fever and other things. In the middle of it all came poor Mrs C. anxiously wishing to know whether she couldn't catch this afternoon's mail and fly to her son. (The infinite goodness of mothers all the world over!) So Mrs Allen bundled out and took her shopping: the poor lady having no thin kit of any kind. Mrs. C. in "reach me downs" will be quaint to look upon. I am sorry for her but seeing what Chesney's constitution is, and knowing how quickly the disease developed itself I don't think that much harm will come to him. God spare him for he was good to look upon that bead-eyed fair haired boy!

And now for the personal aspect of the question. See saw is a fool to it. Parke can't hold on beyond the 15th at the outside for he is aw'fly seedy. On the other hand there is that brute Kay for whom I have no sort of sympathy, and on top of all comes the urgent necessity of the Simla work being done. Kay won't knock under if he can possibly help it for he has completed the tale of his sins by over-staying his leave, and then going sick after a visit to an unhealthy station – Darjeling to wit.

Allen says that if anything happens he'll go down but I feel sure that Lahore just now would kill him – it's no place for an old man and tho' he is strong he can't go the ten hour "two-twenty" on the office chair.

I'd feel mean if I let him go and would never forgive myself if aught happened to him. On the other hand what the deuce is to be done about Parke. Hensman, who is dying to get back to Simla says: – "I'll go down, inspect P. send him off for his leave at once and be assured that I shan't want *you* at Allahabad till the 15th. Up till then use my office and do my work up here: but *don't* volunteer for Lahore."

Allen won't hear of my going and would sooner shift P. to Lahore and send me down to Allahabad. You may imagine how I loathe the idea of returning to the Punjab and you know how I detest the work. So far, I'm safe here till the 15th but we must wait the wire from Lahore. I can't be in two places at once, like Sir Boyle Roche's bird[3] and I go my full pile on the N.W.P.

All I can say is Thank *Heaven* it didn't happen before and this is my consolation. But for poor Chesney I – and all of us – are glad that the smash has come as it proves what we all felt long ago that we were undermanned, and if it all ends in our getting a couple more men on the *Pi*, well and good.

Anyhow the rest of my holiday has been stopped for whether I stop here or go down to Lahore (which God forbid) I must put my shoulder to the wheel.

"We'll give you more leave in September or October" says Allen. "Can't afford it" says I, and if I once quit Simla I am sure as nails that I don't go back. "Go to Naini Tal"[4] says the mother – "but these holidays at the end of a string aren't good enough." And that's my own idea – not only for holidays but as regards the work generally. It is *not* good enough – at least it will not be and I am more than ever set in my determination to go home and quit the *Pi*. (But this is still a confidence most particular). The leading paper in India is an excellent thing but there are many things better in this world and I must strike out and find 'em. From a financial point of view this disgusting mess means at least three hundred rupees for me whether in Simla or the plains but I have lost my old savage hunger for the money which means independence.

If you never prayed before, pray now that Kay may mend his health as he declares that he means to do. The impertinence more than the misfortune of his lapse, collapse, relapse or whatever it is to be called, makes me wroth.

And several new features of a peculiar and festive kind are introduced into the arena by this. Hensman takes my rooms at the Allens when he goes down, and that means rootling around for quarters somewhere when I follow. Also he is told off for the Black Mountain Expedition[5] which starts in October. Wherefore assuming that C. makes the speediest of recoveries, Park and I will have to run the rag certainly till December, and I shan't be set free for Bhamo[6] anyhow till the end of the year.

What do you think of it all? There's always the Club to fall back upon I suppose and I cannot say that the delay grieves me though I simulated a decent regret when it was announced at tiffin, only let all go straight till the 15th and whatever comes afterwards will touch me but very lightly.

As a fitting finale to a dark day, the twilight has brought roaring rain, mist and cloud spume and it is almost too dark to see to write. I'd give something to be assured that this was the beginning of the rains. What have you at Mussoorie and what does your husband think of it? Pukka[7] or a passing storm merely. Ask him.

Except this ravel of my own affairs little has happened since yesterday. Went to Viceregal Lodge this morning and met all the Council coming away. Years ago in a moment of levity I wrote that when councillors died they transmigrated into the bodies of the great gray Langurs.[8] Looking upon the grey, hairy monkeyish faces today I see that my words were true. They are *very* like apes are our legislators – all except the Chief who is neat and clean. The year has brought many changes and of all the gang there were only three or four that I knew and to the others I was sadly introduced. The Viceroy wasn't visible, Mackenzie Wallace[9] executing a sort of official war dance between him and the [outer][10] world to keep off the profane crowd. A good watch dog is the faithful Donald, and when he is on duty he refuses to unbend. However his master says that he is coming to tea with us next week, and if he doesn't forget I dare say he'll be round. He has just made a discovery – or he pretends that he has – and tells the tale (with a sombre twinkle in the one eye that he can see out of) as one who is genuinely pained and astonished. "Do you know" says H.E. "that there are gentlemen – Indian Civilians – who write – ah yes – *write* to me suggesting – ah yes – *asking* that they should be decorated because they have done the state some service." Then he paused and went on gravely "And quite the hardest part of my official labours is replying to those letters!" I should think so; for I know some of the men who had pestered him last Queen's birthday on spec.[11] But the way he put up his eyebrows and mourned over the degeneracy of these "gentlemen – Indian Civilians" was irresistibly funny.

7: p.m. Out of darkness light. Here comes your letter, unlooked for, unhoped for and most welcome. How shall I thank you for it? By giving news about the Crusher? Verily I know naught and have asked you, only yesterday, to tell me what *you* knew. I spoke to Mrs. N. about him but she denied all knowledge of his whereabouts and showing me his latest photo said briefly: – "bloated some"; for she is an *exigeante* little lady. "These violent delights have violent ends"[12] as Shakespeare says and the Lord in his Infinite Mercy wisely arranges a hook for the jaws of nearly every shark that swims in our muddy sea of life, so it is possible that the Crusher has gone with the rest and is hooked by a "pretty penniless little girlie" what a foul and vile word is that last!

All good wishes go with you for your anniversary over which you did not fast and, indeed, why should you? That is for the likes o' me and – I don't care to be chaffed, for I have a hide which is not so thick as it ought to be. But never mind, I dare say you didn't mean it.

Can't say that I envy the miserable Pike.[13] Guess if I had a wife to tote along in this weather I'd put her into the dog-box with a seer[14] of ice on her head and say to the guard: – "Now if you let that critter out on the platform 'tween this and the end of the journey, there will be trouble." But some men think otherwise.

Your sketch of the Allahabad of the Rains isn't a pretty one. Prickly heat tempered by the occasional glimpse of Miss Brodhurst![15] I have a misty recollection of her face. Her mother kept her in a brown holland cover – or else it was the sofa but they were both so alike that I've forgotten. The Rains are sure to break ere long – Elliott[16] goes about wagging his head and looking like a boiled owl; so something is sure to happen and the rain here has a distinctly monsoonish drip! Pity me I've got to go out to dinner through it.

Doesn't Simla dance? That's all. I told you of last night's hop and there's another on the 5th and another on the 9th, I think but I'm not sure, and after the 15th there will be any amount of 'em but I shall not be there. Simla will *not* mourn spite o' all.

Received a letter from Kay this night, which I opened with fear and trembling. "Had I seen any trace of an album with photoes in his rooms". Then I who-ooped and put care behind me. Another letter informed me that he stuck pretty steadily to his billiards. 'T all events a man must stand up to play billiards and while a man can stand he can run a paper as I know to my sorrow. Let us hope that the acuteness of his malady has been – no not exaggerated – merely edited which is a prettier word.

Beyond the fine and fluent swing of your handwriting which told me that you were in a hurry, your letter had little of news in it save your refusal to take a new frock to the club dance. Solomon lied or else someone else did when he said: – "Can a maid forget her ornaments or a Bride her attire?",[17] for behold you have falsified all Ecclesiastes and filled me with profound respect and admiration. How in the name of Fortune could you have the heart to do it? That a mere man with a claw hammer coat should retire from the giddy throng is explicable – *mais* . . . you of all people!

Great Scott! It's half past seven and I'm due at a quarter past eight. I must hurry into my bottle green wedding garments. If there's anything amusing at dinner I'll report when I come back. So far Harry Allen[18] is the only other guest I know of.

Midnight. Save me from the British dinner party as adorned with music and recitations. Of course I met the one woman in all Simla whom I was most anxious to avoid. Had to take in an arrogant *chee-chee*[19] girl who talked about keeping Diwalli[20] as though it were some sort of festival of the church and confided to me that she had been brought up in a school at Mussoorie. In sheer desperation I clung to her with great fervour talking at random till after the uncomfortable meal was ended and the men were left. The evening closed with an idiotic recitation by a half-German, half-English girl[21] who emphasized all her conjunctions and jumped bad words such as "zounds" "hussy" and the like. You may guess the extreme age of the verses she gurgled, from this little fact. I had time to think while she was jabbering – getting more and more German in her accent as her nervousness increased – and my notion was How ghastly it would be if all this mournful and grotesque gathering of twelve were suddenly compelled to clamour about their secret woes, griefs and aspirations. I knew nearly all the people and, on my faith, there was enough dynamite floating free to have lifted the roof off the house. But nothing happened. The recitation came to an end and we nodded and smirked and grinned at each other and assured our hostess that we had spent a most delightful evening and then we departed each one taking his own burden as, except in very rare cases, is the custom of this world. The rain had stopped and the night was a dull drippy depressing one. I came back to the hotel firmly convinced that I was one of the most unlucky people in the world, that every thing was going badly and that K.R. was even then on the point of giving up the ghost. But nothing seemed to be much affected by my sorrow (it was too cloudy to see the stars) and the mood passed as I sat me down again to this letter. Had I known whom I should ha' met wild horses should not have taken me to that dinner. I wasn't uncomfortable – only intensely and unreasonably irritated, much as I was earlier in the day when *Vixen*, who had been turned out because of her muddy feet, came in through the window and insisted on curling up to sleep in my bed. There was not one good sentence or happy answer born of that dinner and, so far as I can see, 't was an evening wasted.

Now, which will you – a longer letter or a day's delay in replying? I'm off to Mashobra[22] tomorrow, if nothing happens, and back again on Saturday morn to take Hensman's work. No – on second thoughts, this letter shall be finished off tonight and I will begin a scrawl from under the pines tomorrow. There won't be much to write about from The Retreat for the house-party will be a small one and between five meals a day one has no time for the higher emotions.

Forgive nearly seven pages of crass stupidity and selfishness but to tell the truth, all these office complications have vexed and bothered me more than I care to admit to any one except to you. Only let no ill befal 'till the end of the 13th of July and the Virgin shall have a candle for every four and twenty hours. Yea, and I will make an offering to the poor also for perhaps Providence which is pitifully human may be bribed to overlook me. Pray thou also for the Rains, and for the clouds that return not after the Rains and for everything else that may seem good to thee.

Write me an answer soon and unless you have grown to fly from the sight of my handwriting, I will reply at length but whether there will be sense in my reply I cannot say. I only know now that I am anxious – anxious and again anxious.

Notes
1. M. H. Park, assistant editor of the *Pioneer*.
2. Howard Hensman (?–1916) went out to India in the 1870s and became correspondent for the *Pioneer* at the headquarters of the government of India. He also represented *The Times*, and was recognised as the main point of connection between officialdom and the press.
3. Roche (1743–1807) was famous for his Irish bulls.
4. In the outer Himalayas in Kumaon, the summer capital of the North-Western Provinces.
5. The Black Mountain tribes lived at the extreme north of the North-West Frontier. The 1888 expedition against them was over by November. RK alludes to the expedition in "A Conference of the Powers" (*Many Inventions*).
6. In northern Burma: see 29–30 May.
7. Genuine. One of Hill's functions was as meteorological reporter to the government of the North-West Provinces.
8. "Simla Notes", *CMG*, 24 June 1885 (uncollected).
9. (Sir) Donald Mackenzie Wallace (1841–1919), foreign correspondent for *The Times* at Constantinople before serving as private secretary to Lord Dufferin when Viceroy of India; he afterwards returned to *The Times* as director of its foreign department.
10. "Other" in copy.
11. RK's "The Fountain of Honour", *CMG*, 4 June (uncollected), makes fun of the scramble for honours.
12. *Romeo and Juliet*, ii.vi.9.
13. H. W. Pike, Assistant Magistrate and Collector, Allahabad.
14. A measure of weight, varying from eight ounces to three pounds; most commonly about two pounds.
15. Daughter of an Allahabad judge, a neighbour of the Hills: see 7 October 1888.
16. (Sir) John Eliot (1839–1908), Meteorological Reporter to the Government of India, 1886–1903; Director-General of Indian Observatories, 1899–1903.
17. Jeremiah 2:32.
18. One of George Allen's sons.
19. Eurasian.
20. Hindu feast of the lantern. RK's article on "The Amritsar Fair", *CMG*, 22 October 1884 (Pinney, *Kipling's India*), describes a Diwali festival.
21. Gussie Tweddell: see [9–10] July 1888.
22. Sir Edward Buck's house, called "The Retreat", at Mashobra, about six miles from Simla. According to Sir Walter Lawrence, Buck kept "open house, and often he would forget how many guests were coming. But his servants never failed, and there was always plenty in that elastic Paradise" (*The India We Served*, p. 52).

To Edmonia Hill, [28 June–1 July] 1888
Text: Copy, University of Sussex

Thursday: Unter den Linden. Seven miles from Simla.
Mashobra 10: p.m.

Sufficient unto the day is the evil thereof. I've made all my arrangements for taking over Hensman's work on Saturday but till then I'm Buck's guest in this delightful country house. I wish you could see the place or form any idea of the beauty of the forest of pine and oak that it stands in. Buck owns roughly speaking the top of a mountain – fancy having all that to do what you like with! – and being a man of artistic bent of mind has cut down trees here and opened up vistas there with the single view of making his domain as fair to the eye as possible. When all the snows of Kulu, the mist, the greenery and the sunshine conspire to help out his ideas, the result may be imagined. He took me all over the hill from his pet rhubarb beds to his more petted orchards, and showed me the glory and the beauty of the land. I had known it for three years but had never been so impressed with it before. One doesn't gnash one's teeth in public because an unsympathetic world would immediately say: – "Fits, by George!" but I gnashed them secretly as I trotted through the underwood – rank willow underwood where the striped cobra-plants stood up like snakes at spring – and heard Buck expatiate on his mushroom beds, his English pears and all the hundred fads and whimsies with which a wealthy bachelor is at liberty to surround himself.

We are a very small house party – only Buck, the Mother and Sister, Mrs. Napier and myself. True it is that Lady Roberts[1] (who from the noise she is making this very minute must be going to bed) occupies the upper flat of the Retreat but she doesn't descend to our atmosphere. One of the funniest things in a small way is to hear a chief's A.D.C. using cuss-words when he has to ride the stony seven miles from Snowdon[2] to Mashobra on the order of Lady "Bobs". I was passed by one today as I came out and the opinion he expressed on the woman's weakness for ruralizing was, I grieve to say, unfit for publication.

I fancy Mrs. N. is not exactly pleased with her outing – so far at least but it will be nicer for her later on. Buck asked me blandly what men ought to be asked out to amuse the ladies. I didn't know anything of the Maiden's affairs but I knew a man whom Mrs. N. liked (such a lovely boy with a positively *holy* smile and they call him Beautiful Jim). His name I suggested promptly and he is coming out on Sunday. I go back to Simla please Heaven, and nothing worse than five hours work a day, on Saturday morning. So that gives me only one day here. It's rather a chance for seeing Mrs. N. close to and I think she'll cut into some first class material. She's a woman who is literally all nerves, who cannot if she tried be disagreeable to anyone, who affects the deepest and most genuine interest in all her surroundings, to whom admiration is as the breath of her nostrils and who in fine is as sincerely insincere as Lord Dufferin. I can't say more than that. Mother and Trix worship her because she is (and this I admit) clever and quickly clever. They stayed with her in Pindi[3] this cold weather. I have my own notions and I'll tell you at the end of tomorrow, if she talks at all. But I have a notion that Beautiful Jim will ride over tomorrow and the two will pluck strawberries or something of the kind. Meantime I am possessed of a great desire to blow up every nook and coppice and pocket on Mashobra Hill with dynamite because it is lovely and so useless.

What skittles am I talking! Let us revisit calmer scenes. Herewith "From the Egg to the Fruit" rechristened The Tents of Kedar. 'Twon't go in the W.N. but, as I said, will follow "Poor Dear Mamma", in the Story of the Gadsbys. Out of your kindness give it a careful check if you will and keep a special eye upon the woman's turns of expression in which I fear I may have made a mistake. You will see too the new ending that I have put in to make it suit Captain Gadsby's case and it rests with you to decide whether the ending be correct or no. Personally it seems to me a little strained and brutal but on the other hand there is hardly any limit to the frank selfishness of a man in Captain G's condition. Pray you, whose good opinion I value, don't think any the worse o' me for writing it. There are certain moods and phases of thought that must be faced boldly and set down unflinchingly so that those who read may know and see the worst that can happen, and in this very knowledge, be strong enough to turn it aside. I want my public to say in effect: – "This is what may be" and, "Now that we know, this is what shall *never* be". Do you think that I shall make it read my lesson aright?

Friday morn. So far there is peace in the hills. *Me voici* settled down in the billiard room which gives on to a finer panorama of Hills than ever you saw in Mussoorie, to go on with the letter. This day, if no other follows it, will be one of idleness. Have been botching up "The Tents of Kedar" all this morn till it looks as you will see, a loathly and spidersome production. Buck has taken Mrs. N. to try over songs on the piano; and the two will be settled there for some time as she is a first class musician and he is just beginning the study. There's nothing in the wide world to tell, and I rather wonder why I'm boring you with the sight of my fist. Here comes Trix (poor little Maiden with her own trouble to bear) to say that there are unlimited wild raspberries and strawberries for the picking on the hill side and that we must go out and eat.

7 p.m. A queer walk and a maddening one through the loveliest glades and dingles all one soft grey green except where the bronze of the mosses showed like snake's hide. In the end the Maiden told me her little store of confidences. That objectionable cuss with whom she had broken,[4] had another last-despairing interview with her yesterday morn, and very naturally with his appeals and protestations had shaken the poor darling grievously though she persists and persisted in her original intent. She talked to me and told me as much about it as a woman would ever tell a man and at last the blessed tears came to her relief and she cried all among the pine-needles while I lacked words that could give her any comfort. Then she pointed out, half crying and half laughing, the uselessness of the beauty of the forest, in which point I heartily agreed with her till she turned upon me with: – "Who else would you like to walk with except me you bad boy?" So we agreed that never since the world began was there any sorrow like to her sorrow and hunted for raspberries till the tears were dried and our fingers blue-red, and we began to steal from each other's vines and throw pine-cones at each other's heads as it was in the very early days. But somehow the fooling was not amusing and when Trix collapsed on a rock and said: – "Oh how miserable I am!" I felt that we could not play at being babies any more. Wherefore we came home solemnly to tea and announced that we had had a riotously jovial afternoon. Ay de mi!

Then the clouds came up welt after welt, thick and brown as smoke and the rain broke furiously and a chill wreath of mist pranced through the house, and as Trixie said, shivering in the conservatory (such a perfect conservatory by the way – great cushioned couches and settees) "Now we're all *quite* happy together".

I said I'd tell you more about Mrs. N. I haven't seen much of her but she came into the billiard-room this morning (so I see I didn't mean to tell at first) and talked *pour passer le temps*, completely disregarding the ostentatious manner in which I was preparing to write to some one. "Fancy coming out here to write" said she. I checked the answer upon my tongue and sat tight while she talked about literature and art, and the emotions. She is a hog on the emotions, and has got some of the catch words and fag ends of the Craft which she knows how to use with effect and the air of immense and sympathetic knowledge. She quoted Novalis – incorrectly; crediting him with something Emerson had written; all with a pretty kittenish air, which said: – "This is nothing to what I could do if I tried." But a double misquotation was about enough for me. This is one funny thing I learned. She announced that she was full of the maternal instinct – passionately fond of her children etc. "Are you so," I thought. "Then I've made a mistake". Like many women she overacted her part for presently entered one of her boys aged five and, instead of following a child's natural instinct and running to his mother, came to me. She petted him very prettily – white jewelled hands on lace collar of kid – kiss on the brow showing bend of neck and all that trick-work – but – but – the boy didn't know what to make of it all! Her part was perfect but every line in the child's attitude, let alone the unveiled surprise in his eyes, showed that this was *not* the manner in which he was normally handled. Then I laughed an unpleasant snicker all to myself for it is always pleasant to detect a lady in a fib – when one is indifferent either to truth or blame. Then she wanted to know how I did my work and – the Devil entered into my soul – I started on a career of unbridled mendacity. I thought that I had lost the hang of it but it came back. I informed her that I had not a single idea in the world beyond my work which I generally did in the very early morning – the one time of the twenty four when I get my best sleep. That I got my information from the clubs by making men so drunk that they began to talk, and taking notes of what they said, and so on and so on. To all of which did Desdemona seriously incline with many "Ohs!" and "Ahs!"[5] expressive of deep interest (for Beautiful Jim was not there and Sir E. is more than fat and forty). Then she began to talk of herself at length; informing me that the men who admired her (the list begins with Lord Dufferin, includes all the subalterns of the K.D.G.'s[6] and ends Deuce knows where) always regarded her as a sort of holy saint and put her on a pedestal. Here I had a vision of Lord Dufferin who believes in neither God, Woman or Man ogling her and telling her this and the thought made me smile. "Ah, you don't believe it then?" she said. "You think they make a mistake?" I did – pretty considerable, but . . . well I fear that my eyes showed my thoughts though my lips denied for she dropped the Holy Saint Pedestal *bundobust* and condescended to drop to Earth again – for the express purpose of saying unkind things about Mrs. Hauksbee whom she knew last year. 'Said Mrs. H. was vulgar! Mrs. H. Audacious if you please and with more wit in her little finger than ever Mrs. N. heard or knew of in her life. I wasn't pleased and took no trouble to disguise it; though by this time Mrs. H. has long since dropped me from her panoramic memory – if a single note (announcing, "I am busy – rushingly busy. Don't ask me what I am doing or why or how – but look in the newspapers") be excepted. As she has given no address I can't ask her what she's up to, but I'll bet a month's pay that certain sentences in Lepel's address alluding to the [importance][7] of courage came from her brain.[8] I think I know the twang of her sentences.

So the Sederunt broke up on the Hauksbee platform and I haven't seen any more of her to date except at tiffin; and tomorrow I shall be gone or ever she is up.

She is in the Inner Circle if you like for D. tells her as much as he ever tells any woman and his women folk are said to be angry over the friendship – it's nothing more. All the matter for a good tale there!

Saturday. Simla once more – but alas Hensman's duftar at Oatlands[9] holds me. It's a snug little room and looks out over a sea of green pines that runs down like a wave of the sea into the rain-mist that overhangs Umballa where I hope they are getting their first taste of the monsoon. I never took so deep an interest in the rains before. I hung over the weather maps for two hours with Buck last night and was rewarded by a tearing storm which came on at two in the morning and nearly drowned me in my bed so badly did the roof leak. This morning I came away with Buck and we walked the seven miles in dripping rain while he told me stories of the Departmental kind that my soul loveth. Notably one of a shifty tricky subordinate who, Buck saw, was a man ordained by Heaven for one particular sort of work. He was a "rejection" from many offices, his own Department hated him, he was an inveterate liar, and everyone prophesied that Buck would never be able to restrain him within decent Department bounds. But he did and told me the story of the business – how he had to drive, coerce, threaten, coax, bully and blarney the man for months, to circumvent his beastly eelsomeness and at last to drive him and hold him on a strong hand as a man holds and drives a horse. "I never saw a man with his powers of work" said Buck in conclusion, "and by God, I never met such a liar! I held his head down on the martingale and – I'm holding it still." He chuckled as he spoke, and I who knew the natures of both men (Buck's cliff-like stolidity and invincible belief in himself and the other man's power of evasion and casuistry) chuckled also for I like above all things to watch the power man has over man and the ways and mazes of the wheels at Simla. Many curious yarns did Buck tell me but they were of an official and rather saw-dusty kind. Some of 'em may serve for material.

Since then I've wired some news to the Pi (hope it'll like it) written a thing for the same rag called His Natural Destiny[10] and eaten an infamous tiffin at Hardinges. Oh for an hour of Wutzler and the sausage rolls of the Charleville. I ought to be doing something now for by this hand I have a Simla letter to send off tomorrow[11] but – but I prefer a Mussoorie one you see. I should really like to know what on earth I'm to send the Pioneer; for I've been nowhere, seen no-one and done nothing since I came up. On the 4th, an all goes well, I shall amuse myself by attending a council meeting, and that will be a sufficiently dreary show in all conscience.

Did I tell you of an idea for a new story, "Mrs. Gypsum's Photographs."[12] Mrs. G: is said to be (this is the plot) the prettiest woman in Simla and by this right has a host of adorers. One of 'em goes down the Hill very suddenly and dies from the effect of a gun-accident – had been handling his rifle incautiously and so shot himself through the head – as any good man may by mischance do, any day. No one knows much about him except a man some ten or fifteen years his senior who took a fatherly interest in the boy while he was alive. Well, a youth of the name of Elliott Danner swells the train of Mrs. G's admirers and goes completely off his head. It is to be remembered that the woman is very much like Mrs. Reiver[13] but vainer if possible. She is photoed at Bourne and Shepherds[14] in all manner of kit from riding-habit to fancy dress and her fancy dress photo she distributes to her admirers and among others young Elliott Danner who is struck by a sort of blur at the back of the chair in which Mrs. Gypsum is sitting. The more and more desperately he goes off his head about her, the more clearly does the blur in the photo come up till at last it shows in the filmy likeness of a man standing at the back of the chair. Mrs. G. has been making Danner, who has not the tact to control his feelings, desperately jealous by frivolling with half a dozen men. At last he says bitterly: – "I suppose it's your nature. Why you can't be even photographed alone, without a man in the background." "What d' you mean?" said Mrs. G. and he shows her the photo whereon the blur is now almost as distinct as the real photo. Mrs. G. screams: – "It's Tom!" and in her hysteria says a good deal more than Elliott Danner cares to hear. Wherefore with the wisdom of youth he goes away, gets most beastly drunk and in this festive condition blurts out his woe and his jealousy to a friend at the Club. A stranger cuts in to the conversation, snatches the photo and says: – "That's the face of Tom Feardon" – the fellow who died from mishandling an express rifle. "Mishandling!" stutters Elliott. "I've kissed the hand that pulled the trigger for him and for me!" Hereon the stranger taking the photo goes to call on Mrs. G. and tells her how much he loved young Feardon; finally taxing her directly with having caused his death. Mrs. G. protests faintly: – "It was an accident. It was an accident. He wrote and told me so himself!" and – the scene closes upon her going – a little white about the lips but as composed and as beautiful as ever – to a dance where Elliott Danner after swearing at her for a murderess ... takes as many dances as she is disposed to give him. It's utterly absurd but maybe, if you'll help me with a hint or two I may "make your flesh creep" as the Fat Boy in *Pickwick* says. Is it worth going on with?

An awe-stricken deputation of menials has just interviewed me with the news that the Viceroy came (to tea as he hoped) and called on us yesterday afternoon at six – when we were all at Mashobra (Mother and Trix are there now). It seems that in his bland blind sort of way he "rode all unarmed and he rode all alone"[15] into the verandah of our weeny weeny house which was not only locked up but deserted. Then he *qui-haied*.[16] Fancy a locked out Viceroy qui-haiing in a damp verandah! Natural result was complete stupefaction on the part of the remaining servants who at last made him understand that the Memsahib was away. Then he retreated. You don't know the geography of our locale.

If you saw it you would roar, with delight. It's like a corkscrew which has been stepped upon.

Sunday. A horrible day – blank as a wall and I've been laboriously grinding out a Simla letter (such rot!) for the Pioneer. My people still at Mashobra and no one had the decency to ask me out to dinner so had to dine at the Hotel for the first time and enjoy the society of a flaxen haired pink and white subaltern whose only adjectives of praise appeared to be "ripping" or "clinking" and who cracked his joints in grisly fashion – because they were not set I suppose.

Never a letter from you and the rain is rattling on the tin roof like peas. I feel lonesome and bad company. Therefore I wind me up this letter and tumble into bed.

Notes
1. Nora (1838–1920), wife of the Commander-in-Chief, Lord Roberts.
2. The official residence of the Commander-in-Chief in Simla.
3. Rawalpindi, where Mrs Napier's husband the Colonel commanded.
4. Jack Fleming: he and Trix were engaged again before the end of the summer.
5. Cf. *Othello*, I.iii.145–6.
6. King's Dragoon Guards, her husband's regiment.
7. The copy reads "the of courage".
8. Griffin made a political speech in London on 5 June in which he stated that the first and highest qualification of an English statesman is courage (*Pioneer*, 26 June 1888).
9. A Simla house, owned by Colonel A. W. Crookshank.
10. *Pioneer*, 10 July (uncollected).
11. "Simla (From Our Own Correspondent)", *Pioneer*, 5 July (uncollected).
12. I have not found any publication of this story.
13. The woman from whom Pluffles was rescued in "The Rescue of Pluffles": she figures in three other of the *Plain Tales*.
14. Photographers with studios in Simla, Bombay, and Calcutta. At least two portraits of RK were made by them.
15. Scott, *Marmion*, v.316.
16. *Qui hai* – "is anyone there?"

To Edmonia Hill, [2–3] July 1888
Text: Copy, University of Sussex

[Simla]

Now may every bad entrée that was ever cooked at the Simla bank, choke the Rose Bush woman! Another time I will fill in my letter with chips from leading articles and monsoon forecasts; and you will "go uninformed to your grave." Frankly I was not comfortable at all but I showed you wherein my discomfort lay. This year three – no two and a half – solid miles of mall lie between the houses and as I'm not riding any they might as well be twenty two and a half. There's a subscription dance tonight which I shall attend in the spirit only because it's now nearly twelve o'clock and I must go out to sit on Elliott's head about the monsoon (he carries it in his pocket), must post my first bale of rubbish to you, must send a wire to the *Pi*, must then go to business tiffin at Allen's, must then meet the Mother and the Maiden coming in from Mashobra and must at dinner delicately but firmly refuse to take the Maiden to the dance. When all that is over, it will be about time [. . .]¹

3.40 p.m. Shelved Allen – and wherefore? Diplomacy and a sudden inspiration, for my dull wits are getting sharper. 'Was down among the offices gathering lies and a man said: – "I'd advise you to look out – Aitken² is awfully anxious to step into your shoes." "What shoes?" said I. "The Editorship of the C & M." "O Hades" said I "is it as bad as all that?" and fled up to Aitken at the new club. Now Aitken is an estimable journalist – a trained man and all that, who is advancing in years and yearns for permanent appointments and specially for the chair of the C & M which means comparative wealth. I found Aitken and to him sweetly addressed myself alluding to Robinson's sickness. "I suppose you'll go down if anything happens" said A. "Not if you can help me to help it" sez I and he blushed enthusiastically for – how strangely do the souls of men vary! – he positively hungers for an appointment which is detestable for me. I explained how a re-transfer to Lahore affected my future career very seriously – in that it w'd deprive me of the time for original writing and the larger fields of the *Pi*. "Quite right" said poor A. anxiously. "I should do the same were I in your place." Then we made a private and unofficial *bundobust* to this effect. If anything happens to K.R., A. is to sail in backed by my good word and all his past connection with the paper while I gently but firmly jib on the grounds that Lahore means extinguishment. "If I get the appointment I'll be grateful to you as long as I live" said A. "It's beyond my power to promise anything" said I "but you may take your oath that I'll help you in every way to get it – even to the supplanting of K.R.; for back to Lahore, with our old home broken up and twelve hours routine a day, I do *not* do [sic: go?]." And this seems to me a good guard for Aitken is just the man for the work, as I shall tell Allen. That is to say if the worst comes to the worst for I have no manner of sympathy for K.R. and would do my best to sacrifice him if thereby my road were made clear before my feet.

Having done what I considered a good morn's work, I was retiring peacefully to the damp shelter of Hardinge's when . . . I was *ordered s'il vous plait* to go to tonight's dance, by a wandering *rickshaw*, who refused to believe that I had given up the show. Some people are a good deal too free with their *hookums*³ and I pointed out humbly that I wasn't going. "But you must and I'll give you some dances." "But I am not and you needn't tie your programme into knots for nothing." "Aren't you well?" "No. I'm deadly sick." "You don't look it." "But I am." "Then I shall put the dances down all the same – four, seven, and eleven." "How much?" "Four, seven, and eleven." "I assure you that you'll only have to get fresh partners at the last minute if you do." "You're rude." "I'm very sorry, if I am, but I really am not coming. I've got another engagement." "That's a fib or you would have said so at first." 'Couldn't stand being called a fibster so I slowly and silently vanished away – chuckling. And all this nonsense was only because I wouldn't come and due to the perversity of your sex. Had I said I was coming I s'pose I should ha' had to beg for dances. As you truthfully observe "This is a strange world."

Aren't some people disgustingly generous? Allen is reiterating his promises about giving me compensatory leave later on. I don't want it and I won't take it. All being well I have not the ghost of notion of going sick and why I should be yanked out of Allahabad just when I'm in the middle of some most important work, I don't quite see. Unless I'm sore mistaken however we shall be shorthanded on the Pi right into the winter.

Hensman won't go back when I go down. He'll be there for a month at least and very probably six weeks. A thousand thanks for your offer which, if absolutely convenient to you, I accept.[4] It will be delightful to me and I assure you that a reintroduction to the privileges of decent society will make me cut short both my allowance of the weed and my waking hours. Aye, even would I abandon tobacco absolutely save in office where an occasional cigar assists the progress of the Empire. It's far too kind of you, since you know what manner of person I am, but I really have been brought up in five years of decent domestic life and all my wanderings in the barren places of the earth have not altogether rubbed the remnants of respectability out of me. Tell your husband this with my *salaams*. Hope he doesn't think that I knock about drawing rooms with a cutty pipe of Cavendish in my mouth. *Comme ça par exemple* [sketch].

Now I must really pretend to do some work for the *Pi* and I think I shall commence by seeing if Mrs Allen can give me a cup o' tea at Walsingham.[5] 'Can't work properly without stimulants you know.

10.30. Went to the fortnightly entertainment of the A[mateur].D[ramatic]. Club (songs recitations and the like,) and heard the Silver Wedding as rendered by Hobday for the 3rd time. I liked it because it reminded me of Allahabad fort but the rest was sadly dreary. I've got to spin a yarn of some sort about it I suppose.[6] Saw Allen there with his preternaturally virtuous son – the fat youth who thinks dancing wicked and for his sins is told off to ride with Miss Edge when Mrs A. doesn't want the Daguerrotype hanging about the place. All his father's lakhs are dearly purchased at this price. Coming out of the crush and the show, an afternoon one, was very crowded, I heard a new riddle which I present to you. "What medicine does a man take who is blessed by an obstreperous wife?" He takes an elixir. It is hardly necessary to write "He takes and he licks her." I got this from Scoble[7] the Councillor Sahib so I s'pose it's pretty stale.

Found the Mother and the Maiden returned from Mashobra this even; both heartily sick of the peace and quiet of the country and *very* glad to get back to the Mall again. Mrs N. it seemed was frankly bored and took small trouble to hide it. The Maiden had been watching that nice lady with two sharp eyes and came to the same conclusion as I did. "She attitudinizes over her children and if she'll act over that she'll act over everything" said the Maiden sweepingly. We compared notes and found that an afternoon in the woods had done for the Maiden what the talk in the billiard room had done for me – *videlicet* disillusioned us both. "Let us leave her to Lord Dufferin" said the Maiden; "*he* won't exact truthfulness – but I'm sorry 'cause I went out to worship her – and it's only an ordinary woman after all." Mother's more in love with her than ever and says she's a sweet and fascinating woman. But then she hadn't played with the little boys as Trix had and learned incidentally the distance between them and their mother. Trix rehearsed some of the gushing "Come-and-be-kissed-my-precious" scenes for my benefit and I found that it was even as I had seen. *Nota bene*, sincerity is Mrs. N's ace of spades. I meet her at dinner at the Scobles on Sunday next. Wah! Wah!

They are dancing like old boots – or should I say new slippers? – at the Town Hall. I can hear 'em going rumtity tumtity – down the middle and back again. If anyone *has* booked "four seven and eleven" there will be a shine in the tents of Ham for "four seven and eleven" is here in his shirt sleeves and Vixen, trying to tell in dog's speech what a good time she had at Mashobra, is curled up on the bed for the night as she fondly imagines.

The Maiden who had been for a ride expressed no desire to go to the dance, for which O be joyful.

How is this for virtue and thrift. Five hundred poor one and four penny dibs[8] going into fixed deposit this month? That is the effect of your advice to me. Never again say that a young man cannot be gently led into paths of good living.

Midnight. If I finish this note tonight, what shall I do tomorrow, and with what rubbish will it not be filled? Therefore I will after kicking Vixen off my bed, she seems to think that she has a right to sleep there, retire into Nirvana and like Mr Micawber wait for something to turn up.

Tuesday. Getting ready for another big storm – but that's about all. Just come from tiffin at the Allens' where I rejoice to see he makes no allusion to my going to Lahore and confines himself to discussing Simla work of which I have had rather a dose today. Have to go out to a function o' sorts in half an hour and this letter has been lingering on the stocks for too long. I'd give something if all this shilly-shally nonsense at Simla were over and I down again in the plains. I hate it – 'cause I'm neither on leave nor off it – and am counting each day until the 13th. That's a nice admission to make. However I have every hope of all going well. Write me an answer soon and forgive me for writing about nothing.

Notes
1. A gap of indeterminate length occurs here in the copy.
2. Ben Aitken, sub-editor of the Calcutta *Englishman* and previously sub-editor of the *Indian Witness*.
3. Orders.
4. Since RK had been displaced from his rooms at the Allens' (see 27 June) the Hills now offered him room in their house, a bungalow called Belvedere House, set in a large garden. RK lived there as a part of the Hill household until the end of 1888, when Mrs Hill's serious illness drove him to other lodgings.
5. All Simla houses had names of this sort.
6. A notice duly appears in RK's Simla letter, *Pioneer*, 9 July (uncollected).
7. (Sir) Andrew Richard Scoble (1831–1916), Legal Member of Council, 1886–91.
8. The current exchange value of the depreciated rupee: one shilling and four pence.

To Edmonia Hill, [4–6] July 1888
Text: Copy, University of Sussex

[Simla]

Wednesday. "Heigho! The wind and the rain!"[1] I've been pretending to do work ever since ten and it is now four in the afternoon and it has been pelting all that time. Yesterday was a day of gloom 'cause the Mother went down with an awful sore throat – her share of the "fun" at Mashobra – and the maiden and I were nervous. However she's improved to-day and hopes to be out of bed tomorrow. It was so dramatically complete in all its wretchedness that the maiden and I couldn't help laughing over it. We pinned the Doctor into a corner and said: – "Look here *is* it Diphtheria?" "No" said he cheerfully – "not yet at all events." He was a cheerful man. Then the maiden who has a good knowledge of nursing and holds ambulance certificates[2] turned to and was a pillar of strength in the room while I was dispatched for medicaments. In the twilight just as the Mother was down with high fever who should turn up except the maiden's rejected lover – off his head completely. "Could she give him a quarter of an hour? Only a quarter of an hour?" "If the Mother's going to be real bad" said the maiden "I'll get rid of this man between a poultice and a poultice." So she dealt with him for the space of fifteen minutes and then he left and she was on the verge of tears but she had said very bitter things, and felt more at ease. We had a grievous little dinner together for we were both horribly worried about the Mother. The Doctor had said that it was *tonsilitis*, a wearing trouble brought on by low condition and our fear was the worser disease. Where the Mother is concerned we are very easily upset. However she had none of the symptoms that heralded it. "It's *not* nice" said the maiden tearfully "to have to make poultices with one hand and stave off an importunate lover with the other. Now if I could clap the poultice on his mouth." . . . Then we laughed and thought of fresh torments for ourselves. The maiden falling off her horse, Robinson collapsing in Lahore and so on till we grew marvelous cheerful though I shivered whenever I thought of my own bothers and I had to go on arranging about *Pi* work too.

However in the morning the fever had gone, and the Mother was more at ease. Says she'll get up tomorrow but unless she really is all right I have a notion that she'll be made to stay in bed. Oh! I forgot to say that on top of all else came a vivid hued letter from the Pater saying Kay was awful ill. However Allen has said nothing so far beyond bothering me with his notions and news. Can't you imagine what a cheerful day yesterday was. I had hoped that some sort of note might come in from you, in which case I should not have cared: but it didn't and I forbore to bother you with my troubles till they were over. I knew the maiden was spring-steel before but I have never seen her behave better – in the teeth of her own worry and vexation of spirit too. The man who gets her to look after his house *en permanence* will get a jewel. Had to attend a function at the town hall last afternoon and to write a "sprightly" letter today.[3] I've sliced out a couple of columns and pitiful stuff it is. Tomorrow, by way of a relish, I've got to deal with and summarize a bit of Finance.[4] Can you imagine me dealing with a Financial question?

Friday. Your letter last night just as I was going to dine with Hobday at the Club. I was late in consequence and by the time I had grasped the fact that you were worried and couldn't write I wasn't at all in the mood to go out. However I had to and for three mortal hours Hobday and St. Leger[5] ran on about the glories of Ali Baba[6] which is to be produced here in September. Then H. took me aside and – read me all four acts of the play from beginning to end; asking me to suggest puns. But what I was thinking of while I pretended to listen to all the babble about Blondin donkeys, ten-foot posters, three ballets and so on[7] was just "worried and can't write today." That's my state this morn and I've let things slide on the *Pi* – so you see how Mussoorie can telegraph to Simla and Simla to Allahabad. By the way your *Pi* was late because the old mail cart broke down – so now you know all about it.

There is – how can you help it though – almost as little news in your letters as there is in mine but I see that you have not received my answer to your last but one so I live in hopes of seeing more of your hand writing tomorrow. Wonder if I shall or whether you will be worried again and unable to write. By all manner of means keep the Tents of Kedar till we meet which should be ere long. I am due in Allahabad on the morning of the fifteenth, tho' Allen talks about staying on a few days longer. I explained to him this morning that I am neither "fish, flesh, fowl nor good red herring" where I am – neither working nor on leave, and that I want to get away to some place where I can work. You may in the expressive language of your countrymen lay all that you are worth that I do not stay in Simla one hour longer than I can possibly help. How can I leave Parke down there??

By the way talking of things in Simla there has been a royal "bust up" among the actors in *"An Unequal Match"*[8] the first performance of which I attend this evening. *Hester Grazebrook* (Mrs. Allen) has to faint and lie fainting till some other woman comes in. At one of the rehearsals she fainted as was proper and was kept waiting for nearly ten minutes ere the other woman (Mrs. Fletcher of Naini Tal fame)[9] put in her appearance. Mrs. A. is not blessed with a soft temper. She rapped out: – "I hope that woman will be quick instead of keeping me lying here like a ridiculous idiot." Now the sentence was overheard and the words "ridiculous idiot" so exactly describe that rouged and raddled Mrs. F. that I was not at all surprised [to] find that she took them to herself. Mrs. A. has at least *savoir faire* and would never have used them in the sense imputed to her. Result – explosion, recrimination, and finally withdrawal (for the rest of the season let us hope) from matters theatrical of Mrs. F. her husband and Colonel P.D. Henderson[10] while the rest of the company sang "Glory Glory Hallelujah!"

That's about all the news going except a little matter that I must tell you about of course. Mrs. N[apier] has an idea – such a good sound reasonable one. "Write a tale specially for me!" This was sent point blank at my head when I met her yesterday forenoon. On my word I meant to be polite but there are occasions when something goes wrong with the works and I simply jerked out: – "No" – just like that. I really meant to wrap up the refusal politely but – somehow I didn't. Then there was an embarrassed pause till she said: – "I should have thought that you would have appreciated the compliment. Most men would." Then I made answer: – "I am a barbarian you see and I only write for my public. It sounds ungracious I know but (I couldn't resist this) get Mackenzie Wallace to write you a book." He was passing at the time but she didn't seem to relish the suggestion,[11] and the refusal made her make a personal issue of it. She recurred to it once or twice and when she rode off said: – "You shall write me that tale before you go down and I'll give you the plot." Now what is the betting? Shall I, within the next seven days, bow down and write her a story – for which I shall be rewarded by a tramp at the side of her *'rickshaw* and the certainty that she will go all round Simla saying casually: – "Yes, he wrote that for *me*, specially," – or shall I just tell you all about it and let it go.

I know which way I shall bet myself to behave and now I've 'fessed. Let me know if you can when you go to Allahabad. Do you break journey or do you accomplish that descent into Hades at one fell swoop? I shouldn't care to do it again. Let me know that I may studiously avoid meeting you on the line of rail where I always look like a discharged platelayer – and not too recently discharged at that. I have *selon le mot* taken, cabbaged, cribbed or whatever it is called a portrait of the maiden who has today pulled the Mother into comparative health. I like – I really like immensely – your assumption of years, grey hairs, and the like, "both so young and living so intensely!" It is really one [of] the most audacious things that I've had the pleasure of hearing and I was thirty seven I think last birthday some weeks ago, and [. . .][12]

Notes
1. *Twelfth Night*, concluding song.
2. Trix attended Dr Beilby's lectures on nursing in Lahore and thought of nursing as a career.
3. The function was the unveiling of a portrait of Sir Charles Macgregor, reported in the *Pioneer* by telegraph, 5 July, and again in RK's "Simla" letter, 9 July.
4. I find nothing in the *Pioneer* to answer this description.
5. Lieutenant Arthur St Leger, King's Royal Rifle Corps.
6. A farce by Hobday: a production of it in Lahore was reviewed – probably by RK – in the *CMG*, 4 March 1884.
7. RK's Simla letter, 18 July (uncollected) reported that "*Ali Baba* . . . is going to be something unprecedentedly gorgeous. There will be three ballets, a Blondin Donkey, unlimited scenery of a novel and startling type, and about three hundred of the vilest puns that even Captain Hobday can perpetrate."
8. By Tom Taylor, 1857.
9. I do not know which of several possible Fletchers this may be.
10. Colonel Philip Durham Henderson (1840–1918), Superintendent for the Suppression of Thuggee and Dacoity, Government of India, Simla.
11. Since Wallace's books were *Russia* (1877) and *Egypt and the Egyptian Question* (1883), Mrs Napier's annoyance is understandable.
12. A note on the copy says that "This letter is unfinished and unsigned."

To John Lockwood Kipling, [5 July 1888?][1]
MS: University of Sussex

[Simla]

          The Letter of Halim the Potter to Yusuf
His Father and Master Craftsman in the walled city of
        Lahore; written on the fifth day of the
               month of the Scales.

Halim the Potter from the rainy Hills, –
Under the diamond coronetted pines,
The dun, rain sodden clouds that jewel them,
The snake plants hooded tongued and venomous
The briers and the orchids – sends his word.
His Greeting to the Father whence he gained
First, life and then such Knowledge of The Craft
As is his portion.
                    For a double gift
A double greeting – though alas! the Reed
But bears the message coldly, and no gift
From Halim's hand to yours accompanies –
Yet he, being set about with many thoughts
Because the Day is lucky (so they hold
Who say Man's Day of trouble is a thing
Not to be disregarded lightly, kept
Year after year whenas the Day returns,
With such observance as the Life demands –
To the great Life great Joy, the Little less.
The work alone is worthy – not the Day
Or Birth or Death or – softly. Who am I,
Halim, to hold a fancy thus?) He searched
For gifts but after saw the thought was vain
Knowing fit weapons of The Craft were thine,
And the Sage Councillor[2] that burns and dies
Within the *chillum*[3] Phoenix fashion, born
Anew in greater labours fresher power
Than the unholpen brain could hope for – this
Was also thine; and so he held his hand
Knowing there were no other gifts. He writes
Instead his letter to the man who made
Him and his knowledge – so the gift returns
In some poor fashion to the giver.

First

Behind the *Purdah* (since I write to thee
Thee only, and the Munshi at my side,
My thumb and two first fingers, cannot blab)
The Mother and the Child – which last e'en now
Toils at her fancies in the lower room,
Weaving a mighty empire out of ghosts
As I red armies from the coarser clay –[4]
Are fain of Thee because they know and feel
How daily upward runs the silver thread
Up from the silver pellet[5] – which the men
Beyond the seas have impiously set
As record of Gehenna's torments. Ay,
The Prophet (blessed in Allah) writes: – "take heed
"Because ye are the chosen, yet all skill
"Concentres not in Islam. Swine and dogs
"Have knowledge of the weather more than ye –
"Learn from them, praising Allah." So they learn
Your torment, written in the accursed tongue
That babbles daily and is past my power
To riddle – for my work is otherwise
Than Munshis babes and Babus.[6] So they learn
Your daily torment and would have you here.
Save that the old distemper of the Hills
When clouds are lowest, holds The Mother fast
A little space. I doubt not that the drugs
Of those who know not Islam (– Read again
The Prophet's sentence, though thou knewest it
Before I knew the platter from the cup –)
Will heal her shortly – all three sides are well
Of our small square but that they lack the fourth.
I mostly O my Father! for what e'er
The women wish, my loss is most of all
Seeing that it is double and I lose
My Master Craftsman with my Father. Look!
Thou knowest (no man better) how the clay
Bends inward on the wheel, bends breaks and falls
If my hand run the pitcher lip too high.
Yea, one nail's width beyond the guide. Thou knowest
How the raw clay – removed the potter's hand –
Falls inward also – whether formed or not
(I can but choose the similes I know)
(And know thou seest the meaning ere I write.)
As with the clay so with the potter. Close –

To John Lockwood Kipling, [5 July 1888?]

Too close the likeness – thus my young mind thinks –
Two months ago I held my skill was mine
Admitting hastily a certain hint
A council here and there. Perhaps one touch
On spout or belly ere we fired the kiln
Thy hint, *thy* council and *thy* touch. No more
Than just so much as made (why blink the truth?)
The bad thing good; the drunken pitcher straight
A thing desirable in the front of the stall.
My workmanship thou saidst – and I believed.
It was so small a touch, so slight a word.
I threw the wet clay – marred it. *Now* I see!
The hand went and the clay thereafter fell
Uncouthly. These two months have shown the truth.
It may be that thou knewest it before.
I learnt it lately, toiling at a vase
To do me credit.[7] For myself alone.
(Was this the cause of failure . . . It may be)
Because I loved the labour and no gold
Should draw it from me. 'Twas a noble vase.
(I recollect *you* gave the first design
A clean and noble fashioning thereto)
The thing has failed – not wholly failed. I learnt
Much that I should have learnt before alas!
The fair lip sprouted into useless length
(Who said I needed mud-banks for *chirags*?[8])
And all the belly blistered 'neath my hands
With shapes of *Afrits, Shaitans Djinns* and *Ghouls*.
"*I* could not help it" so I told myself
And knew I lied. – Thou knowest more than I.
But the distorted vessel still remains
Against your coming. Does not Yusuf say
"Even the marred and unclean clay keep thou
"As record of past error. Hand and brain
"May both take warning?" I have kept my work
For judgement. I can only see the faults.
The Remedy is hidden. It may be
My pitcher lip exceeds the nail's breadth. This
At least is certain that the raw clay bends
Into ignoble shapes without thy hand.
The vase has taught me. O! make haste and come.
I can but mar the good, grey, clay till then
And know I mar it, and would mar it more
But for past councils.
      Halim, Yusuf's Son.

Notes

1. The day before JLK's birthday. Professor Andrew Rutherford assigns this verse letter to 1885 (*Early Verse*, p. 269). The evidence for either 1885 or 1888 seems inconclusive.
2. Tobacco, to which RK and JLK were equally addicted.
3. The part of a hookah containing the tobacco and coals.
4. Presumably the stories of *Soldiers Three*: perhaps "Private Learoyd's Story", *Week's News*, 14 July, or "With the Main Guard", *Week's News*, 4 August.
5. The mercury in a thermometer.
6. Generally, a term of respectful address; specifically, a native clerk who writes English.
7. *The Story of the Gadsbys* was RK's most ambitious work so far, and was still in process; but possibly he means *Soldiers Three*, or even "Mother Maturin".
8. Earthenware lamps.

To Edmonia Hill, [7–8] July 1888
Text: Copy, University of Sussex

[Simla]

It begins here because I didn't turn the sheet round Saturday. 12:

Just back from dinner at the L[ieutenant]. G[overnor].'s[1] – a portentous dull affair for which I arrived late 'cause your letter insisted upon coming in at 7.45 and I was invited for 8:15: all dull people except a terrible girl I sat next to. She was a daisy and frivolled with one of the Chief's A.D.C.'s in the regulation Simla style. She talked of "Jawin' the servants" "rotten stuff" etc. etc. It was quite a relief when I could smoke and bring a wholesome stench into the room after she had taken her departure. Mrs. N[apier]. was there and young Clandeboye[2] hung round her adoringly. What a thing it must be to possess the affections of two generations of Viceroys! I came home by her 'rickshaw; she having decided upon the plot of the yarn which *we* were to write. Before I got to the Khaibar Pass, a pass in the hills close to the L.G.'s, the 'rickshaw had gone on because it had discovered that it took two to make the "we" of a story and one of 'em was jibbing. So I came home smoking a great cheroot – the only decent thing at all the dinner – and with many vast plans rolling in my head which had not the least connection with Mrs N.

Which reminds me. You say that an you *do* me the honour of letting me share your menage, I shall flee in disgust. I see myself scudding up the avenue my spectacles glinting in the moonlight, because you are suffering from a desperate headache. Among the many experiences of my short life has been that of seeing a man die from hydrophobia. Can you startle me worse than that? I've been cutting in and out of a sickroom today and yesterday and the day before, occupied by the Mother in acute personal discomfort because she said, her tonsils had caught fire and were slowly (!) burning to ashes! In all sincerity, if you offer me the choice between civilization and the horrors of Clubland *is* it likely that – mirrors or no mirrors – I should refuse; yea though your husband pound mercury developer on my hair while you screamed aloud in the agonies of neuralgia!

Just after I sent off my last letter to you I made an awful discovery, which turned my hair grey. I wrote *selon l'habitude* two sheets and when the letter was gone there was one sheet unposted! But I know that I sent you two sheets. Consequently you must have got something out of some one else's letter or a lump of copy. Which is it, please let me know as I am rather troubled about it.[3] Luckily the second sheet was not sent off to any one else, so all is yet well. But what *have* I sent you?

Do you know what it is like to live in a Turkish bath for three days at a stretch? The weather here is hot steamy and muggy and when one goes for a ride with a lady who wears a fringe the effect is curious. At five o'clock the hair is beautifully frizzed and curled on the forehead and you think: – "This is the very brow of Diana." At seven the hair has uncurled and is bulging low down above the eyebrow in unsightly wisps and smears and – the forehead is like the forehead of a servant girl. This happened to me the other day and the effect was exactly that of a curtain being let down on a pretty scene.

Your life at Mussoorie seems a full one indeed but – after that the deluge of stagnation at Allahabad. Won't you find it awfully dull? My fear is that you will, some fine day, discover that I am a most undesirable critter to take into domestic life – and that fear makes me uncomfortable.

On my faith I have but little to tell you save that I am counting the days to the end of my leave – so called. On Friday I went to see the *Unequal Match* and alas and alack realized that Mrs A[llen]. has grown stout. Pity it is when a matronly figure assumes the frolicsomeness of nineteen – in short frocks. It accentuates the outlines. The play was a dull and a moral one and Simla didn't quite know where to look. 'Tain't used to be preached at. I found myself next to Mrs Fred Atkinson – a painted atrocity – and the last time we had met in the theatre was almost exactly a year before when we were acting together in The Scrap of paper – a dull play which fell flat.[4] I was aware of a still small voice saying in my ear: – "This is almost as bad as we were" but a virtuous husbandman or blacksmith on the stage began to preach a sermon and Mrs Atkinson said quickly: – "No – we never – *never* thumped a tub." I'm afraid that I've slated the play in my critique[5] but I had a reason for it. I don't want to praise any one at all – at all. It was almost wholly tub-thumping. I am rather amused at your audacity in claiming that Mussoorie sets Simla the lead in her plays. *The Vilikins and Dinah* of your particular suburb is not at all likely to resemble the Metropolitan Article – as prepared and adapted by Hobday.[6] Mercifully he had not taken me into his confidence about it – so I can't tell you what the splendours will be like. Why [what?] mean your dark and dismal allusions to "second leave" to Simla. I am the last person in the world who will take it for Simla has been an "abomination" to me this season. There's a dance at the L.G.'s tonight to which I am not going of course; and after that another subscription.

Sunday. And all the church bells a ringin' horrid! I shan't be down in Allahabad till after you are and as soon as ever the date is settled I'll let you know. No. I have not told the Mother because I wasn't sure that the thing was settled – and I am loath to believe in too much good fortune. It's unspeakably kind of you and – anyhow pen and ink is a bad medium to convey thanks in. I'll keep them till we meet which will be ere long.

This forenoon produced a pretty note from the Viceroy asking whether I had seen the last *Saturday Review* as it might interest me. I scudded up to the library and found no end of a good review of the P.T.'s in it.[7] Nearly a column, I think it was, and they had quoted some of the Privates' most uncivilized sentiments. Among the many papers that you take in is the *Saturday* one? It's a great piece of good luck as I never got the "Old Woman" to speak before and – oh it's all toward clearing the way for the homeward flight. Therefore I rejoice and – what do you think? Is it well?

11.30. p.m. Just in from a dreary dull dinner at Scoble's – the Councillor man. He himself was delightful and told me many things worth the remembering – notably the Supreme Govt's attempt to stultify as far as possible the ends and aims of Ripon's "lokil sluff"[8] scheme, and also a lot of interesting personalities about the Viceroy's way of doing work. Herein I was in luck for Mrs N. tells me quaint things about H[is].E[xcellency].'s private life and past experiences so that I get a certain amount of information on both sides. Scoble was not enthusiastic about education in India and said one or two very bitter things on the native press. Met also a man who knew Philadelphia well wherefore I was interested in him and spake sweetly to him. There were no other nice people to talk to.

This morning a deputation of "log rollers" came to sit upon my head about the petroleum well-sinking concession in the Punjab. They were too beastly affable for anything and I finally came to the conclusion that some sort of swindle was going to be worked. However this is for your private ear only and – won't interest you.

I am not – how shall I put it? – equable except in a few important matters, and I'm not several things that I ought to be – Indeed I am not! and I can only throw myself upon your charity and beg you to overlook them.

By the way, we give ourselves up to prying into the future by cards at Simla. A young lady told me my fortune the other day and said that I should shortly enjoy a piece of luck and later come unexpectedly into the possession of money. She said many other very curious things too and some of her statements were startlingly near the truth. I ain't superstitious and least of all after dinner.

Have attempted a new and slightly audacious form of criticism of The Unequal Match. Instead of writing a laboured review vowing that every one could not have been better I stuck four people into Peliti's balcony and made 'em talk over the play as they naturally would. I fear, as I said, that the result is slightly acid and I fancy that G.W.A[llen]. won't be over and above anxious to retain me as a dramatic critic.

Will you forgive a short letter because there are really no trivialities to talk about and graver matters cannot be discussed. x x x x x Oh my Sainted Aunt! What am I to do. The dak is just in and brings me a letter from an old friend beginning in this awful fashion: – "Dear Cuss. Allow me to congratulate you on your engagement which I heard of some time ago" etc. and ending with "When are you going to be spliced?" Isn't it infamous! Never as long as I live will I forgive Miss P[arry].L[ambert]. for this foul slander, and as soon as I have settled this letter to you I will, with my pen, proceed to take the scalp off my too confiding friend at Evalkote.

By the way, that young woman – I wish you could gaze upon her – is shrinking and coy and from what I can gather I fancy that her young female friends have about chaffed her head off in regard to that "engagement." Her Mamma – the original of the Venus Annodomini – reproaches me with not coming to call and I protest that I have to be in office all day. I'm in office now, and you will see that I am writing steadily.

Hensman tells me today that "Chesney is as strong as a horse but will be in quarantine for the next three weeks." The Staff don't appear to take small-pox very badly – too hardened I suppose. I made a curious discovery about my friend Hensman some days ago and have withdrawn my idea that he is a "rough diamond." A lady with whom he is on platonically intimate terms sent him "The Garden of Eden" for an opinion and he wrote her an eight page estimate of it which she after he had gone down the hill showed to me. He didn't approve of the thing a bit but that is neither here nor there. He simply wrote a beautifully delicate and subtle (fancy H.H. being either!) summary of the main question that the Garden of Eden touched upon. I was amazed when I read it and something more than amazed when I arrived at this sentence: – "for work of that kind however good and lifelike the imitation may be, a man must either have cooed to his own mate or some one else's and Rud has done neither the one nor the other. He has drawn not only on his reserve of imagination but on the books that he has read." "Amen" said I handing back the letter "I had no notion that Howard was so acute a judge of character." And I had known him on and off for four years. Wasn't it strange.

Now, as the children say, I must finish here. There's nothing in this chit and it's a short one but mine is not the only one. Pray you write again as swiftly as may be and if you imagine for a moment that I deem you not "quickly clever"[9] (wish you wouldn't throw my own arrangements of adjectives back at me) remember what you said against the Faith that moves mountains – and doesn't put them back again. You know how clever that was. It grows as you consider it. Adios! The noble Arab champs at my door or he would champ if he wasn't so horrid wet and uncomfortable to call on Kings y'know. Write.

Notes
1. Sir James Broadwood Lyall. Simla was the summer capital of the Punjab as well as of the Supreme Government of India.
2. Archibald (1863–1900), eldest son of Lord Dufferin; styled Lord Clandeboye. He died of wounds in the Boer War.
3. Part of a letter to Margaret Burne-Jones: see [9–10] July.
4. At Simla in September 1887: RK played "Brisemouche".
5. "An Unequal Match", *Pioneer*, 11 July (uncollected).
6. *Vilikins and His Dinah* had been given at Mussoorie on 6 July; it was scheduled for the first week of September at Simla with "new dresses, scenery and appointments" (*Pioneer*, 9 and 11 July).
7. In 9 June 1888, praising the humour and versatility of the writer, a "born story-teller". The review was by Herbert Stephen (Stephen, "W. E. Henley", *London Mercury*, February 1926, p. 391).
8. "lokil sluff", the derisive name, from native pronunciation, for "local self-government" in India, a policy established by Lord Ripon's government.
9. RK's phrase for Mrs Napier: [28 June–1 July] 1888.

To Edmonia Hill, [9–10] July 1888
Text: Copy, University of Sussex

[Simla]

Monday night. Your letter of yesterday – how near that seems doesn't it? – bringing news of death among other things lovelier and more desirable. There are very few things stronger than death – I know of one only – unless it be the blank indifference with which we regard it. I am sorry in that it gave you pain, as I am sorry for all things that distress you.

My last letter will have told you that I knew that I'd made a mistake in the posting of my last news letter. Never mind 'twas only a note to a cousin o' mine Madge Burne-Jones congratulating her on her marriage, to a portentous prig by the way[1] Thanks for returning it to me; and now to matters personal.

In the first place when I expressed a mild demand for news 'twas news about yourself. D'you s'pose it interests me to know that Captain King[2] has been photoed staring languidly at Mrs T? He might be painted in that interesting – attitude – or standing on his head for matter o' that. Nor can I say that I am wildly delighted to learn that the large red subaltern Logan[3] is "giving you a tea" as you put it. *I* feel as though I also should be assisting at that tea and it grieves me that I am not.

And now to other matters. This even at dinner I said to the mother: – "You know what manner of ruffian I am in the bosom o' my family, d'you think that it would be wise o' me to chum with a family?" Then I explained your suggestion. "Well" said the mother judicially "I should have said yes a year ago on your *own* merits. Now I say that it would be good for you because, you'll have to be moderately genial and interested in things. I don't know what the Hills are like but I don't think they'll tolerate your moods and blue-devils and falling into clouds. Yes, you'll have to be civil." "All right" said I. "Proceed *mon amie*." And the mother warming to her subject laid down the advantages of the arrangement. "In the first place you'll get your meals prettily served" said she "and then you won't be alone. I believe that living alone has made you so old and uninterested this year. Then, the great thing is that you can see as much or as little of the people in the house as you want to. Don't be dependent on them for amusements and don't hang round the lady of the house at odd hours or she'll hate you." "That"s wisdom" thinks I to myself "seems easy to carry out too." "You can, when you come in from office always have your tea taken in to your own room unless she is about and offers it you. You need never meet them except at dinner when you all happen to be dining together, and you can always flee from them by saying that you have work to do." "You speak like a book, *mon amie*" said I "then on the whole you'd recommend me to try the experiment?" "Yes" said the mother "and for your sake I should like it to be a success. You'd better write to Mrs Hill and say that, if she will, you'll try for a month and see if they don't get sick of you."[4] So I, taking the mother's advice write: – "For a month and see if you don't get sick of me." *Placetne domini.*[5] The gross and vulgarian details which will make both you and I laugh we will hold over till we meet and then we'll settle 'em. The mother's complaint with me is that I am so "disgustedly self-centred" and uninterested in anybody outside myself. And indeed she has reason. A fair maiden (they tell me she's lovely) called "Gussie Tweddell"[6] met me at dinner the other night and confided to me that she wrote. Today she sent me all her verses and M.S.S. and I was mean enough to declaim them aloud for the benefit of the Maiden who was unsympathetic. The mother dropped on us both for hard hearted cynics. "There's a girl that Ruddy ought to fall head over ears in love with and that the Maiden ought to ask to tea – instead of which I find you both laughing at her poor little versifications. How did I ever bring you two into the world." Trix pranced about the room spouting poor "Gussie's" ravings in rhyme and vowing in between the lines that such an idiot should never come to her girl's teas while I sprawled on the sofa and grinned. "There's a girl that you might marry" said the Mother "she's just your sort." "She's engaged to a subaltern officer – a redolent Italian" shrieked Trix "and this is how she mourns his loss – listen!" So she caught up the M.S. and read with appropriate action a livid poem entitled "He is gone." I contented myself with shouting: – "O Great!" from time to time and bellowing applausively at the more excruciating sentiments. Naturally our poor dear little lady grew furious and said she'd ask Gussie (why does that suggest a torn gown) to dinner. Matters are now *in statu quo* because T. says she shall giggle. She has no patience with girls who moan, over penny-farthing love affairs, in vile verse. Both of 'em have decided that my complaint is overwork and that I need thorough change of scene and life. "You *must* go home next year" they say "and go home round the world. You're blue-moulded with India – fagged, dull and self centred." Perhaps they know best. T. says I'm sickening for smallpox 'cause I don't dance and glares at me daily – for the spots!

Had a gay day today receiving congratulations on the *Saturday's* review. Of course it don't appeal to you but with us – oh *why* are we of two different countries – the favour of the "Old Woman" is reckoned something. The Viceroy was awfully sweet about it and so were one or two others. I'm going to have a shot at Chatto and Windus, with my soldier yarns on the strength of it.[7] The Pater who is *not* a sanguine soul says "that clears the way for the home public. Run an edition of the P.T.'s at home." I may or I may not as I have time.[8] Mrs N was amusingly fulsome on the subject. No, she's not trying to rival Mrs Hauksbee, she's working another tack that I have known before – she is a thorough-paced cynic believing neither in God nor man and meets me on this ground telling me that "there is nothing new, nothing true and it don't signify."[9] She certainly has sapped my faith in Lady Dufferin (for goodness sake don't repeat) and in every body else that she knows I know; and she lies like a fiend. So much for the creature that is "put on a pedestal and worshipped" by her admirers. What her motive may be in taking the trouble to take notice of me when she governs "all sorts and conditions of men"[10] I cannot quite see. My idea is that it is to "complete establishment" and add a writer-man to the horde of civilians and dragoons. Excellent from her point of view *mais je m'en fiche*! When I went to tea the other evening I found her in an exhausted condition. "What has happened?" said I. "Oh there was a man" she gasped. "He came to say goodbye. He came at twelve and he left at a quarter to five!" It was then a quarter past. "Was it a soulful and heartrending interview?" I said. "Yes" she began "an awful trouble." Here I laughed. "Confess that you flirted all you knew and only discarded him because I was coming to tea." "You never will take me seriously" said she, but she laughed also, and admitted that she believed anything that I said as little as I believed anything that she said. "We are both liars" she concluded cheerfully "and which do you think is the biggest?" "*You*" said I promptly "because you're the elder." And this is the woman on the Pedestal. I met her out with Beautiful Jim this evening and he was looking into her eyes adoringly. He goes down on the 15th and is heartbroken at the prospect. She will then take some one else and get him to put her on a pedestal. Forgive me if I am brutal but Simla always makes me savage and this year more than any other of my five seasons.

In regard to what you tell me about your movements I shall not even try for the Saturday morning. Neither you nor I will be in any sense fit to look upon the other; but I shall try and try most urgently to get away on the 15th; reaching A[llahabad] on the 17th. To my extreme disgust Allen professes himself pleased with my idiotic Simla letter[11] and I must – I must get away. My method of getting to office, which you appear to regard as a difficulty, will be all right. I shall get a trap. No distance is too short for a trap and you may rest assured that so far as "independence" is concerned I shall wear any fetters that you may please to impose, with a light heart. I know – have known every year since '83 – what the "desolate freedom of the wild ass" is like but until you have become a man and seen what one evening at the club is like you will never be able to understand its infinite dreariness. You see, there are no latch keys in India and that simplifies matters immensely. Nor am I in the habit of staying out to riotous and unseemly hours and coming home with my arm around the *sais's* neck and a cheerful jodel upon my lips. I have lived and moved among men who did these things and a year of it was about enough for me.

As concerns the question you ask I can give no answer here. I have a notion what the end of my work ought to be and unless I am betrayed it will be good work.

Tuesday Morn. The rain in earnest since midnight. I've just sent the amiable "Gussie Tweddell" (Beautiful name for a comic opera) a sugar-plum sort of antique [critique?]. Trix says she'll have her in to tea and preach to her some afternoon when I'm out.

I haven't done a scrap o' work for the Pi for two days – this is voluntary – and Allen who is always adjuring me, when he wants to get anything out of me, not to overwork myself is not pleased. I'm going to see him today and tell him that Simla don't suit me. He knows that already but it is well to rub it in to him. By the way after the concert yesterday a lady managed to put her foot into it divinely. As you know Mrs. A. was "Hester Grazehook"[12] in the *Unequal Match* and Dick[13] her lover let her down in not playing up to her. He was an almighty stick. About twenty of us were gossiping round the Town Hall door and this misguided little lady turned on Allen who was staring liverishly into the clouds with the gushing remark: – "Oh, why didn't Mrs Allen get a nicer husband." "Thanks" said Allen taking off his hat. "It's pleasant to hear the truth now and then, I shan't trouble her much longer." We all exploded and the woman made matters worse by explaining that she didn't mean the husband of real life. Allen's face was worth watching.

Today brings yet more letters of congratulation on the *Saturday Review* – it's almost as bothersome as being engaged I should think, and the worst of it is that every one who has known me more than a year says "I always said so" with an air of proprietorship as if they themselves had written the review.

Education does not progress rapidly in the Hills. Yesterday afternoon the sandwich-man who should have been parading the notice of *Vilikins and his Dinah* on the Mall, stumped about between the pathetic announcements, on front and back, that "Gentlemen are particularly requested not to smoke in the Foyer." You saw men and women shaking with laughter as he went by. I spoke to him about it. He said that it was a hookum (order) and the Babu had given him the boards to carry. I said: – "Well done thou good and faithful servant. Get along with you." This really concerns your husband's department.

Ah me! What pubbles and prabbles[14] I'm writing. Don't be wrathful Marm. What can one do. I'll go out and kill time by walking. It's a very weary world and – no I wouldn't get out of it, on any terms.

Notes
1. Margaret's marriage to Mackail did not take place until 4 September.
2. Perhaps Captain W. F. King, R.A., Fort Lahore.
3. Lieutenant F. C. L. Logan, North Lancashire Regiment.
4. Mrs Hill's note on this is: "The mother's estimate of the boy was so true – he was impossible at times – but we knew him quite well before he came, and so could make allowances. We also could 'flee'."
5. "Does it please you, my masters?"
6. The daughter of Colonel Francis Tweddell, 31st Bengal Infantry, and a German mother: Trix remembered her as "a pretty girl with beautiful grey eyes . . . Ruddy used to dance with her – and teaze her." She died *c*. 1936 (Trix to Elsie Bambridge, 25 January 1937: MS, Sussex).

7. RK specifies Chatto and Windus perhaps because they were the publishers of his admired Besant; if he made the offer there is no record of it.
8. The first English edition of *Plain Tales* was published in June 1890 by Macmillan.
9. See also 28 November 1885–11 January 1886 for this phrase.
10. *Book of Common Prayer*, Prayer for All Conditions of Men.
11. Either that of the 5th or the 9th in the *Pioneer* (uncollected).
12. Thus in copy, for Grazebook.
13. Lieutenant A. R. Dick, 2nd Punjab Cavalry, played the lover's role of Arncliff.
14. Quarrels, squabbles. RK probably wrote "pribbles and prabbles": see, for example, *Merry Wives of Windsor*, 1.i.56.

To Augusta Tweddell, [10 July 1888]
ALS: University of Sussex

[Simla] *Tuesday*

Dear Miss Tweddell

I have read the poems and M.S. which you so kindly sent me and – what shall I say? You see I have hardly the right or the experience to give advice: and I pray you not to be offended with me if I speak plainly.

You have power certainly – and in one or two places, notably in the story of the Subaltern's brown paper bride a sense of humour which is not common among lady-writers. But on the other hand you, like all beginners, have not the strength of hand to carry out even one tithe of what your brain plots. For instance in the story of a mad-woman you have tried deliberately to be terrible and to fill the reader with awe. To yourself, reading the M.S. over, you are sufficiently ghastly because your mind goes back unconsciously to the mood which affected you when you were writing and bridges over gaps and flaws in the work. But you must remember that the average reader is altogether beyond the influence of these considerations and regards passages which to you seem well thought out as "stilted", and emotions which you intended to be passionate as simply "jerky." Am I too brutal in saying this? I wouldn't do it if I didn't think that you could do something good.

And now will you submit to be preached at for a while? It is Longfellow who says: –

> "That is best which lieth nearest
> Shape from that thy art."[1]

Don't try to invent or fly off into other worlds. That is beginning at the wrong end. If you have invention, and believe me that it is a very rare faculty, all the realities of all this world won't put it out. Go simply and deliberately at the reality of this life as you see it, first. Note faces, turns of expression, and conversations exactly as you would put down sketches of tree-boles or gate posts. Then as you feel your power to reproduce these in pen and ink, take the story of some one you know and write it out until you are assured in your own mind – "this is the truth." Keep on doing this – it doesn't sound nice does it? – and have no fear of attempting to describe anything and everything that lies in the pale of human life. You will fail horribly – as I fail week by week and month by month – but every failure will show you the extent of your own powers. Then if you have invention a time will come when you will find that you are no longer a copyist but a teller of tales – a writer who can make men and women move and speak and think and love like men and women. That time will not be till you have had experience larger than you at present own; and you will find that each experience through which you pass gives a broader scope to your pen. Your diction at present contains a good many German turns of speech (get rid of these by reading good models) and your poetry some very pretty German turns of thought. Keep these by all means but accustom youself to write rhyming poetry. The restraint of dancing in fetters will teach you more thoroughly how to write prose than any thing else; and verse you know is only the stepping stone to good prose. I should recommend you to get and read thoroughly every one of Besant's novels for he to my mind is master of the art of writing about men and women. If you don't know 'em pray ask at the Library for *Ready Money Mortiboy, This Son of Vulcan, By Celia's Arbour, With Harp and Crown, My little girl* and best of all, *All Sorts and Conditions of Men*. Read and reread them unless [until?] you pass from mere reading to criticism and begin to see how they are put together and what means the author uses to produce certain effects. Also (this sounds queer I know) read the Bible thoroughly and see how much can be said in how few words. I regard the Book as a great help to literary composition. There is any amount of loose slipshod English in the world and its influence has affected my style incurably but do you avoid it. Write and rewrite and when you have rewritten put away the sheets even for so short a time as a fortnight and you will be surprised to see how many new ideas have grown up in that short space. If you want relaxation or amusement try a wild and mad story occasionally and you will find that the more you know of human life (which is the wildest and maddest thing of all) the more *grotesquerie* and horror will you be able to put into this sort of work.

Forgive this lofty sermon. I do not pretend to practice what I preach but that doesn't prevent me from preaching does it? From a business point of view not one of the things you have sent me is worth the paper it's written on: but some of them are valuable as showing future promise. If you care to go on writing – remember that ink once in the blood is a subtle poison and destroys a good many pretty illusions and some of the capacities for enjoyment – send me anything you like and as soon as it is fit for anything you may be assured that I will do my best to get it put into a print frock for you. I know most of the papers and weeklies in India. If you care to send me a real life tale I'll get it, at least, set up in type and you will be astonished to see how bald and crude it looks in the merciless clear speaking of print.

Yours very sincerely
Rudyard Kipling

P.S. On second thoughts I won't return you your M.S. yet because I have a strong notion that Trix would like to talk 'em over with you. She also is a girl who writes and I think that in these matters as in many others a maid is a better councillor for a maid than a hide-bound newspaper hack like myself who has been in the rough and tumble of journalism and may very possibly in his desire to give help, such as it is, do a great deal of harm by blundering plain speaking. Talk to my sister and I fancy she'll tell you pretty much what I have.

R.K.

Note
1. Longfellow, "Gasper Becerra", concluding lines: "Shape from that thy work of art."

To Edmonia Hill, [11?] July 1888
Text: Incomplete copy, University of Sussex

[Simla]

So I have turned aside from the appointed path have I? and am wasting my substance on profligate Jerseys[1] at one fifty apiece? If I didn't know that you knew better I should hire a fresh pen and begin a sermon which would anything but relieve you; assuming that you wished to be relieved. I am a person of austere life and profound convictions and one of the profoundest of my beliefs is that a shift to Lahore would be dearly purchased at any price, and I should not think of moving under eight-hundred for the month's work. That shows a generous and noble spirit doesn't it? You are quite right. The end of life is amassing of *pice*. I only wavered for a little because I set some things higher than money. Howbeit I recognize that there is nothing like independence of papers with sickly staffs and *Kutcha*[2] arrangements and this week's mail takes home letters and "copy" which haply may find a niche in London.³ All of this is black treachery to Allen who wishes me to live and die in his service. "Journalism" sez he and, inferentially, "me for your Lord God Almighty." "Literature" sez I and, though this does not concern him, "a divinity of my own choosing." Do I do well. [. . .]⁴ to finish this letter which like the monsoon promises to be a long one. It's raining heavily and I've got to stop [slop?] about in the muck in a mackintosh. And *this* is journalism! [sketch] This is not the smoke of Hardinge's chimneys but a cloud.

The wall [mall?] is very lively just now!

Notes
1. I cannot explain the reference.
2. The antithesis of *pukka*: temporary, flimsy, substitute, etc.
3. Perhaps the approach to Chatto and Windus about RK's soldier stories mentioned in [9–10] July.
4. A gap of indeterminable length occurs here in copy.

To Edmonia Hill, [12] July 1888
Text: Copy, University of Sussex

Simla:

Thursday morn.

The briefest of notes to tell you how very very sorry I am for your trouble and to apologize for being such a brute as to bother you with Simla frivolities when I ought to have known that you would be in no mood to hear them. You know that I am sorry. What is actually the matter with your husband? I don't like to hear of a man going down at a hill-station. That isn't the place for seediness.

Moreover I cannot understand what in the world you mean about unanswered letters. I have answered all as they came – including the one wherein I posted you an English letter by mistake.

So far I am in Simla and shall remain here until I go down and pray you to write to me here when you have time.

Bother the Saturday Review – let me know when your own anxieties are lightened. Mine can keep. They are not worth bothering you with just now.

The Mother has had a relapse and is in bed again – worse luck and I'm suffering from all the agonies of a vaccinated arm so you see all the world goes a sorrowing. This is merely a line put in hastily to save post and contains nothing beyond: – "I'm sorry" – tho' goodness knows that won't help Alec. Let me know how he is as soon as may be and I dare say you in your business will forgive short note. I write tomorrow but just now I can't. Simla is dripping with rain and I am as savage as a bear with a sore head. That must be the arm.

To Edmonia Hill, 13 July 1888
Text: Copy, University of Sussex

[Simla]

Friday morn.

Were you very much surprised at getting that skimpy note from me yesterday? I thought that I'd wait further news before I rushed into the inkpot and yesterday came your letter showing that things were not so bad after all. It was good and kind of you to write – but why oh why do you allude to "three unanswered letters". I've answered, as I said before, every one of 'em and with one single exception answered 'em with interest.

I have several matters to discuss but, before all, don't you dare to say that I am gallivanting about Simla. Never man led a quieter life than I do up here and only last night I refused a dinner invitation for the express purpose of bearing my mother company. Maybe the fact that your letter was late had something to do with it. Anyhow I sent a jhampani[1] off at the last moment with a note explaining that I was "unavoidably detained by business." The only advantage of my accursed craft is that one can always take refuge behind it. Howbeit I shall have a bad five minutes with my hostess if I meet her.

No, seriously, *mon amie*, I do not gallivant and I tell you every single thing I do.

Which reminds me of a curious walk I took yesterday. There is a huge – an enormous – woman up here – a Mrs. Beauclare[2] – who acted *Lady Jane* in Calcutta the other day. And she has a notion that India is improperly governed. We met once or twice before and talked "politics". heaven help that woman! And yesterday she asked me to tea at the Hotel and a walk afterwards. The tea was all right and so was the walk as long as she stuck to her 'rickshaw. At least her size was not undecently noticeable. But she wanted to get out and walk and I was sorry that I hadn't brought my horse. However I turned the 'rickshaw into an unfrequented path of surpassing vileness, and steepness and said mendaciously: – "This is the prettiest road in Simla." She rolled out and in half an hour her boots were cut to pieces, she was blowing like a grampus and was wearied. Just fancy if this Glumdalclitch[3] had walked with me on the Mall. She was simply gigantic. At first she talked very cleverly and I fancied that she was really nice. Then I got her to talk about other women and – the veil fell and I saw that she was like the others. So far as I know you are the only woman who refuses point blank to talk about other women and I admire you for it. But you would have laughed to have seen the woman struggling up the bed of a young watercourse that had cut the path to pieces. It was all that I could do to keep a stiff upper lip.

Never mind about the second sheet which was never sent.[4] 'Twas only filled with the foolishest of Simla gossip. How could you help reading the other letter – if the likeness between the two closely written sheets deceived me into putting it in. Don't trouble to make excuses. It was, as I told you, to my cousin in England a maiden whom I knew since I was six but who lived in an entirely different life from mine – all among the aesthetic folk and the writer-men of Oscar Wilde's epicene stamp. Now she has married a scholar of Balliol and from the height of her happiness looks down on me. I wrote her a rather cynical letter in February[5] when I was in Bengal in reply to hers telling me of her engagement and assuring me that whatever my views were I too should come in time to find my consolation. I did *not* write "Don't think the worse of me whatever I may do" but "do not altogether forget your cousin whatever he may do." I go home next year with a new book or two under my arm to make my place and to make it soft enough. That means cutting about among the old writing sets and so on, and so on – you don't know how quaint the London literary *salons* are – and as soon as I am fixed up with the regular papers to take my regular work, a lien on the Pioneer for English letters[6] which ought to be a sure prop of £200 a year, I shall rest content to be forgotten by all the sets – they never care when a man drops out of the ring as Allan Cunningham[7] did many years ago – and to live my life in my own way. As many theatres as ever we[8] can afford – I am hungry for the theatres because I have yet to write my play – and long summer days at Richmond, Datchet, Virginia water, and rests on the borders of Epping forest,[9] perhaps the most beautiful in all the world. Then there is the whole of North Devon that I used to know and love, and all the beauty of Yorkshire mine own country and above all, rattling London with some place to go to every night if one cares to. If not the peace of one's own place or the quiet of the parks. I don't know what you would think of such a life. Like all others it would have its drawbacks but from what I know of it 't would have more compensations. And that is what I purpose to do – to dive into London and break with all the folk I know. If all goes well I shall marry there.

Don't credit me with every vile thing in the *Pi. No* I didn't write that leader about the Beauty Show and I do know what Ninth and Arch means[10] tho' I am rather at a loss to see how you knew that I knew. But I believe that you know everything.

I'd give a good deal to be allowed to s s s scrrrratch! My arm has begun to take already and oh how I detest the Black Baby to whom I am indebted for my torments. The doctor said that it was a first-class healthy Black Baby, but I am of opinion that it is a Little Beast. I've written a thing for the C & M about him[11] and begin to feel quite friendly to all little Black babies in consequence. But I'd like to smack mine all the same. Don't believe that a calf would have hurt half so much.

Ah me! Here comes a thundering Govt resolution about education. I must wire an abstract to the Pioneer and write a skit on it afterwards[12] though I'd much rather go on with this letter. A thousand thanks for what you said about "we and the world." I shall remember it long. My date of going down is not yet settled but it will be after Monday at any rate. Write me back an answer as soon as may be and I'll be grateful. This 'ere is no sort of a letter.

Notes
1. The carrier of a *jampan* or sedan chair.
2. Not identified.
3. The giant girl in *Gulliver's Travels*, Book II.
4. Of the letter that got mixed with one to Margaret Burne-Jones: see [9–10] July.
5. That of 25 January–24 March 1988.
6. This suggests that RK had already reached an agreement with Allen for such work. He continued to contribute to the *Pioneer* through 1890 and to the *CMG* through 1892.
7. Cunningham (1784–1842), after publishing two volumes of poems and working as a London journalist, served for twenty-seven years as secretary to the sculptor Chantrey, writing his own work only in the evenings.
8. Mrs Hill's note is: "The beloved girl is still in his thought. I can't say at this late date, but I suppose he still hoped to win the mother's consent."
9. Where RK spent the summer of 1877 following his deliverance from Mrs Holloway: he may also be thinking of its use as idyllic background in Besant's *All in a Garden Fair*.
10. "Forty Lively Ladies", a leader in the *Pioneer*, 10 July, is about a beauty show in Philadelphia at the "Ninth and Arch Museum".
11. "Little Tobrah", *CMG*, 17 July (*Life's Handicap*). The hero's parents die of smallpox and his sister is blinded by the disease.
12. "The Educational Policy of the Indian Government", *Pioneer*, 17 July (uncollected) is followed by RK's "O Baal, Hear Us!", *Pioneer*, 19 July (Rutherford, *Early Verse*).

To Edmonia Hill, 15 July 1888
Text: Incomplete copy, University of Sussex

[Simla]

[. . .] where he couldn't see her and she was making pathetic little attempts to be cheerful and moping because she wouldn't see him. Under these circumstances I shook her gently but firmly, and demanded explanations. When I got 'em my heart smote me for it seemed that I was keeping two loving souls apart and who was I to do that? "Only let him see me" said the Maiden "and try not to hate him so and then – if there is another quarrel it will be all over – indeed it will." The Mother said: – "Let them see each other and get to understand each other and perhaps they won't care so much." "Great Heavens" I said "Have I been unconsciously acting the stern Parient [sic] all this while!" So I trotted out and caught him and explained that while I hated him just as much as ever (poor brute, he was *so* humble) I liked my sister's peace of mind more and consequently he wasn't to stay at the Club making a gibbering baboon of himself but to come down to see the maiden now and again with the assurance that I would not regard him as a burglar and as an assassin. He was awfully grateful and I shook hands with him and felt that if ever anyone had secured his own happiness by this concession *I* was that man. You see the maiden is very dear to me and after all, the poor innocents only wanted to know each other better for three months – there was to be no engagement oh no – only could they meet? As the Mother explained the situation to me I gasped and then as I have said, I climbed down. Maybe under other circumstances I should have been more hard-hearted and backed up my father.[1] Isn't the heart of a maid a curious thing.

I always thought that the maid was so wise and sensible. But she said to me: – "In these things I'm no wiser than anyone else – and I care for him ever so much." I give it up. I have done my best to smooth things for her and my conscience is clear. I never had to deal with one of the maiden's many suitors before – in that way – and it was rather a quaint experience – don't you think so. I am making arrangements for my departure which will be in a few days whereof I will inform you anon.

You never told me that there was any trouble about your sister. For goodness sake don't let us both devastate our respective belongings with sickness. The Mother is better – much – and I am worse – for the Black Baby is giving me trouble – headache, heavy eyes and all the rest of it. I know what the symptoms are and the doctor seems to think that I am in for a "beautiful arm" as he calls it. I myself fancy that it won't give me any trouble after tomorrow when things begin to look brighter.

This again is merely a note because I am hampered with work of every kind and can only get through it by systematically discarding dinner and the engagements which have no great charm for me. Write me a line when you can spare time. Despite my arm I am jubilant though to end with what I began with. I am more than sorry that you so thoroughly misunderstood my report of the talk with the Mother.² It's raining cats and dogs but I can write *au revoir* instead of *good bye*.

Notes
1. JLK disapproved of Fleming because, although "a model young man", his tastes were not those of Trix (to Edith Plowden, 1888: Baldwin, *Macdonald Sisters*, p. 130).
2. In [9–10] July.

To Edmonia Hill, 5 October 1888
Text: Incomplete copy, University of Sussex

[Allahabad]

Friday:
[. . .] Scarcely had I set foot in the sarcophagus – it's Belvidere really but just now it's like a coffin¹ – before I was aware of the sounds of subdued music of the Asian kind thus: – "Lumpty-tumpty tumpty-tum!" and then over again backwards: – "Tum tumpty, tumpty, lumpty!" "This" said I to myself "means more than appears on the surface." And I sat me down and mourned at the table so: –

[sketch]

There was too much table and too little me but I got the *is se accha chiz*² and . . . did I drink beer. No matter. 'Bout cheroot and coffee time the faithful K[adir].B[aksh]. came to me

> clasped hands and the petitionary grace
> "of Khitmatgars subdued me ere he spake."³

"Sahib" said K.B.
"Grrmph" said I.
"The Ayah"⁴ said K.B.
"Well" said I. "Leave her alone" and then I drank coffee. The punkah ceased to pull and I saw through the door that the verandah was full of white robed ghosts.
K.B. threw a glance towards the listening populace as one who said: –

"Behold how I manage *this Sahib*! Observe, O Barbarians how I twist him round my little finger!"

I drank some more coffee.

"It's a petition" said K.B.

"The deuce it is" said I. "Petish!"

"The ayah says she wants to hold a nautch."[5]

"Oh" said I.

"And a burra khana"[6] said K.B.

"Anything else?" said I.

"No . . . but there'll be music speaking in the night time" said K.B.

"Well?" said I.

The crowd without increased and the punkah was still unswung. K.B. looked round for applause and coughed.

"She wants your orders" said K.B.

"Does she expect me to come and nautch with her?" said I. "Because I'm not in the mood for nautching."

"But you are the *malik*"[7] said K.B.

"What has that to do with her" said I.

"She wants your permission" said K.B.

"*Is* she my ayah?" said I.

"God forbid" said K.B. "but she doesn't want to inconvenience you."

"Then let her not nautch" said I.

"But it is on account of her son" said K.B.

"Then let her nautch" said I.

"And the Burra Khana?" said K.B.

"Let her Burra-Ka" said I. "It's none of my business."

"The ayah will be very grateful" said K.B.

"The ayah will be very sick" said I "and if she is ill when the Memsahib returns she will be made sicker."

The crowd at the doors dispersed, the punkah pulled and the music of the tom toms was resumed. The ayah is going to do things in style. The dance comes off tonight and the dinner tomorrow so I shall have diversion in my leisure hours. But they'll all be dead or well by the time you return.

On the strength of the hand of the government being removed I did this morn horribly oversleep myself and eat too heavy a breakfast which led *me* to write a pasquinade in the *Pi* on the text of a telegram from Bombay.[8] Tiffin was a dreary wilderness and they had very appropriately decorated the table with a funeral cross of hybiscus (is that how you spell it?). I did the hybiscussing on my own account for even the best of Bombay all-blaze[9] and great chunks of primrose hued butter console not for the everpresent desolation.

You shouldn't have taken me in, dear people, and showed me what a happy home is like. It makes one exacting.

The brougham departed this morn to the place of Resurrection and I fancy from certain evidences about the place that the whitewash men will be around shortly. In the midst of all these distressing events the parrot is the only one who is calm. He woke me up this morn with shrieks and drunken whoops for the which I did not bless him.

One immediate result of your departure has been the appearance (as you'll see in the *Pi*), of the sea-serpent in the bay of Bengal.[10] Same old samp[11] – tea cup eyes, etc. etc. I *knew* they'd have to do something to fill up the gap caused by your flitting but I didn't think it would be anything half so common and devoid of originality as the sea-serpent.

Tonight I go in state to the Band and so help me that's the whole of all that has to be told. I trust you escaped without a headache and will not develop one while you are away.

Yours always
RK

P.S. Is this the sort of letter you wanted.

Notes
1. Hill, who was weather reporter to the Government of India, had gone on a tour of inspection of weather-reporting services to Pachmarri, in the Satpura Hills of the Central Provinces, taking Mrs Hill with him. The house was to be cleaned and white-washed in their absence, while RK remained as tenant.
2. Something better.
3. Cf. Tennyson, "The Brook", ll. 112–13.
4. Lady's maid.
5. Dance performed by women.
6. A feast, big dinner.
7. Lord.
8. "The Dignity of It", *Pioneer*, 6 October (uncollected): burlesquing the desire of the native members of the Bombay municipality for high-sounding titles.
9. A stew; ("ala-blaze" in *Hobson-Jobson*): RK praises Mrs Hill's Bombay all-blaze in "A Celebrity at Home" (MS, Library of Congress).
10. It is reported in the *Pioneer*, 6 October, with "two large eyes the size of teacups". RK wrote a note in the *CMG* two years earlier beginning "the sea-serpent has returned" (25 August 1886: uncollected).
11. Snake.

To Alexander and Edmonia Hill, [6] October 1888
Text: Copy, University of Sussex

[Allahabad] Saturday morn. 10.30. p.m. [*sic*]

Dear People –

So you arrived in state and ancientry[1] at Jubbulpore[2] and found

Captain Silver[3] there. Now it may be merely a matter o' taste that I personally would do much before I made a pilgrimage, to meet one of Captain Silver's like, so long as yourn. Howbeit I am *not* making pilgrimages. The daub overleaf will show you in what manner I purpose to spend the day and another daub enclosed will show you a very common incident in my daily life.

Saturday night. 10.p.m.

Now what happened in betweens, I can not quite remember. Certain it is that I went to sleep and equally certain it is that somewhere or another I captured the beginnings of a cold – a very fine and large cold which I shall cherish carefully against your return.

The ayah has really had a fine old time of it. Last night was vocal, instrumental and melodious. Strange ekkas jingled down the avenue by two and threes and through all the hum of voices came for four mortal hours the *tchink* of a woman's anklets and the wail of a sitar. I only hope the ayah – beg her pardon, the hostess – changed the performer once in a while. Mere flesh and blood legs couldn't stand the strain.

I went to sleep at two but the show was still in swing. Really I had no notion that forty poor rupees could create such a devilment for so long!

Today as I said I did naught except copy out *The World Without*[4] and reflect long upon the letters that I had received. Forgive my boring you with my Home affairs but I have learned that Trix will be married in May or June next! "Didn't you know?" writes the mother as though I had received a printed notification with every issue of the *Pi* for the last month. No madam, I did *not* know and I ain't one little bit pleased, but console myself with Mrs Kipling's practical philosophy. Here it is. "The older I get the less inclined am I to bother about the future until it becomes the present. The future generally arranges itself." So far good but how about the futures of other people – sisters par example – which are arranged it would appear by detestable irrepressible subalterns. But enough of Jack!

I really and sincerely pity you in the wilderness. I do so every meal time. Never was a graceless boy in thicker clover. *You* are in all likelihood eking out an uncertain and headachy existence on cookies – crumbly ones. *I* fare sumptuously on egg soup, cunning stews, roast fowl with all the liver and plantain fritters followed by coffee set upon a table handed to the blue couch, the reading lamp gently moderated thereover and my noble sole encased in raw yellow slippers. "It amounts to something being captain of this raft" as Huck Finn saith.[5] The servants take a wicked delight in pressing beer upon me (there are more bottles in the house than are dreamt of in your philosophy). I say *Peg lao* very firmly and they respond by saying Han! *beer shrab*:[6] which is to me a poignant insult. I wonder how long my Resolution will hold out.

Was at the Club this even. Not lively – "a party sitting in a parlor all silent and all damned"[7] but that through the green baize door I could catch the eldritch shrieks of the ladies of Allahabad. It scared me till I saw that the husbands were not alarmed.

I wage nightly war with a sandy red cat who seems to be wanting something. She found a shoe last night and it shocked her deeply. The cutter-grass is being repaired but as the machine man said "Bahut accha"[8] whenever I opened my lips to point out its diseases I fancy he doesn't know much about the case.[9]

Notes
1. Old-fashioned style.
2. Jubbulpore, in the Central Provinces, was on the road to Pachmarri.
3. Captain G. Silver, of the East Surrey Regiment at Allahabad, was now Adjutant of the Bengal-Nagpur Railway Volunteer Corps, Nagpur, in the Central Provinces.
4. Written for the book form of *The Story of the Gadsbys*, of which it forms the second part.
5. "It *amounted* to something being a raftsman on such a craft as that" (ch. 16).
6. *Shrub* means any wine, spirit, or prepared drink, hence Port-shrub, Sherry-shrub, beer-shrub.
7. Cf. Wordsworth, "Peter Bell", part 2, 516ff (1819 edn).
8. All right; very good.
9. The rest of the copy – two short paragraphs and a detached sentence – is, from clear internal evidence, part of a letter or letters to Mr Hill later than 6 October. They read thus:
    "What has come to three chits I wrote, one announcing Conybeare's engagement to the female Brod? Mrs. Hill says she hasn't received 'em and one of 'em contained a vernacular version of Humpty Dumpty which I sent to you" [*c*. 12? October 1888].
    "Let me know fixedly on what date the Lady of the House returns that I may make my dispositions accordingly. I do not gather from her letter that you twain are having a specially brilliant holiday. There seems to have been less joy and more toil in climbing to Pachmarri than she had anticipated" [*c*. 7? October 1888].
    A note at the end of the letter says that "On the following page are two sketches. At the top of the second page are three lines of apparent imitation of a young boy's writing, etc. – 'P.S. Thare is sum more of this letter somewhere but I cannot write upon the picture page, so it will come after.'"

To Alexander and Edmonia Hill, 7 October 1888
Text: Copy, University of Sussex

[Sketch signed R.K. del.]

[Allahabad] Oct. 7. 88.

Sunday Night: Dear People
Another day over in *sturm und drang* for I've had to write against time

in the Irish dialect, as you will see in today's *Pioneer*.[1] They seem to be getting it warm on the Border for Beley[2] whom I knew well is slain and Crookshank[3] whom I knew better is wounded. I wonder before all is done, how many men with whom I have eaten and drank will be accounted for!

What shall I write about. Would that I had written what I meant to write last night but I thought it too frivolous for recording until I read your letter this morn and was rather struck by the accident. On Friday night then I having gone to bed in a normal frame of mind dreamed my dream which was this. I was stung on the hand by a snake – a little snake that bit at me three times and on the string[4] after many unpleasant matters followed the sickness of death which you have described. It was all I could do to wake and when awake to persuade myself that I had not been stung. I was sweating with apprehension and as wearied as though I had in real truth gone through the deadly faintness. Wasn't that funny? I *wish* I had written of it then. Pray you what led to your death in your dream? My trouble was indigestion as yours I make no doubt was antipyr-indigestion? It lowers the action of the heart I believe.

The morn's dak brought a funny little note from Miss or Mrs. B.M. Croker –[5] she wrote *Pretty Miss Neville* did she not – expressing the pleasure the P.T.'s seem to have given her. Somehow the turning of the phrases irresistibly reminded me of Jane Austen or Harriet Beecher Stowe and I laughed. She lives at the Nilgiri depot Wellington and this is news to me for I thought she was at home in England.

The abominable Park[6] was this afternoon smitten with a strange desire to go to the telegraph office (the one close to the Railway) and wire messages. Would I drive him down? I turned out the Pig and Whistle[7] and drove wondering why when Abana and Pharphar[8] the office of the Pioneer stood close by he should bother himself to journey to distant parts. After the wire was despatched he suggested an adjournment to the Railway Station (at 5.30 p.m. remember) to meet the Calcutta mail (which comes in at 6.30 p.m.) on the grounds that Allahabad Station was a sort of club and gathering place on Sundays for the lower classes. I was not much of a hog on the lower classes but one place was about as good to me as another so I consented and surveyed mankind in the shape of fat Eurasian women and slatternly half caste girls tramping tramping, everlastingly tramping up and down the platform or clustering in groups and giggling until a lamp wagon dispersed them. One huge brown buffalo wore (I am not exaggerating) a full carte de visite photo under glass as a brooch. It glared like an engine lamp when the sun shone upon it. But about six the real "Society" began to arrive and arrange itself round the little tables of the refreshment room. There was a round fat man in dirty white clothes who fed a piquant damsel on coffee and maraschino, a deserted wife who plowtered[9] up and down the platform while her husband drank with Kellner's Manager and lastly there was Bechtler's spectacled assistant and the ever popular and graceful Wingrave of Sheneff's.[10] I assure you we don't know half that young man's versatility. You should see him in his Sunday best doing the honours of two whisky pegs and one of his own cheroots. It was like a glimpse into the new world for me and I was well content to watch though the mail was 20 min. late. Park didn't meet his friend whoever it was but I found a man (one of the many) who knew all about me and talked volubly of Lahore for ten minutes while I grinned with an air of overstrained intelligence and tried to fish remembrance out of wits that had altogether gone wool-gathering. But I failed and came away at 7.15 having filled in the evening little to P's satisfaction and less to mine.

Don't the life seem small and trivial when looked at from afar? I spend the bulk of my time meditating with my heels higher than my head. Tain't pretty but it's conducive to thought. Just as I write your garden and the church compound is ringing with the noise of *chor chor*.[11] All the chowkidars[12] are taking up the cry until it dies out away by the Brods.[13] Your chowkidar planted himself in the front verandah and there stolidly shouted chor as one performing a solemn religious rite. I have cautioned him to cough tonight with excessive zeal. Can I give more convincing proof of my devotion to your interests. I'm going to bed. It's a weary weary world and the cold weather is coming in by leaps and bounds.

A Dieu.

Notes
1. "The Way av Ut", *Pioneer*, 8 October (Rutherford, *Early Verse*): RK calls this "today" presumably because he means to mail the letter on the 8th.
2. Captain C. H. H. Beley, 25th Bengal Infantry, killed at Hazara, 5 October.
3. Colonel A. C. W. Crookshank, 34th Bengal Infantry, Mian Mir; he died on 24 October.
4. Thus in the copy.
5. Mrs Bithia Mary Croker (?–1920), prolific writer of novels (one entitled *The Road to Mandalay*, 1917); *Pretty Miss Neville* (1883) was her first. With her husband, Lieutenant-Colonel John Croker, she spent fourteen years in India and Burma.
6. M. H. Park, assistant editor of the *Pioneer*.
7. RK's name for his horse and trap.
8. See 2 Kings 5:12.
9. A Scotticism: to dabble, to splash, or to wade messily; or to fuss about purposely, to idle.
10. Thus in copy, for Shirreff. Kellner's was a Calcutta firm owning the dining rooms along the East Indian Railway; Bechtler's was a firm of jewellers in Allahabad. Wingrave is identified by the *India Directory* as an assistant in the firm of Lyell, druggists and photographic dealers in Allahabad; perhaps they were connected with Shirreff's, photographic chemists and photographic apparatus manufacturers (S. A. Hill, a keen photographer, would have known the local trade well).
11. "Thief, thief". "The long-drawn cho-or – choor! (thief! thief!) that sets the serai ablaze of nights" (*Kim*, end of ch. 1).

12. Watchmen.
13. The Honorable Maynard Brodhurst, Puisne Judge of the High Court, Allahabad, lived with his family at 10 Church Road: the Hills' house was no. 9.

To Edmonia Hill, [8] October 1888
Text: Copy, University of Sussex

[Allahabad]

Monday: night

Such a campaign of tossed and tangled M.S. all round me this even! Soldiers Three is nearly all in type praise the Lord and I'm giving last touches to the other three.[1] First a whiff at the pipe, then an alteration; then another whiff and then a realteration. Those beautiful speckless sheets on which you pasted my poor prose will be sair grubby by the time you've done your wanderings. Oh by the way I presume you know the news. I found it out from Malcolmson[2] at the club this evening, who said that he had heard it from Mrs. Cowie if that be the name of Mrs. Pike's mamma and *her* informant was Mrs. Brod herself.[3] I have no special reason to credit M's word so I said "Shucks!" at a venture but then Conybeare[4] came in radiant and chirpy moving with the short and nervous gait affected by men in like calam-felicities. I saw man after man go up and shake him by the hand, the while he was babbling merrily looking over their heads, into the ceiling and round the bar as is his embarrassing wont. So after a space I thought I'd go up and shake hands too. I caught him in the lobby just as I was going home. "When do the Hills return?" quo' he (I guess he's yearning for a confidante.) "I'm not quite sure" I said. "Have I the right to congratulate you?" and I timidly extended my fragile fist. He shook it, marm. He shook it as tho' I had been his dearest and nearest friend and I babbled of the platitudes usual at such feasts. "Yes" he said "it was only settled a very short time ago – tho' I have been game for some months." There was an engaging frankness about this but next minute when Park came up he was babbling with lighted eyes of the difficulty of getting volumes of the *Enc. Britt.* out of the library. He talked with joy and delight and old Park stood and looked on grimly. Then the Pig and Whistle came round the corner. "By Jove" said Conybeare "that's a nice little turn out. I must get something like that." I nearly exploded as I clambered in. Park merely looked back at him and muttered *et tu in Arcadia vixisti*.[5] Whence I argue that he was thinking of his time past. I am the more confirmed in the idea because on the road home he swore with many oaths to save up money and marry a wife. Anyhow, Conybeare is all right and happy and I hope and I hope and I hope that no one has forestalled me with this little piece of news. Of course the entire club discussed the matter with engaging frankness from every possible point of view; some men averring that she had been driven into it by her mamma and others cheerfully recording the times when C. was wont to hang round other girls. The general opinion of the N.W.P. Club as represented by six peg glasses seems however to be that the match is an eminently suitable one. It amuses C. which after all is all that we are entitled to expect.

And that's all the outside khubber[6] that I've been able to gather. I've sent to the C & M a second section of my exercises in administration[7] and have been generally horribly busy; but I have unearthed some Indian renderings of English nursery rhymes which ought to amuse your husband. They are by Bignold:[8] – the "successful competitor" – now passed into a land where competition is not allowed. Let the great Philotogistischulekafel-meister be merciful if I have not reproduced the proper spelling of the Aryan version of Humpty Dumpty.

> Hamti Damti chargya chhat
> Hamti Damti girya phat
> Raja ka pulton, Taja ka ghori
> Hamte Damte Kabhi nahin jori[9]

I quote it from memory only. It moved me to childish laughter when I read it.

This morn brought no letter from you whence I argue that you spent the Sabbath at the heels of unbridled ponies, while I was eating pillau of a lovely kind. Colonel Stewart[10] called this afternoon. I saw his eyebrows flashing in the sun as he drove away and that, deed deed and double deed, is all that I have seen save the bare walls of the office and the chairs of the Club. If I can nerve myself for the ordeal I go to call on Mrs. Pike next Saturday. Does a bride wear her wedding dress when she receives. Will I have to wreath my bald patch with roses and prance into her presence singing a song? Enlighten![11]

Notes
1. *Soldiers Three* was published late in 1888; the "other three" were the next three numbers in the Indian Railway Library series, *The Story of the Gadsbys*, *In Black and White*, and *Under the Deodars*.
2. R. Malcolmson, attorney, High Court, Allahabad.
3. Mrs Cowie was the wife of the Deputy Accountant General at Allahabad, Henry George Cowie; Mrs Pike, wife of the Assistant Magistrate and Assistant Collector, H. W. Pike; and Mrs Brodhurst, wife of the Judge.

4. Henry Crawford Arthur Conybeare (1853–1916), in the Indian Civil Service since 1871; Joint Magistrate, North Western Provinces from 1885; afterwards a commissioner. He married Amy Maxwell, daughter of Judge Brodhurst, in February 1889.
5. Cf. the traditional "et in Arcadia ego".
6. News.
7. *CMG*, 12 October; the first part appeared on 15 September (both uncollected).
8. Thomas Frank Bignold (1838–88), who entered the Indian Civil Service in the first days of competitive examination. He died while his book, *Leviora, Being the Rhymes of a Successful Competitor* (Calcutta, 1888), was in press.
9. RK later sent these verses to *St Nicholas* (see 15 October 1892), where they appeared in the January 1893 number. The texts in this letter, in the MS of 15 October 1892, and in *St Nicholas* all differ.
10. Possibly Colonel James Calder Stewart, commanding the 7th Bengal Cavalry at Bareilly.
11. Pike must have lost the wife mentioned in 27 June 1888 and have taken a new one.

To Edmonia Hill, 10 October 1888
Text: Copy, University of Sussex

[Allahabad]

Wednesday

Something has gone wrong somewhere – How? There was a letter ye writ on Friday night, Saturday night, Sunday night, and Monday night. On Tuesday night (last night) this child feeling himself singularly aggrieved in that he had received no letters for two nights curled up his legs upon the sofa and smoked contemptuous. Later on he became penitent and finished The Celebrity at Home[1] but he didn't feel like a celebrity – nary a bit. He felt unpleased for it was in his imagination that the stately prancing *byle*[2] had fallen over a khud[3] or the wild tonga pony had run away into the Central provinces and that the end of these things would be telegrams. Howbeit your letter – what a gay and giddy pleasuring you're having – came this morn and put things straighter. It did not improve the chaos in the house for I was dining in your bed room and the chut[4] of the little verandah was being torn over by a coolie. By the way that bold bad man from the height of a step ladder beheld me in my sainted bath this morn and I cried.

So you return on Monday morn and I am to seek the seclusion which the Club has given me aforetime. Be it so. I am at your disposal.

Don't be alarmed if I suddenly refuse to exchange a word with you again. 'Tis not on personal grounds madam, but national. A horrid low thief of an American publisher has pirated the P[lain].T[ale].'s and is going to publish 'em in his disgusting country![5] What a people it is. They steal your books and they steal – but I will be calm. You'll hear more about international copyright when you return than ever you have heard before. Fancy cubbing⁶ that little beast of a book. They might ha' left it alone. But I will be revenged upon them – see if I don't! Has this week's mail brought you good news? I was startled by the apparition of a letter in a handwriting which puzzled me for some time and which I now forward to you for perusal. Shall I answer it? – Asiatic quarterly and all? There's a cool insolence about the preamble which left me gasping, and an intimate knowledge of my movements which tickled me immensely. She must be awfully hard up for amusements or she would not have written to me.⁷

Another curious little item of intelligence made me laugh. You know the verses I write about Hunter?⁸ Well it seems that he himself took 'em to Sir G. Brodwood⁹ in the India office and read them aloud to him. Brodwood writes me that Hunter is really in earnest and should not be "flouted." If there be one thing more than another deadly certain to set me a "flouting" it would be Hunter's pretence of earnestness. Only let me find a handle to take hold of and – Academy¹⁰ notwithstanding – there shall be yet more lampoons. I am as cross as a bear with a sore head and demand blood.

Old Pig and Whistle is trying to fall lame in his "behime feet" as Uncle Remus saith and I am forestalling him by putting him aside against your return and pattering about in the dust, to my infinite weariness and discontent. Life, believe me, is a tremendously over-rated affair just at present and I'd like to get rid of it for a little time. Don't mind this temporary lashing out. You know my way of sinking genially into gulfs of dark despair.

What may I tell you about? The only matter of note that I remember since you left is this. Yesterday while walking in the road I saw a lady turning in to the Club. I truthfully did! I don't know what her name was but she was a large lady and I remembered the fact distinctly because it's the only one I've seen except the coffee-coloured ones at the Station since you went away. 'Say tho! I'd like to know where the mischief an' all them letters have goed to. Two of 'em had pictures in 'em and one told you about Conybeare's engagement. Perhaps the pony's ate them on the road. Tell me if you get them and when and in what state.

I see with pain and sorrow that R. L. Stevenson has been writing heresies against art in Scribners¹¹ reducing the worker in literature to his own base level – one writing to please only. I wish you could catch me that Scribner because I've only summaries seen in the other papers.

Heigho! It's a horrid weary world and the dak's going out so I must e'en come to an end. My fist is not very clear but its old pie to the fist that accompanies. Mrs. Hauksbee was ever an evil writer. On Monday at seven in the morning!

My you'll be tired though and dirty and hungry.

                                                     Yours ever
                                                            R.K.

Notes

1. A MS now in the Library of Congress. It is a description of Mr and Mrs Hill and Belvedere House, and parodies a series of this title then running in *The World*. It has been imperfectly reprinted in Harbord, *Readers' Guide*.
2. Bullock.
3. Steep hillside.
4. Cloth ceiling.
5. This edition, if it was in fact produced, has not been identified.
6. Thus in copy: "cribbing"?
7. Mrs Burton is meant: see the end of the letter.
8. "To the Address of W.W.H.": see [25–7] May 1888.
9. Thus in copy, for Birdwood. Sir George Birdwood (1832–1917) began as a doctor in Bombay and was active there in the University, the Museum, and other institutions. Returning to England in 1868 he became a leading interpreter of Indian culture to England.
10. Hunter had given a long and laudatory review to *Departmental Ditties* in *The Academy*, 1 September 1888: "the first English review that ever came to me" RK called it (see 15 January 1897).
11. "Letter to a Young Gentleman Who Proposes to Embrace the Career of Art", *Scribner's*, IV (September 1888) 377–81. The artist is numbered with "dancing girls and billiard markers."

To Edmonia Hill, [11] October 1888
Text: Copy, University of Sussex

                                                [Allahabad] *Thursday night*

                To the wake av Tim O'Hara
                   came company –
                All St. Patrick's alley
                   was there to see –
                Wid the friends an' kinsfolk
                   of the family.[1]

which being translated into the English meaneth that at 5. this afternoon when I was offering myself for a desolate walk little Alston[2] dropped in with the news that the Wrights[3] from Bombay would be coming into [Allahabad] tomorrow morn at a quarter to eight. *Nota bene*. The house is a howling quagmire of whitewash complicated with scaffolding in the dining room. But after a moment my gigantic intellect grasped the situation in all its vast and complicated bearings. To leap into my raiment and to howl for K[adir].B[aksh]. was the work of one minute. To light a cheroot puckrao bushna[4] and give my orders the work of ten. Take out my kit and shove it into the Sahib's dressing room and be careful that not a fraction of tobacco remains in the room – not a vestige. These things were under way when I departed straight to the Club to write you a letter.

I go down to the station tomorrow and catch 'em and send 'em to the house where they will have *chota hazri*[5] and arrange themselves while I come on with the luggage to spare them pain and discomfort. Something will have to be done to the eating-room that's flat but what it is I have not yet determined. I must see tonight. Mrs. W. will want to go over to Mrs. Couri's[6] where all her luggage and effects lie and I'll put the pig and whistle at her service (the brougham ain't back yet) and pray her to regulate her own hours in the matter of meals. That will be all right, won't it? I'll keep over to the duftar[7] and give as little sign of my presence as in me lies but believe me I'll do all I can to make them comfy in your house. Wright has to be at Benares on the 18th so I can not say for certain how long they will abide here but I daresay you will know more about these things than I. An they stay over the Monday methinks that even the eagle-eye of the Brod could detect naught wrong in my remaining under the same roof as you. Howebeit these be matters entirely for your own disposal and in the which I am your servant. The main point is to get 'em housed and fed comfily without mixing the whitewash in their food. That's all I have to tell you. Write me any instructions that the occasion may demand. I'm off with this to the station on the offchance of its catching the Jubbalpur mail.

R K

[sketch: "Study of a domestic crisis."]

Notes
1. Robert Buchanan, "The Wake of Tim O'Hara", *London Poems*, 1866; the first four lines are the epigraph to "Black Jack" (*Soldiers Three*).
2. (Sir) Charles Ross Alston (1862–1937), advocate, High Court of Allahabad, practised in India from 1885; Judge of Allahabad High Court, 1909.
3. William Henry Wright (1840?–1926) had been on the faculty of Muir College with Hill, where he was Professor of English Literature; he was now returning from leave to take up the position of Principal of Queen's College, Benares.
4. Perhaps the copyist's error for "puchrao buchna" – roughly equivalent for "taking it carefully".
5. Early tea.
6. Thus in copy, probably for Cowie (see [8] October 1888).
7. Office: the room "to the right of the drawing room as you enter" Belvedere, used by the Hills as a study and described in "A Celebrity at Home".

To Edmonia Hill, 12 October 1888
Text: Copy, University of Sussex

Allahabad.

The Blow has fallen as you will have guessed from my letter and wire but I don't quite see where the evil of it lies as you appear to do.

As I told you by tar[1] I went down to the station and found Wright and the memsahib looking at your telegram. Now I hadn't shifted out of my room for nothing so I simply took them to Belvidere gave 'em tea, washed 'em and had breakfast at ten from which breakfast I am but this instant come away.

The case stands thus. I am settled in the dressing room (your husband's) and will be shot if I let you have it. The Wrights have my room, the dining room will be fit for use tomorrow. Meantime the room which was your bedroom has been converted into a dining room. There isn't a trace of litter in your husband's duftar because I have slinked everything out of sight. When the dining room is repaired and they are working hard at it, everything will be put back there and your room will be made ready for you. I am *not* going to permit you to be turned out on my account. I am perfectly comfortable and can manage for the Wrights without the least trouble until you return on Monday morn at 7.45. a.m. It's all absolutely teek[2] as it can be and there won't be the least trouble. Neither Booj[3] nor any one else is in the faintest degree incommoded; only return on Monday and see for yourself. It's too late for me to shift back into my own room even had I desired to do so on receipt of your letter, because (1) there are seven boxes with the W's, and (2) your room is the dining room so there is no where to put them, (the W's). I consider that I have managed *uncommonly well* as you will see for yourself when you return. I do not think that I shall despatch Kulub Ali to the station but that remains to be seen. I have taken the liberty of putting your brown horse into my ghari (at least he will be put in if Mrs W. wants him as old Pig and Whistle is still a bit gummy in his near hind leg.) Need I tell you how much I look forward to your return on Monday?

R K

I fancy that the Wrights will stay till Wednesday certainly not longer as he has to be in Benares by Thursday. That means for me only three nights in the dressing room after your return and that is not likely to kill me.

You seem to be having a gay and festive season at Pachmarri – pray you let not the picnics destroy you utterly. So joyous are you that you refuse to acknowledge my letters which in itself is sufficient proof that you are busy with the distractions of the hour; though it is hardly pleasant for me.

Mulvaney "came" with a rush on the couch in the blue room and if I walked one mile up and down as I was hacking it out I walked three.[4] It would ha' been better if you had been there. Now Chesney has gone away to Naini Tal to insult the L.G. on high affairs of State. Park and I are alone and I have (O shame!) to write scraps.[5] To this pleasing duty will I now address myself. Adios for three days.

P.S. Never saw a man so changed by England as W.H.W. He's 20 years younger, talks continuously, is spry active and genial and she, for her, is radiant and communicative. Just Heaven! By all the laws of proportion if the recipe has the same effect on you and your husband you ought to return from your home trip the one in short frocks and the other in Eton jackets. They both want to see you.

R K

Notes
1. Telegram.
2. Exact, precise.
3. Mrs Hill's cook.
4. "Black Jack", the only one of the stories in *Soldiers Three* not already published.
5. None of these can be positively identified. Those in the *Pioneer* for 12 October include items on technical education in India, mosquitoes in Bombay, and the Black Mountain expedition; for the 13th, on an attack on Lord Dufferin, and (a favourite topic for RK) the state of the drains in Bombay.

To Cormell Price, 4 December 1888
ALS: Library of Congress

Allahabad. / Dec 4 / 88:

Dear Uncle Crom:

Please see enclosed "Ed" of mine and make remark.[1] They are raising the question (all along o' exchange) of a school in *India* for gentlemen's sons. The matter is being fought on the Bombay side and the *Times of India* the paper which raised it makes many allusions to the Old Coll. which it apparently knows.[2] You'll see I've also dragged it in to strengthen the opposition. 'Seems to me that the notion is suicidal and my prejudice is based on observation of the country bred boy who is an abnormally lewd little beast, insolent, domineering and used up ere he is thirty through sheer lack of stamina. Don't you think you could see your way either to favour us or the *Times of India* with a letter on the subject or lay the matter before your own Board of Control and point out which way the tide is setting in India. It is impossible for men with Rs 1,000 a month, i.e. £660 sterling thanks to exchange, to keep up his married establishment out here and to educate say even one son at rates as cheap as those Westward Ho! offers. Your £800 means Rs 1200 exclusive of holiday expenses and it is a very strong man that can keep his married expenses down to Rs. 500 a month, keeping up insurance, at the same time. As most families by reason of the infirmity of humanity are not limited to one son the problem becomes harder.[3] Westward Ho! has done a great deal for the sons of Anglo Indians though alas! in my own case I did not profit by any special teaching. Is there no chance of its doing more? If these fools are induced to put two or three lakhs into an Indian Educational scheme the Lord help their issue. It would ease the fathers maybe but 't wouldn't be fair on the boys. Of course I have no notions of my own on the subject so I lay the matter before you. There is a certain amount of depreciated silver available for Schools out here. It ought to be drawn to England.

Your exceeding short and business like notes have been received by me and the advts inserted.[4] I see that the Chronicle has been good enough to review me.[5] My thanks to my brother Editor therefore. I'm up to my eyes in new books, stories and journalistic ventures and begin to hope that I have made the beginnings of a reputation. Can you imagine a University regretting that I was not a fellow – ye Gods! one of its Fellows! Tell that to W.C.C[rofts]. and watch him squirm. Can you imagine me bothered to set papers for an examination? I refused on the broad grounds that I hadn't time but in reality I quaked at the idea of such presumption.[6] My best love to all the Common Room. I'll send you some books ere long.

Yours always
Ruddy.

Notes

1. An untitled note, *Pioneer*, 19 November, beginning "A first step has been made on the Bombay side towards the permanent expatriation of the Englishman in India" and arguing pretty much as the letter does about the "country bred boy" (uncollected).
2. The discussion began with a letter signed "Self Help", *The Times of India*, 14 November, and ran through the next ten days. RK's note of 19 November (see preceding note) was reprinted in *The Times of India* on 21 November.
3. USC was already in financial trouble, in part through the decline of the rupee: "Boys were taken away from 1888 onwards, and by 1891 the school was losing money" (Richard Maidment, "Imagination and Reality in Rudyard Kipling's View of Education: A Literary Study", MA thesis, University College of Swansea, 1981, p. 125).
4. An advertisement for the school ran in the *Pioneer* weekly for many weeks from

November; it emphasised that "the expenses are as low as they can be kept compatibly with efficiency" (17 November).
5. The third edition of *Departmental Ditties* is reviewed in the USC *Chronicle,* 29 October 1888.
6. I do not know what this alludes to.

To Stephen Wheeler, 12 December 1888
ALS: Dalhousie University

Allahabad. / Dec. 12 / 88.

Dear Wheeler,

After these many months, Salaam. I fancied I recognized your sweet roman hand in the review of the St. James's on my verses.[1] Can you do me yet another favour. I am sending to the St. James's by this mail two small volumes of this accursed land's manufacture (*Soldiers Three* and *The Story of the Gadsbys*). One seems to me unwholesome; the other isn't, but I tried to put good work into both. Can you lend them a fostering hand? *Don't* review 'em. You know *too* much or if you do, let me down easily and your petitioner will ever pray etc.[2]

They are selling well out here, and the Barrack room book might take at home.

Yours,
Ruddy.

Notes
1. After his return to England in 1887 Wheeler worked for a time on the *St James's Gazette.* I have not found the review of *Departmental Ditties.*
2. The *St James's Gazette* reviewed the Indian Railway Library stories 6 July 1889: see 16 September 1889. RK sent copies of his Indian Railway Library stories to other English correspondents about this time in hopes of arousing interest in his work before his arrival in England (to the editor of the *Academy,* 12 December 1888 [ALS, Berg Collection]; to George Hooper, January 1889 [ALS, Syracuse University]).

Part Three
The Road Back to England
1889

INTRODUCTION

The serious illness of Mrs Hill at the beginning of 1899 seemed, for a time, to threaten the plans that Kipling had made to accompany the Hills as they went off on leave and he ventured to London to make his name. By the end of January she was recovering, and their plans went ahead quickly. After a brief farewell visit to his parents in Lahore, Kipling sailed with the Hills on 9 March, travelling via Rangoon, Singapore, Hong Kong, to Japan, where the three spent nearly a month. On 11 May they sailed for San Francisco, arriving on 28 May. The Hills went on to her Pennsylvania home, leaving Kipling to make his way after them through the American west. He had arranged to pay his way by writing a series of travel letters for the *Pioneer*, and it was thus necessary for him to see the sights for the sake of the copy they furnished. By the end of July Kipling reached Beaver, Pennsylvania, the home of Mrs Hill's parents. From there he visited the major eastern American cities. At the end of September Kipling sailed for London with Mrs Hill, her sister Caroline, and four Taylor relatives; the party arrived in England on 4 October, almost seven months after Kipling had set out on his journey from India.

The record of his travels is written out in the thirty-nine letters that Kipling sent back to the *Pioneer*, a series later collected, in much revised form, in the book called *From Sea to Sea* (1899). The American *From Sea to Sea* letters are amusingly supplemented by the letters he sent to Mrs Hill in the course of his travels across the continent. In the public letters, Kipling stresses the violence and danger of American life: murderous traffic, crazily-constructed railways, unrestrained drinking, unashamedly corrupt politics, and, in the west at any rate, the ever-present threat of death from the firearms that he supposed most Americans carried. In writing to the American Mrs Hill, he drops these themes and, though not inclined to flatter, turns his attention to the variety, the energy, and the comedy of American life.

Once in England, Kipling caught on almost at once as a writer; some echo of the excitement that his work had created in India had preceded him in England, and once editors saw his work they could not get enough. In his autobiography, Kipling recalls that at this period he "stepped into a sort of waking dream" in which he was dealt "fantastic cards". As at the beginning of his Indian career, when he was instantly transformed from schoolboy to hardworking and responsible adult, so now he was instantly transformed from unknown provincial to eagerly sought-after writer.

In the three weeks that elapsed between their arrival in England and the departure of Mrs Hill for India, Kipling became engaged to her sister, Caroline Taylor, who was to accompany Mrs Hill to India. Nothing is known of the history of this affair, and we can only guess at how it is bound up with the tangle of his emotions towards Mrs Hill herself. The year ended for Kipling in contradictory feelings, the euphoric effect of his spectacular literary success contrasting to the misery of his separation from Mrs Hill. As he wrote to her on Christmas day, 1889, "there are five million people in London this night and saving those who starve I don't think there is one more heartsick or thoroughly wretched than that 'rising young author' known to you as / Ruddy."

To Edmonia Hill, [January? 1889]
Text: Copy, University of Sussex

[Allahabad]

Dear Lady,

Good morning. I hear that you are better.[1] I rejoice with a great joy. You must get better soon because I am going round the world writing letters to the Pioneer and the Civil and Military.[2] I leave the *Pi* about the middle of March or perhaps a little earlier. Dare[3] has just now settled the matter with me, so if you play on the road to Singapore you will let me catch you up.[4] *Please* get well.[5]

RK

Notes
1. Mrs Hill had been ill since late December and by mid January was in critical condition with fever and other symptoms. This letter is presumably from early January.
2. That is, the long series of travel letters for the *Pioneer*, partly collected in *From Sea to Sea*, and the miscellaneous contributions to "Turnovers" in the *CMG*, collected in *Abaft the Funnel*.
3. William John Dare, general manager of the *Pioneer* press; it must have been Dare who said to RK on paying him his last wages, "Take it from me, you'll never be worth more than four hundred rupees a month to anyone" (*Something of Myself*, p. 75). Dare was, RK recalled, "a natural as well as a semi-educated brute" but added "I don't recall that he ever did me any harm" (to Sir James Walker, 15 October 1911: ALS, Dalhousie).
4. Some time after this letter RK and the Hills agreed to travel together through the Orient to America.
5. A note on the copy says: "Letter printed, not script".

To Edmonia Hill, [26? January? 1889?]
Text: Copy, University of Sussex

[Allahabad] Saturday night:

Dear Lady:

A note from Alex: this even saying that I shall hear tomorrow how you have passed the night: wherefore I write this on the assumption that you have passed a good night: As I told you just now nothing has happened and I can only write again and again and yet again how sorry

I am that you are not well. I met when I was coming to Belvidere this even, your nurse who impressed me as a kind and capable body. She and I confabulated at the head of the drive and she told me that you were "getting on nicely thank you, Sir:" and ought to pick up in a few days. Later on, after I had left you and returned to the Club I met Irwin[1] who said that my turn out (the Pig and Whistle) was just the thing he wanted to buy if he had the dibs. He also told me that you were progressing marvellously well and seemed to think much of the docile manner in which you had responded to his treatment.

I am sitting now just behind young Porter[2] and an American-looking native both of whom appear to have been at Oxford together and who are now passing the evening in exchanging reminiscences. Porter is a nice young man but as the bulk of his jokes are pointed with a Latin quotation (generally from the more obscure of the Ancient Authors) his effect on the club is that of a cultured wet-blanket. Digby[3] was the next man to me at dinner and he poured flattery upon me in a manner that I did not understand. I guess he must want to get something out of me.

The Club is a very dreary place. I ravage the Library every night after dinner and am "shocked" to see the sort of twaddle that the ladies read. No wonder that they cackle and shriek so behind the baize doors.

Did I tell you when I talked to you purdah-nashin of the long talk that Bayless[4] and I had together? The thing (next to his *Fiancée*) that he appears to value most is a Winchester repeating rifle which I got hold of and which to my intense alarm he insisted on "showing off" to me in his rooms. It is a loathsome weapon which fires off four cartridges without reloading and flicks out the empty cases into your eye just like a sort of murderous human being. Bayless gave me a lot of letters of introduction for the American tour, which I have a notion will be of much value to me. He says that I am to hunt for his Papa and Mamma. "If they are not at Santa Barbara, you'll be sure to find 'em somewhere in California," says he. Rather like hunting for a needle in a bundle of hay, isn't it?

This week's mail brings me a letter from my cousin Margaret to whom I have not written for the better part of a year. She wants to know what has become of me, and why I have held my peace for so long. In reply I have asked: "What in the world do you who have not sent me a line for *three* parts of a year mean by asking me a question like that?" Another relative one of my aunts the wife of Poynter the R.A.[5] says that she will be happy to put me up when I arrive in London. I wonder when and how far hence that time will be! My old school-master also writes me a long letter and tells me nothing. My people at Lahore have behaved awfully. They haven't sent me a letter for nearly a week past. I have sent up an indignant protest against such treatment.

Talking of letters reminds me that Captain Bayless desires me to convey his apologies to you for not coming to enquire after your health. He has been stuck on the range from dawn to dusk, he says, and his time is not his own. As a matter of fact I believe that he spends his time writing enormous letters to his lady love and, 'pon my word, I do not blame him. She is not lovely to look upon – all raw and undeveloped if her photo speaks the truth but he seems to be immensely fond of her. He told me a lot about her this afternoon.

And now, as the little children say, I must say "Good bye." I wish I could have written a more interesting letter but that's impossible as I go nowhere and do nothing in these days. Tomorrow evening if all is well I will try and write you a more amusing chit, on the strict understanding that you get better in order to read it.

Ever yours
Rudyard Kipling

Notes
1. J. M. Irwin, MB, surgeon at the Station Hospital, Allahabad, and Hill's physician.
2. Wilfrid King Porter (1865?–?) BA, Balliol, 1888; barrister of Gray's Inn and Indian Civil Service, 1888; advocate before the court, Allahabad. He disappears from the *India Directory* in 1890.
3. Captain T. E. Digby, Executive Engineer, Military Works, Allahabad.
4. That is, Captain E. G. Bayliss: see [22] April [1888]. He was Instructor in Army Signalling in the East Surrey Regiment.
5. Aunt Aggie.

To Edmonia Hill, [6? February] 1889

Text: Copy, University of Sussex

[Allahabad] Wednesday Night

Dear Lady and most Enquired-after Invalid,

To you on your couch of discomfort, salutation!

Indeed this morning Alex wrote suggesting that I should write you a note; but I reflected that it would not be seemly to bother you with overmany communications from the outside world (which, after all, is but a second rate and chilly sort of arrangement) and so I refrain my pen even from good words. Now a note this evening tells me that you are displeased; and I sit down in a deserted club-room to make amends.

There is no news to tell you. How could there be any with the light of your countenance withdrawn from the station? Behold the ordering of my day.

In the morning at nine I rise up and disport myself in my tub (once upon a gusty morning the *Kanât*[1] of the bathroom fell down and left me gazing, after the manner of Lady Godiva of blessed memory, upon the road) and partly walk upon my legs and partly am driven to office, where I stay till 4.30. when I make inquisition as to your health from Alex and walk from thence to the Club. That regularly takes me to 5:30. Then I change and walk from the Club to the little stone pillar which is over against the bandstand and back again. That usually brings me to 6:30 when I again repair to the Club and read old bound numbers of *Vanity Fair, Punch* and the *Cornhill Magazine,* till dinner. After dinner I smoke the pipe of reflection and go to bed. Can you imagine a life less uneventful than mine (if I except only yours at the present moment).

I have been told a great deal about the prospects of the Civil Service Cup.[2] I dare say 'twas vastly interesting to those who "take delight in the legs of a horse"[3] but I only listened with half an ear and said: – "Oh yes, of course" at inopportune moments. Even my wild attempt at gambling in the Cup Lottery at the Club was a failure. I took three tickets and Gordon[4] the Secretary presented me with a box like a camera with the inside knocked out and said: – "You must help to draw tickets." So I drew numbered gun-wads from this camera for three mortal hours and that was all the profit I ever got out of the show.

Yesterday evening at half past five when I reached the Club I found a *chit* from Mrs. Colvin[5] asking me to come to tea at five that evening. So you see even though I could not accept the invite I might have moved in the height of society. The Colvins' have red badminton nets when they give parties. I saw them blazing from afar.

Within the past ten days I have seen Mrs. Irwin,[6] also from afar, – a back view of her in a cart. Also Mrs. Lawrence,[7] same view, and once Mrs. Ross driving in a barouche. They were all too high and mighty to take any notice of me. And the more so because when I took off my hat to Mrs. Ross the lining of it stayed on my head! I thought I was more or less of a philosopher up till that hour but I tell you Marm to have your well-considered politeness spoilt by a leather fillet round your noble brows like the wreath of a sacrificial bull is trying – very trying.

Talking of critters reminds me that I have the honour to know one of the funniest little bull terrier pups that ever chewed a boot. He is all head and paws and grin – belongs to Porter who owns the next tent to me and is an abiding delight to me – comes in and helps me to dress by slobbering over my boots and hanging on to the end of my braces as they trail. But I grieve to say that my over much kindness has bred in him a belief that I am personally interested in his career. Consequently he turns up with mouldy bones and fragments of garbage unspeakable and chews 'em in the centre of my tent, not because they afford him any nourishment but simply to show that he is a real "man-pup". Then I flick him with a towel and he starts a lamentable howling. I dropped him into my tub this morning and you never saw a small dawg so horrified in his life.

You have seen or read the reviews up to date.[8] There is a copy of the Phantom Rickshaw[9] awaiting your royal pleasure as soon as you care to take it and I have the honour to report that one half of Wee Willie Winkie[10] is in type. Also that the Native Press are pointing out with great glee that I, and not Mr. Chesney ought to have been whacked by Hearsey.[11] Hall[12] tells me that that same gentleman is now in Naini maturing plans that shall sweep the *Pi* off the face of the earth. He isn't supposed to work as his sentence means only simple imprisonment. Consequently from the time he gets up till 4. p.m. he is supplied with a Bible and left to his own base devices. After 4. p.m. is supposed to be the period of recreation and then his mind seeks refreshment in a novel. Rather a queer way of putting in time isn't it?

Didn't you once say that you didn't like Mills?[13] He improves on acquaintance. Is a lonely, lopsided, three cornered sort of chap with a passion for music which he can't gratify, and all a young man's violent notions and prepossessions about the world and all that is therein. I have seen a good deal of him lately and it seems that he will supply goodish material.

All the letters from the Mother are full of much sorrow for you – it swamps the other news – and the Pater, bless him, moralizes sagely about malaria and such like. They are only just scraps of notes. One encloses a rough thumbnail of the design for Wee Willie Winkie.[14] It will be different from all the others I fancy and quite the quaintest. Now there is no more to tell. You see I haven't been going about the place at all and since all the gossip or else gossip lies, is to be found among the ladies of the station, and since I only hear them whooping and squealing on the other side of the green baize door, all the contents of my budget come to but little.

Get well I pray you and let me have the pleasure of taking you for a scoot in the Pig and Whistle once more ere I depart for the North to have my sea-going kit overhauled by the Mother. Here's all our little universe out of gear for lack of a gracious lady to illumine it and make it *chel*[15] properly. Of course you are entitled to have your fling ere quitting India but, most revered Madam, surely this fling has lasted long enough. If you are sufficiently restored to lie upon your little bed and use hard words about me, come forth and say what you have to say openly. If you can't or won't hit one of your own size at least let the smitten have a chance of reply.

I gather though I have not seen her that the good woman who looks after you is of a kind and tender and beneficent disposition and this cheers me. Irwin also, upon whose remarkably handsome lips I hang daily, says pleasant things about you and your progress.

In your own good time, come out of the darkened room and revisit the glimpses of the moon.[16] There will be no one more glad to see you of all your hundred friends without than

Yours ever –
Rudyard Kipling.

P.S. I'm blissfully idle these days. 'Ain't got a writable notion in my brain and don't intend to get one until we're in blue water.

Notes
1. The side wall of a tent or canvas enclosure. The bachelor accommodation of the North West Provinces Club, where RK was staying, appears to have consisted of tents.
2. Run at Lucknow, 7 February: "The great race of Northern India" (*Pioneer*, 9 February).
3. Cf. Psalms 147:10.
4. Perhaps Donald Clunes Gordon, Examiner of Public Works Accounts for the North-West Provinces.
5. The wife of (Sir) Walter Mytton Colvin, brother of Sir Auckland Colvin and the leading lawyer of Allahabad; he married Annie Money in 1873.
6. The doctor's wife (see [26? January? 1889?]).
7. The former Susan Edwardes, wife of Alexander John Lawrence, Commissioner, Allahabad Division.
8. Of the volumes so far published in the Indian Railway Library. The first two numbers – *Soldiers Three* and *The Story of the Gadsbys* – were reviewed at once in the *Englishman*, *Times of India*, *CMG*, and *Indian Planters' Gazette*, with uniform high praise.
9. Fifth of the six volumes of the Indian Railway Library, published in January.
10. Sixth and last of the Indian Railway Library series.
11. On 4 January a Captain Andrew Hearsey assaulted George Chesney with a whip in the offices of the *Pioneer* for an insulting phrase in RK's "A Study of the Congress", *Pioneer*, 1 January (uncollected). On 25 January Hearsey was sentenced to a month's imprisonment (*Pioneer*, 26 January).
12. G. C. Hall was Superintendent of Naini Jail, Allahabad, the central prison.
13. A. S. Mills, Assistant Accountant General, Allahabad, a probationer in the Financial Department. He soon disappears from the *India Directory*.
14. All the covers for RK's volumes in the Indian Railway Library were the work of JLK, though modestly attributed to the "Mayo School of Art".
15. Go.
16. Cf. *Hamlet*, i.iv.53.

To Edmonia Hill, [9? February] 1889
Text: Copy, University of Sussex

[Allahabad] Sat.

Dear Lady,

Need I tell you how rejoiced I was to see your handwriting once more. The direction was beautifully written and the inside was in a new and strange caligraphy. But I was mightily glad. This morning coming over to the office I saw Irwin's gharri going in to the house so I gathered that you were still being watched over. Yesterday I learn that you ate a "dinner of three courses." It sounds lordly but I daresay it wasn't much when you came to look in to it. That again made me rejoice.

There is nothing in the wide world to tell. The weather is lovely and should go far to bringing you into the world again. I have seen no one and done nothing beyond trying to write the finale for the sixth book[1] which is now more than half completed. The Pater sent me the cover of Wee Willie Winkie for some remarks. It was a noble cover but he had made Wee Willie Winkie a Frenchified little brat and I wrote: – "Just you make him a good deal fatter ma Pa," and sent the cover away post haste. You will get the first copy as soon as ever it is ready. I am now going off to tiffin with Bayless and for the life of me cannot remember whether he is at the Fort or the E. Surrey. I shall go to the East Surrey and if he is not there I shall catch a subaltern and make him feed me.

Colonel Dodd[2] tells me that a Colonel Lang[3] (locality unknown) won the album of photographs. I hope he may be worthy of the trouble taken over it. Don't you.

This is merely a scrap of a note but if you are well and Alex approves I will send you another this afternoon or evening or tomorrow morning.

Remember you have naught to do save to lie still and get well and I am always

Yours sincerely
R.K.

P.S. What's the use of a Saturday if you can't enjoy it. I meant to get up this morning at 10 but slept till eleven. Then it didn't seem worth while to toddle over to the Club and I called for my breakfast in bed and filled my bed with crumbs. When I was tubbing the bull pup put his foolish head round the corner and I caught him by the ears and for the second time gave him a gratis *guzal*.[4] He'll learn manners in time.

Notes
1. *Wee Willie Winkie*: the "finale" would be "The Drums of the Fore and Aft", the last story in the volume and the only one not previously published.
2. Lieutenant-Colonel C. A. Dodd, Superintendent of the Government Press, Allahabad.
3. Perhaps Colonel A. M. Lang, Deputy Commissioner at Amritsar. A note by Mrs Hill explains that she had made two books of photographs to be raffled at an Allahabad bazaar in February 1889. RK wrote a "A Ballade of Photographs" for the albums (in two versions), one of which was raffled and the other kept by the Hills. They contain also some verse captions by RK. Both are now in the Library of Congress. See Rutherford, *Early Verse*, pp. 450–2.
4. Bath.

To Edmonia Hill, [c. 10? February? 1889]
Text: Copy, University of Sussex

[Allahabad]

Holy Caesar! What *am* I to do dear Lady? Here you go and anoint yourself with strange and powerful visuants[1] (*I could have told you that iodine is a raging fire when it is laid upon the tender flesh with a trowel*) and when I pay a flying visit I hear you moaning, and see Alex with a face as long as Tiglath Pileser's[2] tail calling heaven and earth to witness that you have developed seventeen new symptoms. I put it to you *is* that sort of conduct the proper way to secure chits from a desolate journalist? I've been trying to write leaders but that has been a failure because there was nothing to write about. This is merely a green ghost of a note to tell you that I am immensely relieved to get the last and latest note and shall now sleep the sleep of the just. I dine at the Colvin's Tuesday night. Will you be well enough to make me a heliotrope buttonhole? The weather is fine, but it seems to me that all the fog in the station settles over Belvidere. I drove through a big belt of it on my way from office.

May the Lord send you a good night. Alex reads this through the curtains.

Yours ever
Rudyard Kipling

Notes
1. Thus in copy: unguents?
2. The Hills' horse, called after the horse in RK's story of the same (biblical) name, *CMG*, 26 October 1888 (*Abaft the Funnel*).

To Margaret Mackail, 11–14 February 1889
ALS: University of Sussex

N.W.P. Club. / Allahabad. / Feb: 11/89:

Dear Margaret ("Wop" is a little out o' date under these circumstances y'know)

You want to know where I am and what I have been doing. It's kind of you. I know that I have been remiss and worse than remiss in answering your letters, and I have further refrained for two weeks from answering your latest. If you had been me you would ha' done the same, out o' mercy to your correspondent. The last month has been to me one long stretch of "fever an' ague" coupled with violent sickness and mental depression, yea even to the verge of hanging myself. It was never bad enough to spoil my work or at least to stop it but it put me "down in a gulf of dark despair."[1] The thing that cured me was a man that I hated telling me that I was going to die. I revived on purpose to disappoint him and won a bet from him into the bargain. He said that I was sickening for small-pox which just now is raging round the station and knocking over good men right and left. I betted him £15 I wasn't and recovered. Howbeit the doctors say that unless I wish to leave my bones in the country – that is their elegant way of putting it – I had better quit. I am going to quit but of that more anon.

I wrote you two letters but they were so gloomy, and suicidal in their tendencies that I tore 'em up for I knew that brighter days would come and I would be unfair to inflict on you the aggravated sorrow of cold black and white that cannot be explained away until the next mail. Behold me therefore much better though still anything but well, and able to take a sounder and more rational view of life. I've gone through a good deal and it hasn't bowled me over yet, but O it has taken the bulk of my top-hair off and I am as bald as a coot: or I shall be soon: and the gray hairs (don't laugh) have begun to come on my temples whence I pluck them in disgust. On top of all my own malaise the wife of the man I'm chumming with, a professor in the Educational Dept, has fallen sick – and deathly sick. Ever since the first of the new year she has been ailing and ill from a hideous development of nervous headaches which she inherited from her father and of which I had seen a good deal. She gave up on the 16th of January for the second time and collapsed – bad malarial fever raving delirium and all the rest of it – I gave up my share in the house to a nurse and then the trouble began. After the fever broke she was off her head and the doctors talked of cerebro-spinal meningitis. (She's a young American who has overworked herself at her books). I told him as energetically as I could that he was a liar and, under God, the event proves that I am correct. We have tided her through the head trouble – the poor wandering wits have come back again and all that she has now is a sharp go of pleurisy. Isn't it a sweet land wherein you can be thankful for mere pleurisy. That however is being rapidly reduced and we expect that she will be out of bed in a few days. The affair has turned her husband into an old man but he and I executed a wild war-dance of satisfaction in the front verandah when the doctors said that she was out of danger. He sticks however to the idea of the brain trouble and thinks that it may crop out again for which I love him not. The great thing however is that she is alive and well and can talk coherently. Three weeks ago she was babbling like an idiot and Hill and I could only look at each other and say: – "Oh Lord, how long!" She had a notion that her father was dead in a railway accident in Pennsylvania and laboured all she could to convince us of the *fact*. It nearly broke me down and it quite smashed up poor Hill. But as I have said before she is now on the highroad to recovery and will ere long be well. You don't know how awful it is to have a brilliantly clever American woman in whose house you have lived for six months, becoming for the time being insane. Except for the joy of her recovery, and the deep delight of proving the doctor wrong, I wouldn't go through the past six weeks for all under Heaven. I'm in charge of a weekly paper in additional work to my daily stuff and in the hour of very deepest darkness (a) the foreman (b) my assistant, and (c) two proof readers went and got most royally drunk. (b) has been on the drink for three weeks and has now got small pox so I must make up my weekly paper alone.

But this tyranny is not for long. In another week I ought to be with the family at Lahore and on the 9th of next month the bows of my steamer ought to be pointing for Rangoon. I am coming home via Singapur, Hon Kong, Japan (where I spend a month in the inland sea) Frisco and America. I've got about a thousand pounds of my own and the *Pi* will take a series of letters on my wanderings. Further they guarantee me £100 a year from the sister paper, the *Civil and Military Gazette*, and at the end of two years claim first refusal of my services at enhanced rates if I don't wish to stay on in England. Also the royalty of my *Plain Tales* is bringing me in £300 a year. Also, though this is not clinched, Moreton Frewen[2] the bimetallist man who is by way of being an enthusiast about my little writings, is doing all he can to arrange for the *Daily Telegraph* and the *New York Sun* to take a series of my letters. He has sent 'em samples of my work and wires to me at Frisco.[3] If not I make other arrangements. My other books are all about the country and are selling like smoke. If I can get good papers in England and America to take my work I can do America as I want to do it. I've got letters to all sorts of out of the way places from gold mines in Montana to polygamous minor sects in Pensylvania and by the help of Heaven I ought to do good work. But you shall see and judge. Next to America Japan interests me most and my month there ought to allow me good time to see the beauties of the fringe thereof. Anyway I ought to be in blue water a month after this and if I have time to stay over a steamer or two I shall go up to Mandalay the capital of our new Burma and see all the old schoolfellows I can.[4] I know nearly every man in those parts.

After all is over and I have readjusted my notions about cities and men I shall come home and see what's to be done. I am absolutely unfit to return to you now, for I'm practically fifteen years older than my age – broken down, bitter and unjust. The doctors say that I want rest and change. A few days' sea will put me in train again and then I can get to my work. The Pioneer has treated me royally and while admitting the wisdom of my going away seems very sorry to lose me. Even the manager though he mourns says I do well. His notion is that another year of my present work will slay me and give me no return for my death. My own co-mates are also very nice and bid me go away and enjoy myself. Had I better health I would have stayed on and got more money but then again the life round me seems choking. I'm too respectable now to mix among the lower-class natives as I used to do and the press of my journalistic duties prevents my doing the work dearest to me. I have seen much "cities and men"[5] and I want to see more – to know more of men and women and to write about them. The end of me when I have done my short studies for practice, will be a novelist; but in the meantime I've learned my trade and have a fair knowledge of a special correspondent's duties. Looking back now on my six and a half years service as a dying man

Feb: 13th There the sentence broke off abruptly. I felt rather too much like a dying man to go on. A doctor who was knocking about the club said, "Go and have a rousing hot bath. It'll either kill or cure." So I went and steamed myself nearly into a fit and the fever has broken. I know I meant to draw some elegant retrospections about my past misspent life but just at present I am more occupied with pleasant things. This afternoon poor Mrs Hill staggered into life and announced herself well enough to see me for a minute or two. I hadn't seen her for six weeks and feared the most awful things from what the Doctor had told me. To my intense delight she was perfectly collected though desperately weak with a distinct memory of all that had gone before her illness and a complete grip on the affairs of this world, remembered exactly how she had fallen ill, remembered some of her delusions and balanced dates and incidents in her head with perfect coolness and precision. Then I sought the doctor and told him that he was a qualified liar. "I am" said he "but I never was so glad to be told so in my life. She's making a most satisfactory recovery." Of course he says that she may break down again but he says that there will be no permanent insanity to be dreaded. She's hysterical and captious and exacting beyond belief but these little incidents are cheap at the price.

She can do anything she darn pleases so long as she keeps her head. This even too I discovered that the doctor who gave me the advice about the bath has himself been smitten down with bad small-pox, and a young barrister who was quite well sixteen days ago is dying of it tonight over the way. I've just been playing a game o' billiards with the man who attends him. So casually are our little epidemics regulated. One of the chaplains is down also and two or three men in the club are feverish and headachy. I guess they'll have it too. If I don't get it, and I have now reached such a blessed Nirvana of utter weariness of soul that I do not care what touches me, I ought to go off to Lahore by Monday next and by Wednesday be with the Mother again if my substitute arrives to relieve me in time. She, the Mother, is very anxious to see me again and I confess that I should like to feel her arms round me once more before I go. I can get as much praise as I want in these parts but love is a scarce commodity and I hold the best is a mother's. Thank your God Madge that you have never had to live alone without help or sympathy except what comes by letter. If I live I see a long stretch of solitary years before me. When I get back my normal tone I'll enjoy 'em. At present the prospect rather wearies me. I've been there before, y'know, and know what it means. As your grandfather said: – "Lord what things I lie here and remember!"[6] I've had a good time. I've tasted success and the beauty of money, I've mixed with fighters and statesmen, administrators and women who control them all, and "much have I seen, cities and men." It was vivid and lively, and gloomy and savage. I've tried to get to know folk from the barrack room and the brothel, to the Ballroom and the Viceroy's Council and I have in a little measure succeeded. My training has been extensive and peculiar and now I'm going to come home by long wanderings to see how it will work. Be merciful to me, Madge, if ever I knock about among your men and womenfolk. Seen from this distance all your life seems so dainty and small and cared for that I feel I should blunder about the ways like a bull in a china-shop. You mourn about Percy Wyndham's house having been fired.[7] Wait till your friends begin to drop round you and you have to sympathize for the loss o' more than blackened furniture and bric-a-brac. Everywhere I turn now some one I liked seems to be bowled over and the new men who take their places, though nice, are not folk I take a deep interest in. I shall be full ready to quit the country. You don't happen to want a neat little phaiton and Arab. I'm trying to sell my turnout at an alarming sacrifice and no one seems to want it.

Feb: 14th: And Today is St. Valentine's day. I wonder where this time next year will find me and in what quarter of this little earth of ours.

Seems to me that if I don't finish up this long and maundering epistle it will be finished in Hiogo[8] or Nagasaki. I'd like to write to you from there but I'm fraid I'll be so desperately busy that I won't have time to write to no one at all. I'll tell the Mother to send you on all my letters in the *Pi*, maybe they'll amuse you.

Just at present I seem to live in the midst of a maze of letters and telegrams settling up all the last links of my chain. Never knew that I had so many dealings with so many people before.

Forgive the general depression of this letter. I ought to be most happy seeing the time that in all human probability I have before me, but somehow or other I am not and shall not be till I leave the land behind me.

All love to you and yours. Uncle Crom writes me great things about Phil, who would be greater if he were stuck on a desert island for a while with nothing but paints and canvass and no Society; tell me some day what you think o' Fleming.[9] He's an unresponsive sort of animal but appears an honest man.

Yours always
Ruddy

Notes
1. As in *Helen's Babies*: cf. 4 April 1884.
2. Frewen (1853–1924) was an irrepressible speculator and adventurer. After a career of hunting and racing in England and cattle raising in Wyoming, he was now in India, having arrived in the train of a deposed vizier of the court of Hyderabad, and was spreading the gospel of bimetallism. Frewen was from an old Sussex family who owned the Brickwall House used in RK's "Gloriana" (*Rewards and Fairies*) and Brede Place, where Frewen later lived as one of RK's Sussex neighbours. He was married to the American Clare Jerome, of New York, sister of Winston Churchill's mother.
3. See [10–11 June 1889].
4. He did not go.
5. Cf. Tennyson, "Ulysses", l. 13; it is quoted again in this letter, below, and in the same adapted form used as the motto to ch. 33 of *From Sea to Sea*.
6. The Revd George Browne Macdonald (1805–68): see Carrington, *Kipling*, p. 13.
7. "Clouds", East Knoyle, near Salisbury, built by Philip Webb for Percy Wyndham only three years earlier, burned on 6 January 1889; some work by Burne-Jones was destroyed with it. The house was rebuilt, and there RK's father was to die.
8. Now part of Kobe.
9. Fleming was evidently in England: see 21 February 1889.

To Edmonia Hill, 20 February 1889
Text: Copy, University of Sussex

Aligarh,[1] 9.50.

Dear Lady.

Have you seen K[adir].B[aksh]. I haven't and he isn't in the train. As he has about Rs 300 of mine in his possession I am a little uncomfy tho' the guard says that since he has taken his ticket he must be coming on. *Nota Bene*. This paralytic seizure of the pencil is due to the fact that the train is trying to go thirty miles an hour while I am trying to write. It isn't due to sickness tho it seems to bear a strong likeness to your more florid style of fist. My stall-companion is a most amusing man – one of Kellner's[2] travelling auditors who has been telling me quaint tales of bad men who defraud the firm. He has just read me the descriptive roll of an enterprising babu who "trades" under the name of K.P. Roy and represents himself as belonging to some royal family. The description ends: – "has a ready address but always looks anxious and takes *goods away with him.*" Isn't that a perfect summary of the vagrant swindler. Here thank goodness occurs a station and now I can return, as the train slows down, to my normal script. In this train are Mr. Halsey, of Amritsar, and Captain Sherston one of the Chief's Aides. As Roberts is in Allahabad Sherston is naturally going to the North and equally of course in charge of horses. One of the critters has a lame – chestnut[3] (Don't you sympathize with him) and Sherston has to hop out at every station and apply linament – an attention the horse resents by kicking vehemently. But he doesn't squeal. (On we go again and I must change at Ghaziabad – all my kit is in hideous disorder and there is no K.B.)

One station before Ghaziabad. I am really concerned about that Aryan. All this stage I've been wrestling with my bedding which seems to swell up like whipped cream as I try to force it into the straps. Pity me when I emerge on the platform followed by seventeen howling coolies. So far, the weather has grown chillier with each turn of the wheel but I only hope for your sake that Allahabad is getting the splendid sunshine we're steering through.

This is merely the ghost of a line (all the pencil marks will be faded by the time it reaches you) to tell you that I am well and to remind you of your promise to get well also. My love to Alex – let's hope he gets his natural sleep, and respex to the estimable Missis Knobs.[4] Write soon and write often and believe me

Yours ever
RK

[note on envelope] Found him at Ghaziabad. All right.

Notes
1. RK was *en route* to Lahore for a last visit before leaving India.
2. The Calcutta firm of provision and wine merchants, and railway restaurant operators.
3. Mrs Hill's note says that "chestnut" meant "legs": "a forbidden topic – as I could not walk".
4. Mrs Knobbs was Mrs Hill's nurse.

To Edmonia Hill, 21 February 1889

Text: Copy, University of Sussex

Lahore:/Feb: 21st/89:

1.p.m. in a small, new, and funny cosy house
Dear Lady.
    Behold me arrived and now sitting in great state and splendour

surrounded by all that an effete civilization can boast. It was a loathely journey from Ghaziabad onward. I was plagued by natives – one of whom insisted on bringing into the compartment a female friend in an aniline *saree* with silver spots. Then they chewed betel together lovingly and spat tastefully about the compartment. I foresaw a Turnover[1] for the C & M and said nothing till a huge Babu with four office boxes came in at Saharanpur – let down the upper bunk, loaded it with his kit and prepared to sleep on *my* seat. I made a lamentable outcry and at the sound of it the engineer of the line and an old acquaintance of mine turned up and said: – "Come along into my traveling carriage!" then I came and from Saharanpur journeyed in great state to Lahore in the sumptuously fitted compartment designed for the special use of the able and energetic engineer who etc. etc. etc. This it is to have friends. I began to meet men I knew at Meerut and Mozafernagar[2] an' kep' on meeting more at each succeeding station.

I can hardly tell you how pleased I am to find the Fambly looking so well. The Pater is a young and frivolous lad by comparison with the weighed-down man I left behind me. The Mother is stronger than I have known her for years, and the child radiant in the hope of Jack's approaching return. You see, you know them so well that I need scarcely apologize for mentioning 'em. The Mother eyed me over and said: – "Well, for a sick man you are looking uncommonly well cared for," and the general verdict was that I had fleshed up some. Wa-affles Ma'am – waa-fles, chicken and tartare sauce and corn dodgers I do assure you. Then I had to explain exactly how you were and by the time I had got to the — chestnuts — "Gout!" said the Mother. "Rheumatic gout. My ankle was swollen at Simla from the same cause and I was lying *in bed* in agony till I tried Belladonna ointment." Of course you are anything but lying in bed these days but if the chestnuts are not quite well by the time this reaches you may I venture to recommend Belladonna ointment to your distinguished consideration. Only please write first and let me know how you are. I've got ten thousand different things on my hands tonight chief of which is to give the Maiden's horse a run. Think of me at five bucketing up and down in the unaccustomed saddle. Luckily we don't set to work on the packing till tomorrow – and the first day's will, if I know my mother, be given up to the: – "Good – Heavens – Ruddy, what *is* this disgusting rag?" business.

The Pater is full of his home trip[3] and I must fly over to his office and make him disgorge more news. By the measure of my delight in seeing my folk, I can faintly guess what will be your pleasure when you return to Beaver.[4] For which laudable purpose get well.

This is only a line "dashed off" as the amateurs say, in the hope of catching the post. Observe the fiendish nature of the punishment. This is addressed to *Alex*. It will come when you are not feeling quite well and you will instantly rise up and write to me that you can be trusted with letters all to your own self. Thus I shall be richer by a note and you will have a lively desire to break my head.

Lahore, as much of it as I have seen, has changed beyond knowledge – not only new houses have grown up but new *streets*, and of course all the names of the people are new and strange.

In my next I will tell you a lovely story about the vaccination panic in Lahore when all Lahore took off its shirt sleeves and ran with one accord for the fatted calf. This *chit* doesn't count. All love to Alex.

Yours ever
Rudyard Kipling

Notes
1. "Turnovers" were the miscellaneous stories inaugurated when RK and E. K. Robinson remodelled the *CMG* in August 1887. The name comes from the fact that the stories started on the last column of the front page and went on – turned over – to the first column of page two.
2. Thus in copy, for Muzaffarnagar, a town in the Meerut division of the United Provinces.
3. JLK had gone to England in August 1888 and returned to India before the end of the year. I do not know what his business was.
4. Mrs Hill's home town in western Pennsylvania.

To Edmonia Hill, 22 February 1889
Text: Copy, University of Sussex

Lahore: Feb. 22/89:

What a demon is exchange! I've been going through that dreary business known as getting letters of credit and I stand horrified at the amount of money that is literally chucked into the sea. Where does it all go to? I read, or rather pretend to read, Mr. Chesney's bimetallic articles[1] and deuce a bit nearer the solution am I. The day (a vilely dull and gloomy day) has been just one whirl of flying round to pay bills and to contract new ones. There is great fun in being in your own land again and I feel a Punjabi indeed when every third man in the street ducks his head and inquires how I am. Horsedealers, clerks (we don't keep babus in these parts) carpenters, coach-builders, and a whole horde of chaprassis and low folk have turned up to pay their respects and I am wearied of grinning at 'em and pretending that the sole desire of my life is to see that they are well and happy.

To Edmonia Hill, 22 February 1889

I've seen Kay Robinson who appears fit and hearty but did not inform me that he was wedded.[2] I didn't pursue the topic as it did not seem to delight him.

Yesterday evening I saw a fat and fluffy man with a red face rolling about outside a horse. When he came nearer I perceived that it was Major Chalmers.[3] Him I chased into the Club where I gathered from him that Lahore was beastly, only he used a stronger word, and that he was longing to get back to Allahabad. He enquired at once after you, and was sorry to find that you had been so ill. D'you know he is really a most cherubic major and his face is as red and as shining as a Norfolk pippin.

Trix has been showing me her photo-books. She seems to have as many of 'em as you have. I daren't tell her that, so far as I can see, when she wasn't taking "Jack," Jack was taking her and so I breathe it in your private ear. Her *fiancé* has hung her about with jewelry from pearl necklaces to curb-chain bangles and one – two – three engagement rings! I walked round and round her till she was dizzy asking: "Where did you get this" and the invariable answer was: – "Oh, Jack gave that to me, ages ago. Didn't you know." I didn't but I perceive now that there is a steady undercurrent of Jack flowing through the house and I gather that the mail is an event. He comes to India on the 22nd of next month. I fancy that I shall begin to see the good points of his nature when the Bay of Bengal and the Straights of Malacca (ain't that their name) lie between us.

Most of the men in the club are consumed with envy and revenge themselves for the splendours of my trip by forecasting that I shall be killed in a brawl in a Colorado rum-shop for refusing to drink with a "miner." I have pointed out that I cannot imagine circumstances under which I would refuse to drink with any created being under the canopy of Heaven, and remind them cheerfully of the heats of June and the watery delights of August.

But these be minor points. The real downright serious one is that you have not written – nor has Alex. Consequently I have dark dreams of your kicking Mrs Knobbs in the mouth and tearing the stuffing out of the sofa, when your foot hurts more than ordinary. But be consoled. The large and healthy Irwin who never had aught worse than fever in his life thinks that it is "all imagination" y'know. Only *think* that and you'll be well. Isn't this brutal. It's all your fault for not writing.

There goes the tiffin bell; and I can hear the mother raging as she turns over my thick clothes. All my thin things are in perfect order but K.B. and I are being wigged for allowing the rust and moth to play the mischief with some of my suits. But I am tranquil. I've stolen the Pater's new travelling bag as I said I would. Trix hunts the house to get me a cheroot or a light and I am allowed to make salad of a disgusting kind.

These be the simple delights of home. This even I go to the Gardens to hear the band, gaze once more upon the ivory tushes of the Boojum,[4] to whom the rumour still persists in saying, I am engaged. *Twice* since I left Simla has the Boojum coyly repeated her question to Trix as to how the maiden would like the B. for a sister. Twice has the maiden grunted. Now the B. is getting fat, to add a finish to her charms. Decidedly I must get away from Lahore as soon as I can or awful things will happen.

Until I reach the sea, please send an occasional line. You must be better y'know – if so say so – if not say why not.

Yours
R K

P.S. You know the Macfarlane girls. I've seen a girl just now twice as tall, three times as thick, and four times as deep through, as *both* the girls put together. "Ye-es" says the Pater "they're all very fine and large in these parts – like the cattle."

Notes
1. These were a standard feature in the *Pioneer*, as George Allen was a convinced bimetallist.
2. Robinson married Florence Theresa Gordon in 1887.
3. Major E. W. Chalmers, 7th Bengal Cavalry.
4. Miss Parry Lambert: see [24–5] June 1888.

To Edmonia Hill, 23 February 1889
Text: Copy, University of Sussex

Lahore: Feb: 23/89:

Good gracious! What new horror is this? Your letter this morn, and bless you for it. How did you manage to get at that ink? I was cheered to see it but the matter of the letter gave me no consolation except when you said that there was no blistering after all. I am certain that your nerves are so smashed up that you would weep under any circumstances and you know how sorry and more than sorry I am for you. *Please* don't cry. Tisn't much longer to hold on before you get to the open sea where the ankles cease from troubling and the blisters are at rest. By the way, wasn't that a delicious little mistake of yours about the blisters? *Fly* not "*Flying*" surely.[1] Made up, they are I believe from the same stuff as that hair developer that you bought for me. And yet *I* never wept when I rubbed it into my pate. Howbeit, blisters notwithstanding, the letter of

To Edmonia Hill, 23 February 1889

yours has cheered me mightily and I stood in need of cheering. The weather here is something awful. Mother says it's stifling hot. I *know* that it's bitter cold. The skies are leaden blue. It rained heavily all the night and the roads are covered with the black viscid mud of the Punjab, which only the Puppy (Vix's daughter) appreciates. Having thoroughly coated herself with it, she is now clamouring to enter society and all the available servants of the establishment seem to be cutting about to bar her path to the drawing room.

Talking of drawing rooms reminds me of your teeth – no I mean tiger-claws. My man in Rajputana says: – "*Do* you expect that I'm going out to Gangoa to kill a tiger just for you." Mother had a complete set of 'em last Spring but on turning 'em out, the insects had eaten 'em into white dust and there isn't enough to make a toothpick of. I'm trying Moolchand in Peshawur and a man in the bazar. By the way I've rooked one fairly decent print for you – unique of its kind, red and black and white with pious sentences from the Koran printed on the borders. The Pater says he'll do what he can for me but the land has been overrun by the T G's[2] and the native workmen under the plethora of orders have, following their immemorial instincts, shut up like so many oysters. They have got enough money for the hot weather so why should they bother? Aren't they a distracting people to deal with – there's a sale-department in [the] Museum where the supply cannot keep pace with the demand. I saw a lovely carved door yesterday priced Rs 65, which I much fear your customs would appraise at five times that value. 'Tis too big to bring away so I shall look for what Mr. Wemmick calls "portable property."[3] I have a peshawari snuff mill and powder horn – rude and barbaric to the last degree but genuine and such as is made on the border to this day. My wicked wish is to get Alex a poshteen[4] but the Winter stock is all worn out and the Kafilas aren't through the passes yet on account of the snows. He'd look imposing in a poshteen and would make Beaver City howl! However we'll see what I can pick up. I am setting the Civil and Military *dafhi*[5] at work on nice soft blocks for writing; making due allowance for the ones that you'll requisish. Talking of snow reminds me that snow has fallen as low as *Rajpur* on the Mussorie road! And within ten miles of Jhelum which is on the plains. Strikes me those who are left behind will have a fairly cool-hot weather. I think we can resign 'em that without a murmur.

Last night was guest night at the Lawrence Hall. I met Major Chalmers who told me that a nice new hickory cart that he bought from Weathrall had been smashed the day before. Two drunken natives came up and hit his sais on the head, (these are no manners of the Punjab) and the mare went home her own sweet way and arrived with the shafts and a buckle or two. I tell you this because I have a notion that you may have ridden in that cart. C. gave me much advice as to kit on the voyage.

D'you know I think *one* trunk and a Gladstone bag will see me out. I shall smile. I leave here on the night of the third and pass through Allahabad on the morning of the 5th. That is settled and now, being a thrifty soul, I'm pass-hunting. I'll get one from here to Delhi and hope to get one from Delhi to the Sea. No use belonging to the press unless one can make use of the Position.

The quietness of our life here is extreme. I've looked at [all?] through T's negatives. She has some beauties of the Thibetans including the celebrated explorer the unknown A.____ K.____. Ask Alex if he has ever heard of that man. I've teased Vixen, smoked baccy, written a Turn-over for the C & M,[6] driven Trixie nearly wild with rude remarks about her cooking – she is doing something with lemon, white of egg and sugar on a stove and she says it's cheese-cake; gone over to the School of Art and played havoc with everything I could find there, twisted the turnstile of the Museum until it registered more people than ever come in one day, and generally made myself a surpassing nuisance. There isn't anything more to do except eat, and try to imitate a new salad dressing that the Mother is proud of. Tisn't as good as tartare sauce with capers – there isn't enough mustard in it – but the idea of it is that onion does *not* go into the salad but is chopped up very, very small in the dressing so that it gives a general impression of onion round the corner. This must be made a note on. I have filled the Mother's heart with envy by describing your short pastry – the stuff that crumbles into white flakes. "But what's the good of you if you can only *gorge* it, and then know nothing of how it's made" says Trixie who is prancing round the house with a spoon in one hand and a cookery book in the other. They are an awful busy couple, those two. Always sewing something or cooking something. One of the first questions the Mother asked when I told her of your illness was: – "*Does* she worry herself about the servants?" So you see you have deep and genuine sympathizers up here in the Black North.

I have been introduced (last night it was) to a woman who is said to be the Loveliest Woman in Lahore. She's a Mrs. Roper and has married absolutely the ugliest and dullest little pig of a man I ever saw.[7] Lahore points to her with admiration and if you say: – "Why oh why does she look as if she were going to be sick" they answer: – "Oh but her husband has only two hundred a month you know." It *does* seem to account for it when you come to think of it, doesn't it? I can't say she impresses me mightily. She is gaunt and hollow eyed, but she is the shibboleth just now and if you don't admire you are a person of no (or low) intellect. Another lady here is the precise image of Mrs Irwin. I looked for Edna[8] when I saw her but she was not.

Last evening I took a fiendish delight in drawing the wife of the dentist to whom you sent me and of whom I told you strange things.

She is a terrible woman, and in the presence of about seventy people at the hall informed me in a loud and ringing voice "My pore old 'ubby 'as soft corns on every *one* of 'is toes and one on the outside." So you see society in Lahore is pretty mixed.

Tell Alex all the schoolboys of the Punjab are mad on cricket. There's a big school tournament on now, Government College, Amritsar Normal School, and every other training institution you can think of. The big Maidan is ringed with a shouting crowd ten deep and you can hear them bellow: – "Wal rân" half a mile away. It's a curious mania and I suppose has a tendency like most manias. Now I will to my tailor myself betake and from him garments on tick procure. Keep, oh, keep yourself well and send me a line the next time you can get at the inkpot. I am always yours expectantly

R. K.

Notes
1. Perhaps Spanish fly (*Cantharides*), used as a blistering agent, is meant?
2. Travelling gentlemen.
3. Dickens, *Great Expectations*, e.g., ch. 24.
4. An Afghan wrapper or cloak of fleece-lined leather.
5. Thus in copy, a word unknown to *Hobson-Jobson*: perhaps the copyist's error for *daftar*: office.
6. Not identified.
7. I have not found them in the Indian directories.
8. Mrs Hill's godchild (born 1885), the daughter of Mrs Irwin, for whom RK wrote "Imperious Wool-Booted Sage" (Rutherford, *Early Verse*).

To Edmonia Hill, [24] February 1889
Text: Copy, University of Sussex

Sunday: Feb: 23/89:

Gott in himmel! An incursion of Austrian maniacs has just swept through the house, gutted the studio and fled, carrying the Pater with 'em to the Museum. There were two of 'em – one a Count something or other – simply wild about India and all that is therein. They had been consigned to us from Bombay and we were first aware of their presence by shrill shrieks from the drive for "Meestare Kipleen." Then they pranced in, one a red bearded tornado with a cracked voice, and t'other a dried up walnut looking sort 'o man who couldn't speak English. They wanted to go to Peshawur. They wanted to see Graeco-Bhuddist sculptures – they wanted to encamp on the Attock;[1] they wanted to embrace the whole blazing East and they wriggled with impatience as they explained their needs. Pater took the wildest and I tackled 'tother in a wild polyglot of French [and?] vernacular. I guess that was a fair enough approximation to Austrian. They tore through the Pater's portfolios; they seemed ready to tear down the pictures from the walls and the big one, backing the Pater into a corner, stood over him while he shouted: – "Tell me now about Alexandare. I am in him mooch interest. *Did* he now come to this place, and where is Taxila." All this as though Alexandare was a brother globe-trotter who had just gone through. It takes a good deal to put the Pater out of countenance (He's my father you know) but he collapsed when he was called upon to give a resumé of Indian archaeology and I chuckled. The other man had got hold of T's photo-studies of men and animals taken to help the Pater's drawings and between gasps of Austrian admiration was wildly appealing to me for duplicates. "I am artist you know" was his explanation and he spoke as who should say: – "I am the Almighty." He could draw more than a little for I went through his note book and saw that he had given names that were neither in Heaven above or the Earth beneath to bits of Lahore. Punjabi translated through the medium of a continental intellect becomes rather queer. Wherefore I corrected his grosser errors of nomenclature and rather wondered what in the world he would call Peshawar if he called the Mosque of Wazir Khan the *"Nazir Masjid."*[2]

They have gone, as I have said, and I am sitting down in the eddies their departure has left to tell you all about it. We certainly do contrive to pick up the rummiest foreigners in the world; and if any man goes to the Pater and says he is "artist," the doors are wide opened.

Talking of this reminds me that yester afternoon the Pater shot me as I was writing; and the result was a lovely pen and ink, and a blue stump sketch – just head and pipe; the former frowning and the latter fuming.[3] It's a great deal more characteristic than any photo; and I'll catch the pen and ink one to show you if you like. I think it's an attitude of mine that you know.

For your sake I trust that your weather has been better than ours. A storm began at three yesterday and kept on with intervals till this morning. Most of the afternoon was pitch dark and I was reduced to drawing in charcoal on the studio wall. Hi! I've made a horrid mess that will be reverently cherished after I've gone.

You can guess that there is nothing and less than nothing to tell. We've all been indoors reading and writing and talking since yesterday. I gather by the way that I have got into a scrape. You remember my verse on Lord Dufferin's farewell to Lord Lansdowne,[4] and my allusion therein to his mother's letters.[5] In his last letter to the mother he assumes that I have written it and begs that if I republish it I'll cut out that allusion which he thinks I must have got from Mother. It came from Mrs Napier who is afraid of losing her place in his heart if he ever gets hold of the source. (These be the penalties of being admired by great men). The Mother has written that it wasn't her that told anyway – she'd scorn the imputation.[6] I rather chuckle; but of course if I republish I'll respect his wishes.[7] Which reminds me, pray you stuff away *windfalls* until we meet again on the morning of the 5th. It won't take up much room and tisn't very long to wait. I wish that you had sent me a line today – I wanted to know something more about those chestnuts and the flying blisters. It wasn't kind of you.

I'm yearning to be on the sea once more and have written a sort of farewell to India, after the manner of Walt Whitman, which I will send to the *Pioneer* as soon as I am fairly on the Seas.[8]

Here Trix dashes in. "Say Ruddy, can you give me the rules for a postage stamp flirtation?"

"No, I can't."

"What's the good of you – a journalist who ought to give answers to correspondents."

"Well, look here, if you can't squeeze all the love you want to send to Jack in a letter, stick crosses in the corner."

"Ruddy, you're a low minded ruffian." Then she fled. It takes her about a week to write to Jack and then . . . . but I haven't yet seen a coolie staggering under the weight of an envelope, so I can't say prezactly how much she sends.

Here comes the sun, and the clouds are racing over the sky like scared white rabbits. May this be an omen from the South, that you are much, much better. When I've seen some one and talked somewhere and generally taken further stock of my surroundings, I'll tell you all about it. At present there's nothing to tell.

All love to Alex.

Yours ever
R. K.

Notes

1. Presumably at Fort Attock, on the far North-West frontier, where the Kabul River joins the Indus.
2. *Masjid* means "mosque". The Austrian has confused *Wazir* (chief minister) with *Nazir* (an officer of the court). The mosque of Wazir Khan, built in 1634, is one of the ornaments of Lahore.
3. The second of these is now at Sussex and has been reproduced in Rutherford, *Early Verse*. The pen and ink sketch has not been located.
4. The fifth Marquess of Lansdowne succeeded Dufferin as Viceroy in 1888.
5. "One Viceroy Resigns", published in the *Pioneer* as "One Word More. In the Manner of R. Br—ng", 7 December 1888. The passage in question reads:

"My mother's letters – that will be a book –

The legend of the Doorkeys, how they bred –
This land spawns Doorkeys."

For Lady Dufferin's letters, see [24–5] June 1888.
6. Alice Kipling's letter to Lord Dufferin, 17 December 1888, is now in the Public Record Office of Northern Ireland, Belfast.
7. When RK reprinted the verses in *Departmental Ditties* (1890) he omitted the reference.
8. I cannot find this in the *Pioneer*.

To Edmonia Hill, 26 February 1889
Text: Copy, University of Sussex

Tuesday / Lahore: / Feb: 26/89:

"Five ladies almost all at once" – says your last letter. Quite enough to account for anything and everything madam. I only wonder that you were spry enough to play go-cart with the drawing room chairs afterwards. Am I making fun of your troubles. God knows I'm not tho' I could not choke a laugh at the idea of the faithful Knobbs (Nobbs?) making experiment as to the strength of the blisters on her own vile corpse. Then I nearly choked when you described your poor pitiful little amble round the drawing room but the wire which Alex sent this morning consoled me. You see there had been silence in the land for a longer space of time than I approved of and – as I said I would – I sent down a wire to explain these things. You certainly didn't hurry your sweet selves to reply. What *can* I do to render my letters more interesting? I'm so sorry that they don't amoose you. I meant 'em to. There is so little that one can write about up here and indeed and indeed, dear Lady, I tell you everything that I do and a good deal of what I think.

Yesterday as you know I didn't send a letter. I thought a *tar* would be more to the point. Well, yesterday I made a new discovery and added unto myself a new sympathy. We live near the flourishing village of Mozang,[1] where little boys do all day long fly kites.

"Have you ever flown a kite?" said the Pater when we were loafing round the garden together.

"Never" said I.

"Then we'll get half a dozen and begin" said the Pater. You never saw anything so funny in your life. There were not more than five hundred people watching me and my awkwardness. My kite went up with a rush and the line cut my hands and the population of Mozang rocked and roared in rows – in battalions. Your Punjabi bellows like a bull when he is amused. Then without warning another kite swooped over mine, ducked and dragged its line across my kite line. There was a twang and my masterless kite pitched head over heels far to leeward while a shouting mob of little boys ran to catch it; the law of kite flying being that whoso first touches a fallen kite is its owner. Then the science of the game became apparent and I went baldheaded into the fun of cutting kite strings. I invested in a ball of glass powdered line (by the same token that cuts the hand) but mean little kites flown with greater skill swept my ventures away and I lost four in the afternoon. 'Tis a most fascinating game and mysterious withal. You do not see and cannot tell who your antagonist is. He may be a quarter of a mile away and the spoils of battle fall to a third person equally unknown to you both. Very much like life isn't it. I am very delighted with the new pastime and this morning cut away a big white butterfly-kite that deliberately challenged me and flew across a high belt of trees to catch me. Isn't it childish and more than childish to indulge in these things? Never you mind. I must do something to fill in the time and to allow me room for thinking. Talking of thinking, reminds me that the more the Mother looks at me, the more she thinks I have been well cared for and she has said that she is sorry she doesn't know you that she may thank you for all your kindnesses to me. Says that my little manners have improved, and that I have an appearance of having been in respectable society, i.e. not run wild at a club. There's for you!

This morning has brought us yet another globe-trotter – a Lady Greville.[2] Seems that she was at the Straights in Allahabad and there incontinently fell sick. She is the most perfect presentment of the French notion of the British Matron I have ever seen – huge aquiline nose, big, slack mouth filled with over many and yellow rabbit teeth, long flat foot, high, raw colour, and a superfluity of angularity which makes it easy to understand why she is not travelling with her husband. She feigns enthusiasm about my books but I guess this is because she wants the Pater to trot her about and offers me on my return from (*) the States the entrée of her Drawing Room (capital D please) where she says I shall find many men and women that will be useful to me. She also professes great intimacy with the *Daily Telegraph* folk and passes in a mild way for a *bas bleu*. I shall hold her to her promise when I reach England and then you'll have some fun in reading my accounts of the "Hupper Sukkles" – if you ever read 'em, as I don't think you will. Last night a couple of queer men dined here, one of whom when amused has a trick of rubbing his face with his hands exactly as a rabbit "fondles his own harmless face."[3] I thought Beck's[4] hysterical chuckles were rather discomposing things to meet at dinner but this dry washing of the face in public almost knocked me over. Luckily I had been forewarned.

Your letters are intensely interesting to me, and don't you forget it,

* Started to say England but erased it [RK's note].

as that incorrigible Yank Bayliss says. Let me know all about everything up to Friday night. I leave Lahore on Sunday evening. That is to say I shall run into Allahabad for breakfast on Tuesday morning – an awful, grimy, dirty, unshaven tracklayer and the great G.W. Allen will perchance come down to the station and blandly burble over me and then go home and tell his friends that my journey is solely undertaken in the interests of the *Pioneer*, and I shall loaf down the platform with an unclean pipe in my mouth and see you comfortably disposed in your carriage and shall wring the necks of the canaries and see if I can be of any use and then we shall be fairly embarked on the way to the high seas. You can't expect to be absolutely well till you snuff blue water. I had no end of a headache yester night. All of which means [   ], or is it [   ]?[5]

Forgive the pun.

R.K.

P.S. Did you read Alex's mournful P.S. to your letter. A moaning tangle of arrears of work – winding up with a wicked word. Tell him that though deeply pained at his profanity (for I myself *never* use it) I sympathize much and shall remember Bonsard's.[6]

R.

Notes
1. Mozang, or Muzang, is just south of the civil station at Lahore.
2. Lady Beatrice Violet Graham (d. 1932), daughter of the fourth Duke of Montrose, married in 1863 the second Baron Greville (1841–1909). She came to Lahore, RK's mother wrote, "out of admiration for Rud's books" and promised to make him "free of her house on his return to England" (to Georgiana Burne-Jones, 5 March 1889: ALS, Bancroft Library).
3. Tennyson, "Aylmer's Field", l. 851.
4. Not identified.
5. Blanks in copy.
6. L. Bonsard was proprietor of the restaurant and Hotel de France in Calcutta, mentioned as a place to eat in RK's "City of Dreadful Night" (*From Sea to Sea*).

To Edmonia Hill, 28 February 1889
Text: Copy, University of Sussex

Lahore:

Dear Lady,

Two at once. Now I wonder what has happened in the post! Your letters have a trick of falling into the C. & M. and turning up at this place after I have given up all hope of getting 'em. It's consoling but when a man waits till the last moment and then goes out desperately to buy shirts and socks and such small beer and then returns to find two letters, he is rather pressed for time to catch the post to answer 'em. I read the Tuesday one first and then I didn't so much mind the wail of the Sabbath though I was awfully sorry for you. Confound those chestnuts! As soon as you get home have 'em both off and get a pair of reliable cork ones. Oh I *am* so sorry. But neither you nor Alex are to be discouraged or I'll descend upon you in fire and flame. It's just this way. As soon as your poor poor feet find that they are "Marching *to* Georgia" they get so interested in the route that they'll recover; and this time next week you will be comfortably established at Calcutta. I think before I go I'll tell Alex to wire Umballa or Saharanpur and give me the latest news of all. Otherwise I shall be uneasy. Never you mind whether I telegraph. I'll telegraph as much as I please an' if yer say much blessed if I don't telegraph *bearing!*[1] Then you'll be sorry you spoke.

Yours is good news about Tiglath – good for you but not for Hughes.[2] I regret that I shall not see that big fat man rolling out of the carriage in an agony of apprehension as Tiglath puts his head in at the door. It'll thin him down before the hot weather ends. I can't draw him properly but he'll have to fan himself with one hand and argue with Tiglath with the other, something as I have indicated.

[sketch]

It is not good for people to hear too flattering opinions of themselves else I should have told you what the folk said about the book.[3] What took the Mother was the way in which the cover had been made. I said something about "tin tacks", which I believed played great part in the mystery and yet they seemed to marvel just the same. That's funny. Because to me the photoes were so much, so much, and I took the cover as one of the operations of nature. In good sooth that book is vastly admired but I'm not going to let him be on the drawing room table.

Last night the Volunteers held their big ball. I was dining at the Club with a long haired professor in the Educational – a literary cuss and journalist, Eric Robertson[4] by name. He said: – "We will go to the ball" and I sat tight. Well, we played one game of billiards and every man in the Club fled away to assist to prance with the daughters of engine drivers and the wives of guards and Robertson and I sat down to talk. I declare we did not talk long but t'was two o'clock in the morning or ever we rose from our seats in front of the fire and then said we with one voice: – "We will go to our respective beds." And so it was I did not attend the ball. Eight hundred people filled it and made the floor quiver again so I am told. But Robertson, in his capacity of an ex-reviewer of the Standard, was preaching unto me the ethics of art – and the canons of criticism. "You're a cold-blooded photographer" said he. "You'll never do any first class work till you have fallen in love, and broken your heart. You're an Ass, and a philistine. You must have an ideal." "Wah! Wah!" said I. "Am I so lost as all that?" "You are" said Robertson and upon this text he preached a sermon of one hour with interruptions for fresh pegs and an occasional cheroot. "Lay yourself out to love" said this large-eyed long haired aesthete; and I proceeded to draw him on this topic insomuch that he made unto me a variety of strange and entertaining confidences. This morning brings over from him a most penitent chit begging me to forget all that he had said about his own private affairs. Then I marvelled at the weakness of this high and lofty critic that had sat in judgment upon me and my works. By the way, can you imagine me wandering around the world in search of an ideal and laying myself out to love! Which reminds me of a wonderful woman we have here about whom I told you stories when I was in Lahore in the prehistoric ages. You can refer to the file of letters which I firmly believe you intend to publish – (This ain't me! Trix did it).[5]

Well, this woman is possessed of a deep bass voice, has the manners of a coal-heaver, and the head of a washer woman. She was confiding her past to Trix and I heard her say, all in one continuous roar: – "I was married when I was fifteen and had eight offers before I was engaged. What is life without love!" I could see T. turn crimson with suppressed laughter and try not to catch my eye. The tone of the confidence was aggresive to say the least of it.

This morn after I got those shirts I went to see a big Freemason Panjandrum who gives me a circular letter to all the Lodges of America. He is the District Grand Master of the Punjab and when he is at home, out of his canonicals that is to say, a very dear friend of mine.[6] His child has been deadly sick – fits, I think – but is now better. "Last week – this time last week we thought he was dying," said the poor fellow and explained to me what sickness in a household meant, winding up with "But you are not acquainted with these things of course." I told him that I sympathized with him deeply but I dare say that he took it as a mere *façon de parler*. How very little one half of the world knows of the life of the other half!

After I had paid that call I went over to Kay Robinson to get some cards printed, and looked at the chair and table where I had sweated through those long hot nights in June, nearly a year ago. It all seemed so strange and so distant. By the way, Kay really is married but, being by nature a brute, he keeps his wife in Amritzar and doesn't tell people up here. Passes as a bachelor and goes down to Amritzar from Saturday till Monday. This is not nice. Seems to me that if a man becomes possessed of a wife, no matter by what strange and accidental means, it is his duty to see that she ranks with him. His own pride ought to make him jam her down the throat of society.

My congratulations to Alex.[7] That's a good review; and wanted. If the world only knew the circumstances under which the second book had been written, they ought to give the writer a laurel wreath of sovereigns. Please make him see that there is no use in being discouraged. If he gives up his leave – he'll collapse flat as an opera hat but not half so pleasantly. Besides you couldn't go home then either by the East or by the West. It will be all right, as I have said before, when you are once upon the steamer. Your going out for drives in the Museum – I mean Brougham – and walking four whole steps is in itself ample proof that you are well and on the mend.

Yesterday I got hold of a red copper open work box which struck me as pretty and I have set it aside for you. The difficulty of getting good prints is something awful in these parts.

Oh my eye! The Chaprassi's going to post. I must stop. Goodbye, and be well.

Yours ever
R K

Notes
1. Thus in copy.
2. The gentleman to whom the Hills had managed to sell their fractious horse: a fat man, according to Mrs Hill's note on the letter.
3. A book of photographs made for Alice Kipling by Mrs Hill (Mrs Hill's note).
4. Robertson (1856?–1926), a graduate of the University of Edinburgh, had been appointed to the Punjab Educational Department early in 1887, so that RK would have known him before leaving Lahore. Robertson became Vice-Principal of Lahore University before returning to England and entering the Church. He did a good deal of literary and editorial work and was made an LL D of St Andrews in 1923.
5. "Refers to blots" according to the copyist's note.
6. Edwin Woodall Parker, District Judge at Lahore.
7. Hill published a number of reports on meteorology between 1876 and 1889, but in serial form, not separately. I do not know what is referred to here.

To Edmonia Hill, [2 March] 1889
Text: Copy, University of Sussex

[Lahore] Saturday

Dear Lady:

Your grievous little note this morn came to upset me in the middle of my packings and just when I had discovered that the trunk had broken its lock. I am sorry – how often have I said that in the course of our correspondence? – and I should be sorrier did I not know what was in store for you. You will feel horrid bad and the symptoms of every malady known to doctors may or may not exist for a few days in your frame but the sea and the rest and the complete change will put that right in a fortnight. When you get home try *massage* and cheerful little things of that nature. What you've got is a trouble of the nerves that is very distressing but people don't die of it, besides the Mother says that you're "a sweet lady" and she hopes to see you "one of these days." You mustn't go playing tricks with yourself this side the seven seas.

Oh please forgive me if ever I boasted about things to be picked up in Lahore. The globe-trotters – bad luck to 'em – have simply swept the country and left it desolate. I've gleaned after them and the whole result of my gleaning is but two pairs of muslin curtains with little cockyolly birds upon 'em which are very coarse and ineffective; a terra cotta plaque of Ganesh[1] which you must hang up in Beaver city for good luck; a Rajah's butter dish (if it can come down without being broken) the other things and some women's bracelets which might possibly be mounted for European use. At present they are all dirty and messy. But you shall see what you shall see, and forgive me that I have not brought better things.

There's nothing to tell you save that I have got a pass from Lahore to Delhi and Delhi to Howrah! Tain't bad that when you come to consider it. It shall travel in state and luxury all through. The last two days have been full of wild hurry and turmoil. Can you imagine how pressed I must ha' been when I tell you that I had absolutely not ten minutes to write you. Just now I am snatching time for this note while a vagrant *mistri*[2] is trying to mend my trunk lock. He may finish the job any minute, so you must forgive my pen flying over the paper in this way. I never was a neat writer.

Saw Major Chalmers last night and gave him your message. He is certainly getting much redder in the face here than ever he was at Allahabad.

You could have written me yet one more letter seeing that I don't leave here till to-morrow night. I fancy about half Lahore will come down to see me off and *Oh shan't* I be glad to go; even the 51 hours to Calcutta do not appal me. I want to see for myself how you are, to preach to you the necessity of being well and to see that you get due supplies of iced water on your way down. Mother has given me a flask holding enough whiskey to float a ship. I don't suppose you'll make many demands on it.

You'll let me know of course anything that I can do for you in Calcutta. I've only got one or two minor matters of financial interest to settle[3] and then I shall wander round that city of stinks as a gentleman at large. Do you know how much baggage I take – one small trunk and one large bag!

Euchred madam, and that's two to me. Which reminds me, I have introduced the game[4] – the first game in the world – to this household and Trix and the Pater have taken to it amazingly. They sat up with me till midnight playing three handed Euchre and – truth compels me to say this – cheating awfully! Trix has a way of playing a card and then revoking which would make a saint swear, but she bids fair to become an accomplished Eucheriste. She is much set up at the thought of a second horse which is coming shortly – a real lively horse says she and one that will give me employment: *Her* boy reaches Bombay on the 9th of March; and I fancy hurries up north as fast as ever he can. From the way in which the Mother talks of wedding cake, and the presents which drift into the house, seems to me that she and Jack will be married some time in April. But this is a deadly and confidential secret, and you mustn't tell anybody – not even Mrs Knobbs.

The hook nosed lady Greville is gone. I went for a drive with her ere she went to Peshawur and she was very funny over the way in which she has been treated on Indian lines by the haughty and arrogant guards. "I do not mind men in sleeping suits" she said "but I will not stand babies and ayahs. Consequently, when I make a fuss about the accommodation in the ladies' compartment the guard says: – 'P'raps, you'd like to get in with the gentlemen,' and I answer: – 'I don't care *where* I go so long as I can lie down.' Then I threaten to run about the platform in my night gown and manage to secure a compartment to myself." Even as she spoke I had a vision of her with her teeth gleaming in the lamplight running about Ghaziabad platform "mit nodings on" and I cease to wonder that the guards fell on their knees and besought her not to put her threat into execution.

Cooke[5] is overwhelming me with circulars and prospectuses of railway lines in America. They are all very fine and large but they are written in an absolutely incomprehensible argot. What's a "st'p 'ff ch'k"? and *if* as I am told it means "Stop off check" what does that mean. Why should I stop off, and if I choose to stop off why should I be checked. Must I visit towns like Tuskarora, Wallibong, Boshville, Skunk Rapids (I quote from memory only) Brigg's Breeches, Anaconda Dam, and so on? Yours may be a great country but it all wants to be christened over afresh. I shall rename the towns when I write to the Pioneer. The inhabitants will know nothing about it, but the people in India will believe that I am in decent places. I *cannot* date a letter from "Forks of Credit." It looks as though I were bankrupt and sitting on the rail waiting for money to arrive.

Be pleased to listen to a perfectly true elephant story which has delighted me mightily. It's all true and says volumes for the wicked wisdom of the elephant.

It may have been on this very Chittagong expedition,[6] that they shipped 'em; but anyhow not long ago they had to ship forty elephants from Calcutta to Burma and they, with infinite trouble, got 'em into a British India steamer in the Hugli stalling them, twenty a side, facing each other down the length of the ship – so! [sketch] Well, as you know a hathi is a fairly long beast and by the time they were installed in the lower hold with all their ropes complete, there was only left a small gangway between the lines of elephants. You had to pass the whole length of the thing to get at the last elephant. Then, when everything was comfy, the mahouts began to take the food down the lines. It was all right so long as the first few elephants were busy with their popattes,[7] but when these had finished and became aware of the further supplies of food *still* passing along under their very noses, the fun began. The mahouts with the fodder had to run the gauntlet of twenty waving trunks, were cuffed on the head, were tripped up and buffeted until they dropped the food which was then shared by the nearest elephant [sketch].

You can see from the above diagram that it was some time before the last elephant could get any grub. So desperate was the case that the mahouts at last had to crawl over the elephants' backs out of reach of their insatiate trunks to convey the food safely.

But that wasn't all. That night the steamer dropped down the river and anchored off Sangor Island in dead calm water. It was a hot night and as still as death, but presently the steamer began to roll. First she rolled a little and then she began to swing through a circle of about a hundred and twenty degrees. Up came the Engineer yelling that his engines were being shaken to pieces; up came the Captain crying that his ship would turn turtle if this went on. Who was responsible? They looked down into the hold and saw the strangest sight in the world. You know how an elephant is never still. He always rocks as if at anchor wherever he is. These big beasts had discovered that if they all rocked together as they stood, one side of the steamer would tilt down and this appeared to amuse 'em. So twenty elephants (which is to say sixty tons) rocked forward, and twenty rocked back and the steamer rolled as if she was on the Madras surf. – Each swing getting larger and larger. The men in command, sent the mahouts down with all speed to make the elephants break step, lie down, do anything that would stop their dangerous game. But the elephants approved of see-saw, and the row below was indescribable. The moment a mahout went away the elephants began rocking again, so the stifling night was filled with the groans of the mahouts begging to be allowed to come up on deck for a little, the curses of the ship's officers keeping 'em down below, and the trumpeting of the defrauded elephants. I've heard of queer ways of losing ships but fancy a living cargo turning one upside down, which was what the elephants did their best to do.

The mistri has gone away, and Mother is calling. All love to you, and goodbye till Tuesday morn.

Yours ever
R K

Notes
1. The elephant-headed Hindu god, remover of obstacles and bringer of good fortune; RK made the head of Ganesh his trademark.
2. Workman.
3. The sale of the copyright in his books in the Indian Railway Library series, for one thing: the agreement is dated 7 March 1889 (Sussex).
4. Euchre, an American card game, reached its greatest popularity at the end of the nineteenth century.
5. Thomas Cook and Son, the travel agents. John Mason Cook, the son of the founder and the great developer of the business, had visited India in 1885 and was acquainted with JLK.
6. Sent out in January to the Burmese borders, where disturbances were constant.
7. Thus in copy: I do not find the word recorded.

To Georgiana Burne-Jones, 31 May 1889
ALS: Bancroft Library, University of California, Berkeley

Frisco:[1] / May: 31: 89:

Dear Aunt Georgy:

As is cold water in thirst so is good news from a far country. I felt very lonesome here in this big raging tearing city till I got your note and then the sky brightened. I read it in the street and on the spot took the cable-car – a contraption of the devil inasmuch as the motive power lies underground – and ran up many steep hills to Mrs. Carr[2] who had just sent me a note. I knew her not but we both knew you and there was Uncle Ned's portrait and photoes of his paintings in the room. So we fell into each other's arms and she told me that she was very well, very busy and happy in her life and the possession of a boy named Mike – ætat seven – a queer mixture of English and American. She lives in a funny little house all of painted wood, (which is the custom in Frisco – and has refined – that is to say, unAmerican – daintinesses about her).

I am to give you all her love and tell you that America has hardened her and she can now watch a street accident or a shooting affray without emotion! I have up to date only seen a passing Chinaman stabbed in the eye. I was rather disgusted, but the populace did not mind.

If you are one tithe as sweet to your friends as you are to your nephew I don't wonder that they rave about you after seven years. Of a surety I will fold my wings at the Grange when I touch England but that will not be for some months. I am working now for three papers and making money as fast as I spend it – nearly. I want to spend my little gains on knocking about the States as I shan't get a second chance like this for long. Wherefore I pray you on receipt of this send all my letters with speed to me at *Chicago*. It's a few thousand miles across the continent but I'll be there in a month or so, watching pigs being slain. – *Post Office Chicago*, then. I could write you much of the beauties of Japan, the wierdness (vile word) of China and the tropical splendours of the Straits but that all my spare time is filled with writing and I am running a lady typewriter to enable me to catch up with the mass of work. Howbeit believe that so far I have had a splendid time and look to have others as good. None the less I love not the Americans in bulk! They spit even as in the time of Dickens[3] and their speech is not sweet to listen to – 'specially the women's.

A telegram from India tells me that Trix is to be married on the 11th of June.[4] But I dare vouch that you are better posted than I in these regards.

Now I must kite round the city and wallow in humanity and eat oysters and strawberry cream. On Monday I dine with Mrs. Carr and some time later take her and Mike out for a picnic. I am up at the Bohemian Club[5] for membership where I am likely to meet some amusing folk – have been interviewed by 4 reporters and described to an admiring world as a "handsome but bashful Englishman." Verily I shall have changed since the old days.

All love to Uncle Ned and Madge and Phil and a heartful to you the sweetest of the Aunts.

Ever your nephew
Ruddy

Notes
1. RK and the Hills left Calcutta on 9 March aboard the SS *Madura* and travelled by way of Rangoon, Penang, Singapore, and Hong Kong to Japan, which they reached on 15 April. On 11 May they sailed from Yokohama on the *City of Peking* for San Francisco, where they landed on 28 May. The Hills must have left for Pennsylvania on 30 May.
2. In an inscription dated June 1889 RK writes her name as Mrs Carmichael-Carr (Stewart-Yeats, *Bibliographical Catalogue*, p. 56). She must therefore be the Mrs Carmichael Carr, teacher of music, residing at 1815 Sacramento (*Langley's San Francisco Directory*, 1889). I have not found any information connecting her with Burne-Jones.
3. The American habit of spitting is a major theme in Dickens, *American Notes* (1842).
4. At Simla, on a day when "the monsoon broke over us" (Trix to W. G. Maitland, 10 June 1939: MS, Library of Congress).

5. The Bohemian Club, founded in 1872 by working newspapermen, aimed to include all those interested in the arts. RK certainly made use of the Club, but there is no evidence in the Club's records that he ever received an honorary membership. He says, however, that he was elected ([7]–9 June).

To [Edmonia Hill], [6 June 1889]
Text: Marguerite Stabler, "An Inside Light on Rudyard Kipling", *Pacific Monthly*, XVIII (November 1907) 562

[San Francisco]

There is no other place like it. Reckless and roaring like nothing you ever saw. The men make money and "break up" with a rush that goes to your head. Everything is done on a large scale, even the coins are not small, two-bits is the smallest piece worthy the notice of a self-respecting citizen. But next to the ocean winds it is the reporter man that most takes you off your feet. Your soul is not your own, neither your secrets, your plans, your private ambitions, when they grapple you. It is knowing their Bohemian Club that makes you know San Francisco. High jinks and low jinks presided over by the Owl makes this body of men to hum.[1] There was a "blow-out" (know you the meaning of that?) given for a great Sahib who had stuck by his ship – he was a fighting Sahib, by the way – when there was a cyclone or something of unusual size.[2] There were speeches and wittles and drink, twenty I should say, then more of both. Then the Man of the Cyclone rose up and said a few modest and harmless little words, whereupon we howls off the roof of the house. The man next me soothes me suddenly by saying, "When we get on our hind legs we do like this. See?" I saw and if I could have induced wealth to rhyme with raiment my turn at a verse might have gone better, but I had to be satisfied with collars, dollars.[3]

Notes
1. For the owl, see [10–11 June]. The Bohemian Club "high jinks" is a serious play put on from time to time by the members; "low jinks" is a musical comedy, produced annually.
2. Lieutenant James W. Carlin of the USS *Vandalia*, a hero of the storm that damaged the German and American fleets at Samoa in March, was honoured at a Bohemian Club dinner on 5 June.
3. See the fourth stanza of RK's verses on the Bohemian Club in [10–11 June].

To Edmonia Hill, [7]–9 June 1889
Text: Copy, University of Sussex

[San Francisco]

Palace Hotel:
Friday: More than one week now since you departed this place and never an answer has come to me. Tisn't the liveliest thing in the world but never mind. I forgive you. You must be looking ahead now far more than backward.

My last told you of the big dinner to Lieut. Carlin and feebly tried to describe the decorations at the Club. I met Carlin again last night at a dinner party given in his honour and it was very pretty to see the hero from Samoa bowing down before a big Kentucky blonde – all strawberries and cream in the face and all foolishness and giggles otherwise. She was a Miss Bissell and told me that she had been nursed by a nigger-nurse and had all the superstitions of the "quarters." The other girls – so funny to go to a party of unmarried girls – kicked up and carried on with young men in a way that I did not like. There was not an ounce of harm in it of course but – well, somehow I didn't feel in the mood for a "frolic." I glowered at the show and increased the reputation of England for insular reserve.

That afternoon I had been to see the richest heiress in 'Frisco – a Miss Haggin.[1] Mrs. Carr took me there – you remember what I told you about my quaint dinner with her and her fat little son. Well Miss Haggin is very plain but clever in a soured and bitter sort of way – a woman would be bitter if she thought every man was making love to her for the sake of her money I fancy. She lived in a palatial house filled with all sorts of shiny glittering things dragged together from the ends of the earth and ranged about the rooms with the catholic ignorance of moneyed barbarism. I felt very sorry for her and she tried to [be] vastly smart and witty.

This evening I've just come back from a "stag" party at Spencer's.[2] He has been a tutor to me throughout. There were eight men and we played whist till 11. I kept a stiff upper lip and returned my partner's lead and I don't think my awful ignorance of the game was made unduly patent. On my way home I dropped in at the Club – my Club i' faith – and frivolled with the President to whom I have sent a set of verses thanking him for my election. But I told you of that. Now I am sitting in my room and recording things for your eyes. I think you know everything I have done since twenty minutes after the time you left Oakland Station. You can see what a high old time I am enjoying – and yet I am not enjoying. One feels so awful lonesome even in the giddiest of the giddy throng. I can't make out the people at home. You know they wired about the wedding. Since then as I told you they sent me my golden silk cummerbund and white jackets but deuce a line of writing. That's the straw that breaks the camel's back. You also are dumb but I can understand how you should be occupied with other and more pleasant things. God bless you. I'm going to turn in.

Sunday morn. Ow! I am just awful sick. This away. Yesterday morn, Brough of the *Breeder and Sportsman*, the young Englishman I told you about who has interviewed me and published the whole of the Broken Link Handicap.[3] Brough, I say, suggested that I should attend a trotting race and dragged me off somewhere to the back of the Park to assist at the dreariest function that ever I clapped eyes on. In the middle of the racing, (such racing!) the Stables got on fire and I got very warm and festive assisting in the general tamasha[4] that followed. Then the wind blew chill; you know how it can be cold in Frisco. That started all my teeth and by evening I was wild. I fled to a dentist who stuffed a tooth and my head began to swell. It is now the size of a healthy pumpkin and throbs. Consequently I am neither fit to be seen nor heard. Pity me. I am *not* happy. At least I have received your telegram telling me that you are back to your mother again and that cheers me. Perhaps by this time you have got my wire adjuring you to write. I can't write myself just now because I am waltzing about with Teeth! But my last letter ought to have broken the U.S. postage for a while and amused you for at least an hour. Don't think from what I said then that I disliked the American girl. All I meant was that she didn't amuse me as much as I had expected. Isn't it strange? And now, pluming your wings in the old nest after your long flight, go and have as good a time as you know how. All luck and pleasure be with you, and in the midst of your happiness don't forget to send an occasional line to me. I'll wire you when my address changes but just now a letter means so much – so much.

Yours always,
The Boy with the Swelled head:

Notes
1. Presumably one of the daughters of the lawyer and landowner, James Ben Ali Haggin (1821–1914).
2. George W. Spencer, insurance man and member of the Bohemian Club. RK had a letter of introduction to Spencer from his Allahabad friend Captain Bayliss; through Spencer he was brought into the Bohemian Club (Harold Orel, ed., *Kipling: Interviews and Recollections*, 1983, p. 181.).
3. The story, originally published *CMG*, 6 April 1887, appeared in the *Breeder and Sportsman*, 8 June 1889, accompanied by an account of racing in India evidently derived from RK. Brough I have been able to identify only as Norman Brough, editor of the *Breeder and Sportsman*, of 305 Bush Street (*San Francisco Directory*, 1889).
4. Show, excitement.

To Edmonia Hill, [10–11 June 1889]
Text: Facsimile and printed text, *Bohemian Club Library Notes*, no. 9 (June 1961) 2–4

[San Francisco]

Palace Hotel:
Monday:

A busy day of revision correction and alteration. But the first part of it was awfully lively. I told you yesterday how my head was swelled beyond its natural size. This morn it had swelled enough to bung up my left eye and with the other I steered my doubtful way to a firm of dentists, for I felt that one mere man would never be able to cope with the agony. One villain looked at me and passed me on to another who after an hour hewed off the end of my toof – and I 'quealed – 'quealed like evvyting – and flung me maimed and quivering on the streets of Frisco. "Tomorrow" said he "we'll fit on a crown." But I thought I was already wearing the martyr's crown of anguish. However the swelling has gone down and I feel twenty per cent happier than I did. Before that I felt awful lonesome and woebegone. The news of today ma'am is that fifteen of the Moreton Frewen letters are done[1] and the rest will be through in a day or two. Now you will understand that I have very little outside news of any kind to tell you. I am or have been self centred on myself. But a confession has to be made. The amber mouthpiece of our pipe broke itself not half an hour ago. I was biting on it with the peculiar viciousness that comes from thinking hard on any one subject and it splintered in my jaws – just the teeny weeny bit of amber at the end. The screw itself is not hurt and I'll get it mended tomorrow. Tomorrow also – it is nearly tomorrow now – sees a signed article of mine in the examiner which I will send along to you as soon as may be.[2] I wonder much whether you will like it. It come to me all of a sudden. I hope you will. In the meantime please look over a copy of the verses I sent to the Bohemian Club when they made me an honorary member. The totem of the club, which you will find throughout its rooms, is an owl. The piece runs: –

>   Men said, but here I know they lied,
>   The owl was of a sullen clan
>   Whose voice upon the lone hillside
>   Forboded ill to mouse and man –
>   A terror noiseless in the flight,
>   A hooknosed hoodlum of the night.

> But I have found another breed,
>   An owl of fine artistic feelings,
> A connoisseur of wine and weed
>   Who flutters under frescoed ceilings
> Nor scorns to bid the passing guest
> Abide a season in his nest.
>
> I saw him on the staircase sit
>   And blandly wink at jibe and joke,
> An arbiter twixt wit and wit,
>   A god enshrined in baccy smoke
> While round his pedestal there beat
> The clamour of his servants' feet.
>
> Some toiled in journalistic fetters
>   And some in stocks – and stand up collars –
> Some worked his will in Art and letters.
>   And some their own with things called dollars.
> Whate'er they ran or wrote or drew
> The owl was monarch of the crew.
>
> With humour bright as Frisco air
>   In speech as dry as Frisco sand,
> He blithely bade me welcome there
>   And stretched a claw to take my hand
> Whereat I found acceptance free
>   Among his jovial company.
>
> A wanderer from East to West
>   A vagrant under many skies,
> How shall a roving rhymster best
>   Requite O owl they courtesies?
> Accept in lieu of laboured stippling
> A simple "Thank you"
>   signed,
>   R. Kipling.

The Club is going to have it hung up and illuminated.[3]

Tuesday. The dentists have been killing me again and I lie in the lowest deeps of despair. It does not console me to know that I am going for a picnic tomorrow with Mrs. Carr and her son, or that by that same lady I have been introduced to a Mrs. Cropper who knew the Burne-Jones at home. Mrs. C. is a big lump of a woman who lounges about on Oriental rugs and weaves her arms into statuesque poses. She is an American who pretends to be very English and is most American when she does so. I was calling on her this evening and she lisped and giggled and simpered till I could ha' killed her dead. When I went away a fat Philadelphia millionaire who has seen me in the hotel took me up to his rooms and introduced me to his wife and three girls. Say I don't like the 'Melican girl much. There's a repellant hardness about her that isn't pretty and when she tries to be smart she succeeds in sailing very near to vulgarity. I have mapped out the skeleton of a trip to Portland, Vancouver, Marysville, the Yellowstone, Salt Lake, Denver, Omaha, Minneapolis and Chicago of which I will[4] give you written and telegraphic details later. But for the fact that I spose I must do it I would much sooner do nothing. I guess it is the tooth that has clean taken the heart out of my life and I don't want to do anything. I've begun Fergus Deakin[5] but I can't go on and written one or two turnovers but they don't interest me. Maybe I'll come all right when I have to think and cut about and look out for things. At present . . . but that's of no consequence as Mr. Toots says.[6] I don't think it is good to be alone in a big hotel. I hate big hotels.

Howbeit I cannot move till I get a letter from you telling me how you are and what you did and what you thought of thinks[7] generally. Do you know it is nearly a fortnight since I've had a line from you. The last you wrote was that letter of introduction to Mare Island. Of course you're very much taken up with the delights of home coming but remember me – for a mere twenty minutes remember me. I have been spoiled and I feel the reaction. Not a line has come to me from India. All I know is that Trix was married this morning. I'm going to bed. Good night and God bless you. Give my best love to your mother.

Yours ever
R.

What do you think of the address. That's the way men sign their names here. I got a *chit* today from a girl – "first family" too – addressed to "Mr. R. Kipling!" Ugh!

Notes

1. These are a mystery. RK mentions (11–14 February 1889) that Frewen was negotiating for publication of RK's letters in New York and London papers. Evidently some positive arrangement was made, but I have found no information beyond the references in RK's letters: see also 3–25 December 1889 where RK says that "Longman has sent the letters to Andrew Lang to read." Perhaps they were to enter into the work to be called *The Book of the Forty-Five Mornings*, announced but never published: see [11 August 1890].
2. This has not been found. A search of the *Examiner* both before and after 11 June reveals nothing to fit RK's statement. The closest thing is an interview with RK in the *Examiner* of 9 June entitled "Snakes and Elephants: A Traveler's Strange Tales of Exciting Scenes in the Heart of India". According to Francis L. H. Noble, then Sunday editor of the *Examiner*, RK offered the paper some of the material later published in the letters to

the *Pioneer*, but Noble turned it down as exaggerated and offensive to San Francisco (*Boston Sunday Globe*, 27 December 1925, reprinted in Orel, *Kipling: Interviews and Recollections*, pp. 191–3).
3. The MS of the poem is not now in the Bohemian Club. According to Bailey Millard, the verses were written in the album of the club and were later torn out by an enraged Club member after he had read Kipling's remarks on San Francisco and the Bohemian Club in the *From Sea to Sea* letters ("How Kipling Discovered America", *The Bookman* (New York) XXVI (January 1908) 488).
4. The facsimile of the manuscript ends here; the rest of the letter is from the printed text, except for the post script, which is written at the head of the first page of the manuscript.
5. Not identified: by RK? or something he is reading?
6. In Dickens, *Dombey and Son*.
7. Thus in copy.

To Edmonia Hill, 15–16 June 1889
Text: Copy, University of Sussex

Palace Hotel:/S: Francisco:/June: 15/89:

Bless you – and again and many times, bless you, I whooped when I got your letter and immediately sent back a wire, just to persuade you that I was not altogether dead. I forgive you. Something must have happened to both our mails that they never arrove at either end for the same dāk that carried my first letter – 8 pages – to you carried also a letter of thanks to your mother. But I must write again to that kind lady. Never mind missing the letters. I ain't lonesome any more now that yours of the 9*th* has come in. My! What a big continent this is! I used to think India big enough and wearisome enough to despatch a letter in but this beats it hollow. This time last year by the way I was at Mussoorie sitting on a hilltop reading you M.S. Today there ain't no one to read my M.S. and no one to help me with my packing and I am awful lonesome all round. How on earth I am ever to get clear o' the place I don't know. It has pleased me immensely that the Mother has written to you. I hope she wrote a proper letter and said you was a sweet lady and the very nicest in the world. Did she? You know do you not that Trix was to have been married on the 11th. I have sent off a telegram of congratulation and . . . . won't it be a lark if the marriage is delayed or anything and my "bless 'em both" drops into the camp before the ceremony!

Some things in your letter pleased me not and I pray you refrain from repeating 'em. You know which they were and you know what sort of answer you would have received had they been said in my ear! I am *not* ill, and thou knowest without the telling that I have not been frivolling. Nor does the "desolate Freedom of the wild ass" seem a desirable thing to me, even did I possess it, which I don't. And I don't want to, an' when I get to Beaver I'll just take an' prove to you I don't. Read thou with the eye of faith before coming to the next paragraph which is purely business.

Tomorrow (Sunday) night I leave by the 7 p.m. train (Pullman car) for a place called Portland in Oregon; thence for Tacoma opposite Vancouver island; then by steamer to Victoria and then back again. (I *won't* go to Alaska). To Bayless's[1] mine in Montana, then to Livingstone to do the Yellowstone Park; then down to Ogden, then Denver, Omaha, Minneapolis and Chicago and then Pittsburgh. Now I'll carefully write out my dates. Oh bother, they are locked up in the dispatch box and I'll have to get at 'em later on. You know by now how much more I would sooner turn up at Pittsburgh direct – you do not luckily know what it has cost me to screw myself down to the trip – but the tour is purely a matter for writing letters and making money and please God it won't take long. Henceforward be prepared for the eruption of casual telegrams into your quiet home – they aren't loaded. They'll merely tell you where to write to. I'll be writing all along and I mean to take good care not to have any missing of connection en route. Again, therefore, expect the telegrams.

Did I tell you of my picnic with Mrs. Carr on the shores of Lake Merritt, just across the bay. Twas the funniest thing imaginable. The dear old lady took out her 7 year old son Michael (He was very grubby before he started) and Michael's chosen school-friend a child who was called Phil, a basket of food and a light heart. I carried the basket. Then I helped the boys to sail their boat, caught little crabs for 'em, tried to 'tice fish, and wound up with a row on the lake: returning to Frisco just about the fashionable hour as dirty as a sweep having filled the boys up with ice-cream soda, peanuts and all manner of unwholesomenesses. Mrs. Carr and I sat under a tree and when the boys did not demand our every attention talked about the old days at the Grange, when all the cousins were young. Mrs. Carr has been introducing me all round the place as a sort of connection but she's so nice and homely an old soul that I can't kick.

They – I refer grandly to the people of San Francisco – have given two receptions in my honour. It was very funny to be the centre of a big drawing room with people waiting to hear what I would say next. Nothing has startled me more than the difference between "Young Kipling of the Pi" and "Rudyard Kipling the Indian Editor." I own I enjoyed it while it lasts, but afterwards it is all dust and ashes in my mouth as I am alone in my room at night with nothing to do but to think. On mature reflection the Lord has not cut me out for a society man and I've split my dress trousers and the buttons are beginning to rot off most my shirts. I try to cobble things together but it's very hard work. I'd sooner write a leading article on the Silver question.

Sunday. Oh how I wish you were here to help me along with my packing. 'Tis the most horrible mess that ever you did see. However here's my route: beginning a week hence:

Saturday: 22: Leave Tacoma @ 6.45
Sunday: 23 in train
Monday: 24. arrive Livingstone
Tuesday ⎫
Wednesday ⎬ In the Yellowstone Park
Thursday ⎪
Friday ⎭
Saturday: 29: Leave Livingston and reach Helena
Sunday – in Helena:

Then follows all a long list of arrivals and departures from Denver and St. Paul till I strike Chicago on July the tenth:[2] Now in all human probability I shall exceed these times but this is only to give you an idea of where I may be wandering. I am not going up to Alaska, because that would take nearly a month, unless I am credibly informed that the thing would pay. Guess I shall have material enough from what I see only: Howbeit the telegram will tell you where to write and when. Of course I shall tell the Palace People to forward the letters as fast as may be. It's lucky that one of us at least stays in the same place.

Now I must return to what I am pleased to call my packing. I have bought a little grip-sack to take along in the train with me. The rest of my luggage I shall check on ahead and pick it up at such places as seem expedient. Once more you do not know how happy your letter has made me. Good bye and God bless you. I'll write the day after tomorrow.

R.

Notes
1. Captain E. G. Bayliss; he had a brother in Montana as well as parents in California.
2. This schedule was altered, as succeeding letters will show. RK did not, for example, leave Tacoma until 30 June; he was in Yellowstone Park 5–11 July; and he did not go to Helena, nor to St Paul.

To Edmonia Hill, 18 June 1889
Text: Copy, University of Sussex

The Gilman House:/Portland/Oregon:

Into what strange place have I tumbled now dear Lady? It is more than 700 miles north of S. Francisco and, by hotel accommodations, at least 2,000 miles distant from anywhere else. But the journey was well worth the roughness. You have crossed the Rockies and slept many times in a Pullman car, consequently my tale will have little of the novel for you. It won't startle you to know that in crossing the Siskyou Mts: into Oregon we dropped 2200 feet in thriteen miles over a series of palpitating trestles, cuts and embankments, and saw miles ahead of us by line but only 500 feet below by bee-line another train. I was glad when those Siskyou mountains ended. I wasn't afraid – not in the least. I couldn't exactly tell how a thing like this [sketch] was going to carry Caesar and his fortunes. Howbeit we came across – at which I have never ceased to wonder. All the time that we were passing the Sacramento River I wanted to get out and stop and fish. The scenery had been lovely but man – man in long boots and a red shirt – was doing his best to defile it with lumber mills and logging camps. But this is beside the matter – what I really wished to impress upon you was my misery in the sleeping car. Y'see I was never made to undress myself lying down – still less to dress in the same manner. Consequently when I had to do both those things in a sweating stuffy bunk I wriggled and kicked and cussed and wound up by falling out flop into the gangway in my pyjamas. I could hear suppressed giggles from all the other bunks and I own I felt hot and very uncomfortable. The heat from San Francisco to Portland rather made me open my eyes. There seemed a lingering touch of the gilded East about it that was quite familiar to me. On the road, everyone was awfully nice to me. I spent most of my time in the smoker swapping stories (which means getting turnovers from the aborigines).[1] One of them a life insurance Secretary and the other a small millionaire[2] steered me to this very horrible hotel where as the house is full I am now sharing a double-bedded room with the Life insurance man. The millionaire is an enthusiastic fisherman and wants me to come to some place 20 miles away and help catch 30 pound trout. Not much, says this child. I have other fish to fry. Mr. Spencer to whom Bayliss gave me letters has given me letters to Portland here and I am threatened with a complete history of the town and all its modern improvements at three this afternoon. As I only came in at 11.30 hot, dusty, unshaved and unwashed you will understand that I am getting in a line to you before I am altogether kilt by the yarns of the oldest inhabitants of this town.

Portland is composed of three streets – two very dirty and one not at all clean. It is built on a river chiefly peopled by rude little boys in boats. It's hackmen are vigorous and muscular and compete for fares as happier nations fight for the dear life. The chief industry of Portland consists in piling bails[3] on the pavements walking round and slowly whistling at them. Real estate rules high on account of the large blocks of the same already secured by the inhabitants who keep them under their finger nails and in their collars. There is one tramway and one horse, and there are no women. The sidewalks are too dirty for their dresses. And this is a truthful account of Portland just as this is a mere scrap of a note to catch the post and to tell you that I am well and fit. I sent you a wire this morn asking you to write to Livingstone near the Yellowstone till the 24th. Heaven sent you understood till the 24th with you, not with me, for in this loneliness, and I am very lonely, I need your letters sorely. Give my best regards to your mother who I trust by this time has received my second letter. Keep thou well above all things and have good times. For me the novelty has worn off long ago and I am not so interested in seeing scenery and people as I ought to be. But I must put the thing through and write about it somehow. Later letters will tell you all about mine self and my doings. I hope to leave here to-morrow and will write from Tacoma if I do so. If not you'll let a chit answer.

Goodbye and keep well.
R.

[sketch]

Notes
1. Four of RK's "Turnovers" contributed to the *CMG* are anecdotes of western American life: "The Shadow of His Hand", "The Bow Flume Cable Car", "A Little More Beef", and "Her Little Responsibility" (*Abaft the Funnel*).
2. According to a letter in the *Portland Oregonian*, 13 March 1928, from C. E. Rumelin (see 23 June 1889), the insurance man was J. L. M. Shatterly, of San Francisco, and the "small millionaire" A. J. Salsbury (or Salisbury) of Hueneme, California.
3. My guess is that this means "wooden bars".

To Edmonia Hill, 23 June 1889
Text: Copy, University of Sussex

[Tacoma] June: 23rd 1889

Forgive me this atrocious paper: but what can I do!
I have just struck my baggage for the first time in a week, and am now resting after a dusty daylong ride to this place. The town is new

and booming, the hotel is new and boominger and the men are the newest and boomingest of all. I am sitting in a big, raw bar reeking of the smell of new paint and fresh sawn timber, lighted by an electric lamp and filled with men all spitting all over the floor and all talking about lumber and town lots and Heaven only knows what other skittles. A savagely naked electric lamp flares and winks at us (we have no gas system) and in the interval between the winks I am sitting down to write to you dear lady.

And you demand account of myself. By the Gods I have both seen and accomplished wonders within the past four days. The old man from California clave to me like the old man of the sea and begged me to come with him by steamer up the Columbia river to a place called the Dalles. Well I went and I was well rewarded. The old man had been waiting four and twenty years, so he told me, for the scenery along the river – a round trip of 220 miles. I only know that I clapped my hands and shouted like a child at the bluffs and the waterfalls as they slid by. All the same in the pauses between my shouting it seemed so strange unnatural and wrong to be seeing all this loveliness alone. I wanted to turn round and find you at my elbow as it was in the Moulmein Pagoda at Penang and Kyoto. But you were not there and – the old man chewed tobacco which was the only flaw in his otherwise estimable character. Well we saw scenery such as I cannot in any way describe – painted rocks, a cascade 890 feet high, and Indian wigwams and remains of old time block houses, sturgeon 130 lbs weight, wicked salmon wheels that caught the poor salmon, tossed him into a barge and kept him there, and canneries where Chinamen (ugh their fingers!) pressed the fish into cans allee same as we eat in the hot weather. That was very nasty but I found it interesting and 'twill certainly make a good letter.[1] We pulled up at a little lonely town called The Dalles and loafed about it in the long Northern twilight that lasts till 9. o'clock, while the cows came home across the meadows and the people sat out in their verandahs and shouted to each other across the street and commented on the beauty of the pears and hollyhocks in their garden. Then we went down the river back to Portland and the trip took us two days. Every step of it was full of incident and emotion. Next day a young man[2] turned up and got into conversation with us (he was a real estate agent) and discovered that we were members of the craft and was more than kind. Finally he told us of a place fifteen miles away where we could get salmon. The old man who is a maniac about fishing hired a team and drove us two out, over the vilest road through lumber forests that ever I saw or felt. When we weren't bounding through a blackberry patch we were skipping (all four wheels in the air) along a corduroy road. But the rich wooded scenery by the way was superb. We pulled up at the house of one James Day a primitive farmer who had not yet degenerated into the "summer boarder" type and who consented to give us food and a roof over our heads withal. His house was on a bluff overhanging a lovely river.[3] Mosquitoes filled it (the house) within and without and it was exactly half an inch thick. Every voice could be heard at the lowest whisper and I was keenly aware ere I had been twenty minutes in the place that the daughter of the house – a lumpy slattern of eighteen – was making things hot for her younger brother, a bare footed boy of eight, because he had ridden five miles to a dressmaker – a dressmaker in that wilderness! – and had returned with the news that the girl's best go-to-meeting dress wasn't ready. Say, human nature is powerful much alike all the world over. But these things be altogether beside the mark. We arrived there at 3 p.m. in blazing sunshine that would have smitten me dead in India but only frizzled my nose in Oregon. When we went down to the river the old man was in luck. I only foul-hooked a water snake which frightened me nearly into a fit but he got a salmon of 11 $\frac{1}{2}$ pounds. Eleven and one half pounds maam! Next morn after a hot and mosquitosome night the real work began and in *six* hours he and I (the young man from Portland did not fish) landed 141 lbs. weight of fish – the smallest being six pounds. The prize catch was 15$\frac{1}{2}$ pounds. The old man caught it but I landed two ten pounders and a twelve pounder on an eight ounce rod! Wah! Wah! I had to play the big one for thirty seven minutes and was dripping with perspiration when I came out the winner and seduced him into shallow water. What do you think of that for a day's fishing. It was magnificent, and in the heart of magnificent scenery – just the spot to camp out in. You wait and see the letter that I will write about it all.[4] The old man begged me to stay on and fish some more but I refused and so he came along with me to Tacoma today. He pretends to have taken a great liking to me and he certainly does everything to match his words. Can you imagine me trapesing about the country with a white-headed langur who chews tobacco owns cattle-ranches and ships and tells the wildest and most improbable anecdotes in the voice of a slightly tired archangel? It's very funny. All his soul is centered on fishing and the industries of the country and he literally oozes anecdotes of every kind. When he landed the fifteen pounder he whooped till the hills rang and danced a wild war dance with me all along the pebbles of the river-shore. All that he regretted he said, was that his wife was not with him to see the catch. I said that every married man would naturally feel like he did. Then he betted that I was married and refused to believe that I wasn't. Verily he is a quaint old man and if I left him to his own devices would pay for us both all along.

Now this even we struck this queer mad town of Tacoma where the lumber lies about the street and the mammoth uncompleted opera house jostles the wooden shanty and the gilded liquor saloon rubs shoulders with the chip and nail barrack of the Salvation Army, and just across the bay the primeval forests come slick down to the water edge. You never saw such woods in your life and *never* such mosquitoes. They are big fat confiding beasts who stay still to be squashed but when you have killed one on your manly brow you feel as if you had upset a bottle of claret there. Our Allahabad 'skeeters are fools to these. I have wandered up and down the unfinished streets till nine o'clock and the dusk was only just beginning to settle down then. Tomorrow I go round Puget Sound and head towards Victoria. A wire will tell you where to write and where and how. I'd give a good deal for a glimpse of one of your letters to cheer me but that I shan't get till I strike the Livingstone and read with the eye of faith. Think of me as a sun-tanned, flannel shirted rascal who eats raspberries and cream and broiled salmon three times a day and carries on his breast – but what do you know what I carry with me? Your Melican hot bread will give me the dyspepsy one of these fine days but not I hope before I have done my work. I am simply choked up with material to write about and only want you to stand behind me with a thick stick and make me work. But really I am doing a good deal, tho' I fall from time to time into horrible moods of depression and general misery. But you know how I am built. I get through the dark hour and take no harm.

My love to the Professor. Ask him how the plates[5] are coming on and give all my regards to your folk whom I feel that I know well. As for myself

I am what I shall always be.[6]

Notes
1. Letters 26 and 27 in *From Sea to Sea*; originally numbers 27 and 28 of the letters in the *Pioneer*, 25, 28, and 31 December 1889.
2. C. E. Rumelin; in his letter to the *Portland Oregonian*, 13 March 1928, on RK's account of this fishing trip in *From Sea to Sea*, Rumelin says he was not a real estate man. He also says that they were a party of four including Shatterley.
3. The Clackamas.
4. Part of Letter 26, *From Sea to Sea*.
5. Hill's photographs intended to illustrate RK's travel letters. At least four sets were made: copies are now in the Library of Congress, the Huntington Library, Cornell and Princeton
6. A hand-written note on the copy adds: "On the envelope, – sketch of R.K. fishing".

To Edmonia Hill, [30 June 1889][1]
Text: Incomplete copy, University of Sussex

[Tacoma]

The Pater has done a lot of illustrations for In Black and White.[2] He writes as tho' he was pleased with the output. The Mother writes me in confidence that they are lovely – particularly a sketch of Lalun leaning out of the window in The City Wall, and another of the old Warden of the ford shaking himself clear of the dead man who had opportunely brought him to land. This seems to me to augur well for the success of the second edition that we corrected – Didn't we.[3] [. . .][4]

Never mind. I'll tell you later on. I too have had a long letter from the Mother and a longer from the Pater full of news. The worst was that the man I dined with in Rangoon is dead – died of heart disease in Pegu while on a shooting excursion; and a man in Lahore, I liked him, died of dysentery. Also a woman, a Mrs. Levett-Yeats[5] lies at the point of death from the same disease and the cholera is rattling all over the Punjab. These be sad things to reflect on. But the better news is that the Spectator has given me a "splendid review" of Soldiers Three with long extracts from the speech of Mulvaney.[6] [. . .]

It is nearly eleven o'clock and I must fly off and rearrange my trunks by the simple "stamp and clamp" method. Tell Aleck that I'll sort over all the pictures when I arrive and worry the soul out of him. Mother speaks of him as the 'Fessor, so I guess that she has been reading the letters.[7] Elliott[8] the P.W.D. Member of Council professes himself specially delighted with 'em and I learn that the public generally take or pretend to take an interest. [. . .]

lot – 45 × 150 feet – on an avenue.[9] Vancouver is a steady little English town where they build in brick and dressed granite and I feel very lordly now that I know I am a landed proprietor! What shall we call the lot – Ruddy's folly? Really it's a very nice little lot and I shall grow mushrooms there.

But a truce to fooling. I *must* fly upstairs.

Keep well, keep well and again keep well.

Notes
1. The text that follows, according to a note on the copy, consists of "two fragments of letters" in an envelope with the Tacoma postmark of 30 June; there is no way of knowing whether the fragments are parts of a single letter or of several, nor whether they belong to 30 June or not. I print them together here as they appear in the copy.
2. These were not published.
3. The first revised text of In Black and White is that published in London (1890), technically not the second edition but the first English. A copy of In Black and White with autograph corrections by RK is described in the Grolier Club Catalogue of the Works of Rudyard

Kipling (New York, 1930) p. 79. It is possible that RK and Mrs Hill collaborated on the work on board ship.
4. The letter, according to Mrs Hill's note, was full of sketches which she cut out and gave away, leaving gaps in the text.
5. Wife of Sidney Kilmer Levett-Yeats, Deputy Examiner, Office of Audit and Account, Public Works Department, Lahore, and a writer of fiction (see 14 December 1895). RK described Mrs Levett-Yeats as best of the company at a costume ball where she appeared as Helen of Troy (*CMG*, 29 December 1886).
6. 23 March 1889, pp. 403–4, calling RK's stories "realistic in the best sense of the word".
7. The "From Sea to Sea" series in which Hill appears as the "Professor" and, occasionally, the "'Fessor".
8. Sir Charles Elliott (1835–1911), a member of the Council of India, in charge of the Public Works Department.
9. RK bought two lots in the Mount Pleasant district of Vancouver and held them until 1928. He travelled to Victoria and Vancouver between 24 and 30 June.

To Alexander Hill, 2 July 1889
Text: Copy, University of Sussex

Livingston, Montana / July: 2/89

Dear Hill,

You at one end of the pole and I at the other. Guess 'twould be about as much as my life was worth to talk about prohibition in these parts. I thought San Francisco drunk but it's an infant sucking in the night compared to Montana. I've been introduced to the cowboy. Mein Gott! Even as he was reeling out his tipsy blasphemies in the reeking bar I was smitten with a wicked thought: – what would happen if this vessel of wrath was transported to Beaver and allowed to reel up and down its sacred streets! They'd try to catch and cage him as the drunken harlot and then – something would happen to Beaver. But seriously, I grieve, my dear friend, to notice in your epistle traces of a certain impatience at having to go round by stealth to get any of your beer. Now I have made extensive experiments and have discovered that you can't get drunk on Milwaukee beer. There is no guile in that brand. I always take it when I am asked – ordered shall I say – to drink. You might mention that little fact to your circle. Milwaukee beer remember. In regard to what you say of Prohibish: Talk it must be, to put it mildly, galling; but was there ever saintly or for matter of that mundane cause in which the losers did not cry: – "Nous sommes trahis." I know from certain lurid reminiscences what my grandmothers' (both of 'em) life and the communion of the Methodist Episcopal Church meant.[1]

You should be with me. I haven't even a kodak and I'm moving among the lordliest scenery in a wilderness of Indians, cow punchers, herds of horses wandering loose over the prairie, pink and blue cliffs, cascades, tunnels and snow clad mountains that would make your very camera's mouth water with envy. Each day I meet some new character madder than the last. My latest is an English dude of four inch collars and very little sense who had made an atrocious fool of himself at home and was wandering around waiting for things to blow over. He confided a lot of queer things to me: and my constant wonder was that his father didn't send him to school instead of letting him loaf about the world in charge of a valet – a valet in America! – even more foolish than himself. Guess he'll go into a book.[2]

I'm more than head and ears over in work but find I can just keep abreast by writing all day in the cars, and looking at the scenery in between times. All the same I am as fit as a whole orchestra of fiddles or else I would be dead of work long ago.

This place Livingstone is about to celebrate the 4th. All the cowboys are in, and they are at present *only* shooting fireworks about the street which is composed of wooden buildings. But a very drunken man is kicking about the streets armed with a Winchester and from the language of the bystanders I gather that he is looking for someone. Isn't it delightful.

The nig waiter here calls me that feller. Sort of *"Hi hem hitherao"*[3] business. I start for the Park tomorrow.

All regards to Mrs. Hill to whom I am writing and above all keep thou well. I'd give something if you were with me. You'd have fun.

Yours ever,
Rudyard Kipling.

[sketch]

Notes
1. Both of RK's grandmothers – Mrs Frances Lockwood Kipling and Mrs Hannah Jones Macdonald – were the wives of Methodist ministers. Beaver College, over which the Reverend Taylor presided, was a Methodist foundation.
2. He appears briefly in Letter 31 of *From Sea to Sea*.
3. "Hi, come here."

To Edmonia Hill, 2 July 1889
Text: Copy, University of Sussex

Livingston: / Mont.

Dear Lady:

The accumulated dâk at Livingston to-day gave me three letters from you – two cheerful and one sad. I can't make out what has been happening to my letters but when I come, letters won't matter. I am tied down now entirely to my work and hardly take my nose off it. The description of the Yellowstone lies before me and that will be the stiffest job I have yet undertaken, and I fancy the most conspicuous failure.[1] I don't like to hear of your larking around with friends and moonlight picnicing because you are anything but strong and you might hurt yourself. Please go slow for my sake. You know what it means to me when you are ill. All the same just you go along and enjoy yourself all you are worth, cause that's good for you. I wish I was around to have a share in all the fun – even tho' it entailed being a rabid prohibitionist. Did Aleck tell you that he has sent me a note the chief portion of which is taken up with a wail over his lost beer. I'm truly sorry for him. But when I come I'll be his companion in misfortune tho' for the last fortnight I've been almost without looking at beer, too busy. Did you get my letters from Tacoma? Did you get and digest all that was in them? I hate this idiotic waiting over of a week or ten days before I can get any answers.

I've got nothing that I can write to you except the fact that I've been seeing wonderful scenery and am now among the Montana cowboys in a ramshackle building designated by dwellers in smaller towns as an "elegant hotel." They call it the Albemarle, and just don't you never come anigh here.

The town is scattered over the rolling prairie and is chiefly occupied in raising the devil and raising horses. They do the former most. I start for the Yellowstone tomorrow and get it over in five days and then begin to head South to Chicago which I shall quit at once. I must stop or else I'll never be able to get abreast of my work. I've such a lot to say to you that I don't know how to put it down, so I must hold it over till I reach you and then you shall hear it all. The last two days have been spent in the train riding mostly and smoking a good deal. You'll see in the letters when I bring 'em to you what sort of a time I've been having.[2] It's mainly descriptions of characters met on the road. God knows they weren't very interesting, but I had to make 'em so, and you know that I've got to go through with it. A good deal of my good name depends on these letters and I want to make 'em worthy of the illustrations. Aydemi!

I can't write any more. My fingers have been on the stilo for eight hours without almost a break. I leave tomorrow at seven o'clock for the Park and must turn in. Take this as only a line to fill in and catch the mail with. I'll be writing tomorrow for sure, if I am anywhere within reach of pen and ink. Good night and goodbye, and all blessing be on you.

Yours always
Ruddy.

Notes
1. Letters 30 and 31 of *From Sea to Sea* describe RK's visit to Yellowstone Park.
2. *From Sea to Sea*, Letter 28, describes RK's journey from Vancouver to Livingston.

To Edmonia Hill, 5 July 1889
Text: Copy, University of Sussex

[Mammoth Hot Springs Hotel, Yellowstone] July: 5th: 1889:

Dear Lady,

I can lay my hand on my sacred heart and honestly declare I am glad that you are not in this trip. It and the Yosemite would have killed you more dead than nails. You know that I have a round ticket for the trip, which is done chiefly in stages – six horse stages under a grilling sun. Well, I have struck a party of trippers – Raymond's excursionists from down East and they have very satisfactorily managed to ruin all my pleasure. There are about three hundred of them; and they are shrieking and laughing and rioting up and down and about this big yellow barn of an hotel till my head aches. They go in herds, each led by a padre of sorts, and they have a notion that their wild and daring trips from Philadelphia to Montana will have a good result in binding the continent more closely together. I heard 'em say this. They appear to be devoid of shame. They go kissing and hugging all about the place just as the fancy takes 'em; and they besiege the unfortunate hotel piano with tunes that they can't quite recollect but work off on one finger.

The Mammoth hot springs is the first step into the Park: and they say the least wonderful. A few hundred yards away from the hotel lies a hill of pure white sugar, streaked with red and pink and cut into white wooly terraces innumerable. You have seen photos of the pink and white terraces at Rantonga [Rotorua?] New Zealand. The Mammoth Springs are a reproduction on a small scale of the white terraces and the excursionists are doing their best to trample it into powder. The springs of purest deepest green water boil and spit all among the terraces, and smell like many boiled bad eggs. The whole place has been a marvel but is now thanks to the defilements of the excursionists nothing more than an exhibition and O the journey from Cinnabar Station to get here. It's only eight miles but the road is not good.

Tomorrow I have to take a 20 mile drive in a stage to go into the Norris Geyser Basin. I shudder at the thought and very much wish that I could return straight away to the South. Entre nous I'll tell you that I haven't been quite well and have had to go slow in consequence. It was just the littlest touch in the world of dysentery but it has almost gone now and I am if anything the better for it. Still owing to that and the absolute necessity of writing up my work, I haven't been able to get forward as swiftly as I could wish. However, I shall cut the visit to Bayless's brother at Marysville when I get out of the Park and run slick down to Denver. I'm very, very lonesome here and I don't think you'll be altogether displeased at seeing me – will you?

Of course I have no news – only I am awful thankful you didn't try this trip. It knocked up three or four women in the stage yesterday and knocked 'em up badly. Even as I bounded about on the box seat I took consolation in the thought that you were not around. The glare off the hills and specially from some white chalky hills just made me wink again.

Yesterday as you may perhaps remember was the Fourth of July and the Raymond trippers had what they called "Exercises" – a patriotic shiveree, on the second story of the hotel. I assisted, with my moral support. They sang to begin with: "My Country 'tis of thee." Don't you remember once singing that over to me. I could have blessed 'em all for it. It is a tune connected in my mind with the 'scursion down the River:[1] Well, then they prayed and orated and read the declaration of Independence and sang poems of their own composition. I only hope that their patriotism was better than their poetry.

Note
1. Perhaps the episode described in "The Strange Adventure of a Houseboat", *CMG*, 16 April 1888 (uncollected).

To Edmonia Hill, 10 July 1889
Text: Copy, University of Sussex

Mammoth Hot Springs, /July. 10 1889

Returned! The skin off my face, most of my clothes ruined and all of my temper. Never go to the Yellowstone Park or try the round trip, as I have done dear Lady. Today I strike the railway line anew and just kite over to Pittsburgh, stopping only for a day at Salt Lake as fast as I can.[1]

I can't describe the things I have seen. They were beyond description. Ask any one of your friends who have been to the Yellowstone and they will tell you of mountains that roared and smoked like boilers under pressure; of pink and blue and green formations as wild as anything that ever scene-painter put on to a theatre for a background to a ballet of fairies. I spent one happy evening all alone by the banks of a river watching a couple of beaver eating their evening meal. They were real live wild beaver, just as tame as rabbits and they owned a real dam and a veritable beaver Lodge of trimmed sticks. Then I felt that I had really travelled. As soon as I get back the use of my eyes and get rid of a foul headache in the back of my head I'll sit down and try to describe it for the Pioneer – and then you'll know; but at present I am only just equal to writing a line to you to tell you I am alive and well. The trip all round the park was an awfully lonesome one. There were crowds of excursionists and they all made up parties and ran about and shrieked – all but me. I didn't want a party, so I stood out and sulked.

As a park, your big wilderness is a failure. I don't like having to drive 150 miles in a buggy to get even a small idea of its many wonders; and I don't like having to sleep in tents when the weather is freezing. On the 8th of July in the Yellowstone Park the water in my ewer froze nearly half an inch. It was awful cold for I had to lie out in a single fold tent and be thankful that I could get it. But the bother was worth the reward of looking down the Cañon – from inspiration point – 1700 feet sheer into the Roaring Yellowstone below. I shall never be able to describe it accurately. But we'll talk it over when I come, as I am now making every arrangement to do, and as swiftly as I know how. Parks are monotonous, and industries do not satisfy me. I want to see you again awful bad. I think you will have no complaint to make about the quality, I mean quantity of work. The quality has sadly deteriorated because you were not there to supply the necessary stimulus. Anyhow I shan't be more than a week from tomorrow before I strike Pittsburgh, unless I am slaughtered on the road. This is an incoherent sort of a note but I'm busy packing up my things to return to the line of railway at Cinnabar, – eight miles away. Goodbye and bless you till we meet again and I don't think that will be long.

Yours ever
Ruddy

Note
1. Leaving Yellowstone for Salt Lake City, RK travelled via Omaha to Chicago and on to Pittsburgh; he reached Beaver on 24 July (Mrs Hill's diary, 1888–90: Cornell). He appears to have spent between two and three weeks in Beaver with the Taylor family.

To Edmonia Hill, 9 August 1889
Text: Copy, University of Sussex

[Lakewood, NY]¹ August 9th 1889:

Excellentissima:

Behold how many things may happen in one short hour. Scarcely had the rustic back view of the Black Maria died away in the rain – scarcely had I taken out my book and begun to flay Chautauqua and all her works² when I was invaded by the apparition of the chambermaid thus: – [sketch]. Her I treated as an ordinary chambermaid and bade her make as little dust as she could avoid. But she had me to understand that she was in no sense a poor girl but sort o' took up this business in her own pleasure. Yea, more, she studied German, and music (Oh the pitiful scrubby little fist with blackened nails) [sketch] and was going to "Yurrup" next year. Then she told me all about her people who were English, and a rich uncle who was the brother of a "Sir Lord" somewhere in far away England and leaned on her broom while she impressed me with the family glories. I observe that a chambermaid who studied German and music is not as clean a duster (from a merely Philistine point of view) as she who has been deprived of these boons. In the midst of our one-sided conversation there appeared a small boy in search of his mother Mrs. Dravo³ of Alleghenny! [sketch] Was she in the cottage. "My name", said the music-Teutonic chambermaid, "is Miss Florence Crandall." "Ugh!" said the charming enfant terrible. "I don't want to know your name. Where's my marmar?" I was mean enough to grin at this. When she left (the girl) the bald headed Manager man entered and bade me remember that I had only promised to stay one night and that a party of ten (10!) were even now on their way to occupy the cottage. They came! I have only put down six of them [sketch]. There wasn't room for the others, two of the party objected to the electric light on the grounds that there was no gas to do their bangs with. I have drawn the bangs. Aunt Keziah (her name must ha' been Keziah): I'd⁴ the almerále⁵ bed in our parlour and said cheerfully: "We can put the children in there." I have depicted one of the children. If Aunt Keziah carries out her awful threat, (she looks quite capable of it) I'm afraid that long boy will have a bad time of it. [sketch] Well, I quit on the instant.

These things have decided me to [sketch] leave for Buffalo tonight with all convenient speed. I am really going to put in work that shall make you not unashamed of me by the time I return. This can be depended upon. My idiotic letter is the expression of good intentions if you can read between the lines and only sent off to try to amuse you for a minute or two and to tell you that I am on hand and ferocious.

The rain strange to say hath not stopped tho' tis quite two hours since you left, by mundane reckoning.

Don't forget about the trunk and the ticket therein.

I'm off for my little dinner. Isn't it a trial, as you say, to have to walk down that long dining room. [sketch]

Always yours

Notes
1. On Lake Chautauqua, home of the celebrated "Chautauqua Institution", a summer programme offering courses in the sciences, arts, and humanities. It grew to be nationwide. According to Mrs Hill, RK "had a bad touch of Indian fever and was confined to bed for several days" at Chautauqua. Mrs Hill, her mother, and her husband were with RK for the first days of this visit ("Extracts from Hill Diaries", typescript, Cornell).
2. Letter 39 in the "From Sea to Sea" series in the *Pioneer*, 1 April 1890, describing RK's visit to the Chautauqua Institute on the shores of Lake Chautauqua, New York, was omitted from the *From Sea to Sea* volume; it appears as "Chautauqued" in *Abaft the Funnel*.
3. The name is that of the prominent family in Mrs Hill's home town of Beaver; RK used the name as "Dravot" in "The Man Who Would Be King" (Edmonia Hill, "The Young Kipling", p. 411).
4. Thus in copy: for "eyed"?
5. Thus in copy: perhaps *almirah*, a wardrobe or chest of drawers.

To Edmonia Hill, 11 August 1889

Text: Copy, University of Sussex

[Buffalo, NY] Aug. 11th

Sometime after supper and – an interview

Dear Lady,

I've had a day and a half or rather two days, for your cousin[1] hath treated me royally. It seems that he went down to meet two trains on Friday morning in the hope that I would come in, and the fear that I would stay with him. But it came to pass that Wells Fargo had managed to derail one of their expresses not far from Lakewood and so the train that should have started at 3:55 from that point got away nearer seven o'clock and I landed in Buffalo at a quarter to ten! I was not pleased but they directed me to a superb new hotel[2] – such gorgery of smoked oak fittings, twisted brass lamps and grey and blue plush, – and I took heart and a welsh rabbit which kept me awake for an hour or two.

Next morn, on Saturday that is to say, I went to the White Building and found Taylor who forthwith tucked me under his wing and took me on a little voyage in a steamer across the bay, so that I might be able to see Buffalo from the water. It's a most picturesque city and not unlike a little Chicago; but I suppose you have seen it. Then we landed and investigated a grain elevator sucking wheat out of the vitals of a big steamer which as Pepys saith "amused me mightily." Thereafter I had lunch and went to the P.O. for letters but found none. At 3:30 Taylor took me around in a buggy to the Fort and the Park and through all manner of quiet streets paved with asphalte where the houses stood like cattle under the shade of big trees and chewed the cud, and the people, from the great quiet of their faces, chewed the cud also.

We had tea at his house when I was introduced to Mrs. McSperran – a pretty woman with large eyes – and where my "accent" made the servant girl burst out laughing at table. After that we (Taylor and I) went to a place where we heard lovely music (a great hall where all the people seem to gather o' nights) and to our wrath saw two boys make two girls hideously drunk (I'm going to describe that in my letters).[3] After this riotous entertainment you won't be surprised to learn that I preferred not to go about today (Sunday) but sat in my tent and finished off the Chautauqua letter (9 full pages and closely written) so you see that I am of some good after all.

This evening a reporter introduced himself to me and interviewed me on behalf of the Buffalo Courier – which see if you want news of me, my thoughts and my sentiments.[4] I am off to Niagara tonight by the 11.50 train in order to see the moonlight on the water and shall stay there for a day or so, as you ordered me. I have bought a little tweed cap for your sister and a soft hat for myself. Methinks the latter addeth not to my style of beauty. I suppose you are up to your eyes in packing. My unused hand is all stiff from the amount of writing I have been doing this day. Forgive so short a note but tis a faithful record of all that has befallen.

My regards to all your folk (How is Miss Carrie's badminton)[5] and tell the Professor to look after himself and not get left behind by an Atlantic liner.[6] (Isn't that mean?)

Ever, yours.

Notes
1. Edgar Taylor; he and other members of his family accompanied Mrs Hill and her sister and RK on their trip to London at the end of September.
2. The Iroquois; according to a note on the copy, this letter was written on the hotel's stationery.
3. The scene appears in the original letters to the *Pioneer* and in the pirated *American Notes* (1891), but not in *From Sea to Sea*.
4. "As Others See Us", *Buffalo Courier*, 12 August.
5. The first mention of Caroline A. Taylor, Mrs Hill's younger sister (see 2 November 1889). Many years later Trix remembered her unkindly as "plump and plain . . . with

none of her sister's charm", a "snub-nosed girl with a cottage-loaf figure" (MS notes, Sussex).
6. Hill returned to India in advance of his wife, travelling via the north of Ireland in order to visit his family.

To Edmonia Hill, 13 August 1889
Text: Copy, University of Sussex

Toronto Aug: 13 1889

Dear Lady:
The hastiest of lines to tell you that I got your note at the P.O. this afternoon about $2\frac{1}{2}$ seconds before I took the cars to Lewiston.[1] I fancy I must have beamed idiotically for the balance of the railway journey inasmuch as many people, to me unknown, turned to stare at me. But perhaps a pocket handkerchief was hanging from my coat-tails. I went away with the happy knowledge of having done Niagara to the extent of four hours and a half. Twas a sore weariness of the flesh but I Maid-of-the-Misted,[2] I went down under the water fall (both sides), went down to the whirlpool rapids, saw the place where Webb[3] was last seen alive, and did everything that ever entered into mind of mortal man to do. I don't think I look pretty in Japanese Court dress, do you? [sketch of RK in oil-skins].
They wanted to photograph me in my oilskins with the falls as a "sort o' back-ground" but I fancy you would hardly care for a more permanent memorial than this. Observe how I have carefully refrained from over accentuating my own puny individuality as compared with the gigantic and over-whelming display of the elementary forces of nature, etc. etc. Seriously, I was not half as impressed as I ought to have been but, and this is of more consequence, I have managed to do some work [sketch of seasick passengers on boat].
This is the first part of a decorative frieze that I designed on the steamer crossing to Toronto. The weather was uneven and we carried 7,642,931 passengers; of these 5,689,447 got awfully sick, 1,724,113 said that they felt as if "they wuz goin' to throw up" and later on they did! We carried 76495 couples newly wed and it was a case of "Kiss me Teddy, I'm going to be sick" all along the decks. You don't know how sublimely foolish a young bridegroom can look till you see him supporting (himself half gone) a seasick bride. I can't reproduce the agony, but I watched it all [sketch]. Thank goodness my bride will never be seasick – not if I know myself. In regard to those things which you did not write – let 'em be. As you know I know and I am accustomed

to much taking of the will for the deed and I know that you meant well. I am grieved about the change being impossible. I should have preferred it and indeed I should not have given much trouble in the house.[4] But we'll let that stand. Tomorrow I start upon the home track and never was a man more glad to return. I hope old Mark Twain is well out of the way in Maine where they say he rusticates[5] and even more do I hope that you will be pleased with the little that I have done. I guessed partly what was the trouble with you because I happened to have a pretty bad head all my own. But as you say 'twould have been worse had I been forced to take it to Buffalo alone at 11.56.

                                                                Yours ever

I'm bringing you back the Witch's Head by Haggard.[6]

Notes
1. Downriver from Niagara Falls.
2. That is, the boat trip below the Falls on the *Maid of the Mist*.
3. Captain Matthew Webb (1848–83), the English swimmer, drowned attempting to swim the rapids below Niagara Falls.
4. RK did not stay in the Taylor house at Beaver but in one of the Beaver College buildings (*The Critic*, xxxv [(October 1899)] 882–3).
5. RK found Mark Twain at his summer home in Elmira, New York; his interview with Twain was first published in the New York *Herald*, 17 August 1890 (*From Sea to Sea*).
6. Rider Haggard, *The Witch's Head* (1885).

To Edmonia Hill, 5 September 1889
Text: Copy, University of Sussex

                                        [Washington, DC] Sept: 5th 1889

Most excellent Lady – such a hot night and such an evil-minded organ grinder on the pavement without! I am sitting in my shirtiest of sleeves with all the windows open longing for a breath of fresh air and – to spit on that organ grinder's head!

But I will to the record of my journey. My train was – of course – delayed by a hot box this time and so struck Washington at 9:10 instead of 7:10. All the better for me as I got a good rest in the sleeper which I rather wanted. Then having washed and fed I took a life[1] hansom and went out to see the Capitol but by the way managed somehow to get entangled with the naval and military department specially the military which I found in a beautiful cool building. I got hold of a man in the A[djutant.G[eneral].'s department who showed me the Infantry, Cavalry and Artillery drill books of the U.S. Army and referred me to a Captain Bourke[2] who had seen much fighting. Him I found sitting enthroned in a Library of the finest with a Colonel West commanding the 6th Cavalry. Well we talked nineteen to the dozen about military subjects and he (the Captain) ended by dragging me off to lunch with him at his house which was simply stuffed with Indian curiosities. It turned out that he had for fifteen years been among the Indians of Arizona and New Mexico and even in the North where he fought 'em on the Powder river. He knew and had worked ethnologically with Custer and was even then deep in a monograph on the less known religious customs of the Mojabe indians.[3] *Les belles esprits se rencontrent.* I unloaded little scraps of Indian folk lore; found he had been corresponding with some men in India that I knew (so small is this big world of ours), put him on the track of other men who would ethnologically be of use to him and altogether had a very delightful time; he, in the end, pressing his pamphlets upon me. These I grieve to say dealt with matters unfitted for private perusal but were quaint and interesting exceedingly.[4] So you see how good and kind all the world is to me. I am more than impressed with Washington. It is my ideal of a Headquarters of administration and goes far towards being a thoroughly beautiful city. The asphalte, the avenues and the refined look of the people on the streets both delight me. I should like to go through a season here. The place smells Simla-ish. And the shops! I assure you I have this afternoon been staring at a bed room suite compared to which the Pittsburgh Exposition one is not a circumstance. Apropos of that queer little Quaint Jones, I thought much upon it with laughter that came very near to tears. It was so [   ][5] and your delight in the burnt almonds was so touching. I trust you properly impressed all your folk at home with the advantage you took of your stop over. Yah! Yah! They hadn't any enterprize. Please thank Miss Carrie with my much thanks for the farewell gift of "One Summer"[6] which took my fancy from the title page to closing line and helped along the journey. The illustrations alone are bad – and not equal to the text of a very charming little book. I trust that she and her sister will not be too offended at the liberties I have taken in sending 'em fings o' sorts for their amusement. Now I must hurry up and write a note to my Parpar and get along with some more Pioneer letters. This is but a note snatched by the scruff of the neck from the employment of the day. I am rather weary but I am with you in whatever spirit remains unto me. Keep well and happy and write to me, to me, as soon as may be.

Yours ever,

O my! There are no stamps in the hotel, so this letter must wait till the morn!

Notes
1. Thus in copy.
2. Captain John Gregory Bourke (1846–96), in military service in Indian country, 1871–83, then appointed to study the south-western Indians.
3. "Notes on the Cosmogony and Theogony of the Mojave Indians of the Rio Colorado Arizona", *Journal of American Folk-Lore* (1889).
4. Doubtless "The Urine Dance of the Zuni Indians of New Mexico" (Ann Arbor, Mich., 1887) and "Compilation of Notes and Memoranda Bearing upon the Use of Human Ordure and Human Urine in Rites of a Religious or Semi-Religious Character among Various Nations" (Washington DC, 1888).
5. Blank in copy.
6. By Blanche Willis Howard (1875).

To Edmonia Hill, [7 September] 1889
Text: Copy, University of Sussex

Philadelphia / Saturday 1889:

Your note I found at the P.O. just now. Being in a hansom I did not dance for joy nor otherwise conduct myself unseemly. A thousand thanks for it and bless you for the writing. No, there were no letters of any kind for me in Philadelphia other than the one I wanted most; but many and curious have been my adventures. I left Washington by the 4:20 last night and beguiled the time by conversation with a Divisional Superintendent of Railways, who told me many amusing things about American lines. When I reached the Lafayette and registered, quoth the Clerk "There are three gentlemen from India here – natives of your country." "Amen" said I and turned up the register to find the names of Allbless, Rustomjee Wazibdar, and Byramjee Ratnagir, all Parsees – and Allbless at least, of a family I knew something about. When I went into supper I found 'em seated at a table and stealing behind 'em spake in the sweetest of vernaculars. Whereat they leaped nearly sky high and fell upon me with devotion. Allbless had studied under Griffiths,[1] my Godfather, in the School of Art which the Pater used to boss in Bombay; and the others all knew the name of Kipling. So we powwowed tremendously – and I and these three jolly Parsees went out on a pleasure trip. They had seen Europe and "Paris Exhibeeshun" and were trying to do America in ten days. They drew imaginary sketches of up country Bunnias[2] asked to pay eight annas for a shave and were more than impressed with the costliness of American life. Then we parted after having talked ourselves out and a newspaper man got hold of me and dragged me down town to look at the public buildings and see his offices. I wasn't introduced to more than two thousand men; among 'em a politician of sorts who swore by the name of Quay.[3] When I casually hinted that I had met the great man and had lived for a month in his township I rose forty five feet in their (the politician and his friend's) estimation – so great an advantage it is to rub shoulders with the great men of the Earth. We visited about five newspaper offices and I guess there's likely to be an interview of sorts knocking round the Phila. papers.[4]

But, bother interviews, I *must* sit down and write out Washington. How I wish you were with me to give me your council. I feel like a rudderless or Ruddyless ship without you and the writing won't flow easily. The Railway Library is increased by Clark Russell's Marooned, The Deemster, and a life of Reade[5] to which I shall draw your distinguished attention when next we meet. But meantime each day hath twenty four weary hours and I must e'en get through 'em as best in this life I can.

Ever your

Notes
1. John Griffiths (1837?–1918), painter, as a young man had worked on the decoration of the South Kensington Museum with JLK. Griffiths and JLK were appointed to the School of Art in Bombay at the same time.
2. Merchant.
3. Matthew Stanley Quay (1833–1904), of Beaver, boss of Pennsylvania Republican politics and US Senator from 1886 until his death. The Taylor family were friends of Quay, whom RK was taken to meet (Isaac R. Pennypacker, "Quay of Pennsylvania", *American Mercury*, ix (November 1926) 358–9).
4. I have not succeeded in finding any such interview.
5. Russell's *Marooned* (1887); Hall Caine, *The Deemster* (1887); Charles L. and Compton Reade, *Charles Reade* (1887).

To Edmonia Hill, 10 September 1889
Text: Copy, University of Sussex

[New York] September: 10th:

What shall I begin with? I came in to New York from Philadelphia night 'fore last having sent you from the City of P. certain remarks of the Saturday Review in regard to my work.[1] My natural modesty (and the haste under which I then laboured) prevented me from adding that the entire article was devoted all to my precious self – or rather our precious selves. Well I left Phila. much impressed with the size of the public buildings and the want of size of the streets and, as I have said, reached New York at 9 p.m. where I hopelessly lost myself and in desperation clomb into the elevated which bore me off to 110th Street and when I said I wanted the Windsor the conductor laughed. Howbeit the Windsor I found and next morn (yesterday) after searchings manifold captured my long lost uncle[2] in a building in Wall Street. It was a queer meeting for we had to talk family affairs for an hour with the ticker reeling off the prices of stock in our ear. As soon as I arrived he handed me an envelope which contained the enclosure, whence you will learn a good deal that mystified me and one fact at least that has horrified me. Chesney must be a damphool to spring my No. 8 on an innocent Anglo-Indian public.[3] Well I talked to a man who hasn't seen my mother for 30 years and horrible sensations of age crept over me. Time has not dealt kindly with him though he seems comfortably well off. That evening I dined with him and his wife[4] who was once a very handsome woman and who even now retains a stern and lofty countenance. I had to tell 'em all about my ways and works – not the novels – I couldn't help letting them continue in the notion that I was a sort of wandering scapegoat. In return they told me much family history which was doubtless very interesting – if I had only listened to it. And so I recemented the alliance with mine uncle.

But that same day I dug up one Lockwood De Forest[5] who was in India nine years ago – an artist living in one of the very luxurioustest houses I've ever seen. He received me for my father's sake literally with open arms and said Harper had been talking about my father only a week ago.[6] Then he gave me a note to Henry Harper[7] saying that I had more literary powers than my father and told me to apply to him if I wanted anything else! Then he fled to Quebec, for a holiday. I am flying off now to take the note to H's – Oh how I wish you were here to help –[8]

Notes
1. Unsigned review, by Andrew Lang, of *In Black and White* and *Under the Deodars*, *Saturday Review*, 10 August 1889. Lang praises both works – "so clever, so fresh, and so cynical" – but prefers the stories of native life to those of Simla.
2. Henry James Macdonald (1835–91), oldest of Mrs Kipling's siblings. He qualified for the Indian Civil Service, but at the last minute he abandoned his Indian appointment and his fiancée and sailed for New York. He did newspaper work there and was for a time financial editor of the New York *World*. He then joined a firm of stockbrokers, where he spent the rest of his working life.
3. Letter 8 of *From Sea to Sea*, published in the *Pioneer*, 18 June 1889, describes the brothel life of Hong Kong.
4. *Née* Caroline Erskine Gold. Her marriage to Henry Macdonald was childless.
5. De Forest (1850–1932), artist, architect, decorator, and traveller; he had been in India in 1881, where he had founded workshops for the revival of wood carving near Bombay, and where he had met JLK at Lahore. He lived at 7 East 10th Street in New York.
6. JLK may have been in negotiations with Harper and Brothers, the publishers, for his book on *Beast and Man in India*, though it was in the event published by Macmillan.

7. Joseph Henry Harper (1850–1938), then head of the literary department of the firm.
8. According to the received story, Harper turned RK away saying "Young man, this house is devoted to the production of literature" (Carrington, *Kipling*, p. 132). See [early September 1890].

To Edmonia Hill, 13 September 1889
Text: Copy, University of Sussex

The Drugstore of Wellesley / September: 13: / 8:20 p.m.
Three quarters of an hour from Boston and a drizzling night.

Excellentissima.

Mop my head with a wet towel – carry me home in a coffin – and stir me up with an electric battery; while Miss Carrie laughs at me! But to begin things decently and in order and to explain for my lack of letter writing. I left New York for Boston on the eve of the first big equinoctial and as I looked at flooded West Street – the sewage and sea water mingling cheerfully in the washed out bar rooms underground – I thanked my stars that we were not going to face it. I did not (for reasons which will appear when you read the papers) I did *not* fare to Boston by the Fall Line Steamers.[1] I went in a train and we were a crowded and loathsome company. Men had come in from Manhattan and Brighton Beaches with awful stories of hotels knocked down houses ripped open and breakwaters turned down by the Sea. These news so wrought upon my spirits that when I reached Boston I became on a sudden muchly sick and spent the day before yesterday and half of yesterday in my little bed at Young's hotel. All might have been cured if you had only written me a line or two to keep my spirits up and my dinner down. Howbeit yesterday afternoon I sought out a cousin of this new uncle of mine – one Lethgow Devens[2] – who, almost and before I could speak made me a member of the Somerset Club and the big new Athletic Club – two vastly luxurious institutions – and had me to dinner with him where I enjoyed myself more or less. He has a wife, she is crossing on the 25th, *but* in the Germanic, Allah a Akbar and I'm pleased.[3] Well, this morn I got up and in what was left of the gale paid a pilgrimage to the tomb of Longfellow at Mount Auburn, saw his house, and all the historical celebrities along the road. As soon as the car-load understood that I was a Britisher they rubbed those historical facts into me point first with a great deal of satisfaction. It must be a pleasant thing to be an American. I explored Mt. Auburn and while in there was overtaken with an attack of "blues" insomuch that I could have knocked out my brains against the nearest vault which was something like this (I'll go bail for it that I never looked so.) [sketch]. However, I did better; I polished off a 'Frisco letter, revised the next three and so sent off four in one lump; managing to make a sad mess of stuffing the M.S. into the envelope whereat I longed more than usual for you. Then being filled with a bold thought I took train to Wellesley to hunt for Miss Colman.[4] Had I known what I had to go through, I should never have done it. To begin with a drunken man in the train would have it that my ignorance of a town called South Reading (his birthplace) was a deep device to cover the fact that I was a card sharper and he adjured several of the men in the train who were playing Whist not by any means to play with me. *Can't* you imagine me playing cards on a train. Then he tapped his nose with wisdom, and intimated that I wasn't going to "play him for a sucker" and fell fast asleep while the rest of the population glared at me reproachfully. Then the train dropped me in a large village entirely inhabited by young girls screaming about their baggage. Wellesley College was collecting itself. I went on down several pretty lanes, the crowd of female girls always increasing, till I found myself opposite a fine tame wilderness overrun with more girls. "Here" thought I "my troubles are at end and Miss Colman is close at hand." But the fun was only just opening. I found some cottages on a hill and remembering Chautauqua gathered up my coat-tails to flee but presently finding the paths so serpentine that escape was impossible I took heart; and a girl in a blazer told me that I should find Miss C. at Stone Hall – a big raw red boil of a building on another hill. I found that place and a fat woman in an apron in front of it. [sketch]. "La!" said she, "this is a dormitory" and pulling out a paper book proved conclusively that there was no such person as Miss Colman in the place. But the word dormitory was enough for me. I ran away through the battalions of girls, yammering for the real Wellesley College. When I found it I sat down in a reception room and girls came and peeked at me. I grew gummy under my hat band. Other girls came and I grew wretched. Miss Colman came with a sort of "Who the devil may you be" look on her face. She didn't of course remember me at Pittsburgh. When I quoted Miss Taylor's name[5] she said she was just then in the agonies of a Council meeting and that I had better stay for dinner. Meantime she would send a Miss Kendal[6] a professor to look after me. So she sent and Miss Kendal came and played with me eruditely making due allowance for my being a man barbarian – and then – oh then – we went to dinner [sketch] and I beheld with agony that I was the one man among four hundred girls – and they all looked at me – looked at me good. By this time I was hardened. The sweat had dried. I looked back. Say the bulk of those girls ought to have been in their beds. They weren't fit for hard work, no how. Half way through dinner Miss C. turned up and after dinner took me to the parlour of the Faculty – a gorgeous room furnished in gold and hangings – to the library soberly sumptuous – and to the reading room. Then this full-statured woman with the imperial eyes and the mouth of eloquence expounded to me the theory of education, the perfectability of woman, and the sweetness of life. Ye Gods! She bewildered me flat and I didn't wonder that your sister fell down before her. I squatted like the toad in the ear of Eve and spake dubersomely of all projects and in return roused Artemis the Queenly to almost a lecture. I guess she must have talked to me for fully an hour and a half. She said that she had seen no one so impressed as I except ____ the Zuni Indians. Whereat I bowed gracefully and grinned. The luxury and beauty of the surroundings undeniably impressed me – [   ].[7] I have my opinion. Then I fled into the grounds and tried to walk my way back to the Depot but the paths serpentined and there was no light and I wandered darkling till a couple of laughing girls set me on the right path and I reached the air of every day life feeling as though I had been bathed in the Princess.[8]

I am writing this in the back room of a druggist's store in Wellesley while I wait for my train and while the small boy in charge waits for "Pap" to come back. A wee fluffy white kitten has climbed up on to my shoulder and is watching my pen travel over the paper and purrs to herself because she does not know how to write or how to do many other things. I return to Boston in a few minutes and go to Concord tomorrow. The days are passing but not very quickly and I have had no letter from you. Write to the N.Y. Post Office and tell me how you fare. Good night and God's best blessings be with you. For myself you know I am what I am and whose I am.

Notes
1. A heavy storm hit the east coast on 10 September: the Fall River Line reported its boats undamaged but noted that the seas were "a source of great discomfort to the passengers" (*New York Times*, 11 September 1889).
2. Thus in copy; Arthur Lithgow Devens, a Boston financier and clubman, is meant.
3. RK too was to sail on the 25th, but on the *City of Berlin*: see 22 September 1889.
4. Katherine Coman (1857–1915), Professor of History and Economics at Wellesley from 1880.
5. After graduating from Beaver College, Caroline Taylor had been a special student at Wellesley.
6. Elizabeth K. Kendall (1855–1952), in the department of history at Wellesley from 1888 to 1920, and a notable traveller.
7. Passage omitted in copy.
8. Tennyson's poem on women's education: referred to also in the next letter.

To Edmonia Hill, 16 September 1889
Text: Copy, University of Sussex

[Somerset Club, Boston] Sept: 16/89:

Dear Lady:
This has been a day of very much writing and therefore I have completed – my Chicago letter.[1] You know our topsy-turvy way of getting at things. Later on I shall describe the College of the Princess Ida and my interview with the fair Miss Colman.[2] More than ever does my glimpse at the great factory of which your sister is so fond, confirm me in my unbelief. But of these things I will tell you when we meet. First of all, rest easy in regard to that tea. If all New York holds a single pound of Kangra Valley[3] that will I get for you to cheer you on your weary way across the Atlantic. Let this be an awful warning to you, how you invest in teas with eccentric titles. No fish is so bad as that you buy by the sea-side.

And now . . . well there is no news to tell you. I have come over to this sumptuously furnished club to tell you all about myself and behold there is nothing.

Yesterday brought me a note from Mrs. De Forest[4] – wife of that artist man I told you about – asking me to come and spend a day with her and her father somewhere in Long Island.[5] The father is a hideous invalid but I guess I must go if it's only to tell the Mother that I have seen her friend. Tomorrow I quit Boston for Concord and, it may be, West Point. I am not going to bother about the other places because it only means my getting more than ever behindhand in my work and that isn't worth the candle.

Apropos of work, I copied you out the other day, a selection of reviews that I found on turning over the files of the papers in this club. Twasn't an elaborate search either and I dare say I shall find more waiting for me in England. What think you of the things? Tell me frankly and with wisdom. Wasn't it worth having – this concensus of appreciation.

Neither the *World*[6] nor the *St. James's*[7] are moved to speak lightly – and yet you see what either says. Give us your congratulations, and not to me be the praise. You did well in steadily advising us to go on with Mother Maturin. I think that's more likely to catch the uncultured British taste than anything of the "chartered Libertine"[8] brand. And as soon as time serves I will get to work on it. I own the reviews have made me foolishly happy but you know as well as I that they are but means to an end. The more that I wander about the world and realize the utter insignificance of literary aims and aspirations except to the very few who are interested in them, the more assured I am that there is only one thing in the world worth having. And that is not Fame.

Write me just what you think would be the best for us to do: and I will husband it and argue with you when we meet. Just at present I dare not lift my eyes off the *Pioneer* letters and they demand all my attention.

I have a half-hearted return of verse-making come upon me and have bought a little book wherein to put down my rough attempts which, please the pigs, shall go to the making of another small volume of verse some day or another. But that's enough of nonsense.

What share did you get of the storm. I trembled for the pear trees when I heard it howling among the chimneys of Boston and went down to the wharves and saw the battered and strained tramps of the sea sneak into harbour. Yet somehow I caught myself wishing that I had been out in it.

Yes, I know – none better – that it is hard for you to leave your folk and woe is me – nothing that I can say can at all lighten your grief. Enjoy all that remains of the time and quietly cut the banjo-strings and punch a hole through the banjo-top: and oh do not forget me. I'm well enough but uncommon hungry.

Yours.

Notes
1. Letter 35 of *From Sea to Sea*.
2. He did not.
3. Tea from the north-eastern Punjab.
4. The former Meta Kemble, who married de Forest in 1880.
5. The de Forests had a house called "Nethermuir" at Cold Spring Harbor.
6. *The World*, 7 August 1889, reviewed RK's stories, especially *Soldiers Three*.
7. Review of the Railway Library stories, *St James's Gazette*, 6 July 1889.
8. Shakespeare, *Henry V*, I.i.48.

To Edmonia Hill, 17 September 1889
Text: Copy, University of Sussex

[Somerset Club, Boston] Sept: 17th.

Dear Lady:

This day I have spent in Concord – and this day has more impressed me with the "might majesty dominion and power"[1] of the Great American Nation than any other. (Let's take a thicker pen). I wonder if you will understand how and why I came very near to choking when I saw "the Minuteman"[2] and realized that I was standing on the first battle field in the very beginning of things. I can't explain the emotion; but there it is for you. Not even the sight of Hawthorne's manse, nor his grave nor Emerson's nor even Louisa M. Allcott's touched me one half so much. And I wonder why.

My spare moments (they are not many) have been taken up by a Literary Scheme which when settled in my mind I will unfold to you. Please don't blame me for not kiting about the country. I've been too busy and a great weariness has come on me. The heat here in Boston, after the storm, is like unto the heat of Bengal. Everybody is complaining about it – and I find it best to lie still. By the way the maddest thing has happened to my hair. I hope it will get better by the time you come. Two patches on the temple have turned light and look as if they had been singed. Rude barbers make unkind remarks about this. I hope it isn't a warning that I am turning grey. It looks very much like it. How would you like me so: – [sketch]. Methinks I would look unseemly. If the trouble spreads I shall begin to dye.

OH! I nearly forgot! I have scoured Boston and secured some Assam tea – not first chop, but I think good enough for the voyage. I chewed up a lot of it and it tasted very nasty so I guess t'will meet your requirements.

This is only a note, snatched out of an evening of scribbling, just to tell you that I am here and thinking of you. Were there anything to tell I would tell it but there ain't, except one deadly secret. Tonight at ten I am going to sup on Welsh Rarebit. I didn't get anything like a square meal at Concord today and mine little tummy yearns for cheese – toasted mostly – as the derelict in Treasure Island said.[3] Which reminds me that I have got R. L. Stevenson's "In the Wrong Box"[4] and laughed over it dementedly when I read it. That man has only one lung but he makes you laugh with all your whole inside. Pray you think of me a little and remember me always as

                                                              Yours.

Notes
1. From the "ascription" used at the end of the Anglican service.
2. The statue by Daniel Chester French erected in 1875 to commemorate the battle of Lexington.
3. Ben Gunn, in ch. 15.
4. *The Wrong Box* by R. L. S. and Lloyd Osbourne (1889).

To [Julia] Taylor,[1] 22 September 1889
Text: Copy, Library of Congress

Lounsbury & Co – H. J. MacDonald –/Sept 22, 1889.

Dear Miss Taylor:
  There has reached me from Pittsburgh its neighbourhood a lamentable outcry about

TEA.

I can't quite understand the rationale of it but it appears that you and Mrs Hill devoured all your Indian tea with soup-ladles and so had nothing left except – so far as concerned yourself – an intense longing for

TEA.

Then I was ordered on pain of death to send some along because you had been poisoned by old Man's Eyebrows.
  New York is a city seventeen miles long and four wide. I have been round it eighteen times and a half on the last trip.
  I secured three pounds of India tea and (what is much more important) the address of the vendor. If you like the stuff his name is Cassidy & Co No 135 Front St N.Y. and he will send you more that you may maintain your strength for badminton. Two more pounds I have kept for the City of Berlin.[2] The actual value of the tea I forget but if your father could, by a mortgage on the house, pay the following incidental expenses I should be much obliged.

IN THE MATTER OF SOME TEA

To 45 elevated r'nd fares @5c (because of tea)	2.25
45 horse car do @ do	2.25
Speaking to 176 Police men for directions @10 per speak	17.60
Being answered rudely by do @ do	17.60
Walking 14 miles @ 10 per furlong	11.20
Visiting coffee warehouse & stepping on a dog	15.42
″ sugar ″ & being cussed by 8 draymen	19.30
Getting mixed up with a grain elevator (in act. tea)	15.0
Pair of boots: (one pair worn out hunting tea)	7.50
One hat destroyed by sugar aforesaid (looking for tea)	5.50
To water trip to Manhattan (in search of tea)	.69
To thirst at Manhattan & else where (caused by tea)	8.20

To chewing tea at Cassidys, Houllugues, Louis Jackson @ 1 per chew	3.0
To exhaustion of nervous system (caused by tea)	1150.
(sd) Rudyard Kipling	1275.61[3]

Notes
1. Julia was the second of the Reverend Taylor's three daughters.
2. The ship on which RK sailed for England on the 25th. It left from Jersey City for Liverpool, and the party, besides RK, Mrs Hill, and Caroline Taylor, included Edgar Taylor, H. L. Taylor of Buffalo, his daughter Jessie, and Miss Maggie Taylor (Mrs Hill, Diary 1888–90: Cornell).
3. I make the sum to be 1275.51.

To John Addington Symonds,[1] 15 October 1889
ALS: University of Bristol

The Grange,[2] */ West Kensington, W. / Oct: 15th / 89:*

Dear Sir

You were kind enough to write me a letter dated June 4th. saying some very undeserved things about a small book of mine. On that date I was in the pine woods of Oregon:[3] and did not reach London till a few days ago,[4] after much wandering through Japan and the States. On my word I cannot see how to thank you for all the generous praise you have seen fit to bestow on an unknown manufacturer of books – a savage from among savages. In regard to my three friends whatever merit lies in my work comes from the fact that I loved 'em – very much, I take it, as you loved a man called Benevenuto Cellini and in your translation[5] showed that love – so that he became alive and swaggered and brawled and beat his way across the pages. Out in India there are no get-at-able rules of work nor any things in the way of sympathy and competition. Moved by my small success I am come to London to start that queer experience known as a literary career. At present the tide goes with me and I hope to bring the three men to the notice of the Englishman.[6] But there is no light in this place, and the people are savages living in black houses and ignorant of everything beyond the Channel. Therefore, of your kindness and when you have time, I pray you write me some words. And if you like, I'll send you samples of stuff that I do, that you may warn me when I slide from decent work. Seven years of the grind of journalism lays a man very open to the scamping and faking of his duty. Some day if God pleases we shall meet. Meantime if there is anything in my power that I can do for you in England from the purchase of cigars to the capture of dogs (forgive me if I do not know your tastes and judge all from my own weaknesses) you may command me and throughout believe me

                              Yours very sincerely
                              Rudyard Kipling

Notes
1. Symonds (1840–93), essayist, critic, poet, historian, and translator, had been reading *Soldiers Three* and wrote to tell RK of his pleasure in it (Phyllis Grosskurth, *The Woeful Victorian*, New York, 1965, p. 306).
2. Burne-Jones's house on North End Road.
3. Palace Hotel, San Francisco, in fact.
4. RK arrived in Liverpool on 4 October and went on to London at once.
5. Symonds's translation of Cellini's *Autobiography* appeared in 1887.
6. The first English edition of *Soldiers Three* was published early in 1890.

To Edmonia Hill and Caroline Taylor, [22 October 1889]
Text: Diary of Mrs Edmonia Hill, 8 March 1888–90, entry for 22 October 1889: MS, Cornell University

                              [London][1]

        I came to see you – as I said –
        But you – confound you! went to bed.
        And since the hour was ten at night
        T'was neither pretty nor polite.
        This makes me wrath. When next I call
        Get up and dress your selves. That's all.

                                              R.K.

Note
1. Mrs Hill's diary records that after she landed at Liverpool on 4 October she went to Belfast (presumably to see her husband's family) before going on to London, where she arrived on 12 October, only to leave on 16 October for Paris. Before that, on 9 October, she notes in the diary: "Carrie engaged to R.K." And on 17 October, in Paris, she notes: "Mr. Kipling came in the early morn." She – and presumably RK – returned to London on 20 October. On 24 October she wrote: "Shopped with Mr. Kipling for his chambers, overlooking the middle of the Embankment" (Cornell University). RK's engagement to Caroline Taylor, from the evidence of Mrs Hill's diary, must have been

arrived at between the 4th, when they all landed in Liverpool, and the 9th, when Mrs Hill notes it. When the arrangement was explicitly broken off is not known, but RK soon knew that he had made a mistake and wanted out at least as early as February 1890 (Carrington, *Kipling*, p. 157).

To Edmonia Hill and Caroline Taylor, 25 October 1889
Text: Copy, University of Sussex

The Grange, West Kensington, W.

The Evening of the Day.[1]

Phil[2] gone out: A lonely dinner eaten in candle-lighted state after a day on foot: Headache to follow.

Verily dear people tis worse for those who are left behind than for those who go. Up till today I believed otherwise. Now I am wiser. When your faces had gone into white blobs and the last twirl of Mrs. Hill's Boa was indistinct (or else there was something in my eyes) my empty tummy heaved within me and there fell upon me a fine and gilt edged misery. I wasn't half so wretched when I went away by myself 7 years ago. Nor indeed was there so much reason, for you had made my life happy and delightful for two years – given me help sympathy encouragement and council and a host of other things of which it is easy to think but not so easy to write down in black and white. Dear people I was wretched and nothing but the more obvious misery of Edgar saved me from breaking down outright. He and I went up to town together talking animatedly about things in which we took no manner of interest – chimney pots and locomotives if I recollect rightly – and sedulously avoiding all the subjects that lay nearest to our hearts. Then I pulled out Ted's[3] letter. Nice girl to do shopping after you had left the country. Nice job you gave me, too. After a muddled inspection of my room[4] (bed, couch and wardrobe, and most of Evans's things had arrived) I kited over to Evans and didn't find the red down pillows so I cussed and went away. I must get it tomorrow somehow I spose. Then I caught a fat old man with a dew drop on his nose who said he was a painter and he's going to paint and varnish what is left of the floor of the room for fifteen bob. You know that room goes so [sketch] and consequently a square carpet won't fit. I bought for my sacred toes a fat white sheep skin rug, and for the bedroom three yards of matting to lead me safe from mine little bed to mine little wash-stand. Also the nice and hollowed chair to w'iggle about in while I works. And now you know all about it. The further developments will be told as they occur.

I've written a note to your mothers – or mother is it? I know I got singularly mixed in my singulars and plurals while writing it. Also I know that I ought to go to a theatre with Edgar tonight but I've got a headache brought on – don't tell – by weeping between lights this afternoon when I had done my day's work. It's all very well to pretend to be festive but I'm miserable and a perfectly illogical soul within is crying out "Come back to me, come back to me!" As tho' I were a little child. I believe I am and a deed fool too. But you go on and have a good time and take care o' Miss Taylor who is going to take care of you and remember that I'm always and always

Your Ruddy.

If this don't catch on at Naples I'll be angry. Just as a relief I'll do some cussing now.

Notes
1. Mrs Hill and Caroline Taylor sailed from London for India on 25 October. They were accompanied to their ship at the Royal Albert Docks by RK and Edgar Taylor.
2. Burne-Jones.
3. Ted = Edmonia.
4. RK had just taken rooms in Embankment Chambers (now called Kipling House), on Villiers Street, between the Embankment and the Strand, in the shadow of Charing Cross Station. Mrs Hill and Caroline Taylor helped him to furnish them.

To Andrew Lang,[1] 26 October 1889
Text: Copy, University of Sussex

The Grange, / West Kensington, W. / Oct: 26. 89

Dear Mr. Lang,
No. There were no adventures. What happened after your tour[2] was told in March 1890 by Bret Harte[3] in the Argonaut in this manner: –

I reside at Table Mountain and my name is Truthful James
I am not versed in lecturin' or other sinful games.
You will please refrain from shooting while my simple lyre I twang
To the tale of Mister Haggard[4] and his partner Mister Lang.

They were high toned litter*a*teurs and two most unhappy men
For they started to enlighten our enlightened citizen
And thanks to the reporter who the interviewing fixed
Mister Lang and Mister Haggard got inextricably mixed.

The Road Back to England, 1889

Now our sunward-gazing nation gets its information slick
From the daily mornin' journal – an' it reads darnation quick
So if that information be inaccurately wild
Some eighty million citizens are apt to be beguiled.

In the ears of Mister Haggard whom they hailed as Mister Lang
The societies of Boston ethnologically sang
And they spoke of creature-legends, and of totem, myth and sign
And the stricter laws of Metre[5] – Mister Haggard answered "*Nein.*"

Then emboldened by his silence which was painful and extreme
They discoursed of gnome and kelpie and the imp that steals the cream
And of pornographic poems (which the same he never knew)
And they bade him chaunt a rondel – Mister Haggard then withdrew.

His subsequent adventures form no part of this concern –
It is to the other person Mister Rangard Hang we turn:
Our sunward-gazing nation fell upon him in a mass
Demanding little stories of his friend Umslōppogas.[6]

The prohibition party made him lecture on the fate
Of the female Cleopatra[7] who imbibed her poison straight
While the Theosophic centres were revolving round his knees
And suggesting further volumes of some forty further "Shes."[8]

But the straw that broke that camel was Chicago's mild request
For a Zulu dance in character – appropriately dressed
And vain is approbation when the path to glory leads
Through a wilderness of war-whoops and a wardrobeful of beads.

In the "Iroquois"[9] at Buffalo that partnership broke up
To the melancholy music of a six-shot boudoir-Krupp
And the waiters on the staircase counted pistol shot and oath
While the partners argued hotly if the States could hold 'em both.

* * * * * * * * * * * *

They collaborate in Yarrup where men know them who from which
And by latest information they are striking of it rich
But when evening lamps are lighted and the evening paper rustles
Still they pick forgotten bullets from each other's gluteal muscles.
       Yours very penitently
        Rudyard Kipling.

Notes
1. Lang (1844–1912), journalist and man of letters, folk-lorist and scholar, the "greatest bookman of his age" (*DNB*). He had been among the first to write about RK in the English press (see 4–5 December 1886 and 10 September 1889), and they were soon acquainted.
2. In publishing this letter Morten Cohen explains that Lang and Rider Haggard, the novelist, had been at work on *The World's Desire*, a romance about Odysseus; RK's verses imagine a lecture tour that Lang and Haggard might make in 1890 to promote the book in the United States and the resulting confusion (*Dalhousie Review*, XLV [1965] 361–4).
3. Harte's "Plain Language from Truthful James" (1870) is the model for RK's verses.
4. (Sir) Henry Rider Haggard (1856–1925), writer of adventure and fantasy fiction, best known for *She* and *King Solomon's Mines*. He took a serious interest in agriculture and in the development of the British empire as well as in his fiction. The attraction between Haggard and RK was immediate and strong, and the two remained friends to the end. RK's correspondence with Haggard has been edited by Morton Cohen, *Rudyard Kipling to Rider Haggard, The Record of a Friendship* (1965).
5. Lang had published *Myth, Ritual, and Religion* (1887), among other works on comparative mythology, and his *Ballads and Lyrics of Old France* (1872) helped reintroduce such forms as the ballade, triolet, and rondeau.
6. That is, Umslopogaas, in Haggard's *Allan Quatermain* (1888).
7. Haggard, *Cleopatra* (1889).
8. Haggard, *She* (1887).
9. Buffalo's newest hotel, where RK stayed on his American tour: see 11 August 1889.

To Edmonia Hill and Caroline Taylor, 1 November [1889][1]
ALS: Huntington Library

[London] Nov. 1:

Have had wee wee touch fever. Also got top hat. Hence am unhappy and homesick. *But* the room progresses beautifully. Only wants a committee of you 'uns to arrange it. No there was no fit pillow for Edgar. Must send it on later as I can.

All serene at present. Dined at Savile am down for it.[2] Besant goes there and everyone seems to know me. St J's Gazette offers regular work.[3] Yah! I have refused (in a poem of extreme levity).[4] The weather is what they call fine – diluted sunshine and ink. I am now much well. Have done next month's poem for Macmillan.[5] Sent you a copy of 1st poem[6] and charge seriously into ink tomorrow. Best love and God bless you all. This is a snatch line on the chance of the regular letter not catching.

Ruddie

Notes
1. This note is written on a postcard addressed to "all the S.A. Hills" on the SS *Gurkha*

at Port Said. RK has drawn on it a caricature sketch of himself wearing a top hat and has ornamented his signature with a tiny pair of spectacles.
2. In Piccadily, much favoured by literary men – Stevenson, Henley, Besant, and Saintsbury among them. RK was not elected until 1891.
3. The *St James's Gazette*, a Conservative daily paper founded in 1880, was now edited by Sidney Low.
4. A fragment of these verses has been preserved and is published in Rutherford, *Early Verse*, p. 469.
5. "The Ballad of East and West", *Macmillan's*, December 1889 (*Barrack-Room Ballads*).
6. "The Ballad of the King's Mercy", *Macmillan's*, November 1889 (*Barrack-Room Ballads*).

To Caroline Taylor, 2 November 1889
Text: Copy, University of Sussex

[Embankment Chambers, London] Nov: 2: 89:

I am an ass. Perhaps you didn't know that before but I am. There lie in my waste paper basket the torn fragments of three long letters to you. Excellent letters they were but I destroyed 'em because I was afraid of the coldly critical eye that would read 'em. Heart o' mine you, as well as I, must have discovered by this time that the writing of love letters is no easy thing. I own that I laughed disrespectfully at the delicious one you sent off by the pilot – happy man was he. (I wonder rather that we didn't go down to his boat and so gain perhaps half a day). Your new Theory of True Affection was the quaintest of all. And there was much truth in it. If a man professes love and behaves as tho' he meant it, when his inside is empty and his feet are chilled by the wet mud of the London docks, there is a certain amount of sincerity about that man. He may be depended upon. And now, what can I tell you. After you had completely gone away into the sea and river neither I nor Edgar felt happy (Oh my goodness. I've dipped into the marking ink by mistake).

10.45. p.m. That was only the beginning of my mistakes. My little beast of a fire has absolutely refused to burn and in my futile attempts to cheer it up has just filled the room with pitchy black smoke (I thought the man in charge was suspiciously anxious to light the bedroom fire in preference to this un). I'll blow him sky high in the morning. To return to my subject. I am indeed perhaps as a consequence of affliction immediately set upon by an old friend of mine – the Indian fever – and made to shake for eighteen hours. It didn't amuse me at the time but I am now perfectly well and don't intend to have any of it anymore. It was a mild attack but it caused me to miss Edgar because when I got well I had to go down to Dorking and stay with Colonel Lavin.[1] That was a queer experience. As you know it brought me into contact with George Meredith. Indeed we drove up together from the station to the sumptuous old English country house (real Ghost, hot and cold water and all the rest of it) just buried in the ling and heather that stretched for miles round Hindhead. Show me no more celebrities for they disillusion me sadly. Imagine an old withered little man very deaf in one ear who, as did Dagonet in the Morte D'Arthur, "skips like a withered leaf upon the floor."[2] He is full to a painful overflowing of elaborated epigrammatic speech which on the first fizz strikes one as deuced good. Five minutes later one cannot remember what on earth it was all about. And neither time, tide, Heaven nor Hell nor the sanctities of five o'clock tea seem to be able to stop that flow of talk. The raucous voice continues; the little old man balances him on his toe-tips like a Shanghai rooster to command attention and that attention *must* be given or he sulks like a child. He brought along a daughter [3] who idolized her father and – woe is me – tried to talk after his manner. The result was not happy.[4]

I went for a walk with him (English girls are not allowed to walk alone with young men. Shocking!) and he fizzed epigrams till I was conscious of a distinct sense of headache. I don't want to see him any more. My host a retired Anglo-Indian was perfectly charming and introduced me to a tableful of whole minor stars whose names and whose aspirations I am not sorry to say I have forgotten. There was a lathely woman in black with white feathers who wrote for the *Pall Mall Gazette*. She and I divided irrevocably on the women's rights questions. She said I was a barbarian; but I knew she was a *pagal*.[5] Ask Ted what that means. But she was mild and merciful compared to the Mrs. Assheton Dilke[6] whom I met at Macmillan's last night. She's on the London County Council (I don't know whether that will convey any notion to you) and her mission in life is to set all mankind right about female education. She manages to do this in a tone that makes you long ardently to kick her round the room forty times. By the way, English publishers live in regal – nay imperial luxury. I begin to see now why authors were created and where go the profits that should rightly be theirs. This makes me sad because I am just now being chased by several publishers. The last firm are very funny. They are a sort of Literary Supply Association and they want me to write tales of adventure suitable for youths.[7] Just at present I reply with great sweetness that my engagements are *complet* and that they had better go and take a walk. Publishers are not used to being treated in this manner and they return to the charge like Jew hawkers with proffers of ready money down. See'st thou the drift of this? It is to make the new man write as swiftly and as largely as possible on the novel subject. Then when he is squeezed dry they heave him away and call the newspapers to witness that there is no originality in the present writers.

I did not come to England to write myself out at first starting – not by a very long sight. This seemeth to me the more perfect way. To go slowly and only do sufficient magazine work to enable me to rub along comfortably while I turn my attention to the novels and the books. A man can fritter himself away on piece work and be only but a very little the richer for it. Whereas if he holds his hand the money and what is of more importance the power of doing fresh and original work comes to him. What thinkest thou? I have burned more than one solitary pipe over the question. Even regarding it from a business point of view the latter method pays better in the long-run. Wherefore I have refused in a brief poem of five stanzas[8] the St. James's Gazette offer of a permanent engagement. Catch me putting my head into that old noose again – and me hardly recovered from the constant surprises of seven years' journalism.

The situation stands thus. I hold work on Macmillan's Magazine up to £300 a year: The Lahore paper stands me for £100 (and that's four hundred); on those two alone therefore without turning my attention to the St. James's, the Spectator, Longmans, and Punch (who all want me) I could devote myself to building up the American connection and going on straight with the books and the poetry. Have I your sanction for these things?

This evening I spent with my cousin Margaret Burne-Jones and her husband Jack Mackail in a funny little-old house in Kensington.[9] It's next door to an old inn that is mentioned in Thackeray's *Esmond* but that's neither here nor there. What impressed me most and set me thinking as I went my homeward way, was the delight and comfort of that quiet little *ménage* of the two young folks.

Notes
1. Thus in copy. Lieutenant-Colonel Thomas Herbert Lewin (1839–1916), of Parkhurst, Abinger Common, Dorking, was a friend of Meredith; his stepdaughter married Meredith's son Will in 1892. Lewin had published books about his service in India.
2. Tennyson, "The Last Tournament", l. 4.
3. Marie Eveleen (Mariette) Meredith, later Mrs Henry Sturgis. Violet Maxse, afterwards Lady Milner, remembered being one of the guests at Colonel Lewin's on this occasion, when she was still a schoolgirl: Meredith, she says, "read aloud from 'One of Our Conquerors'" (Lady Milner's diary, 18 January 1936: Kent County Archives).
4. The rest of the text of this letter is taken from a copy at Sussex dated 7 February 1890 but clearly by mistake for 2 November 1889.
5. Lunatic, fool.
6. Margaret Mary Cooke, Mrs Ashton Dilke (1857–?), published *Women's Suffrage* (1885).
7. Probably the McClure Syndicate: see [January 1890].
8. The verses referred to in the preceding letter.
9. 27 Young Street, described in Angela Thirkell, *Three Houses* (Oxford, 1931).

To [Caroline Taylor], [*c.* early November 1889]
Text: Copy, University of Sussex

[Embankment Chambers]

Yes, dear, the chambers are very comfy tho 'tis a sore trial to keep things neat and I hate having to brush my own clothes. I get up at 8:a.m. (*this is true*) and wallow in a luxurious tub. Then simply but elegantly dressed in a blue serge suit, a tennis jacket, the Japanese dressing gown and my monkey skin slippers I devour the frugal bloater and the merry rasher. The morning pipe and the morning mail waft me gently to my labours. From ten till four I drive the festive quill across the bounding foolscap and reply to the notes of the pressing publisher. I have lunch at two by my side. At four, new shaven, and in a glossy hat, I go forth to take the air and think of you. Generally a desire for tea drives me to Aunt Georgie's where I am made much of; but I have very many friends at whose houses I am certain of welcome as warm as the food. Also I am much persecuted with dinners. If I don't dine out, I sally forth at eight and catch a meal in one of the merry restaurants which line the Strand. Then I return and do a little work and a little thinking and go to bed. Never was life at once so utterly isolated and yet so immediately in touch with all the world. I must confess I enjoy it, tho' there are times between the lights, when I feel unutterably lonely – too lonely to take comfort in seeing any body, but then I can watch the fire and weave tales and dream dreams. Today I have been lunching at the Savile Club with Margaret's husband and so am taking tea alone. Here's to your health sweetheart in a cup of Kangra Valley. Make me a kettle holder some day. The blamed old tea pot burns like uenkil![1] My latest purchase is a huge baccy jar about a hundred and twenty years old – price 25 cents. I want to keep my litter as small as possible but somehow things roll up and do much accumulate. Aunt Georgie is giving me a cat. I say is giving advisedly for the little sinner is yet too tiny to rough it in bachelor chambers being of a tender and squashy age and mewing hideously. Except for a run of small social events there is nothing much to tell. One's life goes quietly when one is alone with one's own thoughts and a sheet of writing paper. I maintain rude and rumbustious health and am fully aware – you needn't rub it into me, O my dear despot – that I am not my own master. I know it and how badly I want you, no words can tell.

[sketch on other side of sheet]

This is a stereoscopic view of my rooms. Them things as wouldn't come into the picture why I twisted 'em round and made 'em fit. Observe the lovely screen with the skeletons my one little extravagance. They cheer me vastly in the evenings.

Note
1. Thus in copy.

To Edmonia Hill, [early November 1889]
Text: Copy, University of Sussex

[London]

Here come the proofs of my yarn The Incarnation of Krishna Mulvaney for next month's Macmillan and I must see what the brutal English printer has done to my Irish dialect. I saw a proof of the poem that goes into Macmillans this month. Next month I try a grimmer subject.[1] Look out in the Civil and Military for two things called "The New Dispensation"[2] which I've just done.

An Australian paper offers me 5 guineas, which is perhaps twenty-five dollars, for anything I choose to write. That's pretty decent and might be thought over but I do want the American connection above all things and I mean to get it.

London is a vile place and Anstey[3] and Haggard and Lang and Co. are pressing on me the wisdom of identifying myself with some "set", while the long-haired literati of the Savile Club are swearing that I "invented" my soldier talk in Soldiers Three. Seeing that not one of these critters has been within earshot of a barrack, I am naturally wrath. But this is only the beginning of the lark. You'll see some savage criticisms of my work before spring. That's what I am playing for.

Notes
1. "The Ballad of the King's Mercy" and "The Ballad of East and West" were the poems that in fact appeared in *Macmillan's* for November and December, but it is not quite certain that RK means these titles: there was some shifting, or at least some thought of shifting, publication arrangements: see, e.g. 8–16 November.
2. *CMG*, 10 and 16 December 1889 (*Abaft the Funnel*).
3. Thomas Anstey Guthrie (1856–1934), humorous writer under the name F. Anstey; he wrote for *Punch* from 1886, and produced a series of comic novels.

To Edmonia Hill, 8–16 November 1889
Text: Copy, University of Sussex

[London] Nov: 8.89.

The Diary of a Bad boy:
Nov: 8: Friday.
Very early this morn found that the hot and cold water was neither hot nor cold and so lay in bed for half an hour waiting for it to warm itself. Consequently as it refused to behave I went without my bath and felt grubby in consequence. After breakfast did some polishing to a ballad called "Kamal"[1] which goes into Macmillan's Mag next month, – but in the middle o' this arrived the proofs of my prose tale for this month called "The Incarnation of Krishna Mulvaney." Found that the British printer had not made an unusual vile hash of my dialect and after correction despatched to the Editor of Macmillan. *Mem*. In future alter the formation of my w's which are printed as double o's: thus giving wild appearances to innocent words. Bolted a hasty lunch of lentil soup (Mem. never eat it again) and boiled beef and fled to confer with Lord Cross's Private Secretary[2] at the India office. This was glory. Proved to him at length that ye India office might be swept off ye face of the earth without anybody in India knowing it at which he was thoughtful and it seemed pained. Then to Sir G. Birdwood about a new assistant for the Pater's school of art. So delighted was B. to find someone he could advise that he promptly dropped the subject of assistants and gave me counsel as to my future literary career. Told me to live at Oxford with the Dons!!! six months! Course of English literature! A bull in a china shop would be easier than I. Accepted advice, refused invitation to lunch next day where was to meet Dadabhoy Navrojee[3] (show this to Alex) and levanted. Am to come in casually and see the chosen assistant (who is a cad possessed of knowledge of art) and subsequently report to the Pater. By the way Alex was near S. Kensington. Doesn't he know any trained youth of decent appearance who w'd jump at Rs 500 a month in India. A man of the schools fit for technical teaching? If so, please communicate. Thence home to my diggings wearied of Birdwood and after rest and smoke did eat mine little chop in the restaurant over against Gatti his Music Hall[4] and so to bed. Mem. that mattress wants tightening.

Nov. 9th. Rose up betimes (at 8) and finished the ballad of Kamal to my no small satisfaction. Received a note from the editor of Macmillan asking me to come over and smoke a cigar over Terence Mulvaney. Guessed there was something in the wind and so fought my way across the thickening crowds gathered so early to see ye Lord Mayor his show, was chased by a mounted policeman and saw much of the humours of the mob and reached Mowbray Morris[5] who complained that Terence was too drunk and so wished my sanction to cutting out some thirty lines thereof. This courtliness is an improvement on the Pi's undiscriminating slashing and I cheerfully agreed. Thereafter read him Kamal which he said was "dee fine" and promptly held over the other poem which has gone to you and ran Kamal in for this month.[6] Stayed for lunch, talked Scott and discussed next month's story.

At four o'clock perceived that the crowd was cutting me off from Villiers Street and so ran into Aunt Aggie's house at Knightsbridge where I had tea and played railway tricks with the small boy Hugh – a late arrived cousin whom I persist in regarding in the light of a nephew.[7] Passed on by special invite to meet my unmarried Aunt Edith Macdonald, Jack Mackail and Margaret at Aunt Georgie's where there was a family gathering only disturbed by the presence of Sidney Colvin[8] (who wrote Keats). The same is an allfired prig of immense water and suffers from all the nervo-hysterical diseases of the 19th Century. Went home with him as far as Charing Cross in a 3rd smoking (wh. made him sick). He recounted all his symptoms and made me sick. A queer beast with match-stick fingers and a dry unwholesome skin. Found a letter from the St. James's at home demanding a "Plain Tale" connected with literature. Lighted a pipe and thought out a notion which I slept upon.[9] Mem. The washing came home, and all the streets were illuminated. This has no connection with the washing but the Prince of Wales's birthday. A row of drunken women under my window at one o'clock. Language Epic but unprintable.

Sunday – Nov. 10th. Rose up. My notion of the literary tale for the Jimmy still hot and disposed myself unto a complete day. Began at ten, stopped for lunch at two and went on till five weaving the yarn of a young man who started in a literary career in London and wrote himself out in the desire to accumulate money. He used and reused his incidents all over again till the public sickened of him and he married a rich wife just in the nick of time. Thought it a grim and fantastic yarn but wondered how it would strike Low,[10] the Editor. Put the polish on and got a quotation and then remembered that I hadn't been shaved and it was Sunday. So ran aimlessly up and down the Strand hunting a barber's shop till I found a kindly hansom man who drove me to a place somewhere near Seven Dials – half bird shop and half barber's where all the customers had nicknames and a small boy rubbed in the lather while his fat father gashed my chin. Felt as tho' I had been newly sand-papered and then, bleeding gently, went off to dinner at the Poynter's, where I made that grim Academician talk and laugh about Japanese architecture. Left early, but young Poynter[11] my cousin aetat 22 came with me to my rooms and he spoke till one in the morning, never so he says having had a soul to talk to before. The trouble is an old one.

Young man in his father's house, just growing up and inheriting his father's nervous temperament, unhappy, lonely, doesn't know quite what he wants. Gave him a sight of good advice – I'd be sorry to follow it all myself – and got him to open his heart down to the deeps and felt sorry for him. He will bear cultivating and he is safer with me than making experiments on his own account. Has promised to come to me when he has anything on his mind and to spend any holiday time in my company. My wisdom astonished myself. Turned him out at 1.a.m. smoked a pipe and went to bed. Mem. That washing isn't to be compared to American washing. Too dirty.

Nov. 11. An evil-evil day. Rose up in the morn at 9 and found the gloom of the Pit upon the land, a yellow fog through which the engines at Charing Cross whistled agonizedly one to the other and I could see the switch-boxes lit up with cheap and yellow gas when the electric light was manifestly needed. These English are fools which things so moved me to despair that I sat down forthwith and wrote a doleful ditty for nothing in particular which I later packed up for the C & M Gazette. It was called *In Partibus*[12] and was the wail of a fog-bound exile howling for Sunlight. The last verse was particularly touching – Chaunt it slowly and note the effect

> The busses run to Islington
>   To Highgate and Soho,
> To Hammersmith and Kew therewith
>   And Camberwell also
> But I can only murmur bus[13]
>   From Shepherds Bush to Bow.

Then there came a fiendish darkness darker than any dust-storm and I had to light my reading lamp before lunch. That about finished me and I did no more but went out to the shop in the basement and got two whopping cherry wood pipes and enfolded myself in the mists of fancy; thinking out subjects to be written and dialogues to be touched up. My thoughts were about as valuable as the baccy smoke. My spirits were most awful low and I was beginning to weep audibly when a knock arrived at the door and Aunt Georgie's housemaid – the cross-eyed one not the pretty one – arrived with a packet of letters from India. Then I whooped. It struck me as queer that the Girl should have come across London to give the letters into my hand when she could have posted 'em. So I made enquiries. "Where's Aunt Georgie?" "Oh she's gone to Rottingdean" said the artless Anne who I dare say desired amusement, and sought it in my chambers. So I treated her with immense distinction – the buttons are beginning to drop off my shirt collars you must understand – and then I gravely gave her tea, and she discussed housekeeping details – coal, wristbands, darning stockings etc. In the end emboldened by much tea, which made her glisten like a newly buttered muffin, she said that it would be fitting and proper for me to settle down and marry a nice steady young woman, because I "kept my things dreadful." With a large smirk she left me to digest the advice – I *do* hope she doesn't mean herself – and the home letters.

They were cheering and festive, giving details of life in Kashmir, Trixie's return pending Jack's absence in Burma and best of all their freedom from anxiety. Something had happened to the Pittsburgh and Chicago letters and they wrote in the dark but as full of love as ever. (Mem. You *must* know 'em. I've told 'em you know all and more too about me in more than one letter). Another packet of letters contained introductions from a man in India to Cassell and Co, Hall Caine[14] and someone else. But everything was spoilt by the old *Pi.* I read my *Arashima* letter and the Kyoto factories one here in the dark.[15] It didn't make me sick – oh no, not in the least. I didn't kick and squirm – Quite to the contrary. Mem. I wish the Pioneer would hurry up with those things and get them over. They hurt.

Dined at an Italian restaurant and felt that the day was not wholly unprofitable when I heard a hot headed young Irishman explode in a furious passion of "You be damneds" when it was pointed out to him that he had ordered oxtail soup from a yesterday's bill of fare and that there was only celery soup about the place. O but he was wrath. He said bills of fare made no difference and he was going to have that soup if all Villiers St. went to perdition. He departed swearing. All through my intense amusement I couldn't help feeling sorry for the poor girl with him. She was conscious that he was making a great ass of himself and her evident humiliation was pitiful to watch.

Since that hour I've been sprawling on the sofa, reading Besant's All in a Garden Fair and energetically tried to persuade myself that I did not in the least resemble Allen the fledgling poet. I own occasionally after my or our glorious burst of travel and larks to feeling lonely but if you are that way for a sufficient length of time you go perforce to the reading desk and write or read something and that's worth the trouble. And now, good folk, good night. You are still on the roaring seas where there is no fog. Ye gods but I wish I were with you. I forgot to say that the Syndicate publishers once mentioned having failed to come to term by letters is now seeking personal interviews with me: which I am loath to grant. Also I have discovered a beautiful print of drunken soldiers coming out of a canteen; all wearing each others' hats which reminds me of good old days gone by. Ah me!

Nov 12th. Sunshine for twenty blessed minutes in the morning, bless the Lord. Real sunshine strained thro' green water. Did some foolish hefling[16] work in the morn of the nature of poesy and then ran out to consult with Armstrong,[17] director of Sciences and Arts at the South Kensington in regard to the Pater's assistant. Found him snugly settled in a tiny conventual office next door to the Brompton Oratory – say, Alex, these educational gentlemen at home seem to enjoy all the good things of life. He entertained me with much civility and had me to lunch in the South Kensington Grill room where he paid me foolish compliments about my work which it seemed he had seen. Then argued hotly about the assistant and got many promises out of him that the man, however intelligent and architectural, should not be a bigger cad than was absolutely necessary. This settled he showed me a new acquisition of the South Kensington – a big fresco – tempera dome [sic] first spotted by Ambo Poynter in the heel of Italy approved by Poynter and purchased. The peeling off of a fresco and its re-erection in London is a quaint thing to watch. Learned incidentally that some of the most priceless Jap. bronzes in the Museum had been found in the forges of a foundry! whither they had been sent by that foolish foolish Jap Govt. to be melted up! Mem. Does this not justify the annexation of Japan. Armstrong entertained me with the grievances of the Educational Dept. in England (they have as many as in India, with the additional delight of Parliamentary interference), and I got away at 4.P.M. Went over to see a Mrs Gilgerd[18] once Miss Welford from New York and an ally of mine seven years ago. Her late father was $\frac{1}{3}$ or $\frac{2}{3}$ of Scribners and she saith that I can either get Scribner or the Century – as I please. Discussed American work for an hour and talked about America. Had to explain at length *why* I hadn't brought you 'uns along to talk to her and so left her – She leaving for the Riviera on Friday. Met there an old friend with a lovely name – a Mrs. Probesting, a raddled wrinkled New Yorker who lives up to every inch of her title. Got home at 6, and dined alone at seven. Felt lonely and wished that Aunt Georgie's little kitten were sufficiently grown up to play with me. Went to bed early and found on my table an invite to dine with one Trevor[19] (once at Hyderabad and brother of the Commissioner of Ajmir) on Sunday at the Universities Club. (Mem. Met on my way to the S. Ken. Major Cooper[20] once Mil. Sec. to the Viceroy when Bill Beresford[21] went home.)

Nov. 13. Natural consequence of going to bed early – lay in bed late. Whitings (their head [bread] crumbed tails in their mouths) cold in consequence at 10.A.M. Saw a fog which led me to write a poem on the subject in Swinburnian metre for Punch.[22] Hope it'll get in. This kept me till after lunch (hot roast beef, but *no* pickles). Mem. Speak to the bottle nosed man, and wish Booj[23] was around. After lunch went to the Arts and Crafts for reasons of mine own, and to get the setting of a [   ][24] which simmers in my head. You shall know anon. Stopped at the Cockspur Street branch of the Oriental Banking Corporation to transfer my account from the inaccessible East End branch. The Manager hailed me with delight seemed to know all about me. Said that Logan (Acct. Gen. Punjab, *your* friend dear lady) had his account there. This impressed me with fear – Logan is not safe in any bank. Came out after a long talk of Anglo-Indians and naturally ran slick into the arms of an old school-fellow, now a lieutenant out of Bombay Cavalry, whom I had not met for ten years. We danced on the pavement. He was coming out of the P and O office having just got his passage for India. He moaned. I offered to swop lots, but the deal was impossible. Besides his uniform wouldn't fit and I'm sure I couldn't ride his horses. After the Arts and Crafts went home and had tea and cussed over a letter from Mobr. Morris who found that Macmillans was two pages over weight and so must cut into my poem. I cut it according. It hasn't done much harm but when one is safely delivered of a child one hates to cut off his little nose and ears. At seven thirty started for Aunt Aggie's (the Poynters) before alluded to. Found Teddy Bell (once an actor now a stage designer married to an American wife) and Malcolm Bell[25] a writer man who wrote a thing called "His Fatal Success." He writes in America but as he explains lives here, so is paid at Melican and lives at English rates. He was fulsomely complimentary. The American bride was nice and we had a talk. She struck me as fresh and girlish. When they were gone Aunt Aggie explained that Teddy had found her a widow and a school marm; her first husband having been drowned five months after date. *Mem.* never judge people off hand. A good dinner but the whipped cream didn't compare with Belvidere's and they had forgotten the bread sauce with the partridges. Yah! Young Poynter who insists on regarding me as his father confessor thrust into my hand on leaving his M.S. volume of poems and A FIVE ACT TRAGEDY IN BLANK VERSE! I shall go to heaven for this. Such a queer pathetic written letter accompanied the thing. Got home at 11.30 and found a letter from Lang telling me that C. Longman[26] had read my Plain Tales and wanted to know if I could let him have *any thing* for Longman's p.d.q. Acknowledged letter and set myself to study the soul of a young man as revealed in his writings of verse. Never before shown to anyone. You shall know the result tomorrow.

Nov. 14th. Mowbray Morris – his hair on end – arrived ere I was up to explain that certain parts of the poem might be saved. I cussed the poem. What is the use of being a poet if you have to bother about your proofs. However methinks I've saved the refrain and that's summat.

Yes, those poems were queer, young Poynter's, I mean and not mine. Most of 'em were translations from the Latin and Greek; and the poor boy had evidently been struggling with religious difficulties thro' it all – complicated with budding flirtations which, most naturally, plunged him further into the maze of doubt and uncertainty. The Sin of the young man of the Nineteenth century appears to be over-self-consciousness and a morbid condition of the nerves. None the less some of the lines of the boy's tragedy which is eminently and even stiffly classical, are fine. He seems to have read Shelley and Shakespeare with great diligence and to have not unskillfully borrowed from 'em both. Very naturally he estimates all his poems *not* by the thing actually put down in black and white but by all the glorious inchoate fancies that flashed through his brain when his pen was in his hand. He wants my verdict not so much on his poems as his psychological condition. If I put it down in writing I shall offend him. I will e'en ask him to dinner – or a pipe – and talk things over – verily the soul of a young man is awful cu'rous.

Sat up till two o'clock reading Ambrose's stuff and got up at 9 with a headache. *Mem.* Never read an aspiring cousin's tragedy any more. Wrote the beginning of a long letter to the Father and Mother telling them all about myself and begging 'em to send along the M.S. of *Mother Maturin*. Then went out to see Longman (Charles) and in a luxurious office in Paternoster Row found a bearded and sympathetic youngish middle aged man, not unlike Aleck, who spoke me fair. Had seen my tales, thought that he could do business with me. Would I send him over some letters of mine called From Sea to Sea and any of the railway books that might be to my hand. In the interval could I see my way to writing him anything for Longmans. Would give 10 guineas for anything I chose to write. I fancied I saw my way to that and left. Lunched at a queer place in Ave Maria Lane called "Ye Salutation Tavern." (Mem. they know how to cook chops there). Then went on to a rascally firm of publishers in Fleet Street with whom my cousin Phil Burne-Jones had got himself mixed up. They were running a mean little rag which professed to publish the lives of "Eminent Workers". With the eternal vanity of the artist Pip had allowed himself to be roped into the show – had forwarded an autobiography and had sat for a likeness!! Struck a queer dirty office in Fleet Street opposite the Pink 'Un.[27] (Ask the man at the Club what the Pink 'Un is like). One glance at the first number of the horrible journal was enough for me. (I saw that old Stewart the Cawnpore boot factory man[28] had written his life there by the way) and I schemed to pull that phool Phil out of the disgraceful horde. Ran back to his studio in Kensington High Street, told him he was an ass, and that he had better give me a power of attorney to interview the unprincipled editor and get Phil's M.S. of his own life back again, since he was in more than shady company and his foes would scoff. Pip promised and carried me off to see Barnum's[29] which is close to the Grange. A howling jam – the monsters made me almost sick. I do not like people without legs or hands and I *hate* a two headed boy. But 'tis a great show: tho' I never saw the tenth of it. Dined with Phil and Burne Jones alone and Uncle Ned presently uncorked himself and became a mine of wisdom on letters and Art. He is one of the best talkers I know when he cares. Home early to pack up selections of my works for Longman.

Nov. 15th. A steady grind. Went ahead at a yarn entitled *For One Night Only*[30] – the story of people who hired a box at a theatre but when they were in it could see nothing save howling chaos – the blank darkness of the Pit – not the theatre Pit. Worked it over and over and sent it to *Longman's* (I'm beginning to mix my mags – 10–10 to me). The Literary Supply Association man, still anxious for "a serial tale of adventure," sent me a note begging me to see him next week and consider his terms. Knocked off at five and went for a walk. Dined at the Italian restaurant and after dinner concluded to go to Gatti's Music Hall. This opened a new world to me and filled me with fresh thoughts – surely the people of London require a poet of the Music Halls.

Found on return a letter from Lady Simon[31] inviting me to dine on Monday. They are a queer crazy old couple and don't allow smoking after dinner. Accepted, and went to bed to dream of the dumb millions of London whose only amusement is the Music Hall.

Nov: 16th. Woke early and lay in bed till the bath was hot ruminating over Music Halls. Then had a luxurious steam and attiring myself in slippers and gown wrote for the C & MG a thing called "A Legend of Great Honour"[32] – an exposition of Music halls which lay very heavy on my heart. I am so sorry for the poor folk who listen to the sad songs and are told by their betters that they are "immoral and vulgar." A note from the W.B. Richmonds[33] the artists inviting me to dinner on the 28th. and made me wroth. They only care because I'm getting on. A note from Walter Besant enclosing prospectus of a sort of Literary Pool. He said he was one of my greatest admirers, could I see my way to writing a tale of 3000 words for his syndicate – to be paid for at Magazine rates on the spot; this only buying serial rights for *one* production. Then at the end of the Series, in which ten or twelve well known authors were to assist, all the profits to be pooled and divided. This looks too mechanical but Besant, whom ye know I have long worshipped, is a man of business – so accepted tentatively and asked ten guineas for my yarn, which in Allahabad I sh'd ha' done for the Weeks News for nothing. Then wrote a letter to Lang to amuse him; he complaining that London was Hell; studied the report of the English Education Commission which Margaret's husband had left me and went out to dine with Emerson,[34] once an architect in Bombay and always a dear friend of my father's, at Barkston Gardens. Met there Mrs. Griffiths, my God-father's wife (wife of the man at the head of the S.T.[35] School of Art at Lahore) leaving for Bombay tomorrow with a big fat wallopping throllopping, daughter whom I remember as a screaming fat pasty babe in short frocks. No one else to amuse except a woman visibly dying of heart disease, with whom I was almost afraid to talk. Stayed late talking of India and am only just home – a heavy fog on London.

Good night and God bless you all. Here's the tale of a week. Unless you stop me p.d.q. you'll get the other weeks in equal detail. Keep well, go slow, be strong and get to know my people as soon as ever and believe that thro' all this chaos I am as I always was

"The Boy."

Notes
1. "The Ballad of East and West".
2. Viscount Cross (1823–1914) was Secretary of State for India, 1886–92; his secretary was Clinton Edward Dawkins (see 3–25 December 1889).
3. Dadabhai Naoroji (1825–1917), first Indian MP (Finsbury, 1892–5); President of the Indian National Congress, 1886, 1893, and 1906.
4. Opposite RK's rooms on Villiers Street, under the arches of Charing Cross Station.
5. Editor of *Macmillan's*: see 3 May–24 June 1886.
6. But, after all, "The Ballad of the King's Mercy" appeared in the November *Macmillan's*, "The Ballad of East and West" in December.
7. (Sir) Hugh Poynter (1882–1968), worked in Turkey before the First World War, and in France, Canada, and Australia afterwards. He lived in Australia, where he was in business, from 1926.
8. Colvin (1845–1927), critic of art and literature, had been director of the Fitzwilliam Museum, Cambridge, and was now keeper of the department of prints and drawings at the British Museum. He published *Keats* in 1887, and is especially remembered as the friend and editor of Stevenson.
9. "The Comet of a Season", *St James's Gazette*, 21 November 1889 (uncollected).
10. (Sir) Sidney Low (1857–1932) succeeded as editor of the *St James's Gazette* in 1888 and was later on the staff of the *Standard*. He wrote much on politics, biography and literature, and was the friend and admirer of many of the imperialist leaders of his generation.
11. Ambrose Poynter (1867–1923), 2nd Baronet, the elder son. He was at school with his cousin Stanley Baldwin, and was best man to his cousin RK. He practised as an architect, but without marked success.
12. *CMG*, 23 December 1889.
13. Hindustani for "enough", "stop!"
14. (Sir) Thomas Henry Hall Caine (1853–1931), novelist, widely popular since publication of *The Deemster* (1887). The letter was from Eric Robertson; Caine recalled that RK was introduced thus: "He has seen everything, he knows everything, and he can do anything. His name is Rudyard Kipling" (*St Andrew's Citizen*, 13 October 1923).
15. Letter 16 of *From Sea to Sea*.
16. I can find no such word recorded. Perhaps RK wrote "trifling"?
17. Thomas Armstrong (1832–1911) succeeded Edward Poynter as Director for Art at the South Kensington Museum in 1881.
18. Thus in copy, for Mrs Gielgud, the former Evelyn Welford; a MS copy of RK's valentine verses to her, *c.* 1883, is in the Morgan Library (Rutherford, *Early Verse*, pp. 179–81). She was the daughter of Charles Welford (d. 1885), an Englishman who joined Scribner as a partner in 1857 and served as the firm's London agent from 1864.
19. Frederick George Brunton Trevor (1838–1924), brother of Colonel George Herbert Trevor, Commissioner of Ajmir.
20. (Colonel) Harry Cooper (1847–1928), ADC to the Viceroy of India, 1884–8.
21. Lord William Beresford (1847–1900), third son of the Marquess of Waterford, was Military Secretary to three successive Viceroys, 1882–94.
22. Nothing of RK's is known to have appeared in *Punch*.
23. Bhoj was Mrs Hill's cook in Allahabad.

24. Blank in copy. The Arts and Crafts Exhibition Society, founded 1888, associated with Morris, Burne-Jones, and Walter Crane.
25. The Bells were nephews of Sir Edward Poynter. Malcolm Bell's *His Fatal Success* appeared in 1888.
26. Charles James Longman (1852–1934) edited *Longman's Magazine*, 1882–1905.
27. The *Sporting Times*, called the Pink 'Un after the paper it was printed on.
28. Colonel John Stewart (1833–1914) established the government harness and saddlery factory at Cawnpore and managed it until 1888.
29. Barnum and Bailey's show opened at the Olympia, Kensington, on 11 November. RK mentions the show in "My Great and Only", the story he began the next day: see n. 32, below.
30. *Longman's Magazine*, April 1890 (Sussex Edition, xxix).
31. Perhaps Lady Rachel Simon, wife of Sir John (1818–97), a prominent barrister and MP, active in Jewish causes.
32. Published as "My Great and Only", *CMG*, 11 and 15 January 1890 (*Abaft the Funnel*).
33. (Sir) William Bell Richmond (1842–1921), son of the distinguished Victorian portrait painter George Richmond and himself a successful painter. One of his sons had been at Westward Ho! (see [29] April 1882).
34. (Sir) William Emerson (1843–1924) went out to Bombay a year before JLK. After his return to England he received important Indian commissions, including the Victoria Memorial, Calcutta. He was President of the Royal Institute of British Architects, 1899–1902.
35. Thus in copy: possibly a misreading of "J.J.", for the Jamsetjee Jeejeebhoy School of Art in Bombay, where Griffiths worked: "Lahore" must be RK's inadvertent error.

To [Walter Besant], 20 November [1889]

ALS: Dalhousie University

Embankment Chambers, / Villiers Street, Strand. / Nov: 20:

Dear Sir:

All thanks for your kind letter. But Mr. Lang was wrong. I am not young – only "an old man spotted with decaying youth" for I have seven years of Indian journalism behind me and they leave one neither happy nor hopeful. Also I have gotten popularity from my own public across the water so that they all know me and I have suffered from the amiable publisher a little. Even now as you say, they profess Love and a terrifying disinterestedness which almost unmans me. Indeed I have signed nothing, promised nothing and pledged nothing since my Indian and Australian connections enable me to wait developments with a vast calm. And further when I was an Editor and required serial matter for my paper I dealt with publishers as one pork butcher with another and so came to know the difference between their buying and selling prices; per running foot of matter [sketch of double-faced figure]. There is a very great difference. I fancy that the agent whom you so kindly suggest[1] will be of service and I feel sure that the Society[2] will.

Could you tell me when I should be required to send in the stuff.[3]

War – bloody war – I expect – will be my simple theme tho' adultery a *partie carrée* has its seductions.

Yours very gratefully
Rudyard Kipling

Notes
1. Alexander Pollock Watt (1835–1914), a Scotsman who had worked for the publisher Alexander Strahan in London before setting up as a literary agent around 1875. Watt was not the first literary agent, but he was the first effective one. RK remained with Watt's firm for the rest of his life.
2. The Society of Authors, founded by Besant in 1884. RK became a member in 1890.
3. Besant had invited RK to contribute to a literary syndicate: see 16 November in 8–16 November 1889.

To Edmonia Hill, 3–25 December 1889
Text: Copy, University of Sussex

[London]

The Diary of a Bad Boy
(Sadly interrupted)

Tuesday: 3rd: Dec: A day of Death and Fog. Did some very bad work and then went down the street to meet 3 Anglo-Indians walking arm in arm, to wit Bullen Smith of the Bank of Bengal, Smith of the Forests and Close of the Bank.[1] With these I foregathered till t'was time to go and lunch with Pollock[2] the Editor of the Saturday in grisly grey chambers in the Albany. Met Saintsbury[3] and Jebb.[4] A vile lunch. No talk. Pollock half asleep and the forks dirty! Dined at 6 (ungodly hour) with Hooper[5] of the Spectator. Met a wild socialist who told me that the workingman was a God. "Then kill him" said I and levanted.

Wednesday: Thurs 4 and 5: Stayed at home and cussed chiefly. Weather black as the Pit.

Friday 6th. Did some work for a change. At 7 turned up young Ambo Poynter whom I fed at the restaurant and took to a Music Hall. A keen tongued cynical young dog. He stayed barking in my rooms till 2:A.M. Turned him out by force: Old Story: All his confidences.

Saturday. A blank in the diary. Probably slept all day.

Sunday. 8th. Lunched at the Poynter's first going over to inspect Poynter's new picture[6] wh. he says will be the masterpiece of his life. It's Old Brer Solomon coming down the steps of his throne to welcome Sis Sheby as she comes along with apes and peacocks and all that truck. I never saw such a blaze of colour or jumble of notions in my life. Sol is in stamped blue and red Peshawurlac cloth. Sheba in Delhi brocade and Kenkab and half the Zanzibar nigs in Amritzar schulkharis![7] "I thought it was oriental" said Poynter "and no one knows any better here." It's mighty curious to see behind an R.A.'s piccy[8] and note the bits of things it is made up of.

He had a set of photoes of Assyrian sculps which w'd ha' delighted Aleck. In my usual genial way I proferred advice and suggestions – two of which were accepted – and as I ran out of the studio (it's one of a great range) I stepped into or onto the tray containing Hamo Thorneycroft's[9] modest lunch. He does his sculpture on milk and rusks. He was not pleased but they shouldn't leave his lunch at his door.

Went at 9.p.m. to supper with the Walkers of the Simla bank who knew all about you 'uns. Met what was left of Fenwick[10] first Editor of the C and M. Ask Alec who he was. Also a girl who knew Emile Moreau[11] (She hates him as much as the Memsahib does): Monday was work.

Tuesday was a day of toil, for a thing for the Contemporary,[12] a view of English politics written by an intriguing Muslim. A whack at the Congress was included.

Wednesday. (11th) Dined at the Poynters. Met a militia subaltern who is qualifying for the Guards (Scots) "because my mother doesn't want me to go on active service y'know." Then with Aunt Aggie (she whom ye saw at tea) went over to a dance at 27 Rutland Gate. Didn't know the hostess's name[13] – didn't care. A tiny drawing room was cleared out – a mournful cornet encouraged a pale violin to battle and a piano arbitrated. A crowded room cannoneered impartially all round. Then even as I looked the whole thing wearied. Arrived at No. 2 danced one waltz with Aunt Aggie who dances lightsomely, saw three girls to whom she purposed introducing me; saw a glimpse of Phil Burne-Jones who showed me another girl. I am I hope strong but their eyes scared me; like this [three sketches] and so quit while No. 4 waltz was beginning and walked home in the night. But Phil found time to tell me one tale which was worth many dances. There was a man last season who, smitten of Heaven for his sins, was suddenly at a crowded dance violently sick over his partner!! He did not commit suicide – not he. He lives but he has no given name. Everyone calls him "The man who was sick." Next morn I explained to Aunt Aggie that I wasn't used to dancing at a bottom of a bucket.

Thursday. 12: Saw my literary Agent A.P. Watt – a nice man who vows that I shall have a princely income. Besant (I told you I think) advised me to put myself in his hands. He does all the business work for Besant, Haggard etc. and its Wilkie Collins's executor. "Hurry up your novel" sez he "and become rich." He took me up on the strength of Plain Tales only. I like him. He takes 10% on all prices: For that he gets you better prices, fights the publisher and sees you reviewed.

Friday: was a long hot day of labour – Barrack Room yarn this time.[14] I see in my rough notes that the word "Damn" is written in front of this day. Most extraordinary thing – Never saw it before. Must mean that I was in a pot about Mulvaney's account of the Courting of Dinah Shadd. O ye Gods how I want you dear folks over here to help, advise suggest and talk. But I shall not weep.

(*Sat. 14th. Dec*) Prelude to a week's unholy carouse. Dined with Dawkins[15] Ex-Sec to Cross now gone over to the Treasury and Goschen's Sec. Met there Wynn,[16] Cross's new Sec. and a man without any features; also a haggard and unkempt Virgin of great age who pretended to be lamb. She was mutton and bazar mutton at that! The hostess Dawkins' wife began talking about my books. "And how did you think of your characters Mister Kipling!" I am sick of this. By the way the cabby drove me somewhere into the Zoo on being told to go to West Brompton. You won't understand the detour – Alec will. But the slovenliness of a young housekeeper's menage made the dinner so late that I arrived as it was ready. Stayed talking with Dawkins (India office shop) till 1.A.M. He told me a tale of Gladstone wh. I sent to the C. & M. See "The Adoration of the Magi".[17] It's quite true!

On the 15th (Sunday) Don't laugh. I went to church (St. Clement Dane's) and then lunched with Hooper, Money editor of the *Times*.[18] Met Justin McCarthy Junior[19] – a child who is also an M.P. and pretends to understand Persian. Cunningham[20] a member of the Alpine Club who is a mimic and gave a lovely account of a meeting between Madame Novikoff (O.K.) and de Blowitz the Times correspondent.[21] The other man was in the legal profession. I found that out when I wound up a tale with "A barrister Judge in nine cases out of ten loses his head." "*I am a barrister Judge*" said the unknown while the men roared. I felt this was no time for half measures. "Then you'll bear me out" said I. This time the laugh was not at me.

Do you recognize this? I thought the other sheets were skimpy.

After tea (6.p.m.) still at Hoopers. Old Hooper his father of the Spectator took me home to a quiet dinner among the old maids with whom I lived in the holidays when I was fourteen years old.[22] They were friends of Leigh Hunt and Carlyle so they be no spring chickens. A nice dinner only drawback having to repeat every remark 3 (three) III times – once for Mrs. Hooper, once for Miss Wynnard, once for Miss Mary. The daughter of the house is a Socialistic-artist.[23] Don't know much about her socialism but her art is bad enough. Played cribbage with old Hooper and left early to do some stuff for the St. James's.[24]

Mon. 16th. Oh what a wet day it was. Worked all day by gas, at Mulvaney. At 6. went over to the Savoy Hotel a sort of stuccoed Grand only with more gilding to dine with Mr and Mrs Walker[25] and two girls of a household wherein the mother is a mad spiritualist and the two children "Budge" and "Bunny" first class little billiard players. (Can beat an average player if he holds his little opponent up to the table to make a difficult cannon.) What queer households there be in the world, baint they? In the middle o' the dinner who should sail in down the room but Mrs Langtry[26] of the 8th Hussars. That seemed sort o' familious like, Allee same Simla in other days. My party had seats at the Gaiety for Ruy Blas, or the Blasé Roué.[27] I quit – theatres ain't my shape. I *can't* stand 'em – and went home to fight with some more Mulvaney.

Tuesday. 17th. O black day! Dined with George Macmillan[28] (brother of the man I told you about at whose house I met Mrs. Assheton Dilke) at 19: Earls Terrace Kensington. An awful dinner with one bright spot o' light. I took in Miss Corbyn[29] a rattling American girl daughter of Corbyn president of the Philadelphia Reading R'y. We talked America while Pater[30] (whip me that master of [prose?][31] with scourges) moaned and frothed and yammered over Blake's poems. Pater's remarkably like a gorilla – no, a *langur*. I heard a fat man laying down the law on Japanese Art – a subject whereof we and we alone (*Have* you unpacked those cases yet, O unhappy people?) know more than a little. Then Mrs. Macmillan told me that India was fit to govern itself and that "we in England" (the ultra liberal idiots always speak of "we") "are very much in earnest about putting things right there."

Hereto I with my engaging frankness. "Oh, that's not earnestness that you're suffering from. That's hysteria. You haven't got enough to divert your mind."

Mrs. Macmillan looked at the ceiling as one who said: – "Just Heavens what barbarian am I entertaining?" and Miss Corbyn giggled. Somehow I thought of a very angry Memsahib 'way back on a Melican Ship and grew homesick and moody. Nothing interested me for a long time till a placid long haired gentleman who said he was an admirer of mine told me tales of cannibals in New Guinea. "I was among them for some time with my friend". "And?" . . . . said I. "Oh they ate my friend?" said he plaintively and I dropped the subject. I couldn't catch his name but I think 'twas Johnson[32] in which case Africa and not New Guinea was the spot. But Alec would know more about this than I. Most of the evening I hung on to Miss Corbyn. Her accent soothed me and she didn't talk about my bl—— blessed books.

Wednesday: 18th: Dined at the Burne Jones's to meet my Uncle Fred Macdonald[33] the Methodist preacher and his Nephew George[34] a weedy sucking solicitor, just going on the Continent for 5 weeks. Fred is the wit of our family and told us queer tales. Aunt Georgie had stuck the pallid boy George with his back to the fire. He was much too polite to ask for a screen so he was! Then he drank two glasses of clinging clammy Saumur. (I love my Aunt Georgie but I don't drink her wines.)

Then when the ladies (represented by Mrs Poynter (Aunt Aggie) and Edith Macdonald the unmarried Aunt) had retreated, George wrapped himself round one of Burne Jones's best Havanas! (I love my Uncle Ned and I *do* smoke his cigars when I can get 'em). That didn't agree with George. He was – not to put too fine a point on it AWFUL SICK! I misremember what occurred but Phil ran for the slop bowl and I ran for the hall. Fred evidently was used to the hair-trigger stomach of his offspring for he left Phil to doctor the poor boy who instead of seeing his loving relatives had to languish limply over two chairs and at parting (blue white) gave us each a clammy hand while the servants burnt incense (pastilles) in the dining room. Now the shame of the performance is this. Ten or eleven years ago when I had last seen George a rickety scrofulous child he was being sick up and down his father's stairs. Today, nothing in the wide world will convince me that he hasn't been continually sick ever since. And yet he must have had some lucid intervals or he would not have passed his examinations! Drove home with Aunt Aggie, saw Young Poynter for a minute and went on to mine own apartments.

Thursday – 19th. Moreton Frewen called in the morning – red and happy as ever; full of new schemes, anxious to do somthing for me – says I'll get £4 each for the letters I sent him,[35] *ca m'est egal*. I'll get more than four quid in the end. Longman has sent the letters to Andrew Lang to read. Don't you fuss yourself my very dear memsahib, we'll smash Arnold[36] into his own lights of Asia yet. Dined at the Poynters to meet (a) the mother of the Militia subaltern, a hooknosed woman with a haggard eye and (b) a Mrs. Norman Grosvenor[37] [sketch]. They both talked about my books, wherefore I left early in the company of Anstey which his real name is Guthrie; talking about music halls and his work in Punch and the slating his last book "*The Pariah*" has been getting. "And I did so want to get out of my dam comic line" wailed little Guthrie. The Norman Grosvenors asked me to tea next day, no I thank you, previous engagements. Dinners is dinners and so's lunches; but tea breaks up the whole of the afternoon and I do not care for taming my conversation to suit the needs of the grain-fed matrons of Belgravia. They show me off and trot me round confound 'em.

Friday 20th. Never mix in second rate company. This day I dined with Justin Macarthy[38] (*pere et fils*) M.Ps., their daughter,[39] a WOMAN with tinted cheeks, and an artist of the name Simpson[40] at Printalis which is a restaurant where they give you good things to eat. Don't know Alec's view but the Irish M.P. appears to be an awful rotter. Old Macarthy was rowling out amazing "crackers", in a rich full up [   ][41] the white headed incarnation of insincerity. The young 'un was talking cheap orientalism to amuse me. I wasn't amused; and the woman with the tinted cheeks was making eyes at the artist, who wrapped himself up in his dinner. Miss McCarthy was a virgin of emancipated lustre. She discussed divorce cases in a manner which made me long to send her to bed for a brazen little hussy. I felt that the sooner I got out o' this sort o' society the better for me so I left early. As long as Providence gives me the instinct to know when I am among second-rate people I am not wholly lost.

Saturday. 21nd. This night I entertained an admirer – such a queer young chap sprung from deuce knows where. He's nineteen and in business but anxious to write. Calls me "Sir" and with the artless adoration of youth tells me that I'm greater than anyone he knows. This is touching. In return I give him much good advice (I can only hope that t'will be accounted to me for righteousness hereafter) and warn him against the perils of this wicked world. Well, I fed him at the Salferino,[42] took him to the Empire which is a sort o' glorified music hall and then brought him to my chambers where he told me (a) all his life (b) all his hopes (c) all his love affairs. You should have seen me sternly frowning on the latter. As he stayed till the last train had gone I had to send him home in a cab.

Sunday 22. Took up Mulvaney at 9.A.M. and fought him till 6.p.m. Then turned over on my sofa and fell deeply asleep till 10. Got up undressed and staggered into bed. But I've fixed "The Courting of Dinah Shadd". Would that I could read it to you.

Mon: 23rd: A business day, first with Thacker Spink[43] about P[lain]. T[ale].'s and royalties. They told me casually of Moreau's agents, (188 Strand). I ran there and found a man who told me Moreau was an unbusinesslike beggar but that Sampson Low and Co were republishing *Soldiers Three* for him (M) and the work w'd be in the market after ten days.[44] As the 4th Edition of the D.D. (£50 worth of new poems added[45]) will be out in a fortnight I shall begin the new year a little better than I had hoped. Everything connected with the Railway Series appears to have been infamously mismanaged, but it's a consolation to learn that one book at least will be got ready. You've no idea of the demand for it in England. John Addington Symonds has started a correspondence with me from Davos Platz. He's a sugary gushing sort of a Johnnie but I fancy I see his tender first in some of the reviews of my performances. The provincial papers including the *Manchester Courier* are beginning to ask "Who is Mr. Rudyard Kipling" even as Mowbray Morris does; and I have received a letter from one journal – *no* you shan't know the name; it made me blush – asking for an interview. I said *NO* awful loud an' strong. Let me win my little measure of success without machinery helps. Monday also brought me a letter from James Payne[46] demanding short stories for the *Cornhill*. I sent the chit on to my agents who will settle the terms. My system is simple – the shorter the yarn the longer the price. And I get it! Wah! Wah! Now I know I dined out somewhere on Monday and for the life o' me I can't remember where. But it's o' no consequence.

Tuesday: 24th. Went out and got a book for Baby Hugh, the Poynter's child. Did a lot of work of no value and paid a flying visit to Aunt Aggie. Baby Hugh (aetat 7) immensely set up with the gift of a real watch and gold chain. "Tisn't enough to wear it in my pocket" said he, "I wish I could wear it on my cheek." That's nice.

Dined with an American girl, she's married now, whose father was part of Scribner and Harper (Welford). She was just coming out of a fortnight's bronchitis and demanded to be played with, so I played and she and her husband laughed. Yet my heart wasn't light. Your letters had come in with no cheering news and the Mother's saying that the Pater was far from well (Lahore bores[47] and general poverty of the blood). Mother said she was writing to you 'uns. I hope she's done it and the Pater sang the praises of "your world-wide charity." That exactly describes it when you think of it. Write to 'em sometimes. I must see Lord Cross about getting the Father out of India somehow. See 'em before they depart[48] and give 'em my heart's best love.

Today is Christmas Day. The streets are nearly empty and those who are in the streets are nearly full. There's a splash of dirty sunlight on the river but I'm not happy. I'm sulking like a bear with a sore head. I dine with Phil and Ned at the Salferino tonight but that doesn't seem to amuse. Oh I wish I was in Belvidere even tho' you were just about to launch into last year's illnesses – wish I was dead. These beasts hereabouts will be sweet and sugary to me just as long as I have any success, but *you'd* be just the same if I turned up without a whole shirt on my back and broken boots. That's why I hate 'em – hate everybody and chiefly myself. This time last year we were dining at the Irwins. *Consequently* last night my hostess was telling me all about Captain Silver's marriage and engagements, insomuch that things got mixed in my mind. But I'm very rich in Xmas cards. Had one from my tailor's London Agents reminding me that I owed him £4–10 and begging me to send it along. That's bliss. I've been trying to work but have only succeeded in swearing copiously. Tell you what Xmas is a beastly season. I thought of sending you a "pome" allee same last year but I couldn't get up either peace or good will.[49]

Midnight. Never mind what I've written. Phil and Ned have just gone from my room after a dreary-lively dinner. Ned tells me of a parcel at the Grange from India ("looks like cheroots" says he). I'll lay my life that's your thoughtfulness, bless you, but we don't seem to get any forwarder as regards expense, the customs make you pay just the same. Therefore don't bother in the future. I have sent you nothing. Anybody can send gifts at Christmas. The great thing is to send 'em at other times. I'll catch something later on and I'll remember about the badminton bats, sure's I'm born. Now I'll end the scrawl and pull myself together to contemplate the hideous fact that I'll be 24 on the 30th of this month. O my, where'll I be next year and what will I be doing with it. My love to you all. I am not in the least pleased with your sister's want of health. It does not amuse me and I fancy you don't like it. Speak to her severely, take away her saddle and kill the horse, till she gets better. There are five million people in London this night and saving those who starve I don't think there is one more heartsick or thoroughly wretched than that "rising young author" known to you as

Ruddy.

Notes

1. L. G. Smith was Assistant Conservator, Forest Department, Chambra Division, Punjab; C. Bullen Smith, Accountant, Bank of Bengal, Lahore; Close I have not been able to identify.
2. Walter Herries Pollock (1850–1926), editor of the *Saturday Review*, 1883–94; the magazine's offices were in the Albany.
3. George Saintsbury (1845–1933), journalist and writer for the magazines at this time, was assistant editor of the *Saturday Review*, 1883–94, and afterwards Regius Professor of English at Edinburgh. Saintsbury's *Notes on a Cellar-Book* (1920), his celebrated account of his career as a *bon buveur*, is dedicated to RK.
4. (Sir) Richard Claverhouse Jebb (1841–1905), Professor of Greek at the University of Glasgow until 1889, when he was appointed Regius Professor of Greek at Cambridge. Like Saintsbury and Pollock, Jebb was a member of the Savile Club with RK.
5. George Hooper (1824–90) a London journalist, had edited the *Bombay Gazette*, 1868–71, when he would have known the Kipling family. He was on the staff of the *Daily Telegraph*, 1872–86, and then on the *Spectator*.
6. "The Queen of Sheba's Visit to King Solomon", finished in 1890 and purchased by the National Gallery at Sydney.
7. *Kenkab* or Kincob is gold brocade: I do not find *schulkharis* in *Hobson-Jobson*.
8. This was the slang term used in Rossetti's circle.
9. (Sir) William Hamo Thornycroft (1850–1925), sculptor.
10. Major George Roe Fenwick (d. 1904), founder of the *CMG* at Simla and its editor at Lahore; editor of the *Broad Arrow* in England.
11. Moreau (1856–1937) was senior partner in the Allahabad firm of A. H. Wheeler, publishers of RK's Indian Railway Library stories. RK sold his copyright in these stories to Moreau two days before leaving India.
12. "One View of the Question" appeared not in the *Contemporary Review* but the *Fortnightly Review*, February 1890 (*Many Inventions*).
13. Mrs George D. Hammond lived at 27 Rutland Gate.
14. "The Courting of Dinah Shadd", *Macmillan's*, March 1890 (*Life's Handicap*).
15. (Sir) Clinton Edward Dawkins (1859–1905), now secretary to Lord Goschen, Chancellor of the Exchequer. He was afterwards financial member of the Council of India.
16. Arthur Watkin Williams Wynn (1856–?).
17. Thus in copy. The "Adoration of the Mage" was published in the *CMG*, 25 January 1890 (uncollected). The anecdote is meant to illustrate the idiot self-importance that RK attributed to Gladstone.
18. Wynnard Hooper (1853–1935), son of George Hooper.
19. Justin Huntly MacCarthy (1861–1936), son of Justin MacCarthy (see n. 38, below), was a journalist, dramatist, novelist, and historian.
20. Carus Dunlop Cunningham (1856–96), wrote *A History of the Swiss Confederation* (1889); a member of the Alpine Club since 1882.
21. Henri de Blowitz (1832–1903), *The Times* correspondent in Paris; Mme Olga Novikoff

(1848–1925), Russian-born political journalist resident in England, published under the initials "O.K."
22. Miss Winnard and Miss Mary Craik: see 28 January 1882. Hooper was Miss Winnard's brother-in-law, and it was through him that arrangements had originally been made for the Ladies of Warwick Gardens to care for the Kipling children.
23. Perhaps Margaret L. Hooper, who exhibited in London c. 1881–1911. RK continued to see her as late as 1910 (Bateman's Visitors Book, Sussex).
24. Perhaps "The Battle of Rupert Square", *St James's Gazette*, 28 December 1889 (*Uncollected Prose*, I, Sussex Edition).
25. James Walker of Simla, one of the *CMG* proprietors.
26. Wife of Colonel Henry Langtry (1841–?), Eighth (King's Royal Irish) Hussars.
27. *Ruy Blas, or the Blasé Roué*, a burlesque that opened at the Gaiety on 21 September starring Nellie Farren.
28. George Macmillan (1855–1936) was the cousin not the brother of Sir Frederick Macmillan; he had been in the firm since 1874; his wife was the former Margaret Helen Lucas.
29. The daughter of Austin Corbin (1827–96), banker and railroad financier, president of the Reading Railroad, 1886–90, and of the Long Island Railroad. He had three daughters, Mary, Isabella, and Anna. I do not know which one RK means. Corbin has been identified as the original of Slatin Beeman, the millionaire alluded to in ch. 2 of *"Captains Courageous"* (W. S. Tower, "Who Was Slatin Beeman?", *Kipling Journal*, September 1975, pp. 10–12).
30. Walter Pater (1839–94), Oxford don, critic, and essayist: the chief guide of the aesthetic movement in England.
31. "Puree" in copy.
32. Sir Harry Hamilton Johnston (1858–1927), had explored in Angola, the Congo, the Niger delta, and Kenya by 1889. A copy of his *The History of a Slave* (1889), inscribed by him to RK, 2 September 1890 is in the Library of Congress. In July 1894 he and RK were the honoured guests at a dinner of the Authors' Club.
33. The Revd Frederic Macdonald (1842–1928), who followed the family tradition, had been in the ministry since 1862 and was President of the Methodist Conference in 1899.
34. George Macdonald (1868–1930), eldest son of Frederic; I do not know why RK calls him "nephew". George was afterwards RK's solicitor.
35. See 10–11 June 1889.
36. Sir Edwin Arnold (1832–1904), journalist, orientalist, and poet, best known for his epic *The Light of Asia* (1879).
37. The former Caroline Wortley married, 1881, Norman Grosvenor (1845–98), insurance director, MP, and amateur composer.
38. Justin MacCarthy, the elder (1830–1912), was a journalist and politician.
39. MacCarthy's only daughter, unmarried, lived with her widowed father to his death.
40. Perhaps Henry Simpson (1853–1921), genre painter, who exhibited at the Royal Academy in the 1880s.
41. Blank in copy.
42. That is, Solferino's, a Soho restaurant popular in W. E. Henley's circle.
43. William Thacker Spink (d. 1928); Thacker, Spink and Co. of Calcutta, and W. Thacker and Co. of London, were the publishers of *Departmental Ditties* from the second edition on, and of *Plain Tales from the Hills*.
44. RK managed to make some slight changes in the text of this, the first English edition of *Soldiers Three* (1890: see Stewart–Yeats, *Bibliographical Catalogue*, p. 45).
45. This was the first English edition; the £50 worth of new poems included the "Prelude", "The Masque of Plenty", "The Song of the Women", "The Ballad of Fisher's Boarding House", and "The Grave of the Hundred Head".
46. Payn (1830–98), novelist, was editor of the *Cornhill*, 1883–96. Nothing of RK's in the *Cornhill* is known.
47. Thus in copy: for "sores"? See 30 July–1 August 1885.
48. They were preparing to return to England in April for a year-and-a-half's leave.
49. The MS of RK's Christmas poem to the Hills in 1888, beginning "Peace upon earth to

people of good will" is in the Library of Congress (Rutherford, *Early Verse*, pp. 442–5).

To Caroline Taylor, 9 December 1889
Text: Copy, University of Sussex

[London] December: 9:

That was indeed a sober letter of great gravity and a proper and commendable one forebye. I thank you for it and the more because you speak casually about yourself and take a little – but not much – anxiety off my mind. Sweetheart you're a casuistical little villain. I must hire an unprejudiced person to tell me about your health.

To reply to what was on your mind, not if this court knows itself. No. Aleck was a little wrong. Your slave, may he be your sacrifice, was baptized in Bombay Cathedral into the Church of England which you call Episcopalian, was brought up as you have read in that church and confirmed by the Bishop of Exeter in Bideford Church in '80 or '81. Does that satisfy, dear, that I am not a veiled adherent of the Church of Rome?

In regard to what I believe you open a door to much discussion. I'll try to explain as clearly as I may.

Imprimis I believe in Carrie and that faith has taught me many things. Chiefly I believe in the existence of a personal God to whom we are personally responsible for wrong doing – that it is our duty to follow and our peril to disobey the ten ethical laws laid down for us by Him or His prophets. I disbelieve directly in eternal punishment for reasons that would take too long to put down on paper. On the same grounds I disbelieve in an eternal reward. As regards the mystery of the Trinity and the Doctrine of Redemption I regard them most reverently but cannot give them implicit belief, accepting them rather as dogmas of the Church than as matters that rush to the heart. I would give much to believe in them absolutely. Now all these are things that I should infinitely have preferred to discuss with you, darling, face to face but since you have asked and you – but you alone – have the right to an answer I explain as baldly and as clumsily as I may. Summarized it comes to *I believe in God the Father Almighty maker of Heaven and Earth and in one filled with His spirit who did voluntarily die in the belief that the human race would be spiritually bettered thereby.*

I believe after having seen and studied eight or nine creeds in Justification by work rather than faith, and most assuredly do I believe in retribution both here and hereafter for wrong doing as I believe in a reward, here and hereafter for obedience to the Law.

There! You have got from me what no living soul has ever done before. The whole skittledom of the R.C. Church interests me immensely – just as the Greek or the Syrian Church would interest me, inasmuch as it shows how the fringe of a living faith can overlap far into the borders of downright idolatry. Had you known me a little better you would scarce have quoted Alec. Ask him if I am the sort of person likely to hand over will and conscience to another's keeping? I know what it was I said that led him to that belief.

So now you know, and the question is how far will you allow that knowledge to influence you in our relations? I will learn from your lips anything that you may see fit to teach me, my Queen. It is sure to be truer and purer than what I have believed hitherto. I had but one talk with you on matters of faith and that was on the stoop. From that I gathered that even you had doubts and questionings. Can you forgive me if I, too, question a little – or is it more than you can overlook. Not even for your sweet sake, Carrie, in matters relating directly to my deepest heart, would I care or dare to perjure myself. I have enough on my conscience already. But this I promise as I honestly can. Neither in word nor in deed will I do anything to sap or divert your faith and if it is so willed "Thy God shall be my God"[1] till we two find out together what manner of Deity we have worshipped on earth. When I see your father I shall tell him exactly what I have told you here and it is for him to give or withold consent. Only – don't *you* give me up sweetheart. You are not a child but a woman, and as a woman I have spoken to you on this matter.

Remains yet another which to speak truth worries me more than any question of creed – 'tis *so* easy to lose the All Father when one is honestly loved by an American Angel –. You wrote, Mademoiselle, some stuff – not to put too fine a point upon it – some ABJECT DRIVELLING ROT – LUNACY – BOSH – ! on the subject of *All in a Garden Fair* and your views about poets and sympathy, culled from the pages of Walter Besant. You feared and then again, you didn't know as how and so forth.

Heart's heart, that sort of thinking about sympathy to be given to me, is like the letting in of waters. In the first place I am not a poet and never shall be – but only a writer who varies fiction with verse.

Never mind what I was going to say you shall hear it next week. But I love you – I love you and again I love you. Good night dear one and bless your dear heart.

Note
1. CF. Ruth 1:16.

To John Addington Symonds, 9 December 1889
ALS: University of Bristol

Embankment Chambers, / Villiers Street, Strand. / Dec: 9: 89.

Dear Mr. Symonds,

Am I a beast for keeping silence over your letter so long? I have been rained upon, befogged, snowed over, frozen and thawed several hundred times within the past few days and this has driven me to my bed not so much from any disease as pure disgust. Altogether I am savage sore and discontented. It is no use to read Italian Sketches[1] with your feet upon the frosty Caucasus or the kitchen fender and a dripping fog without. Why did you write them and what is that thing called sunshine you speak of so often in the book?

It is good to think that you liked some of the stories. Would that I could show you the line and sepia illustrations for *In Black and White* drawn by my father[2] who being an artist knows how to draw the natives he has lived among for a quarter of a century and having bred me knows exactly what my pen's driving at better than all the world. All the unwritten chapters of On the City Wall are contained in a sepia sketch of the young man Wali Dad.

If you see Macmillan's you may find that Yussuf[3] has been writing border ballads – which is me – and that Mulvaney has reappeared. Frankly I don't think much of him. He seems to lack a great deal of his old spirit. The uninitiate whom I meet out at dinner hold up to me as desirable the poesies of "Yussuf" and bid me go and do likewise. This makes me laugh all to mine self. Your Colonel is right about the Afghans – no Pathan stands unless he is vastly superior in numbers or is cornered – but wrong about the soldier. They didn't I suppose have regular musketry instruction when he was a subaltern but it is on the range and at the butts that Thomas, waiting for his turn to shoot, blossoms like a lotos. Half my canteen talk I've picked up on long hot lazy afternoons lying on the range in the dry dust watching the shadow of the targets get longer and the shooting wilder as the sun went down. But Thomas does not exactly bandy wit with his Colonel.

And now I go to fight with the beasts in Paternoster Row. You will have, without my written wish, a merry Christmas because you have the sun over there. I shall eat the plum pudding of the British in fog.

All good fortune go with you and yours – how much I value your sympathy I need hardly say.

Yours ever
Rudyard Kipling

Notes
1. RK may mean Symonds's *Sketches in Italy and Greece* (1874), *Sketches and Studies in Italy* (1879), or *Italian Byways* (1883).
2. See [30 June 1889].
3. The four "border ballads" that RK contributed to *Macmillan's* between November 1889 and February 1890 are all signed "Yussuf" – "Joseph", as RK had been baptised.

To Henry Rider Haggard, [late 1889?]
ALS: Library of Congress

Embankment Chambers, / Villiers Street, Strand.

Dear Mr. Haggard,

Forgive a Junior's impertinence but this thing was picked up the other day across some drinks and it seemed – but of course you know it.

There was first one Englishman and one Mummy. They met in Egypt and the live man bought the dead for it was a fine dead. Then the dead was unrolled and in the last layers of cloth that malignant Egyptian had tucked away a commination service of the most awful kind to the address of any man who disturbed him. He should die horribly in the open as a beast dies at the hand of a beast and there should not be enough of him to put into a matchbox – much less a Mummy case. Whereat they laughed and of course later the Englishman went to your country and became "fey" insomuch that he was weak enough to fire a shot gun into an elephant's trunk. Then he was dealt with after the manner of elephants till he was black-currant jam but the rest of the camp would have taken what remained to the sea so they cachéd it with great care and put a watcher on it, and there came in the night a Beast such a Hyæna as never was and raked out that corpse and gave tongue to all the other beasts and – nothing remained or it might have been that (as happened not long since in India) the elephant returned to find her dead and battered the corpse afresh into the earth. These things the native watcher told when the camp returned with the coffin. Were the Mummy not in it I could and would take the thing and play with it. But there is a King in Egypt already and so I bring the body to his feet – for what it is worth.[1]

Yours sincerely
Rudyard Kipling

Note
1. Haggard did not use the story.

Register of Names and Correspondents

A full index will be published at the end of the fourth volume. For the convenience of the reader in the interim this list is provided of RK's correspondents and contemporaries identified in this volume. The page references are to the notes in which the identifications are made.

Aitken, Ben, 231
Alikhanoff, General, 181
Allen, Sir George, 77
Allen, Mrs George, 206
Alston, Sir Charles Ross, 267
Armstrong, Major Richard, 123
Armstrong, Thomas, 367
Arnold, Sir Edwin, 377

Baldwin, Alfred, 5
Baldwin, Louisa Macdonald, 5
    letters to: [December? 1872?]; 24 January 1886
Baldwin, Stanley, 5
    letter to: 20 December 1878
Baugh, Major Mackenzie Walcott, 117
Bayliss, Lieutenant Eustace Granville, 159
Beames, Lieutenant David, 188
Beames, John, 195
Beley, Captain C. H. H., 261
Beresford, George Charles, 11
Beresford, Lord William, 367
Berney, Captain Thomas Hugh, 123
Besant, Sir Walter, 214
    letter to: 20 November [1889]
Bielby, Dr Elizabeth, 112
Bignold, Thomas Frank, 264
Birdwood, Sir George, 266
Boileau, Lieutenant-Colonel Herbert Edward, 116
Bonsard, L., 302
Booj (Bhoj), cook, 269
Boucher, Revd Charles Estcourt, 123
Bourke, Captain John Gregory, 338
Brodhurst, Amy Maxwell, 264

Brodhurst, Maynard, 262
Brodhurst, Mrs Maynard, 263
Brough, Norman, 313
Buck, Sir Edward, 207
Burne-Jones, Georgiana, 111
    letter to: 31 May 1889
Burne-Jones, Margaret: see Mrs J. W. Mackail
Burne-Jones, Philip, 5
    letter to: [c. 1883?]
Burton, Major Francis Charles, 144
Burton, Mrs Isabella, 144
    letter to: 26 October 1887

Caine, Hall, 367
Campbell, Henry Vincent, 33
Carlin, Lieutenant James W., 311
Carmichael-Carr, Mrs, 310
Chalmers, Major E. W., 294
Chesney, George, 130
Cheyne, Lieutenant Charles, 123
Clandeboye, Lord, 242
Colvin, Sir Auckland, 87
Colvin, Sidney, 367
Colvin, Sir Walter, 282
Colvin, Lady, 282
Coman, Katherine, 343
Connaught, Duke of, 81
Conybeare, Henry, 264
Cook, John Mason, 309
Cooper, Colonel Harry, 367
Corbin, Austin, 377
Corbin, Miss, 377
Coxen, Miss, 74
    letter to: 2 September 1884
Craik, Geogiana, 14

Craik, Mary, 14
Craster, Shafto Longfield, 32
Crawford, Charles Edward Gordon, 144
Crawford, Mrs Charles Edward Gordon, 144
Crofts, William Carr, 46
    letters to: 14 November 1883; 20 December 1885; 18–27 February 1886; 14 September 1886
Croker, Mrs Bithia Mary, 261
Crookshank, Colonel A. C. W., 261
Cross, Viscount, 367
Cunliffe, Brigadier-General Frederick, 123
Cunningham, Carus Dunlop, 376

Dare, William John, 277
Davey, Elizabeth, 78
    letter to: 2 October 1884
Davies, Colonel Charles Henry, 117
Dawkins, Sir Clinton, 376
De Blowitz, Henri, 376
De Forest, Lockwood, 340
De Forest, Mrs Lockwood, 345
Devens, Arthur Lithgow, 343
Dick, Lieutenant A. R., 247
Digby, Captain T. E., 279
Dilke, Mrs Ashton, 356
Dodd, Lieutenant-Colonel C. A., 283
Dodge, Mary Mapes, 8
    letter to: 22 August 1879
Drake, Lieutenant F. R., 96
Dufferin, Hariot, Marchioness of, 162
Dufferin, first Marquess of, 162
Dunsterville, Lionel Charles, 11
    letter to: 30 January 1886
Dury, Lieutenant Robert, 117

Edge, Ethel Laura, 202
Edge, Sir John, 210
Edge, Lady, 210
Edwardes, Stanley Malcolm, 15
Edwards, Tom, 207
Eliot, Sir John, 220
Elliott, Sir Charles, 326
Emerson, Sir William, 368

Fenton, Raymond Rooke, 32
Fenwick, Major George Roe, 376
Fleming, Lieutenant-Colonel John, 155

Fleming, Mrs John (Alice Kipling, "Trix", RK's sister), 14
    letters to: 28 January 1882; [c. early February 1882]
Frewen, Moreton, 289

Garrard, Florence Violet, 10
Geary, Grattan, 112
Gielgud, Mrs, 367
Gordon, Donald Clunes, 282
Graham, Lady Beatrice Violet, 302
Green, Charles Douglas, 123
Green, Ernest Frederick, 123
Griffin, Sir Lepel Henry, 169
Griffiths, John, 339
Grimston, Sir Rollo, 32
Grosvenor, Mrs Norman, 377
Guthrie, Thomas Anstey, 358

Haggard, Sir Henry Rider, 353
    letter to: [late 1889?]
Haggin, Miss, 313
Hall, G. C., 282
Harper, Joseph Henry, 341
Hawthorne, Dr R., 200
Hearsey, Captain Andrew, 282
Henderson, Colonel Philip Durham, 234
Hensman, Howard, 220
Hill, A. P., 144
Hill, Edmonia, 149
    letters to: [late December 1887?]; [22] April [1888]; [24? April 1888]; [c. 25 April 1888]; 30 April 1888; 8 May [1888]; [9–11?] May 1888; [12–14] May 1888; 15 May 1888; 19–21 May 1888; [25–7] May 1888; 29–30 May 1888; [1] June 1888; [5–6] June 1888; 12 June [1888]; 22 June 1888; [24–5] June 1888; [25–6] June 1888; 27 June 1888; [28 June–1 July] 1888; [2–3] July 1888; [4–6] July 1888; [7–8] July 1888; [9–10] July 1888; [11?] July 1888; [12] July 1888; 13 July 1888; 15 July 1888; 5 October 1888; [6] October 1888; 7 October 1888; [8] October 1888; 10 October 1888; [11] October 1888; 12 October 1888; [January? 1889]; [26? January? 1889?]; [6? February] 1889; [9? February] 1889; [c. 10? February? 1889]; 20 February

Hill, Edmonia – *continued*
 letters to – *continued*
  1889; 21 February 1889; 22 February 1889; 23 February 1889; [24] February 1889; 26 February 1889; [2 March] 1889; [6 June 1889]; [7]–9 June 1889; [10–11 June 1889]; 15–16 June 1889; 18 June 1889; 23 June 1889; [30 June 1889]; 2 July 1889; 5 July 1889; 10 July 1889; 9 August 1889; 11 August 1889; 13 August 1889; 5 September 1889; [7 September] 1889; 10 September 1889; 13 September 1889; 16 September 1889; 17 September 1889; [22 October 1889]; 25 October 1889; 1 November [1889]; [early November 1889]; 8–16 November 1889; 3–25 December 1889
Hill, Samuel Alexander, 149
 letters to: 7 October 1888; 2 July 1889
Hobday, Colonel Edmund, 210
Hooper, George, 376
Hooper, Margaret, 377
Hooper, Wynnard, 376
Hunter, Sir William Wilson, 195

Irwin, Edna, 297
Irwin, J. M., 279

Jebb, Sir Richard, 376
Johnston, Sir Harry, 377

Kadir Baksh, 166
Kendall, Elizabeth K., 343
King, Captain W. F., 246
Kipling, Alice Macdonald: *see* Alice Kipling Fleming
Kipling, John Lockwood
 letter to: [5 July 1888?]
Kishore, Munshi Newal, 176
Koenig, F., 156
 letter to: 22 March 1888

Lang, Colonel A. M., 283
Lang, Andrew, 353
 letter to: 26 October 1889
Langtry, Mrs, 377
Lansdowne, fifth Marquess of, 299
Lawrence, Mrs Alexander, 282
Lawrence, Sir Walter Roper, 130
Lawrie, Dr E., 27
Levett-Yeats, Sidney Kilner, 326

Levett-Yeats, Mrs Sidney, 326
Lewin, Lieutenant-Colonel Thomas Herbert, 356
Logan, Lieutenant F. C. L., 246
Longman, Charles James, 368
Low, Sidney, 367
Lyall, Sir James Broadwood, 176

MacCarthy, Justin, 377
MacCarthy, Justin Huntly, 376
Macdonald, Andrew, 77
 letter to: [February? 1886]
Macdonald, Edith, 9
 letters to: [c. January 1881?]; 24 December 1882; [May? 1883?]; 12–13 June 1883; 14–17 August 1883; [December 1883]; [26–8 January 1884]; 4 February 1884; 4 April 1884; 28 April 1884; 2–7 June [1884]; [10–14] July [1884]; 14 August 1884; 17 September 1884; 21 November 1884; 30 July–1 August 1885; 4–5 December 1886
Macdonald, Revd Frederic, 377
Macdonald, George, 214
Macdonald, George (RK's cousin), 377
Macdonald, Henry James, 340
Macdonald, Mrs Henry, 340
Mackail, John William, 156
Mackail, Mrs John William (Margaret Burne-Jones), 52
 letters to: [c. 1883?]; 10 June 1884; [27] September 1885; 28 November 1885–11 January 1886; 3 May–24 June 1886; 25 January–24 March 1888; 11–14 February 1889
Macmillan, George, 377
Marsh, Mrs H., 176
Masson, Sir David Parkes, 27
Maunsell, Colonel John Richardson, 143
Maunsell, Mrs, 143
 letter to: 10 June 1887
Maxwell, Lieutenant-Colonel William, 123
Meredith, Marie Eveleen, 356
Mills, A. S., 282
Molesworth, Lieutenant George, 124
Moreau, Emile, 376
Murray, John Henry, 32

Naoroji, Dadabhai, 367

Napier, Mrs, 206
Nicholson, Mrs W. G., 214
Novikoff, Olga, 376

Park, M. H., 220
Parker, Edwin Woodall, 305
Parry-Lambert, Miss, 188
Parry-Lambert, Mrs, 195
Parry-Nisbet, Lieutenant-Colonel Robert, 214
Pater, Walter, 377
Payn, James, 377
Perry, John Tavenor, 11
Perry, Mrs John Tavenor, 11
  letters to: 25 January 1882; 31 January–1 February 1882; 9 March 1882; [29] April 1882; 22 May 1882; 28 May [1882]
Pike, H. W., 220
Plowden, Edith, 9
  letter to: [August 1881]
Pollock, Walter Herries, 376
Porter, Wilfrid King, 279
Poynter, Ambrose, 367
Poynter, Agnes Macdonald, 16
Poynter, Sir Edward John, 16
Poynter, Hugh, 367
Powell, Sidney Henry, 30
Price, Cormell, 29
  letters to: 30 December 1882; 18 March 1883; 19–21 May 1883; 1 June 1883; 29 August 1883; 19 February 1884; 19 September 1885; 26 April 1888; 4 December 1888
Pugh, Matthew Henry, 123
Pullen, Kitty, 61

Quay, Matthew, 339

Ranken, Colonel George, 123
Reuther, A. M., 196
Richmond, Francis George, 20
Richmond, Sir William Bell, 368
Ripon, First Marquess of, 58
Roberts, Lord, 227
Roberts, Nora, Lady, 227
Robertson, Eric, 305
Robinson, Edward Kay, 124
  letter to: 30 April 1886
Robinson, Philip Stewart, 124
Ross, Mrs G. E. A., 159
Rumelin, C. E., 324

Saintsbury, George, 376
Salsbury, A. J., 321
Sandys, Captain E. C. C., 87
Scoble, Sir Andrew, 231
Shatterly, J. L. M., 321
Silver, Captain G., 259
Simon, Lady Rachel, 368
Simon, Sir John, 368
Simpson, Henry, 377
Sims, R. Proctor, 116
Smith, C. Bullen, 376
Smith, L. G., 376
Sparks, James Noel, 87
Sparks, Lieutenant-Colonel John Barnes, 87
Spencer, George W., 313
Spink, William Thacker, 377
Stead, William Thomas, 123
Stewart, Colonel James Calder, 264
Stewart, Colonel John, 368
Stockwell, Colonel George, 123
Straight, Mrs Douglas, 161
Straight, Sir Douglas, 161
Stratton, Wallace Christopher, 32
Symonds, John Addington, 349
  letters to: 15 October 1889; 9 December 1899

Taylor, Caroline, 334
  letters to: [22 October 1889]; 25 October 1889; 1 November [1889]; 2 November 1889: [c. early November 1889]; 9 December 1889
Taylor, Edgar, 334
Taylor, Julia
  letter to: 22 September 1889
Thornycroft, Hamo, 376
Trevor, Frederick, 367
Turner, Sir Charles Arthur, 214
Tweddell, Augusta, 246
  letter to: [10 July 1888]

Walker, Sir George Casson, 44
Walker, Sir James, 40
Walker, Mrs James, 44
  letter to: [September? 1883]
Wallace, Sir Donald Mackenzie, 220
Watt, A. P., 369
Webb, Captain Matthew, 336
Welford, Charles, 367

Wheeler, Stephen, 27
   letter to: 12 December 1888
Willes, Arthur Herbert, 32
Willes, Francis Charles, 32
Willes, Rev George, 26
   letters to: 17-[18] November 1882; 24 April 1883
Wilson, Lieutenant-General Thomas, 195

Winnard, Miss, 14
Wright, William Henry, 267
Wutzler, H., 203
Wynn, Arthur Watkin Williams, 376

Young, Arthur Frederick, 116
Young, Colonel George Gordon, 214
Young, Norman Edward, 32